SLOGANS

SLOGANS

First Edition

A Collection of More Than 6,000 Slogans,
Rallying Cries, and Other Exhortations Used in
Advertising, Political Campaigns, Popular Causes and
Movements, and Divers Efforts to Urge People to Take
Action, the Entries Representing a Broad Spectrum of
Time and Origin yet Conveniently Arranged by Thematic
Categories and Identified as to Source, the Whole
Enhanced by a Specially Prepared Foreword and
Introduction and by the Inclusion of Detailed Indexes

Laurence Urdang, Editorial Director
Ceila Dame Robbins, Editor

GALE RESEARCH COMPANY
BOOK TOWER • DETROIT, MICHIGAN 48226

Editorial Staff:

Laurence Urdang, *Editorial Director*

Ceila Dame Robbins, *Editor*

Frank R. Abate, *Managing Editor*

Peter M. Gross, Linda M. D. Legassie, and Charles F. Ruhe, *Editorial Assistants*

Typographic and Systems Design by Laurence Urdang

Programming, Data Processing, and Typesetting by
Alexander Typesetting, Inc., Indianapolis, Indiana

Library of Congress Cataloging in Publication Data

Main Entry under title:

Slogans.

"A collection of more than 6,000 slogans, rallying
cries, and other exhortations used in advertising,
political campaigns, popular causes and movements, and
divers efforts to urge people to take action, the
entries representing a broad spectrum of time and
origin yet conveniently arranged by thematic categories
and identified as to source."
    Includes indexes.
    1. Slogans.   2. Political slogans.   I. Urdang,
Laurence.   II. Robbins, Ceila Dame.
HF6135.S57   1984   659.13'22   84-10197
ISBN 0-8103-1549-1

Printed in the United States of America

Contents

Foreword 17

Introduction 23

How To Use This Book 27

Slogans, Arranged by Categories 31–371

Index I

  Slogans & Categories Listed Alphabetically 375

Index II

  Source Information Listed Alphabetically 497

Table of Thematic Categories and Cross References

N.B.: *In the following table, both actual categories used in the text and synonyms are listed, with cross references shown for each. The categories are preceded by numbers, the synonyms are not.*

"See also" references are to other categories of possibly related interest; "See" references are from synonyms to actual categories used in the book.

1. ADHESIVES 31

2. ADVERTISING 31

3. AEROSPACE 33
    See also 4. AIR TRAVEL AND CARGO; 38. ELECTRONICS
      INDUSTRY.
    AGRICULTURE ... See 42. FARMING SUPPLIES AND
      EQUIPMENT.
    AIR CONDITIONING ... See 58. HEATING AND AIR
      CONDITIONING.

4. AIR TRAVEL AND CARGO 35
    See also 3. AEROSPACE; 119. TRAVEL.
    AIRPLANES ... See 3. AEROSPACE.
    ALCOHOLIC BEVERAGES ... See 14. BEER AND ALE;
      71. LIQUORS; 125. WINES.
    ALE ... See 14. BEER AND ALE.
    APPLIANCES ... See 60. HOME APPLIANCES AND
      EQUIPMENT.

Contents 6

5. AUDIO EQUIPMENT 39
   See also 38. ELECTRONICS INDUSTRY; 78. MOVIES AND
      ENTERTAINMENT; 97. RECORDINGS.

6. AUTOMOBILE RENTAL SERVICES 42
   See also 7. AUTOMOBILES.

7. AUTOMOBILES 42
   See also 6. AUTOMOBILE RENTAL SERVICES;
      8. AUTOMOTIVE PARTS AND PRODUCTS;
      9. AUTOMOTIVE SERVICE.

8. AUTOMOTIVE PARTS AND PRODUCTS 47
   See also 7. AUTOMOBILES; 9. AUTOMOTIVE SERVICE;
      114. TIRES.

9. AUTOMOTIVE SERVICE 51
   See also 7. AUTOMOBILES; 8. AUTOMOTIVE PARTS AND
      PRODUCTS; 88. PETROLEUM PRODUCTS.

10. BABY PRODUCTS 52
   See also 47. FOOD, MISCELLANEOUS; 106. SOAP; 118. TOYS
      AND GAMES.

11. BAKED GOODS AND BAKING SUPPLIES 52
   See also 47. FOOD, MISCELLANEOUS; 68. KITCHEN
      PRODUCTS AND UTENSILS.
   BANKS ... See 43. FINANCIAL INSTITUTIONS AND SERVICES.

12. BATH ACCESSORIES 55
   See also 104. SHAVING SUPPLIES; 106. SOAP;
      116. TOILETRIES.
   BATHING SUITS ... See 109. SWIMWEAR.
   BATTERIES ... See 60. HOME APPLIANCES AND EQUIPMENT.
   BEAUTY AIDS ... See 116. TOILETRIES.

13. BEDS AND BEDDING 56
   See also 50. FURNITURE.

14. BEER AND ALE 58
   See also 15. BEVERAGES, MISCELLANEOUS; 71. LIQUORS;
      125. WINES.

15. BEVERAGES, MISCELLANEOUS 66
   See also 14. BEER AND ALE; 27. COFFEE; 33. DAIRY
      PRODUCTS; 47. FOOD, MISCELLANEOUS; 71. LIQUORS;
      107. SOFT DRINKS; 110. TEA; 125. WINES.

16. BOATS AND BOATING EQUIPMENT 67
   See also 102. SEA TRAVEL AND CARGO.
   BOOKS ... See 94. PUBLISHING.

17. BROADCASTING 68
   See also 95. RADIO EQUIPMENT;
      111. TELECOMMUNICATIONS; 112. TELEVISIONS.

18. BUILDING SUPPLIES 69
   See also 55. HARDWARE; 65. INTERIOR DECORATION;
      75. METALS INDUSTRY; 82. PAINT AND PAINTING
      SUPPLIES.

19. BUS LINES 75
See also 119. TRAVEL.
BUSINESS MACHINES . . . See 28. COMPUTER EQUIPMENT;
81. OFFICE EQUIPMENT AND SUPPLIES.
CAMPAIGN SLOGANS . . . See 91. PRESIDENTIAL
CAMPAIGNS.
CAMPING EQUIPMENT . . . See 98. RECREATIONAL
EQUIPMENT.
20. CANDY AND GUM 76
See also 47. FOOD, MISCELLANEOUS.
CARGO . . . See 4. AIR TRAVEL AND CARGO; 96. RAIL TRAVEL
AND CARGO; 102. SEA TRAVEL AND CARGO.
CARPETS . . . See 46. FLOOR COVERINGS.
CARS . . . See 7. AUTOMOBILES.
CASSETTES . . . See 97. RECORDINGS.
CERAMICS . . . See 52. GLASS AND CERAMICS.
21. CEREALS 80
See also 47. FOOD, MISCELLANEOUS.
22. CHEMICAL INDUSTRY 82
See also 24. CLEANING AND LAUNDRY PRODUCTS; 86. PEST
CONTROL.
23. CHINA 84
See also 52. GLASS AND CERAMICS; 68. KITCHEN
PRODUCTS AND UTENSILS.
CIGARETTES . . . See 115. TOBACCO PRODUCTS.
CIGARS . . . See 115. TOBACCO PRODUCTS.
24. CLEANING AND LAUNDRY PRODUCTS 85
See also 22. CHEMICAL INDUSTRY; 106. SOAP.
25. CLEANING SERVICES 90
CLOCKS . . . See 124. WATCHES AND CLOCKS.
26. CLOTHING, MISCELLANEOUS 90
See also 48. FOOTWEAR; 61. HOSIERY; 109. SWIMWEAR;
121. UNDERWEAR; 123. WARDROBE ACCESSORIES.
27. COFFEE 98
See also 15. BEVERAGES, MISCELLANEOUS; 110. TEA.
COMMUNICATIONS . . . See 111. TELECOMMUNICATIONS.
COMPANIES . . . See 31. CORPORATIONS, MISCELLANEOUS.
28. COMPUTER EQUIPMENT 102
See also 37. ELECTRICAL PRODUCTS AND SERVICE;
38. ELECTRONICS INDUSTRY; 81. OFFICE EQUIPMENT
AND SUPPLIES.
29. CONDIMENTS AND SPICES 106
See also 47. FOOD, MISCELLANEOUS.
CONFECTIONS . . . See 20. CANDY AND GUM.
CONSTRUCTION . . . See 18. BUILDING SUPPLIES;
73. MACHINERY.
COOKING FUELS . . . See 59. HEATING AND COOKING FUELS.

Contents

COOKWARE ... See 11. BAKED GOODS AND BAKING
  SUPPLIES; 68. KITCHEN PRODUCTS AND UTENSILS.

30. COPYING EQUIPMENT 109
  See also 81. OFFICE EQUIPMENT AND SUPPLIES.

31. CORPORATIONS, MISCELLANEOUS 109

32. COSMETICS 112
  See also 54. HAIR CARE; 116. TOILETRIES.
  CRUISE SHIPS ... See 102. SEA TRAVEL AND CARGO.
  CUTLERY ... See 55. HARDWARE.

33. DAIRY PRODUCTS 116
  See also 15. BEVERAGES, MISCELLANEOUS; 47. FOOD,
    MISCELLANEOUS.

34. DENTAL CARE 119
  See also 116. TOILETRIES.
  DEODORANTS ... See 116. TOILETRIES.
  DETERGENTS ... See 24. CLEANING AND LAUNDRY
    PRODUCTS.
  DISHES ... See 23. CHINA.

35. DRUGS AND REMEDIES 121
  See also 56. HEALTH AND FITNESS.
  DRY GOODS ... See 103. SEWING AND KNITTING SUPPLIES.
  EARTHMOVERS ... See 73. MACHINERY.

36. ECONOMIC DEVELOPMENT 129
  See also 119. TRAVEL.

37. ELECTRICAL PRODUCTS AND SERVICE 130
  See also 38. ELECTRONICS INDUSTRY; 58. HEATING AND
    AIR CONDITIONING; 60. HOME APPLIANCES AND
    EQUIPMENT; 70. LIGHTING PRODUCTS.
  ELECTRICITY ... See 93. PUBLIC UTILITIES.

38. ELECTRONICS INDUSTRY 132
  See also 3. AEROSPACE; 5. AUDIO EQUIPMENT;
    17. BROADCASTING; 28. COMPUTER EQUIPMENT;
    37. ELECTRICAL PRODUCTS AND SERVICE; 95. RADIO
    EQUIPMENT; 111. TELECOMMUNICATIONS;
    112. TELEVISIONS; 122. VIDEO EQUIPMENT.

39. ELEVATORS 133

40. EMPLOYMENT AGENCIES 133
  ENERGY ... See 59. HEATING AND COOKING FUELS;
    88. PETROLEUM PRODUCTS; 93. PUBLIC UTILITIES.
  ENTERTAINMENT ... See 78. MOVIES AND
    ENTERTAINMENT.

41. EYEGLASSES 134
  See also 123. WARDROBE ACCESSORIES.
  FABRICS INDUSTRY ... See 103. SEWING AND KNITTING
    SUPPLIES.

42. FARMING SUPPLIES AND EQUIPMENT 135
    See also 73. MACHINERY; 120. TRUCKS AND TRUCKING
        INDUSTRY.
    FASHION ACCESSORIES ... See 26. CLOTHING,
        MISCELLANEOUS; 32. COSMETICS; 123. WARDROBE
        ACCESSORIES.
    FEED ... See 42. FARMING SUPPLIES AND EQUIPMENT.
    FERTILIZER ... See 42. FARMING SUPPLIES AND
        EQUIPMENT.
    FILM ... See 89. PHOTOGRAPHIC EQUIPMENT.
43. FINANCIAL INSTITUTIONS AND SERVICES 138
    See also 64. INSURANCE; 66. INVESTMENT.
    FINISHES ... See 82. PAINT AND PAINTING SUPPLIES.
44. FIREARMS 141
45. FISHING SUPPLIES 143
    See also 98. RECREATIONAL EQUIPMENT; 108. SPORTING
        GOODS.
    FITNESS ... See 56. HEALTH AND FITNESS.
    FLATWARE ... See 23. CHINA; 67. JEWELRY AND SILVER.
    FLAVORINGS ... See 29. CONDIMENTS AND SPICES.
46. FLOOR COVERINGS 145
    See also 18. BUILDING SUPPLIES; 65. INTERIOR
        DECORATION.
47. FOOD, MISCELLANEOUS 147
    See also 10. BABY PRODUCTS; 11. BAKED GOODS AND
        BAKING SUPPLIES; 15. BEVERAGES, MISCELLANEOUS;
        20. CANDY AND GUM; 21. CEREALS; 29. CONDIMENTS
        AND SPICES; 33. DAIRY PRODUCTS; 49. FRUITS AND
        NUTS; 74. MEATS; 87. PET FOOD AND PRODUCTS;
        99. RESTAURANTS.
48. FOOTWEAR 152
    See also 26. CLOTHING, MISCELLANEOUS; 123. WARDROBE
        ACCESSORIES.
    FRAGRANCES ... See 84. PERFUMES AND FRAGRANCES.
    FRUIT DRINKS ... See 107. SOFT DRINKS.
49. FRUITS AND NUTS 162
    See also 47. FOOD, MISCELLANEOUS.
    FUEL ... See 9. AUTOMOTIVE SERVICE; 59. HEATING AND
        COOKING FUELS; 88. PETROLEUM PRODUCTS;
        93. PUBLIC UTILITIES.
50. FURNITURE 164
    See also 13. BEDS AND BEDDING; 65. INTERIOR
        DECORATION.
    GAMES ... See 118. TOYS AND GAMES.
    GARDEN PRODUCTS ... See 69. LAWN AND GARDEN
        PRODUCTS.
    GARTERS ... See 61. HOSIERY.

Contents 10

GASOLINE ... See 88. PETROLEUM PRODUCTS.
GAUGES ... See 63. INSTRUMENTS AND GAUGES.
GEMS ... See 67. JEWELRY AND SILVER.

51. GIFTS AND GREETINGS 168
52. GLASS AND CERAMICS 168
See also 23. CHINA.
GLASSES ... See 41. EYEGLASSES.
GLOVES ... See 123. WARDROBE ACCESSORIES.
GLUE ... See 1. ADHESIVES.
53. GOVERNMENT SERVICE 169
See also 92. PUBLIC SERVICE.
GREETINGS ... See 51. GIFTS AND GREETINGS.
GUM ... See 20. CANDY AND GUM.
GUNS ... See 44. FIREARMS.
54. HAIR CARE 170
See also 32. COSMETICS; 116. TOILETRIES.
HANDBAGS ... See 123. WARDROBE ACCESSORIES.
HANDKERCHIEFS ... See 123. WARDROBE ACCESSORIES.
55. HARDWARE 172
See also 18. BUILDING SUPPLIES; 117. TOOLS.
HEALTH AND BEAUTY AIDS ...
See 32. COSMETICS; 116. TOILETRIES.
56. HEALTH AND FITNESS 174
See also 35. DRUGS AND REMEDIES; 98. RECREATIONAL
EQUIPMENT; 108. SPORTING GOODS.
57. HEARING AIDS 175
58. HEATING AND AIR CONDITIONING 175
See also 37. ELECTRICAL PRODUCTS AND SERVICE;
60. HOME APPLIANCES AND EQUIPMENT.
59. HEATING AND COOKING FUELS 178
See also 88. PETROLEUM PRODUCTS.
HERBS ... See 29. CONDIMENTS AND SPICES.
60. HOME APPLIANCES AND EQUIPMENT................. 180
See also 58. HEATING AND AIR CONDITIONING;
68. KITCHEN PRODUCTS AND UTENSILS.
HOME MAINTENANCE ... See 24. CLEANING AND
LAUNDRY PRODUCTS; 86. PEST CONTROL.
61. HOSIERY 188
See also 26. CLOTHING, MISCELLANEOUS; 48. FOOTWEAR;
121. UNDERWEAR; 123. WARDROBE ACCESSORIES.
62. HOTELS AND MOTELS 190
See also 119. TRAVEL.
INSECTICIDES ... See 86. PEST CONTROL.
63. INSTRUMENTS AND GAUGES 192
64. INSURANCE 193
See also 43. FINANCIAL INSTITUTIONS AND SERVICES;
66. INVESTMENT.

65. INTERIOR DECORATION 200
See also **18. BUILDING SUPPLIES; 46. FLOOR COVERINGS;
50. FURNITURE; 82. PAINT AND PAINTING SUPPLIES.**

66. INVESTMENT 201
See also **43. FINANCIAL INSTITUTIONS AND SERVICES;
64. INSURANCE.**

JETS . . . See **3. AEROSPACE; 4. AIR TRAVEL AND CARGO.**

67. JEWELRY AND SILVER 202
See also **123. WARDROBE ACCESSORIES.**

JOB PLACEMENT . . . See **40. EMPLOYMENT AGENCIES.**

JUICES . . . See **15. BEVERAGES, MISCELLANEOUS.**

68. KITCHEN PRODUCTS AND UTENSILS 205
See also **11. BAKED GOODS AND BAKING SUPPLIES;
23. CHINA; 60. HOME APPLIANCES AND EQUIPMENT.**

KNITTING SUPPLIES . . . See **103. SEWING AND KNITTING
SUPPLIES.**

LAMPS . . . See **70. LIGHTING PRODUCTS.**

LAUNDRY PRODUCTS . . . See **24. CLEANING AND LAUNDRY
PRODUCTS.**

69. LAWN AND GARDEN PRODUCTS 206
See also **86. PEST CONTROL.**

70. LIGHTING PRODUCTS 208
See also **37. ELECTRICAL PRODUCTS AND SERVICE;
60. HOME APPLIANCES AND EQUIPMENT; 65. INTERIOR
DECORATION.**

LINENS . . . See **13. BEDS AND BEDDING.**

LINGERIE . . . See **121. UNDERWEAR.**

71. LIQUORS 210
See also **14. BEER AND ALE; 15. BEVERAGES,
MISCELLANEOUS; 125. WINES.**

LOCKS . . . See **55. HARDWARE.**

72. LUGGAGE 218
See also **119. TRAVEL.**

LUMBER . . . See **18. BUILDING SUPPLIES.**

73. MACHINERY 220
See also **37. ELECTRICAL PRODUCTS AND SERVICE;
42. FARMING SUPPLIES AND EQUIPMENT; 120. TRUCKS
AND TRUCKING INDUSTRY.**

MAGAZINES . . . See **85. PERIODICALS AND NEWSPAPERS.**

MAINTENANCE . . . See **24. CLEANING AND LAUNDRY
PRODUCTS.**

MAKE-UP . . . See **32. COSMETICS.**

MARKETING . . . See **2. ADVERTISING.**

MEASURING DEVICES . . . See **63. INSTRUMENTS AND
GAUGES.**

74. MEATS 222
See also **47. FOOD, MISCELLANEOUS.**

Contents 12

MEDICATIONS ... See 35. DRUGS AND REMEDIES.

75. METALS INDUSTRY 224
    See also 18. BUILDING SUPPLIES.

76. MISCELLANEOUS 226
    MOTELS ... See 62. HOTELS AND MOTELS.
    MOTOR OIL ... See 88. PETROLEUM PRODUCTS.

77. MOTORCYCLES 226
    See also 7. AUTOMOBILES; 98. RECREATIONAL EQUIPMENT.

78. MOVIES AND ENTERTAINMENT 226
    See also 5. AUDIO EQUIPMENT; 17. BROADCASTING;
        89. PHOTOGRAPHIC EQUIPMENT; 112. TELEVISIONS;
        122. VIDEO EQUIPMENT.

79. MOVING AND STORAGE 227
    See also 120. TRUCKS AND TRUCKING INDUSTRY.

80. MUSICAL INSTRUMENTS 228
    NAUTICAL SUPPLIES ... See 16. BOATS AND BOATING
        EQUIPMENT.
    NEWSPAPERS ... See 85. PERIODICALS AND NEWSPAPERS.
    NOTIONS ... See 103. SEWING AND KNITTING SUPPLIES.
    NUTS ... See 49. FRUITS AND NUTS.

81. OFFICE EQUIPMENT AND SUPPLIES.................. 231
    See also 28. COMPUTER EQUIPMENT; 30. COPYING
        EQUIPMENT; 83. PAPER PRODUCTS; 126. WRITING
        INSTRUMENTS.
    OUTBOARD MOTORS ... See 16. BOATS AND BOATING
        EQUIPMENT.
    OUTDOOR SUPPLIES ... See 98. RECREATIONAL
        EQUIPMENT; 108. SPORTING GOODS.
    OVENS ... See 60. HOME APPLIANCES AND EQUIPMENT.

82. PAINT AND PAINTING SUPPLIES 235
    See also 65. INTERIOR DECORATION.

83. PAPER PRODUCTS 239
    See also 68. KITCHEN PRODUCTS AND UTENSILS;
        81. OFFICE EQUIPMENT AND SUPPLIES.
    PENCILS ... See 126. WRITING INSTRUMENTS.
    PENS ... See 126. WRITING INSTRUMENTS.

84. PERFUMES AND FRAGRANCES 244
    See also 12. BATH ACCESSORIES; 32. COSMETICS;
        104. SHAVING SUPPLIES; 116. TOILETRIES.

85. PERIODICALS AND NEWSPAPERS 245
    See also 94. PUBLISHING.

86. PEST CONTROL... 263
    See also 22. CHEMICAL INDUSTRY; 69. LAWN AND GARDEN
        PRODUCTS.

87. PET FOOD AND PRODUCTS............................. 264
    See also 47. FOOD, MISCELLANEOUS; 86. PEST CONTROL.

13   **Contents**

88. PETROLEUM PRODUCTS 265
    See also 9. AUTOMOTIVE SERVICE; 59. HEATING AND
       COOKING FUELS.
    PHARMACEUTICAL PRODUCTS ... See 35. DRUGS AND
       REMEDIES.
    PHONOGRAPHIC EQUIPMENT ... See 5. AUDIO
       EQUIPMENT.
    PHONOGRAPHS ... See 5. AUDIO EQUIPMENT.
89. PHOTOGRAPHIC EQUIPMENT 270
    See also 78. MOVIES AND ENTERTAINMENT.
    PHYSICAL FITNESS ... See 56. HEALTH AND FITNESS.
    PIPES ... See 105. SMOKING ACCESSORIES.
    PLUMBING SUPPLIES ... See 55. HARDWARE.
90. POLITICAL ISSUES 272
    See also 91. PRESIDENTIAL CAMPAIGNS.
    POTTERY ... See 52. GLASS AND CERAMICS.
91. PRESIDENTIAL CAMPAIGNS 272
    See also 90. POLITICAL ISSUES.
92. PUBLIC SERVICE 299
    See also 53. GOVERNMENT SERVICE.
93. PUBLIC UTILITIES 300
94. PUBLISHING 301
    See also 85. PERIODICALS AND NEWSPAPERS.
95. RADIO EQUIPMENT 302
    See also 5. AUDIO EQUIPMENT;
       111. TELECOMMUNICATIONS.
96. RAIL TRAVEL AND CARGO 306
    See also 119. TRAVEL.
    RANGES ... See 60. HOME APPLIANCES AND EQUIPMENT.
97. RECORDINGS 310
    See also 5. AUDIO EQUIPMENT.
    RECORD PLAYERS ... See 5. AUDIO EQUIPMENT.
    RECORDS ... See 97. RECORDINGS.
98. RECREATIONAL EQUIPMENT.......................... 311
    See also 16. BOATS AND BOATING EQUIPMENT;
       44. FIREARMS; 45. FISHING SUPPLIES; 56. HEALTH AND
       FITNESS; 77. MOTORCYCLES; 108. SPORTING GOODS;
       109. SWIMWEAR; 118. TOYS AND GAMES.
    REFRIGERATORS ... See 60. HOME APPLIANCES AND
       EQUIPMENT.
    RELISHES ... See 29. CONDIMENTS AND SPICES.
    REMEDIES ... See 35. DRUGS AND REMEDIES.
99. RESTAURANTS 312
    See also 47. FOOD, MISCELLANEOUS.
100. RETAIL STORES 312
    SCALES ... See 63. INSTRUMENTS AND GAUGES.
101. SCHOOLS 314

Contents   14

102. SEA TRAVEL AND CARGO 315
     See also 16. BOATS AND BOATING EQUIPMENT;
        119. TRAVEL.
     SEEDS . . . See 42. FARMING SUPPLIES AND EQUIPMENT.

103. SEWING AND KNITTING SUPPLIES 317
     See also 113. TEXTILES.
     SHAMPOO . . . See 54. HAIR CARE.

104. SHAVING SUPPLIES 318
     See also 12. BATH ACCESSORIES; 84. PERFUMES AND
        FRAGRANCES; 106. SOAP; 116. TOILETRIES.
     SHIPPING . . . See 3. AEROSPACE; 96. RAIL TRAVEL AND
        CARGO; 102. SEA TRAVEL AND CARGO; 120. TRUCKS
        AND TRUCKING INDUSTRY.
     SHOES . . . See 48. FOOTWEAR.
     SILVER . . . See 67. JEWELRY AND SILVER.
     SILVERWARE . . . See 67. JEWELRY AND SILVER.
     SKIN CARE . . . See 32. COSMETICS; 116. TOILETRIES.

105. SMOKING ACCESSORIES 321
     See also 115. TOBACCO PRODUCTS.

106. SOAP 323
     See also 10. BABY PRODUCTS; 12. BATH ACCESSORIES;
        24. CLEANING AND LAUNDRY PRODUCTS; 104. SHAVING
        SUPPLIES; 116. TOILETRIES.
     SOCIAL ISSUES . . . See 90. POLITICAL ISSUES.
     SOCKS . . . See 61. HOSIERY.
     SODA . . . See 107. SOFT DRINKS.

107. SOFT DRINKS 325
     See also 15. BEVERAGES, MISCELLANEOUS; 27. COFFEE;
        110. TEA.
     SOFTWARE . . . See 28. COMPUTER EQUIPMENT.
     SPICES . . . See 29. CONDIMENTS AND SPICES.

108. SPORTING GOODS 328
     See also 16. BOATS AND BOATING EQUIPMENT;
        44. FIREARMS; 45. FISHING SUPPLIES; 56. HEALTH AND
        FITNESS; 98. RECREATIONAL EQUIPMENT;
        109. SWIMWEAR; 118. TOYS AND GAMES.
     STATIONERY SUPPLIES . . . See 81. OFFICE EQUIPMENT
        AND SUPPLIES; 83. PAPER PRODUCTS; 126. WRITING
        INSTRUMENTS.
     STEREOS . . . See 5. AUDIO EQUIPMENT.
     STOCKINGS . . . See 61. HOSIERY.
     STORAGE . . . See 79. MOVING AND STORAGE.
     STOVES . . . See 60. HOME APPLIANCES AND EQUIPMENT.
     SUNGLASSES . . . See 41. EYEGLASSES.
     SWEETS . . . See 20. CANDY AND GUM.

109. SWIMWEAR 330
    See also 26. CLOTHING, MISCELLANEOUS;
        98. RECREATIONAL EQUIPMENT; 108. SPORTING
        GOODS.
    TABLEWARE ... See 23. CHINA; 67. JEWELRY AND SILVER.
    TAPE DECKS ... See 5. AUDIO EQUIPMENT.
    TAPES ... See 97. RECORDINGS.
110. TEA 331
    See also 15. BEVERAGES, MISCELLANEOUS; 27. COFFEE;
        107. SOFT DRINKS.
111. TELECOMMUNICATIONS 332
    See also 17. BROADCASTING; 95. RADIO EQUIPMENT.
112. TELEVISIONS 334
    See also 38. ELECTRONICS INDUSTRY; 60. HOME
        APPLIANCES AND EQUIPMENT; 78. MOVIES AND
        ENTERTAINMENT; 122. VIDEO EQUIPMENT.
113. TEXTILES 335
    See also 65. INTERIOR DECORATION; 103. SEWING AND
        KNITTING SUPPLIES.
    TIMEPIECES ... See 124. WATCHES AND CLOCKS.
114. TIRES 337
    See also 8. AUTOMOTIVE PARTS AND PRODUCTS.
115. TOBACCO PRODUCTS 338
    See also 105. SMOKING ACCESSORIES.
116. TOILETRIES 348
    See also 12. BATH ACCESSORIES; 32. COSMETICS;
        34. DENTAL CARE; 54. HAIR CARE; 84. PERFUMES AND
        FRAGRANCES; 104. SHAVING SUPPLIES; 106. SOAP.
117. TOOLS 350
    See also 55. HARDWARE.
    TOOTHPASTE ... See 34. DENTAL CARE.
    TOURISM ... See 119. TRAVEL.
118. TOYS AND GAMES 352
    See also 10. BABY PRODUCTS; 98. RECREATIONAL
        EQUIPMENT; 108. SPORTING GOODS.
    TRACTORS ... See 42. FARMING SUPPLIES AND EQUIPMENT.
    TRANSPORTATION ... See 4. AIR TRAVEL AND CARGO;
        19. BUS LINES; 96. RAIL TRAVEL AND CARGO; 102. SEA
        TRAVEL AND CARGO; 120. TRUCKS AND TRUCKING
        INDUSTRY.
119. TRAVEL 354
    See also 4. AIR TRAVEL AND CARGO; 6. AUTOMOBILE
        RENTAL SERVICES; 19. BUS LINES; 36. ECONOMIC
        DEVELOPMENT; 62. HOTELS AND MOTELS;
        72. LUGGAGE; 79. MOVING AND STORAGE; 96. RAIL
        TRAVEL AND CARGO; 102. SEA TRAVEL AND CARGO.

Contents   16

TRAVELERS CHECKS . . . See 43. FINANCIAL INSTITUTIONS
AND SERVICES; 119. TRAVEL.

120. TRUCKS AND TRUCKING INDUSTRY 357
See also 42. FARMING SUPPLIES AND EQUIPMENT;
73. MACHINERY; 79. MOVING AND STORAGE.

TYPEWRITERS . . . See 81. OFFICE EQUIPMENT AND
SUPPLIES.

UMBRELLAS . . . See 123. WARDROBE ACCESSORIES.

121. UNDERWEAR 359
See also 26. CLOTHING, MISCELLANEOUS; 61. HOSIERY.

UTENSILS . . . See 68. KITCHEN PRODUCTS AND UTENSILS.

VARNISH . . . See 82. PAINT AND PAINTING SUPPLIES.

122. VIDEO EQUIPMENT 362
See also 78. MOVIES AND ENTERTAINMENT;
112. TELEVISIONS.

WALLETS . . . See 123. WARDROBE ACCESSORIES.

123. WARDROBE ACCESSORIES 362
See also 41. EYEGLASSES; 48. FOOTWEAR; 61. HOSIERY;
67. JEWELRY AND SILVER.

124. WATCHES AND CLOCKS 364

WHISKEY . . . See 71. LIQUORS.

125. WINES 367
See also 14. BEER AND ALE; 15. BEVERAGES,
MISCELLANEOUS; 71. LIQUORS.

126. WRITING INSTRUMENTS 369
See also 81. OFFICE EQUIPMENT AND SUPPLIES.

Foreword

Throughout history, as long as language has been employed in any form, slogans have been formulated and promulgated. As a means of focusing attention and exhorting to action they long have been and still remain most effective; as an aspect of language they are illustrative of the intimate relationship of thought, word, and deed. Although the word *slogan* itself takes its origin from the Gaelic *sluagh-ghairm* 'host-cry,' a battle cry of the Scottish clans, its meaning has broadened to include the catchwords and phrases used by religious, political, and other groups. Recently we have witnessed a huge proliferation of slogans with a commercial purpose, saturating print and electronic media. But in fact slogans have been exploited and made popular for many centuries, in different cultures, and with a variety of intentions, as the following list indicates:

Let my people go. (Exodus 5:1)

Know thyself. (Inscription from the oracle at Delphi)

Delenda est Carthago. 'Carthage must be destroyed.' (Cato the Censor's unswerving opinion given during any discussion he joined in the Roman senate)

Love thy neighbor as thyself. (Exodus 19:18, Matthew 19:19, *et al.*)

Liberté! Égalité! Fraternité! 'Liberty! Equality! Brotherhood!' (rallying cry of the French Revolution)

Remember the *Maine.* (used to incite warlike fervor at the time of the Spanish-American War)

Drink Coca-Cola. (simple but effective, translated into many languages)

These examples are all famous, perhaps obvious. But many other verbal combinations, not normally thought of as slogans, are in fact, or have been used as such. Consider, for instance, the Ten Commandments and the Beatitudes, the phrase *God save the king,* even song titles such as

Love makes the world go 'round and *Give peace a chance*—all have characteristics common to effective slogans.

My own definition of a slogan is a group of words that promise a reward in a dramatic way: easy to read, easy to say, and easy to remember. To explore the nature of this linguistic phenomenon, let us look at slogans used in advertising and promotions.

Powerful enough to kill a rabbit.

This is the first slogan I can remember. It appeared in a small advertisement for a super slingshot and instantly ignited my imagination. It promised a reward that I simply could not resist, especially at that hunting age of ten.

Make your own ruts.

These four words appeared on road signs on a clam shell road between Charleston, South Carolina and Folly Beach. They challenged drivers to make their own ruts instead of driving down the old ones and making them deeper. Surprisingly enough the slogan worked and the clam shells were crushed into one smooth surface. Years later I used this story in my talks to young people about choosing their careers. I urged them to "make your own ruts" in life.

Little did I realize at the time that some day I would be deeply involved in writing advertising and slogans. Although my ambition had been to write for motion pictures, I ended up in 1933 as a copywriter in an advertising agency. I shall never forget the huge photo mural of a crowd which dominated the reception room of Ruthrauff & Ryan. Under it was this slogan:

To sell them, you must know them.

R&R's philosophy was to speak to people in the language they could understand. Use simple words. Use the words that wear in and don't wear out. No big words. R&R's house advertisements and promotional booklets reflected this philosophy:

Slow down the bandwagon, the elephants can't keep up.

Now you can beat the drum, Junior, here comes the commercial.

The agency was already well known for creating the "B.O." (body odor) advertisements in magazines and newspapers for Lifebuoy Health Soap. This was at a time when radio was just beginning to catch the public's attention as well as mine. Soon I switched from print advertising to creating and editing radio copy and slogans.

One Monday morning after a foggy weekend, Pete Barnum, a radio producer, shuffled into my office complaining that he had been unable to sleep over the weekend. Asked why, he said that a foghorn had kept him half-awake blasting away what sounded to him like B...O...! It was the birth of the B.O. foghorn for Lifebuoy radio commercials. Crowds chanted it, youngsters imitated it. Radio gave a new dimension to the slogan "Beware of B.O." and multiplied its effectiveness. Sales soared.

Such success as this one made other advertisers shift to radio because they thought they could see a pot of gold over the horizon. Showmanship, however, was but half the story. In their zeal, advertisers often forgot the other half: salesmanship. Thus many slogans created tremendous attention but failed to sell the product. To draw attention to our own success we developed the slogan:

Entertain them, yes, but don't forget to sell them!

It has been my experience that the most effective slogans for advertising emerge only after a thorough study of the product, what the product will do for the consumer, and which consumers are the best prospects. The effective advertising slogan is really a synthesis of these and comes out of the roots of the product itself. Similar criteria can be used to test any sort of slogan.

The *staging* of a slogan is tremendously important and can make a big difference in its success or failure.

In print, does the type talk?

In radio, does the sound reinforce the words?

In television, does the picture strengthen the sales story?

Of course, there are many, many, more considerations in the production of a slogan, whatever medium is used.

The happy little washday song added tremendously to Rinso-White, the sonovox train to Bromo-seltzer, and the "sing it again" song to Virginia Dare. These successes with slogans at R&R attracted that great merchant and legendary salesman, George Washington Hill, President of the American Tobacco Company. He loved to sloganize his sales pitch for his products. His overall sales philosophy is best illustrated by two of them.

Quality of product is essential to continuing success.

Not how much ... but how well.

These he had made in bronze plaques for his executives. When I started working on his account he gave them to me. I still have both on my desk.

Our first assignment was for Pall Mall Famous Cigarettes. Mr. Hill had been running spectacularly beautiful color advertisements for this brand without the sales results he expected. We persuaded him to dramatize his sales story in radio with the now famous commercials containing the slogan:

Modern design makes the big difference as America moves ahead .... on land ... in the air ... and on the sea.

The sound effects were attention-getting, particularly the destroyer whistle that ended with "beep, beep, BEEP!"

To his slogan:

Pall Mall's greater length travels the smoke further ...

We added:

... gets rid of heat and bite on the way.

When we presented the latter copy change he simply said, "Gentlemen, you have put the pants on my copy."

The sales success of Pall Mall encouraged Mr. Hill to outbid the competitors for the services of the Jack Benny Show, which had the largest audience in radio. We spent a summer preparing commercials for the new season, but just before the show returned to the air, Mr. Hill decided to shift Lucky Strike cigarettes to the Jack Benny spots. Pall Mall was off the air and off the cigarette counters.

Lucky Strike green has gone to war.

Mr. Hill assigned us the Jack Benny Show and then challenged us to come up with some new copy to make his investment pay off. What a challenge it was! Talented writers had been working on Lucky copy for years:

Reach for a Lucky instead of a sweet.

Luckies are kind to your throat.

LS/MFT... Lucky Strike means fine tobacco.

So round, so firm, so fully packed—so free and easy on the draw.

What an assignment to top those slogans!

The last night before our presentation to Mr. Hill we had nothing worthwhile to show and we were desperate about the outcome of the meeting. To break the tension I told a story about my college roommate who smoked a pipe and was under 5′3″ with Adler Elevators. He would inhale until he was bursting with smoke, hold the smoke in his lungs for a minute or two and then exhale; for the next few minutes he was enveloped in smoke. Looking back on this recollection, I said, "I have never seen anyone drag smoke so deep-down—" I stopped. The idea flashed in our collective minds:

For deep-down smoking enjoyment smoke that smoke of fine tobacco—Lucky Strike.

I never had it typed. I showed it to Mr. Hill in my handwriting on yellow paper. For several minutes he was silent. Then he got up from his desk, took off the hat he always wore—the one with the salmon fly attached—dusted the floor with it as he bowed, and said, "Mr. Bayles, that is the greatest idea since Mr. Lasker gave me 'Luckies are kind to your throat' Congratulations!"

Following a season of the Jack Benny Show I decided in 1946 to start a new advertising agency with Ray Sullivan, Don Stauffer and Bob Colwell known as Sullivan, Stauffer, Colwell & Bayles, Inc., later shortened to SSC & B. With the war over I felt there was a new challenge ahead to get back to writing advertisements instead of valentines. One of our first accounts was Arrid deodorant and it was in deep trouble. The market consisted of deodorants that stop odor and anti-perspirants that stop perspiration. Consumers did not distinguish the difference. Arrid did both and it was our job to educate them. We tested hundreds of copy ideas and finally hit on:

Don't be half-safe. Be completely safe. Use Arrid—to be sure.

In print it made the point; in radio the echo chamber dramatized it and the "Volga Boatman" made it singable. Sales took off. The slogan "Don't be half-safe" started us on our way to building our new agency and a number of accounts signed with us.

On Good Friday 1948, I was alone in our offices at the Marguery Apartments on Park Avenue when a call came in from Mr. Paul Hahn, President of the American Cigarette & Cigar Company, a subsidiary of the American Tobacco Company. He asked if I could locate Don Stauffer and come down to see him at two o'clock at 111 Fifth Avenue. With some difficulty I got in touch with Don and we arrived together at Mr. Hahn's office at two o'clock sharp. His first question was, "Don and Heagan, are you still interested in handling the Pall Mall account?" Stunned, we answered, "Yes, we most certainly are." He simply said, "Gentlemen, you have the Pall Mall account."

The sales of Pall Mall were increasing at a satisfactory rate and Mr. Hahn wanted us to be extra careful about what we did. Once again we shifted out of print, this time to television, where we thought we could dramatize the filtering story with this slogan:

Filters the smoke on the way to your throat—filters the smoke and makes it mild.

Then we developed the animated puff chart to illustrate another slogan:

Puff by puff Pall Mall's greater length of fine mellow tobaccos filters the smoke on the way to your throat ... filters the smoke and makes it mild.

The real breakthrough came when we hit upon the negative slogan:

Guard against throat-scratch!

and combined it with our positive story of filtering "Puff by puff ..." All of this was capped with the slogan:

Outstanding ... and they are mild.

Pall Mall sales climbed and climbed until Pall Mall Famous Cigarettes became the leading brand in the U.S. and set the stage for filter-tip cigarettes and their filtering action.

In analyzing various businesses and their products over the years we wrote two slogans to express the philosophy of our agency:

The facts that built a business are often forgotten.

The High Cost of Goofing.

These two brief statements served over the years as constant reminders to those in our agency of the need for productivity and "doing homework." They encapsulized ideas and principles that we considered essential to our doing business properly, and as such proved to be very effective slogans.

One could go on for many more pages with analysis and commentary on the history and effectiveness of slogans, but we prefer to offer the suggestions that we have and allow the reader to use them and his own ideas while perusing the thousands of examples contained in *Slogans*. We hope that what is offered here will help the reader better appreciate slogans, both in their contribution to the impact of advertising on sales and, in another light, as effective and affective elements of language.

S. Heagan Bayles, Founder Chairman
Sullivan, Stauffer, Colwell & Bayles, Inc.

Introduction

Slogans is a compilation of more than 6,000 entries, the majority from American commercial advertising, with a substantial number of additional slogans having political and social intent. Such a sizable collection, originating over a broad span of time and from diverse provenances, may seem at first a bit difficult to bring into focus. Indeed, browsing through the book will reveal slogans both familiar and obscure, inspired and matter-of-fact, ludicrous and deadly serious, each with its own intended purpose. In order to provide some insight into the character, breadth, and potential usefulness of *Slogans*, we offer below several selections with comments to illustrate particular points of interest.

Among the many thousands of slogans from commercial advertising, particular ones are notable for being exceptionally popular and enduring. Some even transcend their original purpose and meaning so far that they become part of the lexicon of English.

For instance:

Breakfast of Champions
—Wheaties breakfast cereal

This slogan has become so familiar that it has been used as the title of a novel; it is also used as a jocular reference to the partaking of beer in the early morning. Similar in its popularity and extended application is:

99 44/100% pure
—Ivory soap

Sometimes with other words taking the place of *pure*, this phrase is commonly used to connote near perfection within human limitations. Other such venerable slogans, all long in use and so well established as to have become the stuff of allusion, are the following:

Cover the earth
—Sherwin-Williams paint (accompanied by the familiar logo of the earth being coated in paint)

23

Hasn't scratched yet
—*Bon Ami cleanser* (with the famous logo of the newly
hatched chick)

His master's voice
—*RCA Victor* (with the familiar logo of the faithful dog
perched attentively before the horn of a Victrola)

Think
—*IBM* (a corporate slogan; now found on placards in
many languages)

When it rains, it pours
—*Morton salt* (originally a proverbial expression, now
more familiar to many as the slogan)

Turning from the renowned slogans, we would be remiss to
ignore the many in the collection that contain a bit of humor,
frequently based upon a pun:

Our business is going to the dogs
—*Champion Animal Food Co.*

Try them on for sighs
—*Strutwear nylons*

What foods these morsels be
—*J. N. Adams Tea Room, Buffalo, N.Y.*

Some have a touch of down-home common sense mixed with humor:

**If Purina chows won't make your hens lay, they
are roosters**
—*Ralston Purina Co.*

**If you think clothes don't make a difference, try
walking down the street without any**
—*Wolf Tailoring*

These examples, which strike us as perhaps funnier than
originally intended, serve to introduce another class of humorous
slogans, those that we find ridiculous:

Every man should wear at least three straw hats
—*National Association of Straw Hat Manufacturers*

Surely they couldn't have meant *at once*? Another entry seems fairly
standard until one reads the name of the company:

**Since 1720, a family heritage of careful boat
building**
—*C. P. Leek & Sons Inc.*

One would think that in their case the owners might have been wiser
not to use the family name for the business. At least the R. A. Flatt
Tire Co. showed some imagination, trying to make the most out of
their seemingly unfortunate name:

Lots of Flatt tires running around

It is difficult, however, to determine the motives of the authors and promulgators of slogans. Clearly, humor can serve to gratify the buying public and help fix the company or product name in the mind. Ridicule may seem a detriment, carrying the humor too far; but perhaps it kindles a spark of sympathy and becomes an *advantage.* If so, then judicious exploitation of self-ridicule through slogans may well function as a marketing device.

Thus far, we have spoken only of the commercial aspects, but there are hundreds of examples of slogans that attract our interest for what they have to say about social and political issues. Every slogan reveals something about its own time, and as a means to catch and hold the public's attention they have been widely used and disseminated throughout American history. Hence, slogans are a part of our culture and can offer a glimpse at history. In them we can see illustration of things as mundane as the fact that products and prices have changed:

The car of a thousand speeds
—Owen Magnetic motor car

All you can eat for a nickel
—Baby Ruth candy bar

Man alive! Two for five!
—Standard Cigar Co.

Slogans may also reflect the attitudes and behavior of our changing society:

For digestion's sake, smoke Camels
—Camel cigarettes

For the one man in 7 who shaves every day
—Glider brushless shave

The gum with the fascinating artificial flavor
—Wrigley's gum

To lighten the burden of womankind
—Crystal washer

The political arena has long exploited the advantages of slogans; examples contained herein document campaigns and causes throughout our history. In fact, the largest single category in *Slogans* is **PRESIDENTIAL CAMPAIGNS**, with more than 400 entries spanning the 19th and 20th centuries. Some of these are quite famous:

Don't swap horses in the middle of the stream
—Abraham Lincoln, 1864

Give-'em-Hell Harry
—Harry S. Truman, 1948

Tippecanoe and Tyler too
—William Henry Harrison, 1840

Others seem unfortunate or a bit bizarre:

> **Adlai and Estes are the bestes**
> *—Adlai Stevenson and Estes Kefauver, 1956*
>
> **Dewey or don't we?**
> *—Thomas E. Dewey, 1948*
>
> **Son of his grandfather**
> *—Benjamin Harrison, 1888* (grandson of W. H. Harrison)
>
> **We Polked 'em in '44, we'll Pierce 'em in '52**
> *—Franklin Pierce, 1852*

A good number within this category reveal the bitterness that can be exchanged in campaigning for the White House:

> **A vote for Coolidge is a vote for chaos**
> *—John W. Davis, 1924*
>
> **Hari-kari with Barry**
> *—Lyndon B. Johnson, 1964*
>
> **Twenty years of treason**
> *—Dwight D. Eisenhower, 1952*
>
> **We want Willkie—third term means dictatorship**
> *—Wendell Willkie, 1940*

Lastly, we note the employment of slogans in campaigns of a more general, social nature, where the purpose is to capture the attention of the public for education or propaganda:

> **Remember Pearl Harbor**
> *—U.S. rallying cry during World War II*
>
> **Only you can prevent forest fires**
> *—public service announcement* (promulgated by the familiar cartoon character, Smokey the Bear)
>
> **We shall overcome**
> *—in support of civil rights for black Americans*

There are, doubtless, other aspects that we could investigate and other interests that may be piqued by the analysis of selections from *Slogans*. This brief introduction can only hint at some of the possible applications of the material in this collection; users of the book will, we trust, explore many avenues of research not yet considered. The editors invite the comments and suggestions of those who make use of *Slogans* with the hope that we might expand and improve upon what has so far been compiled.

Frank R. Abate

Essex, Connecticut
April 1984

How To Use This Book

The information presented in *Slogans* has been organized with the intention of providing the utmost accessibility, versatility, and ease of use. The text offers an organization of the slogans by categories, similar to that of a thesaurus, bringing together material of a related nature. This allows for comparison and contrast that is difficult or impossible with dictionary format; thus, the inherent usefulness and interest of such a sizable compilation is greatly enhanced. At the same time, the advantages of dictionary order are not overlooked: detailed indexes, including, in one alphabetic order, all slogans and categories (in Index I), as well as their sources (in Index II)—product, company, individual, and institutional names—furnish the opportunity for alphabetic access to all pertinent information.

Under each of the 126 category sections used in the text can be found the appropriate slogans, listed in alphabetic order, along with source information as complete as could be verified by our research. In addition, all categories are numbered, as are the slogans under each, allowing handy numerical reference from the indexes to the text. The numbered list of categories appears in the Contents, where there can also be found ample cross references, both between related categories and from synonymous terms to the actual categories used in the book. For further convenience, the cross references have been included in the text at the appropriate places.

SLOGANS

A

1. ADHESIVES

1. **A million and one uses**
   —Fix-All Liquid Cement Co.
2. **Best glue in the joint**
   —(*Elmer's Glue All*) Borden Chemical Div., Borden Inc.
3. **Holds the world together**
   —H. B. Fuller Co.
4. **Join with Bostik for better bonding**
   —B. B. Chemical Div., United Shoe Machinery Corp.
5. **Leader in adhesive technology**
   —H. B. Fuller Co.
6. **Mends everything but a broken heart**
   —Fix-All Liquid Cement Co.

2. ADVERTISING

1. **Action people**
   —(*Yellow Pages*) AT&T
2. **Advertise and realize**
   —Pencil Specialty Co.
3. **Advertise for action**
   —(*Yellow Pages*) AT&T
4. **Advertising is the power of an idea multiplied**
   —D'Arcy Advertising Co.
5. **Advertising that follows through to sales**
   —Lithographers National Association.
6. **Advertising with a basic idea**
   —J. Walter Thompson Co.
7. **An agency is known by the clients it keeps**
   —Gottschalk-Humphrey.
8. **A true expression of heart-felt sympathy**
   —Florists Association.
9. **Better business is our aim**
   —Business Advertising Agency.
10. **Bright by day, light by night**
    —Pyrograph Advertising Sign Corp.

31

2. **ADVERTISING** *cont.*

11. **Built on bedrock**
—Johnson, Read & Co.

12. **Creators of direct mail literature**
—D. H. Ahrend Co.

13. **Displays that move goods**
—Julian Maas Co.

14. **Find it faster in the Yellow Pages**
—AT&T

15. **Idea Creators, not just illustrators**
—Martin Ullman Studios.

16. **In Federation there is power**
—Federal Advertising Agency.

17. **Let your fingers do the walking**
—(*Yellow Pages*) AT&T

18. **Merchandise well displayed is half sold**
—Russell H. Spoor Co.

19. **Meredith moves merchandise**
—Meredith Publishing Co.

20. **More for the money**
—J. Walter Thompson Co.

21. **No matter what kind or what priced merchandise you make, the Plain Dealer alone will sell it**
—*Cleveland Plain Dealer.*

22. **Put it up to men who know your market**
—Federal Advertising Agency.

23. **Repetition makes reputation**
—Emil Brisacher & Staff.

24. **Service beyond the contract**
—Haas & Howell.

25. **Signs of long life**
—Artkraft Sign Co.

26. **Teaching the millions to buy**
—Millis Advertising Co.

27. **The backbone of New York advertising**
—*Sunday American.*

28. **The interrupting idea**
—Federal Advertising Agency.

29. **Thematic advertising**
—Grey Advertising Agency.

30. **The right angle in advertising**
—Collin Armstrong Inc.

2. **ADVERTISING** *cont.*

   31. **The shortest distance between two points**
                                —J. L. Arnold Co.

   32. **Think of it first**
                                  —Ideas Inc.

   33. **To sell millions, tell millions**
                         —National Transitads Inc.

   34. **True salesmanship in print**
                            —Lord & Thomas.

   35. **We'll make you believe in signs**
                —Frederick Advertising & Display Co.

   36. **We stick up for everybody**
                   —(*bill posters*) McClintock Co.

   37. **Where the sun never sets on an unfilled order**
                —Western Newspaper Union.

3. **AEROSPACE**
    See also **4. AIR TRAVEL AND CARGO, 38. ELECTRONICS INDUSTRY**

   1. **Accustomed to the finest . . . you'll find it in a Beechcraft**
                         —Beech Aircraft Corp.

   2. **America's most useful personal planes**
               —(*Stinson*) Consolidated Vultee.

   3. **Built for permanence, calibrated for performance**
                —Bendix Aviation Corp.

   4. **Capability has many faces at Boeing**
                          —Boeing Co.

   5. **Easy to buy, easy to fly**
               —(*Stinson*) Consolidated Vultee.

   6. **Family car of the air**
                     —Cessna Aircraft Co.

   7. **First in creative engineering**
                    —Bendix Aviation Corp.

   8. **Garrett *is* experience**
            —Garrett AiResearch, The Garrett Corp.

   9. **In the air or outer space Douglas gets things done**
                —Douglas Aircraft Co. Inc.

  10. **Look to Lockheed for leadership**
                      —Lockheed Corp.

  11. **Look to the leader for good safe planes you can afford to buy and fly**
                    —Piper Aircraft Corp.

3.   AEROSPACE *cont.*

12. **More people buy Cessna twins than any other make**
—Cessna Aircraft Co.

13. **More people fly Cessna airplanes than any other make**
—Cessna Aircraft Co.

14. **More people have bought Pipers than any other plane in the world**
—Piper Aircraft Corp.

15. **North American Aviation is at work in the fields of the future**
—North American Aviation Inc.

16. **Pacemakers of aviation progress**
—Bell Aircraft Corp.

17. **The business jet that's backed by an airline**
—(*Fan Jet Falcon*) Business Jets Div., Pan American World Airways Inc.

18. **The future is building now at Garrett**
—Garrett AiResearch, The Garrett Corp.

19. **The jet that justifies itself**
—(*Sabreliner*) North American Rockwell Corp.

20. **The modern magic carpet**
—(*helicopters*) Bell Aircraft Corp.

21. **The world is smaller when you fly a Beechcraft**
—Beech Aircraft Corp.

22. **This one means business**
—(*The DH 125*) Hawker Siddeley Group Ltd.

23. **World's first family of jets**
—Boeing Co.

24. **World standard**
—Bell Helicopter Co.

25. **Years ahead in the science of flight**
—Lockheed Corp.

26. **Your personal plane IS HERE**
—Aeronca.

AGRICULTURE ... See 42. FARMING SUPPLIES AND
EQUIPMENT

AIR CONDITIONING ... See 58. HEATING AND AIR
CONDITIONING

4. AIR TRAVEL AND CARGO

See also **3.** AEROSPACE, **119.** TRAVEL

1. **A friend of the family**

   —Air Canada.

2. **A great name in aviation**

   —Pacific Northern Airlines.

3. **Air-freight specialists**

   —Flying Tiger Line Inc.

4. **Airline of the professionals**

   —American Airlines Inc.

5. **All over the world BOAC takes good care of you**

   —British Overseas Airways Corp.

6. **America's favorite way to fly**

   —Eastern Airlines Inc.

7. **America's leading airline**

   —American Airlines Inc.

8. **"A most remarkable airline"**

   —Continental Air Lines Inc.

9. **Australia's round-the-world jet airline**

   —Qantas.

10. **Coast to coast overnight**

    —American Airlines Inc.

11. **Coast to coast to coast**

    —National Airlines Inc.

12. **Delta is ready when you are**

    —Delta Air Lines Inc.

13. **Determined to serve you best**

    —Eastern Airlines Inc.

14. **Don't go to a warm place cold**

    —Eastern Airlines Inc.

15. **Europe's foremost airline**

    —British European Airways.

16. **Europe's most helpful airline**

    —Sabena Belgian World Airlines.

17. **First across the Pacific; first across the Atlantic; first throughout Latin America**

    —Pan American World Airways Inc.

18. **First airline in the Americas**

    —Avianca.

19. **First in airfreight with airfreight first**

    —Flying Tiger Line Inc.

4. **AIR TRAVEL AND CARGO** *cont.*

20. **First in Latin America**
—Pan American World Airways Inc.

21. **First on the Atlantic**
—Pan American World Airways Inc.

22. **First on the Pacific**
—Pan American World Airways Inc.

23. **First 'round the world**
—Pan American World Airways Inc.

24. **Fly anywhere in Europe via Air France.**
—Air France.

25. **Fly the friendly skies of United**
—United Air Lines Inc.

26. **Fly the planes that fly the U. S. Flag**
—Airlines of the U. S.

27. **Gets there first**
—Air Express.

28. **Golden nugget jet service**
—Alaska Airlines Inc.

29. **Great people to fly with**
—Pakistan International Airlines.

30. **Great People to ship with**
—Pakistan International Airlines.

31. **Nationwide, worldwide depend on . . .**
—Trans World Airlines Inc.

32. **Over the Atlantic and across the world**
—British Overseas Airways Corp.

33. **Pan Am Makes the going great**
—Pan American World Airways Inc.

34. **Proud bird with the golden tail**
—Continental Air Lines Inc.

35. **Á votre service**
—Air France.

36. **Sailing the South Pacific skies**
—UTA French Airlines.

37. **See how much better an airline can be**
—Eastern Airlines Inc.

38. **Serving America's billionaires**
—Northwest Airlines Inc.

39. **Specialists in international jet service to Texas or South America**
—Braniff Airways Inc.

4. **AIR TRAVEL AND CARGO** *cont.*

40. **Speedbird service**
—British Overseas Airways Corp.

41. **Swisscare. Worldwide**
—Swiss Air Transport Co. Ltd.

42. **The airline run by fliers**
—Transcontinental & Western.

43. **The airline that knows the South Pacific best**
—Air New Zealand.

44. **The airline that measures the midwest in minutes**
—Ozark Air Lines Inc.

45. **The airline that treats you like a maharajah**
—Air-India.

46. **The airline with the big jets**
—Delta Air Lines Inc.

47. **The Alaska flag line**
—Pacific Northern Airlines.

48. **The calm beauty of Japan at almost the speed of sound**
—Japan Air Lines.

49. **The *Extra Care* Airline**
—United Air Lines Inc.

50. **The fan-jet airline**
—Northwest Airlines Inc.

51. **The friendly way, C. P. A.**
—Canadian Pacific Air Lines.

52. **The jet with the extra engine**
—Western Air Lines Inc.

53. **The main line airway**
—United Air Lines Inc.

54. **The nation's largest airline**
—United Air Lines Inc.

55. **The pioneer of low fares to Europe**
—Icelandic Airlines.

56. **The things we do to make you happy**
—Trans World Airlines Inc.

57. **The unbeatable way to jet home**
—Western Air Lines Inc.

58. **The way to get there**
—Iberia Air Lines of Spain.

59. **The world's largest airline**
—Air France.

4. **AIR TRAVEL AND CARGO** *cont.*

60. **The world's largest independent airline**
—World Airways Inc.

61. **Up up and away**
—Trans World Airlines Inc.

62. **We know where you're going**
—Air France.

63. **Welcome aboard**
—United Air Lines Inc.

64. **We pamper passengers throughout mid-central U.S.A.**
—Lake Central Airlines Inc.

65. **We've earned the trust of American Business**
—Emery Worldwide.

66. **Where only the plane gets more attention than you**
—Iberia Air Lines of Spain.

67. **Why fool around with anyone else?**
—Federal Express.

68. **World's friendliest airline—Panagra**
—Pan American-Grace Airways Inc.

69. **World's largest air cargo carrier**
—Pan American World Airways Inc.

70. **World's largest charter airline**
—World Airways Inc.

71. **World's most dependable air freight service**
—Airborne Freight Corp.

72. **World's most experienced airline**
—Pan American World Airways Inc.

73. **Your air commuter service in 12 busy states**
—Allegheny Airlines Inc.

74. **You're better off with Pan Am**
—Pan American World Airways Inc.

75. **You're not just flying. You're flying the friendly skies.**
—United Air Lines.

76. **You want it. You got it.**
—Purolator Courier.

AIRPLANES ... See 3. AEROSPACE

ALCOHOLIC BEVERAGES ... See 14. BEER AND ALE, 71. LIQUORS, 125. WINES

ALE ... See 14. BEER AND ALE

APPLIANCES ... See **60.** HOME APPLIANCES AND
EQUIPMENT

5. AUDIO EQUIPMENT
See also **38.** ELECTRONICS INDUSTRY, **78.** MOVIES AND
ENTERTAINMENT, **97.** RECORDINGS

1. **Anything else is a compromise**
—(*car stereos*) Concord.

2. **Auto stereo**
—(*car speakers*) Visonik.

3. **Because the music matters**
—(*Pioneer Audio Systems*) Pioneer Electronics (USA) Inc.

4. **Be finicky**
—(*cartridges*) Shure.

5. **Discover what sound is all about**
—James B. Lansing Sound Inc.

6. **Don't just tape it. TDK it.**
—(*cassettes*) TDK Electronics Corp.

7. **Feature rich**
—(*Aiwa*) Selectron International Co.

8. **For those who can hear the difference**
—Pickering and Co. Inc.

9. **Getting closer to the source**
—(*speakers*) EPI.

10. **Great sound starts with the source**
—(*speakers*) Pyle Driver.

11. **His master's voice**
—RCA Corp.

12. **Innovation. Precision. Integrity.**
—(*cartridges*) Audio Technica.

13. **Is it live? Or is it Memorex?**
—(*Memorex recording cassettes*) Memorex Corp.

14. **It speaks for itself**
—(*Audiotape*) Audio Devices Inc.

15. **Just slightly ahead of our time**
—Panasonic.

16. **Kenwood: the sound of leadership**
—(*receivers*) Kenwood Electronics Inc.

17. **Made in Japan by fanatics**
—(*tape decks*) Teac.

18. **Maxell. It's worth it.**
—(*recording tape*) Maxell Corp.

5. **AUDIO EQUIPMENT** *cont.*

19. **Move at the speed of sound**
—(*car stereos*) Clarion.

20. **Our state-of-the-mind is tomorrow's state-of-the-art**
—Harman-Kardon Inc.

21. **Our woofers bark, but don't bite**
—(*car speakers*) Maxima.

22. **Plays all records, natural as life**
—Vitanola Talking Machine Co.

23. **Portable phonographs of distinction**
—Caswell Mfg. Co.

24. **Power & Grace**
—(*speakers*) Electro-Voice Inc.

25. **Products to care for your music**
—Discwasher Inc.

26. **Putting more pleasure in sound**
—(*receivers*) Sansui.

27. **Quality. Technology. Value.**
—(*car stereos*) Maxima.

28. **Setting new standards in sound**
—Electro-Voice Inc.

29. **Simply, the best**
—O'Sullivan Industries Inc.

30. **Sound shapers have no equal**
—(*equalizers*) ADC.

31. **Studio sound for the home**
—(*equalizers*) Numark.

32. **That's life**
—(*cassette decks*) Sanyo.

33. **The answer to all your tape needs**
—(*recording tape*) Maxell Corp.

34. **The choice of professionals**
—(*cartridges*) Stanton.

35. **The leader in solid-state high-fidelity components**
—Harman-Kardon Inc.

36. **The longer you play it, the sweeter it grows**
—Cheney Talking Machine Co.

37. **The most trusted name in sound**
—RCA Corp.

38. **The name that means MUSIC to millions**
—(*Wurlitzer phonograph*).

39. **The one & only**
—(*receivers*) Sony Corp. of America.

5. **AUDIO EQUIPMENT** *cont.*

40. **The phonograph of marvelous tone**
—Vitanola Talking Machine Co.

41. **The phonograph with a soul**
—Edison.

42. **The Science of Sound**
—(*Technics*) Matsushita Electric Corp. of America.

43. **The sound approach to quality**
—Kenwood Electronics Inc.

44. **The sound of excellence!**
—(*amplifiers*) SAE Two.

45. **The tapeway to stereo**
—Sony Corp. of America.

46. **The world leader in tape technology**
—(*recording tape*) TDK Electronics Corp.

47. **The world's "first family" of changers and tape decks**
—BSR (USA) Ltd.

48. **True in every sound**
—Victor Talking Machine Co.

49. **We take you there**
—JVC America Inc.

50. **We want you to hear more music**
—Harman-Kardon Inc.

51. **What you want is a Wollensack**
—(*tape recorders*) Revere-Wollensack Div., Minnesota Mining and Mfg. Co.

52. **When its the sound that moves you**
—(*car stereos*) Jensen.

53. **When you like your music enough**
—(*receivers*) Kenwood Electronics Inc.

54. **Win their way by their play**
—(*phonograph sound boxes*) F. C. Hunt Co.

55. **World's most perfect high fidelity components**
—Empire Scientific Corp.

56. **World's most wonderful phonograph**
—Aeolian Vocalion.

57. **You never heard it so good**
—(*receivers*) Akai.

58. **Your assurance of quality in tape components**
—Viking of Minneapolis Inc.

6. **AUTOMOBILE RENTAL SERVICES**
   See also **7. AUTOMOBILES**

1. **America's largest leasing system**
   —Ford Authorized Leasing System.

2. **Anywhere in the wide world**
   —Hertz Corp.

3. **A pioneer in the leasing field**
   —Emkay Inc.

4. **Car plan management and leasing specialists**
   —Peterson, Howell and Heather.

5. **Let Hertz put *you* in the driver's seat**
   —Hertz Corp.

6. **The biggest *should* do more. It's only right.**
   —Hertz Corp.

7. **The customer is always No. 1**
   —National Car Rental System Inc.

8. **We try harder**
   —Avis Inc.

7. **AUTOMOBILES**
   See also **6. AUTOMOBILE RENTAL SERVICES,**
   8. AUTOMOTIVE PARTS AND PRODUCTS,
   9. AUTOMOTIVE SERVICE

1. **A car for every purse and purpose**
   —General Motors Corp.

2. **A car you can believe in**
   —Volvo of America Corp.

3. **All that's best at lowest price**
   —(*Chevrolet*) General Motors Corp.

4. **America's favorite fun car**
   —(*Mustang*) Ford Motor Co.

5. **America's finest motor car for America's finest families**
   —Pierce-Arrow Motor Car Co.

6. **America's first car**
   —Haynes Automobile Co.

7. **America's first truly fine small car**
   —Marmon Motor Car Co.

8. **America's friendliest factory**
   —Studebaker Corp.

9. **America's lowest-priced fine car**
   —(*Pontiac*) General Motors Corp.

7. AUTOMOBILES *cont.*

10. **America's most distinguished motorcar**
—(*Lincoln Continental*) Ford Motor Co.

11. **America's most luxurious motor car**
—(*Stearns-Knight*) Willys-Overland Inc.

12. **America's smartest car**
—(*Ranier*).

13. **A more enlightened approach**
—(*Mercury*) Ford Motor Co.

14. **As fine as money can build**
—(*Chrysler*) Chrysler Corp.

15. **Ask the man who owns one**
—(*Packard*) Studebaker-Packard Corp.

16. **A twentieth century expression of the French civilization**
—(*Renault*) Renault Inc.

17. **Bared to its bones, it's still the "beauty"**
—(*Buick*) General Motors Corp.

18. **Beautiful beyond belief**
—(*Hudson*) American Motors Corp.

19. **Best bet's Buick**
—(*Buick*) General Motors Corp.

20. **Best built, best backed American cars**
—(*Plymouth*) Chrysler Corp.

21. **Best of all ... it's a Cadillac**
—(*Cadillac*) General Motors Corp.

22. **Best year yet to go Ford!**
—Ford Motor Co.

23. **Better buy Buick**
—(*Buick*) General Motors Corp.

24. **Big-car quality at lowest cost**
—(*Chevrolet*) General Motors Corp.

25. **Body by Fisher**
—(*Fisher automobile bodies*) General Motors Corp.

26. **"Built tough for you"**
—Toyota Motor Distributors Inc.

27. **Dedicated to excellence**
—American Motors Corp.

28. **Driving in its purest form**
—(*Porsche*) Volkswagen of America Inc.

29. **Engineered like no other car in the world**
—(*Mercedes-Benz*) Mercedes-Benz of North America Inc.

7. **AUTOMOBILES** *cont.*

30. **Escape from the ordinary**
—(*Oldsmobile*) General Motors Corp.

31. **Ford has a better idea**
—Ford Motor Co.

32. **Get your hands on a Toyota . . . you'll never let go**
—Toyota Motor Distributors Inc.

33. **Have you driven a Ford . . . lately?**
—Ford Motor Co.

34. **Honda . . . we make it simple**
—(*Honda*) American Honda Motor Co. Inc.

35. **Inexpensive. And built to stay that way.**
—(*Subaru*) Subaru of America Inc.

36. **It's the going thing**
—Ford Motor Co.

37. **Let yourself go . . . Plymouth**
—(*Plymouth*) Chrysler Corp.

38. **Mark of excellence**
—General Motors Corp.

39. **Nothing else is a Volkswagen**
—(*Volkswagen*) Volkswagen of America Inc.

40. **One drive is worth a thousand words**
—(*Thunderbird*) Ford Motor Co.

41. **Only in a Jeep**
—(*Jeep CJ-7*) Jeep Corp.

42. **Probing deeper to serve you better**
—Ford Motor Co. Research Laboratories.

43. **Putting you first, keeps us first**
—(*Chevrolet*) General Motors Corp.

44. **Smart to be seen in, smarter to buy**
—(*Studebaker*) Studebaker Corp.

45. **Socially, America's first motor car**
—(*Packard*) Studebaker-Packard Corp.

46. **So new! So right! So obviously Cadillac!**
—(*Cadillac*) General Motors Corp.

47. **Spend the difference**
—(*Ford*) Ford Motor Co.

48. **Standard of the world**
—(*Cadillac*) General Motors Corp.

49. **Strength, safety, style and speed**
—(*Hudson*) American Motors Corp.

50. **Switch to Dodge and save money**
—(*Dodge*) Chrysler Corp.

7. AUTOMOBILES *cont.*

51. **Take the Studebaker third degree road test**
                    —Studebaker Corp.

52. **Taking charge**
                    —(*Chevrolet*) General Motors Corp.

53. **Technology never felt so comfortable**
                    —(*Ford Tempo*) Ford Motor Co.

54. **Test drive total performance '65**
                    —Ford Motor Co.

55. **The beauty and distinction of custom car styling**
                    —(*Kaiser*) Kaiser-Frazer Corp.

56. **The car of a thousand speeds**
                    —(*Owen Magnetic Motor Car*).

57. **The car of no regrets**
                    —(*King Motor Car*).

58. **The car of the year in eye appeal and buy appeal**
                    —(*Studebaker*) Studebaker Corp.

59. **The car that has everything**
                    —(*Oldsmobile*) General Motors Corp.

60. **The car that is complete**
                    —(*Chevrolet*) General Motors Corp.

61. **The car with a longer life**
                    —(*Westcott*) Westcott Motor Car Co.

62. **The car with the foundation**
                    —(*Commonwealth*).

63. **The difference is valves**
                    —(*Datsun*) Nissan Motor Co.

64. **The great highway performers**
                    —(*Corvair, Monza*) General Motors Corp.

65. **The line is drawn for the future**
    —(*Honda Civic Hatchback*) American Honda Motor Co.
                    Inc.

66. **The Mazda experience**
                    —Mazda Motors of America.

67. **The mini-brutes**
                    —(*Opel Kadett*) General Motors Corp.

68. **The more you look, the more you like**
                    —Mazda Motors of America.

69. **The most intelligent car ever built**
                    —(*Saab*) Saab-Scania of America Inc.

70. **The New England solution**
                    —(*Subaru*) Subaru of America Inc.

7. AUTOMOBILES *cont.*

71. **The one to watch**
—(*AMC/Renault*) Renault Inc.

72. **There is no saturation point for honest value**
—(*Dodge*) Chrysler Corp.

73. **There's a Ford in your future**
—Ford Motor Co.

74. **The rocket action car**
—(*Oldsmobile*) General Motors Corp.

75. **The sensible spectaculars**
—American Motors Corp.

76. **The smaller fine car**
—(*Allen*).

77. **The sportsman's car**
—(*BMW*) Bavarian Motor Works.

78. **The spotlight car of the year**
—(*Studebaker*) Studebaker Corp.

79. **The style leader**
—(*Lincoln Zephyr*) Ford Motor Co.

80. **The superfine small car**
—(*Templar*).

81. **The tuned car**
—(*Buick*) General Motors Corp.

82. **The universal car**
—(*Ford*) Ford Motor Co.

83. **The "unstoppables"**
—Kaiser Jeep Corp.

84. **The world's 100,000-mile durability champion**
—(*Mercury Comet*) Ford Motor Co.

85. **Tomorrow's car today**
—(*Durant Star*).

86. **Total performance**
—Ford Motor Co.

87. **Unchallenged for quality**
—(*Cadillac*) General Motors Corp.

88. **Unique in all the world**
—(*Thunderbird*) Ford Motor Co.

89. **Watch the Fords go by**
—Ford Motor Co.

90. **We are Dodge, an American Revolution**
—(*Dodge*) Chrysler Corp.

91. **We are driven**
—(*Datsun*) Nissan Motor Corp.

7.   AUTOMOBILES *cont.*

92.   **We build excitement**
—*(Pontiac)* General Motors Corp.

93.   **When better cars are built, Buick will build them**
—*(Buick)* General Motors Corp.

94.   **Where friend meets friend**
—*(Chevrolet)* General Motors Corp.

95.   **Where quality is built in, not added on**
—American Motors Corp.

96.   **Wide-track**
—*(Pontiac)* General Motors Corp.

97.   **Winning and holding good will**
—*(Oakland)* Oakland Motor Car Co.

98.   **With an engine you'll never wear out**
—*(Willys-Knight)* Willys-Overland Inc.

99.   **Work horse of the world**
—*(Jeep)* Jeep Corp.

100.   **World's safest low-priced car**
—*(Plymouth)* Chrysler Corp.

101.   **Wouldn't you really rather have a Buick?**
—*(Buick)* General Motors Corp.

102.   **You get the good things first from Chrysler Corp.**
—Chrysler Corp.

103.   **You'll be ahead with Chevrolet**
—*(Chevrolet)* General Motors Corp.

104.   **You'll be ahead with Nash**
—*(Nash)* America Motors Corp.

105.   **Your money goes farther in a General Motors car.**
—General Motors Corp.

8.   **AUTOMOTIVE PARTS AND PRODUCTS**
See also **7.** AUTOMOBILES, **9.** AUTOMOTIVE SERVICE,
114. TIRES

1.   **Adds miles to tire life**
—Tirometer Valve Corp.

2.   **All steel and a car wide**
—*(bumpers)* Stewart-Warner Corp.

3.   **America's supreme ignition system**
—Bosch Corp.

4.   **An eye for your gas tank**
—*(Ford gas gauge)* Marquette Mfg. Co.

5.   **A real magnetic horn**
—North East Electric Co.

8. **AUTOMOTIVE PARTS AND PRODUCTS** *cont.*

6. **As necessary as brakes**
—(*windshield wipers*) Bosch Corp.

7. **Assurance of quality**
—National Automotive Parts Association.

8. **Beauty, service and comfort**
—(*motor car bodies*) Haynes-Hunt Corp.

9. **Best anti-freeze since mink**
—(*Zerex*) Du Pont.

10. **Brake inspection is your protection**
—Asbestos Brake Lining Assn.

11. **Built stronger to last longer**
—Powell Muffler Co.

12. **Control with Dole**
—Dole Valve Co.

13. **Dependable spark plugs**
—Champion Spark Plug Co.

14. **Divides the road in half**
—(*headlights*) Saf-De-Lite Sales Corp.

15. **Eyes of the night**
—(*Ilco headlight*) Indiana Lamp Corp.

16. **FEL-PRO sets the standards for the gasketing industry**
—Felt Products Mfg. Co. Inc.

17. **First for fast service**
—Federal-Mogul Corp.

18. **First name in tire valves for original equipment and replacement**
—A. Schrader's Son.

19. **Harrison cooled, the mark of radiator satisfaction**
—Harrison Radiator Corp.

20. **Ignition starts with P and D**
—P and D Mfg. Co.

21. **In products, performance, purpose . . . Essex measures up!**
—C-P Fittings Div., Essex Wire Corp.

22. **Install confidence . . . install Thermoid**
—Thermoid Div., H. K. Porter Co. Inc.

23. **Made for the professional!**
—Permatex Co. Inc.

24. **Made to stay brighter longer**
—(*Mazda auto lamps*) General Electric Co.

8. **AUTOMOTIVE PARTS AND PRODUCTS** *cont.*

25. **Makes every road a boulevard**
—(*shock absorbers*) E. V. Hartford Inc.

26. **Master of road and load**
—Russel Motor Axle Co.

27. **Maximum capacity**
—(*CãPac*) Wells Mfg. Corp.

28. **McCord is go . . . go with it**
—McCord Corp.

29. **Means safety made certain**
—(*brake linings*) Staybestos Mfg. Co.

30. **Moog means more under-car business**
—Moog Industries Inc.

31. **Never lets go**
—Hammer Blow Tool Co.

32. **Number 1 in acceptance**
—Airtex Products Inc.

33. **Overcome skidding, nerve strain and muddy roads**
—American Chain Co.

34. **Performance as great as the name**
—(*Edison-Splitdorf spark plugs*).

35. **Performance insurance**
—(*CãPac*) Wells Mfg. Corp.

36. **Permits daylight speed at night**
—Saf-De-Lite Sales Corp.

37. **Puts the "go" in ignition!**
—Tungsten Contact Mfg. Co.

38. **Puts the steady hum in motordom**
—Carter Carburetor Corp.

39. **"Quality parts for the auto *makers* and *owners*"**
—Holley Carburetor Co.

40. **Quality seals build the reputation of professional mechanics**
—Chicago Rawhide Mfg. Co.

41. **Re-equip/Equip and profit with . . .**
—Bear Mfg. Co.

42. **Right bearing for every car**
—Bearing Co. of America.

43. **Safe driving is a frame of mind**
—(*Lee tires*).

44. **Simply say Delco**
—(*storage batteries*) General Motors Corp.

8. AUTOMOTIVE PARTS AND PRODUCTS *cont.*

45. **Since 1921 ... the engine builders source!**
—Muskegon Piston Ring.

46. **Sold by more dealers than any other brand**
—(*mufflers*) A. P. Parts Corp.

47. **Specify Spicer**
—Spicer Div., Dana Corp.

48. **Temperatures made to order**
—Harrison Radiator Div., General Motors Corp.

49. **The aristocrat of auto jacks**
—Duff Mfg. Co.

50. **The big three lines of defense**
—(*bumpers*) Sheldon Axle & Spring Co.

51. **The crown jewels of ignition**
—Filko Ignition.

52. **The gold standard**
—(*filters*) Wix Corp.

53. **The headlight that floodlights the road**
—Indiana Lamp Corp.

54. **The heart of a tune-up**
—Champion Spark Plug Co.

55. **The line that moves**
—Murray Corp.

56. **The long-life battery for your car**
—Electric Battery Co.

57. **The only 100% coverage line for cars, trucks, tractors, stationary engines**
—Victor Manufacturing and Gasket Co.

58. **The perfect anti-freeze**
—(*Prestone*) Du Pont.

59. **The quality equipment line**
—Bishman Mfg. Co.

60. **The resiliency is built in the wheel**
—Sewell Cushion Wheel Co.

61. **The seal mechanics see most, use most**
—Chicago Rawhide Mfg. Co.

62. **The shock absorber that shifts gears**
—Struthers Mfg. Co.

63. **The starter that is built to order**
—Wagner Electric Corp.

64. **The straight-talk tire people**
—B. F. Goodrich Co.

8. AUTOMOTIVE PARTS AND PRODUCTS *cont.*

65. **The superior brake fluid**
—Wagner Electric Corp.

66. **To feel new power, *instantly*, install new Champions now and every 10,000 miles**
—Champion Spark Plug Co.

67. **World leader on highway and speedway**
—Monroe Auto Equipment Co.

68. **World's foremost heavy-duty ignition line**
—(*Blue Streak*) Standard Motor Parts Inc.

69. **World's foremost rebuilders of automotive parts**
—Kimco Auto Products Inc.

70. **World's largest maker of V-Belts**
—Gates Rubber Co.

71. **World's largest producer of automotive wheels, hubs and drums**
—Kelsey-Hayes Co.

9. AUTOMOTIVE SERVICE
See also **7. AUTOMOBILES, 8. AUTOMOTIVE PARTS AND PRODUCTS, 88. PETROLEUM PRODUCTS**

1. **As you travel ask us**
—Standard Oil Div., American Oil Co.

2. **At the sign of friendly service**
—Mobil Oil Corp.

3. **Come to Shell for answers**
—Shell Oil Co.

4. **For more good years in your car**
—(*Goodyear service*) Goodyear Tire and Rubber Co.

5. **Keep that great GM feeling**
—(*GM service*) General Motors Corp.

6. **Localized for you**
—(*Texaco Sky Chief*) Texaco Inc.

7. **The sign of extra service**
—Esso.

8. **Trust the Midas touch**
—Midas Mufflers.

9. **Trust your car to the man who wears the star**
—Texaco Inc.

10. **Uh, Oh, better get Maaco**
—(*body repair*) Maaco Enterprises Inc.

11. **Why go anywhere else?**
—(*transmission service*) Aamco Transmissions.

B

10. **BABY PRODUCTS**
     See also **47. FOOD, MISCELLANEOUS, 106. SOAP,**
     118. TOYS AND GAMES

1. **"Babies are our business . . . our only business"**
                              —Gerber Products Co.

2. **Baby's best bed builders**
                              —Gem Crib and Cradle Co.

3. **"Baby talk" for a good square meal**
                    —(*Biolac*) Borden's Prescription Prods.

4. **Best for baby, best for you**
     —(*Johnson's baby powder*) Johnson & Johnson Baby
                                        Products Co.

5. **If babies were born trained, they wouldn't need**
     Diaparene Baby Powder
                              —Breon Laboratories Inc.

6. **Strained for babies, chopped for young children**
                              —(*Clapp's baby foods*).

7. **The food that builds bonnie babies**
                    —(*Glaxo*) Jos. Nathan & Co., Ltd., London.

8. **The strained foods baby really likes**
                              —(*Stokely*).

9. **Wash easier, dry faster, absorb more, wear longer**
              —(*Curity diapers*) Textile Div., The Kendall Co.

11. **BAKED GOODS AND BAKING SUPPLIES**
     See also **47. FOOD, MISCELLANEOUS, 68. KITCHEN**
     PRODUCTS AND UTENSILS

1. **A quality loaf for quality folks**
                              —Baby Bear Products Corp.

2. **A sack of satisfaction**
                              —(*Bewley's flour*).

3. **As good as the best you ever ate**
                    —(*Drake's cake*) Drake Bakeries Inc.

4. **Bakers of America's finest bread**
                              —Langendorf United Bakeries.

5. **Bakes right because it is made right**
                              —(*Made-Rite flour*).

6. **Balanced for perfect baking**
                              —The Pillsbury Co.

11. BAKED GOODS AND BAKING SUPPLIES *cont.*

7. **Best by test**
   —Calumet Baking Powder Co.

8. **Better biscuits made the better way**
   —Sawyer Biscuit Co.

9. **Bread is your best food, eat more of it**
   —Fleischmann Co.

10. **Chewy, gooey, homemade good**
    —(*Duncan Hines cookie mix*) Procter & Gamble Co.

11. **Completes the feast**
    —(*National fruit cake*) National Biscuit Co.

12. **Costs more, worth more**
    —(*Occident flour*) Peavey Co.

13. **Don't ask for crackers, say Snow Flakes**
    —Pacific Coast Biscuit Co.

14. **Eat Johnston Cookies, the taste that thrills**
    —R. A. Johnston Co.

15. **Every bite a delight**
    —Grennan Cake Co.

16. **Famous for its its flavor**
    —(*Flavor flour*) Anglo-American Mill Co.

17. **Favorite of housewives for 150 years**
    —(*Baker's cocoa*) General Foods Corp.

18. **For fresher bread tomorrow, buy Taystee Bread today**
    —Purity Bakeries.

19. **Good flours make good bakers better**
    —Federal Mill.

20. **Helps build strong bodies 12 ways!**
    —(*Wonder Bread*) Continental Baking Co. Inc.

21. **Hot biscuits in a jiffy**
    —Abilene Flour Mills Co.

22. **I'se in town, honey**
    —(*Aunt Jemima pancake flour*) Quaker Oats Co.

23. **It raises the dough**
    —Codville Co. Ltd.

24. **It's blended to better your best in baking**
    —Fisher Flouring Mills Co.

25. **It splits in two**
    —(*Tak-hom-a-biscuit*) Loose-Wiles Biscuit Co.

26. **Its purity shows in everything you bake**
    —(*Dainty flour*) Food Suppliers Inc.

11. BAKED GOODS AND BAKING SUPPLIES *cont.*

27. **It tastes good to the last crumb**
    —(*pumpernickel*) Geo. F. Stuhmer Co.

28. **It wouldn't be America without Wonder**
    —(*Wonder Bread*) ITT Continental Baking Co. Inc.

29. **Keep that "youthful" look with Safe-T cones**
    —Illinois Baking Corp.

30. **Made in the bakery of a thousand windows**
    —(*Sunshine Biscuits*) Sunshine Biscuits Inc.

31. **Makes baking taste better**
    —Valier & Spies Milling Co.

32. **Makes fine, better cakes**
    —(*Swans Down*) General Foods Corp.

33. **Makes more loaves of better bread**
    —(*Robin Hood flour*) Cascada SA.

34. **Makes pancakes mother's way**
    —Armour Grain Co.

35. **Mmm, Ahhh, Ohhh, Poppin' Fresh Dough**
    —(*Poppin' Fresh Dough*) The Pillsbury Co.

36. **Ninety golden brown biscuits from each package**
    —Abilene Flour Mills.

37. **Nobody doesn't like Sara Lee**
    —Sara Lee Foods.

38. **Nothing tastes as good as Ritz, but RITZ**
    —(*Ritz crackers*) National Biscuit Co.

39. **Old Homestead Bread makes little bodies gain**
    —Old Homestead Bakery.

40. **Only a good cracker is fit to eat**
    —Biscuit & Cracker Mfrs. Assn.

41. **Pure and white as Rainier's snows**
    —(*flour*) Novelty Mills Co.

42. **Quality product for every chocolate use**
    —(*Baker's cocoa*) General Foods Corp.

43. **Rich as butter, sweet as a nut**
    —(*Franz Butter-Nut bread*) U. S. Bakery.

44. **Right in the mixing bowl, light from the oven**
    —(*Clabber Girl baking powder*) Hulman & Co.

45. **Southern cakes for southern tastes**
    —Southern Biscuit Works.

46. **Strength is the foundation of all good baking**
    —Valier & Spies Milling Co.

47. **That ole southern flavor**
    —Abilene Flour Mills.

11. BAKED GOODS AND BAKING SUPPLIES *cont.*

48. **The aristocrat of package cocoa**
—E. & A. Opler Inc.

49. **The baking aid that nature made**
—Falk American Potato Flour Corp.

50. **The flavor you can't forget**
—(*bread*) Baby Bear Products Corp.

51. **The flour of a thousand uses**
—Jenny Wren Co.

52. **The flower of fine flour**
—(*Bisquick*) General Mills Inc.

53. **The heart's in it**
—(*flour*) Elam Mills Inc.

54. **The perfect sour milk biscuit flour**
—Thomas Page Mill Co.

55. **The power behind the Dough**
—(*KC baking powder*) Jacques Mfg. Co.

56. **The saving flour, it goes farther**
—Hecker H-O Co. Inc.

57. **They just don't wilt**
—(*Ritz crackers*) National Biscuit Co.

58. **Triply protected for oven-time freshness**
—(*Rumford baking powder*) The Rumford Co.

59. **Use the wheat and spare the meat**
—Fisher Flouring Mills Co.

60. **You can have your cake and drink it, too**
—(*ground chocolate*) Guittard Chocolate Co.

BANKS ... See **43. FINANCIAL INSTITUTIONS AND SERVICES**

12. BATH ACCESSORIES
See also **104. SHAVING SUPPLIES, 106. SOAP,
116. TOILETRIES**

1. **Coordinated fashions for bed and bath**
—Fieldcrest Mills Inc.

2. **Correct in every weigh**
—(*Counselor bathroom scales*) The Brearley Co.

3. **Royal family of home fashions**
—(*towels*) Cannon Mills Co.

4. **The personal bathroom scale**
—(*Detecto*) Jacobs Bros. Co. Inc.

5. **Twin names in quality towels**
—(*Martex, Fairfax*) West Point Pepperell.

12.   **BATH ACCESSORIES** *cont.*

> 6.   **World's largest producer of bath scales**
> —(*Counselor bathroom scales*) The Brearley Co.

BATHING SUITS ... See **109.** SWIMWEAR

BATTERIES ... See **60.** HOME APPLIANCES AND EQUIPMENT

BEAUTY AIDS ... See **116.** TOILETRIES

13.   **BEDS AND BEDDING**
> See also **50.** FURNITURE

> 1.   **America's largest manufacturer of custom day beds and sofa beds**
> —M. Mittman Co.

> 2.   **A pillow for the body**
> —Sealy Mattress Co.

> 3.   **A quality for every purse and purpose**
> —(*Thomaston sheets*) Thomaston Mills Inc.

> 4.   **Enjoy the rest of your life**
> —(*Koolfoam pillows*) American Latex Products Corp.

> 5.   **Famous overnight**
> —Eclipse Sleep Products Inc.

> 6.   **Fine combed, fine count percale sheets**
> —(*Utica*) Stevens & Co. Inc.

> 7.   **First name in towels is the last word in sheets**
> —(*Cannon towels & sheets*) Cannon Mills Co.

> 8.   **For controlled warmth**
> —(*thermostatic blankets*) Fieldcrest Mills Inc.

> 9.   **For the best in rest**
> —(*Southern Comfort mattress*) Charleston Mattress Mfg. Co.

> 10.   **Guest-room luxury for every bed in your house**
> —(*Pepperell sheets*) West Point Pepperell.

> 11.   **If you'd walk without a care do your sleeping on Spring-Air**
> —(*mattresses*) The Spring Air Co.

> 12.   **Invest in rest**
> —Better Bedding Alliance of America.

> 13.   **Just everyday things for the home made beautiful by Stevens**
> —Stevens & Co. Inc.

> 14.   **Like sleeping on a cloud**
> —(*Sealy mattress*) Sealy Inc.

13. **BEDS AND BEDDING** *cont.*

15. **Made stronger, wear longer**
—(*Pequot sheets*) Springs Mills Inc.

16. **Makers of the world's only electronic blanket**
—Simmons U.S.A.

17. **Nature's sweet restorer**
—(*mattresses*) Simmons U.S.A.

18. **No sag in any WAY**
—Minneapolis Bedding Co.

19. **One third of your life is spent in bed**
—Simmons U.S.A.

20. **Proven best for rest during 73 years test**
—Ostermoor & Co.

21. **Real restful rest on steel feathers**
—(*Hercules bed spring*).

22. **Recline on Eclipse and the rest is easy**
—Eclipse Sleep Products Inc.

23. **Rest assured**
—(*Marshall mattress*).

24. **Rest assured on "Shur Rest" bedding**
—Greenpoint-Southern Co.

25. **Sleeping on a Sealy is like sleeping on a cloud**
—Sealy Inc.

26. **The bedspring luxurious**
—Rome Co.

27. **The finest name in sleep**
—Englander Co. Inc.

28. **The first name in custom bedding**
—Hein and Kopins Inc.

29. **The mattress that feels so good**
—(*Spring-Air*) The Spring Air Co.

30. **The mattress that will never grow old**
—United Mfg. Co.

31. **The one bed frame people ask for by name**
—Harvard Mfg. Co.

32. **There is only one In-A-Dor bed, the Murphy**
—Murphy Dor Bed Co.

33. **Warm as sunshine, light as floating clouds**
—(*Torfeaco bedding*).

34. **Words to go to sleep by**
—(*Perfect Sleeper*) Serta Inc.

35. **World's largest mattress maker**
—Simmons U.S.A.

13. **BEDS AND BEDDING** *cont.*

   36. **World's most comfortable mattress**
            —(*Beautyrest*) Simmons U.S.A.

   37. **You know the quality when it's King-Fisher made**
            —King-Fisher Mattress Co.

   38. **Your morning is as good as your mattress**
            —Sealy Inc.

   39. **You sleep ON it, not IN it**
            —(*Serta Perfect Sleeper mattress*) Serta Inc.

14. **BEER AND ALE**
      See also **15.** BEVERAGES, MISCELLANEOUS, **71.** LIQUORS,
      125. WINES

   1. **A beer is no better than its ingredients**
            —Hammerschlag Refining Co.

   2. **Actually aged longer**
            —Leisy Brewing Co.

   3. **Add a Dutch of class to your next party**
            —(*Grolsch lager*) Grolsch Importers Inc.

   4. **Aged by Father Time himself**
            —Hyde Park Breweries Assn.

   5. **Aged extra long for extra flavor**
            —Breidt Brewing Co.

   6. **A glass of Guinness is a cheerful sight**
            —(*Guinness Stout*) Guinness-Harp Corp.

   7. **A Guinness a day is good for you**
            —(*Guinness Stout*) Guinness-Harp Corp.

   8. **Always in good company**
            —Standard Brewing Co.

   9. **America has gone Budweiser**
            —(*Budweiser*) Anheuser-Busch Inc.

  10. **America's beverage of moderation**
            —U. S. Brewers Assn.

  11. **America's oldest lager beer**
            —(*Schaefer*) F. & M. Schaefer Brewing Co.

  12. **America's original sparkling malt liquor**
            —(*Champale*) Metropolis Brewery of New Jersey, Inc.

  13. **America's premium quality beer**
            —Falstaff Brewing Corp.

  14. **Any time is STANDARD time**
            —Standard Brewing Co.

  15. **As good as it looks**
            —Bavarian Brewing Co.

14. **BEER AND ALE** *cont.*

16. **Ask your doctor**
—(*All-American Premium Beer*).

17. **As of yore**
—Harvard Brewing Co.

18. **As tonic as sunshine itself**
—Aetna Brewing Co.

19. **A taste sells a case**
—Pacific Brewing & Malting Co.

20. **Backed by a century of brewing experience**
—Gerhard Lang Brewery.

21. **Be ale-wise**
—Old Colony Brewing Co.

22. **Beer belongs, enjoy it**
—U. S. Brewers Foundation.

23. **Beer is as old as history**
—(*Budweiser*) Anheuser-Busch Inc.

24. **Beer that grows its own flavor**
—(*Edelbrew*).

25. **Beer that made Milwaukee famous**
—Jos. Schlitz Brewing Co.

26. **Best beer by far at home, club, or bar**
—Jacob Hornung Brewing Co.

27. **Born in Canada, now going great in the 48 states**
—(*Carling's ale*) Carling National Breweries Inc.

28. **Breidt's for TIME, the part of beer you taste but never see**
—Breidt Brewing Co.

29. **Brewed in the British manner**
—Connecticut Valley Brewing Co.

30. **Brewed** *only* **in Milwaukee**
—(*Miller High Life*) Miller Brewing Co.

31. **Brew that holds its head high in any company**
—(*Senate beer*) Heurich Brewing Co.

32. **Brew with a head of its own**
—(*Krueger*) Narragansett Brewing Co.

33. **Bring out your best**
—(*Bud Light*) Anheuser-Busch Inc.

34. **Budweiser . . . King of Beers**
—(*Budweiser*) Anheuser-Busch Inc.

35. **Come to think of it, I'll have a Heineken**
—(*Heineken*) Van Munching & Co. Inc.

14. **BEER AND ALE** *cont.*

36. **Delicious, deLIGHTful, demand it**
　　　　　　　—(*Piel's*) Piel Bros. Inc.

37. **Don't say beer, say Falstaff**
　　　　　　　—Falstaff Brewing Corp.

38. **Everything you always wanted in a beer . . . and less**
　　　　　　　—(*Lite*) Miller Brewing Co.

39. **Experts pronounce it best**
　　　　　　　—(*Krueger*) Narragansett Brewing Co.

40. **Famous for five generations**
　　　　　　　—Oil City Brewing Co.

41. **Fit for a king**
　　　　　　　—Kings Brewery.

42. **Foaming with flavor**
　　　　　　　—(*Eichler*).

43. **For all you do, this Bud's for you**
　　　　　　　—(*Budweiser*) Anheuser-Busch Inc.

44. **From one beer lover to another**
　　　　　　　—(*Stroh's*) The Stroh Brewing Co.

45. **From the land of sky blue waters**
　　　　　　　—(*Hamm's*) Theo. Hamm Brewing Co.

46. **G-B means Great Beer**
　　　　　　　—Grace Bros.

47. **Get that golden glow with Rheingold**
　　　　　　　—Liebmann Breweries.

48. **Give me another Central Royal Beer**
　　　　　　　—Central Breweries Inc.

49. **Good old Munich and it's good for you**
　　　　　　　—Buckeye Producing Co.

50. **Good taste suggests it**
　　　　　　　—Peter Fox Brewing Co.

51. **Guinness and oysters are good for you**
　　　　　　　—(*Guinness Stout*) Guinness-Harp Corp.

52. **Have a glass of Guinness when you're tired**
　　　　　　　—(*Guinness Stout*) Guinness-Harp Corp.

53. **Head for the mountains**
　　　　　　　—(*Busch*) Anheuser-Busch Inc.

54. **If you've got the time, we've got the beer**
　　　　　　　—(*Miller*) Miller Brewing Co.

55. **It lives with good taste everywhere**
　　　　　　　—(*Budweiser*) Anheuser-Busch Inc.

14. BEER AND ALE *cont.*

56. **It's a dynamite taste**
    —(*Colt 45 Malt Liquor*) Carling National Breweries Inc.

57. **It's always Fehr weather**
    —Frank Fehr Brewing Co.

58. **It's a real glass of beer**
    —Flanagan Nay Brewery.

59. **It's beer as beer should taste**
    —(*Rheingold*) Liebmann Breweries.

60. **It's better, not bitter**
    —(*Carling's ale*) Carling National Breweries Inc.

61. **It's better than it used to be, and it used to be the best**
    —(*Horton Pilsener*).

62. **It's blended, it's splendid**
    —(*Pabst Blue Ribbon*) Pabst Corp.

63. **It's flavoripe**
    —Globe Brewing Co.

64. **It's good to get home to a Guinness**
    —(*Guinness Stout*) Guinness-Harp Corp.

65. **It's jubilating**
    —Bruckmann Co.

66. **It's one of the three great beers**
    —(*Krueger*) Narragansett Brewing Co.

67. **It stands on top**
    —Flock Brewing Co.

68. **It's the water**
    —(*Olympia*) Olympia Brewing Co.

69. **It's worth it ... it's Bud**
    —(*Budweiser*) Anheuser-Busch Inc.

70. **John L, the best bet for every round**
    —James Clark Distilling Corp.

71. **Just the kiss of the hops**
    —Jos. Schlitz Brewing Co.

72. **Keeps a head**
    —General Brewing Corp.

73. **King of bottled beer**
    —(*Budweiser*) Anheuser-Busch Inc.

74. **Light beer of Broadway fame**
    —(*Trommers*) Piel Bros. Inc.

75. **Lives with good taste**
    —(*Budweiser*) Anheuser-Busch Inc.

14. **BEER AND ALE** *cont.*

76. **Lunch time is Guinness time**
—(*Guinness Stout*) Guinness-Harp Corp.

77. **Made like, tastes like fine imported beer**
—(*Trommers*) Piel Bros. Inc.

78. **Made on honor, sold on merit**
—Narragansett Brewing Co.

79. **Made the old-fashioned way ... slowly ... naturally**
—Wm. Gratz Brewing Co.

80. **Makes every bite a banquet**
—(*Iron City Beer*) Pittsburgh Brewing Co.

81. **Maryland's Masterpiece**
—(*National Premium beer*) Carling National Breweries
Inc.

82. **Millions remember Doelger, a glass will tell you why**
—(*Doelger*).

83. **Milwaukee's choice**
—(*Braumeister beer*) Huber Brewing Co.

84. **Milwaukee's most exquisite beer**
—(*Blatz*) Heileman Brewing Co. Inc.

85. **Mountain water makes the difference**
—(*Old Export beer*) Cumberland Brewing Co.

86. **Nationally famous for good taste**
—Goebel Brewing Co.

87. **Ohio's favorite brew since 1862**
—Leisy Brewing Co.

88. **Old friends are best**
—Rubsam & Horrmann.

89. **One luxury all can enjoy**
—Piel Bros. Inc.

90. **Our hand has never lost its skill**
—F. & M. Schaefer Brewing Co.

91. **Preferred ... for mellow moments**
—(*Hamm's beer*) Theo. Hamm Brewing Co.

92. **Quality brew since 1852**
—Potosi Brewing Co.

93. **Real gusto in a great light beer**
—(*Schlitz*) Jos. Schlitz Brewing Co.

94. **Remember the name, you'll never forget the taste**
—Rubsam & Horrmann.

95. **Retains all the esters**
—Buckeye Producing Co.

14. **BEER AND ALE** *cont.*

96. **Schaefer is the one beer to have when you're having more than one**
—(*Schaefer*) F. & M. Schaefer Brewing Co.

97. **Seldom equalled, never excelled**
—Hyde Park Breweries Assn.

98. **Slow aged for finer flavor**
—(*Ruppert*).

99. **Smooth sailing with Old Anchor Beer**
—Brockenridge Brewing Co.

100. **Something more than a beer, a tradition**
—(*Budweiser*) Anheuser-Busch Inc.

101. **Some things speak for themselves**
—(*Michelob*) Anheuser-Busch Inc.

102. **Strength ... in a glass by itself**
—(*Guinness Stout*) Guinness-Harp Corp.

103. **Tailored to taste**
—(*cream ale*) Genesee Brewing Co.

104. **Taste without waist**
—(*Black Label beer*) Brewing Corp. of America.

105. **That Bud ... that's beer!**
—(*Budweiser*) Anheuser-Busch Inc.

106. **That old-time ale with the old-fashioned flavor**
—Aetna Brewing Co.

107. **The all-American ale**
—Cleveland-Sandusky Brewing Corp.

108. **The beer for good cheer**
—Potosi Brewing Co.

109. **The beer of friendship**
—Jax Brewing Co.

110. **The beer that made Milwaukee famous**
—Jos. Schlitz Brewing Co.

111. **The beer that made the nineties gay**
—Potosi Brewing Co.

112. **The beer that made the old days good**
—(*Jacob Ruppert*).

113. **The beer that makes friends**
—Lubeck Brewing Co.

114. **The beer that's brewed the natural way, aged the natural way**
—Breidt Brewing Co.

115. **The beer that wins awards**
—Jacob Hornung Brewing Co.

14. **BEER AND ALE** *cont.*

116. **The beer with millions of friends**
—Hyde Park Breweries Assn.

117. **The beer with the flavor as different as day from night**
—Breidt Brewing Co.

118. **The beer with the 4th ingredient**
—Breidt Brewing Co.

119. **The best has a taste all its own**
—(*Bud Light*) Anheuser-Busch Inc.

120. **The best tonic**
—Pabst Corp.

121. **The blond beer with the body**
—(*Tecate*) Tecate Importers.

122. **The bottled beer with the draught beer flavor**
—Globe Brewing Co.

123. **The brew that brings back memories**
—Pabst Corp.

124. **The brew with small bubble carbonation**
—Heurich Brewing Co.

125. **The champagne of bottle beer**
—(*Miller High Life*) Miller Brewing Co.

126. **The choice of all who know one beer from another**
—Forest City Brewing.

127. **The choicest product of the brewer's art**
—(*Falstaff*) Falstaff Brewing Corp.

128. **The head of the class**
—Brewing Corp. of America.

129. **The Luxury Beer**
—Barbey's Inc.

130. **The maker's name proclaims its quality**
—Pabst Corp.

131. **The most popular beer the world has ever known**
—(*Budweiser*) Anheuser-Busch Inc.

132. **The new big name in beer**
—(*Brewer's Best*).

133. **The next one tastes as good as the first**
—Central Breweries Inc.

134. **The peer of beers**
—Rubsam & Horrmann.

135. **The perfect glass**
—(*Ballantine*) Narragansett Brewing Co.

14. BEER AND ALE *cont.*

136. **The Prince of Ales**
    —(*Busch Pale Dry*) Anheuser-Busch Inc.

137. **There is as much satisfaction in the brewing of a good beer as in the drinking of it**
    —(*Blatz*) Heileman Brewing Co. Inc.

138. **The tang of good old ale**
    —Haffenreffer & Co.

139. **The taste of the nation**
    —Brewery Corp. of America.

140. **The toast of the coast**
    —Aztec Brewing Co.

141. **Thirst come, thirst served**
    —Erlanger Brewery.

142. **33 fine brews blended into one great beer**
    —Pabst Corp.

143. **Too good to forget**
    —(*Tech beer*) Pittsburgh Brewing Co.

144. **Unmistakably ... America's premium quality beer**
    —Falstaff Brewing Corp.

145. **Weekends were made for Michelob**
    —(*Michelob*) Anheuser-Busch Inc.

146. **Welcome to Miller time**
    —(*Miller*) Miller Brewing Co.

147. **We'll rest our case on a case**
    —Liebmann Breweries.

148. **When you say Budweiser, you've said it all**
    —(*Budweiser*) Anheuser-Busch Inc.

149. **Where there's life ... there's Bud**
    —Anheuser-Busch Inc.

150. **Wieland's extra pale is always extra good**
    —Pacific Brewing & Malting Co.

151. **You feel you've had something worth drinking when you've had a Guinness**
    —(*Guinness Stout*) Guinness-Harp Corp.

152. **You get more out of Hampden**
    —Hampden Brewing Co.

153. **Your first taste tells you and sells you**
    —Pacific Brewing & Malting Co.

15. BEVERAGES, MISCELLANEOUS

See also 14. BEER AND ALE, 27. COFFEE, 33. DAIRY
PRODUCTS, 47. FOOD, MISCELLANEOUS,
71. LIQUORS, 107. SOFT DRINKS, 110. TEA,
125. WINES

1. **Adds 70% more nourishment to milk**
—(*Cocomalt*) R. B. Davis Co.

2. **A pippin of a drink**
—Virginia Fruit Juice Co.

3. **Appollinaris mixes best with holiday spirits**
—(*Appollinaris carbonated water*).

4. **Avoid teeter-totter vitality**
—Horlick's Malted Milk Corp.

5. **Builds brain, nerves and body**
—(*Ovaltine*) Wander Co.

6. **Builds for the years ahead**
—(*Maltcao*) Merckens Chocolate Co.

7. **Children like it better than milk**
—(*Ghirardelli's hot chocolate*) Ghirardelli Chocolate Co.

8. **Contains no caffeine or other harmful stimulants**
—(*Postum*) General Foods Corp.

9. **Drink a bunch of quick energy**
—(*Welch grape juice*) Welch Grape Juice Co.

10. **Drink a glass of health**
—(*malted milk drink*) S. Gumpert & Co.

11. **Drink your apple a day**
—S. Martinelli & Co.

12. **Drink your prunes**
—California Prune & Apricot Growers Assoc.

13. **Even a child can tell the difference**
—Reichardt Cocoa & Chocolate Co.

14. **Fagged? Drink a bunch of quick energy**
—(*Welch grape juice*) Welch Grape Juice Co.

15. **Feel fine, go alkaline**
—Saratoga Vichy Spring Co.

16. **Health . . . your happiness, our business**
—Mountain Valley Water.

17. **It beats the Dutch**
—(*Philips cocoa*).

18. **It's good for you, America**
—(*Ocean Spray cranberry drinks*) Ocean Spray Cranberries Inc.

15. **BEVERAGES, MISCELLANEOUS** *cont.*

19. **Keeps YOU sparkling, too**
—(*White Rock water*) White Rock Products Corp.

20. **Ochee beverages make friends on taste**
—Ochee Spring Water Co.

21. **Picked with pride, packed with skill since 1869**
—(*Welch grape juice*) Welch Grape Juice Co.

22. **See it made**
—(*Sunkist fresh fruit drinks*) Sunkist Growers Inc.

23. **That marvelous mixer**
—(*Waukesha mineral water*).

24. **The champagne of table waters**
—(*Perrier*) Health Waters Inc.

25. **The cup that cheers**
—Reichardt Cocoa & Chocolate Co.

26. **The earth's first soft drink**
—(*Perrier*) Great Waters of France Inc.

27. **The fountain of youth**
—Horlick's Malted Milk Corp.

28. **The good things of milk and malt**
—(*malted milk tablets*) Horlick's Malted Milk Corp.

29. **The *natural* lift**
—(*Instant Postum*) General Foods Corp.

30. **The new sparkling water**
—(*Evervess*).

31. **The prune juice with the fruit juice appeal**
—(*Del Monte*) California Packing Corp.

32. **The real thing from Florida**
—(*orange juice*) Florida Citrus Commission.

33. **The sign of better taste**
—(*Mott's apple juice*) Duffy-Mott Co. Inc.

34. **The world's best table water**
—(*White Rock water*) White Rock Products Corp.

35. **Tops the meal**
—(*peach cordial*) Jung & Wulff Co.

36. **We know what we CAN 'cause we can what we grow**
—(*Donald Duck orange juice*) Citrus World Inc.

16. **BOATS AND BOATING EQUIPMENT**
See also **102.** SEA TRAVEL AND CARGO

1. **America's most popular boats**
—Starcraft Co.

16. BOATS AND BOATING EQUIPMENT *cont.*

2. **Another carefree Johnson**
   —(Johnson) Outboard Marine Co.

3. **Built on reputation**
   —Ditchburn Boats Ltd.

4. **Cruiser of tomorrow**
   —(Richardson Ranger) Richardson Boat Co.

5. **Dependable in any weather**
   —(Baltzer boats).

6. **Evinruding is rowboat motoring**
   —Evinrude Motor Co.

7. **First in dependability**
   —(Johnson) Outboard Marine Co.

8. **First in marine propulsion**
   —(Keikhaefer Mercury) Brunswick Corp.

9. **First in outboards**
   —Evinrude Motor Co.

10. **It's a winner**
    —(PlastiCraft motorboat).

11. **Matchless in outdoor excellence**
    —(Mercury outboard motor) Brunswick Corp.

12. **Missing the boat? Own an Owens**
    —Owens Yacht Co.

13. **Precision-built, water-tight**
    —(Johnson "sea-worthy" boats).

14. **Since 1720, a family heritage of careful boat building**
    —C. P. Leek and Sons Inc.

15. **Starts with a quarter turn**
    —(Elto outboard motors).

16. **The greatest name in yachting**
    —(Consolidated yachts).

17. **The new standard of performance**
    —(Martin outboard motors).

BOOKS . . . See **94.** PUBLISHING

17. BROADCASTING

See also **95.** RADIO EQUIPMENT,
   111. TELECOMMUNICATIONS, **112.** TELEVISIONS

1. **Give us 20 minutes and we'll give you the world**
   —WINS Radio.

2. **Parade of Stars**
   —National Broadcasting Co.

17. **BROADCASTING** *cont.*

    3. **Where what you want to know comes first**
       —(*CBS radio network*) Columbia Broadcasting System Inc.

    4. **Wide world of entertainment**
       —American Broadcasting Co.

    5. **You're tuned to 88 . . . WCBS . . . All news radio**
       —WCBS Radio.

18. **BUILDING SUPPLIES**

    See also **55. HARDWARE, 65. INTERIOR DECORATION, 75. METALS INDUSTRY, 82. PAINT AND PAINTING SUPPLIES**

    1. **Always one step ahead of the weather**
       —(*Rusco windows*) R. C. Russell Co.

    2. **America's finest basement door**
       —Bilco Co.

    3. **Amerock makes it authentic**
       —Amerock Corp.

    4. **A name to remember**
       —Pen Metal Co. Inc.

    5. **Anchors like a rock**
       —Chicago Steel Post Co.

    6. **A quality name in forest products**
       —Long-Bell Lumber Co.

    7. **Asbestos cannot burn**
       —Asbestos Shingle, Slate and Sheathing Co.

    8. **Back-bone of better plastering**
       —Milwaukee Corrugating Co.

    9. **Beautiful birch for beautiful woodwork**
       —Northern Hemlock Mfrs. Assn.

    10. **Beauty and economy burned in**
       —Common Brick Mfrs. Assn. of America.

    11. **Best way to close an opening**
       —(*doors*) Cookson Co.

    12. **Bird takes the burden out of keeping up your home**
       —Bird & Son Inc.

    13. **Board of 100 uses in 1000 places**
       —The Upson Co.

    14. **Building for the ages**
       —Queenston Limestone.

    15. **Build right, with Insulite**
       —The Insulite Co.

18.	BUILDING SUPPLIES *cont.*

16.	Build the nation securely with the nation's building stone
—Indiana Limestone.

17.	Built like fine furniture
—(*kitchen cabinets*) Coppes Bros. & Zook.

18.	Built to weather the years
—Rust Sash and Door Co.

19.	Carry the weight, save freight
—Atlas Plywood Corp.

20.	Chief of the mouldings
—Ponderosa Mouldings Inc.

21.	Cork-lined houses make comfortable homes
—Armstrong Cork & Insulation Co.

22.	Creative ideas in glass
—American Saint Gobain Corp.

23.	Depend on Potlatch for everything in quality lumber
—Potlatch Forests Inc.

24.	Duraflake makes *only* particleboard and only the best
—Duraflake Co.

25.	Easy to spread, hard to beat
—National Mortar & Supply Co.

26.	Everything to build anything
—Dower Lumber Co.

27.	First in epoxies … in the age of ideas
—CIBA Products Co.

28.	First with better ways to build
—(*Gold Bond*) National Gypsum Co.

29.	For quality Western lumber products, look to T, W, and J
—Tarter, Webster and Johnson Div., American Forest Products Corp.

30.	For the beautiful point of view
—(*windows*) Woodco Corp.

31.	Gently as a whisper
—(*door checks*) Sargent & Co.

32.	History tells which line excels
—Ohio Brass Co.

33.	Home builders to the nation
—(*Readi-cut houses*) Aladdin Co.

34.	Insulate as you decorate
—Certigrade Red Cedar Shingles.

18. **BUILDING SUPPLIES** *cont.*

35. **It's built to sell when it's built of wood**
     —National Lumber Manufacturers Association.

36. **John Lees keeps you in trim**
     —Cullman Products Corp.

37. **Just a "shade" better**
     —(*Thorpe awnings*).

38. **Keep heat where it belongs**
     —Mason Fibre Co.

39. **Keep the weather out**
     —Ceco Weatherstrip Co.

40. **King of the walk**
     —Tri-Lok Co.

41. **Leadclad fences make good neighbors**
     —Leadclad Wire Co.

42. **Leader in prefinished hardwoods**
     —E. L. Bruce Co.

43. **Let the "kitchen maid" be your kitchen aid**
     —(*cabinets*) Wassmuth-Endicott Co.

44. **Look to MFG for the shape of things to come**
     —Molded Fiber Glass Companies Inc.

45. **Made by the mile, sold by the foot**
     —(*sectional steel buildings*) Liberty Prods.

46. **Makes products better, safer, stronger, lighter**
     —Fiber Glass Div., PPG Industries Inc.

47. **Make your windows avenues of health**
     —Vita Glass Corp.

48. **Manufacturers of creative building products**
     —Caradco Inc.

49. **Manufacturers of quality hardwood products since 1872**
     —Connor Lumber and Land Co.

50. **Men who build America trust this trade mark**
     —(*Arro-lock shingles*).

51. **Monarch out-strips them all**
     —Monarch Metal Weatherstrip Co.

52. **More savings with Symons**
     —Symons Mfg. Co.

53. **Nature makes Douglas fir durable**
     —Fir Door Institute.

54. **Never renew, yet ever new**
     —Associated Tile Mfrs.

18. BUILDING SUPPLIES *cont.*

55. **Niedecken Showers give refreshing hours**
                              —Hoffmann & Billings.

56. **No better built than Durabilt**
                              —Durabilt Steel Locker Co.

57. **Once in a lifetime**
                              —New Jersey Zinc Co.

58. **One of the many fine products that comes from 40
     years of thinking new**
                              —(*Gold Bond*) National Gypsum Co.

59. **One of the many quality home-improvement
     products made by J. M.**
                              —Johns-Manville Corp.

60. **Only the rich can afford poor windows**
                              —Andersen Corp.

61. **PPG makes the glass that makes the difference**
                              —PPG Industries Inc.

62. **Products of wood technology for construction and
     industry**
                              —Pope and Talbot Inc.

63. **Put your house in the pink**
          —(*Fiberglas insulation*) Owens-Corning Fiberglas Corp.

64. **Quality products for quality living**
                              —Mirawal Co.

65. **Resists fire and rot**
                              —California Redwood Assn.

66. **Rightly put together to fight both time and weather**
                              —Ohio Brass Co.

67. **Saving ways in doorways since 1895**
                              —Kinnear Corp.

68. **Sells easy ... sells fast ... makes resales**
          —Insulite Div., Minnesota and Ontario Paper Co.

69. **Sell Simpson and be sure**
                              —Simpson Timber Co.

70. **Slate—consider its uses**
                              —National Slate Assn.

71. **Small cost for great richness**
                              —Algoma Panel Co.

72. **Smooth as a kitten's ear**
                              —Hammond Cedar Co.

73. **Step inside a Yankee Barn. You many never want
     to live in a house again.**
                              —Yankee Barn Homes.

18. BUILDING SUPPLIES *cont.*

74. **Symbol of quality**
—Potlatch Forests Inc.

75. **The action line**
—Evans Products Co.

76. **The aristocrat of American roofing**
—American Sea Green Slate Co.

77. **The aristocrat of building materials**
—Indiana Limestone Quarrymen's Assn.

78. **The birch line**
—Kitchen Kompact Inc.

79. **The brightest name in aluminum**
—Nichols Aluminum Co.

80. **The builder's selection for unfailing protection**
—American Tar & Chemical Co.

81. **The cabinet-wood of the elect**
—American Walnut Mfrs. Assn.

82. **The choice of the crew and the big boss, too**
—Ohio Brass Co.

83. **The classic name in the building field**
—Bird & Son Inc.

84. **The crowning touch of quality**
—Red Cedar Shingle and Handsplit Shale Bureau.

85. **The easiest way out**
—(*automatic treadle-operated door*) National Pneumatic Co.

86. **The greatest name in building**
—United States Gypsum Co.

87. **The hardest hardwoods grow in the north**
—Northern Hard Maple Mfrs.

88. **The home with the silver lining**
—(*insulation*) Reynolds Corp.

89. **The kitchen cabinet that saves miles of steps**
—Hoosier Mfg. Co.

90. **The line and design for creative window planning**
—Malta Mfg. Co.

91. **The mark of a good roof**
—Celotex Corp.

92. **The mark of the well-built house**
—Flax-li-num Insulating Co.

93. **The master wood of the ages**
—Mahogany Assn. Inc.

18. BUILDING SUPPLIES *cont.*

94. **The material difference in building**
—(Geon Vinyls) B. F. Goodrich Co.

95. **The most beautiful kitchens of them all**
—H. J. Scheirich Co.

96. **The nation's building stone**
—Indiana Limestone Quarrymen's Assn.

97. **The noblest of all cabinet woods**
—American Walnut Mfrs. Assn.

98. **The one-man, one-hand shingle**
—Bird & Son Inc.

99. **The original masonry wall reinforcement with the truss design**
—(Dur-O-Wal) Cedar Rapids Block Co.

100. **The pavement that outlasts the bonds**
—National Paving Brick Mfrs.

101. **The paving that's saving**
—Jennison-Wright Co.

102. **The pick o' the pines**
—Western Mfrs. Assn.

103. **The post everlasting**
—Long-Bell Lumber Co.

104. **The red nylon ring of reliability**
—Elastic Stop Nut Corp. of America.

105. **There is one best in everything**
—Johns-Manville Corp.

106. **The roof of ages**
—(red cedar shingles) West Coast Lumbermen's Assn.

107. **The roof without a regret**
—Hawthorne Roofing Tile Co.

108. **The silent servant with a hundred hands**
—(kitchen cabinets) Hoosier Mfg. Co.

109. **The sovereign wood**
—Hardwood Mfrs. Institute.

110. **The sun never sets on Hammondtanks**
—Hammond Iron Works.

111. **The superior interior**
—(Upson Board) The Upson Co.

112. **The supreme structural wood of the world**
—Southern Pine Assn.

113. **The wood eternal**
—Southern Cypress Mfrs. Assn.

18.   BUILDING SUPPLIES *cont.*

114. The world's largest manufacturer of fine kitchen cabinets
—Colonial Products Co.

115. Use redwood, it LASTS
—California Redwood Assn.

116. Verified insulation performance
—Owens-Corning Fiberglas Corp.

117. Walls of character
—Hachmeister Lind Chemical Co.

118. We fool the sun
—Indianapolis Tent & Awning Co.

119. When you think of asbestos, think of Johns-Manville
—Johns-Manville Corp.

120. Where quality is a tradition
—Dierks Forests Inc.

121. Where your sealing is unlimited
—Standard Products Co.

122. Window beauty is Andersen
—Andersen Corp.

123. Withstands the test of time
—Barber Asphalt Co.

124. Wood that nature armed against decay
—Red Cedar Lumber Mfrs. Assn.

125. Wood that weathers every storm
—National Oak Lumbermen's Assn.

126. Wood that you would and should use
—National Oak Lumbermen's Assn.

127.   World's largest roof truss system
—Sanford Truss Inc.

128. Your windows are the lamps which light your rooms by day
—Columbia Mills Inc.

19.   BUS LINES
See also **119.** TRAVEL

1. Easiest travel on earth
—Continental Trailways Bus System.

2. Leave the driving to us
—Greyhound Lines Inc.

3. Roll south into summer this winter
—Greyhound Lines Inc.

19. **BUS LINES** *cont.*

    4. **Trailways serves the nation at "scenery level"**
       —Continental Trailways Bus System.

    BUSINESS MACHINES . . . See **28.** COMPUTER EQUIPMENT,
    81. OFFICE EQUIPMENT AND SUPPLIES

C

CAMPAIGN SLOGANS . . . See **91.** PRESIDENTIAL
        CAMPAIGNS

CAMPING EQUIPMENT . . . See **98.** RECREATIONAL
        EQUIPMENT

20. **CANDY AND GUM**
        See also **47.** FOOD, MISCELLANEOUS

    1. **A breathless sensation**
                    —(*Pioneer mints*) Strong, Cobb & Co.

    2. **A delicious health confection**
                    —(*Post's Bran Chocolates*) Postum Cereal Co. Inc.

    3. **After every meal**
                    —(*Wrigley's gum*) William Wrigley Jr. Co.

    4. **A gift to remember**
                    —(*Princesse de Conde chocolates*).

    5. **A grand slam favorite**
                    —American Chewing Products Corp.

    6. **Aids digestion**
                    —(*Beech-nut gum*) Life Savers Inc.

    7. **All you can eat for a nickel**
                    —(*Baby Ruth candy bar*) Curtis Candy Co.

    8. **Always refreshing**
                    —(*Beech-nut gum*) Life Savers Inc.

    9. **A message of purity**
                    —(*Angelus marshmallows*) Crackerjack Co.

    10. **An agreeable chewing digestant**
                    —Bi-Car Gum Co.

    11. **An American institution since 1840**
                    —(*Park & Tilford candy*).

    12. **As sweet as love songs**
                    —(*butterscotch*) Kerr Bros.

    13. **A sweet among sweets**
                    —(*butterscotch*) Kerr Bros.

20. **CANDY AND GUM** *cont.*

14. **A woman never forgets the man who remembers**
—(*Whitman's chocolates*) Pet Inc.

15. **Be Chic—Chew Chicks**
—American Chewing Products Corp.

16. **Best nickel candy there iz-z-z**
—(*Whiz*) Paul F. Beich.

17. **Be sweeticular**
—Imperial Candy Co.

18. **Candies of character**
—Wallace & Co.

19. **Candies of distinctive quality**
—Tiffin Products Inc.

20. **Candy has energy and taste**
—(*Rebbor candies*).

21. **Candy makers to the American nation**
—Curtis Candy Co.

22. **Confections that win affections**
—(*Funke*).

23. **Cut to fit the mouth**
—(*salt water taffy*) James Bros.

24. **Dandy candy**
—(*Yankee Toffee*) Brown & Haley.

25. **Dear to your heart but not to your purse**
—(*candy mint*) Strong, Cobb & Co.

26. **Eat candy for energy**
—National Confectioners' Assn.

27. **Exclusive makers of the original old-fashioned molasses candy in delightful modern flavors**
—Bishop Candy Co. Inc.

28. **For beauty exercise**
—(*Wrigley's gum*) William Wrigley Jr. Co.

29. **Freedent's the one that took the stick out of gum, and put the fresh in your breath**
—(*Freedent chewing gum*) William Wrigley Jr. Co.

30. **Give Whitman's Chocolates, it's the thoughtful thing to do**
—(*Whitman's chocolates*) Pet Inc.

31. **Good candy for all the family**
—(*Chuckles*) Fred W. Amend Co.

32. **Happiness in every box**
—United Retail Candy Stores.

20. **CANDY AND GUM** *cont.*

33. **Have you had your fruit today?**
—(*SunKist Fruit Rolls*) Sunkist Growers Inc.

34. **High as the Alps in quality**
—Peter Cailler Kohler Swiss Chocolate Co.

35. **Leaves you breathless**
—(*gum*) L. P. Larson, Jr. Co.

36. **Life Savers . . . a part of living**
—(*Life Savers*) Life Savers Inc.

37. **Love at first bite**
—(*Suchard chocolate bars*) Wilbur-Suchard Choc. Co.

38. **Make it a habit, take "her" a bar**
—Mary Lincoln Candies Inc.

39. **Make the greeting sweeter**
—(*Quaker Maid candies*).

40. **Making the world sweeter**
—(*Nut Tootsie Rolls*) Sweets Co. of America.

41. **Mellow as moonlight**
—Vogan Candy Co.

42. **Nestle's makes the very best**
—(*Nestle's chocolates*) Nestle Co. Inc.

43. **Old England's finest chocolates**
—Cadbury's Ltd.

44. **Only natural flavors last longer, naturally**
—(*Topps gum*) Topps Chewing Gum Inc.

45. **Packed with good taste**
—(*Clark's Teaberry gum*) Philip Morris Inc.

46. **Perfection in a confection**
—Confections Inc.

47. **Popular at contract or auction games**
—American Chewing Products Corp.

48. **Pure as the mountain air**
—D. L. Clark Co.

49. **Refreshing as the rising sun**
—American Chewing Products Corp.

50. **Satisfies you**
—(*Snickers candy bars*) Mars Inc.

51. **Served by modern hostesses**
—American Chewing Products Corp.

52. **Talk of the town**
—(*Park & Tilford candy*).

53. **That good Pittsburgh candy**
—Reyner & Bros. Inc.

20.   CANDY AND GUM *cont.*

54.   **The butter in Bamby makes it better**
—Cushman's Sons Inc.

55.   **The candy mint with the hole**
—(*Life Savers*) Mint Products Co.

56.   **The chewing gum bon bon**
—(*Vi-lets*) F. H. Fleer Corp.

57.   **The chocolates with the wonderful centres**
—(*Liggett's chocolates*).

58.   **The confection of the fairies**
—Liberty Orchards Co.

59.   **The finest chocolate in the world**
—Bachman Chocolate Mfg. Co.

60.   **The gift candy of America**
—Huyler's Inc.

61.   **The gum with the fascinating artificial flavor**
—(*Wrigley's gum*) William Wrigley Jr. Co.

62.   **The handy candy**
—(*mints*) Beechnut Packing Co.

63.   **The life of the party**
—Boston Confectionery Co.

64.   **The milk chocolate melts in your mouth. Not in your hands.**
—(*M & M Candies*) Mars Candy Company.

65.   **The more you eat, the more you want**
—(*Crackerjacks*) Rueckheim Bros. & Eckstein.

66.   **The nickel lunch**
—Planter's Nut & Chocolate Co.

67.   **The one and only one cocktail gum**
—(*Warren's chewing gum*).

68.   **The perfect candy for smart entertaining**
—(*Brach*) B.J. Brach & Sons.

69.   **The South's most famous confection**
—(*Creole pralines*) Hotel Grunewald.

70.   **The welcome partner**
—American Chewing Products Corp.

71.   **Untouched by human hands**
—(*Sweet Message chocolates*).

72.   **When you crave good candy**
—Milky Way Co.

73.   **Wholesome sweets for children**
—(*Laura Secord candy*) Laura Secord Candy Shops Ltd.

20. **CANDY AND GUM** *cont.*

74. **You bet your Life Savers**
—(*Life Savers*) Life Savers Inc.

CARGO ... See 4. AIR TRAVEL AND CARGO, 96. RAIL
TRAVEL AND CARGO, 102. SEA TRAVEL AND CARGO

CARPETS ... See 46. FLOOR COVERINGS

CARS ... See 7. AUTOMOBILES

CASSETTES ... See 97. RECORDINGS

CERAMICS ... See 52. GLASS AND CERAMICS

21. **CEREALS**
See also 47. FOOD, MISCELLANEOUS

1. **A full meal in two biscuits**
—Shredded Wheat Co.

2. **A hot weather hot cereal**
—(*Zoom*) Fisher Flouring Mills Co.

3. **America's best-liked cereal assortment**
—The Kellogg Co.

4. **America's grandest cereal assortment**
—The Kellogg Co.

5. **America's new breakfast banquet of shredded whole wheat**
—(*Cubs cereal*) National Biscuit Co.

6. **America's popular year 'round breakfast**
—Quaker Oats Co.

7. **An ounce of prevention for everybody, everyday**
—(*Post's Bran Flakes*) General Foods Corp.

8. **Best because it's pan-dried**
—(*Robin Hood*) Rapid Oats.

9. **Breakfast of champions**
—(*Wheaties*) General Mills Inc.

10. **Famed for flavor**
—Purity Oats Co.

11. **Food shot from guns**
—(*Puffed Wheat, Puffed Rice*) Quaker Oats Co.

12. **For a livelier life**
—(*Cubs cereal*) National Biscuit Co.

13. **For bracing up digestion, nerves, and appetite**
—Quaker Oats Co.

14. **Fresh as the morning**
—(*Campbell's corn flakes*).

21. **CEREALS** *cont.*

15. **Fresh from the mill to you**
     —(*Livingstone's oats*).

16. **Fresh to you each morning**
     —The Kellogg Co.

17. **Had your Wheaties today?**
     —General Mills Inc.

18. **Health and growth for boys and girls**
     —Ralston Purina Co.

19. **Health without hazard**
     —(*Kellogg's All-Bran*) The Kellogg Co.

20. **Help yourself to health**
     —The Kellogg Co.

21. **Here's a thrill for breakfast**
     —(*Grape Nuts Flakes*) General Foods Corp.

22. **Join the "regulars" with Kellogg's All-Bran**
     —The Kellogg Co.

23. **Keep going with Pep**
     —(*Pep Bran Flakes*) The Kellogg Co.

24. **Life is swell when you keep well**
     —(*Post's Bran Flakes*) General Foods Corp.

25. **Light, white and flaky**
     —Comet Rice Co.

26. **Makes kids husky**
     —(*Three Minute cereals*) The National Oats Co.

27. **New to look at, new to taste**
     —(*Corn Kix*) General Mills Inc.

28. **Now you'll like bran**
     —Postum Cereal Co. Inc.

29. **One delicious flavor in two delicious forms**
     —(*Grape Nuts, Grape Nuts Flakes*) General Foods Corp.

30. **Parade of the immortals**
     —The Kellogg Co.

31. **Ready to eat**
     —(*Wheaties*) General Mills Inc.

32. **Shot from guns**
     —Quaker Oats Co.

33. **Stay crisp in milk or cream**
     —(*Post Toasties*) General Foods Corp.

34. **Tastes so good and so good for you**
     —(*Cream of Rice*) Grocery Store Products Co.

35. **The best to you each morning**
     —The Kellogg Co.

21. CEREALS *cont.*

36. **The cereal you can serve a dozen ways**
—(Shredded Wheat) National Biscuit Co.

37. **The delicious whole wheat cereal**
—The Wheatena Co.

38. **The great American family cereal**
—(Cream of Wheat) Nabisco Inc.

39. **The nation's breakfast food**
—(Amerikorn) Chas. A. Krause Milling Co.

40. **The original corn flakes**
—The Kellogg Co.

41. **The plus food for minus meals**
—(Kellogg's All-Bran) The Kellogg Co.

42. **There's a meal in every Muffet**
—Muffets Corp.

43. **The right road to health**
—(Old York cereal).

44. **They're Grrrr-eat!**
—(Kellogg's Sugar Frosted Flakes) The Kellogg Co.

45. **To keep happy, keep well**
—(Kellogg's All-Bran) The Kellogg Co.

46. **Top of the morning**
—(Cream of Wheat) Nabisco Inc.

47. **Whatever you do, eat Krumbles**
—The Kellogg Co.

48. **What the big boys eat!**
—(Wheaties) General Mills Inc.

49. **Wheat shot from guns is elegant eatin'**
—(Sparkies) Quaker Oats Co.

50. **Won its favor through its flavor**
—The Kellogg Co.

51. **Yours for a good morning**
—(Carnation Albers cereals) Albers Bros. Milling Co.

22. **CHEMICAL INDUSTRY**
See also **24.** CLEANING AND LAUNDRY PRODUCTS,
86. PEST CONTROL

1. **Another example of how Monsanto moves on many fronts to serve you**
—Monsanto Co.

2. **Anticipating tomorrow's needs today . . .**
—Enjay Chemical Co. Div., Humble Oil and Refining Co.

3. **A skilled hand in chemistry . . . at work for you**
—Nopco Chemical Co.

22. CHEMICAL INDUSTRY *cont.*

4. **Basic chemicals and cost-cutting ideas**
—PPG Industries Inc.

5. **Basic producers from mine to finished product**
—Tennessee Corp.

6. **Basic provider of chemicals in volume**
—Abbott Laboratories.

7. **Basic to America's progress**
—Allied Chemical Corp.

8. **Best-selling aerosols are powered with Freon propellents**
—(*Freon*) Du Pont.

9. **Better things for better living through chemistry**
—Du Pont.

10. **Energy chemicals**
—Cities Service Co.

11. **Go where you get choosing range**
—United States Borax and Chemical Corp.

12. **Houdry means progress … through catalysis**
—Houdry Process and Chemical Co.

13. **In home, health, farm and industry, science in action for you**
—American Cyanamid Co.

14. **In industry world-wide**
—Swift & Co.

15. **Interested personal service – always – when you buy from Eastman**
—Eastman Chemical Products Inc.

16. **Let us help put Armour idea chemicals to work for you**
—Armour and Co.

17. **Look for more from Morton**
—Morton Chemical Co.

18. **Pioneers in hydride chemistry**
—Metal Hydrides Inc.

19. **Plus values**
—Chemical Div., General Mills Inc.

20. **Progressive products through chemical research**
—Dexter Corp.

21. **Putting the "push" in America's finest aerosols**
—(*Genetron*) Allied Chemical Corp.

22. **Special chemicals for industry**
—Carlisle Chemical Works Inc.

22. **CHEMICAL INDUSTRY** *cont.*

23. **Specialists in making water behave**
—Anderson Chemical Co. Inc.

24. **The bright new silicates for industry**
—Allegheny Industrial and Chemical Co.

25. **The one to watch for new developments**
—Goodrich-Gulf Chemicals Inc.

26. **To gladden hearts and lighten labor**
—Dow Chemical Co.

27. **Use-engineered for cleaning, protecting and processing**
—Dubois Chemicals.

28. **Watch Highson ... for progress through creative research**
—Highson Chemical Co.

29. **Where *experience* guides *exploration***
—Dow Corning Corp.

30. **Where flame technology creates new products**
—Cabot Corp.

31. **Where what's happening gets its start**
—Amoco Chemicals Corp.

23. **CHINA**
See also **52. GLASS AND CERAMICS, 68. KITCHEN PRODUCTS AND UTENSILS**

1. **China by Iroquois for the hosts of America**
—Iroquois China Co.

2. **Don't wait to inherit Spode**
—Spode Inc.

3. ***Fine* dinnerware**
—(*Vernonware*) Vernon Div., Metlox Mfg. Co.

4. **Finest in china since 1735**
—(*Richard Ginori*) Pasmantier Inc.

5. **Know the best by this mark**
—Jackson China Co.

6. **The beginning of taste**
—Syracuse China Corp.

7. **The world's most beautiful china**
—Meakin & Ridgway.

8. **True to its tone**
—(*china*) Onondaga Pottery Co.

CIGARETTES ... See 115. TOBACCO PRODUCTS

CIGARS ... See 115. TOBACCO PRODUCTS

24. CLEANING AND LAUNDRY PRODUCTS
See also **22.** CHEMICAL INDUSTRY, **106.** SOAP

1. **A good broom sweeps cleaner and lasts longer**
   —American Broom & Brush Co.

2. **America's favorite bleach and household disinfectant**
   —(*Clorox bleach*) Clorox Co.

3. **A shine in every drop**
   —Black Silk Stove Polish Works.

4. **Avoid "tattletale gray"**
   —(*Fels Naphtha soap*) Purex Corp.

5. **A wipe and it's bright**
   —(*porcelain cleaner*) B. T. Babbitt Inc.

6. **Breaks the static barrier**
   —(*Fab*) Colgate-Palmolive Co.

7. **By the world's largest maker of dishwasher detergents**
   —(*Electrasol*) Economics Laboratory Inc.

8. **Cascade eliminates drops that spot**
   —(*Cascade*) Procter & Gamble Co.

9. **Chases dirt**
   —(*Old Dutch cleanser*) Cudahy Packing Co.

10. **Cleans as it polishes**
    —(*O-Cedar polish*) Channel Chemical Co.

11. **Cleans easier, works faster, won't scratch**
    —(*Sunbrite cleanser*) Swift & Co.

12. **Cleans in a jiff**
    —(*washing powder*) Dif Corp.

13. **Cleans like a *white tornado***
    —(*Ajax*) Colgate-Palmolive Co.

14. **Cleans so well so easily, and for so little**
    —(*Mystic foam upholstery cleaner*) American Cyanamid Co.

15. **Cleans the impossible washload**
    —(*Dynamo detergent*) Colgate-Palmolive Co.

16. **Clean up with S. O. S. It's easy**
    —(*S. O. S. Magic scouring pads*) Miles Laboratories Inc.

17. **Complete household soap**
    —(*Oxydol*) Procter & Gamble Co.

18. **Cuts dishpan time in half**
    —(*Washington powder*) Dif Corp.

24. CLEANING AND LAUNDRY PRODUCTS *cont.*

19. **Doesn't scratch**
    —(*Old Dutch cleanser*) Cudahy Packing Co.

20. **Don't ask for "polish," demand Brite-Lite**
    —Britelite Co.

21. **Don't be bullied by your bowl, Bully your bowl instead**
    —(*Bully toilet bowl cleaner*).

22. **Double action, single cost**
    —(*Sunbrite cleanser*) Swift & Co.

23. **Duz does everything**
    —(*Duz washing powder*) Procter & Gamble Co.

24. **Eats everything in the pipe**
    —(*drain pipe cleaner*) John Sunshine Chemical Co.

25. **Every granule licks dirt 8 ways**
    —(*Noctil*) Rumford Chemical Works.

26. **Famous for products that really work**
    —Glamorene Products Corp.

27. **Fast for dishes yet kind to your hands**
    —(*Duz washing powder*) Procter & Gamble Co.

28. **Faultless starch lightens laundry labor**
    —Faultless Starch Co.

29. **First in quality, performance, preference**
    —(*Clorox bleach and disinfectant*) Clorox Co.

30. **Get brighter windows with Windex**
    —(*Windex window cleaner*) The Drackett Co.

31. **Give your dishwasher the best**
    —(*Cascade*) Procter & Gamble Co.

32. **Gleaming armor for your floors**
    —(*Old English No Rubbing Wax*) A. S. Boyle Co.

33. **Good soap is good business**
    —Procter & Gamble Co.

34. **Good washing wins good will**
    —Cowles Detergent Co.

35. **Grease just vanishes from pots, pans, dishes**
    —(*Rinso*) Lever Bros. Co.

36. **Hasn't scratched yet**
    —(*Bon Ami cleanser*) Bon Ami Co.

37. **Home-care know-how ... at your doorstep!**
    —Amway Corp.

38. **Hurts only dirt**
    —(*Kitchen Klenzer*) Fitzpatrick Bros.

24. CLEANING AND LAUNDRY PRODUCTS *cont.*

39. **If it's a question of cleaning/conditioning ... ask Oakite**
—Oakite Products Inc.

40. **If it's lovely to wear it's worth Ivory Flakes care**
—(*Ivory Flakes*) Procter & Gamble Co.

41. **If it's safe in water, it's safe in Lux**
—(*Lux soap*) Lever Bros. Co.

42. **If you're not using Vano, you're working too hard**
—Chemicals Inc.

43. **Isn't it worth it?**
—(*Lysol disinfectant spray*) Lehn and Fink Consumer Products.

44. **It makes a dust magnet of your dust mop or cloth**
—(*Endust*) The Drackett Co.

45. **It's always a shade better**
—(*Bulldog Venetian blind cleaner*).

46. **It's scratchless, it's matchless**
—(*cleaner*) Swift & Co.

47. **It's sudsy**
—Gold Dust Corp.

48. **It's the tops for kitchen tops**
—(*asbestos pads*) Weiss & Klau Co.

49. **Ivory-mild for safety; granulated for speed**
—(*Ivory Snow*) Procter & Gamble Co.

50. **Keep your floors beautiful always**
—Raynorshyne Products.

51. **Keep your furniture beautiful always**
—(*polish*) Raynorshyne Products.

52. **Kindness to hands, speed in the dishpan**
—(*Ivory Snow*) Procter & Gamble Co.

53. **Let the Gold Dust Twins do your work**
—(*soap powder*) N. H. Fairbank Co.

54. **Makes cotton look and feel like linen**
—(*Linit laundry starch*) CPC International Inc.

55. **Makes hard water soft**
—(*Gold Dust soap powder*) N. H. Fairbank Co.

56. **Makes old things new, keeps new things bright**
—(*polish*) Britelite Co.

57. **Makes water wetter**
—(*PN-700 washing powder*) Service Industries.

24. **CLEANING AND LAUNDRY PRODUCTS** *cont.*

58. **Mar-VEL-ous for dishes, stockings, lingerie, woolens**
> —(*Vel soap*) Colgate-Palmolive Co.

59. **Melts dirt away**
> —(*Old English powdered cleaner*).

60. **More than a polish**
> —Raylo Corp.

61. **No purer soap was ever made**
> —(*Chiffon soap flakes*) Armour Co.

62. **Norco way is the easiest and best way to polish silverware**
> —F. F. Horst Co.

63. **Of paramount importance to the housewife**
> —Arcraft Broom Co.

64. **Old floors look new in six to nine minutes**
> —(*Aerowax*) Midway Chemical Co.

65. **Out of the blue comes the whitest wash**
> —(*Reckitt's blue*) Reckitt & Colman Ltd.

66. **Preferred in fine homes for many years**
> —(*Hawes floor wax*) American Home Products Corp.

67. **Removes the film of dirt and smudge**
> —(*Keyspray*) Keystone Chemical Co.

68. **Rougher on dirt, easiest on clothes**
> —(*Oxydol soap*) Procter & Gamble Co.

69. **Scours the pan, not your hands**
> —(*GLO soapy scouring pads*) J. H. Rhodes Co.

70. **Scratches disappear as you polish**
> —(*Old English scratch removing polish*) Boyle-Midway.

71. **"Sheeting action"**
> —(*Cascade*) Procter & Gamble Co.

72. **Simply the business of homekeeping**
> —Fuller Brush Co.

73. **Sold by the carload, used by the drop**
> —(*Mrs. Stewart's bluing*) Luther Ford & Co.

74. **Sombre silver dulls more than the dinner**
> —(*Wright's silver cream cleaner*) Caswell-Massey Co.

75. **Something to crow about**
> —Supreme Polish Co. Ltd.

76. **Spray that cleans windows without water**
> —(*Windex window cleaner*) The Drackett Co.

77. **Spreads like good news**
> —(*Satinwax*) Economics Laboratory Inc.

24. CLEANING AND LAUNDRY PRODUCTS *cont.*

78. Static is stuck on you
　　　　—(*Static Guard*) Alberto-Culver Co.

79. Stop window washing
　　—(*Whiz mirror and glass cleaner*) Hollingshead Corp.

80. Stronger than dirt
　　　　—(*Ajax detergent*) Colgate-Palmolive Co.

81. Suds in a jiffy
　　　　—(*Jif soap flakes*).

82. Sunbrite, the cleanser with a spotless reputation
　　　　—Swift & Co.

83. Sure is strong
　　　　—(*lye*) Wm. Schield Mfg. Co.

84. Takes TOIL out of toilet cleaning
　　　　—Globe Laboratories.

85. The blue of spotless reputation
　　　　—(*Mrs. Stewart's bluing*) Luther Ford & Co.

86. The complete first suds detergent
　　　　—(*Prime soap*) Beach Soap Co.

87. The finest dye that money can buy
　　　　—(*dye*) Rit Products Corp.

88. The greatest name in housekeeping
　　　　—(*O-Cedar products*) Channel Chemical Co.

89. The meanest chore is a chore no more
　　　　—(*Sani-flush*) Boyle-Midway.

90. The products with a million friends
　　　　—(*wax, polish*) Midway Chemical Co.

91. There's not a cleaner like it
　　　　—Monarch Cleaner Corp.

92. The shine shines through
　　　　—(*Ajax all-purpose cleaner*) Colgate-Palmolive Co.

93. The washday miracle
　　　　—(*Tide*) Procter & Gamble Co.

94. The white line is the Clorox line
　　　　—(*Clorox bleach and disinfectant*) Clorox Co.

95. The woman who uses it, knows
　　　　—(*E-Z polish*) Martin & Martin.

96. The world's finest name in silver care
　　　　—W. J. Hagerty and Sons, Ltd. Inc.

97. This is a good place for a Stickup
　　　　—(*Stickup room deodorant*).

98. Thoughtfully designed with a woman in mind
　　　　—(*Bowlene*) The Climalene Co.

24. **CLEANING AND LAUNDRY PRODUCTS** *cont.*

   99. **Tide's in, dirt's out**
                                —(*Tide*) Procter & Gamble Co.

  100. **Tintex tints in the rinse**
                                  —(*dye*) Tintex Co. Inc.

  101. **When all soaps fail, Flash cleans**
                                  —Flash Chemical Co.

  102. **Wipes off dirt and grease, as easy as dusting**
                         —(*Old English household cleaner*).

  103. **Wizard of wash**
                    —Maid-Easy Cleansing Products Corp.

  104. **You'll find the woman's touch in every Purex product**
                                     —Purex Corp.

  105. **Your biggest bargain in cleanliness**
                      —(*Soilax*) Economics Laboratory Inc.

25. **CLEANING SERVICES**

    1. **And away go troubles down the drain**
                               —Roto-Rooter Corp.

    2. **Clothes do help you win, dry clean them oftener**
                     —American Laundry Machinery Co.

    3. **Send it to the dry cleaner**
                     —American Laundry Machinery Co.

    4. **The cleaning people who care**
                                 —Servicemaster

    5. **The laundry does it better**
                     —Laundry Industry of Seattle.

CLOCKS . . . See 124. WATCHES AND CLOCKS

26. **CLOTHING, MISCELLANEOUS**
    See also **48. FOOTWEAR, 61. HOSIERY, 109. SWIMWEAR, 121. UNDERWEAR, 123. WARDROBE ACCESSORIES**

    1. **A hat for every face**
                                  —Sam Bonnart Inc.

    2. **All the new ones all the time**
                          —Rothschild Bros. Hat Co.

    3. **Always virgin wool**
                          —Pendleton Woolen Mills.

    4. **America lives in R and K Originals**
                        —R and K Originals Inc.

    5. **America's finest fitting outercoats**
                          —Barron-Anderson Co.

26. CLOTHING, MISCELLANEOUS *cont.*

6. **America's first name in formal wear**
                                   —Rudofker's Sons

7. **America's only known-priced clothes**
                —(*Styleplus*) Henry Sonneborn & Co.

8. **A miracle in the rain**
        —(*Koroseal raincoat*) Goodrich General Products Co.

9. **A "must" for every wardrobe**
                —(*Sportleigh briefer coat*).

10. **A national buyword**
                —(*Georgiana frocks*).

11. **Apparel without parallel**
                —(*Ellesse clothing*) Ellesse U.S.A. Inc.

12. **A 'round the year coat**
                —(*Alligator rainwear*).

13. **A shade better than the rest**
                —(*straw hats*) Superior Hat Co.

14. **A sweater is better if it's a Huddlespun**
                —Herald Knitwear Co.

15. **As western as the setting sun**
                —(*Frontex shirts*).

16. **Balanced tailoring makes Timely Clothes look better—longer**
                —Timely Clothes Inc.

17. **Because it might rain**
                —(*Harbor Master*) Jonathan Logan.

18. **Belcraft Shirts, your bosom friend**
                —Belcraft Shirt Co.

19. **Berkley Ties the world**
                —Berkley Knitting Co.

20. **Be Scotch, get your money's worth**
                —Doniger & Co.

21. **Born in America. Worn round the world**
                —John B. Stetson Co.

22. **Brilliant as the sun**
                —(*Lustray shirts*) Lustberg-Nast Co.

23. **Buy overalls from the inside out**
                —Crown & Headlight.

24. **By this sign you shall know them**
                —Currick, Leiken & Bandler.

25. **Clothes in the New York manner**
                —Weber & Heilbroner.

26.   CLOTHING, MISCELLANEOUS *cont.*

26.   **Clothes that enhance your public appearance**
—House of Worsted-Tex.

27.   **Coolest hat under the sun**
—Cardine Hat Co.

28.   **Cut out for a long career**
—(*Washwear*) Elder Mfg. Co.

29.   **Danskins are not just for dancing**
—Danskin Inc.

30.   **Definitely Glenoit for happy persons**
—Glenoit Mills Inc.

31.   **Designed to be lived in**
—(*sweaters*) Irwill Knitwear Corp.

32.   **"Designs for the world's best dressed"**
—Mr. John.

33.   **Does something for you**
—(*Style-Mart suit*) Merit Clothing Co.

34.   **Don't forget that Koveralls Keep Kids Klean**
—Levi Strauss & Co.

35.   **Don't get wet, get Palmer**
—Palmer Asbestos & Rubber Corp.

36.   **Dry back or money back**
—(*outdoor clothing*) Lewis M. Weed Co.

37.   **Every man should wear at least three straw hats**
—National Association of Straw Hat Mfrs.

38.   **Every style worth while**
—Louis Meyers & Son Inc.

39.   **Everything to wear**
—Genesco Inc.

40.   **Expensive shirts ought to look it**
—(*Excello*) Kayser-Roth Corp.

41.   **Fashion in action**
—(*ranch togs*) Wrangler's.

42.   **Faultless since 1881—The nightwear of a nation**
—Faultless Nightwear Corp.

43.   **Feel the fabric and you'll feel the difference**
—(*Botany shirts*).

44.   **Fifty per cent more wear**
—H. D. Lee Mercantile Co.

45.   **Follow the ARROW and you follow the style**
—(*shirts*) Cluett, Peabody & Co. Inc.

46.   **For goodness sake wear Buckeye Shirts**
—Buckeye Shirt Co.

26. CLOTHING, MISCELLANEOUS *cont.*

47. **For men who care what they wear**
                              —Pioneer Suspender Co.

48. **For that good-looking feeling**
                              —Doris Miller Clothes.

49. **For the elegant petite**
                         —(*coats, suits*) Lilli-Ann Corp.

50. **For the man on the move**
                              —McGregor-Doniger Inc.

51. **For the nicest youngsters you know**
                              —Mason Clothes.

52. **For the rest of the night**
                         —(*pajamas*) Steiner & Son.

53. **For the typical American size**
                              —Leslie Fay Inc.

54. **For those friskie years**
                —(*Spree Togs for children*) Tri-Parel Corp.

55. **For younger young men**
                         —Leopold, Solomon & Eisendrath.

56. **For young men and men who stay young**
                —(*Society Brand clothes*) Alfred Decker.

57. **From mill to millions**
                         —(*overalls*) Hamilton Carhartt.

58. **Fur goodness sake try Kruskal**
                         —(*furs*) Kruskal and Kruskal.

59. **Furs that reflect youth**
                              —Zimmerman-Scher Co.

60. **Guaranteed, the hardest working workwear**
                              —H. D. Lee Co. Inc.

61. **Hats made so fine that all others must be compared to them**
                              —Knox the Hatter.

62. **Help build personality**
                —(*Stadium clothes*) Woodhull, Goodale & Bull Inc.

63. **If you think clothes don't make a difference, try walking down the street without any**
                              —Wolf Tailoring.

64. **I look my best in a Hardeman**
                              —Hardeman Hat Co.

65. **"Important occasion dresses"**
                              —Lorrie Deb Corp.

66. **Internationally known mark of quality**
                              —Manhattan Industries Inc.

26. CLOTHING, MISCELLANEOUS *cont.*

67. **It pays to show the name they know**
—Kleinert's Rubber Co.

68. **It's in the fit**
—Schwartz Bros. Dress Co.

69. **It's not Jockey brand if it doesn't have the Jockey boy**
—Jockey Menswear Div., Coopers Inc.

70. **Just wear a smile and a Jantzen**
—Jantzen Inc.

71. **Largest immediate delivery fur house**
—Samuel Katz.

72. **Lead the Ship 'n Shore life**
—(*blouses*) Ship 'n Shore Inc.

73. **Learn about little women from us**
—Schwartz Bros. Dress Co.

74. **Let them grow up in Kaynee**
—The Kaynee Co.

75. **Let us tan your hide**
—(*furs*) Crisby Frisian Fur Co.

76. **Made in America for little Americans**
—R. Solomon Knitting Mills.

77. **Made to stand the gaff**
—Nogar Clothing Mfg. Co.

78. **Make the children happy**
—(*Yankiboy play clothes*) Sackman Bros.

79. **Mix 'em and match 'em**
—Buster Boy Suit Co.

80. **Most admired, most desired for cool comfort**
—(*Marlboro shirts*).

81. **Neatness lasts from breakfast to bedtime**
—Essley Shirt Co.

82. **"Never wear a white shirt before sundown," says Hathaway**
—C. F. Hathaway Co.

83. **Not the biggest—but the best!**
—(*Seven Seas slacks*) Anthony Gesture.

84. **Official tailors to the West**
—H. D. Lee Co. Inc.

85. **Oshkosh, b'gosh**
—(*overalls*) Oshkosh Overall Co.

86. **Overhead economy**
—(*hats*) John B. Stetson Co.

26. **CLOTHING, MISCELLANEOUS** *cont.*

87. **Peak value of the year**
—Dickinson Clothes Inc.

88. **Right for Sunday Morning**
—(*hats*) John B. Stetson Co.

89. **Rub 'em, tub 'em, scrub 'em, they come up smiling**
—Jack Tar Togs.

90. **Rugged as the west**
—Black Mfg. Co.

91. **Seen in the best of company**
—(*Vanity hats*) Noname Hat Mfg. Co.

92. **Slip into a Bradley and out-of-doors**
—Bradley Knitting Co.

93. **Soft and silky as a kitten's purr**
—(*Society Brand clothes*) Alfred Decker.

94. **Soft as kitten's ears**
—(*Melbroke ties*) Spiegel Neckwear Co. Inc.

95. **So-o soft, so-o smooth, so-o comfortable**
—Eclipse Sleep Products Inc.

96. **Sportswear for sportsmen**
—Jantzen Inc.

97. **Step out with a Stetson**
—(*hats*) John B. Stetson Co.

98. **Strong for work**
—Jobbers Overall Co.

99. **Styled for young fellows, worn by all fellows**
—Chas. Levy's Sons.

100. **Style without extravagance**
—(*men's clothes*) Dreyfous & Lang.

101. **Takes the guessing out of dressing**
—Wembley Ties Inc.

102. **Tate-made is Rite-made**
—(*industrial uniforms*) Tate Mfg. Co.

103. **The aristocrat of polyester neckwear**
—Wembley Ties Inc.

104. **The aristocrat of shirtings**
—Sea Island Mills.

105. **The best name in all-weather coats and rainwear**
—The Alligator Co.

106. **The boy's suit built for wear**
—J. J. Preis & Co.

107. **The brand with loyalty to quality**
—(*Billy the Kid slacks*) Hortex Mfg. Co.

26. CLOTHING, MISCELLANEOUS *cont.*

108. **The coats for every wear, everywhere**
 —International Duplex Coat Co.

109. **The "Color Guide" tie**
 —Wembley Ties Inc.

110. **The easiest name for a man to remember**
 —(*shirts*) Wilson Bros.

111. **The finest habit a man can have**
 —Merchant Tailors Society.

112. **The finest human hands can achieve**
 —Langrock Clothing Co.

113. **The friend-making work shirt**
 —McCawley & Co. Inc.

114. **The furmost line**
 —Wells-Treister Co.

115. **The hat corner of the world**
 —Knox the Hatter.

116. **The hat of silent smartness**
 —Lamson & Hubbard Co.

117. **The hat that goes with good clothes**
 —Mallory Hat Co. Inc.

118. **The kind of clothes gentlemen wear**
 —Kahn Tailoring Co.

119. **The kind real boys wear**
 —(*Perfection clothes*) H. A. Seinsheimer Co.

120. **The label mothers know and trust**
 —(*children's suits*) Minneapolis Knitting Works.

121. **The label to ask for**
 —Davidow Suits Inc.

122. **The mark of modern pajamas**
 —(*Dot snappers*) United-Carr Inc.

123. **The mark of the world's most famous hat**
 —John B. Stetson Co.

124. **The million dollar overall**
 —Crown Overall Mfg. Co.

125. **The most comfortable hat made**
 —(*Resistol self-conforming hats*) Byer-Rolnick.

126. **The name to remember in rainwear**
 —(*Weatherbee*) Triangle Raincoat Co.

127. **The national summer suit for men**
 —(*Keep-Kool*) Snellenburg Cloth Co.

128. **The pattern people**
 —Simplicity Patterns Co. Inc.

26. CLOTHING, MISCELLANEOUS *cont.*

129. The perfect brace that stays in place
—(*suspenders*) Sidley Co.

130. The rage of the college age
—(*Sidley cords*).

131. The rainy day pal
—(*Reflex slicker*) A. J. Tower Co.

132. There are no dudes in our duds
—(*Man-O-West slacks and pants*) Freeman Mfg. Co.

133. There can be no compromise with quality
—Langrock Clothing Co.

134. There's a Lee for every job
—(*Lee work clothes*) H. D. Lee Co. Inc.

135. There's a Merton cap or hat for every sport
—C. S. Merton & Co.

136. There's something about them you'll like
—(*Fleurette frocks*) Einhorn Bros.

137. The rest is easy
—(*nightshirts, pajamas*) E. Simons Mfg. Co.

138. The right hat for real men
—Langenberg Hat Co.

139. The secret of California casualness
—(*men's sportswear*) H. & L. Black.

140. The shirt house of America
—F. Jacobson & Sons.

141. The skier's tailor since 1929
—White Stag Mfg. Co.

142. The stiff brim straw with the soft brim fit
—(*hats*) M. S. Levy & Sons.

143. The world's smartest collar
—Phillips-Jones Corp.

144. They fit royally
—(*shirts*) Phillips-Jones Corp.

145. They hold their shape
—(*Travelo knit jackets and vests*) Peckham-Foreman.

146. They must make good or we will
—Oshkosh Overall Co.

147. Tropical suit that "breathes" fresh air
—(*Northcool suits*) Sagner Inc.

148. Wares that men wear
—Stone Bros.

149. Watch the wear
—(*overalls*) H. W. Carter & Sons.

26. **CLOTHING, MISCELLANEOUS** *cont.*

150. **We are what others pretend to be**
—Izod Lacoste.

151. **Wears like a pig's nose**
—(*men's overalls*) W. M. Finck & Co.

152. **We don't insure status . . . only quality**
—(*Hang Ten clothing*) Ram Knitting Mills.

153. **When appearance counts**
—David Adler & Sons.

154. **When in Broderick suits your class is dressed, each girl's inspired to play her best**
—Tom Broderick Co.

155. **When the sun goes down**
—Berkeley Square Clothes.

156. **Wherever you go you look better in Arrow**
—Cluett, Peabody & Co. Inc.

157. **Work clothing that conquers hard wear**
—Cowden Mfg. Co.

158. **World's finest mink**
—United Mink Producers Assn.

159. **You can't knock the crease out**
—(*Digby slacks*) Digby Inc.

160. **Younger by design**
—(*Van Heusen*) Phillips-Van Heusen Corp.

161. **Your shoulders will thank you**
—Pioneer Suspender Co.

27. **COFFEE**
See also **15.** BEVERAGES, MISCELLANEOUS, **110.** TEA

1. **All the good left in**
—Cheek-Neal Coffee Co.

2. **Always in good taste**
—(*Royal Blend*) Granger & Co.

3. **Always the same, always good**
—(*Old Reliable*) Dayton Spice Mills Co.

4. **Always the same good coffee**
—The Haserot Co.

5. **America's largest selling high grade coffee**
—(*Maxwell House*) Cheek-Neal Coffee Co.

6. **America's No. 1 Mountain Grown Coffee**
—(*Folger's*) Folger and Co.

7. **A mountain of flavor in every spoonful**
—(*Folger's*) Folger and Co.

27. **COFFEE** *cont.*

8. **As delicious as coffee can be**
                              —Hanley & Kinsella Coffee Co.

9. **Be coffee-wise not coupon-foolish**
                              —Merchants Coffee Co. of New Orleans.

10. **Beginning a second century of leadership**
                      —(*Chase & Sanborn*) Standard Brands Inc.

11. **Better coffee every time with S & W**
                              —S & W Fine Foods.

12. **Celebrate the moments of your life**
    —(*General Foods International Coffees*) General Foods
                                                      Corp.

13. **Chock Full O' Nuts is that heavenly coffee**
                —(*Chock Full O' Nuts*) Chock Full O' Nuts Corp.

14. **Coffee from the magic mountains**
                              —(*Folger's*) Folger and Co.

15. **Coffee rich enough to be served in America's finest
    restaurants**
                      —(*Folger's instant*) Procter & Gamble Co.

16. **Coffee, the American drink**
                      —Joint Coffee Trade Publicity Committee.

17. **Cream of the coffees**
                              —Albert Ehlers Inc.

18. **Drink it and sleep**
                              —(*Sanka*) General Foods Corp.

19. **Every cup's a cup of joy**
                              —American Coffee Co.

20. **Fall in love with coffee all over again**
                —(*High Point decaffeinated*) Procter & Gamble Co.

21. **Fill it to the rim with Brim**
                —(*Brim decaffeinated*) General Foods Corp.

22. **For goodness sake buy Admiration Coffee**
                              —Duncan Coffee Co.

23. **For people who love coffee, but not caffeine**
                —(*Sanka decaffeinated*) General Foods Corp.

24. **Get more out of life with coffee**
                              —Pan-American Coffee Bureau.

25. **Good to the last drop**
                      —(*Maxwell House*) General Foods Corp.

26. **Has 'em all beat**
                              —International Coffee Co.

27. **Healthful and good**
                              —Kaffee Hag Corp.

27. **COFFEE** *cont.*

28. **Hold on tight to your dreams**
—National Coffee Council.

29. **It more than satisfies, it agrees**
—Coffee Products of America.

30. **Its high quality makes it economical**
—(*Folger's*) Folger and Co.

31. **Just as you'd expect, right EVERY way**
—(*Del Monte*) California Packing Corp.

32. **Learn the economy of quality in Solitaire Coffee**
—Morey Mercantile Co.

33. **Life begins at breakfast with McLaughlin's Coffee**
—(*McLaughlin's*).

34. **Look for the date on the tin**
—(*Chase & Sanborn*) Standard Brands Inc.

35. **Made in the cup at the table**
—(*George Washington*).

36. **Maxwell House, too, is part of the American scene**
—Cheek-Neal Coffee Co.

37. **More cups of better coffee**
—Griggs Cooper Co.

38. **More flavor per cup, more cups per pound**
—(*Albert Ehlers*) Brooke Bond Foods.

39. **Morning's first thought**
—(*Royal Blend*) Granger & Co.

40. **One good cup deserves another**
—(*Beechnut*).

41. **Roaster-fresh coffee made in the cup**
—(*Nescafe*) Nestle Co. Inc.

42. **Seven great coffees in one**
—(*Del Monte*) California Packing Corp.

43. **So good you want a second cup**
—(*Savarin*) S. A. Schonbrunn & Co. Inc.

44. **Start the day right with Yale Coffee**
—Steinwender-Stoffregen Coffee Co.

45. **The best drinking coffee in the world**
—Lowry Coffee Co.

46. **The coffee-er coffee**
—(*Savarin*) S. A. Schonbrunn & Co. Inc.

47. **The coffee of inspiration**
—Schwabacher Bros.

48. **The coffee served at the Waldorf-Astoria**
—(*Savarin*) S. A. Schonbrunn & Co. Inc.

27. **COFFEE** *cont.*

49. The coffee that lets you sleep
—Kaffee Hag Corp.

50. The coffee without a regret
—(*Barrington Hall*) Baker Importing Co.

51. The coffee with the flavor advantage
—(*Folger's*) Folger and Co.

52. The cup of southern hospitality
—Duncan Coffee Co.

53. The first taste tells you it's good to the last drop
—(*Maxwell House*) Cheek-Neal Coffee Co.

54. The first thought in the morning
—(*Folger's*) Folger and Co.

55. The flavor sensation that sold the nation on coffee made in the cup
—(*Nescafe*) Nestle Co. Inc.

56. The friendly drink from good neighbors
—Pan-American Coffee Bureau.

57. The Good Coffee Folks
—P. W. Eastham & Co.

58. The Guest Coffee
—(*Yuban*) General Foods Corp.

59. The only instant coffee that's caffeine-free
—(*Instant Sanka*) General Foods Corp.

60. We roast it, others praise it
—(*Big Horn*).

61. Where only the best will do
—Hanley & Kinsella Coffee Co.

62. Wings of the morning
—(*Schilling coffee*) McCormick and Co. Inc.

63. Without grounds for complaint
—Alexander Balart Co.

64. You can't describe it until you've tried it
—Ronnoco Coffee Co.

65. You'll appreciate the flavor
—Crescent Mfg. Co.

66. You might as well have the best
—W. S. Quimby Co.

67. You never had coffee like this before
—(*Borden's instant*) Borden Inc.

COMMUNICATIONS . . . See **111.** TELECOMMUNICATIONS

COMPANIES . . . See **31.** CORPORATIONS, MISCELLANEOUS

28. **COMPUTER EQUIPMENT**
>   See also **37. ELECTRICAL PRODUCTS AND SERVICES,**
>   **38. ELECTRONICS INDUSTRY, 81. OFFICE EQUIPMENT**
>   **AND SUPPLIES**

1. **Announcing the state of the smart**
    > —(*personal computers*) IBM.

2. **A printer for every need and every speed**
    > —(*printers*) Printronix.

3. **A tool for modern times**
    > —(*personal computers*) IBM.

4. **Automation is economical**
    > —Fusion Inc.

5. **Brains & Beauty**
    > —(*Olivetti M20 personal computer*) Olivetti Corp.

6. **Celebrating the future**
    > —National Cash Register Co.

7. **Command the powers of Adam**
    > —(*Adam Computers*) Coleco.

8. **COMPAQ PLUS, the first high-performance portable personal computer**
    > —Compaq Computer Corporation.

9. **Computers for people**
    > —Atari.

10. **Confidence in every package**
    > —(*General Ledger*) Software International, General Electric Information Services Co.

11. **Data General. A Generation ahead.**
    > —Data General Corp.

12. **Designers of innovative systems for the information worker**
    > —(*terminals*) Lee Data Corp.

13. **Discover the Dysan difference**
    > —(*disks*) Dysan Corp.

14. **Everybody makes terminals. Only we make Lear Sieglers.**
    > —(*terminals*) Lear Siegler Inc.

15. **Everything a computer's supposed to be. Except expensive.**
    > —Alpha Micro.

16. **Excellence in software technology**
    > —Cincom Systems Inc.

17. **Family computer history is about to be written**
    > —Coleco.

28. **COMPUTER EQUIPMENT** *cont.*

18. **Glare/Guard: A difference you can see**
—(*anti-glare panels*) Optical Coating Laboratory Inc.

19. **High performance matrix printers**
—(*printers*) Datasouth Computer Corporation.

20. **ICOT . . . the data communications company**
—(*terminals*) ICOT Corp.

21. **Information. Not automation.**
—Sperry Corp.

22. **Leader in computer graphics**
—(*Cal Comp*) California Computer Products Inc.

23. **Machines that make data move**
—Teletype Corp.

24. **Make the Wyse decision**
—Wyse Technology.

25. **Maxell. It's worth it.**
—(*disks*) Maxell Corp.

26. **MDS Hero will make a hero out of you**
—Mohawk Data Sciences.

27. **Meeting the communications challenge of the 80's**
—(*printers*) Paradyne Corp.

28. **MicroComputers for DataCommunications**
—Micom Systems Inc.

29. **NEC and me**
—(*printers*) NEC Information Systems Inc.

30. **Never forgets**
—(*disks*) Elephant Memory Systems.

31. **Nothing is better than a Verbatim response**
—(*disks*) Verbatim Corp.

32. **Now that the world relies on computers it needs a computer it can rely on**
—(*software*) Stratus.

33. **One language. One solution.**
—(*FOCUS software*) Information Builders Inc.

34. **Our business is the intelligent use of computers**
—Electronic Data Systems.

35. **Our windows reflect the way you work**
—(*Desq software*) Quarterdeck Office Systems.

36. **Powerful Software Solutions**
—Software AG of North America Inc.

37. **Qume printers. Your best investment in productivity.**
—(*printers*) Qume Corp.

28. **COMPUTER EQUIPMENT** *cont.*

38. **Ramis II . . . the leader by design**
—(*Ramis II software*) Mathematica Products Group, Martin Marietta Data Systems Co.

39. **SAS saves time**
—(*software*) SAS Institute Inc.

40. **Setting you free**
—(*Hewlett-Packard personal computers*) Hewlett-Packard Co.

41. **Simware delivers**
—(*software*) Simware Inc.

42. **Specialists in digital technology**
—(*Cal Comp*) California Computer Products Inc.

43. **Standard of the plotting industry**
—(*Cal Comp*) California Computer Products Inc.

44. **Strategic solutions to storing, sharing and moving data**
—(*data storage*) Masstor Systems Corp.

45. **Stratus: Continuous processing**
—(*software*) Stratus.

46. **Tandem. NonStop transaction processing.**
—Tandem Computers Inc.

47. **Teletype: value sets us apart**
—(*terminals*) Teletype Corp.

48. **The automated answer to the paper explosion**
—Remington Office Systems Div., Sperry Rand Corp

49. **The dawn of a new era in personal computing**
—(*Tandy personal computers*) Radio Shack.

50. **The first computer**
—(*Univac*) Sperry Rand Corp.

51. **The First line in printers**
—(*printers*) Printronix.

52. **The friendly computer**
—Commodore.

53. **The future . . . without the shock**
—(*Exxon office systems*) Exxon Corp.

54. **The hardest working software in the world**
—(*Lotus software*) Lotus Development Corp.

55. **The industrial bar code experts**
—(*terminals*) Intermec.

56. **The key to information center productivity**
—(*FOCUS software*) Information Builders Inc.

28. **COMPUTER EQUIPMENT** *cont.*

57. **The most complete software company in the world.**
—University Computing Co.

58. **The natural language query system**
—(*Intellect software*) Artificial Intelligence Corp.

59. **The network you can control**
—(*networks*) M/A-COM Linkabit Inc.

60. **The office automation computer people**
—(*Wang VS computers*) Wang Laboratories Inc.

61. **The optimum software for data center management**
—Value Computing Inc.

62. **The other computer company**
—Honeywell

63. **The power is within your reach**
—Timex/Sinclair.

64. **The printer company**
—(*printers*) Dataproducts Corporation.

65. **The problem solvers**
—General Electric Co.

66. **The Smart Desk from IBM**
—(*personal computers*) IBM.

67. **The technology leader in data communications**
—(*Networking Microplexer*) Timeplex Inc.

68. **The user friendly company**
—(*software*) Sterling Software Marketing.

69. **The world's largest independent manufacturer of computer interfaces**
—MDB Systems Inc.

70. **Together, we can find the answers.**
—Honeywell.

71. **Tomorrow's software. Here today.**
—Hogan Systems.

72. **Tomorrow's software today**
—(*software*) McCormack & Dodge Corp.

73. **Univac is saving a lot of people a lot of time**
—Sperry Rand Corp.

74. **Visual . . . See for yourself**
—(*terminals*) Visual Technology Inc.

75. **We don't make computers. We make them better.**
—(*Quadram System*) Texas Instruments Inc.

76. **We make networks work**
—(*networks*) Interlan Inc.

28. **COMPUTER EQUIPMENT** *cont.*

77. **We make the addition easy**
—(*computer systems*) PHAZE Information Machines Corp.

78. **We make the right decisions**
—(*printers*) Decision Data Computer Corporation.

79. **We make your systems fault tolerant from end to end**
—(*matrix switching*) Data Switch.

80. **We sparked the revolution**
—(*networks*) Datapoint Corp.

81. **We stretch your budget. Not the truth.**
—Alpha Micro.

82. **Where imagination leads**
—(*Lasergrafix 1200 printer*) Quality Micro Systems Inc.

83. **Where service and software come together**
—(*software*) Sterling Software Marketing.

84. **Where the data movement started and startling moves are made**
—Teletype Corp.

85. **Where the Solutions Come First**
—Perkin-Elmer.

86. **You're not just playing, you're learning**
—Texas Instruments Inc.

29. **CONDIMENTS AND SPICES**
See also **47. FOOD, MISCELLANEOUS**

1. **America's favorite for thick, rich catsup**
—(*Heinz catsup*) H. J. Heinz Co.

2. **America's favorite mayonnaise**
—(*Hellmann's*) CPC International Inc.

3. **A salt for every purpose**
—International Salt Co.

4. **Better than mayonnaise, yet costs less**
—(*Miracle Whip salad dressing*) Kraft Foods.

5. **Bring out the Hellmann's and bring out the best**
—(*Hellmann's mayonnaise*) Best Foods.

6. **Come rain or fog there's no shaker-clog**
—International Salt Co.

7. **Costs less when used**
—(*Dr. Price's vanilla*).

8. **First aid for clever cooks**
—(*Derby steak sauce*) Derby Foods Inc.

29. CONDIMENTS AND SPICES *cont.*

9. **Flavor so delicious only your figure knows they're low calorie**
     —(*Wish Bone salad dressing*) Thos. J. Lipton Inc.

10. **Flows freely, dissolves readily, develops food flavor**
     —(*Diamond Crystal salt*) Diamond Crystal Salt Co.

11. **For the well-dressed salad**
     —Seidner's Mayonnaise.

12. **Free running**
     —(*Regal salt*).

13. **Good things to eat come from 1 Mustard St.**
     —The R. T. French Co.

14. **Halves the cost and doubles the satisfaction**
     —(*True-Taste mayonnaise*).

15. **Health in every jar**
     —(*Blue Ribbon mayonnaise*) Richard Hellman Inc.

16. **It's as good as the best and better than the rest**
     —(*Queens Health salt*).

17. **Its favor has grown through flavor alone**
     —McCormick and Co. Inc.

18. **It's in the bag**
     —(*rock salt*) International Salt Co.

19. **It's no secret … Schilling flavor makes all the difference in the world!**
     —Schilling Div., McCormick and Co. Inc.

20. **It stays on the salad**
     —(*French dressing*) A. E. Wright Co.

21. **It takes the best to make the best**
     —Worcester Salt Co.

22. **Less than a cent's worth will flavor a cake**
     —(*Shirriff's vanilla*).

23. **Made in the home-made way**
     —(*mayonnaise*) Richard Hellman Inc.

24. **Make good foods taste better**
     —(*tomato catsup*) H. J. Heinz Co.

25. **Makes every meal an event**
     —(*Premier salad dressing*) F. H. Leggett.

26. **Makes good food taste better**
     —(*salt*) General Foods Corp.

27. **Mellowed in wood to full strength**
     —(*vinegar*) H. J. Heinz Co.

28. **New Orleans' most famous sauce**
     —(*Remoulade*).

29. **CONDIMENTS AND SPICES** *cont.*

29. **Pass the salt for better livestock**
—(*Sterling salt*) International Salt Co.

30. **Rain or shine, it will always run**
—(*Purity salt*) Purity Condiments Inc.

31. **Salt of the Covenant**
—(*kosher salt*) Ohio Salt Co.

32. **Silent partners in famous foods**
—(*coloring, flavoring*) Stange Co.

33. **The added touch that means so much**
—(*Lee & Perrin's sauce*).

34. **The catsup with the big tomato taste**
—(*catsup*) Hunt-Wesson Foods Inc.

35. **The chef's flavor in home cooking**
—Kitchen Bouquet Inc.

36. **The dash that makes the dish**
—(*A-1 sauce*) Heublein Inc.

37. **The house of flavor**
—McCormick and Co. Inc.

38. **The pick of pickles**
—(*pickles*) Crosse & Blackwell.

39. **There *are* imitations—be sure the brand is *Tabasco***
—(*Tabasco sauce*) McIlhenny Co.

40. **The salt cellar of America**
—Barton Salt Co.

41. **The salt of the earth**
—Morton Salt Co.

42. **The seasoning supreme**
—(*Tabasco sauce*) McIlhenny Co.

43. **The season's best and the best of seasoning**
—(*ketchup*) H. J. Heinz Co.

44. **The way to a man's heart**
—(*Log Cabin syrup*) General Foods Corp.

45. **This is no place for "second best"**
—(*Hellmann's mayonnaise*) Best Foods Div., CPC International Inc.

46. **When it rains, it pours**
—Morton Salt Co.

47. **When it's wet it's dry**
—Worcester Salt Co.

48. **Word to the wives is sufficient**
—Carey Salt Co.

29. CONDIMENTS AND SPICES *cont.*

49. **You know it's fresh, it's dated**
> —Dated Mayonnaise Inc.

50. **Ze dash zat makes za dish**
> —(*A-1 sauce*) Heublein Inc.

CONFECTIONS ... See **20. CANDY AND GUM**

CONSTRUCTION ... See **18. BUILDING SUPPLIES, 73. MACHINERY**

COOKING FUELS ... See **59. HEATING AND COOKING FUELS**

COOKWARE ... See **11. BAKED GOODS AND BAKING SUPPLIES, 68. KITCHEN PRODUCTS AND UTENSILS**

30. COPYING EQUIPMENT
See also **81. OFFICE EQUIPMENT AND SUPPLIES**

1. **As easily as the sun shines**
> —(*Blue Reprint machines*) Wicker Bros.

2. **Copies for communication throughout the world**
> —American Photocopy Equipment Co.

3. **Electro-Copyst, a photo-copying machine for every office**
> —(*Electro-Copyst*).

4. **For imagination in communication, look to 3M business product centers**
> —Minnesota Mining and Manufacturing Co.

5. **Look to 3M for imagination in image-making**
> —Minnesota Mining and Manufacturing Co.

6. **New advances in office copying keep coming from Kodak**
> —Eastman Kodak Co.

7. **Now everybody can have Xerocopies**
> —Xerox Corp.

8. **Quickest way to duplicate**
> —(*Ditto duplicator*) Duplicator Manufacturing Co.

9. **The most beautiful copies of all**
> —Chas. Bruning Co.

10. **You can't buy a multigraph unless you need it**
> —Multigraph Co.

31. CORPORATIONS, MISCELLANEOUS

1. **A company of uncommon enterprise**
> —Dravo Corp.

31. CORPORATIONS, MISCELLANEOUS *cont.*

2. **An eye to the future, an ear to the ground**
    —General Motors Corp.

3. **Applying advanced technology to bring you
    exciting new products**
    —Eaton, Yale and Towne Inc.

4. **A step ahead of tomorrow**
    —Zurn Industries Inc.

5. **Building business is our business**
    —Tenneco Inc.

6. **Check with Koppers**
    —Koppers Co. Inc.

7. **Dedicated to the pursuit of excellence**
    —Rohr Corp.

8. **Diversified-worldwide**
    —Singer Co.

9. **Does a lot for you**
    —Scovill Manufacturing Co.

10. **Doughboy does it better ... for a wide range of
    industries**
    —Doughboy Industries Inc.

11. **8 Companies running hard**
    —Trans Union Corp.

12. **... Helping people communicate**
    —Addressograph-Multigraph Corp.

13. **In metals, plastics and paper Budd works to make
    tomorrow ... today**
    —Budd Co.

14. **Mannesmann builds for the future**
    —Mannesmann-Export Corp.

15. **North American Rockwell and the future are made
    for you**
    —North American Rockwell Corp.

16. **Progress for industry worldwide**
    —Combustion Engineering Inc.

17. **Progress is our most important product**
    —General Electric Co.

18. **Progress through precision**
    —Torrington Co.

19. **Putting ideas to work ... in machinery, chemicals,
    defense, fibers and films**
    —FMC Corp.

31. CORPORATIONS, MISCELLANEOUS *cont.*

20. **Reliability in rubber, asbestos, sintered metal, specialized plastics**
—Raybestos-Manhattan Inc.

21. **Specialists in process and energy control**
—The Foxboro Co.

22. **The discovery company**
—Union Carbide Corp.

23. **The Foodpower people**
—Central Soya Co. Inc.

24. **The great engineers**
—Borg-Warner Corp.

25. **The growing world of Libby-Owens-Ford**
—Libby-Owens-Ford Co.

26. **The growth company**
—Georgia-Pacific Corp.

27. **"The Innovators"**
—Torrington Co.

28. **The *name* is Crane**
—Crane Co.

29. **The people movers**
—Budd Co.

30. **The 21st century company**
—Gulf and Western Industries Inc.

31. **We're synergistic**
—Sperry Rand Corp.

32. **We understand how important it is to listen**
—Sperry Corp.

33. **We've just begun to grow**
—Keene Corp.

34. **What's new for tomorrow is at Singer today**
—Singer Co.

35. **Where great ideas are meant to happen**
—Arvin Industries Inc.

36. **Where ideas unlock the future**
—Bendix Corp.

37. **Wherever you look ... you see Budd**
—Budd Co.

38. **World-wide engineering, manufacturing and construction**
—Dorr-Oliver Inc.

39. **You can be sure if it's Westinghouse**
—Westinghouse Electric Corp.

32. COSMETICS

See also **54.** HAIR CARE, **116.** TOILETRIES

1. **A beautiful skin is adored**
   —Nu-Art Laboratories.

2. **Adds life to years rather than years to life**
   —(*face cream*) B. S. Boss.

3. **A fountain of youth for your skin**
   —(*Balm-o-Lem*) Jean Jordeau Inc.

4. **Always at your fingertips**
   —(*nail polish*) Lorr Laboratories.

5. **A personalized service that comes to your home**
   —(*Avon cosmetics*) Avon Products Inc.

6. **Beautiful skies now and forever**
   —Charles of the Ritz Group Ltd.

7. **Beautiful skin begins with Noxema**
   —(*Noxema Skin Cream*) Noxell Corp.

8. **Beauty in every box**
   —(*face powder*) Celebrated Products Sales.

9. **Beauty *is* only skin deep; Luminiere controls the skin**
   —En-Ve Inc.

10. **Beauty's master touch**
    —(*Oriental cream*) F. L. Hopkins & Son.

11. **Because lips that feel lifeless aren't worth a look**
    —(*Blistex lip balm*) Blistex Inc.

12. **Be kind to your skin**
    —Beaver-Remmers-Graham Co.

13. **Buy your beauty needs from beauticians**
    —Contoure Laboratories.

14. **Devoted to beauty**
    —Princess Pat Ltd.

15. **Don't be a pale face**
    —The Coppertone Corp.

16. **Doubles your face value**
    —(*Dreskin cosmetics*) Campana Corp.

17. **Enchanting ladies choose Dorothy Gray**
    —Lehn and Fink Consumer Products

18. **Ends that painted look**
    —(*Tangee lipstick*) Luft-Tangee Inc.

19. **Eyes of youth**
    —(*eye creams*) Gertrude Shyde.

32. COSMETICS *cont.*

20. **Filters sun, speeds tan**
—(*Sutra lotion*).

21. **For all important occasions, wear Dura-Gloss**
—Lorr Laboratories.

22. **For "dream hands," cream your hands**
—(*Paquins hand cream*).

23. **For matching lips and fingertips**
—(*lipstick, nail polish*) Revlon Inc.

24. **For smooth white hands tomorrow use Thine Hand Creme tonight**
—Frailey Prods.

25. **For that "come hither" look**
—(*Angelus lipstick*).

26. **For that smart sun-tan look**
—(*Max Factor make-up*) Max Factor & Co.

27. **For the private world of the bath**
—House of Wrisley Inc.

28. **For the women who can afford the best. Even though it costs less**
—(*Hazel Bishop*) Bishop Industries Inc.

29. **For women whose eyes are older than they are**
—John Robert Powers Products Co.

30. **For youthful hands, to have and to hold**
—(*hand lotion*) Montclair Laboratories.

31. **From the world's most renowned cosmetic research laboratories**
—Revlon Inc.

32. **Get the winning feeling**
—(*Vaseline Intensive Care Lotion*) Chesebrough-Pond's Inc.

33. **Good to your finger tips**
—(*nail polish*) Strathmore Products Co.

34. **Guard your youth with Youth Garde**
—(*Youth Garde Moisturizer*).

35. **Incense of flowers**
—(*Black and White face powder*) Plough Inc.

36. **It can help you look younger too**
—(*Oil of Olay*) Olay Corp.

37. **Just to show a proper glow**
—(*Ingram's rouge*) F. F. Ingram Co.

38. **Keep Dura-Gloss always on hand**
—Lorr Laboratories.

32. COSMETICS *cont.*

39. **Keep kissable with Flame-Glo Lipstick**
                              —Flame-Glo Cosmetics.

40. **Keeps your face fit**
                              —(*Aqua Velva cream*) J. B. Williams Co. Inc.

41. **Keep the stars in your eyes**
                              —(*eye lotion*) Sales Affiliates Inc.

42. **Liquid jewelry**
                              —(*nail polish*) Lorr Laboratories.

43. **Living face make-up and living face cosmetics**
                              —(*Marinello*) Sales Affiliates Inc.

44. **Makes dull faces shine**
                              —Keystone Emery Mills.

45. **Makes the skin like velvet**
                              —Mystic Cream Co.

46. **Never before did 10¢ do so much for a woman**
                              —(*nail polish*) Lorr Laboratories.

47. **No more sticky fingers**
                              —(*Soft Sense skin lotion*)

48. **Only a liquid can cleanse to the depths of the pores**
                              —E. Burnham Inc.

49. **Personality face powder**
                              —Celebrated Products Sales.

50. **Personalized cosmetic services**
                              —Luzier Inc.

51. **Powdered perfume for the complexion**
                              —(*Velveola Souveraine face powder*).

52. **Promotes a tan while it protects your skin**
                              —Dorothy Gray.

53. **P. S. And it's especially great as a hand lotion**
                              —(*Dermassage*) S. M. Edison Chemical Co.

54. **Refresh, revive that sleepy skin**
                              —Dorothy Gray.

55. **Removes the freckles, whitens the skin**
                              —Stillman Co.

56. **Saves the face of the nation**
                              —(*lotion*) Fife Products Corp.

57. **Screens out burn and makes you brown**
                              —(*sun oil*) Dorothy Gray.

58. **Sheer make-up for sheer beauty**
                              —(*Houbigant*) Houbigant Inc.

59. **She has it made**
                              —Clairol Inc.

32. COSMETICS *cont.*

60. **Sifted through silk**
—(*Pussywillow face powder*) Henry Tetlow Co.

61. **Skol tan keeps you "outdoor lovely"**
—(*Skol sun oil*) J. B. Williams Co. Inc.

62. **Smoothest powders in the world**
—Melba Mfg. Co.

63. **... So glamorous you have to be *told* they're hypo-allergenic**
—(*Almay*) Schieffelin and Co.

64. **Specialists in skin care**
—Chap Stick Co.

65. **Stay pretty in the sun**
—(*sun oil*) Elizabeth Arden.

66. **Stays on till you take it off**
—(*Coty 24 Hour lipstick*) Chas. Pfizer and Co. Inc.

67. **Tartan lets you TAN, never burn**
—(*Tartan sun oil*) McKesson & Robbins.

68. **The authority in the exciting world of beauty**
—Max Factor & Co.

69. **The body cosmetic**
—(*Cashmere Bouquet talcum*) Colgate-Palmolive Co.

70. **The eye make-up in good taste**
—Maybelline Co.

71. **The famous skin softener**
—(*Campana Balm*) Campana Corp.

72. **The girl with the beautiful face**
—Clairol Inc.

73. **The girl with the beautiful mouth**
—Clairol Inc.

74. **The kind that keeps**
—(*cold creams*) Daggett & Ramsdell.

75. **The light moisturizing bath oil for dry skin**
—(*Tender Touch*) Helene Curtis Industries Inc.

76. **The lipstick without the dye**
—Ar-ex Products Inc.

77. **The most elegant name in cosmetics**
—(*DuBarry*) Lambert-Hudnut Mfg. Labs Inc.

78. **The most prized eye cosmetics in the world**
—Maybelline Co.

79. **The nail enamel your manicurist recommends**
—(*nail polish*) Revlon Inc.

32. COSMETICS *cont.*

80. The perfect cold cream
—Daggett & Ramsdell.

81. There is beauty in every jar
—(*milkweed cream*) F. F. Ingram Co.

82. Tomorrow's skin care—today
—(*Coty*) Chas. Pfizer and Co. Inc.

83. When a Studio Girl enters your home a new kind of beauty brightens your life
—Helene Curtis Industries Inc.

84. Where beautiful young ideas begin
—Helene Curtis Industries Inc.

85. Windblown through silk
—(*Pompeian beauty products*) Pompeian Inc.

86. Your complexion's best friend
—Campana Corp.

87. Your face never had it so clean!
—(*1006 lotion*) Bonne Bell Inc.

88. Zephyr-screened face powder
—Sales Affiliates Inc.

CRUISE SHIPS...See **102.** SEA TRAVEL AND CARGO

CUTLERY...See **55.** HARDWARE

D

33. DAIRY PRODUCTS
See also **15.** BEVERAGES, MISCELLAENOUS, **47.** FOOD, MISCELLANEOUS

1. A cut above the commonplace
—Danish and Blue Cheese.

2. Always churned from sweet cream
—(*butter*) June Dairy Products Co.

3. Baby's milk must be safe
—(*Challenge milk*) Challenge Foods Co.

4. Be certain with Certified Milk
—Certified Milk Producers of Southern California.

5. Borden's just has to be good
—Borden Inc.

6. Cheese; zest at its best
—American Dairy Association.

33. **DAIRY PRODUCTS** *cont.*

   7. **Churned from sweet (not sour) cream**
                                  —Land O' Lakes Creameries Inc.

   8. **Country charm quality**
                                  —Dean Foods Co.

   9. **Cream's rival**
                                  —Sego Milk Products Co.

  10. **Digestible as milk itself**
                                  —(*Velveeta*) Kraft Inc.

  11. **Fit for a golden spoon**
                                —(*Lady Borden ice cream*) Borden Inc.

  12. **Fresh as a daisy**
                                —(*butter*) June Dairy Products Co.

  13. **Fresh milk; drink it once a day**
                              —Fresh Milk Industry of Southern California.

  14. **Fresh milk; have you had your glass today?**
                                —Fresh Milk Industry.

  15. **From contented cows**
                                —Carnation Co.

  16. **Gives cream and butter flavor**
                                —Pet Milk Co.

  17. **Have more milk 'cause milk's got more**
                                —American Dairy Association.

  18. **How to make a muscle**
                                —National Dairy Products.

  19. **Ice cream for health**
                                —National Association of Ice Cream Mfrs.

  20. **Ice cream, one of the good things of life**
                                —Esmond Gundlach & Co.

  21. **If it's Bordens, it's got to be good**
                                —Borden Inc.

  22. **It is better and you can prove it**
                                —Borden Inc.

  23. **It slices, it cooks, it keeps**
                                —Kraft Inc.

  24. **It's still smart to be healthy**
                                —(*Quality ice cream*) Maple Island Inc.

  25. **King of cheese**
                                —Purity Cheese Co.

  26. **Know your milkman**
                                —Twin City Milk Producers Association.

  27. **Look for this famous name in the oval**
                                —(*Philadelphia Brand Cream Cheese*) Kraft Inc.

33. **DAIRY PRODUCTS** *cont.*

28. **Made in the milky way**
    —Ohio Butterine Co.

29. **Milk is the fresher refresher**
    —American Dairy Association.

30. **Milk that cuts the cost of cooking**
    —(*condensed milk*) Borden Inc.

31. **Mother's first thought for every milk need**
    —(*White House evaporated milk*).

32. **Naturally it's delicious ... it's made by Bordens**
    —Borden Inc.

33. **Nature forgot vitamin D, but Dean's didn't**
    —Dean Milk Co.

34. **No matter how diluted, it is never skimmed milk**
    —Pet Milk Co.

35. **Pure country milk with the cream left in**
    —(*evaporated milk*) Borden Inc.

36. **Taste the difference**
    —(*Breyer's ice cream*) Kraft Inc.

37. **The aristocrat of ice creams**
    —(*Crane's*).

38. **The butter that betters the meal**
    —Falfurrias Dairy Co.

39. **The cheese most people like**
    —(*Brookfield*) Swift & Co.

40. **The cheese with the paper between the slices**
    —N. Dorman and Co.

41. **The finest of natural cheeses—naturally from Kraft**
    —Kraft Inc.

42. **The first hands to touch it are yours**
    —(*Elkhorn cheese*) J. L. Kraft & Bros.

43. **The milk every doctor knows**
    —Carnation Milk Products Co.

44. **The smile follows the spoon**
    —Poinsettia Ice Cream Co.

45. **Voice of the dairy farmer**
    —American Dairy Association.

46. **Watch your children thrive on it**
    —(*chocolate malted milk*) Borden Inc.

47. **You can depend on the name**
    —Borden Inc.

48. **You eat it with a smile**
    —(*ice cream*) Seale-Lilly Ice Cream Co.

33. **DAIRY PRODUCTS** *cont.*

49. **You'll fall in love with Jersey Maid**
—*(ice cream)* Jersey Maid Ice Cream Co.

34. **DENTAL CARE**
See also **116.** TOILETRIES

1. **A clean tooth never decays**
—*(Pro-phy-lac-tic toothbrush)* Pro-phy-lac-tic Brush Co.

2. **A leader in dental research**
—Squibb Beech-Nut Inc.

3. **A massage for the gums**
—*(Gum-rub)* Dental Lab. Prods. Co.

4. **A name you can trust**
—*(dental cream)* Squibb Corp.

5. **Beauty bath for your teeth**
—*(Listerine tooth paste)* Lambert Pharmacal Co.

6. **Be good to your gums**
—*(Pro-phy-lac-tic toothbrush)* Pro-phy-lac-tic Brush Co.

7. **Bent like a dentist's mirror to reach more places**
—*(Squibb toothbrush)* Squibb Corp.

8. **Be true to your teeth or they'll be false to you**
—*(Medisalt)* Carey Salt Co.

9. ***Beware Of Smokers Teeth***
—*(tooth paste)* Bost Inc.

10. **Cleans as it fizzes**
—*(denture cleanser)* Fizzadent Corp.

11. **Cleans inside, outside and between the teeth**
—*(toothbrush)* The Western Co.

12. **Easy to use**
—*(Listerine tooth paste)* Lambert Pharmacal Co.

13. **For lazy people**
—*(Listerine tooth paste)* Lambert Pharmacal Co.

14. **For the smile of beauty**
—*(Ipana)* Bristol-Myers Co.

15. **Good for tender gums**
—*(Ipana)* Bristol-Myers Co.

16. **Good habits that last a lifetime**
—*(Aim toothpaste)* Lever Bros. Co.

17. **Guard your mouth**
—Dental Hi-gene Products Inc.

18. **It cleans your breath while it cleans your teeth**
—*(Colgate dental cream)* Colgate-Palmolive Co.

19. **Just rub it on the gums**
—*(Dr. Hand's teething lotion)* Colorado Chemical Co.

34.   DENTAL CARE *cont.*

20. **Keeps breath pure and sweet 1 to 2 hours longer**
        —(*Pepsodent antiseptic*) Lever Bros. Co.

21. **Leaves that clean taste in your mouth**
        —(*Amerdent tooth paste*) Raelin Prods.

22. **Lovely to look at, pleasant to use**
        —(*Tek toothbrush*) International Playtex Corp.

23. **Makes your teeth feel smooth as silk**
        —Otis Clapp & Son.

24. **More dentists use Lavoris than any other
     mouthwash. Shouldn't you?**
        —(*Lavoris*) Vick Chemical Co.

25. **Now, no bad breath behind his sparkling smile**
        —(*Colgate dental cream*) Colgate-Palmolive Co.

26. **"Okaze" your plates, "okaze" your breath**
        —(*dental cleanser*) Staze Inc.

27. **Prescription for your teeth**
        —(*Listerine tooth paste*) Lambert Pharmacal Co.

28. **Recommended by dentists surveyed 9 to 1 over all
     toothpastes combined**
        —(*Polident*) Block Drug Co. Inc.

29. **Recommended by more dentists than any other
     denture cleaner**
        —(*Polident*) Block Drug Co. Inc.

30. **Removes the dingy film**
        —(*Pepsodent*) Lever Bros. Co.

31. **Sign of a healthy mouth**
        —(*Amerdent mouth wash*) Raelin Prods.

32. **The correct toothpaste**
        —Orphos Co.

33. **The dentifrice that made fine teeth fashionable**
        —(*Dr. Lyons*) Glenbrook Laboratories.

34. **The first dental preparations made especially for
     children**
        —Clinical Lab.

35. **The *green* cleans in-between ... the *white* polishes
     bright**
        —Pro-phy-lac-tic Brush Co.

36. **The perfect powder for dentures**
        —Corega Chemical Co.

37. **The powder that penetrates between the teeth**
        —McKesson & Robbins.

38. **There's beauty in every drop**
        —(*Teel mouth wash*).

34. DENTAL CARE *cont.*

39. **The safe modern way to clean plates and bridges**
—(*Polident*) Block Drug Co. Inc.

40. **The smoker's friend**
—(*Bost tooth paste*) Bost Inc.

41. **The smooth tooth paste**
—(*Chlorax*) Nulyne Laboratories.

42. **The toothsome paste**
—Red Gum Products Co.

43. **To keep teeth clean use Saltine**
—Saltine Co.

44. **Tooth powder in paste form**
—Sunny Smile Products Co.

45. **Twice a day and before every date**
—(*Colgate Ribbon dental cream*) Colgate-Palmolive Co.

46. **Use BOST, and get a good paste in the mouth**
—Bost Inc.

47. **Wake up lazy gums with Ipana and massage**
—Bristol-Myers Co.

48. **Water-proofed against sogginess**
—(*Dr. West's toothbrushes*) Cooper Laboratories.

49. **Your daily dentist**
—(*tooth paste*) Prof. Research Labs.

50. **Your mouth will sing its praises**
—(*Worcester Salt tooth paste*).

51. **Your strongest line of defense against gum disease**
—(*Johnson & Johnson dental floss*) Johnson & Johnson

52. **Your teeth are only as healthy as your gums**
—Forhan's Co.

DEODORANTS . . . See **116.** TOILETRIES

DETERGENTS . . . See **24.** CLEANING AND LAUNDRY
PRODUCTS

DISHES . . . See **23.** CHINA

35. DRUGS AND REMEDIES
See also **56.** HEALTH AND FITNESS

1. **Ah, there's the rub**
—Somerville Co.

2. **America's physic**
—(*Pluto Water*) French Lick Springs Co.

35. DRUGS AND REMEDIES *cont.*

3. **Another clinical-strength medication from Warner-Lambert**
   —Warner-Lambert Pharmaceutical Co.

4. **A precious bit more than a laxative**
   —(*Alonzo*) Bliss Medical Co.

5. **At the first sneeze, Vick's VapoRub**
   —(*VapoRub*) Vick Chemical Co.

6. **Bayer works wonders**
   —(*Bayer aspirin*) Glenbrook Laboratories

7. **Be as regular as a clock**
   —(*Serutan laxative*) Healthaids Inc.

8. **Be bright. Feel right. Take Eno**
   —(*antacid*) Beecham Products Inc.

9. **Better medicines for a better world**
   —Parke, Davis & Co.

10. **Better than a mustard plaster**
    —(*Musterole*) Plough Inc.

11. **Better than whisky for a cold**
    —Dr. Miles Medical Co.

12. **Casco kills colds**
    —Casco Co.

13. **Children cry for it**
    —(*Fletcher's Castoria*) Glenbrook Laboratories.

14. **Chlorine ointment, better than iodine**
    —Minox Chemical Corp.

15. **Corn-free happy feet**
    —(*corn salve*) Kohler Mfg. Co.

16. **Does not harm the heart**
    —(*Bayer aspirin*) Glenbrook Laboratories.

17. **Easy doses, no fishy taste, no bad after-taste**
    —(*Caritol*) S. M. A. Corp.

18. **Easy to use, just shake in your shoes**
    —(*Allen's Foot Ease*).

19. **Everything will come out all right**
    —(*laxative*) The Dill Co.

20. **Famous name in pain relief**
    —(*Sloan's instant balm*) W. R. Warner & Co.

21. **Feel it heal**
    —(*Noxema skin cream*) Noxell Corp.

22. **Fights colds and sore throats**
    —(*Listerine*) Lambert Pharmacal Co.

35. **DRUGS AND REMEDIES** *cont.*

23. **First aid for the family**
—Sodiphene Co.

24. **First thought, first aid and Astyptodyne**
—Astyptodyne Chemical Co.

25. **For a good night's sleep**
—(*Nytol*) Block Drug Co. Inc.

26. **For FAST headache help**
—(*Bromo Seltzer*) Warner-Lambert Pharmaceutical Co.

27. **For penetrating relief get Hall's Vapor Action**
—(*Hall's Mentho-Liptus*) American Chicle Co.

28. **For relief you can trust**
—(*Tylenol pain reliever*) McNeil Consumer Products Co.

29. **For these symptoms of stress that can come from success**
—(*Alka-Seltzer*) Miles Laboratories Inc.

30. **For the tummy**
—(*Tums*) Norcliff Thayer Inc.

31. **For your stomach's sake**
—Eatonic Remedy Co.

32. **Get at that corn today, forget that ouch tomorrow**
—(*corn salve*) Kohler Mfg. Co.

33. **Gets the red out**
—(*Visine eye drops*) Leeming/Pacquin.

34. **Give your cold to Contac. Real medicines for real colds.**
—(*Contac cold medicine*) Menley & James Laboratories.

35. **Great aches from little corns grow**
—(*Blue Jay corn plaster*) The Kendall Co.

36. **Handiest thing in the house**
—(*Vaseline*) Chesebrough-Pond's Inc.

37. **Helping a nation to avoid severe colds**
—Vick Chemical Co.

38. **Helps nature cure your cough**
—(*Pertussin*) Chesebrough-Pond's Inc.

39. **How do you spell relief?**
—(*Rolaids antacid*) American Chicle Co.

40. **Ideal laxative for young and old**
—(*Beechalex laxative*).

41. **In the service of medicine for over three decades**
—Drug Products Co.

42. **It happens in two seconds**
—(*Bayer aspirin*) Glenbrook Laboratories.

35. DRUGS AND REMEDIES *cont.*

43. **It's the little daily dose that does it**
—(*Krushen salts*).

44. **It's your guarantee of quality**
—(*Contac cold medicine*) Menley & James Laboratories.

45. **Join the regulars**
—(*Ex-Lax*) Ex-Lax Distributing Co. Inc.

46. **Just rub on, inhale the vapors**
—(*VapoRub*) Vick Chemical Co.

47. **Keep fighting, keep working, keep singing, America**
—E. R. Squibb & Sons.

48. **Keep it handy**
—(*Sloan's liniment*) W. R. Warner & Co.

49. **Keeps you going**
—(*Contac cold capsules*) Menley & James Laboratories.

50. **Kondon's kills kolds**
—Kondon Mfg. Co.

51. **Largest selling pain reliever**
—(*Anacin analgesic*) Whitehall Labs Div., American Home Products Co.

52. **Laugh it off with a "Jest"**
—(*alkalizer*) Jests Inc.

53. **Makers of medicines prescribed by physicians**
—Parke, Davis & Co.

54. **Makes you feel fit faster**
—(*Bromo Seltzer*) Warner-Lambert Pharmaceutical Co.

55. **Medicamenta vera**
—Parke, Davis & Co.

56. **My lips are sealed with Chap Stick**
—(*Chap Stick*) The Merchandising Co.

57. **Never neglect a break in the skin**
—Newskin Co.

58. **Never neglect the tiniest cut**
—(*Band-Aid*) Johnson & Johnson.

59. **Never upset an upset stomach**
—(*Pepto-Bismol*) Norwich-Eaton Pharmaceuticals.

60. **Next to safety first, first aid**
—Johnson & Johnson.

61. **Nip-it with Sip-It**
—(*Sip-It cough remedy*).

62. **No water needed**
—(*Phillips' Milk of Magnesia tablets*) Glenbrook Laboratories.

35. DRUGS AND REMEDIES *cont.*

63. NR tonight, tomorrow all right
—(*Nature's Remedy laxative*) Norcliff Thayer Inc.

64. Original research serving the physician
—Sandoz Inc.

65. Pat it on the face, wop it on the body
—(*Pat-&-Wop*) Allied Drug Products.

66. Pharmaceuticals of assured accuracy
—J. S. Airhart.

67. Prescription medicines around the world
—Eli Lilly and Co.

**68. Priceless ingredient of every product is the honor
and integrity of its maker**
—Squibb Corp.

69. Products you can trust from people you know
—(*dressings*) Will Ross Inc.

70. Put one on, the pain is gone
—(*Zono pads*).

71. Quality is paramount to price
—Johnson & Johnson.

72. Real medicine for throats too sore to ignore
—(*Chloraseptic*) Norwich-Eaton Pharmaceuticals.

73. Relief is just a swallow away
—(*Alka-Seltzer*) Miles Laboratories Inc.

74. RELy on REL for real RELief
—Maryland Pharmaceutical Co.

75. REMember this REMarkable REMedy ... REM
—Maryland Pharmaceutical Co.

76. Research in the service of medicine
—G. D. Searle & Co.

77. Rolaids spells relief
—(*Rolaids antacid*) American Chicle Co.

78. Rub your cold away
—(*Mistol rub*) Oakhurst Co.

79. Safe for every cough
—(*Pertussin*) Chesebrough-Pond's Inc.

80. Safe for the little folks, too
—The New-Syn Co.

81. Serutan spelled backwards spells "Nature's"
—(*Serutan laxative*) Healthaids Inc.

82. Service to medicine
—Wyeth Laboratories Div., American Home Products
Corp.

35. **DRUGS AND REMEDIES** *cont.*

83. **Sharing the responsibilities of modern medicine**
—Stanlabs Inc.

84. **So gentle for children, so thorough for grown-ups**
—(*Phillips' Milk of Magnesia*) Glenbrook Laboratories.

85. **Soothes. Cleanses. Refreshes.**
—(*eye drops*) Murine Co. Inc.

86. **Speedy is its middle name**
—(*Alka-Seltzer*) Miles Laboratories Inc.

87. **Stay fit for fun with Phillips**
—(*Phillips' Milk of Magnesia*) Glenbrook Laboratories.

88. **Stop that tickle**
—(*cough drops*) Bunte Bros.

89. **Swift relief follows the swallow**
—Neo-Syn Co.

90. **Take two, pain's through**
—Neo-Syn Co.

91. **Taste as good as they make you feel**
—(*Tums*) Lewis-Howe Co.

92. **Teaching a nation to avoid severe colds**
—Vick Chemical Co.

93. **That Kruschen feeling**
—(*salts*) E. Griffiths Hughes.

94. **That's all. Nothing else.**
—(*Comtrex Cold Reliever*) Bristol-Myers Co.

95. **The aspirin of quality**
—Smith, Kline & French Co.

96. **The bandage that breathes**
—(*Sealtex*).

97. **The beauty laxative**
—(*Dr. Edward's Olive tablets*) Oakhurst Co.

98. **The best aid is first aid**
—Johnson & Johnson.

99. **The best in tapes has "Able" on the label**
—Arno Adhesive Tapes Inc.

100. **The candy-mint alkalizer**
—(*Alkaid*) F. & F. Laboratories Inc.

101. **The cheapest health insurance in the world**
—(*cough drops*) Smith Bros.

102. **The cod liver oil with the plus value**
—(*Scott's emulsion*) Beecham Products Inc.

103. **The criminal within**
—(*Eno laxative*).

35. DRUGS AND REMEDIES *cont.*

104. **The different antacid**
—(*Gelusil*) Warner-Lambert Pharmaceutical Co.

105. **The doctor in candy form**
—(*Partola*) Partola Products Co.

106. **The doctor's prescription**
—(*Father John's medicine*) Medtech Laboratories Inc.

107. **The family liniment**
—(*Sloan's*) W. R. Warner & Co.

108. **The first real improvement since the spoon**
—(*Contac cough capsules*) Menley & James Laboratories.

109. **The first thought in burns**
—(*Unguentine*) Norwich-Eaton Pharmaceuticals.

110. **The great penetrative liniment**
—(*Omega Oil*) Block Drug Co. Inc.

111. **The great regulator**
—(*Beecham's pills*) Beecham Products Inc.

112. **The little nurse for little ills**
—The Mentholatum Co.

113. **The mineral salt laxative**
—(*Sal Hepatica*) Bristol-Myers Co.

114. **The national rub down**
—(*Mifflin alcohol*) The Mifflin, McCambridge Co.

115. **The one more pediatricians give their own children**
—(*Children's Tylenol*) McNeil Consumer Products Co.

116. **The one that coats is the only one you need**
—(*Pepto-Bismol*) Norwich Pharmacal Co.

117. **The original chocolate laxative**
—(*Ex-Lax*) Ex-Lax Distributing Co. Inc.

118. **There's no beating deep heating**
—(*Mentholatum Deep Heating Rub*) The Mentholatum Co.

119. **The safe antiseptic with the pleasant taste**
—(*Listerine*) Lambert Pharmacal Co.

120. **The salve with a base of old-fashioned mutton suet**
—(*Penetro*) Plough Inc.

121. **The scientific corn ender**
—Bauer & Black.

122. **The sniffling, sneezing, coughing, aching, stuffy head, so you can rest medicine**
—(*Nyquil cold medicine*) Vick Chemical Co.

123. **The tested treatment for infectious dandruff**
—(*Listerine*) Lambert Pharmacal Co.

35. DRUGS AND REMEDIES *cont.*

124. **The world over**
—(*Mothersill's seasick remedy*).

125. **They cure the tickle**
—(*mentholated drops*) Dean Medicine Co.

126. **Time it when you take it**
—(*Pasmore's 2-minute aid*).

127. **To fly high in the morning, take Phillips at night**
—(*Phillips' Milk of Magnesia*) Glenbrook Laboratories.

128. **Tomorrow's medicines from today's research**
—Nupercainal.

129. **Tonight at bedtime**
—(*Lee's Magnesia*) Lee-Strauss Co. Inc.

130. **Touches the spot**
—(*ointment*) Homocea, Ltd., England.

131. **Trust Band-Aid brand to cover you better**
—(*Band-Aid*) Johnson & Johnson.

132. **Wake up your liver**
—(*Carter's pills*) Carter-Wallace Inc.

133. **Warmth works wonders**
—(*Radway's Ready Relief*) Radways & Co.

134. **We cover the earth with drugs of worth**
—Meyer Bros. Drug Co.

135. **When nature forgets, remember EX-LAX**
—(*Ex-Lax*) Ex-Lax Distributing Co. Inc.

136. **When nature won't, Pluto will**
—(*Pluto Water*) French Lick Springs Co.

137. **Where today's theory is tomorrow's remedy**
—Merck, Sharp and Dohme Div., Merck and Co. Inc.

138. **Wide range of therapeutic usefulness**
—(*Donnatal medicine*) A. H. Robins Co. Inc.

139. **Will cure a cold in one night**
—(*Carter's Compound Extract*) Brown Medicine Co.

140. **Worth a guinea a box**
—(*Beecham's pills*) Beecham Products Inc.

141. **You're always safe with Baker's Magdolite**
—(*Baker's Magdolite*).

DRY GOODS ... See 103. SEWING AND KNITTING SUPPLIES

E

EARTHMOVERS ... See **73.** MACHINERY

36. ECONOMIC DEVELOPMENT
     See also **119.** TRAVEL

1. **A great state in which to live and work**
                            —Rhode Island.

2. **Come to Kentucky! It's a profitable move!**
                    —Kentucky Dept. of Commerce.

3. **Dallas is the door to Texas**
                            —Dallas, Texas.

4. **Discover the new in New York State**
                    —New York State Dept. of Commerce.

5. **Growing city within a growing city**
                    —W. Seattle Community Adv.

6. **Industrious Maine, New England's big stake in the future**
                —Maine Dept. of Economic Development.

7. **Industry is on the move to Iowa**
                    —Iowa Development Commission.

8. **Industry's friendliest climate**
                    —Public Services of Indiana Inc.

9. **It is profitable to produce in Massachusetts**
                    —Commonwealth of Massachusetts.

10. **Jersey City has everything for industry**
                            —Jersey City, N. J.

11. **Keep Missouri in the center of your thinking**
            —Missouri Commerce and Industrial Development
                                    Commission.

12. **Land of perpetual prosperity**
                            —Oklahoma City.

13. **Logical locale for new business**
                —Massachusetts Development & Industry Comm.

14. **Make the capital choice**
                —Port Authority of the City of St. Paul.

15. **Michigan, state of happiness for everyone**
                                    —Michigan.

16. **Minnesota brainpower builds profits**
                —Minnesota Dept. of Business Development.

36. **ECONOMIC DEVELOPMENT** *cont.*

17. **Ship from the center, not from the rim**
>—St. Louis, Mo.

18. **The city that does things**
>—Norfolk, Va.

19. **The dynamo of Dixie**
>—Chattanooga, Tenn.

20. **The land of elbow room and elbow grease**
>—Omaha Public Power District.

21. **The port of personal service**
>—Wilmington, Del.

22. **"We like it here"**
>—Wisconsin Div. of Economic Development.

23. **Where big things are happening**
>—Commonwealth of Kentucky.

24. **Where free enterprise is still growing**
>—Indiana Dept. of Commerce.

25. **Where good government is a habit**
>—North Carolina Dept. of Conservation.

26. **Where nature helps industry most**
>—Los Angeles, California.

37. **ELECTRICAL PRODUCTS AND SERVICE**
See also **38. ELECTRONICS INDUSTRY, 58. HEATING AND
AIR CONDITIONING, 60. HOME APPLIANCES AND
EQUIPMENT, 70. LIGHTING PRODUCTS**

1. **At your service**
>—New York Edison.

2. **A Yale battery for every battery need**
>—Yale Electric Corp.

3. **Better light brings better living**
>—Consumers Public Power District.

4. **Big name in batteries**
>—(*Ray-O-Vac batteries*) ESB Inc.

5. **Cook electrically and enjoy the difference**
>—(*Reddy Kilowatt*) Reddy Communications.

6. **Electricity gives you matchless cooking**
>—Los Angeles Bureau of Power and Light.

7. **Everything electrical for home and industry**
>—Canadian Westinghouse Co.

37. ELECTRICAL PRODUCTS AND SERVICE *cont.*

8. **Everything electrical for the theatre**
—Major Equipment Co.

9. **From the tiniest to the mightiest**
—*(electric motors)* General Electric Co.

10. **Give Red Bands your hard job**
—Howell Electric Motors Co.

11. **In electricity, it's Edison from start to finish**
—Edison-Splitdorf Corp.

12. **Instantly known when blown**
—*(Royal Crystal fuse plug)* Royal Electric Co.

13. **Live better electrically**
—Edison Electric Institute.

14. **Live electrically and enjoy the difference**
—*(Reddy Kilowatt)* Reddy Communications.

15. **Longest life by owners' records**
—Gould Storage Battery Co.

16. **Makers of things more useful**
—Benjamin Electric Mfg. Co.

17. **More than horse-power**
—*(electric motors)* Louis Allis Co.

18. **Motorized power, fitted to every need**
—General Electric Co.

19. **Name that means everything in electricity**
—Westinghouse.

20. **No damp amps**
—Cincinnati Elec. Prods. Co.

21. **Off when it's on, on when it's off**
—Gould Storage Battery Co.

22. **Plug in, I'm Reddy**
—*(Reddy Kilowatt)* Reddy Communications.

23. **Portable power for progress**
—Battery Div., Sonotone Corp.

24. **"Power to spare"**
—*(Eveready batteries)* Union Carbide Corp.

25. **Responsiveness of a well-trained servant**
—North East Electric Co.

26. **See the difference**
—*(Eveready batteries)* Union Carbide Consumer Products Co.

27. **Stay fresh for years**
—*(Ray-O-Vac batteries)* ESB Inc.

37. ELECTRICAL PRODUCTS AND SERVICE *cont.*

28. **The ABC of radio satisfaction**
    —(*Ray-O-Vac batteries*) French Battery Co.

29. **The biggest name in little engines**
    —(*Super-Cyclone*).

30. **The faithfulness of an old friend**
    —North East Electric Co.

31. **The motor's the thing**
    —Herschell-Spillman Motor Co.

32. **They keep a-running**
    —(*electric motors*) Century Electric Co.

33. **They show when they blow**
    —(*Trico fuse*) Trico Mfg. Co.

34. **Wherever wheels turn or propellers spin**
    —(*Delco battery*) Delco Products.

ELECTRICITY ... See **93. PUBLIC UTILITIES**

38. ELECTRONICS INDUSTRY
See also **3. AEROSPACE, 5. AUDIO EQUIPMENT,
17. BROADCASTING, 28. COMPUTER EQUIPMENT,
37. ELECTRICAL PRODUCTS AND SERVICE,
95. RADIO EQUIPMENT, 111. TELECOMMUNICATIONS,
112. TELEVISIONS, 122. VIDEO EQUIPMENT**

1. **An extra measure of quality**
    —Hewlett-Packard Co.

2. **A reputation through innovation**
    —Whelen Engineering Company Inc.

3. **A world of experience**
    —Collins Radio Co.

4. **Builders of the tools of automation**
    —Reliance Electric and Engineering Co.

5. **Creating a new world with electronics**
    —Hughes Aircraft Co.

6. **Creating useful products and services for you**
    —Texas Instruments Inc.

7. **From sharp minds come Sharp products**
    —Sharp Electronics Corp.

8. **In touch with tomorrow**
    —Toshiba America Inc.

9. **Just slightly ahead of our time**
    —(*Panasonic*) Matsushita Electric Corp. of America.

10. **Manning the frontiers of electronic progress**
    —Autonetics Div., North American Rockwell Corp.

38. **ELECTRONICS INDUSTRY** *cont.*

11. **New ideas in automation control**
—Photoswitch Div., Electronics Corp. of America.

12. **New leader in the lively art of electronics**
—Motorola Inc.

13. **The first and greatest name in electronics**
—General Electric Co.

14. **The "light" touch in automation and control**
—Clairex Corp.

15. **The most trusted name in electronics**
—RCA Corp.

16. **The world's most broadly based electronics company**
—RCA Corp.

17. **We're the guys who get the information around . . . PIW . . . the interconnect people**
—(*coaxial cable*) Philadelphia Insulated Wire Co. Inc.

39. **ELEVATORS**

1. **From pit to penthouse**
—Otis Elevator Co.

2. **Morning uplift**
—Otis Elevator Co.

3. **The budget sets the pace**
—Otis Elevator Co.

4. **The safe, swift, silent "lift"**
—Turnbull Elevator Co.

40. **EMPLOYMENT AGENCIES**

1. **Good people**
—Olsten Temporary Services.

2. **Kelly can do**
—Kelly Services Inc.

3. **Office help—temporary or permanent**
—American Girl Service.

4. **100% guaranteed temporary office help**
—Kelly Services Inc.

5. **One source, one standard—nationwide**
—Kelly Services Inc.

6. **The very best in temporary help**
—Manpower Inc.

7. **When you need the best, call the best**
—Dunhill Temporaries.

ENERGY ... See 59. HEATING AND COOKING FUELS,
88. PETROLEUM PRODUCTS, 93. PUBLIC UTILITIES

ENTERTAINMENT ... See 78. MOVIES AND
ENTERTAINMENT

41. **EYEGLASSES**
See also 123. WARDROBE ACCESSORIES

1. **Better vision for better looks**
—Better Vision Institute.

2. **Don't say sunglasses—say C'Bon**
—Polaroid Corp.

3. **For better eyesight**
—American Optical Co.

4. **For everything "under the sun"**
—(*Willsonite sunglasses*).

5. **Grace the face and stay in place**
—(*glasses*) E. Kirstein & Sons.

6. **Isn't that you behind those Foster Grants?**
—(*sunglasses*) Foster Grant Co.

7. **Life looks brighter**
—(*Univis glasses*).

8. **Like pearl temples behind the ears**
—(*spectacles*) No-Ease Co.

9. **Seeing is believing**
—(*Oculens sunglasses*) Comptone Co.

10. **Since 1833 ... better vision for better living**
—American Optical Co.

11. **Styled for the stars**
—(*Grantley sunglasses*) Foster Grant Co.

12. **That eyes may see better and farther**
—Bausch & Lomb Optical Co.

13. **To greater vision through optical science**
—Bausch & Lomb Optical Co.

F

FABRICS INDUSTRY ... See 103. SEWING AND KNITTING
SUPPLIES

42. FARMING SUPPLIES AND EQUIPMENT
See also **73.** MACHINERY, **120.** TRUCKS AND TRUCKING
INDUSTRY

1. A better yield in every field
—York Chemical Co.

2. Allis-Chalmers does its share to help *you* share in a better future
—Allis-Chalmers Mfg. Co.

3. As necessary as the rain
—Buhner Fertilizer Co.

4. Backed by research, proved by use
—(*farm feed*) Kasco Mills.

5. Beware where you buy your bee-ware
—G. B. Lewis Co.

6. Bred, not just grown
—Associated Seed Growers.

7. Builders of tomorrow's feeds ... today!
—(*Wayne feeds*) Allied Mills Corp.

8. Can lay their weight in gold
—(*baby chicks*) Ken-La Farms.

9. Consistently good year after year
—(*corn seeds*) Funk G. Hybrids.

10. Creators of farm wealth
—Hart-Parr Co.

11. Dependability in the field ... safety for the operator
—Tryce Mfg. Co. Inc.

12. Don't just fertilize ... Spencerize
—Spencer Chemical Div., Gulf Oil Corp.

13. Easier to handle, lighter draft, more durable
—(*plow*) E. B. Foot Lift Plow.

14. Engineered for longer life
—Minneapolis-Moline Inc.

15. Farm Implements with a future - yours!
—Brillion Iron Works Inc.

42. **FARMING SUPPLIES AND EQUIPMENT** *cont.*

16. **Feeds and seeds to meet your needs**
—Crabbs Taylor Reynolds Elevator Co.

17. **Field-tested fertilizers**
—F. S. Royster Guano Co.

18. **First in grassland farming**
—New Holland Div., Sperry Rand Corp.

19. **First in powered equipment since 1918**
—Bolens Div., FMC Corp.

20. **First to serve the farmer**
—International Harvester Co.

21. **Food producers for the world**
—(*tractors*) Hart-Parr Co.

22. **From the tractor people who make the big ones**
—(*tractors*) Allis-Chalmers Mfg. Co.

23. **Good enough to eat**
—(*poultry feed*) American Agricultural Chemical Co.

24. **Hen's only rival**
—103 Degree Incubator Co.

25. **If Purina chows won't make your hens lay, they are roosters**
—Ralston Purina Co.

26. **In garden or in fields, Schell's seeds produce best yields**
—(*Schell's seeds*)

27. **Iron horse quality**
—Matthews Co.

28. **Keeps cows contented from sunrise to sunset**
—Usol Fly Spray.

29. **Lowest cost, per yard, per hour, or per mile**
—(*tractors*) Cleveland Tractor Co.

30. **Makes every acre do its best**
—(*Armour's fertilizer*).

31. **Man, that's corn**
—Pfister Associated Growers.

32. **More acres of corn, more corn per acre**
—Pfister Associated Growers.

33. **More corn, less cob; it's bred that way**
—Pfister Associated Growers.

34. **Practical in design. Dependable in action.**
—New Holland Div., Sperry Rand Corp.

35. **Seeds you can trust**
—Ferry-Morse Seed Co.

42. FARMING SUPPLIES AND EQUIPMENT *cont.*

36. **Serving the businessman in the blue denim suit**
—(*Master Mix feeds*) Central Soya Co. Inc.

37. **Since 1886 ... scientifically designed for practical use**
—John Blue Co. Inc.

38. **So easy, a child can steer it**
—(*tractors*) Cleveland Tractor Co.

39. **Something to crow about**
—American Agricultural Chemical Co.

40. **Southern Fertilizers for the southern farmer**
—The Barrett Co.

41. **Specialists in farmstead mechanization**
—New Holland Div., Sperry Rand Corp.

42. **Team of steel**
—(*tractors, threshers*) Minneapolis Steel & Machinery Co.

43. **The Cletrac way makes farming pay**
—(*tractors*) Cleveland Tractor Co.

44. **The corn with husk ability**
—Pfister Associated Growers.

45. **The corn with yield ability**
—Pfister Associated Growers.

46. **The courage to change. The strength to grow**
—International Harvester Co.

47. **The feeder's silent partner**
—(*Tuxedo feeds*) Early & Daniel Co.

48. **The national soil sweetener**
—Kelley Island Lime & Transport Co.

49. **The people who bring you the machines that *work***
—International Harvester Co.

50. **The second best nurser in the world**
—Eveready Nurser.

51. **The sign of a new prosperity in agriculture**
—H. Ferguson Farm Equipment.

52. **The tractor people, Allis-Chalmers**
—(*tractors*) Allis-Chalmers Mfg. Co.

53. **They moo for more**
—(*cottonseed meal*) Ashcraft-Wilkinson Co.

54. **Where bold new ideas pay off for profit-minded farmers**
—New Idea Farm Equipment Co.

55. **Where quality is a family tradition**
—Gehl Bros. Mfg. Co.

42. FARMING SUPPLIES AND EQUIPMENT *cont.*

56. **World champions of worth!**
> —Hesston Corp. Inc.

57. **World's first mass produced tractor**
> —(*tractors*) Ford Tractor Div., Ford Motor Co.

58. **You can depend on the integrity and quality of Smith-Douglass**
> —(*fertilizer*) Smith-Douglass Div., Borden Chemical Co.

59. **Your way of life depends upon your day of work**
> —(*tractors*) Morrison Tractor.

FASHION ACCESSORIES ... See **26. CLOTHING, MISCELLANEOUS, 32. COSMETICS, 123. WARDROBE ACCESSORIES**

FEED ... See **42. FARMING SUPPLIES AND EQUIPMENT**

FERTILIZER ... See **42. FARMING AND SUPPLIES EQUIPMENT**

FILM ... See **89. PHOTOGRAPHIC EQUIPMENT**

43. FINANCIAL INSTITUTIONS AND SERVICES
See also **64. INSURANCE, 66. INVESTMENT**

1. **A bank of personal contact**
> —Interstate Trust Co.

2. **A distinguished banking connection**
> —Bank of the United States.

3. **All the bank you'll ever need in Texas**
> —Texas National Bank of Commerce of Houston.

4. **All your banking under one roof**
> —Mellon National Bank.

5. **A tower of strength**
> —Bankers Trust Co.

6. **Bank of personal service**
> —First Trust & Deposit Co.

7. **Behind the enduring institution, successful customers**
> —Farmers Deposit Bank.

8. **Be SURE you save at a savings bank**
> —Savings Bank Association.

9. **Be thrifty and be happy**
> —Baldwin National Bank & Trust Co.

10. **Better banking, better service, better join us**
> —Reliance State Bank.

43. FINANCIAL INSTITUTIONS AND SERVICES *cont.*

11. **"Better than money"**
>—(*travelers checks*) First National City Bank.

12. **Building with Chicago and the nation since 1863**
>—First National Bank of Chicago.

13. **Call on Central**
>—Central National Bank & Trust Co.

14. **Constantly building for community usefulness**
>—New First National Bank.

15. **Courtesy, efficiency, service**
>—Manufacturers Trust Co.

16. **Distance is no barrier to our service**
>—Citizens Trust Co.

17. **First in banking**
>—Bank of America.

18. **First in loans to business and industry**
>—Chase Manhattan Bank.

19. **First Pennsylvania means business**
>—First Pennsylvania Banking and Trust Co.

20. **Forward with Miami's oldest bank**
>—Bank of Bay of Biscayne.

21. **For Wilmington, the Carolinas, and the South**
>—Murchison National Bank.

22. **For you—every banking service**
>—Times Square Trust Co.

23. **Founded by merchants for merchants**
>—Merchants National Bank.

24. **Full service bank**
>—Foundation for Commercial Banks.

25. **Get the First National habit**
>—First National Bank at Pittsburgh.

26. **Good for money wherever money means anything**
>—Bankers Trust Co.

27. **Help yourself financially without financial help**
>—Illinois National Bank.

28. **... It's good to have a great bank behind you**
>—Manufacturers Hanover Trust Co.

29. **Keep your income coming in**
>—American National Bank.

30. **Nationwide system of thrifty spending**
>—Christmas Club.

31. **No account too large, none too small**
>—Citizens & Southern Bank.

43. **FINANCIAL INSTITUTIONS AND SERVICES** *cont.*

32. **Oldest Trust Company in Connecticut**
    —Hartford Conn. Trust Co.

33. **One of the Northwest's largest financial institutions**
    —Seattle First National Bank.

34. **Partners in progress around the world**
    —First National City Bank.

35. **People's Trust is the people's bank**
    —People's Trust & Guaranty Co.

36. **Save as you spend with Christmas Club Thrifties**
    —Christmas Club.

37. **Save for a sunny day**
    —First National Bank, Boston.

38. **Security with no ifs**
    —America's Banks.

39. **South Florida's east bank**
    —1st National Bank of Tampa.

40. **Spendable everywhere**
    —(*travelers checks*) American Express Co.

41. **Strength, safety, service**
    —National City Savings Bank & Trust Co.

42. **Systematic saving spells success**
    —Old Colony Co-operative Bank.

43. **The bankers who do a little more for you**
    —United California Bank.

44. **The bank for all the people**
    —Cleveland Trust Co.

45. **The bank for bankers and businessmen**
    —Irving Trust Co.

46. **The bank for me in '43**
    —Mass. Co-operative Bank League.

47. **The bank that means business in California**
    —Crocker-Citizens National Bank.

48. **The bank that works hardest for you**
    —Chemical Bank, New York.

49. **The bank where you feel at home**
    —Central Trust & Savings Co.

50. **The bank with the international point of view**
    —Bank of the Southwest.

51. **The branch around the corner can serve you around the world**
    —National City Bank.

43.   FINANCIAL INSTITUTIONS AND SERVICES *cont.*

52.   **The kind of a bank you will enjoy doing business with**
                              —U. S. National Bank.

53.   **The little bank with a large circle of friends**
                         —1st National Bank of Pleasanton.

54.   **The Oil Bank of America**
                              —National Bank of Tulsa.

55.   **The personal service bank**
                         —Anglo-California Trust Co.

56.   **"The place where you keep your checking account"**
                         —Foundation for Commercial Banks.

57.   **Thrift brings happiness**
                              —Roosevelt Savings Bank.

58.   **Under the old town clock**
                         —Fidelity National Bank & Trust Co.

59.   **Where all street cars meet**
                         —Utica Trust & Deposit Co.

60.   **Where banking is a pleasure**
                              —Trust Co. of Georgia.

61.   **Where people make the difference**
                         —Toronto-Dominion Bank.

62.   *Where* **you save** *does* **make a difference**
                         —The Savings and Loan Foundation Inc.

63.   **You have a friend at Chase Manhattan**
                              —Chase Manhattan Bank.

64.   **You've got the card**
                         —(*American Express card*) American Express.

FINISHES . . . See **82. PAINT AND PAINTING SUPPLIES**

44.   **FIREARMS**

1.   **A gun for every American shooting need**
                              —Marlin Firearms Co.

2.   **A load for every purpose and a shell for every purse**
                              —U. S. Cartridge Co.

3.   **As easy as pointing your finger**
                         —Colt Patent Fire Arms Mfg. Co.

4.   **Choice of champions**
                              —Western Cartridge Co.

5.   **Expert's choice . . . since 1880**
                              —Ithaca Gun Co. Inc.

44. **FIREARMS** *cont.*

6. **Favorite shells satisfy good shooters**
    —Federal Cartridge Corp.

7. **First in sporting arms**
    —Browning Arms Co.

8. **For clean hits and clean barrels**
    —(*Remington shells*) Du Pont.

9. **For more than 25 years the authority on gun cleaning**
    —F. A. Hoppe Inc.

10. **Hits where you aim**
    —United States Cartridge Co.

11. **If it's Remington, it's right**
    —(*cartridges*) Du Pont.

12. **Largest manufacturer of shotguns in the world**
    —Savage Arms Corp.

13. **Mossberg for accuracy**
    —O. F. Mossberg and Sons Inc.

14. **"On the range"**
    —Williams Gun Sight Co.

15. **Out-sells because it out-shoots**
    —(*guns*) Western Cartridge Co.

16. **Pioneering better guns and greater values since 1864**
    —(*Stevens arms*) Emhart Corp.

17. **Power without powder**
    —Crosman Arms Co.

18. **Proven best by government test**
    —Colt Patent Fire Arms Mfg. Co.

19. **Symbol of accuracy since 1870**
    —Marlin Firearms Co.

20. **The arms that protect American farms**
    —Iver-Johnson Arms and Cycle Works.

21. **The balanced load shells**
    —Winchester Repeating Arms Co.

22. **The custom crafted shotgun**
    —(*shotguns*) Charles Daly.

23. **The gun that knows no closed season**
    —Crosman Arms Co.

24. **The most complete line of firearms in the world**
    —Savage Arms Corp.

25. **They better your aim**
    —Lyman Gun Sight Corp.

44. FIREARMS *cont.*

26. **When you get a shot, you get a duck, with Super X**
                              —Western Cartridge Co.

27. **World's champion ammunition**
                              —Western Cartridge Co.

28. **World's largest producer of non-powder guns and ammo**
                    —Daisy/Heddon Div., Victor Comptometer Corp.

29. **World's most complete line of sporting arms and accessories**
                                   —Emhart Corp.

45. FISHING SUPPLIES
           See also **98.** RECREATIONAL EQUIPMENT, **108.** SPORTING
                    GOODS

1. **Adds science to fisherman's luck**
                              —True Temper Corp.

2. **A great name in tackle**
                                      —Pflueger.

3. **America's finest fishing rods**
                              —Browning Arms Co.

4. **"Bait of champions"**
                              —Fred Arbogast Co., Inc.

5. **Best bait for fishing since fishing first began**
                              —George W. Julian.

6. **Creating world-famed fishing tackle since 1893**
                    —South Bend Tackle Co., Div. Gladding Corp.

7. **First choice in fishing tackle hardware**
                                   —Allan Mfg. Co.

8. **First in world records**
                    —Ashaway Line and Twine Mfg. Co.

9. **First on famous waters**
                                   —Johnson Reels Inc.

10. **Fish "Heddon" and fish better**
                              —James Heddon's Sons.

11. **Fishing tackle for every kind of fishing**
                    —South Bend Tackle Co., Div. Gladding Corp.

12. **If Weber makes it, a fish takes it**
                              —Frost Fishing Tackle Co.

13. **Make your own luck with Heddon**
                              —James Heddon's Sons.

14. **Pick a Perrine today!**
                              —Aladdin Laboratories Inc.

45. FISHING SUPPLIES *cont.*

15. **Precision fishing reels since 1883**
—Martin Reel Co.

16. **Put a Burke where they lurk!**
—Flexo-Products Div., McClellan Industries.

17. **Right in shape, temper and finish**
—(*fish hooks*) O. Mustad & Sons.

18. **"Service guaranteed for life!"**
—The Garcia Corp.

19. **Serving the fishermen's needs for over 100 years**
—Fish Net & Twine Co.

20. **The fish hook people**
—O. Mustad & Sons.

21. **The most respected name in fishing tackle**
—Zebco Div., Brunswick Corp.

22. **The reels of champions**
—Penn Fishing Tackle Mfg. Co.

23. **The river-runt does the stunt**
—(*fishing tackle*) James Heddon's Sons.

24. **The rod with the fighting heart**
—James Heddon's Sons.

25. **Think system**
—Scientific Anglers Inc.

26. **Veteran reel for veteran fisherman**
—Meiselbach Mfg. Co. Inc.

27. **"Weavers of the world's finest netting"**
—Victory Sports Net Div., The Fishnet and Twine Co.

28. **Where the action is!**
—Zebco Div., Brunswick Corp.

29. **World's largest exclusive fly line manufacturer**
—Scientific Anglers Inc.

30. **World's most wanted lure**
—Rapala Div., Nordic Enterprises Inc.

FITNESS ... See **56. HEALTH AND FITNESS**

FLATWARE ... See **23. CHINA, 67. JEWELRY AND SILVER.**

FLAVORINGS ... See **29. CONDIMENTS AND SPICES**

46. FLOOR COVERINGS
See also **18.** BUILDING SUPPLIES, **65.** INTERIOR DECORATION

1. **A generation of worldwide acceptance**
   —Torginol of America Inc.

2. **America's finest power-loomed rug**
   —Karastan Rug Mills.

3. **Artistry in carpets**
   —Painter Carpet Mills, Inc., Div. Collins and Aikman.

4. **A rug for every room**
   —Bird & Son Inc.

5. **A title on the door rates a Bigelow on the floor**
   —Bigelow-Sanford Inc.

6. **Beauty basis for your home**
   —(*Mohawk rugs and carpets*) Mohasco Corp.

7. **Brighten your home at little expense**
   —(*Congoleum rugs*) Congoleum Corp.

8. **Burlington, the scatter rug of beauty**
   —Lack Carpet Co.

9. **Carpets of distinction**
   —Patcraft Mills Inc.

10. **Distinctive floor coverings since 1917**
    —Ernest Treganowan.

11. **Fashion loomed to last**
    —Magee Carpet Co.

12. **Feels like walking on velvet**
    —Clinton Carpet Co.

13. **First in fashion**
    —Patcraft Mills Inc.

14. **Floor with maple, beech or birch**
    —Maple Flooring Mfrs. Assn.

15. **For every floor in the house**
    —(*linoleum*) Armstrong Cork Co.

16. **Holmes rugs for artistic homes**
    —Archibold Holmes & Son.

17. **Look for the spinning wheel label**
    —Magee Carpet Co.

18. **Loomed by American labor to beautify American homes**
    —Magee Carpet Co.

46.   FLOOR COVERINGS *cont.*

19.   **More ideas from the Armstrong world of interior design**
>   —Armstrong Cork Co.

20.   **Originators of prefinished hardwood flooring**
>   —The Cromar Co.

21.   **Outlast the factory**
>   —(*Kreolite floors*) Jennison-Wright Co.

22.   **People who know buy Bigelow**
>   —Bigelow-Sanford Inc.

23.   **Quality since 1846**
>   —Philadelphia Carpet Co.

24.   **Resilient floors for every need**
>   —Bonded Floors Co.

25.   **Styled in California, applauded by all America**
>   —(*Pabco linoleums*) Fibreboard Corp.

26.   **The answer is wool . . . it costs less in the long run**
>   —Wool Carpets of America.

27.   **The floor of enduring beauty**
>   —Congoleum Corp.

28.   **The magic of Masland Carpets**
>   —C. H. Masland and Sons.

29.   **The wonder rug of America**
>   —(*Karastan rugs*) Karastan Rug Mills.

30.   **They wear and wear and wear**
>   —Armstrong Cork Co.

31.   **Think original, think Dellinger**
>   —Dellinger Inc.

32.   **Those heavenly carpets by Lees**
>   —James Lees and Sons Co.

33.   **We care about color**
>   —Simon Manges and Son Inc.

34.   **Wholesale floor coverings of distinction**
>   —Manuel Feldman Co. Inc.

35.   **World's largest maker of tufted carpets and rugs**
>   —E. T. Barwick Industries Inc.

36.   **Woven with a warp of honesty and a woof of skill**
>   —Magee Carpet Co.

37.   **Years of wear in every yard**
>   —(*Congoleum*) Congoleum Corp.

47. FOOD, MISCELLANEOUS

See also **10. BABY PRODUCTS, 11. BAKED GOODS AND BAKING SUPPLIES, 15. BEVERAGES, MISCELLANEOUS, 20. CANDY AND GUM, 21. CEREALS, 29. CONDIMENTS AND SPICES, 33. DAIRY PRODUCTS, 49. FRUITS AND NUTS, 74. MEATS, 87. PET FOOD AND PRODUCTS, 99. RESTAURANTS**

1. **A cube makes a cup**
   —(*Steero cubes*) Schieffelin and Co.

2. **All fresh-fruit good!**
   —(*jellies, preserves*) Kraft Foods.

3. **A lordly touch for simple menus**
   —(*Campbell's soups*) Campbell Soup Co.

4. **America's first, finest and favorite pork and beans**
   —Stokely-Van Camp Inc.

5. **America's most famous dessert**
   —(*Jell-o*) General Foods Corp.

6. **America's supreme dessert**
   —(*plum pudding*) Richardson & Robbins.

7. **A nation's health is a nation's strength**
   —Loma Linda Food Co.

8. **A pip of a chip**
   —(*Jays potato chips*) Jays Foods Inc.

9. **Aristocrat of the breakast table**
   —(*marmalade*) Chivers & Sons Ltd.

10. **As a change from potatoes**
    —(*macaroni*) C. F. Mueller Co.

11. **As good as can be**
    —Stouffer Foods.

12. **As good as it tastes**
    —American Rice Products Co.

13. **As they eat 'em in New England**
    —(*brick-oven beans*) Burnham & Morrill Co.

14. **A treasure for eating pleasure**
    —(*canned vegetables*) Country Gardens Inc.

15. **Because it's sweet, not bitter**
    —(*marmalade*) Welch Grape Juice Co.

16. **Best cooks know foods fried in Crisco don't taste greasy!**
    —Procter & Gamble Co.

17. **Better buy Birds Eye**
    —Birds Eye Div., General Foods Corp.

47. **FOOD, MISCELLANEOUS** *cont.*

18. **Canned food is grand food**
  —American Can Co.

19. **Catch them yourself or buy Fowler's**
  —Fowler Sea Products Co.

20. **Choosey mothers choose Jif**
  —(*Jif peanut butter*) Procter & Gamble Co.

21. **Close. But no lumps.**
  —(*Heinz Home Style gravy*) H. J. Heinz Co.

22. **Cooking up ideas**
  —(*Campbell foods*).

23. **Cooks in nine minutes**
  —(*macaroni, noodles*) C. F. Mueller Co.

24. **Delicious in flavor, rich in nutrition**
  —Corn Products Refining Co.

25. **Different, delicious, digestible**
  —Doughnut Corp. of America.

26. **Each grain salutes you**
  —(*rice*) Uncle Ben's Foods.

27. **Easy, delicious . . . versatile, nutritious**
  —Rice Council.

28. **Energy eggs from happy hens**
  —New Jersey Egg Market Committee.

29. **Every bite a rarebit**
  —(*Chicken of the Sea tuna*) Ralston Purina Co.

30. **Everything's better with Blue Bonnet on it**
  —(*margarine*) Standard Brands Inc.

31. **Everything you've ever wanted in a fish fillet**
  —(*Mrs. Paul's fish fillets*) Mrs. Paul's Kitchens.

32. **Feels like it's time, Cup-A-Soup time**
  —(*Cup-A-Soup*) Lipton Inc.

33. **57 Varieties**
  —H. J. Heinz Co.

34. **Finest imported from Italy**
  —(*olive oil*) A. Guiflani & Bro.

35. **Food of the gods**
  —(*honey*) Arthur W. Hoffman.

36. **For good food and good food ideas**
  —Kraft Foods.

37. **For quicker meals, packed with flavor, your best bet is Universal Minute-Savor**
  —Landers, Frary & Clark.

47. **FOOD, MISCELLANEOUS** *cont.*

38. **For the lightest, fluffiest popcorn there's only one, Orville Redenbacher**
     —(*Orville Redenbacher Gourmet Popping Corn*) Hunt-
     Wesson Foods Inc.

39. **Fresh as a spring morning**
     —(*Little America frozen foods*).

40. **Fresh as dewy dawn**
     —Pacific Egg Producers.

41. **From flower to bee to you**
     —(*Airline honey*) A. I. Root Co.

42. **Glowing with health, brimming with flavor**
     —(*Campbell's soups*) Campbell Soup Co.

43. **Good to eat and good for you**
     —Original Ry-Krisp Co.

44. **Great Grapes, what a flavor**
     —(*grape jelly, grapeade*) Welch Grape Juice Co.

45. **Hunt for the best**
     —Hunt-Wesson Foods Inc.

46. **If you like peanuts, you'll like Skippy**
     —(*Skippy peanut butter*) CPC International Inc.

47. **In everything you fry or bake**
     —(*Crisco shortening*) Procter & Gamble Co.

48. **It's all in this little yellow box**
     —(*Velveeta*) Kraft Inc.

49. **It's like homemade**
     —(*Soup Di Pasta*).

50. **It's not just any snack**
     —(*Nacho Cheese Doritos*) Frito-Lay Inc.

51. **It's uncanny**
     —(*Knorr soups*) CPC International Inc.

52. **It tastes good because it is good**
     —(*Mrs. Paul's fish fillets*) Mrs. Paul's Kitchens.

53. **Just form and fry**
     —(*codfish cakes*) J. W. Beardsley's sons.

54. **Like grandma's, only more so**
     —General Foods Corp.

55. **Like little meat pies in sauce**
     —(*ravioli*) American Home Foods Inc.

56. **Look-alikes aren't cook-alikes**
     —Idaho Potato Growers Inc.

57. **Look to Libby's for perfection**
     —Libby, McNeil & Libby.

47. FOOD, MISCELLANEOUS *cont.*

58. **Made from a rare old recipe**
$\qquad$ —(*Shirriff's marmalade*).

59. **Makes eyes sparkle and mouths water**
$\qquad$ —(*Mazola salad oil*) CPC International Inc.

60. **Makes fish day a red letter day**
$\qquad$ —(*Chicken of the Sea tuna*) Ralston Purina Co.

61. **Man's greatest food**
$\qquad$ —(*potato*) Maine Development Commission.

62. **Mazola makes good eating sense**
$\qquad$ —(*margarine*) Corn Products Co.

63. **Measure of quality**
$\qquad$ —(*rice*) Uncle Ben's Inc.

64. **Moist as homemade**
$\qquad$ —(*Duncan Hines cake mixes*) Procter & Gamble Co.

65. **More Ummm, Ummm after every crunch**
$\qquad$ —(*Planters Cheese Balls*) Planters Peanuts.

66. **Move over, Bacon**
$\qquad$ —(*Sizzlean*) Swift & Co.

67. **New foods, new ideas for a better world**
$\qquad$ —General Mills Inc.

68. **Nothing to do but fry**
$\qquad$ —(*Gorton's codfish cakes*) The Gorton Corp.

69. **Not just good … but wonderful**
$\qquad$ —Ward Foods Co.

70. **Packed with the wiggle in its tail**
$\qquad$ —New England Fish Co.

71. **People who talk about good food talk about General Foods**
$\qquad$ —General Foods Corp.

72. **Picked at the fleeting moment of perfect flavor**
$\qquad$ —(*Green Giant peas*) Green Giant Co.

73. **Pick of the pack, picked at the peak of perfection**
$\qquad$ —(*Polar Frosted Foods*).

74. **Quality food products used with confidence**
$\qquad$ —Procter & Gamble Co.

75. **Reach for the Campbell's. It's right on your shelf**
$\qquad$ —Campbell Soup Co.

76. **Seven cents a glass**
$\qquad$ —(*jelly*) La Vor Products Co.

77. **Short lengths, easy to eat**
$\qquad$ —(*macaroni, noodles*) C. F. Mueller Co.

47. **FOOD, MISCELLANEOUS** *cont.*

78. **Shrimply elegant**
—(*shrimp*) Treasure Isle Inc.

79. **Some like 'em big, some like 'em little**
—(*peas*) Bozeman Canning Co.

80. **Start with—stay with Knox**
—Chas. Knox Gelatine Co.

81. **Stir up the Campbell's . . . soup is good food**
—Campbell Soup Co.

82. **Sugar's got what it takes**
—Sugar Information Inc.

83. **Sure to delight your appetite**
—(*food products*) The Haserot Co.

84. **Sweeten it with Domino**
—American Sugar Refining Co.

85. **"Table Grade" Margarine**
—Miami Margarine Co.

86. **Tastes twice as good as ever before**
—(*Jell-o*) General Foods Corp.

87. **That's Italian**
—(*Ragu Spaghetti Sauce*) Ragu Foods Inc.

88. **The better spread for our daily bread**
—(*Interstate cotton oil*).

89. **The big cheese of potato chips**
—(*Pringle's Cheesum*) Procter & Gamble Co.

90. **The brands that made tuna famous**
—(*Chicken of the Sea tuna*) Ralston Purina Co.

91. **The brand that always puts flavor first**
—(*Del Monte fruit cocktail*) Del Monte Corp.

92. **The brand they ask for first**
—(*Allsweet margarine*) Swift & Co.

93. **The economical energy food**
—(*macaroni, spaghetti, noodles*) Quaker Maid Co.

94. **The famous family of Gorton's sea foods**
—Gorton-Pew Fisheries Co.

95. **The flavor is sealed in the flavor bud**
—(*Shirriff's Lushus jelly*).

96. **The highest quality for health**
—Chas. Knox Gelatine Co.

97. **The last word in sea food**
—Oyster Growers & Dealers Assn.

98. **The most asked-for brand of all**
—(*Allsweet margarine*) Swift & Co.

47. **FOOD, MISCELLANEOUS** *cont.*

   99. **The most experienced food processor in the world**
      —Libby, McNeill & Libby.

  100. **The name you can trust in margarine**
      —(*Mazola*) Best Foods Div., Corn Products Co.

  101. **The San Francisco Style Snack Thins**
      —(*Better Cheddars*) Nabisco Inc.

  102. **The soup most folks like best**
      —Campbell Soup Co.

  103. **The tender-textured gelatin**
      —(*Royal*) Standard Brands Inc.

  104. **The world's largest and finest**
      —Lindsay Ripe Olive Co.

  105. **They always eat better when you remember the soup**
      —Campbell Soup Co.

  106. **They're not just breadcrumbs**
      —(*4C Breadcrumbs*).

  107. **They're smackin' good**
      —(*Tater flakes*) The Tater-Flakes Co.

  108. **To bid you good morning**
      —(*Shirriff's marmalade*).

  109. **Trim is in**
      —(*Trim Cup-A-Soup*) Lipton Inc.

  110. **Whenever a recipe calls for gelatine, think of Knox**
      —Chas. Knox Gelatine Co.

  111. **When it's Domino Sugar, you're *sure* it's *pure*!**
      —American Sugar Refining Co.

  112. **When only the best will do, say Uncle**
      —(*Uncle Ben's rice*) Uncle Ben's Foods.

  113. **Where food grows finest, there Libby packs the best**
      —Libby, McNeil & Libby.

  114. **Young America spreads it on thick**
      —(*marmalade*) Welch Grape Juice Co.

  115. **Your best food from the sea**
      —Oyster Growers of North America.

48. **FOOTWEAR**
     See also **26. CLOTHING, MISCELLANEOUS,**
       123. WARDROBE ACCESSORIES

    1. **Absorb shocks and jars**
      —(*Massagic air cushion shoes*) Weyenberg Shoe Mfg. Co.

48. FOOTWEAR *cont.*

2. **Action shoes for boys and girls**
    —(*Red Goose shoes*) International Shoe Co.

3. **A foot nearer perfection**
    —G. R. Kinney Co.

4. **A foot of comfort means miles of happiness**
    —Ault Williamson Shoe Co.

5. **Always a step ahead in style**
    —Connolly Shoe Co.

6. **Always first with all that's new**
    —Winthrop Shoes.

7. **A man's first choice**
    —Weyenberg Shoe Mfg. Co.

8. **American gentlemen shoes designed for the American man**
    —Hamilton Brown Shoe Co.

9. **American lady shoes designed for the American woman**
    —Hamilton Brown Shoe Co.

10. **America's best-known shoes**
    —W. L. Douglas Co.

11. **America's No. 1 heel**
    —O'Sullivan Rubber Co.

12. **America's smartest walking shoes**
    —(*Enna Jetticks*) Dunn & McCarthy Inc.

13. **A million Americans can't be wrong**
    —(*Father & Son shoes*) Endicott Johnson Corp.

14. **Ankle-fashioned shoes**
    —Nunn-Bush Shoe Co.

15. **Any Palizzio is better than no Palizzio**
    —Palizzio Inc.

16. **Art in footwear**
    —Laird, Schober & Co.

17. **A shoe with a talking point**
    —Teeple Shoe Co.

18. **A style for any taste, a fit for any foot**
    —Florsheim Shoe Co.

19. **A sure sign they're good**
    —(*Hood rubbers*) B. F. Goodrich Co.

20. **A wealth of value in Fortune Shoes**
    —Richland Shoe Co.

21. **Beauty treatment for your feet**
    —(*Red Cross shoes*) Krohn Feckheimer Co.

48. **FOOTWEAR** *cont.*

22. **Bends with your foot**
—(*Red Cross shoes*) Krohn Feckheimer Co.

23. **Best for rest**
—(*house slippers*) S. Rauh & Co.

24. **Better little shoes are not made**
—Mrs. Day's Ideal Baby Shoe Co.

25. **Breathin' brushed pigskin**
—(*Hush Puppies*) Wolverine World Wide Inc.

26. **Built-in quality in every shoe**
—D. Myers & Sons.

27. **Calendar of fashion**
—International Shoe Co.

28. **Connolly shoes are comfortable shoes**
—Connolly Shoe Co.

29. **Cushion every step**
—Weyenberg Shoe Mfg. Co.

30. **Designed for going places in style, in comfort**
—(*Pediforme shoes*).

31. **Double welt means double wear**
—Shaft-Pierce Shoe Co.

32. **Every pair is full of wear**
—(*Kinder-Garten shoes*) Wallace Shoe Co.

33. **Every pair made to wear**
—(*Gutta Percha rubbers*) PPG Industries Inc.

34. **Every pair shows the care of the shoemaker's hand**
—(*Bostonian*) The Commonwealth Shoe & Leather Co.

35. **Faithful to the last**
—Nunn, Bush & Weldon Shoe Co.

36. **Famous shoes for women**
—(*Queen Quality shoes*) Thos. G. Plant Co.

37. **Fashioned by master craftsmen**
—Nunn-Bush Shoe Co.

38. **Fashion forecasters**
—International Shoe Co.

39. **Fashion-over-the-shoe**
—(*U. S. Gaytees rubbers*) Uniroyal Inc.

40. **Fashion's favored footwear**
—Washington Shoe Mfg. Co.

41. **Feel the air cushion**
—Weyenberg Shoe Mfg. Co.

42. **Fine bootmakers since 1876**
—Charles A. Eaton Co.

48. **FOOTWEAR** *cont.*

43. **First always, finest all ways**
—Florsheim Shoe Co.

44. **First in quality!**
—Nunn-Bush Shoe Co.

45. **Fit for every foot**
—G. R. Kinney Co.

46. **Fit right, feel right, they're walk-fitted**
—Bostonian Shoe Co.

47. **Fits on the foot like a glove on the hand**
—F. Blumenthal Co.

48. **Fits the foot in action or repose**
—United States Shoe Co.

49. **Fit to be tried**
—Musebeck Shoe Co.

50. **Flexible where you want it, rigid where you need it**
—United States Shoe Co.

51. **Florsheims afoot mean comfort ahead**
—Florsheim Shoe Co.

52. **Foot insurance for the future**
—Julian & Hokenge Co.

53. **Footwear for all occasions**
—Latterman Shoe Mfg. Co.

54. **For any wear and everywhere**
—Florsheim Shoe Co.

55. **For every walk in life**
—Melville Shoe Corp.

56. **For men who measure value in terms of quality alone**
—Florsheim Shoe Co.

57. **For the active woman of today**
—F. Mayer Shoe Co.

58. **For the winning edge**
—(*Dr. Scholl's Odor Eaters*) Scholl Inc.

59. **Friendly to the feet**
—Jarman Shoe Co.

60. **From first step to fourteen years**
—Fargo-Hallowell Shoe Co.

61. **Gives joy complete to women's feet**
—Dunn & McCarthy Inc.

62. **Give your feet young ideas**
—Weyenberg Shoe Mfg. Co.

48. **FOOTWEAR** *cont.*

63. **Good feet are the foundation of good health**
—Burns Cuboid Co.

64. **Great shoes for little Americans**
—(*Little Yankee*).

65. **Half the fun of having feet**
—(*Red Goose shoes*) International Shoe Co.

66. **He won't change from shoes to slippers because he's enjoying Massagic comfort**
—Weyenberg Shoe Mfg. Co.

67. **Honest wear in every pair**
—Marston & Brooks Co.

68. **If it's new, Saks has it**
—Saks Shoe Corp.

69. **In step with fashion**
—Lampe Shoe Co.

70. **In the California manner**
—Gude's Inc.

71. **It takes leather to stand weather**
—J. Edwards & Co.

72. **It takes on added beauty in the shoe**
—Surpass Leather Co.

73. **Keep children's feet as nature made them**
—Shaft-Pierce Shoe Co.

74. **Keep good feet healthy**
—Gilbert Shoe Co.

75. **Keep in step with Paris**
—Enzel-of-Paris Inc.

76. **Keep in step with youth**
—Burdett Shoe Co.

77. **Keeps the foot well**
—(*Arch Preserver shoes*) Shelby Shoe Co.

78. **Keep young feet young**
—Simplex Mfg. Co.

79. **Keep your shoes beautiful always**
—Raynorshyne Products.

80. **Keyed to the mode and mood of romance**
—Stix-Altman-Weiner Inc.

81. **Kiddies' feet are safe in Kinney's hands**
—G. R. Kinney Co.

82. **Kid flatters the foot**
—(*Kid Group*) Tanners Council of America.

48.   **FOOTWEAR** *cont.*

83.   **L'Echo de Paris**
—(*shoes*) Murphy & Saval Co.

84.   **Lets the feet grow as they should**
—(*Educator shoes*) Rice & Hutchins.

85.   **Like walking on air**
—Weyenberg Shoe Mfg. Co.

86.   **Little shoes for little devils**
—Faust Shoe Co.

87.   **Look at your shoes, others do**
—Florsheim Shoe Co.

88.   **Look for the red ball**
—Mishawaka Rubber Co. Inc.

89.   **Looks good from any angle**
—(*Naturalizer shoes*) Brown Shoe Co.

90.   **Made stronger to wear longer**
—Fargo-Hallowell Shoe Co.

91.   **Made-to-measure fit in ready-to-wear shoes**
—W. B. Coon Co.

92.   **Makers of fine shoes for men and women**
—Florsheim Shoe Co.

93.   **Makes life's walk easy**
—L. A. Crossett Co.

94.   **Makes shoes wear longer**
—(*Red-line-in*) Farnsworth Hoyt Co.

95.   **Make you want to walk**
—Nature-Tread Mfg. Co.

96.   **Men wear them everywhere**
—Florsheim Shoe Co.

97.   **Mighty good shoes for boys**
—Teeple Shoe Co.

98.   **Miles ahead**
—Converse Rubber Co.

99.   **More by the pair, less by the year**
—Stetson Shoe Co.

100.   **Moulded to your foot**
—(*Aid-A-Walker shoes*).

101.   **Not made to a price, but a perfect product**
—Mrs. Day's Ideal Baby Shoe Co.

102.   **Not the price per pair, but the cost per mile**
—Stacy-Adams Co.

48. **FOOTWEAR** *cont.*

103. **Praise for Biltrite comes from the heart but the comfort and long wear come from the sole**
—Biltrite Rubber Co.

104. **Prince of soles**
—Alfred Hale Rubber Co.

105. **Put your feet on easy street**
—Weyenberg Shoe Mfg. Co.

106. **Quality at your feet**
—Brown Shoe Co.

107. **Scientifically correct shoes for juveniles**
—H. W. Merriam.

108. **Shaped to fit like your stockings**
—(*Foot Saver shoes*) Shortback's.

109. **Shaped to your foot in action**
—Noned Corp.

110. **She walks in beauty**
—Brauer Bros. Shoe Co.

111. **Shoes of character**
—Volman Lawrence Co.

112. **Shoes of worth**
—A. E. Nettleton Co.

113. **Shoes that often leave everyone natty**
—(*Koorc Spat shoes*).

114. **Since 1857 . . . the standard of excellence in men's footwear**
—(*Foot-Joy*) Brockton Footwear Inc.

115. **Slipper-free where the foot bends**
—Bates Shoe Co.

116. **Slippers of merit**
—Kozy Komfort Shoe Mfg. Co.

117. **Smart shoes for beautiful feet**
—Julian & Hokenge Co.

118. **Soft shoes for hard wear**
—Jumping-Jacks Shoes Inc.

119. **Soft shoes for tender feet**
—J. J. Grover's Sons Co.

120. **Sole of fashion**
—(*Neolite soles*).

121. **Specialists in children's good shoes since 1892**
—Shaft-Pierce Shoe Co.

122. **Stay put**
—Tweedie Boot Top Co.

48. FOOTWEAR *cont.*

123. **Step into a Fortune, your key to a wealth of satisfaction**
—(*Fortune shoes*) Richland Shoe Co.

124. **Sticks like a barnacle**
—Sperry Footwear.

125. **Stronger than the law**
—(*shoes*) Roberts, Johnson & Rand.

126. **Sturdy to the last**
—Merriam Shoe Co.

127. **Style that stays**
—Commonwealth Shoe & Leather Co.

128. **Take it easy and breezy**
—(*Walk-Over Koolies*) George E. Keith Co.

129. **The big house for little shoes since 1900**
—(*Edwards shoes*) The Stride Rite Corp.

130. **The boot with the muscles**
—Beacon Falls Rubber Co.

131. **The comfort shoe of tomorrow**
—McLaughlin-Sweet Inc.

132. **The easiest kind because skeleton lined**
—Florsheim Shoe Co.

133. **The easiest shoe for women**
—Utz & Dunn Co.

134. **The fashion shoe**
—(*Mademoiselle*) Genesco Inc.

135. **The heel that won't peel**
—F. W. Mears Heel Co.

136. **The heel with nine lives**
—(*Cat's Paw*) Foster Rubber Co.

137. **The high mark on leather**
—Alexander Bros.

138. **The jewel of patent leather**
—Lawrence Leather Co.

139. **The last fits, the fit lasts**
—Goding Shoe Co.
—Stacy Adams Co.

140. **The leather is there in every pair**
—Peters Shoe Co.

141. **The life of leather**
—Bergmann Shoe Mfg. Co.

142. **The man's styleful shoe on a real chassis**
—E. T. Wright & Co.

48. FOOTWEAR *cont.*

143. **The most comfortable shoe in the world**
—Ground Gripper Shoe Co.

144. **The most powerful shoe in America**
—Theo. Bergman.

145. **The most salable shoe in America**
—(*Red Cross shoes*) Krohn Feckheimer Co.

146. **The perfected corrective shoe**
—(*Fairy Foot*) Walker-Knaier Shoe Corp.

147. **The prettiest thing on two feet**
—Carlisle Shoe Co.

148. **The proudest name in shoes**
—(*Keith Highlanders*) George E. Keith Co.

149. **The quality is higher than the price**
—Juvenile Shoe Corp.

150. **There are no finer shoes**
—A. E. Nettleton Co.

151. **There's double wear in every pair**
—Dryden Rubber Co.

152. **The shoe everybody knows, and almost everybody wears**
—Melville Shoe Corp.

153. **The shoe of champions**
—Keds Corp.

154. **The shoe that holds its shape**
—W. L. Douglas Shoe Co.

155. **The shoe that's different**
—Field & Flint Co.

156. **The shoe that's standardized**
—(*Educator shoes*) Rice & Hutchins.

157. **The shoe with a memory**
—(*Johnston and Murphy*) Genesco Inc.

158. **The shoe with the beautiful fit**
—(*Naturalizer*) Brown Shoe Co.

159. **The shoe with the mileage**
—W. H. Walker & Co.

160. **The shoe with the youthful feel**
—(*Air Step shoes*).

161. **The walk of the town**
—Simon Bros.

162. **The washable shoes**
—Keds Corp.

48. FOOTWEAR *cont.*

163. **They neither crimp your roll nor cramp your style**
—Bob Smart Shoe Co.

164. **The young point of view in shoes**
—(*Life Stride*) Brown Shoe Co.

165. **They're tops for the bottoms**
—Musebeck Shoe Co.

166. **They've got to be Stetson to be snappy**
—Stetson Shoe Co.

167. **They walk with you**
—Melville Shoe Corp.

168. **They win your feet**
—United Shoe Mfrs.

169. **Time will tell, wear Sundial Shoes**
—Morse & Rogers.

170. **Today's most scientific shoes**
—W. B. Coon Co.

171. **Turns sidewalks into soft carpets**
—(*Air Step shoes*) Brown Shoe Co.

172. **Two feet of comfort in every step**
—W. H. Walker.

173. **Watch your feet**
—(*foot health aids*) Scholl Inc.

174. **Wear tested for your comfort**
—(*Jarman*) Genesco Inc.

175. **When you pay for quality, why not get the finest**
—Florsheim Shoe Co.

176. **When you're out to beat the world**
—(*tennis shoes*) Converse Rubber Co.

177. **Where thrift meets style**
—(*shoes*) J. Edwards & Co.

178. **World's Fair feet**
—Selby Shoe Co.

179. **Worn with pride by millions**
—Freeman Shoe Corp.

180. **You can't wear out their looks**
—J. P. Smith Shoe Co.

181. **Your feet are worth Fortunes**
—Richland Shoe Co.

182. **Your feet are your fortune**
—Musebeck Shoe Co.

183. **Your friend**
—Thom McAn Shoe Co.

48. FOOTWEAR *cont.*

   184. Your personal pedestal
   —(*Adler elevator shoes*).

   185. You walk on cushions when you walk in Osteo-path-iks
   —Allen-Spiegel Shoes.

FRAGRANCES . . . See **84. PERFUMES AND FRAGRANCES**

FRUIT DRINKS . . . See **107. SOFT DRINKS**

49. FRUITS AND NUTS
   See also **47. FOOD, MISCELLANEOUS**

   1. All good things come in pears
   —Oregon-Washington-California Pear Bureau.

   2. All they're cracked up to be
   —(*walnuts*) California Walnut Growers Assn.

   3. An apple a day is Doc Apple's way
   —Pacific Northwest Fruits Inc.

   4. Awful fresh
   —MacFarlane Nut Co.

   5. Best for juice and every use
   —(*oranges*) Sunkist Growers Inc.

   6. Blue Goose stands today, as always, for quality
   —American Fruit Growers.

   7. Buy them by the dozen for their many uses
   —(*lemons*) Sunkist Growers Inc.

   8. Come on over to the right light
   —(*Del Monte Light fruit*) Del Monte Corp.

   9. Crackin' good walnuts
   —(*walnuts*) California Walnut Growers Assn.

   10. Eat more apples, take less medicine
   —(*apples*) Virginia Horticultural Society.

   11. Every day in some way
   —(*prunes*) United Prune Growers of California.

   12. Flavor first
   —(*fruits*) Del Monte Corp.

   13. Full of sunshine and good health
   —California Prune & Apricot Growers.

   14. Good to the core
   —Pacific Northwest Fruits Inc.

   15. Had your iron today?
   —Sun-Maid Raisin Growers Assn.

49. FRUITS AND NUTS *cont.*

16. **If you could see inside oranges, you'd buy Sunkist every time**
—(*oranges*) Sunkist Growers Inc.

17. **Keep regular the healthful way**
—(*lemons*) Sunkist Growers Inc.

18. **Make Sunsweet your daily good health habit**
—Sunsweet Growers Inc.

19. **One taste is worth a thousand words**
—MacFarlane Nut Co.

20. **Only three calories a squeeze**
—(*Sunkist oranges*) Sunkist Growers Inc.

21. **Peel a bite of health**
—Fruit Dispatch Co.

22. **Red apples for red cheeks**
—Hood River Apple Growers Assn.

23. **The final touch to a tasty dish**
—Liberty Cherry & Fruit Co.

24. **The name for quality**
—(*peanuts*) Planters Peanuts.

25. **The nuts that get noticed**
—(*walnuts*) Diamond Walnut Growers.

26. **The way the best lemons sign their name**
—(*lemons*) Sunkist Growers Inc.

27. **They make ordinary occasions special**
—(*dry roasted peanuts*) Planters Peanuts.

28. **They must be good**
—(*prunes*) Sunsweet Growers Inc.

29. **They're wonderful so many ways**
—(*California cling peaches*).

30. **This is the walnut age**
—(*walnuts*) American Walnut Mfrs. Assn.

31. **Tune the meal and tone the system**
—Florida Citrus Exchange.

32. **We take the nut very seriously**
—(*packaged nuts*) Fisher Nut Company.

33. **When you take cold, take lemons**
—(*lemons*) Sunkist Growers Inc.

FUEL...See **9.** AUTOMOTIVE SERVICE, **59.** HEATING AND COOKING FUELS, **88.** PETROLEUM PRODUCTS, **93.** PUBLIC UTILITIES

50. **FURNITURE**
> See also **13.** BEDS AND BEDDING, **65.** INTERIOR
> DECORATION

1. **A handy kitchen means living room leisure**
> —Marsh Furniture Co.

2. **A living tradition in furniture**
> —Heritage Furniture Inc.

3. **America's most distinguished source for fine English furniture**
> —Wood and Hogan.

4. **America's oldest and largest showroom distributor of fine decorative furniture**
> —Knapp and Tubbs Inc.

5. **Another fine creation by Krueger**
> —Krueger Metal Products Co.

6. **At home with your young ideas**
> —Bassett Furniture Industries Inc.

7. **At White, fine furniture making is a lost art we never lost**
> —White of Mebane.

8. **A world of furniture made in a way that makes a world of difference**
> —Kroehler Mfg. Co.

9. **Best buy Boling**
> —Boling Chair Co.

10. **Better your home, better your living**
> —Drexel Heritage Furnishings.

11. **Built to sustain a reputation**
> —Handy Chair & Table Co.

12. **Built to take it ... beautifully**
> —Daystrom Furniture Div., Daystrom Inc.

13. **Buy Castle Furniture for your castle**
> —Castle Furniture Co.

14. **By design ... furniture distinguished for value since 1904**
> —Thomasville Furniture Industries Inc.

15. **Carefree furniture**
> —Viko Furniture.

16. **Chairs for all business**
> —Boling Chair Co.

17. **Come take a trip around our Castle**
> —Castle Furniture Co.

50. FURNITURE *cont.*

18. **Craftsmen of fine solid wood furniture**
                              —Davis Cabinet Co.

19. **Definitive modern furniture**
                              —Founders Furniture Inc.

20. **Enduring masterpieces**
                              —Kiel Furniture Co.

21. **Fine cabinetmakers since 1886**
                              —Karges Furniture Co.

22. **For every room in the house**
                              —Michigan Seating Co.

23. **For more than a century makers of fine furniture in traditional and modern idiom**
                              —John Widdicomb Co.

24. **For the REST of your life**
                              —(*Slumber Chair*) C. F. Streit Mfg. Co.

25. **For those who value excellence**
                              —Henredon Furniture Industries Inc.

26. **Furniture of timeless beauty**
                              —Romweber Industries.

27. **Furniture that's fun to live with**
                              —H. T. Cushman Mfg. Corp.

28. **If it folds ... ask Howe**
                              —Howe Folding Furniture Inc.

29. **If it's chairs ... it's Miele!**
                              —Ralph A. Miele Inc.

30. **Importers and makers of fine furniture**
                              —Leopold Colombo Inc.

31. **In a word ... it's Selig**
                              —Selig Mfg. Co. Inc.

32. **Inspired by originals for homes for distinction**
                              —(*Earl's Court Collection*) Lane Furniture.

33. **It's the very finest because it's Rubee**
                              —Rubee Furniture Mfg. Corp.

34. **... Keeping tradition alive**
                              —Meldan Co. Inc.

35. **Leather: An investment in pleasure**
                              —Roche-Bobois Furniture.

36. **Made by the makers of fine furniture**
                              —Tennessee Furniture Corp.

37. **Making the world safe for baby**
                              —Trimble Nurseryland Furniture Inc.

50. **FURNITURE** *cont.*

38. **Master craftsmen since 1890**
                              —Biggs Antique Co. Inc.

39. **More than a cedar chest, a piece of fine furniture**
                              —Tennessee Furniture Corp.

40. **Oak for charm and livable character, furniture for your children's children**
                              —Oak Service Bureau, Hardwood Institute.

41. **One if by day, two if by night**
                              —(*Sofa-niter*) Charlton Co.

42. **One name in furniture everybody knows**
                              —Kroehler Mfg. Co.

43. **Preferred for America's most distinguished homes**
                              —Romweber Industries.

44. **Prevent schoolroom slouch**
                              —American Seating Co.

45. **Push the button back—recline**
                              —Royal Easy Chair Co.

46. **Quality shows through**
                              —Drew Furniture Co.

47. **Replete with hidden values, free from hidden dangers**
                              —Snyder's Sani-Bilt Furniture.

48. **Sag Pruf will never let you down**
                              —(*Sag Pruf furniture foundation*).

49. **Solid and true, walnut clear through**
                              —(*Gibbard furniture*).

50. **Solid comfort seating**
                              —Hampden Specialty Products Co.

51. **Specialists in seating—and seating only—since 1927**
                              —Harter Corp.

52. **Strong enough to stand on**
                              —(*Samson folding table*).

53. **Style authority in wrought iron**
                              —Lee L. Woodward and Sons Inc.

54. **The chair of amazing comfort**
                              —Jamestown Upholstery Co.

55. **The chair that stands by itself**
                              —Stakmore Co. Inc.

56. **The convertible sofa with accordion action**
                              —(*Sofa-niter*) Charlton Co.

57. **The costume jewelry of the home**
                              —Mersman Tables.

50. FURNITURE *cont.*

58. The folding furniture with the permanent look
—Stakmore Co. Inc.

59. The line with the go
—Conewango Furniture Co.

**60. The more living you do, the more you need
Samsonite**
—Samsonite Corp.

61. The most famous name in rattan furniture
—Ficks Reed Co.

62. The most trusted name in furniture
—Drexel Enterprises Inc.

63. ... The name for fine rattan furniture
—Whitecraft Inc.

64. The present with a future
—(*West Branch cedar hope chest*).

65. There's a quality about a home with Henredon
—Henredon Furniture Industries Inc.

66. The South's oldest makers of fine furniture
—White Furniture Co.

67. Tomorrow is a friend of Dunbar
—Dunbar Furniture Corp.

68. We brush aside all competition
—Hegel Furniture Co.

69. Where pride of craftsmanship comes first
—Empire Furniture Corp.

70. World's greatest table makers
—Imperial Furniture Co.

G

GAMES ... See 118. TOYS AND GAMES

GARDEN PRODUCTS ... See 69. LAWN AND GARDEN
  PRODUCTS

GARTERS ... See 61. HOSIERY

GASOLINE ... See 88. PETROLEUM PRODUCTS

GAUGES ... See 63. INSTRUMENTS AND GAUGES

GEMS ... See 67. JEWELRY AND SILVER

51. **GIFTS AND GREETINGS**
  1. **America's best-loved greeting cards**
                                —Norcross Inc.
  2. **Greeting Cards of character**
                          —Rust Craft Greeting Cards Inc.
  3. **Replace fear with cheer. Send Christmas cards this
     year**
                          —Greeting Card Association.
  4. **Say it with flowers**
                          —Society of American Florists.
  5. **Say it with flowers, by wire**
                    —Florists Telegraph Delivery Association.
  6. **Scatter sunshine with greeting cards**
                          —Greeting Card Association.
  7. **Send your thoughts with special FTD care**
                    —Florists Transworld Delivery Association.
  8. **What I'm really giving you is a part of me**
                    —(*greeting cards*) Hallmark Cards Inc.
  9. **When you care enough to send the very best**
                    —(*greeting cards*) Hallmark Cards Inc.

52. **GLASS AND CERAMICS**
  See also 23. CHINA
  1. **A famous brand in glass**
                          —Latchford Glass Co.
  2. **Born of the breath of man, Waterford is life's child**
                          —(*Waterford crystal*).
  3. **Everyday good ... glass with flair**
                          —Anchor Hocking Glass Corp.

52. GLASS AND CERAMICS *cont.*

  4. **Get it in glass**
        —Glass Containers Manufacturers Institute.

  5. **Glassware of distinction**
        —Czechoslovak Glass Products Co.

  6. **Pioneers in colored glass technology**
        —Houze Glass Corp.

  7. **Treasured American glass**
        —Viking Glass Co.

  8. **Vitrified pottery is everlasting**
        —Franklin Pottery.

  9. **World's largest manufacturer of glass tableware**
        —Anchor Hocking Glass Corp.

GLASSES ... See **41.** EYEGLASSES

GLOVES ... See **123.** WARDROBE ACCESSORIES

GLUE ... See **1.** ADHESIVES

53. GOVERNMENT SERVICE
See also **92.** PUBLIC SERVICE

  1. **Be all that you can be**
        —U.S. Army.

  2. **I Want You**
        —U.S. Army.

  3. **The Few. The Proud. The Marines.**
        —U.S. Marines.

  4. **The toughest job you'll ever love**
        —Peace Corps.

GREETINGS ... See **51.** GIFTS AND GREETINGS

GUM ... See **20.** CANDY AND GUM

GUNS ... See **44.** FIREARMS

H

54. **HAIR CARE**
    See also **32. COSMETICS, 116. TOILETRIES**

1. **A little dab will do ya**
    —(*Brylcreem*) Beecham Products Inc.

2. **Approved by professional hair colorists**
    —(*Nestle Color Tint*) Nestle-LeMur Co.

3. **Beautiful hair**
    —John H. Breck Inc.

4. **Beautiful hair is as easy as HQZ**
    —(*hair preparations*) HQZ Laboratories.

5. **Beauty begins with the hair**
    —(*permanent wave*) Gabrieleen Co.

6. **Beauty insurance**
    —(*cocoanut oil shampoo*) R. L. Watkins Co.

7. **Brush the cobwebs from your beauty**
    —(*Kent brushes*).

8. **Brush your hair to loveliness**
    —(*plastic brush*) Du Pont.

9. **Clairol is going to make someone beautiful today**
    —(*hair color*) Clairol Inc.

10. **Clean hair means a healthy scalp**
    —(*Ace combs*) American Hard Rubber Co.

11. **Color cocktails for your hair with Loxol extra**
    —Sales Affiliates Inc.

12. **Colors hair inside, as nature does**
    —Inecto Inc.

13. **Does she . . . or doesn't she**
    —Clairol Inc.

14. **Everyone knows, if it's Caryl Richards, it is just wonderful for your hair**
    —Caryl Richards Inc.

15. **For silken-sheen hair easy to arrange**
    —(*Kreml shampoo*) J. B. Williams Co. Inc.

16. **For twenty-five years, first in professional hair care**
    —Rayette-Faberge Inc.

17. **Guardians of good grooming**
    —(*hair brushes*) Owens Brush Co.

54. HAIR CARE *cont.*

18. **Hair color so natural only her hairdresser knows for sure**

—Clairol Inc.

19. **If you don't look good, we don't look good**

—Vidal Sassoon.

20. **I'm worth it**

—(*Preference by L'Oreal hair color*) Cosmair Inc.

21. **It puts the sunshine in your hair**

—(*Pine Tree shampoo*).

22. **It washes your dandruff away**

—(*Fitch shampoo*) Bristol-Myers Co.

23. **Keep hair-conditioned**

—The Nawa Co.

24. **Keep it under your hat**

—(*shampoo, hair cream*) Lan-O-Tone Products.

25. **Keep your bob at its best**

—(*bobby pins*) Marcus-Lesoine Inc.

26. **Lets your hair shine like the stars**

—(*Drene shampoo*).

27. **Makes your husband feel younger, too . . . just to look at you!**

—(*Loving Care*) Clairol Inc.

28. **Never let your hair down**

—(*Scoldy Lox bobby pin*) Scolding Locks Corp.

29. **One shampoo convinces you**

—(*Dr. Chas. E. Shiffer shampoo*).

30. **Only your hairdresser knows for sure**

—(*Clairol hair color*) Clairol Inc.

31. **Precious little aids to beauty**

—Sta-Rite Hair Pin Co.

32. **Professional cosmetics for lovelier hair color**

—Roux Labs Inc.

33. **Reveals all your hair's natural beauty**

—(*Alberto VO5 hairspray*) Alberto-Culver Co.

34. **Reveals the hidden beauty of your hair**

—(*Halo shampoo*) Colgate-Palmolive Co.

35. **Sparkling hair that thrills men**

—(*Lustre-Cream shampoo*) Colgate-Palmolive Co.

36. **The colorfast shampoo**

—Clairol Inc.

37. **The cream shampoo for true hair loveliness**

—(*Lustre-Cream shampoo*) Colgate-Palmolive Co.

54. HAIR CARE *cont.*

38. **The deliciously perfumed hair lacquer**
   —(*Nestle Hairlac*) Nestle-LeMur Co.

39. **The hair net that sits true**
   —Sitroux Importing Co.

40. **The master hair coloring**
   —Rap-I-Dol Mfg. Co.

41. **There's no telling who uses it**
   —(*Grecian Formula 16*) Combe Inc.

42. **Tints gray hair any shade**
   —Kenton Pharmacal Co.

43. **To grow healthy hair, keep your scalp clean**
   —(*Jeris hair tonic*) Ar. Winarick Inc.

44. **Used by more men today than any other hair tonic**
   —(*Vaseline*) Chesebrough-Pond's Inc.

45. **Venida rules the waves**
   —(*hair net*) Roser Co.

46. **Wakes up your hair**
   —(*Admiration soapless shampoo*).

HANDBAGS . . . See **123.** WARDROBE ACCESSORIES

HANDKERCHIEFS . . . See **123.** WARDROBE ACCESSORIES

55. HARDWARE
See also **18.** BUILDING SUPPLIES, **117.** TOOLS

1. **America's largest selling residential locksets**
   —Kwikset Div. Emhart Corp.

2. **Are you annoyed by a drip?**
   —Peerless Plumbers Corp.

3. **Ask for K-V** . . . it's a *k*nown *v*alue!
   —Knape & Vogt Mfg. Co.

4. **Be seated by** . . . **Bemis**
   —(*plumbing fixtures*) Bemis Mfg. Co.

5. **Built like a bank vault door**
   —(*laminated padlocks*) Master Lock Co.

6. **Built to wear without repair**
   —(*plumbing fixtures*) H. Mueller Mfg. Co.

7. **Cammillus has the edge**
   —(*cutlery*) Cammillus Cutlery Co.

8. **Choice of three generations**
   —Brown & Sharpe Mfg. Co.

9. **Crane beauty in the open; Crane quality in all hidden fittings**
   —(*plumbing fixtures*) Crane Co.

55. HARDWARE *cont.*

10. ... Creating better ways to hold things together
—National Screw and Mfg. Co.

11. Easily distinguished by the yellow back
—(*faucet washer*) Foss Mfg. Co.

12. Everything hinges on Hager
—Hager Hinge Co.

13. Famous for their razor-sharp edges
—(*cutlery*) Remington Arms Co.

14. Faucets without a fault
—H. Mueller Mfg. Co.

15. First family in drapery hardware since 1903
—Newell Mfg. Co.

16. For every piping system
—Crane Co.

17. Genie keeps you in the driver's seat!
—(*garage-door openers*) Alliance Mfg. Co. Inc.

18. Hardware is the jewelry of the home
—McKinney Mfg. Co.

19. Helps you do things right
—(*Stanley hardware*) The Stanley Works.

20. If it's Speakman, it's quality
—(*fixtures*) Speakman Co.

21. Locks recommended by the world's leading lock experts
—(*locks*) Yale & Towne.

22. Mac-It endurance, your best insurance
—(*screws*) Strong, Carlisle & Hammond Co.

23. Making strong the things that make America strong
—Russell, Bursdall & Ward Bolt & Nut Co.

24. Manufacturers of quality drapery hardware since 1903
—Silent Gliss Inc.

25. Master crafted
—Eljer Plumbingware Div., Wallace-Murray Corp.

26. More doors fold on Fold-Aside than any other kind!
—Acme Appliance Mfg. Co.

27. No sash hardware installs faster than Grand Rapids Hardware
—Grand Rapids Hardware.

28. Serving the nation's health and comfort
—(*plumbing fixtures*) American Standard.

55. HARDWARE *cont.*

29. Since 1904 fine plumbing fixtures
—Eljer Plumbingware Div., Wallace-Murray Corp.

30. Stop that leak in the toilet tank
—Ross Mfg. Co.

31. The best seat in the house
—(*plumbing fixtures*) C. F. Church Div., American Standard Inc.

32. The easiest line to sell
—(*cutlery*) J. Wiss & Sons.

33. The first name in seats—the last name in quality
—(*plumbing fixtures*) Beneke Corp.

34. The safe way out
—Von Duprin Div., Vonnegut Hardware Co. Inc.

35. The shovel with a backbone
—Union Fork & Hoe.

36. The silent drapery track
—Silent Gliss Inc.

37. The Tiffany of the bolt and nut business
—R. I. Tool Co.

38. "Unlocking new concepts in architectural hardware since 1839"
—(*keys*) Russwin-Emhart Corp.

39. We took the splash out of the kitchen
—(*Union brass faucet*) Union Brass & Metal Manufacturing.

40. We want to help you do things right
—(*Stanley hardware*) The Stanley Works.

41. Where quality is produced in quantity
—Sterling Faucet Co.

42. World's leading padlock manufacturers
—(*locks*) Master Lock Co.

43. World's strongest padlocks
—(*locks*) Master Lock Co.

44. Yale marked is Yale made
—(*locks*) Yale & Towne.

HEALTH AND BEAUTY AIDS ... See 32. COSMETICS, 116. TOILETRIES

56. HEALTH AND FITNESS
See also 35. DRUGS AND REMEDIES, 98. RECREATIONAL EQUIPMENT, 108. SPORTING GOODS

1. A natural energy, food and body builder
—Canada Health Foods Ltd.

56. HEALTH AND FITNESS *cont.*

2. **Body by Soloflex**
   　　　—(*Soloflex home fitness system*).

3. **Consult your doctor about your weight problems**
   　　　—(*Sego*) Milk Products Div., Pet Inc.

4. **Consult your physician on matters of weight control**
   　　　—(*Metrecal*) Mead Johnson and Co.

5. **Keep your health in tune**
   　　　—(*Harmony vitamins*) A. S. Boyle Co.

6. **Look for the label with the Big Red "1"**
   　　　—(*One-a-Day vitamins*) Miles Laboratories Inc.

7. **More precious than gold for good health**
   　　　—(*Z-Bec Vitamins*) Robins Co. Inc.

8. **No appetite control capsule works harder to help you lose weight**
   　　　—(*Dexatrim weight loss capsules*) Thompson Medical Co. Inc.

9. **The best friend your willpower ever had**
   　　　—(*Slim-Mint Gum*) Thompson Medical Co. Inc.

10. **The modern aid to appetite control**
    　　　—(*Slim-Mint Gum*) Thompson Medical Co. Inc.

11. **The sugar free taste of sugar**
    　　　—(*Nutrasweet*) G. D. Searle & Co.

12. **Vitamins you can trust**
    　　　—(*Benefax*).

13. **World's leading direct-by-mail vitamin and drug company**
    　　　—Hudson National Inc.

57. HEARING AIDS

1. **Better hearing longer**
   　　　—(*Mini-Max hearing-aid devices*).

2. **Hear more, carry less**
   　　　—(*Otarion singlepack hearing aid*).

3. **There IS a difference in hearing aids**
   　　　—Western Electric.

58. HEATING AND AIR CONDITIONING
　　See also **37. ELECTRICAL PRODUCTS AND SERVICES,**
　　　60. HOME APPLIANCES AND EQUIPMENT

1. **Always save money in the end**
   　　　—Keith Furnace Co.

2. **An above-the-floor furnace**
   　　　—(*parlor furnace*) Allen Mfg. Co.

58.   HEATING AND AIR CONDITIONING *cont.*

3.   **A single match is your year's kindling**
                                        —Bryant Heater Co.

4.   **Beauty and warmth**
                                        —National Radiator Co.

5.   **Brings a touch of the tropics**
                —(*Flamingo gas heaters*) Jackes-Evans Mfg. Co.

6.   **Built like a watch**
                        —(*oil burners*) S. T. Johnson Co.

7.   **Chases chills from cold corners**
                                        —Perfection Stove Co.

8.   **Come home to comfort**
                                        —Bryant Heater Co.

9.   **Comfortable heat when you want it, where you want it, at a price you can afford**
                                        —Oilray Safety Heater Inc.

10.   **Cozy comfort for chilly days**
                                        —American Gas Machine Co.

11.   **Cradled silence**
                —(*Doe Oil Burner*) Oil-Elec-Tric Engineering Corp.

12.   **Don't be satisfied with less than Lennox**
                                        —Lennox Industries Inc.

13.   **Easiest and cheapest way to heat your home**
                                        —Electrol Inc.

14.   **First, from the very first**
                                        —Ray Oil Burner Co.

15.   **For *any* air conditioning**
                                        —Trane Co.

16.   **For comfort and pleasure all through the house**
                        —(*heaters*) Arvin Industries Inc.

17.   **Furnace freedom**
                                        —Penn Electric Switch Co.

18.   **Furnace heat for every home**
                                        —Monitor Stove Co.

19.   **Guardian of the nation's health**
                        —(*water heater*) A. O. Smith Corp.

20.   **Healthful warmth**
                        —(*steel furnace*) Langenburg Mfg. Co.

21.   **Heat alone is not comfort**
                                        —Holland Furnace Co.

22.   **Heat, how and when you want it**
                                        —Home Appliance Corp.

58. HEATING AND AIR CONDITIONING *cont.*

23. **Heat like the rays of the sun**
—American Gas Machine Co.

24. **Heat plus beauty**
—(*Florence heaters*) Central Oil & Gas Stove Co.

25. **Heats every room, upstairs and down**
—Estate Stove Co.

26. **Hot water all over the house**
—(*gas water heaters*) Ruud Mfg. Co.

27. **Hot water at the turn of a faucet**
—Humphrey Co.

28. **Indoor weather as you want it, with a weatherator**
—(*Premier warm air heater*).

29. **It's nature's freshness – indoors**
—Lennox Industries Inc.

30. **It takes more than a flame and a casting to make a good fast-fired circulation heater**
—The Moore Corp.

31. **Kalamazoo, direct to you**
—Kalamazoo Stove Co.

32. **Keep cold away with Magnavox**
—(*heaters*) Magnavox Co.

33. **Keeps step with the weather**
—(*oil burners*) Northern Machinery Co.

34. **Keeps you in hot water**
—Humphrey Co.

35. **Leaders go to Carnes for the newest in air distribution equipment**
—Carnes Corp.

36. **Lets your pup be your furnace man**
—Bryant Heater Co.

37. **Let the furnace man go . . . forever**
—May Oil Burner Corp.

38. **Makes its own gas, use it anywhere**
—(*radiant heater*) Coleman Lamp Co.

39. **Make warm friends**
—Holland Furnace Co.

40. **Making houses into homes**
—(*stokers, heaters*) Rheem Mfg. Co.

41. **Modern heat with oldtime fireside cheer**
—(*parlor furnace*) Allen Mfg. Co.

42. **More heat, less care**
—(*Florence heaters*) Central Oil & Gas Stove Co.

58. HEATING AND AIR CONDITIONING *cont.*

43. **More people put their confidence in Carrier air conditioning than in any other make**
—Carrier Corp.

44. **Most heat per dollar**
—(*oil burners*) Gilbert & Barker Mfg. Co.

45. **Nothing to shovel, nothing to explode**
—Motorstoker Corp.

46. **Performance speaks louder than price tags**
—Ruud Heater Co.

47. **Pioneers in smokeless combustion**
—Utica Heater Co.

48. **Round the calendar comfort**
—Lennox Industries Inc.

49. **See what air-conditioning is doing now ... See Gardner-Denver**
—Gardner-Denver Co.

50. **Silent as the rays of the sun**
—Silent Glow Oil Burner Corp.

51. **Since 1928—industry leadership in heating and air conditioning**
—Fraser and Johnston Co.

52. **The hotter the water, the whiter the wash**
—(*gas water heaters*) Ruud Mfg. Co.

53. **The noiseless oil burner**
—Silent Automatic Corp.

54. **The one you've heard so much about**
—Utica Heater Co.

55. **The quality line since eighty-nine**
—(*gas water heaters*) Ruud Mfg. Co.

56. **The quality name in air conditioning and refrigeration**
—York Corp.

57. **World's largest manufacturer of household electric heating appliances**
—Edison-Splitdorf Corp.

58. **World's largest selling air conditioners**
—Fedders Corp.

59. HEATING AND COOKING FUELS
See also **88. PETROLEUM PRODUCTS**

1. **A bear for heat**
—Fraker Coal Co.

**59.	HEATING AND COOKING FUELS** *cont.*

2.	**Always 2000 pounds to the ton**
—Apex Coal Corp.

3.	**America's fastest growing fuel**
—Thermogas Inc.

4.	**Chief of West Virginia high volatile coals**
—Red Jacket Coal Sales Co.

5.	**Do it tomorrow's way ... with gas**
—American Gas Association.

6.	**For heating and cooling ... gas is good business**
—American Gas Association.

7.	**Gas makes the big difference**
—American Gas Association.

8.	**Gas, the comfort fuel**
—Philadelphia Gas Works Co.

9.	**Hard soft coal**
—Lumaghi Coal Co.

10.	**If it's done with heat, you can do it better with gas**
—American Gas Association.

11.	**It's always coal weather**
—Stearns Coal & Lumber Co.

12.	**Keep the home fire burning**
—(*coal*) American Ice Co.

13.	**Laugh at winter**
—Kopper Gas & Coke Co.

14.	**Live modern for *less* with gas**
—American Gas Association.

15.	**No long waits, no short weights**
—North Memphis Coal Co.

16.	**Of America's great sources of energy, only National serves you in so many ways**
—National LP-Gas Market Development Council.

17.	**Reduce the cost but not the heat**
—Victor-American Fuel Co.

18.	**Solution of the power problem**
—(*white coal*) Wellman-Seaver-Morgan Co.

19.	**Stays dustless until the last shovelful**
—Giese Bros. Coal Co.

20.	**The anthracite that serves you right**
—Deering Coal & Wood Co.

21.	**The clean, convenient fuel**
—Sterno Corp.

59. HEATING AND COOKING FUELS *cont.*

22. **The fuel without a fault**
—(*coke*) Semet-Solvay Co.

23. **The new smokeless coal from Old Virginia**
—Red Jacket Coal Sales Co.

24. **To heat right, burn our anthracite**
—Anthracite Mining Association.

25. **You can do it better with gas**
—American Gas Association.

HERBS . . . See **29.** CONDIMENTS AND SPICES

60. HOME APPLIANCES AND EQUIPMENT
See also **58.** HEATING AND AIR CONDITIONING,
68. KITCHEN PRODUCTS AND UTENSILS

1. **A bright new world of electric housewares**
—(*Norelco*) North American Philips Corp.

2. **A choice of over a million women**
—(*stoves*) The Moore Corp.

3. **A cup for two or two for you**
—(*percolator*) Metal Ware Corp.

4. **A good reputation has to be earned**
—(*Blu-Cold refrigerators*) Lehigh Mfg. Co.

5. **A life preserver for foods**
—Alaska Refrigerator Co.

6. **All that the name implies**
—(*vacuum cleaners*) General Electric Co.

7. **America's leading washing machine**
—(*A. B. C. Super Electric*).

8. **A million in service ten years or longer**
—(*refrigerators*) General Electric Co.

9. **A roller rolls and there's ice**
—(*refrigerators*) Norge Co.

10. **As simple as touching the space-bar of a
typewriter, quick as the action of a piano key**
—(*Savage ironer*) Savage Arms Corp.

11. **Backed by a century-old tradition of fine
craftsmanship**
—Amana Refrigeration Inc.

12. **Backed by a century-old tradition of fine
craftsmanship**
—Amana Refrigeration Inc.

13. **Banishes ironing drudgery**
—Proctor Electric Co.

60. HOME APPLIANCES AND EQUIPMENT *cont.*

14. **Battery with a kick**
    —(*Prest-O-Lite*) The Prestolite Co.

15. **Better always better**
    —(*refrigerators*) Kelvinator Co.

16. **Better because it's gas ... best because it's Caloric**
    —Caloric Corp.

17. **Better products for a better world**
    —(*refrigerators*) Norge Co.

18. **Brings happiness to homework**
    —(*washer*) Bluebird Appliance Co.

19. **Build-in satisfaction ... build-in Frigidaire**
    —(*Frigidaire*) General Motors Corp.

20. **Built for connoisseurs of refrigeration**
    —Kelvinator Co.

21. **Built like the finest automobile**
    —(*Whirlpool washer*) 1900 Washer Co.

22. **Built right for over forty years**
    —(*ice boxes*) Belding-Hall Electric Corp.

23. **Built with integrity, backed by service**
    —Sunbeam Corp.

24. **Buy your last refrigerator first**
    —Jewell Refrigerator Co.

25. **Cataraction, the only real figure-8 movement**
    —(*Cataract washer*).

26. **Change work to play three times a day**
    —Standard Electric Stove Co.

27. **Cleans without beating and pounding**
    —(*vacuum cleaners*) United Electric Co.

28. **Cold and silent as a winter night**
    —(*Sparton refrigerator*).

29. **Come on, breeze, let's blow**
    —(*electric fans*) Wagner Electric Corp.

30. **Cooking is just a SNAP in an Estate electric range**
    —Estate Stove Co.

31. **Cook into the future with electronics from Farberware**
    —(*Farberware Ultra Chef*) Farberware.

32. **Cooks with the gas turned off**
    —(*stoves*) Chambers Corp.

33. **Defrosts itself, saves shut-downs**
    —(*refrigerators*) Belding-Hall Electric Corp.

60. **HOME APPLIANCES AND EQUIPMENT** *cont.*

34. **Designed by women for women**
—(*Hotpoint ranges*) General Electric Co.

35. **Electrical refrigeration, a way to better living**
—Society for Electrical Development.

36. **Empties with a thumb pressure**
—Bissell Carpet Sweeper Co.

37. **Even the collars and cuffs are clean**
—(*Coffield washer*).

38. **Everybody appreciates the finest**
—(*Radi-Oven*) Knapp-Monarch Co.

39. **Fastest in the world**
—(*washer*) Savage Arms Corp.

40. **First with the features women want most**
—(*Hotpoint*) General Electric Co.

41. **For better living**
—(*refrigerators*) General Electric Co.

42. **Gets the dirt, not the carpet**
—(*Eureka vacuum cleaner*) The Eureka Co.

43. **Get the best things first, get Kelvinator**
—(*refrigerators*) Kelvinator Co.

44. **GE . . . We bring good things to life**
—General Electric Co.

45. **Gifts long remembered**
—(*Hotpoint appliances*) Edison Mfg. Co.

46. **Give her a Hoover and you give her the best**
—(*Hoover vacuum cleaner*) The Hoover Co.

47. **Glenwood Ranges make cooking easier**
—Glenwood Range Co.

48. **Ice cubes instantly, tray to glass**
—(*refrigerators*) Inland Mfg. Co.

49. **If it doesn't sell itself, don't keep it**
—(*Maytag washer*) Maytag Co.

50. **If it is a Garland, that is all you need to know about a stove or range**
—Michigan Stove Co.

51. **If you can afford a washer, you can afford a Bendix**
—(*Bendix washer*).

52. **Irons while it steams**
—Elder Co. Inc.

53. **Is your refrigerator a Success?**
—Success Mfg. Co.

60. HOME APPLIANCES AND EQUIPMENT *cont.*

54. It beats, as it sweeps, as it cleans
—(*Hoover vacuum cleaner*) The Hoover Co.

55. It is a mark of intelligent housekeeping to possess a Simplex Ironer
—(*Simplex ironer*).

56. It's fun to own a gift by Rival
—Rival Mfg. Co.

57. It's the woman-wise range
—Estate Stove Co.

58. Jet action washers
—(*Frigidaire*) General Motors Corp.

59. Keeps things to eat good to eat
—Sunshine Ice Co.

60. Kelvination, cold that keeps
—(*refrigerators*) Kelvinator Co.

61. Kitchenaid. For the way its made.
—(*Kitchenaid appliances*) Hobart Manufacturing Co.

62. Made a little better than seems necessary
—Rhinelander Refrigerator Co.

63. Make it yourself on a Singer
—(*Singer sewing machine*) Singer Co.

64. Making your world a little easier
—(*Whirlpool appliances*) Whirlpool Corp.

65. Matchless cooking
—(*Norge ranges*) Norge Co.

66. Matchless quality ... superior service ... enduring excellence
—Electrolux Corp.

67. Mighty monarch of the Arctic
—(*refrigerators*) Grisby-Grunow.

68. Millions of women have their hearts set on a new Maytag
—(*washer*) Maytag Co.

69. More and better things for more people
—(*refrigerators*) General Motors Corp.

70. New ideas for happier homemaking
—The West Bend Co.

71. Nobody knows more about microwave cooking than Litton
—(*Litton Microwave ovens*) Litton Systems Inc.

72. No Jewett has ever worn out
—Jewett Refrigerator Co.

60. HOME APPLIANCES AND EQUIPMENT *cont.*

73. **No watching, no turning, no burning**
 —(*toaster*) Waters-Genter Co.

74. **Originator and perfecter of the garbage disposer**
 —In-Sink-Erator Mfg. Co.

75. **Originator of insulated ranges**
 —Chambers Corp.

76. **Peak of quality for more than 30 years**
 —(*Apex vacuum cleaner*).

77. **Put your sweeping reliance on a Bissell appliance**
 —Bissell Carpet Sweeper Co.

78. **Quality you can trust. Value you can recognize**
 —Iona Mfg. Co.

79. **Restful ironing**
 —(*Savage ironer*) Savage Arms Corp.

80. **Rigid as an oak**
 —(*Sturdee folding ironing table*) Tucker & Dorsey Mfg.
 Co.

81. **Rinses as it whirls, dries as it whirls, needs no wringer**
 —(*Geo. Dunham washer*).

82. **'Round and 'round and over and over**
 —(*Whirlpool washer*) 1900 Washer Co.

83. **Rubbermaid means better made**
 —Rubbermaid Inc.

84. **Sanitary, safe, durable, economical**
 —(*ashcans, garbage cans*) Witt Cornice Co.

85. **Sanitize your dishes sparkling clean!**
 —(*Frigidaire*) General Motors Corp.

86. **Saves food, chills water**
 —Illinois Refrigerator Co.

87. **Servants for the home**
 —(*Hotpoint appliances*) General Electric Co.

88. **Set it and forget it**
 —(*refrigerators*) Kelvinator Co.

89. **Seven leagues ahead**
 —(*ranges*) Thermador Electrical Mfg. Div., Norris
 Industries Inc.

90. **Since 1876, the servant of the well-dressed woman**
 —(*White sewing machine*) White Consolidated Industries
 Inc.

91. **So beautifully practical**
 —(*ranges*) Jenn-Air Corp.

60.   HOME APPLIANCES AND EQUIPMENT *cont.*

92. **Stay-satisfactory range**
—Malleable Iron Range Co.

93. **Takes the burns out of broiling**
—(*Moore's Hi-Lo broiler*) The Moore Corp.

94. **The aristocrat of electric ranges**
—Benjamin Electric Mfg. Co.

95. **The aristocrat of refrigerators**
—Herrick Refrigerator Co.

96. **The Bendix does the wash without you**
—(*Bendix washer*).

97. **The best dealer in town sells Norge**
—(*refrigerators*) Norge Co.

98. **The complete line of electric cooking apparatus**
—(*Toastmaster*) McGraw-Edison Co.

99. **The crisp dry cold of a frosty night**
—Iroquois Electric Refrigeration Co.

100. **The dependability people**
—Maytag Co.

101. **The *dependable* automatics**
—Maytag Co.

102. **The dry constant cold of the mountain top**
—General Refrigeration Co.

103. **The Eden cleans by gentle means**
—(*washer*) Brokaw-Eden Mfg. Co.

104. **The electric range with the safety top**
—(*Presteline*).

105. **The gas range with the life-time burner guarantee**
—Magic Chef Inc.

106. **The gas range you want**
—Caloric Corp.

107. **The house of magic**
—General Electric Co.

108. **The iron with the cool blue handle**
—Coleman Lamp Co.

109. **The modern bed of coals**
—(*electric range*) Tampa Electric Co.

110. **The name known in millions of American homes**
—Nutone Inc.

111. **The name that means everything in electricity**
—Westinghouse.

112. **The oldest name in electric refrigeration**
—Kelvinator Co.

60. **HOME APPLIANCES AND EQUIPMENT** *cont.*

113. **The only iron that banishes ironing fatigue forever**
—Proctor Electric Co.

114. **The original drawer type freezer**
—Portable Elevator Mfg. Co.

115. **The ranges that bake with fresh air**
—Estate Stove Co.

116. **The range with the Centra-cook top**
—Roberts & Mander.

117. **The record is trouble-free**
—(*refrigerators*) Kelvinator Co.

118. **There is no substitute for experience**
—(*refrigerators*) Kelvinator Co.

119. **There's a Hotpoint electric range for every purse and purpose**
—Edison-Splitdorf Corp.

120. **The seam that sells the garment**
—Willcox & Gibbs Sewing Machine Co.

121. **The silent servant**
—National Refrigerating Co.

122. **The simplest electric refrigerator**
—Electro-Kold Corp.

123. **The simplified electric refrigerator**
—(*ElectrICE*) American ElectrICE Corp.

124. **The store that never closes**
—(*Coldspot freezers*) Sears, Roebuck & Co.

125. **The toaster you've always wanted**
—Waters-Genter Co.

126. **The *very* best in floor care products**
—Eureka Williams Co.

127. **The *very* good washer**
—(*RCA Whirlpool*) Whirlpool Corp.

128. **The washer with the backbone**
—Fletcher Works Inc.

129. **The world's fastest cook stove**
—American Gas Machine Co.

130. **Toast to your taste, every time**
—General Electric Co.

131. **To lighten the burden of womankind**
—(*Crystal washer*).

132. **Useful products for family living**
—Hamilton Cosco Inc.

60. HOME APPLIANCES AND EQUIPMENT *cont.*

133. **Washer of tomorrow is the Barton of today**
—Barton Corp.

134. **Washes and dries without a wringer**
—Laundryette Mfg. Co.

135. **We're cooking at the table now**
—(*table appliances*) Chase Brass & Copper.

136. **When it's a Shamrock, you've got the best**
—(*hamper*) Meese Inc.

137. **When it's time to change, get a Glenwood Range**
—Glenwood Range Co.

138. **When the mercury soars, keep happy**
—(*Arctic electric fan*).

139. **Where the nicest people meet the nicest things**
—Stanley Home Products Inc.

140. **Working for today, planning for tomorrow**
—(*refrigerators*) Norge Co.

141. **World's oldest and largest manufacturer of electric blankets**
—Northern Electric Co.

142. **Worthy of the name**
—Gray & Dudley Co.

143. **Year in, year out, the perfect servant**
—(*refrigerators*) Copeland Products.

144. **Years from now you'll be glad it's Norge**
—(*Norge*) Borg-Warner Corp.

145. **You cook better automatically with a Tappan**
—Tappan Co.

146. **You live better automatically with Tappan**
—Tappan Co.

147. **You'll always be glad you bought a General Electric**
—(*refrigerators*) General Electric Co.

148. **You never have to lift or tilt it**
—(*electric iron*) Proctor Electric Co.

149. **You're money ahead with a Maytag**
—(*washer*) Maytag Co.

150. **You're twice as sure with Frigidaire**
—(*Frigidaire refrigerators*) General Motors Corp.

151. **Yours for leisure**
—(*Eureka vacuum cleaner*) The Eureka Co.

HOME MAINTENANCE . . . See 24. CLEANING AND LAUNDRY PRODUCTS, 86. PEST CONTROL

61.   HOSIERY

> See also **26. CLOTHING, MISCELLANEOUS, 48. FOOTWEAR,
> 121. UNDERWEAR, 123. WARDROBE ACCESSORIES**

1. **All that its name implies**
   —True Shape Hosiery Co.

2. **A mile of silk, inspected inch by inch**
   —Berkshire Knitting Mills.

3. **As you like it**
   —J. R. Baston Co. Inc.

4. **Background of beauty**
   —Virginia Maid Hosiery Mills Inc.

5. **Because you love nice things**
   —(*silk stockings*) Van Raalte Co. Inc.

6. **Be sporty in '40**
   —C. H. Roth Co.

7. **Finer seamless stockings**
   —Oleg Cassini Inc.

8. **For every walk in life**
   —(*socks*) Monarch Knitting Co., Ltd.

9. **For good and FITTING reasons**
   —(*Kayser gloves and hosiery*) Kayser-Roth Glove Co. Inc.

10. **For sheer loveliness wear Chatelaine Silk Hosiery**
    —St. Johns Silk Co.

11. **For the loveliest legs in the world**
    —Berkshire Knitting Mills.

12. **Free from "rings" and "shadows"**
    —(*No-Sha-Do hosiery*).

13. **Hanes knows how to please him**
    —(*hosiery*) Hanes Corp.

14. **Hosiery fashion on five continents**
    —Berkshire International Corp.

15. **In the California manner**
    —Gude's Inc.

16. **It lox the sox**
    —Pittsburgh Garter Co.

17. **Knit to fit with the comfort foot**
    —Burson Knitting Co.

18. **Legsize stockings**
    —(*Belle-Sharmeer*) Wayne Gossard Corp.

19. **Leg-size stockings for leg-wise women**
    —(*Belle-Sharmeer hosiery*).

61. HOSIERY *cont.*

20. **Longer wear in every pair**
—Blue Moon Silk Hosiery Co.

21. **Long mileage Hosiery**
—Phoenix Hosiery Co.

22. **Made the strongest where the wear is hardest**
—Durham Hosiery Mills Inc.

23. **No metal can touch you**
—(*Paris garters*) A. G. Stein Co.

24. **Nothing beats a great pair of L'eggs!**
—(*L'eggs pantyhose*) L'eggs Products Inc.

25. **Rollins answers the gift question**
—Rollins Hosiery Mills.

26. **Sheath the leg in loveliness**
—(*Cameron nylons*).

27. **Sheer, sheer, Berkshire**
—Berkshire Knitting Mills.

28. **Sings its own praise**
—Rosenberg & Brand.

29. **Take to water like a duck**
—(*Adler socks*) Burlington Industries Inc.

30. **That's all you need to know about stockings**
—(*Mojud*) Kayser-Roth Hosiery Co. Inc.

31. **The eye line of smartness**
—St. Johns Silk Co.

32. **The greatest name in socks**
—Interwoven Stocking Co.

33. **The leg of nations, before the court of the world**
—(*men's garters*) Sidley Co.

34. **The new air-rolled garter**
—Novelty Rubber Sales Co.

35. **The one that won't bind**
—(*E. Z. garters*) Thos. P. Taylor Co.

36. **There's longer wear in every pair**
—Largman Gray Co.

37. **The smartest thing on two feet**
—(*Esquire socks*) Kayser-Roth Hosiery Co. Inc.

38. **The sock America wears to work**
—Nelson Knitting Co.

39. **The support of a nation**
—(*Paris garters*) A. G. Stein Co.

40. **The utmost in luxury at moderate prices**
—Real Silk Hosiery Mills.

61. HOSIERY *cont.*

41. **The vital 1/4 of your costume**
—(*Runstop hosiery*) Rollins Hosiery Mills.

42. **They do things for your legs**
—Rollins Hosiery Mills.

43. **They fit**
—(*Round-the-Clock*) National Mills Div., U. S. Industries.

44. **They're wear-conditioned**
—Monmouth Hosiery Mills.

45. **To uphold your sox, trousers and dignity**
—(*Barrthea garters and suspenders*).

46. **Try them on for sighs**
—(*Strutwear nylons*) Kayser-Roth Hosiery Co. Inc.

47. **Warm toes in Fox River Hose**
—(*Fox River Hose*).

48. **Wash them any way you like, we guarantee the size**
—(*Adler socks*) Burlington Industries Inc.

49. **Wear Kayser, you owe it to your friends**
—(*gloves and hosiery*) Kayser-Roth Corp.

50. **Will not kink**
—(*Milo hose*) Boston Woven Hose Co.

51. **You just know she wears them**
—McCallum Hosiery Co.

52. **You're asking for a good sock**
—(*Westminster socks*).

53. **You're sure of yourself in Phoenix**
—(*Phoenix Vita Bloom hosiery*) Kayser-Roth Hosiery Co.
Inc.

54. **Your legs will thank you**
—(*Brighton Wide-Web garters*) Pioneer Suspender Co.

62. HOTELS AND MOTELS
See also **119.** TRAVEL

1. **Aglow with friendliness**
—Hotel Fort Shelby, Detroit.

2. **A home away from home**
—Park Central Hotel, New York.

3. **A homey hotel for home folks**
—The Westminster, New York.

4. **All that is best**
—Biltmore Hotel.

5. **America's business address**
—Hilton Hotels Corp.

62. HOTELS AND MOTELS *cont.*

6. **America's smartest resort hotel**
—Ritz-Carlton, Atlantic City, N. J.

7. **An hotel of distinction**
—Mayfair House, New York.

8. **At the crossroads of the world**
—Hotel Astor, New York.

9. **Boston's most famous hotel**
—Parker House.

10. **Coast to coast, we give the most**
—Milner Hotels.

11. **Convenient to everywhere**
—Rittenhouse Hotel, Philadelphia.

12. **Downtown St. Louis at your doorstep**
—Hotels Mayfair and Lennox, St. Louis.

13. **First choice in food, lodging and services nationwide!**
—Holiday Inns of America Inc.

14. **Go international . . . with all the comforts of Hilton**
—Hilton Hotels Corp.

15. **Has the quiet refinement of an exclusive club**
—Mayfair House, New York.

16. **Holiday Inn is Number One in people pleasin'**
—Holiday Inns of America Inc.

17. **House of hospitality**
—Hotel Lincoln, New York.

18. **In keeping with a fine old tradition**
—The Coronado Hotel, St. Louis.

19. **In San Francisco it's the Palace**
—Palace Hotel.

20. **Largest in the northwest**
—Curtis Hotel, Minneapolis.

21. **Live in the atmosphere of an exclusive club**
—Hotels Mayfair and Lennox, St. Louis.

22. **"Luxury for less"**
—Ramada Inns Inc.

23. **One of the world's great hotels**
—Bellevue Stratford, Philadelphia.

24. **Plump on the Boardwalk**
—Alamac Hotel, Atlantic City, N. J.

25. **Register socially**
—Hotel Delmonico, New York.

62. **HOTELS AND MOTELS** *cont.*

26. **"Sign of happy travel"**
—Downtowner Corp.

27. **South's supreme hotel**
—Atlanta Biltmore, Atlanta, Ga.

28. **The big hotel that remembers the little things**
—New Yorker, New York.

29. **The desert resort by the sea**
—Playa de Cortes, Guaymas, Mexico.

30. **"The fine old innkeeping tradition in a modern setting"**
—Holiday Inns of America Inc.

31. **The friendly world of Hilton**
—Hilton Hotels Corp.

32. **The nation's innkeeper**
—Holiday Inns of America Inc.

33. **The Plaza pleases**
—Plaza Hotel, New York.

34. **They all speak well of it**
—DeWitt Clinton Hotel, Albany, New York.

35. **This is living ... this is Marriott**
—Marriott Motor Hotels Inc.

36. **Where good cheer abides**
—Hotel Touraine, Buffalo, New York.

37. **Where quality is a tradition**
—Bismarck Hotel, Chicago.

38. **Where southern hospitality flowers**
—Atlanta Biltmore, Atlanta, Ga.

39. **Where the best costs less**
—Hotel New Yorker, New York.

40. **Where your "resort dollar" buys more**
—Stardust Hotel and Golf Club.

I

INSECTICIDES ... See **86.** PEST CONTROL

63. **INSTRUMENTS AND GAUGES**

1. **Always accurate**
—Guarantee Liquid Measure Co.

2. **Always on the level**
—The Liquidometer Corp.

63. INSTRUMENTS AND GAUGES *cont.*

3. **A time-honored name in scales**
   —Fairbanks-Morse.

4. **It is accurate and it stays accurate**
   —National Meter Co.

5. **It will tell your eyes before your eyes tell you**
   —(*sight meter*) Tampa Electric Co.

6. **Laboratory accuracy at a toolroom price**
   —(*Hoke gauges*) Pratt & Whitney.

7. **Longest lived micrometer that can be bought**
   —J. T. Slocomb Co.

8. **No springs, honest weight**
   —Toledo Scale Co.

9. **Taylor instruments mean accuracy first**
   —Taylor Instrument Co.

10. **Tell the truth**
    —(*scientific measuring instruments*) A. E. Moeller Co.

11. **There's a Tycos or Taylor Thermometer for every purpose**
    —Taylor Instrument Co.

12. **The right way to weigh right**
    —Stimpson Computing Scale Co.

13. **The weigh to profits**
    —Stimpson Computing Scale Co.

14. **To measure is to economize**
    —(*Brown pyrometers*) Brown Instrument Co.

15. **Watches your weight**
    —(*scale*) Jarcons Bros. Inc.

16. **Weigh the loads and save the roads**
    —Black & Decker Mfg. Co.

64. INSURANCE
   See also **43.** FINANCIAL INSTITUTIONS AND SERVICES,
   66. INVESTMENT

1. **Aetna, I'm glad I met ya**
   —Aetna Life & Casualty.

2. **Always worth par when misfortune strikes**
   —Fireman's Fund Insurance Co.

3. **A man who can't remember his last hailstorm is likely to get one he will never forget**
   —Rain & Hail Insurance Bureau.

4. **An emblem of security, a pledge of service**
   —Hanover Fire Insurance Co.

64. **INSURANCE** *cont.*

5. **An idea whose time has come!**
—Harlan Insurance Co.

6. **A policy for every purse and purpose**
—Home Life Insurance Co.

7. **As solid as the granite hills of Vermont**
—National Life Insurance Co. of Vermont.

8. **At the head of the nation**
—Equitable Life Insurance Co.

9. **"Because there *is* a difference"**
—The Northwestern Mutual Life Insurance Co.

10. **Be sure, insure in INA**
—Insurance Co. of North America.

11. **Burglars know no season**
—Standard Accident Insurance Co.

12. **Buy protection, not policies**
—"America Fore" Insurance & Indemnity Group.

13. **Call your Investors man—today!**
—Investors Diversified Services Inc.

14. **Cheaper insurance is easier to purchase but harder to collect**
—Standard Accident Insurance Co.

15. **Enduring as the mountains**
—Western Life Insurance Co.

16. **Everyone needs the Sun**
—Sun Insurance Co.

17. **Extra service without extra cost**
—W. B. Joyce & Co.

18. **Fire insurance is as old as the Sun**
—Sun Insurance Co.

19. **First in life, first in death**
—Detroit Life Insurance Co.

20. **For all kinds of insurance in a single plan, call your Travelers man**
—Travelers Insurance Co.

21. **For a sure tomorrow—insure enough today!**
—American Hardware Mutual Insurance Co.

22. **For doctor bills**
—Blue Shield.

23. **Get a piece of the Rock**
—Prudential Insurance Co.

24. **Get the best in the world**
—World Fire and Marine Insurance Co.

64. **INSURANCE** *cont.*

25. **"Good people to do business with"**
—Employers Mutual Liability Insurance Co. of Wisconsin.

26. **Guardian of American families for 80 years**
—Guardian Life Insurance Co.

27. **Guardian will enrich and safeguard your retirement years**
—Guardian Life Insurance Co.

28. **"Hot-Line" claim service**
—Imperial Auto Insurance.

29. **If it's insurable, we can insure it**
—J. A. Montgomery Inc.

30. **Industry-owned to conserve property and profits**
—Factory Mutual Insurance Co.

31. **"Inspection is our middle name"**
—Hartford Steam Boiler Inspection and Insurance Co.

32. **Insure today to save tomorrow**
—Rain & Hail Insurance Bureau.

33. **Insurors of energy systems**
—Hartford Steam Boiler Inspection and Insurance Co.

34. **Inventor and scientist make dreams come true; the insurance man keeps nightmares from happening**
—Fireman's Fund Insurance Co.

35. **It is better to have it and not need it than to need it and not have it**
—Columbia Casualty Co.

36. **It pays to know when to relax**
—Metropolitan Life Insurance Co.

37. **Keep a roof over your head**
—North British & Mercantile Insurance Co.

38. **Leader in business insurance**
—New York Life Insurance Co.

39. **Let us protect your world**
—The Hartford Insurance Group.

40. **Lifelong security through programmed protection**
—Monarch Life Insurance Co.

41. **Light that never fails**
—Metropolitan Life Insurance Co.

42. **Like a good neighbor, State Farm is there**
—State Farm Insurance Co.

43. **Live and die with Assurance**
—Maryland Assurance Corp.

64. **INSURANCE** *cont.*

44. **Look ahead with living insurance**
—Equitable Life Assurance Society of the United States.

45. **Looks out for you**
—Sentry Insurance Co.

46. **Make insurance understandable**
—Employers Mutual of Wausau.

47. **Make tomorrow pay, Standardize today**
—Standard Life Insurance Co.

48. **MONY men care for people**
—Mutual of New York.

49. **More than you expect or pay for**
—Auto Owners Insurance Co.

50. **Most protection when protection is most needed**
—Sun Life Insurance Co.

51. **Named for those it serves**
—Auto Owners Insurance Co.

52. **Nationwide is on your side**
—Nationwide Insurance Co.

53. **No man's debts should live after him**
—Morris Plan Insurance Society.

54. **Nothing else like it**
—Prudential Insurance Co.

55. **Our business is insuring people's dreams**
—Trans America Insurance Company.

56. **Our concern is people**
—Aetna Life & Casualty.

57. **Our savings are your profits**
—American Mutual Liability Insurance Co.

58. **Owned by the policyholders**
—Mutual Life Assurance of Canada.

59. **Policies "Good as Gold"**
—London Life Insurance Co.

60. **Procrastination is the highest cost of life insurance. It increases both your premium and your risk**
—The Union Central Life Insurance Co.

61. **Protecting the American home**
—National Life Insurance Co.

62. **Protecting the nation – through hometown agents**
—Great American Insurance Co.

63. **Protection for employer and employee**
—American Mutual Liability Insurance Co.

64. **INSURANCE** *cont.*

64. **Protection in a new light**
—Monumental Life Insurance Co.

65. **Protection in depth**
—Liberty Mutual Insurance Co.

66. **Protection with profit**
—Great West Life Assurance Co.

67. **Protect what you have**
—Insurance Co. of North America.

68. **Provident Mutual for stability, safety, security**
—Provident Mutual Life Insurance Co.

69. **P. S.—Personal Service**
—Aetna Life & Casualty.

70. **Restituimus—"We restore" . . . since 1854**
—Phoenix of Hartford Insurance Co.

71. **Safe and sound**
—Peoples Fire Insurance Co.

72. **Safety is always the first consideration, nothing else is so important**
—New York Life Insurance Co.

73. **Security is our business**
—United of Omaha.

74. **Security is the keynote today, and every day**
—Northern Insurance Co.

75. **"Serves you first"**
—Independent Insurance Agents.

76. **Serving you around the world . . . around the clock**
—The St. Paul Insurance Co.

77. **Six and a half billion dollars of protection for our policyholders**
—Great West Life Assurance Co.

78. **Solid as the continent**
—North American Life.

79. **The Aetna-izer, a man worth knowing**
—Aetna Life & Casualty.

80. **The Blue Chip company**
—Connecticut Mutual Life Insurance Co.

81. **The choice of businessmen lets you choose with confidence**
—Aetna Life & Casualty.

82. **The company with the partnership philosophy**
—American United Life Insurance Co.

64. **INSURANCE** *cont.*

83. **The finest protection available for your family, your property and your business**
—Fireman's Fund Insurance Co.

84. **The fourth necessity**
—Metropolitan Life Insurance Co.

85. **The future belongs to those who prepare for it**
—Prudential Insurance Co.

86. **The "good hands" people**
—Allstate Insurance Co.

87. **The good things of life**
—Bankers Life Insurance Co. of Nebraska.

88. **The greatest name in health insurance**
—Mutual of Omaha Insurance Co.

89. **The home of human security**
—Provident Life and Accident Insurance Co.

90. **The largest multiple life insurance organization in the world**
—Travelers Insurance Co.

91. **The man with the plan**
—Employers' Group Insurance.

92. **The name again ... Nationwide Life**
—Nationwide Insurance Co.

93. **The New York Agent in your community is a good man to know**
—New York Life Insurance Co.

94. **The policy back of the policy**
—Hardware Mutual Casualty Co.

95. **The power of the pyramid is working for you**
—Trans America Insurance Company.

96. **The Prudential has the strength of Gibraltar**
—Prudential Insurance Co.

97. **There's no obligation ... except to those you love**
—Metropolitan Life Insurance Co.

98. **The seal of certainty upon an insurance policy**
—Hartford Fire Insurance Co.

99. **The small business that got big serving small business**
—Sentry Insurance Co.

100. **The tower of strength in Dixie**
—Lamar Life Insurance Co.

101. **To better serve the Golden West**
—Unity Mutual.

64. INSURANCE *cont.*

102. **Today's need for tomorrow is life insurance**
—Western Life Insurance Co.

103. **"Value" is a *good* word for Benefit Trust Life.**
—Benefit Trust Life Insurance.

104. **We aim to humanize the science of insurance**
—Manufacturers Liability Insurance Co.

105. **We can help you here and now. Not just hereafter.**
—John Hancock Companies.

106. **We work to keep you safe**
—Liberty Mutual Insurance Co.

107. **Where people and ideas create security for millions**
—Connecticut General Life Insurance Co.

108. **Wise men seek wise counsel**
—Employers Liability Assurance Corp.

109. **With everything American, tomorrow is secure**
—American Insurance Co.

110. **You can bank on Bankers**
—Bankers Accident Insurance Co.

111. **You can count on Kemper care under the Kemper flag**
—Kemper Insurance Co.

112. **You can get all types of insurance under the Travelers umbrella**
—Travelers Insurance Co.

113. **You're in good hands with Allstate**
—Allstate Insurance Co.

114. **Your friend in the home, on the highway, where you work**
—Liberty Mutual Insurance Co.

115. **Your future is our business today**
—Great West Life Assurance Co.

116. **Your guardian for life**
—Guardian Life Insurance Co.

117. **Your Hartford agent does more than he really has to**
—The Hartford Insurance Group.

118. **Your helping hand when trouble comes**
—American Mutual Insurance.

119. **Your life plan deserves expert guidance**
—Penn Mutual Underwriter Insurance.

120. **Your peace of mind is worth the premium**
—National Surety Co.

65. INTERIOR DECORATION

See also **18.** BUILDING SUPPLIES, **46.** FLOOR COVERINGS,
50. FURNITURE, **82.** PAINT AND PAINTING SUPPLIES

1. **A heritage of quality, craftsmanship, service**
    —Virginia Mirror Co.

2. **America's foremost manufacturer of decorative accessories since 1890**
    —Syroco Div., Dart Industries Inc.

3. **A shade is only as good as its rollers**
    —Stewart Hartshorn Co.

4. **Creators of 1001 products for home decorating**
    —Conso Products Co., Consolidated Foods Corp.

5. **"Custom of course"**
    —Lew Smith Beads.

6. **Dare you move your pictures?**
    —(*Sunworthy wallpapers*) Reed Ltd.

7. **Designs that dreams are made of**
    —M/B Designs Inc.

8. **First with the finest in wallcoverings ... always!**
    —Timbertone Decorative Co. Inc.

9. **For connoisseurs by connoisseurs**
    —Mottahedeh and Sons.

10. **For the decorator touch**
    —(*Best Pleat Nip-tite*) Conso Products Co.,
    Consolidated Foods Corp.

11. **Oldest in permanent type wall coverings**
    —Frederic Blank and Co. Inc.

12. **Quality-made by Illinois Shade**
    —Illinois Shade Div., Slick Industrial Co.

13. **Styles for every room in the house**
    —(*Sanitas wall covering*) American Cyanamid Co.

14. **The great name in American ceramics**
    —Haeger Potteries Inc.

15. **The look of quality**
    —La Barge Mirrors Inc.

16. **The most beautiful curtains in America**
    —Robertson Factories Inc.

17. **The surprise of Formica products**
    —Formica Corp.

18. **The wipe-clean wall covering**
    —Columbus-Union Oil Cloth Co.

65. **INTERIOR DECORATION** *cont.*

19. **Tone the sunlight with window shades just as you tone the electric light with lamp shades**
—(*window shades*) Columbia Mills Inc.

20. **Tops everything for lasting beauty**
—(*Nevamar*) National Plastics Products Co.

21. **Wipe off the dust**
—(*Sanitas wall covering*) Standard Textile Products Co.

22. **World's largest manufacturer of mirrors**
—Carolina Mirror Corp.

66. **INVESTMENT**
See also **43.** FINANCIAL INSTITUTIONS AND SERVICES, **64.** INSURANCE

1. **A profit for every investor**
—Reed Service Inc.

2. **Bonds that grow in security**
—Baker, Frentress & Co.

3. **Complete brokerage service in the world's markets**
—Fenner, Beane, & Co.

4. **Depression spells opportunity for the real investor**
—Sloat & Scanlon.

5. **. . . Helping people and business help themselves**
—Commercial Credit Co.

6. **Help yourself as you help your country**
—United States Savings Bonds.

7. **Instant news service**
—Dow Jones and Co.

8. **Lots of satisfaction**
—Miami Realty Co.

9. **Merrill Lynch . . . A breed apart**
—Merrill Lynch Pierce Fenner and Smith.

10. **Merrill Lynch is bullish on America**
—Merrill Lynch Pierce Fenner and Smith.

11. **Minds over money**
—(*Shearson/American Express*) American Express Co.

12. **Over one billion dollars annually for industry**
—Walter E. Heller and Co.

13. **Own your share of American Business**
—New York Stock Exchange Members.

14. **Promoting high standards in the public interest**
—New York Stock Exchange.

15. **Safe as America**
—United States Savings Bonds.

66. **INVESTMENT** *cont.*

16. **Save the easy, automatic way; buy U. S. Bonds**
—United States Savings Bonds.

17. **Since 1808, a tradition in factoring and financing**
—William Iselin and Co. Inc.

18. **Smith Barney. They make money the old-fashioned way . . . they earn it.**
—Smith Barney.

19. **Specialists in financing**
—Associates Investment Co.

20. **Take stock in America**
—U.S. Savings Bonds.

21. **The growth fund**
—National Investors Corp.

22. **Trust us to make it work for you**
—(*Sears Financial Network*) Sears, Roebuck & Co.

23. **When E. F. Hutton talks, people listen**
—E. F. Hutton.

24. **Where your dollar works harder . . . grows bigger!**
—Insured Savings and Loan Associations.

25. **Working funds for industry**
—Walter E. Heller and Co.

26. **You look like you just heard from Dean Witter**
—Dean Witter Reynolds.

27. **Your investment success is our business**
—Francis I. duPont and Co.

J

JETS . . . See **3.** AEROSPACE, **4.** AIR TRAVEL AND CARGO

67. **JEWELRY AND SILVER**
See also **123.** WARDROBE ACCESSORIES

1. **A diamond is forever**
—DeBeers Consolidated Mines Ltd.

2. **America's leading silversmiths since 1831**
—Gorham Div., Textron Inc.

3. **Art in diamond rings**
—B. & E. J. Gross Co.

4. **Bejeweled by Gaylin**
—Gaylin Jewelry Co.

67. **JEWELRY AND SILVER** *cont.*

5. **Beloved by brides for almost a century**
—(*ArtCarved rings*) ArtCarved Inc.

6. **Best-known name in sterling**
—Gorham Div., Textron Inc.

7. **Could it be the real thing?**
—(*pearls*) Marvella Inc.

8. **Diamonds win hearts**
—Loftis Bros. & Co.

9. **Express your individuality**
—Continental Jewelry Co.

10. **Fine fashion Jewelry**
—Sarah Coventry Inc.

11. **For gifts that last consult your jeweler**
—National Jewelers Publicity Association.

12. **For that breath-taking moment**
—(*Lady Crosby diamond rings*).

13. **From generation to generation**
—(*Heirloom Sterling*) Oneida Ltd.

14. **Give the girl of your choice the ring of her choice**
—A. H. Pond Co.

15. **Grows more beautiful with use**
—Wallace Silversmiths

16. **Here and there it's sterling**
—(*silverplate*) Holmes & Edwards Silver Co.

17. **It is sterling, more cannot be said**
—Sterling Silversmiths of America.

18. **It's smart to choose the finest sterling**
—Reed and Barton.

19. **Jewelers to the sweethearts of America for three generations**
—Loftis Bros. & Co.

20. **Jewelry of tradition for the contemporary man**
—Swank Inc.

21. **Leading direct sellers of fine fashion jewelry**
—Sarah Coventry Inc.

22. **Let's make it for keeps**
—(*Community silver*) Oneida Ltd.

23. **Mark of excellence**
—Oneida Ltd.

24. **Master jeweler**
—Monet Jewelers.

67. **JEWELRY AND SILVER** *cont.*

25. **Modern silver with the beauty of old masterpieces**
—(*Watson sterling*) Wallace Silversmiths.

26. **Never a love so true, never a ring so cherished**
—(*Keepsake diamond ring*) Lenox Inc.

27. **Protected where the wear comes**
—Holmes & Edwards Silver Co.

28. **Serve it in silver**
—Benedict Mfg. Co.

29. **Silver with a past, a present, and a future**
—International Silver Co.

30. **Solid silver where it wears**
—Holmes & Edwards Silver Co.

31. **Sterling of lasting good taste**
—(*Lunt silverware*) Lunt Silversmiths.

32. **The best at the price**
—Wm. Rogers Mfg. Co.

33. **The choice you make once for a life-time**
—(*sterling*) Wallace Silversmiths

34. **The family plate for seventy years**
—International Silver Co.

35. **The originator of cultured pearls**
—K. Mikimoto Inc.

36. **There is no finer sterling silver than Fine Arts**
—(*Fine Arts sterling silver*).

37. **The world's most precious simulated pearls**
—Majorca.

38. **World's finest reproductions**
—(*pearls*) Deltah Inc.

39. **Wrought from solid silver**
—International Silver Co.

JOB PLACEMENT ... See **40. EMPLOYMENT AGENCIES**

JUICES ... See **15. BEVERAGES, MISCELLANEOUS**

K

68. KITCHEN PRODUCTS AND UTENSILS
See also **11. BAKED GOODS AND BAKING SUPPLIES,**
23. CHINA, 60. HOME APPLIANCES AND EQUIPMENT

1. **Better meals by the minute**
   —(*pressure cooker*) Landers, Frary & Clark.

2. **50 years of brighter tasting meals**
   —(*Corning Ware*) Corning Glass Works.

3. **For better and faster cooking**
   —(*Pyrex cookware*) Corning Glass Works.

4. **From generation to generation**
   —(*aluminum ware*) Wagner Mfg. Co.

5. **Kitchen tested utensils**
   —Foley Mfg. Co.

6. **Liquids or solids they keep hot or cold**
   —(*vacuum bottle*) Cannon Oiler Co.

7. **Makes that long haul to the curb seem shorter**
   —(*Baggies trash bags*) Colgate-Palmolive Co.

8. **Never before utensils like these**
   —(*Reynolds lifetime aluminum*) Reynolds Metals Co.

9. **No-stick cooking with no-scour clean-up**
   —(*Teflon*) Du Pont.

10. **Nothing else stacks up to it**
    —(*Microwave Cookware*) Rubbermaid Inc.

11. **Now, more WEAR than EVER**
    —(*Wear-Ever aluminum*) Wear-Ever Aluminum Inc.

12. **Reflects good housekeeping**
    —(*Mirro aluminum*) Aluminum Goods Mfg. Co.

13. **Rome polished copperware makes cooking easy for the home**
    —Rome Mfg. Co.

14. **The aluminum ware with the smooth finish**
    —Buckeye Aluminum Co.

15. **The best cooks use aluminum**
    —Aluminum Ware Association.

16. **The can opener people**
    —Dazey Products Co.

17. **The finest food preparer for the home**
    —(*Kitchenaid mixer*) Hobart Corp.

68. **KITCHEN PRODUCTS AND UTENSILS** *cont.*

18. **The line that's fine at cooking time**
—(*cooking utensils*) Griswold Mfg. Co.

19. **The pressure cooker people**
—National Presto Industries Inc.

20. **There's no better way to protect your investment**
—(*Ziplock storage bags*) Dow Chemical Co.

21. **To bring you permanent cooking satisfaction**
—(*kitchen ware*) Rome Mfg. Co.

22. **Worthy to become heirlooms**
—(*kitchen ware*) Rome Mfg. Co.

23. **Your kitchen companion since 1899**
—Dazey Products Co.

KNITTING SUPPLIES...See **103. SEWING AND KNITTING SUPPLIES**

L

LAMPS...See **70. LIGHTING PRODUCTS**

LAUNDRY PRODUCTS...See **24. CLEANING AND LAUNDRY PRODUCTS**

69. **LAWN AND GARDEN PRODUCTS**
See also **86. PEST CONTROL**

1. **A complete plant food, not just a stimulant**
—Olds & Whipple.

2. **A home is known by the lawn it keeps**
—Associated Seed Growers.

3. **A midget in size, a giant in power**
—Gravely Motor Plow & Cultivator Co.

4. **Be wiser—buy Keiser**
—(*shears*) Keiser Mfg. Co.

5. **Famous for power mowers for over 50 years**
—(*Toro*) Wheel Horse Products Co.

6. **Father of tree surgery**
—Davey Tree Expert Co.

7. **For everything green that grows**
—Loma Plant Food.

8. **For growing satisfaction**
—Associated Seed Growers.

69. LAWN AND GARDEN PRODUCTS *cont.*

9. **For lovely lawns in sun or shade**
    —Associated Seed Growers.

10. **Grow what you eat**
    —(*seeds*) S. L. Allen & Co.

11. **It's not a home until it's planted**
    —Hillsdale Nurseries.

12. **Kill lawn weeds without killing grass**
    —(*Weedone*) Union Carbide Agricultural Products Co.

13. **Leaders in lawn research**
    —O. M. Scott and Co.

14. **Lets you take weekends easy the year around**
    —(*garden tractor*) Deere and Co.

15. **Make every plot a garden spot**
    —Best Seed Co.

16. **Next best to rain**
    —Double Rotary Sprinkler Co.

17. **Nothing runs like a Deere**
    —John Deere Tractors.

18. **Old English lawn seed makes better lawns**
    —Philadelphia Seed Co.

19. **Power tiller of a hundred uses**
    —(*Rototiller*).

20. **Quickly kills garden pests**
    —(*Snarol*) Antrol Laboratories.

21. **Reo Reliables ... the powerful performers**
    —Wheel Horse Products Co.

22. **Seeds of satisfaction**
    —Associated Seed Growers.

23. **Sign of the leader in lawn/garden equipment**
    —Wheel Horse Products Co.

24. **Spray "Jake" for safety sake**
    —(*insecticide*) Elkay Products Corp.

25. **The grass people**
    —O. M. Scott and Co.

26. **The ideal complete plant food**
    —Olds & Whipple.

27. **The lawn people**
    —O. M. Scott and Co.

28. **The modern way to grow**
    —(*sprinkler*) National Rain Bird Sales and Engineering Corp.

69. LAWN AND GARDEN PRODUCTS *cont.*

29. **The oldest and largest tree saving service in the world**
     —Davey Tree Expert Co.

30. **The properly balanced organic plant food**
     —Olds & Whipple.

31. **There's simply nothing else quite like it under the sun**
     —(*Garden Way Sun Room/Solar Greenhouse*) Garden Way Research.

32. **The weed exterminator**
     —(*herbicide*) Reade Mfg. Co.

33. **The year 'round insecticide**
     —McCormick & Co.

34. **World's number one weed killers**
     —(*Weedone*) Union Carbide Agricultural Products Co.

35. **Yours for growing satisfaction**
     —Neosho Nurseries.

70. LIGHTING PRODUCTS
     See also **37.** ELECTRICAL PRODUCTS AND SERVICE,
         60. HOME APPLIANCES AND EQUIPMENT,
         65. INTERIOR DECORATION

1. **After sunset, Lightoliers**
    —Lightolier Inc.

2. **A full package of light**
    —Hygrade Sylvania Corp.

3. **American dark chaser**
    —(*lamps and lanterns*) American Gas Machine Co.

4. **America's first name in lighting**
    —Lightolier Inc.

5. **America's largest manufacturer of lighting productions**
    —Ruby Lighting Corp.

6. **A penny a night for the finest light**
    —Coleman Lamp Co.

7. **Beauty mark of fine Lighting**
    —Champion Mfg. Co. Inc.

8. **Bores a 300-foot hole in the night**
    —Niagara Searchlight Co.

9. **Brayco Light makes all things clear**
    —Bray Screen Products.

10. **Brightens the night**
    —Fullerton Electric Co.

70. **LIGHTING PRODUCTS** *cont.*

11. **Brite-Lite has a brilliant future**
> —Britelite Co.

12. **Built for a palace, priced for a cottage**
> —Moe-Bridges Co.

13. **Buy a How searchlight today, you may need it tonight**
> —How Lamp & Mfg. Co.

14. **Daylight's only rival**
> —Silverglo Lamps Inc.

15. **Decorate with artistic lighting equipment**
> —Artistic Lighting Equipment Association.

16. **Experts know these lamps**
> —Hygrade Sylvania Corp.

17. **Eye-ease at the snap of the switch**
> —Silverglo Lamps Inc.

18. **Give long-lasting light, bullet-fast**
> —(*Winchester flashlight*).

19. **Guardian lighting**
> —Guardian Light Co.

20. **Holophane directs light scientifically**
> —Holophane Glass Co.

21. **"Jewelry for the home"**
> —Greene Bros. Inc.

22. **Kind to the eyes**
> —(*Emeralite desk lamp*) H. G. McFadden & Co.

23. **Lamps for see-ability**
> —Westinghouse Electric Corp.

24. **Lamps of elegance**
> —Frederick Cooper Lamps Inc.

25. **Lighting from concealed sources**
> —National X-Ray Reflector Co.

26. **Lighting over a million homes tonight**
> —Aladdin Mfg. Co.

27. **Lights the home, lightens the works**
> —Gray & Davis Inc.

28. **Notice the lighting fixtures**
> —Associated Lighting Industries.

29. **Put your lighting up to Whiting**
> —H. S. Whiting Co.

30. **Safe as sunshine**
> —(*lanterns*) R. E. Dietz Co.

70. **LIGHTING PRODUCTS** *cont.*

   31. **The double duty searchlight**
                             —F. W. Wakefield Brass Co.

   32. **The handiest light in the world**
                             —Bussman Mfg. Co.

   33. **The lamp that chases gloom and glare**
                             —Silverglo Lamps Inc.

   34. **The lamp with the 1500-hour guarantee**
                             —Solex Co., Ltd.

   35. **The lantern with the blue porcelain top**
                             —American Gas Machine Co.

   36. **The light that always shines welcome**
                             —Coleman Lamp Co.

   37. **The light that never fails**
                             —Rapid Mfg. Co.

   38. **The light to live with**
                             —Duplex Lighting Works of General Electric.

   39. **The line of beauty**
                             —(*Lemar lamps*) Lee-Marion Co.

   40. **The modern light conditioning bulb**
                             —Wabash Appliance Corp.

   41. **The name you know in lamps**
                             —Westinghouse Electric Corp.

   42. **The "one stop" creative lighting source**
                             —Petelco Div., Pyle-National Co.

   43. **The royalty of lamps**
                             —The Stiffel Co.

   44. **The standard of residential lighting**
                             —E. N. Riddle Co.

   45. **The sunshine of the night**
                             —Coleman Lamp Co.

   46. **Turns night into day**
                             —Gleason Tiebout Glass.

LINENS ... See **13.** BEDS AND BEDDING

LINGERIE ... See **121.** UNDERWEAR

71. **LIQUORS**
     See also **14.** BEER AND ALE, **15.** BEVERAGES,
       MISCELLANEOUS, **125.** WINES

   1. **A blend of all straight whiskies**
                             —(*Paul Jones whiskey*) Summit Sales Co.

   2. **Aged for 8**
                             —(*Bell's Blended scotch*) Heublein Inc.

71. **LIQUORS** *cont.*

3. **A gentleman's drink**
—(*Cutty Sark Whiskey*) Berry Bros. & Co.

4. **A glorious beginning**
—(*Pinch scotch*) Renfield Importers Ltd.

5. **A heritage to remember**
—(*Philadelphia whiskey*).

6. **A luxury blend for the "carriage trade"**
—(*Gallagher & Burton whiskey*) Four Roses Distillers Co.

7. **Always smoother because it's slow-distilled**
—(*Early Times bourbon*) Brown-Forman Distillers Corp.

8. **America's finest whiskey regardless of age or price**
—(*Four Roses whiskey*) Four Roses Distillers Co.

9. **America's luxury whiskey**
—(*Park & Tilford*) Park & Tilford Distillers Co.

10. **America's most famous bouquet**
—(*Four Roses whiskey*) Four Roses Distillers Co.

11. **America's social-light whiskey**
—Ben Burk Inc.

12. **An American gentleman's whiskey since 1860**
—(*Hunter whiskey*) Four Roses Distillers Co.

13. **A new high in whiskey smoothness**
—(*Ten High whiskey*) Hiram Walker Inc.

14. **"An inch of Pinch, please."**
—(*scotch*) Renfield Importers Ltd.

15. **A noble Scotch**
—Train & McIntyre Ltd.

16. **A rainbow of distinctive flavors**
—(*cordials*) Hiram Walker Inc.

17. **Aristocrat of blended Scotch-type whiskey**
—(*Royal Banquet Whiskey*).

18. **Arrow means quality in any language**
—Arrow Liquors Co.

19. **As different as day and night**
—(*Old Overholt whiskey*) National Distillers and Chemical Corp.

20. **A singular experience**
—(*Tanqueray gin*) Somerset Importers Ltd.

21. **A truly great name among America's great whiskies**
—(*Old Crow*) National Distillers and Chemical Corp.

22. **A whiskey for every taste and purse**
—Park & Tilford Distillers Co.

71. **LIQUORS** *cont.*

23. **Best buy in rye**

—Kasko Distillers Corp.

24. **Blended whiskey of character**

—Carstairs Bros.

25. **Born in 1820 ... still going strong!**
—(*Johnnie Walker Red Label scotch*) Somerset Importers Ltd.

26. **Born where a king of France was born**

—(*Otard cognac*).

27. **Break away from the ordinary**

—(*Seagram's V.O.*) Seagram's Distillers.

28. **Charcoal mellowed drop by drop**

—Jack Daniels Distillery.

29. **Cheerful as its name**

—(*Old Sunny Brook whiskey*).

30. **Clean clear through**

—(*rye*) Continental Distilling Corp.

31. **Clear heads call for Calvert**
—(*Calvert blended whiskey*) J. E. Seagram & Sons Inc.

32. **Designed for your pleasure today, tomorrow and always**

—J. E. Seagram & Sons Inc.

33. **Don't be vague ... ask for Haig and Haig**

—Renfield Importers Ltd.

34. **Drink moderately, insist on quality**

—James Clark Distilling Corp.

35. **Dutch name, world fame**
—(*Bols liqueurs*) Brown-Forman Distillers Corp.

36. **Enjoyable always and *all* ways**

—(*rum*) Bacardi Imports Inc.

37. **Excellence doubly safeguarded**

—(*Beefeater gin*) Kobrand Corp.

38. **Excitement you can taste**
—(*Hazelnut Liquor*) Avon Liquors Company.

39. **Famous. Smooth. Mellow.**
—(*Old Crow*) National Distillers and Chemical Corp.

40. **Fine coffee liqueur ... from sunny Mexico**
—(*Kahlua*) Jules Berman and Associates Inc.

41. **Fine whiskey on the *mild* side**
—(*Corby's*) Jas. Barclay and Co. Ltd.

42. **First among fine whiskies**

—(*Three Feathers*).

71. **LIQUORS** *cont.*

43. **Fond of things Italiano? Try a sip of Galiano**
—Liquor Div., McKesson & Robbins Inc.

44. **For a man who plans beyond tomorrow**
—J. E. Seagram & Sons Inc.

45. **For men of distinction**
—(*Calvert blended whiskey*) J. E. Seagram & Sons Inc.

46. **For men who know fine whiskies**
—(*Kentucky Tavern*) Glenmore Distilleries Co.

47. **For the king of old-fashioneds**
—(*King whiskey*).

48. **For the man who cares**
—(*White Seal whiskey*) Carstairs Bros.

49. **Gentle as a lamb**
—(*scotch whiskey*) Train & McIntyre Ltd.

50. **Gets a hand in any land**
—Arrow Liquors Co.

51. **Give your guest what he wishes**
—National Distilleries.

52. **Have the genius to chill it**
—(*Chartreuse*) Schiefflin and Co.

53. **Head of the bourbon family**
—(*Old Grand-Dad bourbon*) National Distillers and Chemical Corp.

54. **If it isn't P. M., it isn't an evening**
—(*P. M. whiskey*).

55. **It leaves you breathless**
—(*Smirnoff vodka*) Heublein Inc.

56. **It's always a pleasure**
—(*I. W. Harper bourbon*) Schenley Industries Inc.

57. **"It's smart to buy right"**
—(*Highland Scotch Mist*) Heublein Inc.

58. **It's the flavor**
—(*Teachers Scotch*) Bacardi Imports Inc.

59. **It's "velveted"**
—(*Imperial whiskey*) Hiram Walker Inc.

60. **Jamaica's legendary liqueur**
—(*Tia Maria*) W. A. Taylor and Co.

61. **Just smooth, very smooth**
—(*Johnnie Walker Red Label scotch*) Somerset Importers Ltd.

62. **Knowledgeable people buy Imperial**
—Hiram Walker Inc.

71.   LIQUORS *cont.*

63. **Known by the company it keeps**
   —(*Seagram's Canadian V.O.*) J. E. Seagram & Sons Inc.

64. **La grande liqueur Française**
   —(*DOM Benedictine*) Julius Wile Sons and Co. Inc.

65. **Let this seal be your guide to quality**
   —Julius Wile Sons and Co. Inc.

66. **Light or dry, in step with the times**
   —(*Maraca rum*).

67. **Needs no chaser**
   —(*Spot Bottle whiskey*) Ben Burk Inc.

68. **No extravagant claims, just a real good product**
   —(*Brown Friar whiskey*).

69. **No Scotch improves the flavour of water like Teachers**
   —(*Teachers Scotch*) Bacardi Imports Inc.

70. **Not a drop is sold till it's seven years old**
   —(*John Jameson whiskey*) John Jameson & Son.

71. **Nothing else quite measures up**
   —(*Walker's DeLuxe bourbon*) Hiram Walker Inc.

72. **Nothing was stirring but Seagram's 7 and . . .**
   —(*Seagram's 7*) Seagram's Distillers.

73. **No wonder Fleischmann's Preferred is PREFERRED**
   —(*whiskey*) Fleischmann Distilling Corp.

74. **One of the world's great whiskeys**
   —(*Bushmill's whiskey*).

75. **Pennies more in cost . . . worlds apart in quality**
   —(*J & B scotch*) James Moroney Inc.

76. **Pride of cognac since 1724**
   —(*Remy-Martin cognac*) Renfield Importers Ltd.

77. **Red stands out. Tastefully.**
   —(*Johnnie Walker Red Label scotch*) Somerset Importers Ltd.

78. **Remember Ronrico, best rum, bar none**
   —Ronrico Corp.

79. **Rich as a symphony**
   —(*Penn Maryland whiskey*).

80. **Robust as old rye**
   —(*Bushmill's whiskey*).

81. **Same great whiskey today as before the war**
   —(*Four Roses whiskey*) Four Roses Distillers Co.

71. LIQUORS *cont.*

82. Same quality throughout the world
　　—(*Johnnie Walker scotch*) Somerset Importers Ltd.

83. Say Seagram's and be sure
　　—(*whiskey*) J. E. Seagram & Sons Inc.

84. Say Seagram's and be sure of pre-war quality
　　—(*whiskey*) J. E. Seagram & Sons Inc.

85. Signed, sealed, and delicious
　　—(*Old Taylor whiskey*) National Distillers and Chemical
　　　　　　　　　　　　　　　　　　　　　　　　Corp.

86. Smart, smooth, sensibly priced
　　—(*Gilbey's vodka*) National Distillers and Chemical Corp.

87. Smooth as silk, but not high hat
　　—(*Kessler's blended whiskey*) The Seagram Co. Ltd.

88. Tangy as old Scotch
　　—(*Bushmill's whiskey*).

89. Taste the magic
　　—(*Bailey's Irish Cream liqueur*).

90. The American whiskey for the American taste
　　—Frankfort Distilleries.

91. The aristocrat of liqueurs
　　—(*Cherristock*) Schenley Industries Inc.

92. "The best in the house" in 87 lands
　　—(*Canadian Club*) Hiram Walker Inc.

93. The brandy of Napoleon
　　—(*Courvoisier cognac*) W. A. Taylor and Co.

94. The centaur ... your symbol of quality
　　—(*Remy-Martin cognac*) Renfield Importers Ltd.

95. The cognac brandy for every occasion
　　—(*Martel cognac*) Joseph Garneau Co. Inc.

96. The crown jewel of England
　　—(*Beefeater gin*) Kobrand Corp.

97. The crystal clear gin in the crystal clear bottle
　　—American Distilling Corp.

98. The drier liqueur
　　—(*DOM B and B*) Julius Wile Sons and Co. Inc.

99. The first taste will tell you why!
　　—Fleischmann Distilling Corp.

100. The gold medal Kentucky bourbon since 1872
　　—(*I. W. Harper bourbon*) Schenley Industries Inc.

101. The gold medal whiskey
　　—(*I. W. Harper bourbon*) Schenley Industries Inc.

71. LIQUORS *cont.*

102. **The grand old drink of the South**
—(*Southern Comfort whiskey*) Southern Comfort Corp.

103. **The greatest name in bourbon**
—(*Old Crow*) National Distillers and Chemical Corp.

104. **The greatest name in vodka**
—(*Smirnoff vodka*) Heublein Inc.

105. **The heart of a good cocktail**
—(*Gordon's gin*) Schenley Industries Inc.

106. **The imported one**
—(*Beefeater gin*) Kobrand Corp.

107. **The incomparable**
—(*Imperial*) Hiram Walker Inc.

108. **The king of blends**
—(*Eagle whiskey*) National Distillers Products Corp.

109. **The man who cares says: "Carstairs White Seal"**
—(*whiskey*) Carstairs Bros.

110. **The measure of perfection**
—(*Wm. Penn whiskey*) G & W Distillers.

111. **The medal Scotch of the world**
—(*Dewar's*) Schenley Industries Inc.

112. **The oldest name in Scotch**
—Somerset Importers Ltd.

113. **The original and largest-selling in the world**
—(*cocktail mixes*) Holland House Brands Inc.

114. **The peak of perfection**
—(*Old Poindexter whiskey*) Franklin County Dist. Co.

115. **The perfection of Scotch whisky**
—(*Teachers Scotch*) Bacardi Imports Inc.

116. **The possibilities are endless**
—(*Gordon's gin*) Renfield Importers Ltd.

117. **The Puerto Rican mountain rum**
—(*Bon Merito rum*).

118. **"There is nothing better in the market"**
—(*Old Forester bourbon*) Brown-Forman Distillers Corp.

119. **The responsibility of being the best**
—(*Wild Turkey bourbon*) Austin, Nichols and Co. Inc.

120. **The right spirit**
—(*Teachers Scotch*) Bacardi Imports Inc.

121. **The rising BARometer of whiskey preference**
—(*Three Feathers*).

122. **The Scotch that circles the globe**
—Continental Distilling Corp.

71. LIQUORS *cont.*

123. **The Scotch with character**
—(*Black and White*) Fleischmann Distilling Corp.

124. **The sportsman's whiskey**
—W. A. Taylor & Co.

125. **The true old-style Kentucky bourbon**
—(*Early Times bourbon*) Brown-Forman Distillers Corp.

126. **The unhurried whiskey for unhurried moments**
—(*Kinsey*).

127. **The very best buy is the whiskey that's dry**
—(*Paul Jones whiskey*) Summit Sales Co.

128. **The whiskey of the gourmet**
—(*Kentucky Tavern*) Glenmore Distilleries Co.

129. **The whiskey that grew up with America**
—Alexander Young Distilling Co.

130. **The whiskey that speaks for itself**
—Oldetyme Distilling Co.

131. **The whiskey with no regrets**
—Oldetyme Distilling Co.

132. **The whiskey you feel good about**
—(*Golden Wedding*) J. S. Finch & Co.

133. **The world knows no better Scotch**
—(*Haig & Haig*) Renfield Importers Ltd.

134. **The world's best climate makes the world's best rum**
—(*Puerto Rican*) Schiefflin and Co.

135. **The world's finest bourbon since 1795**
—James B. Beam Distilling Co.

136. **Think before you drink, say Seagram's and be sure**
—(*whiskey*) J. E. Seagram & Sons Inc.

137. **Those in the know ask for Old Crow**
—(*Old Crow*) National Distillers and Chemical Corp.

138. **Time works wonders**
—(*Seagram's whiskey*) J. E. Seagram & Sons Inc.

139. **12 kinds—better than most people make**
—(*Heublein cocktails*) Heublein Inc.

140. **Two scotches of exceptional character**
—(*Black and White*) Fleischmann Distilling Corp.

141. **Wed in the wood**
—(*Old Thompson whiskey*) Glenmore Distilleries Co.

142. **Welcomed in the best homes**
—(*Royal Banquet whiskey*) Glenmore Distilleries Co.

71. **LIQUORS** *cont.*

143. **We'll wait. Grant's 8**
—(*scotch*) Austin, Nichols and Co. Inc.

144. **When you would serve the best**
—(*Johnnie Walker scotch*) Somerset Importers Ltd.

145. **Wherever you go, there it is**
—(*Hiram Walker bourbon*) Hiram Walker Inc.

146. **"Yes, I know ... Marie Brizard"**
—Schiefflin and Co.

147. **Your key to hospitality**
—(*Old Fitzgerald*) Stitzel-Walker Distillery Inc.

LOCKS ... See **55. HARDWARE**

72. **LUGGAGE**
See also **119. TRAVEL**

1. **America's best traveling companion**
—(*trunks*) Mendel-Drucker.

2. **America's greatest luggage value**
—(*Lady Baltimore*) Baltimore Luggage Co.

3. **Best today, still better tomorrow**
—(*Firestone luggage*).

4. **Built to fit the trip**
—(*Miller luggage*).

5. **Built to last through every trip**
—(*Rennus luggage*).

6. **Created to carry your belongings in perfection throughout your lifetime**
—(*Halliburton travel cases*).

7. **Creators of distinctive luggage**
—(*Unique luggage*).

8. **Fashion luggage**
—(*Lady Baltimore*) Baltimore Luggage Co.

9. **For people who travel ... and expect to again and again**
—(*Stafflight*) The Sardis Luggage Co.

10. **For those who go first class**
—Horn Luggage Co.

11. **If you have an instinct for quality**
—(*Amelia Earhart luggage*) Baltimore Luggage Co.

12. **It makes its way by the way it's made**
—(*Bridgeport luggage*).

13. **Look for the Hartmann Red on the trunk you buy**
—Hartmann Trunk Co.

72. **LUGGAGE** *cont.*

14. **Luggage you will love to travel with**
—Rauchbach-Goldsmith Co.

15. **So high in fashion ... so light in weight**
—Ventura Travelward Inc.

16. **Someone's always looking at your luggage**
—Amelia Earhart Luggage Co.

17. **Takes the "lug" out of luggage**
—(*Karry-lite luggage*).

18. **Take your travel lightly**
—Horn Luggage Co.

19. **The last word in fine leather luggage**
—Edw. Freeman.

20. **The luggage that knows its way around the world**
—Samsonite Corp.

21. **The luggage that sets the pace for luxury**
—Samsonite Corp.

22. **The name that means everything in luggage**
—Rauchbach-Goldsmith Co.

23. **There is only one "old faithful"**
—(*Rugged luggage*).

24. **The sterling of leatherware**
—(*Rumpp luggage*) Aristocrat Leather Products.

25. **The trunk with doors**
—Winship & Sons.

26. **Travel begins with Everwear**
—(*trunks, luggage*) Rauchbach-Goldsmith Co.

27. **Travel light, travel right**
—(*Val-A-Pak luggage*) Atlantic Products Corp.

28. **Travel with Everwear; Everwear travels everywhere**
—Rauchbach-Goldsmith Co.

29. **Trunks may come and trunks may go, but Everwear goes on forever**
—Rauchbach-Goldsmith Co.

30. **We evolved the styles that the world admires**
—Ideal Leather Case Co.

LUMBER ... See **18. BUILDING SUPPLIES**

M

73. **MACHINERY**
    See also **37.** ELECTRICAL PRODUCTS AND SERVICE,
    42. FARMING SUPPLIES AND EQUIPMENT,
    120. TRUCKS AND TRUCKING INDUSTRY

1. **All work and no play**
                           —Timken Roller Bearing Co.

2. **Always *right* on the job**
                           —The Bowdil Co.

3. **A team of specialists**
                           —Cameron Machine Co.

4. **Better products at lower cost through better methods**
                           —Standard Tool and Mfg. Co.

5. **Blue brutes**
                           —Worthington Pump & Machinery Corp.

6. **Commitment to quality**
                           —Bucyrus-Erie Co.

7. **Creators of dependability**
                           —Geartronics Corp.

8. **Dependable power, absolute safety**
                           —Troy Engine & Machine Co.

9. **Designed for your industry, engineered for you**
                           —Coppers Engineering Corp.

10. **First in automation**
                           —The Cross Co.

11. **For your pressing needs**
                           —Hydraulic Press Mfg. Co.

12. **Handle it mechanically**
                           —Jeffrey Mfg. Co.

13. **HEAD work always wins over HARD work on pay day**
                           —Chicago Engineering Works.

14. **In design and performance, always a year ahead**
                           —Prodex Div., Koehring Co.

15. **It's wise to conveyorize**
                           —Rapids-Standard Co. Inc.

16. **Known by the companies we keep**
                           —(*industrial machinery*) Baker Bros. Inc.

73. MACHINERY *cont.*

17. Machines at work around the world
—Joy Mfg. Co.

18. Machines for total productivity
—Ghisholt Machine Co.

19. Machines that build for a growing America
—Caterpillar Tractor Co.

20. Miles ahead
—(*road machinery*) The Galion Iron Works and Mfg. Co.

21. More goods for more people at lower cost
—National Machine Tool Builders Assn.

22. Moves the earth
—Euclid Road Machinery Co.

23. Portable pony power
—(*Johnson Iron Horse gas engine*).

24. Powered by Howard
—(*motors*) Howard Industries Inc.

25. Precision machinery since 1880
—Warner & Swasey Co.

26. Progress begins with digging
—Marion Power Shovel Co.

27. Roberts keeps you years ahead
—Roberts Co.

28. Roberts value keeps you years ahead
—Roberts Co.

29. Strong where strength is needed
—Athol Machine & Foundry Co.

30. The all-purpose one-man crane
—Byers Machine Co.

31. The electric hoist that operates in the minimum
—American Engineering Co.

32. The imperial line of road machinery
—Sawyer-Massey.

33. The leader around the world
—Cocker Machine and Foundry Co.

34. The long line of construction machinery
—Allis-Chalmers Mfg. Co.

35. The performance line
—HPM Div., Koehring Co.

36. The pump of compulsory accuracy
—Milwaukee Tank Works.

37. There should be a Lee in your future
—Lee Machinery Corp.

73. **MACHINERY** *cont.*

    38. **The strong arm of industry**
          —Electric Hoist Manufacturers' Association.

    39. **Today's ideas ... engineered for tomorrow**
          —Powermatic Inc.

    40. **Who changed it?**
          —H. K. Porter Co. Inc.

MAGAZINES ... See **85. PERIODICALS AND NEWSPAPERS**

MAINTENANCE ... See **24. CLEANING AND LAUNDRY PRODUCTS**

MAKE-UP ... See **32. COSMETICS**

MARKETING ... See **2. ADVERTISING**

MEASURING DEVICES ... See **63. INSTRUMENTS AND GAUGES**

74. **MEATS**
    See also **47. FOOD, MISCELLANEOUS**

    1. **A Kansas product from Kansas farms**
          —Butzer Packing Co.

    2. **All the taste without the waste**
          —(*Council meats*) Indian Packing Corp.

    3. **America's first choice for flavor**
          —Armour & Co.

    4. **A square meal from a square can**
          —(*Broadcast Redi-Meat*).

    5. **Folks favor Fromm's flavor**
          —(*sausage, meat products*) Fromm Bros.

    6. **Food purveyors to the nation**
          —Swift & Co.

    7. **For those who really like to eat**
          —Smithfield Ham & Products Co. Inc.

    8. **Fresh from sunshine and pure air**
          —(*Council meats*) Indian Packing Corp.

    9. **Fresh ideas in meat ... from Hormel**
          —Geo. A. Hormel and Co.

    10. **From the goodness of Louis Rich**
          —(*Louis Rich cold cuts*) Dykstra's Food Service.

    11. **From the tall corn country**
          —(*Dubuque ham*) Dubuque Packing Co.

    12. **Hygrade in name. Hygrade in fact**
          —Hygrade Food Products Co.

74. MEATS *cont.*

13. **If this Gold Seal is on it — there's better meat in it**
—Wilson and Co. Inc.

14. **Meals without meat are meals incomplete**
—Theobald Industries.

15. **Nobody knows chicken like the folks at Weaver**
—(*Weaver Chicken Rondelets*) Weaver Inc.

16. **Our wurst is the best**
—(*Mickelberry's sausage*) Mickelberry Corp.

17. **Pick the polka dot package**
—Swift & Co.

18. **Say Skinless when you say frankfurters**
—Visking Corp.

19. **Smoked with hickory**
—(*ham*) Rath Packing Co.

20. **Smoke that never varies from fires that never die**
—Swift & Co.

21. **Taste the taste**
—(*deviled ham*) William Underwood.

22. **The best and nothing but the best is labeled Armour**
—Armour & Co.

23. **The best-lookin' cookin' in town**
—Armour & Co.

24. **The ham what am**
—(*Star ham*) Armour & Co.

25. **The meats that wear the Armour star are the meats the butcher brings home**
—Armour & Co.

26. **The sandwich spread of the nation**
—(*deviled ham*) Wm. Underwood Co.

27. **The taste tells**
—Cudahy Packing Co.

28. **The two most trusted names in meat**
—(*Swift's Premium*) Swift & Co.

29. **The Wilson label protects your table**
—Wilson and Co. Inc.

30. **Traditionally preferred throughout our land**
—(*bacon*) Swift & Co.

31. **Try it a week; you'll use it for life**
—Swift & Co.

32. **With that sweet smoke taste**
—(*bacon*) Swift & Co.

74. **MEATS** *cont.*

    33. **You can trust the man who sells this brand**
        —(*Swift's Premium*) Swift & Co.

MEDICATIONS ... See **35. DRUGS AND REMEDIES**

75. **METALS INDUSTRY**
    See also **18. BUILDING SUPPLIES**

    1. **A bronze as strong as nickel steel**
        —American Manganese Bronze Co.

    2. **America's foremost producer of custom steels**
        —Sharon Steel Corp.

    3. **America's pioneer manufacturer of prefinished metals**
        —American Nickeloid Co.

    4. **Change for the better with Alcoa Aluminum**
        —Aluminum Co. of America.

    5. **Developers and producers of extraordinary materials**
        —The Beryllium Corp.

    6. **Die casting is the process ... zinc, the metal**
        —St. Joseph Lead Co.

    7. **First and finest in copper and brass ... Fully integrated in aluminum**
        —Revere Copper and Brass Inc.

    8. **First name in cast steel!**
        —Farrell-Cheek Steel Co.

    9. **For almost any product, aluminum makes it better and Kaiser aluminum makes aluminum work best**
        —Kaiser Aluminum and Chemical Corp.

    10. **For strength where the stress comes**
        —International Nickel Co.

    11. **From mine to market**
        —La Belle Iron Works.

    12. **Growth leader of the aluminum industry**
        —Consolidated Aluminum Corp.

    13. **If you see rust, you'll know it's not aluminum**
        —Reynolds Metals Co.

    14. **Imagination in steel for the needs of today's architecture**
        —Granco Steel Products Co.

    15. **In a word, confidence**
        —The Carpenter Steel Co.

75. **METALS INDUSTRY** *cont.*

16. **In stainless, too, you can take the pulse of progress at Republic**
    —Republic Steel Corp.

17. **Look ahead with lead**
    —Lead Industries Association

18. **Metal, the fifth medium**
    —Mathews Industries Inc.

19. **Metalurgy is our business**
    —Vanadium-Alloys Steel Co.

20. **More people want more aluminum for more uses than ever before**
    —(*Alcoa*) Aluminum Co. of America.

21. **Nickel ... its contribution is quality**
    —International Nickel Co.

22. **Nothing equals stainless steel**
    —United States Steel Corp.

23. **Service that never sleeps**
    —Reynolds Aluminum Supply Co.

24. **The company for precious metals**
    —Handy and Harman.

25. **The house of experience**
    —Mirro Aluminum Co.

26. **The most progressive name in steel**
    —Nippon Kokan.

27. *The* **specialist in plate steels**
    —Lukens Steel Co.

28. **The** *specialty* **steel company**
    —Latrobe Steel Co.

29. **The steels with the Indian names**
    —Ludlum Steel Co.

30. **Think copper**
    —(*Anaconda*) American Brass Co.

31. **Value engineering favors zinc**
    —American Zinc Institute.

32. **What next from Alcoa!**
    —Aluminum Co. of America.

33. **Where big ideas turn into aluminum extrusions**
    —Superior Industries Inc.

34. **Where new ideas take shape in aluminum**
    —Reynolds Metals Co.

35. **Where the big idea is innovation**
    —United States Steel Corp.

75. **METALS INDUSTRY** *cont.*

    36. **You can count on Continental to take care of you**
        —Continental Steel Corp.

76. **MISCELLANEOUS**

    1. **Laugh at zero**
        —(*Globe radiator shutters*) Globe Mach. & Stamping Co.

    2. **Masterpieces in plastic**
        —Columbia Protektosite Co.

    3. **Trust in Phillips is world-wide**
        —Phillips Research Laboratories.

    4. **You're in the money**
        —(*Coins of All Nations*) Franklin Mint.

MOTELS . . . See **62. HOTELS AND MOTELS**

MOTOR OIL . . . See **88. PETROLEUM PRODUCTS**

77. **MOTORCYCLES**
    See also **7. AUTOMOBILES, 98. RECREATIONAL EQUIPMENT**

    1. **Follow the leader, he's on a Honda**
        —(*Honda*) American Honda Motor Co. Inc.

    2. **Kawasaki lets the good times roll**
        —Kawasaki Motors Corp.

    3. **World's biggest seller!**
        —(*Honda*) American Honda Motor Co. Inc.

    4. **Yamaha—the way it should be**
        —Yamaha Motor Corp., U.S.A.

78. **MOVIES AND ENTERTAINMENT**
    See also **5. AUDIO EQUIPMENT, 17. BROADCASTING, 89. PHOTOGRAPHIC EQUIPMENT, 112. TELEVISIONS, 122. VIDEO EQUIPMENT**

    1. **A King can have no more**
        —(*movies*) Paramount Pictures Corp.

    2. **Ars gratia artis**
        —Metro-Goldwyn-Mayer.

    3. **Create happy hours**
        —Selznick Pictures Corp.

    4. **Gems of the screen**
        —Columbia Pictures Corp.

    5. **If it's a Paramount picture, it's the best show in town**
        —Paramount Pictures Corp.

78. **MOVIES AND ENTERTAINMENT** *cont.*

6. **Morally straight, physically strong, mentally awake**
—Hygienic Productions.

7. **Moral pictures most mothers approve**
—Hygienic Productions.

8. **More stars than there are in heaven**
—Metro-Goldwyn-Mayer.

9. **Motion pictures are the nation's relaxation**
—Royal Pictures.

10. **Movies make many merry moments**
—Royal Pictures.

11. **Only the best can cut it here**
—Ice Capades.

12. **Real or reel, Royal is best**
—Royal Pictures.

13. **Royal releases release your worries**
—Royal Pictures.

14. **The greatest show on earth**
—Ringling Brothers and Barnum & Bailey Circus.

15. **We are your movie star**
—(*cable television movie service*) Cinemax.

79. **MOVING AND STORAGE**
See also **120. TRUCKS AND TRUCKING INDUSTRY**

1. **America's most recommended mover**
—(*Mayflower*) Aero Mayflower Transit Co. Inc.

2. **America's number 1 mover**
—Allied Van Lines Inc.

3. **Dedicated to people on the move**
—U. S. Van Lines Inc.

4. **Families that move the most call the world's largest mover**
—Allied Van Lines Inc.

5. **Leaving the *moving* to us**
—Greyhound Lines Inc.

6. **Let Lyon guard your goods**
—Lyon Van Lines Inc.

7. **Moving with care . . . everywhere**
—United Van Lines Inc.

8. **The *gentlemen* of the moving industry**
—North American Van Lines Inc.

9. **The people who care about people who move**
—Fernstrom Storage and Van Co.

79. MOVING AND STORAGE *cont.*

10. **The professionals**
                    —Bekins Van and Storage Co.

11. **United Moves the people that move the world**
                    —United Van Lines Inc.

12. **We move families, not just furniture**
                    —Allied Van Lines Inc.

80. MUSICAL INSTRUMENTS

1. **A beautiful piano with a magnificent tone**
                    —(*Betsy Ross spinet*).

2. **Acknowledged the world's best piano**
                    —Wm. Knabe & Co.

3. **Choice of the masters**
                    —(*organ*) George Kilgen & Son.

4. **Choose your piano as the artists do**
                    —Baldwin Piano & Organ Co.

5. **Cultivate your musical bump**
                    —C. G. Conn Inc.

6. **Drum makers to the profession**
                    —Ludwig Drum Co.

7. **Easy to play, pay and carry**
                    —Clark Harp Mfg. Co.

8. **For the home that enjoys home life**
                    —Conn Organ Corp.

9. **Harp-maker to the world since 1889**
                    —Lyon-Healy Co.

10. **Heirloom quality pianos since 1896**
                    —Kohler and Campbell Inc.

11. **If it's a Steger, it's the most valuable piano in the world**
                    —Steger & Sons.

12. **Instruments of quality by one family for 100 years**
                    —(*spinet*) Story and Clark Piano Co.

13. **Instruments worthy of the masters since 1857**
                    —(*pianos, organs*) Kimball International.

14. **Keyboard of the nation**
                    —(*pianos*) Kimball International.

15. **Little piano with the big tune**
                    —Miessner Piano Co.

16. **Made by masters, played by artists**
                    —Buescher Band Instrument Co.

17. **Made by OUR family for YOURS**
                    —(*pianos*) Sohmer & Co.

80. **MUSICAL INSTRUMENTS** *cont.*

18. **Made with the extra measure of care**
—(*Cordova guitars*) David Wexler and Co.

19. **More music for the money**
—Kay Musical Instrument Co.

20. **Most famous name on drums**
—Ludwig Drum Co.

21. **Music's most glorious voice**
—Hammond Organ Co.

22. **No other instrument so richly rewards the efforts of the beginner**
—Hammond Organ Co.

23. **One chord is worth a thousand words**
—(*pianos*) Sohmer & Co.

24. **Popular as music itself**
—(*pianos, player pianos*) Winter & Co.

25. **Since 1874 stringed instrument house of the masters**
—William Lewis and Son.

26. **The difference is quality**
—(*guitars*) Epiphone Inc.

27. **The drum standard of the world**
—Ludwig Drum Co.

28. **The foremost in drums**
—Slingerland Drum Co.

29. **The Hammond is the largest-selling organ in the world**
—Hammond Organ Co.

30. **The instrument of the immortals**
—(*pianos*) Steinway & Sons.

31. **The master's fingers on your piano**
—Auto-Pneumatic Action Co.

32. **The most valuable piano in the world**
—Steger & Sons.

33. **The name to remember in flutes**
—(*Armstrong flutes*) Chicago Musical Instrument Co.

34. **The one and only**
—Hammond Organ Co.

35. **The piano of international fame**
—Steinway & Sons.

36. **The sound investment**
—D. H. Baldwin Co.

37. **The tone heard 'round the world**
—Wm. S. Haynes Co.

80. **MUSICAL INSTRUMENTS** *cont.*

38. **The voice of the cathedrals**
—Liberty Carillon.

39. **"The world's finest"**
—Goya Guitars Inc.

40. **The world's most beautiful organs**
—Story and Clark Piano Co.

41. **Total quality**
—(*pianos, organs*) Kimball International.

42. **We challenge comparison**
—Vose & Sons Piano Co.

43. **With all the grace and beauty of its name**
—(*Minute Model Gulbransen piano*) Gulbransen
Industries Inc.

44. **World's largest builder of organs and pianos**
—Wurlitzer Co.

45. **World's most respected accordion**
—(*Nunziola accordion*).

46. **Wurlitzer means music to millions**
—Wurlitzer Co.

47. **You can bank on a Frank**
—(*trumpet*) Wm. Frank Co.

N

NAUTICAL SUPPLIES...See **16.** BOATS AND BOATING EQUIPMENT

NEWSPAPERS...See **85.** PERIODICALS AND NEWSPAPERS

NOTIONS...See **103.** SEWING AND KNITTING SUPPLIES

NUTS...See **49.** FRUITS AND NUTS

O

81. OFFICE EQUIPMENT AND SUPPLIES
See also **28.** COMPUTER EQUIPMENT, **30.** COPYING EQUIPMENT, **83.** PAPER PRODUCTS, **126.** WRITING INSTRUMENTS

1. **A complete source for fine office furniture**
—Desks Inc.

2. **A finer typewriter at a fair price**
—(*Oliver typewriter*).

3. **A machine for every purpose**
—(*typewriters*) Remington Rand.

4. **A million yards of good will**
—(*gummed paper moistener*) A. C. Hummel Co.

5. **A real safe, not a pretense**
—(*safes*) J & J Taylor.

6. **Built like a skyscraper**
—(*steel filing cabinets*) Shaw-Walker Co.

7. **Built to last a business lifetime**
—Monroe Calculating Machine Co.

8. **Correct mistakes in any language**
—(*erasers*) Weldon Roberts Rubber Co.

9. **Cutting costs is our business**
—Addressograph-Multigraph Corp.

10. **Dictate to the Dictaphone**
—Columbia Graphophone Co.

11. **Distinguished furniture for distinguished offices**
—Stow and Davis Furniture Co.

81. **OFFICE EQUIPMENT AND SUPPLIES** *cont.*

12. **Don't write, Voice-O-Graph**
     —(*voice recorder*) International Mutoscope Corp.

13. **End the day with a smile**
     —(*Royal typewriters*) Royal Typewriter Co. Inc.

14. **Every business form for every form of business**
     —Baltimore Salesbook.

15. **Every year, more Royal typewriters are bought in America than any other brand**
     —(*Royal typewriters*) Royal Typewriter Co. Inc.

16. **First and foremost in microfilming since 1928**
     —Recordak Corp.

17. **First name in filing**
     —Oxford Filing Supply Co.

18. **First name in paper punches**
     —Mutual Products Co. Inc.

19. **For those who must make best impressions**
     —(*typewriter supplies*) Shallcross Co.

20. **Get your man, no waiting, no walking**
     —Dictograph Products Corp.

21. **Hermes means Swissmanship . . . a step beyond craftsmanship**
     —Paillard Inc.

22. **Holding better business with better business forms**
     —Baltimore Salesbook.

23. **IBM . . . Dedicated to the office: where it is now and where it will be**
     —IBM.

24. **Innovation is what makes Supreme supreme**
     —(*files*) Supreme Equipment & Systems Corp.

25. **Insure clerical efficiency and profit protection, use multiple copy forms**
     —Malady & MacLauchlan.

26. **Insure your profits, use Stimpson products**
     —(*Stimpson computing scale*).

27. **Lifetime office equipment**
     —Shaw-Walker Co.

28. **Look and listen**
     —Fairchild-Wood Visaphone Corp.

29. **Look to Eberhard Faber for the finest . . . first!**
     —Eberhard Faber.

30. **Machines should work. People should think**
     —IBM.

81. OFFICE EQUIPMENT AND SUPPLIES *cont.*

31. **Make no mistake about figurework: call Friden**
—Friden Div., Singer Co.

32. **Many typewriters in one**
—Hammond Typewriter Co.

33. **Master of mathematics**
—Marchant Calculating Machine Co.

34. **Modern business forms for modern business systems**
—Baltimore Salesbook.

35. **Most modern of lightweight typewriters**
—Royal Typewriter Co. Inc.

36. **Precision typewriters**
—Olympia Div., Inter-Continental Trading Corp.

37. **Push the button and run**
—Diebold Safe Co.

38. **Put errors out of business**
—Victor Computer Corp.

39. **Puts its quality in writing**
—Eberhard Faber.

40. **Puts you ahead in offset duplicating**
—(*Kodak Ektalith*) Eastman Kodak Co.

41. **Record systems that talk facts fast**
—(*filing system*) Diebold Safe Co.

42. **Specialists in filing supplies and equipment since 1894**
—The Weis Mfg. Co.

43. **Speed. Simplicity. Versatility.**
—(*business machines*) Dura Corp.

44. **The choice when you want quality, too**
—All-Steel Equipment Inc.

45. **The company of specialists**
—(*filing equipment*) Watson Mfg. Co. Inc.

46. **The company with the "know-how"**
—Metropolitan Furniture Adjusters.

47. **"The finest pads have purple bindings"**
—The Universal Pad and Tablet Corp.

48. **The first name in business systems**
—Remington Rand.

49. **The machine to count on**
—(*Ohner adding machine*).

50. **The machine you will eventually buy**
—(*Underwood typewriters*) Olivetti Corp.

81. **OFFICE EQUIPMENT AND SUPPLIES** *cont.*

51. **The name indicates the quality**
—Keener Rubber Inc.

52. **The quick brown fox**
—SCM Corp.

53. **The retailer's line**
—National Blank Book Co.

54. **"The right business form for every form of business"**
—Moore Business Forms Inc.

55. **The safe investment**
—Gary Safe Co.

56. **The touch of tomorrow in office living**
—The Globe-Wernicke Co.

57. **The trend to dictaphone swings on**
—Columbia Graphophone Co.

58. **The world's safest safe**
—Safe-Cabinet Co.

59. **They express success**
—Cutler Desk Co.

60. **Think**
—IBM.

61. **Think ahead—think SCM**
—SCM Corp.

62. **Typewriter leader of the world**
—(*Underwood typewriters*) Olivetti Corp.

63. **We pave the way to save delay**
—(*office equipment*) Currier Mfg. Co.

64. **Wherever money is handled or records are kept**
—National Cash Register Co.

65. **World's largest manufacturer of staplers for home and office**
—Swingline Inc.

66. **World-wide voice writing service**
—(*Ediphone*).

67. **You can pay more, but you can't buy more**
—(*Royal typewriters*) Royal Typewriter Co. Inc.

68. **You're better off with Bostitch**
—Bostitch Div., Textron Inc.

69. **Your one-source solution to every filing problem**
—The Smead Mfg. Co.

OUTBOARD MOTORS ... See **16.** BOATS AND BOATING EQUIPMENT

OUTDOOR SUPPLIES...See **98. RECREATIONAL
EQUIPMENT, 108. SPORTING GOODS**

OVENS...See **60. HOME APPLIANCES AND EQUIPMENT**

P

82. PAINT AND PAINTING SUPPLIES
   See also **65. INTERIOR DECORATION**

1. **A better-wearing brush for every use**
    —Osborn Mfg. Co.

2. **A liquid finish that decorates as it preserves**
    —Colfanite Prods. Co.

3. **A little varnish makes a lot of difference**
    —O'Brien Varnish Co.

4. **All you need to know about paint**
    —Sherwin-Williams Co.

5. **A right kind for every purpose**
    —Montauk Paint Mfg. Co.

6. **Beautifies before your eyes**
    —Hilo Varnish Corp.

7. **Beauty by the brushful**
    —Brooklyn Varnish Co.

8. **Beauty that protects**
    —Atlantic Drier & Varnish Co.

9. **Between wood and weather**
    —Jewel Paint & Varnish Co.

10. **Carter White Lead is concentrated paint**
    —Carter White Lead Co.

11. **Challenges the elements**
    —(*paint*) S. Friedman & Sons.

12. **Clean around the world**
    —Empire Brush Works.

13. **Coatings, colors and chemicals for industry**
    —Sherwin-Williams Co.

14. **Color or white you're always right with Martin-
Senour**
    —(*paints*) Martin-Senour Co.

15. **Cover the earth**
    —Sherwin-Williams Co.

82. **PAINT AND PAINTING SUPPLIES** *cont.*

16. **Decorates as it preserves**
—Colophane Corp.

17. **Defies the elements**
—Flint Paint & Varnish Ltd.

18. **Don't put it off, put it on**
—Kuehnle-Wilson.

19. **Dries before your eyes**
—Hilo Varnish Corp.

20. **Easy to thin, tint and spread**
—Carter White Lead Co.

21. **Eats paint and bites varnish**
—(*Bulldog paint remover*) W. M. Barr & Co.

22. **Everlastingly beautiful**
—Egyptian Lacquer Mfg. Co.

23. **Everywhere on everything**
—(*paints, varnishes*) Glidden Co.

24. **First because it lasts**
—(*paint*) Felton, Sibley & Co.

25. **First on the finish**
—(*Regatta yacht paints*) Baltimore Copper Paint.

26. **Fresh paint is better paint**
—Bradley & Vrooman Co.

27. **Good paint costs nothing**
—Bradley & Vrooman Co.

28. **Heelproof, marproof and waterproof**
—(*varnish*) Pratt & Lambert.

29. **Hit it with a hammer**
—(*varnish*) Pratt & Lambert.

30. **Houses painted with Carter White Lead stay painted**
—Carter White Lead Co.

31. **If you prize it . . . Krylonize it**
—Krylon Dept., Borden Chemical Co.

32. **It costs less to pay more**
—John Lucas & Co.

33. **It's all in the finish**
—American Cyanamid Co.

34. **It's the finish that counts**
—(*paint*) Carpenter-Morton.

35. **Laughs at time**
—Du Pont.

82. PAINT AND PAINTING SUPPLIES *cont.*

36. **Light in the darkest corner**
—Gardco Paint Co.

37. **Makes every house a White House**
—Mineral Refining & Chemical Co.

38. **Makes your house a White House**
—O'Brien Varnish Co.

39. **Make the home look cheerful**
—Dozier & Gay Paint Co.

40. **Master of color since 1858**
—Martin-Senour Co.

41. **More years to the gallon**
—(*Dutch Boy*) Pigments and Chemicals Div., National Lead Co.

42. **Neighbor tells neighbor**
—Foy Paint Co.

43. **No one knows wood as good**
—(*Formby's wood finishing products*) Richardson-Merrell Inc.

44. **No other paint stays brighter under the sun**
—Felton, Sibley & Co.

45. **Pacemaker in paints**
—Glidden Co.

46. **Paint for profit instead of expense**
—Nason Paint Co.

47. **Paint is at its best only when it is properly mixed**
—Springfield Tool Co.

48. **Paints and disinfects, dries white**
—Carbola Chemical Co.

49. **Paint saves the surface, zinc saves the paint**
—New Jersey Zinc Co.

50. **Paints fast as man walks**
—Tennessee Tool Works.

51. **Paint with the two bears, it wears**
—Baer Bros.

52. **Proved throughout industry for over 40 years**
—Rust-Oleum Corp.

53. **Right on the floor**
—Jewel Paint & Varnish Co.

54. **Rust-Oleum quality runs deep**
—Rust-Oleum Corp.

55. **Save the surface and you save all**
—Paint and Varnish Association.

82. **PAINT AND PAINTING SUPPLIES** *cont.*

56. **Shows only the reflection**
—(*varnish*) Pratt & Lambert.

57. **Simply brush it on**
—(*Kyanize*) Boston Varnish Co.

58. **Since 1910, America's No. 1 scratchproof wood finish**
—Minwax Co.

59. **Start with the finish**
—(*paint products*) I. F. Laucks Inc.

60. **Stops rust!**
—Rust-Oleum Corp.

61. **Tested in the waters of the world**
—(*Valspar paints*) Valspar Corp.

62. **The bristles are sealed, the brush will last**
—Selastic Co.

63. **The coat with nine lives**
—National Paint Co.

64. **The disinfecting white paint**
—Carbola Chemical Co.

65. **The king of shine for surface fine**
—F. F. Horst Co.

66. **The lacquer finish that stays new**
—Zapon Co.

67. **The lead with the spread**
—Carter White Lead Co.

68. **The lifelong paint**
—Murphy Paint Co.

69. **The life of paint**
—(*linseed oil*) Spencer, Kellogg & Sons.

70. **The maker who is proud of what he makes, uses Egyptian Lacquer**
—Egyptian Lacquer Mfg. Co.

71. **There's a Jewel for every use**
—(*paints, varnishes*) Wadsworth Howland.

72. **The sign of paint success**
—Acme White Lead & Color Works.

73. **The skill is in the can**
—(*paint*) Bradley & Vrooman Co.

74. **The varnish invulnerable**
—The Morgan Co.

75. **The varnish that won't turn white**
—Valentine & Co.

82. PAINT AND PAINTING SUPPLIES *cont.*

76. **Tough as the hide of a rhinoceros**
                    —(*Rhino enamel*).

77. **Voice of quality**
                    —(*paints, varnishes*) Martin-Senour Co.

78. **Waterproofs everything**
                    —Atlantic Drier & Varnish Co.

79. **Weather armour for homes**
                    —(*Valspar paints*) Valspar Corp.

80. **Weathers our weather**
                    —Utley Paint Co.

81. **Whiter, finer, softer, Carter**
                    —Carter White Lead Co.

82. **You may dent the wood, but the varnish won't crack**
                    —Pratt & Lambert.

83. **You're money ahead when you paint with White Lead**
                    —Lead Industries Association.

83. PAPER PRODUCTS
        See also **68. KITCHEN PRODUCTS AND UTENSILS,**
        81. OFFICE EQUIPMENT AND SUPPLIES

1. **A dynamic force with paper**
                    —Kimberly-Clark Corp.

2. **A good business letter is always better ... written on a Gilbert paper**
                    —Gilbert Paper Co.

3. **All that the name implies**
                    —Stationers Loose Leaf Co.

4. **Always correct**
                    —Eaton Paper Co.

5. **Always makes good printing better**
                    —Northwest Paper Co.

6. **America's cities are Bergstrom's forests**
                    —Bergstrom Paper Co.

7. **America's most used products away from home**
                    —Fort Howard Paper Co.

8. **An international value**
                    —International Paper Co.

9. **Any mail for me?**
                    —Eaton Paper Co.

10. **Ask your printer, he KNOWS papers**
                    —Rising Paper Co.

83. **PAPER PRODUCTS** *cont.*

11. **A world of paper products—from frozen food cartons to printing paper**
—International Paper Co.

12. **Brain-built boxes**
—Milwaukee Paper Co.

13. **Chillicothe papers make the best impressions**
—Chillicothe Paper Co.

14. **Consider paper**
—Champion Papers Inc.

15. **Consider the power of paper used with imagination**
—Champion Papers Inc.

16. **Constant excellence of product**
—S. D. Warren Co.

17. **Famous for generations**
—Eaton Paper Co.

18. **Fine letter papers**
—Eaton Paper Co.

19. **First in carbonless papers**
—National Cash Register Co.

20. **Flat folded stationery**
—American Register Co.

21. **For better results, always use the best paper**
—Nekoosa-Edwards Paper Co.

22. **For every business need**
—Nekoosa-Edwards Paper Co.

23. **For every occasion of social correspondence**
—White & Wyckoff Mfg. Co.

24. **For serving . . . it's Erving**
—Erving Paper Mills.

25. **For special industrial requirements**
—Nekoosa-Edwards Paper Co.

26. **For those letters you owe**
—White & Wyckoff Mfg. Co.

27. **Functional papers**
—Thilmany Pulp and Paper Co.

28. **Good papers for good business**
—W. C. Hamilton & Sons.

29. **H & D delivers the goods**
—(*shipping boxes*) Hinde & Dauch Paper Co.

30. **If it's an envelope, we make it**
—Northwest Envelope Co.

83. PAPER PRODUCTS *cont.*

31. **If it's paper**
—Dillard Paper Co.

32. **If you can't fight, you can write**
—Eaton Paper Co.

33. **Invest in memory insurance**
—Standard Diary Co.

34. **Lace papers of character**
—Milwaukee Lace Paper Co.

35. **Lasting impressions begin with Oxford papers**
—Oxford Paper Co.

36. **Letters are victory weapons**
—Eaton Paper Co.

37. **Look for the watermark**
—Hammermill Paper Co.

38. **Made strong to work hard**
—(*tissues, paper towels*) Scott Paper Co.

39. **No "peeping Tom" can decipher the contents**
—(*window envelopes*) Magill-Weinsheimer.

40. **No. 1 source of gummed papers**
—Dennison Mfg. Co.

41. **Our word of honor to the public**
—Hammermill Paper Co.

42. **Packed to attract**
—Hinde & Dauch Paper Co.

43. **Paper engineering**
—Paper Center Inc.

44. **Paper is part of the picture**
—Strathmore Paper Co.

45. **Paper makers of America**
—The Mead Corp.

46. **Papers for the printer who puts quality first**
—Scott Paper Co.

47. **Pioneers in polycoatings**
—H. P. Smith Paper Co.

48. **Put it on paper**
—Wahl Co.

49. **Quality papers for industry since 1889**
—Sonoco Products Co.

50. **ScotTissue is soft as old linen**
—Scott Paper Co.

51. **Scott makes it better for you**
—Scott Paper Co.

83. **PAPER PRODUCTS** *cont.*

52. **"Send me a man who reads!"**
—International Paper Co.

53. **Simplicity and a Strathmore paper**
—Strathmore Paper Co.

54. **Softness is Northern**
—*(toilet paper)* Marathon Div., American Can Co.

55. **That reminds me**
—Ever Ready Calendar Mfg. Co.

56. **The aristocrat of tissues**
—Golden Fleece Corp.

57. **The best known name in paper**
—Hammermill Paper Co.

58. **The complete paper house**
—Chicago Paper Co.

59. **The correct writing paper**
—Eaton, Crane & Pike Co.

60. **The envelope is the first impression**
—Standard Envelope Mfg. Co.

61. **The first name in American stationery**
—Puritan Stationery Co.

62. **The house that service built**
—Continental Envelope Corp.

63. **The line with the carbon gripper**
—Codo Mfg. Co.

64. **The mark that is a message in itself**
—*(Crane's papers)* Crane & Co. Inc.

65. **The merchant-minded mill with variety and reliability**
—Riegel Paper Corp.

66. **The nation's business paper**
—Howard Paper Co.

67. **The nation's printing papers**
—Howard Paper Mills Div., St. Regis Paper Co.

68. **The new way to do prestige advertising**
—Strathmore Paper Co.

69. **The paper people**
—Brown Co.

70. **The quicker picker upper**
—*(Bounty paper towels)* Procter & Gamble Co.

71. **There is no ration on letters**
—Eaton Paper Co.

83. PAPER PRODUCTS *cont.*

72. **The right paper for the purpose**
—American Writing Paper Co.

73. **They last longer**
—National Fiberstock Envelope Co.

74. **To get a letter, write a letter**
—Eaton Paper Co.

75. **Transos envelope the world**
—Transo Envelope Co.

76. **Two layers of softness ... and one is purest white**
—(*Aurora toilet paper*) Marathon Div., American Can Co.

77. **Value-engineered papers from the mills of Mosinee**
—Mosinee Paper Mills Co.

78. **We believe in the power of the printed word**
—International Paper Co.

79. **Westvaco inspirations lead to new value in paper and packaging**
—Westvaco Corp.

80. **Whenever good impressions count, rely on carbonizing papers by Schweitzer**
—Peter J. Schweitzer Div., Kimberly-Clark Corp.

81. **Where departments unite to make service right**
—Schwabacher-Frey Stationery Co.

82. **Where quality is traditional**
—Old Colony Envelope Co.

83. **World's largest manufacturer of fine carbonizing papers**
—Peter J. Schweitzer Div., Kimberly-Clark Corp.

84. **Write often, write cheerfully, WRITE**
—Eaton Paper Co.

85. **Writing papers that create an impression**
—Montag, Inc., Div. Westab Inc.

86. **Writing paper that welcomes the pen**
—White & Wyckoff Mfg. Co.

87. **Your letterhead is the voice of your business**
—Rag Content Paper Mfrs.

88. **Your printer's performance starts with fine papers**
—Crocker Hamilton Papers Inc.

89. **You save with paper**
—Universal Paper Products Co.

PENCILS ... See **126. WRITING INSTRUMENTS**

PENS ... See **126. WRITING INSTRUMENTS**

84. **PERFUMES AND FRAGRANCES**
See also **12.** BATH ACCESSORIES, **32.** COSMETICS,
104. SHAVING SUPPLIES, **116.** TOILETRIES

1. **A new talc with a new odor**
—Pompeian Inc.

2. **Anything can happen when you wear Fame**
—Parfums Corday Inc.

3. **As different from all other perfumes as you are from all other women**
—(*Emir*) Dana Perfumes Corp.

4. **Be swept away to another world**
—(*Senchal perfume*) Charles of the Ritz Group Ltd.

5. **Cherished as one of the world's seven great fragrances**
—(*Intimate*) Revlon Inc.

6. **Deliberate witchery**
—(*Menace perfume*) Evyan Ltd.

7. **England's choicest lavender**
—Potter & Moore.

8. **Every woman alive wants Chanel No. 5**
—Chanel Inc.

9. **Fashions in fragrance**
—Roger & Gallet.

10. **For high moments in distinguished living**
—Lucieu Lelong Parfums Corp.

11. **For the woman who dares to be different**
—(*Emeraude*) Coty Div., Chas. Pfizer and Co. Inc.

12. **High fashion in fragrance from France**
—Carven Parfums.

13. **Indispensable to the creative perfumer**
—(*Dow aromatics*) Dow Chemical Co.

14. **It's all in fun**
—(*Skylark fragrance*).

15. **Languid splendour set to fragrance**
—(*Lentheric*) Yardley of London Inc.

16. **Perfumes of youth**
—Cheramy Inc.

17. **Potent essence of desire to touch**
—(*White Shoulders perfume*) Evyan Ltd.

18. **Prelude to adventure**
—(*Gay Diversion perfume*) Evyan Ltd.

84. PERFUMES AND FRAGRANCES *cont.*

19. **Promise her anything but give her Arpege**
    —Lanvin-Charles of the Ritz Inc.

20. **Spirited new scent of the sixties**
    —(*Richard Hudnut Sportsman*) Warner-Lambert Pharmaceutical Co.

21. **Surround your life with fragrance**
    —Mary Chess.

22. **The American symbol of feminine charm**
    —House of Tre-Jur.

23. **The daytime fragrance**
    —(*Lentheric*) Yardley of London Inc.

24. **The fashionable fragrance**
    —V. Vivaudou Inc.

25. **The 'forbidden' fragrance**
    —(*Tabu*) Dana Perfumes Corp.

26. **The fragrance of youth**
    —(*April Showers perfume*) Houbigant Inc.

27. **The gay-hearted fragrance**
    —Yardley of London Inc.

28. **The jewel of perfumes**
    —Ybry Inc.

29. **The line of least resistance**
    —House of Tre-Jur.

30. **The most treasured name in perfume**
    —Chanel Inc.

31. **The perfume of romance**
    —(*Chanel No. 22*) Chanel Inc.

32. **The perfume of the Egyptian queens**
    —Grenville Inc.

33. **Tussy really cares about the sorcery**
    —Lehn and Fink Consumer Products.

85. PERIODICALS AND NEWSPAPERS
See also **94.** PUBLISHING

1. **A brisk magazine of Parisian life**
   —*Paris Nights.*

2. **A business journal of furnishing and decoration**
   —*Good Furniture Magazine.*

3. **A business paper for the farm chemical industry**
   —*Crop Life.*

4. **A Clean Home newspaper**
   —*Press-Telegram*, Long Beach, California.

85. **PERIODICALS AND NEWSPAPERS** *cont.*

5. **A good newspaper**
—*Chicago American.*

6. **A human interest newspaper**
—*Evening Graphic*, New York.

7. **A journal for all who write**
—*Writer's Monthly.*

8. **A liberal church journal**
—*The Churchman.*

9. **A live picture tabloid newspaper for all the family**
—*Daily Mirror*, New York.

10. **All the facts, no opinion**
—*United States Daily*, Washington, D. C.

11. **All the flexibility of a newspaper with the coverage of a national magazine**
—*United States Daily*, Washington, D. C.

12. **All the news that's fit to print**
—*New York Times.*

13. **All the news while it is news**
—*Automotive Daily News.*

14. **Always first, always fair**
—*Indianapolis Star.*

15. **Always in the lead**
—*Detroit News.*

16. **Always reaches home**
—*Newark Evening News.*

17. **Always reliable**
—*Philadelphia Record.*

18. **A magazine for all Americans**
—*American Legion Monthly.*

19. **A magazine for farm and home**
—*Grain Growers Guide*, Winnipeg, Canada.

20. **A magazine for farm women**
—*Farmer's Wife.*

21. **A magazine for southern merchants**
—*Merchants Journal and Commerce.*

22. **A magazine of better merchandising for home finishing merchants**
—*Furniture Record.*

23. **A magazine of good, clean humor**
—*Laughter.*

24. **A magazine only a homemaker could love**
—*Family Circle.*

85. PERIODICALS AND NEWSPAPERS *cont.*

25. **A magazine with a mission**
—Hearst's Magazine.

26. **America's best read weekly**
—Liberty Magazine.

27. **America's biggest home magazine**
—Better Homes & Gardens.

28. **America's biggest selling weekly magazine**
—T. V. Guide.

29. **America's biggest suburban home market**
—Better Homes & Gardens.

30. **America's family magazine**
—Look.

31. **America's investment weekly**
—Financial World.

32. **America's largest dairy magazine**
—The Dairy Farmer.

33. **America's largest Polish newspaper**
—Everybody's Daily, Buffalo.

34. **America's leading power boat magazine**
—Power Boating.

35. **America's magazine for the outdoorsman**
—Field & Stream.

36. **America's most potent editorial force**
—Life.

37. **America's number one sportman's magazine**
—Field & Stream.

38. **America's quality magazine of discussion**
—Forum.

39. **A monthly business paper for chain store executives**
—Chain Store Age.

40. **A monthly magazine devoted to more profitable painting**
—American Painter and Decorator.

41. **An American institution**
—Saturday Evening Post.

42. **A national magazine for dry goods and department stores**
—Dry Goods Merchants Trade Journal.

43. **A national publication devoted to ship operation and shipbuilding**
—Marine Review.

85. **PERIODICALS AND NEWSPAPERS** *cont.*

44. A national publication for the wholesale grocer
                                                  —*Groceries.*

45. A newspaper for everybody; it goes into the home
                                          —*Boston Traveler.*

46. A newspaper for the makers of newspapers
                                            —*Fourth Estate.*

47. An illustrated weekly of current life
                                                  —*Outlook.*

48. An independent newspaper
                                  —*Los Angeles Evening Herald.*

49. An international daily newspaper
                            —*Christian Science Monitor,* Boston.

50. A powerful constructive force in the development of Georgia
                    —*The Georgian and Sunday American,* Atlanta.

51. A proud paper for a proud industry
                                              —*Tavern Weekly.*

52. As national as agriculture
                                                 —*Farm Life.*

53. A story-telling pictorial of stage, art, screen, humor
                                          —*American Beauties.*

54. Authority of industry, national and international
                                          —*Iron Trade Review.*

55. A weekly for the whole family
                                                   —*Liberty.*

56. A weekly magazine of philately
                                                    —*Stamps.*

57. A weekly newspaper of insurance
                                      —*National Underwriter.*

58. Baltimoreans don't say newspaper, they say SUNpaper
                                             —*Baltimore Sun.*

59. Best bet in Baltimore
                                                 —*News-Post.*

60. Better your home, better your living
                                            —*House Beautiful.*

61. Biggest, brightest, best magazine for boys in all the world
                                               —*American Boy.*

62. Biggest in the country
                                             —*Farm Journal.*

85. PERIODICALS AND NEWSPAPERS *cont.*

63. **Canada's greatest newspaper**
—Montreal Daily Star.

64. **Canada's national farm journal**
—Family Herald and Weekly Star.

65. **Canada's national magazine**
—Maclean's Magazine.

66. **Canada's national newspaper**
—Toronto Globe.

67. **Capitalist tool**
—Forbes.

68. **Central Pennsylvania's greatest daily**
—Harrisburg Telegraph.

69. **Chicago's best and cleanest paper**
—Evening Post.

70. **Chicago's only illustrated tabloid newspaper**
—Illustrated News.

71. **Chronicle of current Masonic events**
—Square and Compass.

72. **Class magazine in a class by itself**
—Harper's Bazaar.

73. **Covers Spokane and the Spokane country like the sunshine**
—Spokesman-Review.

74. **Covers the country intensively**
—American Press Association.

75. **Dallas is the door to Texas**
—Dallas Morning News.

76. **"Dedicated to serving the families of the West and Hawaii . . . no one else"**
—Sunset.

77. **Deep in the heart of Dixie**
—Commercial Appeal and *Evening Appeal,* Memphis.

78. **Detroit's home newspaper**
—Detroit News.

79. **Devoted to the best interests of South Florida**
—Palm Beach Times.

80. **Dominate Philadelphia**
—The Bulletin.

81. **Don't say "paper," say "Star"**
—St. Louis Star.

82. **Each week the facts add up to success**
—Sports Illustrated.

85. **PERIODICALS AND NEWSPAPERS** *cont.*

83. **Edited by yachtsmen for yachtsmen**
—Yachting.

84. **Everything in Baltimore revolves around the Sun**
—Baltimore Sun.

85. **Fileworthy**
—Post-Dispatch, St. Louis, Mo.

86. **First, by merit**
—Milwaukee Journal.

87. **First for the South**
—Times-Picayune, New Orleans.

88. **First in Chicago**
—Daily News.

89. **First in Cleveland**
—Cleveland Press.

90. **First in Dayton, third in Ohio**
—Daily News.

91. **First in film news**
—Film Daily.

92. **First in the farm field**
—Farm Journal.

93. **First in the field**
—Moving Picture World.

94. **First magazine for women**
—McCall's.

95. **First to last, the truth: news, editorials, advertisements**
—Herald-Tribune, New York.

96. **Florida's great home daily**
—Tampa Daily Times.

97. **Florida's most important newspaper**
—Miami Herald.

98. **Follow the journal and you follow the oil industry**
—Oil and Gas Journal.

99. **For business people who think for themselves**
—(Inc. Magazine) Inc. Publishing Co.

100. **For busy business men**
—Forbes.

101. **For home lovers in cities, towns, and suburbs**
—Better Homes & Gardens.

102. **For more than 25 years the national magazine of the furniture trade**
—Furniture Record.

85. PERIODICALS AND NEWSPAPERS *cont.*

103. **For oil marketing**
                    —National Petroleum News.

104. **For the men in charge**
                    —Fortune.

105. **For the smart young woman**
                    —Mademoiselle.

106. **Fortune means business**
                    —Fortune Magazine.

107. **For you and your town**
                    —Kansas City Kansan.

108. **Founder of better homes in America**
                    —Delineator.

109. **Gateway to the Jewish market**
                    —Daily Forward, New York.

110. **Getting results in rural America is *Farm Journal's* business**
                    —Farm Journal.

111. **Give light and the people will find their own way**
                    —Scripps-Howard.

112. **Go as a travel adventurer**
                    —Travel Adventures.

113. **Goes home and stays home**
                    —Baltimore News-Post.

114. **Goes to the home, stays in the home**
                    —Cincinnati Enquirer.

115. **Greatest concentration in the world's richest farm region**
                    —Successful Farming.

116. **Great national shoes weekly**
                    —Boot and Shoe Recorder.

117. **Growing just like Atlanta**
                    —The Georgian and Sunday American, Atlanta.

118. **Hitch your wagon to a conteSTAR**
                    —National Contest Bulletin.

119. **If you love words, You'll love VERBATIM**
                    *—(*VERBATIM, *The Language Quarterly*) Laurence Urdang Inc.

120. **Important to important people**
                    —Advertising Age.

121. **Industry Spokesman to CPI management**
                    —Chemical Week.

85. PERIODICALS AND NEWSPAPERS *cont.*

122. In Philadelphia nearly everybody reads the Bulletin
—*Philadelphia Evening Bulletin.*

123. Iowa's greatest evening paper
—*Evening Tribune,* Des Moines.

124. Is the Telegram on your list?
—*World-Telegram,* New York.

125. It costs no more to reach the first million first
—*National Geographic Magazine.*

126. It is our business to help your business
—*Building Supply News.*

127. It pays to be in the news
—*Architectural and Engineering News.*

128. It's the life they lead, it's the book they read
—*Better Homes & Gardens.*

129. It takes Emotion to move merchandise ... Better Homes & Gardens is PERPETUAL EMOTION
—*Better Homes & Gardens.*

130. Largest daily circulation in Brooklyn of any Brooklyn newspaper
—*Brooklyn Standard Union.*

131. Largest evening circulation in America
—*Evening Journal,* New York.

132. Leading business and technical journal of the world in printing and allied industries
—*Inland Printer.*

133. Leading clay journal of the world
—*Brick and Clay Record.*

134. Leads among the leaders of today ... and tomorrow
—*Legion Magazine.*

135. Made to order for America's business farmer and his wife
—*Successful Farming.*

136. Magazine of the paper industry
—*Paper Trade Journal.*

137. Magazine of the radio trade
—*Radio Merchandising.*

138. Magazine of today and tomorrow
—*American.*

139. Management publication of the housing industry
—*House and Home.*

140. More than a magazine, a national institution
—*Maclean's Magazine,* Toronto.

85. PERIODICALS AND NEWSPAPERS *cont.*

141. **More than a magazine, an institution**
                              —Christian Herald.

142. **National magazine for mothers of infants**
                              —American Baby.

143. **National voice of the shoe trade**
                         —Boot and Shoe Recorder.

144. **National weekly newspaper devoted to the fraternal interpretation of the World's current events**
                         —The Fellowship Forum.

145. **Never underestimate the power of a woman**
                         —Ladies Home Journal.

146. **New England's greatest Sunday newspaper**
                         —Sunday Advertiser, Boston.

147. **News and management monthly of the graphic arts**
                         —Printing Magazine.

148. **News of consequence for people of consequence**
                    —U. S. News and World Report.

149. **New York's picture newspaper**
                              —Daily News.

150. **Nothing to serve but the public interest**
                         —Des Moines Capital.

151. **Ohio's greatest home daily**
                         —Columbus Dispatch.

152. **Oklahoma's greatest newspaper**
                              —Tulsa World.

153. **One hundred years young**
                         —Youth's Companion.

154. **One of America's great weeklies**
                              —Railway Age.

155. **One of the West's great newspapers**
                         —Oakland Tribune.

156. **Only one magazine edited for rural women exclusively**
                              —Farmer's Wife.

157. **On rearing children from crib to college**
                              —Parents.

158. **Our readers manage the country**
                         —Successful Farming.

159. **People have faith in *Reader's Digest***
                              —Reader's Digest.

160. **Power farming is profit farming**
                              —Power Farming.

85. PERIODICALS AND NEWSPAPERS *cont.*

161. **Practical poultry paper for practical poultry people**
—*American Poultry Advocate.*

162. **Predominant with the 18 to 30 age group**
—*Photoplay Magazine.*

163. **Prosperity follows the plow**
—Agricultural Publishers Association.

164. **Published in the heart of America: most prosperous district of the world**
—*Kansas City Post.*

165. **Published to promote good farming and right living**
—*Nor'West Farmer,* Winnipeg.

166. **Put your money where the market is**
—*Modern Machine Shop.*

167. **Reaches the mother through her child**
—*Child Life.*

168. **Reach her when home is on her mind**
—*American Home.*

169. **Reaching influential America**
—*United States Daily,* Washington, D. C.

170. **Read and preferred by construction men**
—*Construction Methods and Equipment.*

171. **Read Time and understand**
—(*Time magazine*) Time-Life Inc.

172. **Salt of the earth, the subscribers to Needlecraft, over one million of them**
—*Needlecraft Magazine.*

173. **San Francisco's leading evening newspaper**
—*San Francisco Call.*

174. **Saskatchewan's only farm magazine**
—*Saskatchewan Farmer,* Regina.

175. **Seattle's only morning newspaper**
—*Post Intelligencer.*

176. **Sell at the decision level**
—*Business Week.*

177. **Selling and advertising to business and industry**
—*Industrial Marketing.*

178. **Sell it in the all-day home newspaper**
—*New York Sunday American.*

179. **Sells hard wherever hardware sells**
—*Hardware Age.*

180. **So long as the rig is on the location**
—*Drilling.*

85. PERIODICALS AND NEWSPAPERS *cont.*

181. **South America's greatest newspaper**
     —*La Prensa.*

182. **Southern Ohio's greatest newspaper**
     —*Cincinnati Post.*

183. **Sports isn't just fun and games**
     —*Sports Illustrated.*

184. **Start enjoying life**
     —(*Life Magazine*) Time-Life Inc.

185. **Starts the day in Detroit**
     —*Free Press.*

186. **Start with the "heart" where farmers are worth 2 for 1**
     —*Successful Farming.*

187. **St. Louis' largest daily**
     —*Globe-Democrat.*

188. **Supreme in the laundry industry**
     —*Laundry Age.*

189. **Talk to the right people in the right places**
     —*Time.*

190. **Tell it in the morning, tell it in the *Philadelphia Inquirer***
     —*Philadelphia Inquirer.*

191. **Texas' oldest newspaper**
     —*Galveston News.*

192. **The aristocrat of music magazines**
     —*Singing.*

193. **The authority of the waterways**
     —*The Work Boat.*

194. **The automotive business paper**
     —*Motor*, New York.

195. **The automotive service shop magazine**
     —*Motor Service.*

196. **The best comedy in America**
     —*College Humor.*

197. **The best of the world's press**
     —*Woman's Digest.*

198. **The blue book of the trade**
     —*Tea & Coffee Trade Journal.*

199. **The Boy Scouts' magazine**
     —*Boys' Life.*

200. **The business magazine of the radio industry**
     —*Radio Retailing.*

85. PERIODICALS AND NEWSPAPERS *cont.*

201. The business management magazine
—*Dun's Review and Modern Industry.*

202. The business paper of the electrical industry since 1892
—*Electrical Record.*

203. The children's own magazine
—*Child Life.*

204. The child's magazine
—*John Martin's Book.*

205. The complete authority of packaging
—*Modern Packaging.*

206. The dairy paper of the New York City milk shed
—*Dairymen's League News.*

207. The dealer's own paper
—*Building Supply News.*

208. The dime that covers the world
—*News Week.*

209. The dominant newspaper of the Great Northwest
—*Minneapolis Tribune.*

210. The dominant newspaper of the rich Montreal and Quebec Province Market
—*La Presse.*

211. The dry goods daily
—*Daily News Record.*

212. The engineering journal of the industry
—*Oil Field Engineering.*

213. The engineering magazine
—*Industrial Management.*

214. The farmer's service station
—*Successful Farming.*

215. The farm paper of service
—*Michigan Business Farmer.*

216. The farm paper with a mission
—*American Farming.*

217. The farm weekly of largest circulation and most influence
—*Progressive Farmer.*

218. The fastest-growing newspaper and fastest-growing city in Texas
—*Houston Post-Dispatch.*

219. The first national newspaper network
—Metropolitan Newspapers, New York.

85. PERIODICALS AND NEWSPAPERS *cont.*

220. **The first really different magazine in a generation**
—*Interlude.*

221. **The gateway to the Chicago market**
—*Herald and Examiner.*

222. **The giant of the South**
—*Southern Agriculturist,* Nashville.

223. **The Globe sells Boston**
—*Boston Globe.*

224. **The great newspaper of the great southwest**
—*Los Angeles Examiner.*

225. **The grinding, polishing and buffing authority**
—*Abrasive Industry.*

226. **The happy medium**
—*Judge.*

227. **The home craft magazine**
—*People's Popular Monthly.*

228. **The home paper of the industrial worker and the farmer**
—*Industrial News.*

229. **The industry's marketplace**
—*Electronics.*

230. **The international authority on visual merchandising**
—*Display World.*

231. **The Jewish market at its best**
—*Workmen's Circle Call.*

232. **The Journal covers Dixie like the dew**
—*Atlanta Journal.*

233. **The journal of diagnosis and treatment**
—*Modern Medicine.*

234. **The key magazine of industry**
—*Manufacturers News.*

235. **The key to happiness and success in over a million farm homes**
—*Comfort Magazine.*

236. **The largest Catholic magazine in the world**
—*Columbia.*

237. **The leading journal of the Episcopal Church**
—*The Churchman.*

238. **The livest lumber journal on earth**
—*Gulf Coast Lumberman.*

85. PERIODICALS AND NEWSPAPERS *cont.*

239. The Louisiana-Mississippi farm paper
—Modern Farming, New Orleans.

240. The magazine farm families depend on
—Farm Journal.

241. The magazine farm people believe in
—Capper's Farmer.

242. The magazine for all manufacturing
—Factory.

243. The magazine for Milady
—Fashionable Dress.

244. The magazine for parents
—Children.

245. The magazine for professional builders
—NAHB Journal of Homebuilding.

246. The magazine of architectural technology
—Building Construction.

247. The magazine of a re-made world
—Red Book.

248. The magazine of broadcast advertising
—Sponsor.

249. The magazine of business
—System.

250. The magazine of business leaders around the world
—Fortune.

251. The magazine of management
—Factory.

252. The magazine of methods, personnel and equipment
—Administrative Management.

253. The magazine of opportunities
—Money Making.

254. The magazine of Romance
—McClure's.

255. The magazine of service
—The Rotarian.

256. The magazine of the American market
—Look.

257. The magazine of the fifth estate
—Photoplay.

258. The magazine of the hour
—Radio Age.

259. The magazine of the toiletries trade
—Good Looks Merchandising.

85. PERIODICALS AND NEWSPAPERS *cont.*

260. The magazine of Western living
—Sunset.

261. The magazine of world business
—International Management.

262. The magazine that brings the outdoors in
—Outdoor Recreation.

263. The magazine that grew up with the industry
—Frozen Foods Magazine.

264. The magazine that moves the men who move the merchandise
—Progressive Farmer.

265. The magazine women believe in
—Ladies Home Journal.

266. The man's magazine
—Beau.

267. The manufacturing and construction journal of the textile industry
—Cotton.

268. The market with the "rainbow round its shoulder"
—Pacific Rural Press and California Farmer, San Francisco.

269. The massive men's market in print
—True.

270. The minister's trade journal since 1899
—The Expositor.

271. The modern farm paper
—Country Gentleman.

272. The most important magazine to the world's most important people
—Time.

273. The most influential hardware paper
—Hardware Age.

274. The most useful magazine in metalworking
—American Machinist.

275. The national broadcast authority
—Radio Digest.

276. The national dairy farm magazine
—Hoard's Dairyman.

277. The national filling station magazine
—Gas Station Topics.

278. The national guide to motion pictures
—Photoplay Magazine.

85. **PERIODICALS AND NEWSPAPERS** *cont.*

279. **The national inspirational monthly for men and women who sell**
—Specialty Salesman Magazine.

280. **The national magazine of sports and recreation**
—Sportlife.

281. **The national magazine of the grocery trade**
—The Progressive Grocer.

282. **The national magazine of the hardware trade**
—Good Hardware.

283. **The national magazine with local influence**
—American Weekly.

284. **The national newspaper of marketing**
—Advertising Age.

285. **The national weekly**
—Collier's.

286. **The national weekly of programs and personalities**
—Radio Guide.

287. **The necessary two million**
—True Story.

288. **The news magazine of art**
—The Art Digest.

289. **The news of the day in the newsiest way**
—Daily Metal Trade.

290. **The newspaper of the buying population**
—Detroit Times.

291. **The news unbiased and unbossed**
—Ohio State Journal, Columbus.

292. **The newsweekly that separates fact from opinion**
—Newsweek.

293. **The no. 1 buy in the design field**
—Product Engineering.

294. **The no. 1 men's service magazine**
—Argosy.

295. **The Northwest's only weekly farm paper**
—The Farmer.

296. **The oldest farm paper in America**
—Southern Planter, Richmond.

297. **The Pacific coast magazine of motoring**
—Motor Land.

298. **The paper that blazes trade trails**
—New York Commercial.

85. PERIODICALS AND NEWSPAPERS *cont.*

299. The paper that IS England
—*Punch*, London.

300. The pioneer farm journal of Western Canada
—*Nor'West Farmer*, Winnipeg.

301. The plumbing and heating weekly
—*Domestic Engineering*.

302. The point of penetration to the shoe market
—*Boot and Shoe Recorder*.

303. The poultry authority
—*Poultry Tribune*.

304. The Printers' Ink of the dental profession
—*Oral Hygiene*.

305. The quality magazine of the boating field
—*Yachting*.

306. The quality magazine of the radio industry
—*Radio Broadcast*.

307. The real magazine of the small towns
—*American Woman*.

308. There's a difference in farm papers
—*Successful Farming*.

309. The retailer's daily newspaper
—*Women's Wear*.

310. The service magazine
—*Architecture*.

311. The South's greatest newspaper
—*Birmingham News*.

312. The South's greatest newspaper
—*Commercial Appeal*, Memphis.

313. The South's standard newspaper
—*Constitution*, Atlanta.

314. The spokesman for the independent paint dealer
—*Paint Logic*.

315. The Star is Kansas City and Kansas City is the Star
—*Kansas City Star*.

316. The state's greatest newspaper
—*Arizona Republican*, Phoenix.

317. The taste that sets the trend
—*Harper's Bazaar*.

318. The text book of the confectionery trade
—*Candy and Ice Cream*.

85. PERIODICALS AND NEWSPAPERS *cont.*

319. The three-cent quality medium of America's greatest market
> —*World,* New York.

320. The trade magazine for independents
> —*Tire Rebuilders News.*

321. The trade paper of the home
> —*Modern Priscilla,* Boston.

322. The trade paper of the tire industry
> —*Tires.*

323. The traveler's world
> —*Venture.*

324. The truth without courting favor or fearing condemnation
> —*Kansas City Post.*

325. The voice of authority
> —(*Business Week magazines*) McGraw-Hill Inc.

326. The voice of the master barber
> —*Barber's Journal.*

327. The weekly journal of the electrical industry
> —*Electrical World.*

328. The weekly news magazine
> —*Time.*

329. The West's great national magazine
> —*Sunset.*

330. The West's great paper
> —*Tribune,* Salt Lake City.

331. The world's greatest Catholic monthly
> —*Extension Magazine.*

332. The world's greatest industrial paper
> —*Iron Age.*

333. The world's greatest newspaper
> —*Chicago Tribune.*

334. The world's greatest travel publication
> —*Golfer's Magazine.*

335. The world's only tourists' magazine
> —*Tourist.*

336. The world's textile authority
> —*Textile World.*

337. They almost talk to you
> —*Pictorial Review.*

338. The young man's magazine
> —*Varsity.*

85. PERIODICALS AND NEWSPAPERS *cont.*

339. Three magazines in one
—*McCall's.*

340. Through pictures to inform
—*Life.*

341. Thundering power in the eye of the market
—*Metalworking News.*

342. To build a stronger nation
—*Physical Culture.*

343. True stories from real life
—*Smart Set.*

344. What's happening. In business. To business.
—*Nation's Business.*

345. Where advertising pays it stays—and grows
—*Boston Herald.*

346. Where important people turn to say important things
—*American Magazine.*

347. Where quality makes sense
—*House Beautiful.*

348. Where telling the world means selling the world
—*Life International.*

349. While there is Life there is hope
—*Life.*

350. With youth, first impressions last
—*Scholastic Magazines.*

351. World's best seller
—*Reader's Digest.*

352. World's largest newspaper
—*Times,* Los Angeles.

353. World's outstanding boxing magazine
—*The Ring.*

354. Written so you can understand it
—*Popular Mechanics.*

355. You ought to be in pictures
—*Parade Magazine.*

86. PEST CONTROL
See also **22. CHEMICAL INDUSTRY, 69. LAWN AND GARDEN PRODUCTS**

1. Better products for man's best friend
—(*Sergeant's*) Polk Miller Products Co.

2. Dead moths eat no holes
—(*Moth-Tox*).

86. **PEST CONTROL** *cont.*

   3. **Doesn't stun 'em, kills 'em**

                           —The Fly-Foon Co.

   4. **Don't get bit, get Flit**

                —*(insect spray)* Exxon Corp.

   5. **Double doom to flies and mosquitoes**

          —*(Fly-Ded insect spray)* Midway Chemical Co.

   6. **Guaranteed moth protection**

                           —The Lane Co.

   7. **It's bug tested**

          —*(Black Flag insect spray)* A. S. Boyle Co.

   8. **Kills ants in the nest**

             —*(Antrol)* Antrol Laboratories.

   9. **Kills bugs dead**

            —*(Raid)* S. C. Johnson & Son Inc.

  10. **Kills bugs wholesale**

               —Colonial Chemical Corp.

  11. **Kills them off and keeps them off**

     —*(Pulvex flea powder)* William Cooper & Nephews Inc.

  12. **Quick, Henry, the Flit**

                —*(insect spray)* Exxon Corp.

  13. **The clean way to kill dirty rats**

       —*(D-Con mouse and rat killer)* D-Con Co. Inc.

  14. **The moth is more destructive than the flame**

              —Keystone Chemical Co.

  15. **Wipe 'em out, don't stir 'em up**

       —*(Sergeant's flea powder)* Miller-Morton Co.

87. **PET FOOD AND PRODUCTS**

    See also **47. FOOD, MISCELLANEOUS, 86. PEST CONTROL**

   1. **A lopsided diet may ruin your canary's song**

                   —The R. T. French Co.

   2. **A song in every seed**

           —*(bird seed)* The R. T. French Co.

   3. **Dog food of champions**

     —*(Ken-L-Biskit)* Ken-L-Products Div., Quaker Oats Co.

   4. **From world leaders in nutrition**

            —*(Friskies)* Carnation Co.

   5. **Help make him all the dog he's meant to be**

     —*(Ken-L-Biskit)* Ken-L-Products Div., Quaker Oats Co.

   6. **Maker of America's number 1 cat food**

         —*(Puss 'n Boots)* Quaker Oats Co.

   7. **Makes its own gravy**

      —*(Gravy Train dog food)* General Foods Corp.

87.　**PET FOOD AND PRODUCTS** *cont.*

8.　**Nothing, but nothing will tear cats away**
　　　　　—(Friskies Buffet cat food) Carnation Co.

9.　**Nourishes every inch of your dog**
　　　　　—(Gaines dog food) General Foods Corp.

10.　**Our business is going to the dogs**
　　　　　—Champion Animal Food Co.

11.　**Pep for your pup**
　　　　　—Min-A-Gro Corp.

12.　**The complete family of dog and cat foods from the world leader in nutrition**
　　　　　—(Friskies) Carnation Co.

13.　**Their choice every time**
　　　　　—(dog food) Perfection Foods Co.

14.　**The taste your dog's been fishing for**
　　　　　—(Sea Dog dog food).

15.　**When it comes to cooking for dogs—Rival has no rival**
　　　　　—Rival Pet Foods Div., Associated Products, Inc.

16.　**Where better goldfish are grown**
　　　　　—Ozark Fisheries.

17.　**Your canary may be overfed, yet undernourished**
　　　　　—The R. T. French Co.

88.　**PETROLEUM PRODUCTS**
　　See also **9. AUTOMOTIVE SERVICE, 59. HEATING AND COOKING FUELS**

1.　**A great name in oil**
　　　　　—Sinclair Oil Corp.

2.　**America's most customer-minded oil company!**
　　　　　—Sunray DX Oil Co.

3.　**America's No. 1 gasoline**
　　　　　—Socony-Vacuum Co.

4.　**A natural resource company**
　　　　　—Cities Service Co.

5.　**An extra quart of lubrication in every gallon**
　　　　　—(motor oil) Quaker State Oil Refining Corp.

6.　**Be *sure* with Pure**
　　　　　—The Pure Oil Co.

7.　**Be thrifty, buy quality**
　　　　　—Valvoline Oil Co., Div. Ashland Oil and Refining Co.

8.　**Better ideas from UOP**
　　　　　—Universal Oil Products Co.

88. **PETROLEUM PRODUCTS** *cont.*

9. **Blue Sunoco, the Over-Drive Motor Fuel**
—Sun Oil Co.

10. **Does four jobs at once**
—(*motor oil*) Shell Oil Co.

11. **Economy gasoline**
—(*Tydol*) Tide Water Oil Co.

12. **Engine life preserver**
—(*motor oil*) Quaker State Oil Refining Corp.

13. **Finest anti-knock non-premium gasoline ever offered at no extra cost**
—Union Oil Co.

14. **Fire up with Firebird**
—The Pure Oil Co.

15. **First choice of experience**
—(*motor oil*) Quaker State Oil Refining Corp.

16. **First in resources/first in capability**
—Enco Div., Humble Oil and Refining Co.

17. **Flows fast, stays tough**
—Pennzoil Co.

18. **Food for speed**
—British Petroleum Co., London.

19. **For a change, try Sohio**
—Standard Oil Co. (Ohio).

20. **For good advice . . . and good products . . . depend on your Mobil dealer**
—Mobil Oil Corp.

21. **For quality you can *depend* on . . . *depend* on Skelgas**
—Skelly Oil Co.

22. **Full powered**
—(*Pomiac gasoline*) Winona Oil Co.

23. **Gasoline, not cut price guessoline**
—Sun Oil Co.

24. **Gives your engine an extra margin of safety**
—Pennzoil Co.

25. **Go *first class* . . . go Phillips 66**
—Phillips Petroleum Co.

26. **Gulf makes things run better**
—Gulf Oil Corp.

27. **Happy Motoring!**
—(*Conoco*) Continental Oil Co.

88. PETROLEUM PRODUCTS *cont.*

28. **Happy motoring**
—Exxon Corp. (formerly Standard Oil Co., New Jersey)

29. **Headquarters for lubricants and lubri-counsel**
—Davis-Howland Oil Corp.

30. **It makes a difference**
—(*Havoline motor oil*) Indian Refining Co.

31. **It pays to be particular about your oil**
—Wolf's Head Oil Refining Co. Inc.

32. **It's a life insurance policy for your engine**
—Valvoline Oil Co., Div. Ashland Oil and Refining Co.

33. **It's a lucky day for your car when you change to Quaker State Motor Oil**
—(*motor oil*) Quaker State Oil Refining Corp.

34. **Keeps your motor clean as a whistle**
—(*motor oil*) Sinclair Consolidated Oil Corp.

35. **Knock out that "knock"**
—Imperial Oil Co.

36. **Lubrication is a major factor in cost control**
—Texaco Inc.

37. **Makes a better motor, keeps your motor better**
—(*Hyvis motor oil*).

38. **Making petroleum do more things for more people**
—Atlantic Richfield Refining Co.

39. **Making things happen with petroleum energy**
—Atlantic Richfield Refining Co.

40. **Miles of smiles**
—Sherwood Bros.

41. **More power to you**
—National Refining Co.

42. **Oil that goes farther, faster, safer**
—Pennzoil Co.

43. **Perfection for new cars; protection for old cars**
—(*Veedol oil*) Getty Refining & Marketing Co.

44. **Pour smoothness into your motor**
—O'Neil Oil Co.

45. **Put a tiger in your tank**
—(*Enco*) Humble Oil and Refining Co.

46. **Puts wings on your car**
—(*Tydol*) Tide Water Oil Co.

47. **Quality … the best economy of all**
—Sun Oil Co.

88. **PETROLEUM PRODUCTS** *cont.*

48. **Quality you can count on**

—Exxon Corp.

49. **Quality you can trust**

—Crown Central Petroleum Corp.

50. **See what happens when you start using American ingenuity**

—Standard Oil Div., American Oil Co.

51. **STP is the racer's edge**

—(*STP oil treatment*) STP Corp.

52. **Superstar power for more car power**

—(*Texaco Super unleaded gasoline*) Texaco Inc.

53. **Take it slow, it's rarin' to go**

—(*N-tane*) Conoco Inc.

54. **The best that can be bought "a quarter a quart." Why pay more?**

—(*motor oil*) Hardwood Bros.

55. **The chevron—the sign of excellence**

—Standard Oil Co. of California.

56. **The choice of champions**

—(*motor oil*) Kendall Refining Co.

57. **The cream of them all**

—El Penn Motor Oil Co.

58. **The distilled motor oil**

—Sun Oil Co.

59. **The extra miles are free**

—Lion Oil Refining Co.

60. **The independent supplier for independents**

—Ashland Oil and Refining Co.

61. **The knock-out fuel, nox out nox**

—Canfield Oil Co.

62. **The oil of a million tests**

—National Refining Co.

63. **The one right oil for Ford cars**

—(*Ivaline-Foralyn*) Winona Oil Co.

64. **The pacemaker of gasolines**

—Texaco Inc.

65. **The pass word of the road**

—Sun Oil Co.

66. **There is no substitute for quality**

—Skelly Oil Co.

67. **There's power in every drop**

—Odol Corp.

88. PETROLEUM PRODUCTS *cont.*

68. **The utmost in lubrication**
—Skelly Oil Co.

69. **200 extra miles of lubrication**
—(*Motorite*) Union Oil Co.

70. **Unsurpassed to help your car last**
—(*motor oil*) Kendall Refining Co.

71. **We take better care of your car**
—Standard Oil Div., American Oil Co.

72. **Where research is planned with progress in mind**
—Universal Oil Products Co.

73. **Wherever shafts move**
—(*motor oil*) National Oil Co.

74. **World's finest petrochemical products**
—Gulf Oil Corp.

75. **World's first—world's finest**
—(*motor oil*) Valvoline Oil Co., Div. Ashland Oil and
Refining Co.

76. **World's most economical motor oil**
—Radbill Oil Co.

77. **Worth changing brands to get**
—The Pure Oil Co.

78. **You can be sure of Shell**
—Shell Oil Co.

79. **You can depend on it**
—National Oil Fuel Institute Inc.

80. **You *expect* more from Standard and you *get* it.**
—Standard Oil Div., American Oil Co.

81. **You need an oil this good**
—(*Quaker State motor oil*) Quaker State Oil Refining
Corp.

PHARMACEUTICAL PRODUCTS...See **35. DRUGS AND
REMEDIES**

PHONOGRAPHIC EQUIPMENT...See **5. AUDIO
EQUIPMENT**

PHONOGRAPHS...See **5. AUDIO EQUIPMENT**

89. **PHOTOGRAPHIC EQUIPMENT**
     See also **78.** MOVIES AND ENTERTAINMENT

1. **A famous camera from camera-famous West Germany**
    —Minox Corp.

2. **Bell and Howell brings out the expert in you (automatically!)**
    —Bell and Howell Co.

3. **Bell and Howell builds photographic instruments a little better than they really have to be**
    —Bell and Howell Co.

4. **Canon meets tomorrow's challenges today**
    —Canon Inc.

5. **Classics of optical precision**
    —(*Schneider lenses*) Burleigh Brooks Inc.

6. **Fine photography for 40 years**
    —Minolta Corp.

7. **. . . for a good look**
    —(*print paper*) Eastman Kodak Co.

8. **Forever yours**
    —(*snapshots*) Eastman Kodak Co.

9. **For superb personal movies**
    —(*film*) Bell & Howell Co.

10. **If it isn't an Eastman, it isn't a Kodak**
    —(*cameras*) Eastman Kodak Co.

11. **I'm gonna get you with the Kodak Disc**
    —(*Kodak Disc camera*) Eastman Kodak Co.

12. **It deserves to be preserved**
    —Dura Pictures Corp.

13. **Kodak as you go**
    —(*cameras*) Eastman Kodak Co.

14. **Life is a movie; Cine-Kodak gets it all**
    —(*movie cameras*) Eastman Kodak Co.

15. **One pictograph tells more than a thousand words**
    —Pictograph Corp.

16. **Only from the mind of Minolta**
    —(*Minolta X100 camera*) Minolta Corp.

17. **"Open me first"**
    —(*cameras*) Eastman Kodak Co.

18. **Perfection in projection since 1909**
    —(*projection screens*) Da-Lite Screen Co. Inc.

89. **PHOTOGRAPHIC EQUIPMENT** *cont.*

19. **Photographs live forever**
—Photographer's Association of America.

20. **Photographs tell the story**
—Photographer's Association of America.

21. **Say it with pictures**
—(*Stereopticon lantern slides*) E. A. Richter.

22. **Say it with pictures**
—Commercial Photo Service Co.

23. **Serving human progress through photography**
—Eastman Kodak Co.

24. **The camera you never leave at home**
—Minox Corp.

25. **The easy ones**
—Eastman Kodak Co.

26. **The more you learn about photography, the more you count on Kodak**
—Eastman Kodak Co.

27. **The name quality made famous**
—(*Zoom 8*) Minolta Corp.

28. **The negative for positive results**
—(*Gevaert film*).

29. **The snapshots you'll want tomorrow, you must take today**
—Eastman Kodak Co.

30. **The state of the art now**
—(*Pentax cameras*) The Pentax Corporation.

31. **Today's finest—designed for tomorrow's needs**
—(*Topcon Super D*) Charles Beseler Co.

32. **We take the world's greatest pictures**
—(*Nikon cameras*) Nikon Inc.

33. **With Graflex, the payoff is in the picture**
—Graflex Inc.

34. **World's second largest manufacturer of cameras and films**
—Agfa-Gevaert Inc.

35. **You press the button, we do the rest**
—Eastman Kodak Co.

PHYSICAL FITNESS . . . See **56. HEALTH AND FITNESS**

PIPES . . . See **105. SMOKING ACCESSORIES**

PLUMBING SUPPLIES . . . See **55. HARDWARE**

90. **POLITICAL ISSUES**
      See also **91.** PRESIDENTIAL CAMPAIGNS

1. **Hell no, we won't go**
> —Vietnam-era draft resisters.

2. *Liberté! Égalité! Fraternité!*
> —rallying cry of the French Revolution.

3. **Never Again**
      —Jewish exhortation forswearing a recurrence of the Nazi
> Holocaust.

4. **No Taxation without Representation**
> —U.S. rallying cry during Revolutionary War.

5. **Remember Pearl Harbor**
> —U.S. rallying cry during World War II.

6. **Remember the *Maine***
> —U.S. rallying cry during Spanish-American War.

7. **We shall overcome**
> —in support of civil rights for black Americans.

POTTERY ... See **52.** GLASS AND CERAMICS

91. **PRESIDENTIAL CAMPAIGNS**
      See also **90.** POLITICAL ISSUES

1. **Abraham Lincoln/Honest Abe of the West**
> —Abraham Lincoln (*Rep.*), 1860.

2. **A chicken in every pot, a car in every garage**
> —Herbert Hoover (*Rep.*), 1928.

3. **A choice for a change**
> —Barry Goldwater (*Rep.*), 1964.

4. **A choice—not an echo**
> —Barry Goldwater (*Rep.*), 1964.

5. **Adlai and Estes are the bestes**
      —Adlai Stevenson (*Dem.*), 1956, with Estes Kefauver, the
> vice-presidential candidate.

6. **Adlai likes *me***
> —Adlai Stevenson (*Dem.*), 1956.

7. **A halo shines as bright as day around the head of
      Henry Clay**
> —Henry Clay (*Whig*), 1844.

8. **A house divided against itself cannot stand**
> —Abraham Lincoln (*Rep.*), 1860.

9. **All I have left is a vote for Willkie**
> —Wendell Willkie (*Rep.*), 1940.

91. **PRESIDENTIAL CAMPAIGNS** *cont.*

10. **All the way with Adlai**
—Adlai Stevenson (*Dem.*), 1952.

11. **All the way with J. F. K.**
—John F. Kennedy (*Dem.*), 1960.

12. **All the way with LBJ**
—Lyndon B. Johnson (*Dem.*), 1964.

13. **Al Smith: up from the street**
—Alfred E. Smith (*Dem.*), 1928.

14. **A man of character**
—Calvin Coolidge (*Rep.*), 1924.

15. **America always**
—Charles Evans Hughes (*Rep.*), 1916.

16. **America calls another Roosevelt**
—Franklin Delano Roosevelt (*Dem.*), 1932.

17. **America cannot be bought**
—Alf Landon (*Rep.*), 1936 (referring to heavy spending of
the New Deal).

18. **America efficient**
—Charles Evans Hughes (*Rep.*), 1916.

19. **America for Americans—no free trade**
—Benjamin Harrison (*Rep.*), 1888.

20. **America needs Eisenhower—Draft Ike in '56**
—Dwight D. Eisenhower (*Rep.*), 1956.

21. **American Republicans! Beware of foreign influence!
Our country first**
—American Republican Party, a nativist, anti-Catholic
group which supported Henry Clay in the presidential
election of 1844.

22. **Americans must rule America**
—the American Party ("Know-Nothings"), 1856.

23. **American wages for American workingmen**
—Benjamin Harrison (*Rep.*), 1888.

24. **A public office is a public trust**
—Grover Cleveland (*Dem.*), 1884.

25. **A republic can have no colonies**
—William Jennings Bryan (*Dem.*), 1900.

26. **A square deal all around**
—Theodore Roosevelt (*Progressive or Bull Moose party*),
1912.

27. **A superb soldier—a model president**
—Gen. Winfield S. Hancock (*Dem.*), 1880.

91.　**PRESIDENTIAL CAMPAIGNS** *cont.*

28.　**A uniform & sound currency: the Sub Treasury**
　　　—Martin Van Buren (*Dem.*), 1840 (referring to Democratic
　　　　　support of the Independent Treasury System).

29.　**Avoid rebel rule**
　　　　　　　　—Rutherford B. Hayes (*Rep.*), 1876.

30.　**A vote for Coolidge is a vote for chaos**
　　　　　　　　　—John W. Davis (*Dem.*), 1924.

31.　**A vote for Roosevelt is a vote against Hoover**
　　　　　　　—Franklin Delano Roosevelt (*Dem.*), 1932.

32.　**Away with the New Deal and its inefficiency**
　　　　　　　　—Wendell Willkie (*Rep.*), 1940.

33.　**Back to Independence**
　　　—Thomas E. Dewey (*Rep.*), 1948 (Independence, Missouri,
　　　　　was the home of his opponent, Harry Truman).

34.　**Back to normalcy**
　　　　　　　　　—Warren G. Harding (*Rep.*), 1920.

35.　**Better a part-time president than a full-time phony**
　　　—Dwight D. Eisenhower (*Rep.*), 1956 (in answer to
　　　concerns raised about Eisenhower's health following a
　　　heart attack he suffered during his first administration).

36.　**Betty's husband for president in '76**
　　　—Gerald R. Ford (*Rep.*), 1976 (Ford's wife, Betty, enjoyed
　　　　　a high level of public support).

37.　**Be vigilant and watchful that internal dissensions
　　　destroy not your prosperity**
　　　　　　　　—Millard Fillmore (*Whig*), 1856.

38.　**Bring back prosperity with a Republican vote**
　　　　　　　　—Herbert Hoover (*Rep.*), 1932.

39.　**Bring us together**
　　　　　　　　—Richard M. Nixon (*Rep.*), 1968.

40.　**Clean house with Dewey**
　　　　　　　　—Thomas E. Dewey (*Rep.*), 1948.

41.　**Cleveland runs well in England**
　　　—Benjamin Harrison (*Rep.*), 1888 (implying that
　　　Cleveland's tariff policies would benefit England while
　　　　　　　　injuring the United States).

42.　**Come home, America**
　　　　　　　　—George McGovern (*Dem.*), 1972.

43.　**Congress has no more power to make a SLAVE
　　　than to make a KING**
　　　—Martin Van Buren (*Free Soil Party*), 1848 (in opposition
　　　to the expansion of slavery into additional states or
　　　　　　　　　territories).

91. PRESIDENTIAL CAMPAIGNS *cont.*

44. Constitution and Union
—James Buchanan (*Dem.*), 1856.

45. Constitution and Union
—John Bell (*Constitutional Union party*), 1860.

46. Coolidge and Dawes—Full dinner pail
—Calvin Coolidge (*Rep.*), 1924.

47. Coolidge and prosperity
—Calvin Coolidge (*Rep.*), 1924.

48. Coolidge of course
—Calvin Coolidge (*Rep.*), 1924.

49. Coolidge or chaos
—Calvin Coolidge (*Rep.*), 1924 (referring to the possibility that lack of a decisive win by one of the three candidates would force a settlement of the election by the House of Representatives).

50. Courage, confidence, and Coolidge
—Calvin Coolidge (*Rep.*), 1924.

51. Crime, corruption, Communism, and Korea
—Dwight D. Eisenhower (*Rep.*), 1952.

52. Cuba must be ours
—John C. Breckinridge (*Southern Dem.*), 1860 (acquisition of Cuba was seen as a means of expanding slave territory and thus the political power of the slave states).

53. Deeds—not words
—Calvin Coolidge (*Rep.*), 1924.

54. Defeat the New Deal and its reckless spending
—Alf Landon (*Rep.*), 1936.

55. Dem-Ike-Crats for Eisenhower
—Dwight D. Eisenhower (*Rep.*), 1952.

56. Democracy is good enough for all
—John C. Breckinridge (*Southern Dem.*), 1860.

57. Democracy prevails throughout the union
—Andrew Jackson (*Dem.-Rep.*), 1828.

58. Democracy, reform, and one presidential term
—William Henry Harrison (*Whig*), 1840 (expressing opposition to re-election of Van Buren for a second term).

59. Democracy stands for bimetallism not monometallism, people not trusts, republic not empire
—William Jennings Bryan (*Dem.*), 1900.

60. Dewey is due in '48
—Thomas E. Dewey (*Rep.*), 1948.

91. PRESIDENTIAL CAMPAIGNS *cont.*

61. **Dewey or don't we?**
> —Thomas E. Dewey (*Rep.*), 1944.

62. **Dewey the racket buster—New Deal buster**
> —Thomas E. Dewey (*Rep.*), 1948.

63. **Don't bump a good man out of the White House**
> —Dwight D. Eisenhower (*Rep.*), 1956.

64. **Don't let them take it away**
> —Harry S. Truman (*Dem.*), 1948.

65. **Don't swap horses in the middle of the stream**
> —Abraham Lincoln (*National Unionist*), 1864 (the election took place in the midst of the Civil War).

66. **Don't swap horses—stand by Hoover**
> —Herbert Hoover (*Rep.*), 1932.

67. **Don't tear down the Statue of Liberty! Refuse dictatorship**
> —Wendell Willkie (*Rep.*), 1940 (referring to the issue of Roosevelt's candidacy for a third presidential term).

68. **Down with free trade**
> —James G. Blaine (*Rep.*), 1884.

69. **Drop LeMay on Hanoi**
> —1968, expressing opposition to George C. Wallace and Gen. Curtis C. LeMay, the candidates of the American Independent Party (LeMay had taken a very aggressive position on the bombing of North Vietnam's capital).

70. **Dump the Hump**
> —1968 (expressing opposition to Hubert H. Humphrey (*Dem*)).

71. **Elect me president—freedom and the reunion of states shall be permanently established**
> —John C. Frémont (*Radical Rep.*), 1864.

72. **Elect none but natives to office**
> —American Republican Party, a nativist, anti-Catholic group which supported Henry Clay in the presidential election of 1844.

73. **Equal & full protection to American industry**
> —Henry Clay (*Whig*), 1836.

74. **Equal rights to all, special privileges to none**
> —William Jennings Bryan (*Dem.*), 1900.

75. **Experience counts: vote Nixon—Lodge for a better America**
> —Richard M. Nixon (*Rep.*), 1960, with Henry Cabot Lodge as the vice-presidential candidate.

91. **PRESIDENTIAL CAMPAIGNS** *cont.*

76. **Fear God and take your own part**
—Charles Evans Hughes (*Rep.*), 1916.

77. **54° 40′ or Fight**
—James K. Polk (*Dem.*), 1844.

78. **First in the hearts of his soldiers**
—George McClellan (*Dem.*), 1864 (who was commander of Union forces until his removal by Lincoln).
—Ulysses S. Grant (*Nat. Rep.*), 1868.

79. **For freedom—Four Freedoms**
—Franklin Delano Roosevelt (*Dem.*), 1944 (referring to his enunciation of ideals for international order).

80. **For God for home and native land—the saloon must go**
—Clinton B. Fisk (*Prohibition party*), 1888.

81. **For the love of Ike vote Republican**
—Dwight D. Eisenhower (*Rep.*), 1952.

82. **Forward together**
—Richard M. Nixon (*Rep.*), 1968.

83. **4-H-Club—help hustle Harry home**
—Thomas E. Dewey (*Rep.*), 1948.

84. **Four more Roosevelt lucky years**
—Franklin Delano Roosevelt (*Dem.*), 1936.

85. **Four More Years**
—Richard M. Nixon (*Rep.*), 1972.

86. **Freedom to all**
—Abraham Lincoln (*Rep.*), 1860.

87. **Freedom to all men—war for the Union**
—Abraham Lincoln (*National Unionist*), 1864.

88. **Free homes for the homeless**
—Abraham Lincoln (*Rep.*), 1860 (referring to Republican support for land grants from the public lands).

89. **Free Kansas—and the Union**
—John C. Frémont (*Rep.*), 1856 (opposing the issue of the extension of slavery into Kansas).

90. **Free land, free speech and free men**
—Abraham Lincoln (*Rep.*), 1860.

91. **Free soil, free men, free speech, and Frémont**
—John C. Frémont (*Rep.*), 1856 (referring to Republican opposition to the expansion of slavery).

92. **Free soil, free speech, free labor, and free men**
—Martin Van Buren (*Free Soil Party*), 1848 (expressing the Free Soil Party's opposition to expansion of slavery into additional states or territories).

91. PRESIDENTIAL CAMPAIGNS *cont.*

93. **Free soil to a free people**
      —Martin Van Buren (*Free Soil Party*), 1848.

94. **Free speech. Free press. Frémont**
      —John C. Frémont (*Radical Rep.*), 1864.

95. **Free territory for a free people**
      —Abraham Lincoln (*Rep.*), 1860.

96. **From the Tow Path to the White House**
      —James Garfield (*Rep.*), 1880 (referring to Garfield's work as a mule driver on the tow paths of the Ohio Canal in his youth).

97. **General amnesty—uniform currency—equal taxes and equal rights**
      —Horatio Seymour (*Dem.*), 1868.

98. **General Taylor never surrenders**
      —Gen. Zachary Taylor (*Whig*), 1848.

99. **Gen. Frank Pierce the statesman & soldier**
      —Franklin Pierce (*Dem.*), 1852.

100. **Gen. Winfield Scott—first in war, first in peace**
      —Gen. Winfield Scott (*Whig*), 1852.

101. **Give-'em-Hell Harry**
      —Harry S. Truman (*Dem.*), 1948.

102. **Give 'em Jessie**
      —John C. Frémont (*Rep.*), 1856 (referring to the candidate's wife, Jessie Benton Frémont).

103. **Give the presidency back to the people**
      —Pre-nomination campaign of Eugene McCarthy (*Dem.*), 1968.

104. **God would not permit a Roman Catholic to be president of the United States**
      —Anti-Smith slogan from the campaign of 1928 (candidate Alfred E. Smith (*Dem.*) was a Catholic).

105. **Goldwater for president—victory over Communism**
      —Barry Goldwater (*Rep.*), 1964.

106. **Goldwater in 1864**
      —Lyndon B. Johnson (*Dem.*), 1964 (his opponent, Barry Goldwater, was often labeled a reactionary).

107. **Good Republicans don't bolt the party ticket**
      —William Howard Taft (*Rep.*), 1912 (referring to Theodore Roosevelt's break from the Republican party to run as a Progressive).

91.　PRESIDENTIAL CAMPAIGNS *cont.*

108. **Go 4th to win the war**
—Franklin Delano Roosevelt (*Dem.*), 1944 (Roosevelt was seeking a fourth term in an election which took place during World War II).

109. **Governments derive their just powers from the consent of the governed**
—William Jennings Bryan (*Dem.*), 1900.

110. **Grandfather's hat**
—Benjamin Harrison (*Rep.*), 1888 (referring to Harrison's grandfather, former president William Henry Harrison).

111. **Grand old party, good as gold**
—William McKinley (*Rep.*), 1896.

112. **Grandpa's pants won't fit Benny**
—Grover Cleveland (*Dem.*), 1888 (the grandfather of Cleveland's opponent, Benjamin Harrison, was former president William Henry Harrison).

113. **Grantism means poor people made poorer**
—Samuel J. Tilden (*Dem.*), 1876.

114. **Grant us another term**
—Ulysses S. Grant (*Rep.*), 1872.

115. **Greeley–Brown & reconciliation**
—Horace Greeley (*Liberal Rep.*), 1872 (the Liberal Republicans favored ending reconstruction in the South).

116. **Grover, Grover, all is over**
—Benjamin Harrison (*Rep.*), 1892.

117. **Had enough?**
—Dwight D. Eisenhower (*Rep.*), 1952.

118. **Harding and prosperity**
—Warren G. Harding (*Rep.*), 1920.

119. **Hari-kari with Barry**
—Lyndon B. Johnson (*Dem.*), 1964 (referring to his Republican opponent, Barry Goldwater).

120. **Hayes, hard money and hard times**
—Samuel J. Tilden (*Dem.*), 1876.

121. **He kept us out of suffrage**
—Anti-Wilson slogan in presidential campaign of 1916 (referring to Wilson's opposition to women's suffrage).

122. **He kept us out of war**
—Woodrow Wilson (*Dem.*), 1916 (stating the major theme of Wilson's campaign, which stressed his success in avoiding direct involvement in the European war which began in 1914).

91. PRESIDENTIAL CAMPAIGNS *cont.*

123. **He leaves the plough to save his country**
—William Henry Harrison (*Whig*), 1840.

124. **Hello Central, give us Teddy**
—Theodore Roosevelt (*Rep.*), 1904 (referring to telephone service, then a new and novel feature of American life).

125. **Help Barry stamp out peace**
—Lyndon B. Johnson (*Dem.*), 1964 (referring to his Republican opponent, Barry Goldwater).

126. **Help Hoover help business**
—Herbert Hoover (*Rep.*), 1928.

127. **Henry Clay for his country feels but Polk would stop our water wheels**
—Henry Clay (*Whig*), 1844 (Clay was portrayed as a friend of industry because of his support for a protective tariff).

128. **Henry Clay, the champion of a protective tariff**
—Henry Clay (*Whig*), 1844.

129. **He proved the pen mightier than the sword**
—Woodrow Wilson (*Dem.*), 1916 (referring to Wilson's successful efforts to maintain American neutrality in the European war which began in 1914).

130. **He's all right**
—John P. St. John (*Prohibition party*), 1884.

131. **He saved America**
—Franklin Delano Roosevelt (*Dem.*), 1936.

132. **Hold on to Hoover**
—Herbert Hoover (*Rep.*), 1932.

133. **Honest days with Davis**
—John W. Davis (*Dem.*), 1924 (alluding to scandals uncovered in the Harding administration).

134. **Honest money, honest government**
—Rutherford B. Hayes (*Rep.*), 1876.

135. **Honesty at home—honor abroad**
—John W. Davis (*Dem.*), 1924.

136. **Honor where honor's due to the hero of Tippecanoe**
—William Henry Harrison (*Whig*), 1840 (referring to Harrison's victory over the Indians at the Battle of Tippecanoe (1811) in Indiana Territory).

137. **Hoover and happiness**
—Herbert Hoover (*Rep.*), 1932.

138. **Hoover and happiness or Smith and soup houses: which shall it be?**
—Herbert Hoover (*Rep.*), 1928.

91. PRESIDENTIAL CAMPAIGNS *cont.*

139. Horrors of war—blessings of peace
—George McClellan (*Dem.*), 1864 (the Democratic platform supported a negotiated end to the Civil War).

140. I ask no favors & I shrink from no responsibility
—Gen. Zachary Taylor (*Whig*), 1848.

141. If I am re-elected president slavery must be abolished with the reunion of states
—Abraham Lincoln (*National Unionist*), 1864.

142. If you liked Hitler, you'll love Wallace
—expressing opposition to the American Independent candidate, George C. Wallace, 1968.

143. If you want a change to better times, vote for Grover Cleveland
—Grover Cleveland (*Dem.*), 1884.

144. I intend to fight it out on this line if it takes all summer
—Ulysses S. Grant (*Nat. Rep.*), 1868 (quoting one of Grant's wartime statements).

145. I like Ike
—Dwight D. Eisenhower (*Rep.*), 1952.

146. I like Ike but I am going to vote for Stevenson
—Adlai Stevenson (*Dem.*), 1952.

147. I'm extremely fond of Barry
—Barry Goldwater (*Rep.*), 1964.

148. I'm on the water wagon now
—in support of continuing Prohibition, presidential campaign of 1932.

149. I'm safe with Ike
—Dwight D. Eisenhower (*Rep.*), 1956.

150. In Hoover we trusted, now we are busted
—Franklin Delano Roosevelt (*Dem.*), 1932.

151. In your guts you know he's nuts
—Lyndon B. Johnson (*Dem.*), 1964 (referring to his Republican opponent, Barry Goldwater).

152. In your heart you know he's right
—Barry Goldwater (*Rep.*), 1964.

153. I propose to move immediately on your works
—Ulysses S. Grant (*Nat. Rep.*), 1868 (quoting a statement made by Grant at Fort Donelson during the Civil War).

154. It might have been worse
—Herbert Hoover (*Rep.*), 1932 (referring to economic depression which began under Hoover).

91. PRESIDENTIAL CAMPAIGNS *cont.*

155. **It's McKinley we trust to keep our machines free of rust**
—William McKinley (*Rep.*), 1896.

156. **James Buchanan—no sectionalism**
—James Buchanan (*Dem.*), 1856.

157. **John and Jessie forever! Hurrah!**
—John C. Frémont (*Rep.*), 1856 (Jessie Benton Frémont was the candidate's wife).

158. **Keep cool with Coolidge**
—Calvin Coolidge (*Rep.*), 1924.

159. **Keep faith with our sons—bring America into the League of Nations—Vote for Cox and Roosevelt**
—James M. Cox (*Dem.*), 1920 (his running mate was Franklin Delano Roosevelt).

160. **Labor is king**
—James G. Blaine (*Rep.*), 1884.

161. **Land for the landless**
—Abraham Lincoln (*Rep.*), 1860 (referring to Republican support for land grants from the public lands).

162. **LBJ for the USA**
—Lyndon B. Johnson (*Dem.*), 1964.

163. **Leadership for a change**
—Jimmy Carter (*Dem.*), 1976.

164. **Leadership for the '50's**
—expressing opposition to the Republican candidate, Richard M. Nixon, 1968.

165. **Leadership for the '60's**
—John F. Kennedy (*Dem.*), 1960.

166. **Let liberty be national & slavery sectional**
—Abraham Lincoln (*Rep.*), 1860.

167. **Let's be done with wiggle and wobble**
—Warren G. Harding (*Rep.*), 1920.

168. **Let's clean house with Ike and Dick**
—Dwight D. Eisenhower (*Rep.*), 1952 (Eisenhower's running mate was Richard M. Nixon).

169. **Let's get another deck**
—Alf Landon (*Rep.*), 1936.

170. **Let's keep what we've got: prosperity didn't just happen**
—Herbert Hoover (*Rep.*), 1928.

171. **Let the people rule**
—William Jennings Bryan (*Dem.*), 1908.

91. PRESIDENTIAL CAMPAIGNS *cont.*

172. **Let the people speak**
—George C. Wallace (*American Independent*), 1968.

173. **Let us continue**
—Lyndon B. Johnson (*Dem.*), 1964.

174. **Let us encourage our own manufactures**
—Henry Clay (*Whig*), 1844 (referring to his support of a protective tariff).

175. **Let us have a clean sweep**
—Samuel J. Tilden (*Dem.*), 1876 (advocating civil service reform in the wake of the scandals under the Grant administration).

176. **Let us have peace**
—Ulysses S. Grant (*Nat. Rep.*), 1868 (urging resolution of issues remaining from the Civil War).

177. **Let well enough alone**
—Calvin Coolidge (*Rep.*), 1924.

178. **Liberty, equality, and fraternity**
—Horace Greeley (*Liberal Rep.*), 1872.

179. **Liberty, equality and no king**
—Pro-Jefferson forces in 1796 (referring to allegedly monarchical tendencies of George Washington and, by implication, the Federalist Party).

180. **Liberty, equality & fraternity, the cardinal principles of true democracy**
—Gen. Lewis Cass (*Dem.*), 1848.

181. **Liberty, justice and humanity**
—William Jennings Bryan (*Dem.*), 1900.

182. **Liberty, union, and victory**
—Abraham Lincoln (*National Unionist*), 1864.

183. **Lincoln and liberty—good for another heat**
—Abraham Lincoln (*National Unionist*), 1864.

184. **Loyalty shall govern what loyalty has preserved**
—Ulysses S. Grant (*Nat. Rep.*), 1868.

185. **Make America happen again**
—George McGovern (*Dem.*), 1972.

186. **Make the White House the Dwight House**
—Dwight D. Eisenhower (*Rep.*), 1952.

187. **Match him**
—Ulysses S. Grant (*Nat. Rep.*), 1868.

188. **McCarthy and peace in '68**
—Pre-nomination campaign of Eugene McCarthy (*Dem.*), 1968.

91. PRESIDENTIAL CAMPAIGNS *cont.*

189. McKinley and the full dinner pail
—William McKinley (*Rep.*), 1896.

190. Millard Fillmore for the whole country
—Millard Fillmore (*Whig*), 1856.

191. Millions for freedom—not one cent for slavery
—Abraham Lincoln (*Rep.*), 1860.

192. Mr. Nixon: how long will this new pose last?
—Anti-Nixon slogan expressing suspicion about the sincerity of the Republican candidate, Richard M. Nixon, 1968.

193. My brand's LBJ
—Lyndon B. Johnson (*Dem.*), 1964.

194. My favorite son is Stevenson
—Adlai Stevenson (*Dem.*), 1952.

195. My pick is Dick
—Richard M. Nixon (*Rep.*), 1960.

196. New leadership—Kennedy and Johnson
—John F. Kennedy (*Dem.*), 1960 (with Lyndon B. Johnson as the vice-presidential candidate).

197. Nixon and Spiro = zero
—Hubert H. Humphrey (*Dem.*), 1968 (referring to the Republican candidates, Richard M. Nixon and Spiro Agnew).

198. Nix on Ike
—Adlai Stevenson (*Dem.*), 1952 (Richard M. Nixon was the running mate of Eisenhower, "Ike").

199. Nix on Nixon
—John F. Kennedy (*Dem.*), 1960 (running against Richard M. Nixon).

200. Nixon now more than ever
—Richard M. Nixon (*Rep.*), 1972.

201. Nixon's the one
—Richard M. Nixon (*Rep.*), 1968.

202. No beer, no work
—Anti-Prohibition, campaign of 1932.

203. No British pauper wages for Americans
—James G. Blaine (*Rep.*), 1884 (referring to the Republican credo that a protective tariff helped to elevate the wages of laborers).

204. No compromise with armed rebels—may the Union flourish
—Abraham Lincoln (*National Unionist*), 1864.

91. PRESIDENTIAL CAMPAIGNS *cont.*

205. No compromise with traitors
—Abraham Lincoln (*National Unionist*), 1864.

206. No crown for Roosevelt
—Wendell Willkie (*Rep.*), 1940 (reflecting concern about Roosevelt's power, as he was seeking an unprecedented third presidential term).

207. No crown of thorns, no cross of gold
—William Jennings Bryan (*Dem.*), 1896 and 1900 (from a famous quote in a speech given by Bryan).

208. No emancipation, no miscegenation, no confiscation, no subjugation
—George McClellan (*Dem.*), 1864.

209. No fourth term either
—Wendell Willkie (*Rep.*), 1940 (referring to Roosevelt's candidacy for a third presidential term).

210. No Franklin the First
—Wendell Willkie (*Rep.*), 1940 (reflecting fears of the power Roosevelt would gain from a third term as president).

211. No man is good three times
—Wendell Willkie (*Rep.*), 1940 (referring to Roosevelt's candidacy for a third presidential term).

212. No more fireside chats
—Wendell Willkie (*Rep.*), 1940 (referring to Roosevelt's broadcast messages to the American people).

213. No more slave states and no more slave territory
—Martin Van Buren (*Free Soil Party*), 1848.

214. No more slave teritory
—Abraham Lincoln (*Rep.*), 1860.

215. No North, no South, but the whole country
—Millard Fillmore (*Whig*), 1856.

216. No North, no South, no East, no West, nothing but the Union
—John Bell (*Constitutional Unionist*), 1860.

217. No North—no South—the Union inseperable
—Horatio Seymour (*Dem.*), 1868.

218. No submission to the North
—John C. Breckinridge (*Southern Dem.*), 1860.

219. No substitute for experience
—Richard M. Nixon (*Rep.*), 1960.

220. Off the rocks with Landon and Knox
—Alf Landon (*Rep.*), 1936 (Knox was Landon's running mate).

91. PRESIDENTIAL CAMPAIGNS *cont.*

221. **Old Abe removed McClellan—we'll now remove Old Abe**
—George McClellan (*Dem.*), 1864 (Lincoln had previously removed McClellan from command of the Union army).

222. **One country, one flag**
—William McKinley (*Rep.*), 1900.

223. **One flag and one Union now and forever**
—George McClellan (*Dem.*), 1864.

224. **One man rule**
—Thomas E. Dewey (*Rep.*), 1944 (referring to the issue of Roosevelt's fourth-term candidacy).

225. **On the right track with Jack**
—John F. Kennedy (*Dem.*), 1960.

226. **Our centennial president**
—Rutherford B. Hayes (*Rep.*), 1876.

227. **Our country and our rights**
—John C. Breckinridge (*Southern Dem.*), 1860.

228. **Our country needs Roosevelt for another term**
—Theodore Roosevelt (*Progressive or Bull Moose party*), 1912.

229. **Our Dewey Special is due**
—Thomas E. Dewey (*Rep.*), 1948.

230. **Out of the red with Roosevelt**
—Franklin Delano Roosevelt (*Dem.*), 1932.

231. **Pass prosperity around**
—Theodore Roosevelt (*Progressive or Bull Moose party*), 1912.

232. **Patient of toil/Serene amidst alarms/Inflexible in faith/Invincible in arms**
—Ulysses S. Grant (*Nat. Rep.*), 1868.

233. **Peace and power with Eisenhower**
—Dwight D. Eisenhower (*Rep.*), 1952.

234. **Peace at any price. Peace and Union**
—Millard Fillmore (*Whig*), 1856.

235. **Peace, freedom, abundance**
—Henry A. Wallace (*Progressive*), 1948.

236. **Peace, jobs, and McGovern**
—George McGovern (*Dem.*), 1972.

237. **Peace with dishonor**
—Abraham Lincoln (*National Unionist*), 1864 (mocking the Democratic platform).

238. **Perhaps Roosevelt is all you deserve**
—Wendell Willkie (*Rep.*), 1940.

91. PRESIDENTIAL CAMPAIGNS *cont.*

239. Phooey on Dewey
—Harry S. Truman (*Dem.*), 1948.

240. Play safe with Hoover
—Herbert Hoover (*Rep.*), 1932.

241. Polk and Texas; Clay and no Texas
—James K. Polk (*Dem.*), 1844 (in which a major issue was expansion into Texas).

242. Polk and the Democratic Tariff of 1842
—James K. Polk (*Dem.*), 1844 (supporting the low-protection tariff law of 1842).

243. Polk, Dallas, Texas, Oregon, and the Tariff of '42
—James K. Polk (*Dem.*), 1844 (expressing support for territorial expansion into Texas and Oregon. Dallas was Polk's running mate).

244. Preserve home industries
—James G. Blaine (*Rep.*), 1884 (referring to Republican support of a high protective tariff).

245. Press onward—enlarge the boundaries of freedom—Young Hickory
—James K. Polk (*Dem.*), 1844 (referring to his support for territorial expansion, and the fact that he was portrayed as the successor to Andrew Jackson, "Old Hickory").

246. Principles, not men
—Gen. Lewis Cass (*Dem.*), 1848.

247. Proclaim liberty throughout the land
—Abraham Lincoln (*National Unionist*), 1864 (the Emancipation Proclamation had defined the abolition of slavery as a goal of the ongoing Civil War).

248. Prosperity at home, prestige abroad
—William McKinley (*Rep.*), 1900.

249. Prosperity is just around the corner
—Herbert Hoover (*Rep.*), 1932.

250. Protection and prosperity
—Benjamin Harrison (*Rep.*), 1888.

251. Protection for home industries
—Benjamin Harrison (*Rep.*), 1888 (Republicans supported a high protective tariff).

252. Protection to all at home and abroad
—Abraham Lincoln (*Rep.*), 1860 (the Republican platform included support for a higher tariff).

253. Protection to American industry—and no extension of slave power
—John C. Frémont (*Rep.*), 1856.

91. PRESIDENTIAL CAMPAIGNS *cont.*

254. **Protection to honest industry**
—Abraham Lincoln (*Rep.*), 1860 (alluding to Republican
support for a higher tariff).

255. **Protection to the working class is an assurance of
success**
—Henry Clay (*Whig*), 1844 (referring to benefits of a
protective tariff for the working man).

256. **Reduce taxation before taxation reduces us**
—Horatio Seymour (*Dem.*), 1868.

257. **Re-elect Roosevelt: his heart's with the people**
—Franklin Delano Roosevelt (*Dem.*), 1936.

258. **Reform is necessary in the civil service**
—Samuel J. Tilden (*Dem.*), 1876.

259. **Reform is necessary to establish a sound currency**
—Samuel J. Tilden (*Dem.*), 1876.

260. **Remember Hoover?**
—Franklin Delano Roosevelt (*Dem.*), 1936.

261. **Remember Teapot Dome**
—John W. Davis (*Dem.*), 1924 (referring to a major
scandal of the Harding administration).

262. **Repeal and prosperity**
—Anti-Prohibition, campaign of 1932.

263. **Repeat with Roosevelt or repent with Willkie**
—Franklin Delano Roosevelt (*Dem.*), 1940.

264. **Repudiate the repudiators**
—Ulysses S. Grant (*Nat. Rep.*), 1868 (referring to a plan
accepted by the Democratic platform to pay off certain
war debts with greenbacks rather than gold coin).

265. **Return the country to the people**
—Franklin Delano Roosevelt (*Dem.*), 1932.

266. **Roosevelt and protection**
—Theodore Roosevelt (*Rep.*), 1904.

267. **Roosevelt and recovery**
—Franklin Delano Roosevelt (*Dem.*), 1932.

268. **Roosevelt and repeal**
—Franklin Delano Roosevelt (*Dem.*), 1932, advocating an
end to Prohibition.

269. **Roosevelt for ex-president**
—Wendell Willkie (*Rep.*), 1940.

270. **Roosevelt—friend of the people**
—Franklin Delano Roosevelt (*Dem.*), 1932.

91. PRESIDENTIAL CAMPAIGNS *cont.*

271. **Roosevelt is robust**
—Franklin Delano Roosevelt (*Dem.*), 1932 (affirming Roosevelt's good health and vigor in spite of his crippling as a result of polio).

272. **Roosevelt? No! No! 1000 times NO!**
—Wendell Willkie (*Rep.*), 1940.

273. **Roosevelt or ruin**
—Franklin Delano Roosevelt (*Dem.*), 1932.

274. **Roosevelt's way is the American way, America needs Roosevelt**
—Franklin Delano Roosevelt (*Dem.*), 1940.

275. **Rough and Ready: the hero of Monterrey**
—Gen. Zachary Taylor (*Whig*), 1848 (referring to his leadership in the Mexican War; Taylor's informal mode of dress earned him the nickname "Old Rough and Ready").

276. **Rum, Romanism, and Rebellion**
—Grover Cleveland (*Dem.*), 1884 (the opposing candidate was James G. Blaine, whose silence at a speech in which the Democratic party was associated with 'rum, Romanism and rebellion' seemed to contribute to his eventual loss).

277. **Safe and sane**
—William Howard Taft (*Rep.*), 1908.

278. **Safe and sane Cool-idge**
—Calvin Coolidge (*Rep.*), 1924.

279. **Safe on third**
—Franklin Delano Roosevelt (*Dem.*), 1940 (referring to Roosevelt's candidacy for a third term).

280. **Save America—don't save beer and wine**
—In support of continuing Prohibition, campaign of 1932.

281. **Save the Constitution—Thurmond for president**
—J. Strom Thurmond (*Dixiecrat Party*), 1948.

282. **Save what's left**
—Thomas E. Dewey (*Rep.*), 1948.

283. **Scott & Graham, union & constitution**
—Gen. Winfield Scott (*Whig*), 1852 (Graham was the vice-presidential candidate).

284. **Scratch a Democrat and you'll find a Rebel under his skin**
—Ulysses S. Grant (*Nat. Rep.*), 1868.

91. **PRESIDENTIAL CAMPAIGNS** *cont.*

285. **Segregation now, segregation tomorrow, and segregation forever**
—George C. Wallace (*American Independent*), 1968.

286. **Shall the people rule?**
—William Jennings Bryan (*Dem.*), 1908.

287. **Sieg Heil ya'll**
—expressing opposition to the American Independent candidate, George C. Wallace, a Southerner who was sometimes labeled a fascist, 1968.

288. **Sixteen to one**
—William Jennings Bryan (*Dem.*), 1896 (the Democratic platform supported unlimited coinage of silver and gold at the ratio of 16 to 1).

289. **60 million people working—why change?**
—Harry S. Truman (*Dem.*), 1948.

290. **Slavery is a moral, social, and political wrong**
—Abraham Lincoln (*Rep.*), 1860.

291. **Soap! Soap! Blaine's only hope**
—Grover Cleveland (*Dem.*), 1884 (*Soap* referred to campaign donations).

292. **Son of his grandfather**
—Benjamin Harrison (*Rep.*), 1888 (grandson of former president William Henry Harrison).

293. **Sound money, expansion, protection, prosperity**
—Theodore Roosevelt (*Rep.*), 1904.

294. **Sound money—good markets**
—William McKinley (*Rep.*), 1900.

295. **Speed recovery—re-elect Hoover**
—Herbert Hoover (*Rep.*), 1932.

296. **Stand pat**
—Theodore Roosevelt (*Rep.*), 1904.

297. **Stand Pat with Nixon**
—Richard M. Nixon (*Rep.*), 1972 (Pat Nixon was the candidate's wife).

298. **Stand up for America—Wallace-LeMay**
—George C. Wallace (*American Independent*), 1968 (Curtis C. LeMay was the vice-presidential candidate).

299. **Steady America**
—Warren G. Harding (*Rep.*), 1920.

300. **Stick with Roosevelt**
—Franklin Delano Roosevelt (*Dem.*), 1940.

301. **Stop all unnecessary taxation**
—Grover Cleveland (*Dem.*), 1888.

91. PRESIDENTIAL CAMPAIGNS *cont.*

302. **Strike three F. D. you're out**
—Wendell Willkie (*Rep.*), 1940 (referring to Franklin D. Roosevelt's candidacy for a third presidential term).

303. **Support 'the Little Giant' who has proved himself the greatest statesman of the age**
—Stephen A. Douglas (*Dem.*), 1860.

304. **The advocate of the American System**
—Andrew Jackson (*Dem.-Rep.*), 1828 (referring to the "American System" of protective tariffs financing internal improvements, proposed by Henry Clay).

305. **The American way with Willkie**
—Wendell Willkie (*Rep.*), 1940.

306. **The Bank must perish**
—Andrew Jackson (*Dem.*), 1832 (referring to the Bank of the United States, opposed by Jackson as unconstitutional and undemocratic).

307. **The Big Stick**
—Theodore Roosevelt (*Rep.*), 1904 (from Roosevelt's admonition "Speak softly and carry a big stick").

308. **The boys in blue will see it through**
—Rutherford B. Hayes (*Rep.*), 1876 (associating the Republican party with the Northern cause the Civil War).

309. **The champion of internal improvements**
—Henry Clay (*Whig*), 1844 (Clay supported a high protective tariff to finance internal improvements).

310. **The champion of popular sovereignty**
—Stephen A. Douglas (*Dem.*), 1860 (Douglas advocated popular sovereignty as the means to resolve the issue of slavery in the territories).

311. **The champion of Republicanism and the American System**
—Henry Clay (*Nat. Rep.*), 1832 (the "American System" proposed a protective tariff to help finance internal improvements).

312. **The Constitution and the flag, one and inseparable, now and forever**
—William Jennings Bryan (*Dem.*), 1900.

313. **The Constitution and the freedom of the seas**
—Gen. Lewis Cass (*Dem.*), 1848 (in opposition to Britain's attempts to stop slave ships flying the American flag).

314. **The Constitution as it is, the Union as it was**
—George McClellan (*Dem.*), 1864.

91. PRESIDENTIAL CAMPAIGNS *cont.*

315. **The Constitution & Union forever**
$\qquad$ —Abraham Lincoln (*Rep.*), 1860.

316. **The country demands his re-election**
$\qquad$ —Martin Van Buren (*Dem.*), 1840.

317. **The firm and fearless advocate of democracy**
$\qquad$ —Martin Van Buren (*Dem.*), 1840.

318. **The flag of a republic forever, of an empire never**
$\qquad$ —William Jennings Bryan (*Dem.*), 1900.

319. **The gallant & successful defender of New Orleans**
—Andrew Jackson (*Dem.-Rep.*), 1828 (referring to Jackson's heroism in the War of 1812).

320. **The great railsplitter of the West must & shall be our next president**
$\qquad$ —Abraham Lincoln (*Rep.*), 1860.

321. **The Happy Warrior**
$\qquad$ —Alfred E. Smith (*Dem.*), 1928.

322. **The hero of Buena Vista**
—Gen. Zachary Taylor (*Whig*), 1848 (referring to a major battle of the Mexican War).

323. **The honest old farmer of Chappaqua**
—Horace Greeley (*Liberal Rep.*), 1872 (Greeley owned a farm in Chappaqua, New York).

324. **The 'I' in Nixon stands for integrity**
$\qquad$ —Richard M. Nixon (*Rep.*), 1968.

325. **The log cabin candidate, the people's choice**
—William Henry Harrison (*Whig*), 1840 (portrayed as a humble man of the soil though actually descended from an elite Virginia family).

326. **The man of the hour**
$\qquad$ —William Howard Taft (*Rep.*), 1908.

327. **The man of the hour is Eisenhower**
$\qquad$ —Dwight D. Eisenhower (*Rep.*), 1952.

328. **The man of the hour—Woodrow Wilson**
$\qquad$ —Woodrow Wilson (*Dem.*), 1916.

329. **The man that can split rails can guide the ship of state**
$\qquad$ —Abraham Lincoln (*Rep.*), 1860.

330. **The men will need their horses to plow with**
—Ulysses S. Grant (*Nat. Rep.*), 1868 (from a statement made by Grant to General Lee at Appomatox).

331. **The mighty tower—Eisenhower**
$\qquad$ —Dwight D. Eisenhower (*Rep.*), 1956.

91. **PRESIDENTIAL CAMPAIGNS** *cont.*

332. **The Natick cobbler–the Galena tanner–there's nothing like leather**
—Ulysses S. Grant (*Rep.*), 1872 (Grant and his running mate, Henry Wilson, had both been involved in leatherwork earlier in their lives, the former in Galena, Ohio, the latter in Natick, Mass.).

333. **The nation needs fixin' with Nixon**
—Richard M. Nixon (*Rep.*), 1972.

334. **The nation needs Richard M. Nixon**
—Richard M. Nixon (*Rep.*), 1960.

335. **The new Nixon**
—Richard M. Nixon (*Rep.*), 1968 (Nixon was portrayed as a man who had undergone drastic and positive change since his defeat in the presidential election of 1960).

336. **The old red bandanna**
—Grover Cleveland (*Dem.*), 1888 (referring to the vice-presidential candidate, Allen G. Thurman, and his ever-present red bandanna).

337. **The party that saved the Union must rule it**
—Ulysses S. Grant (*Nat. Rep.*), 1868.

338. **The pen is mightier than the sword**
—Horace Greeley (Liberal Rep.), 1872 (Greeley was editor of the New York *Tribune).*

339. **The people against the bosses**
—William McKinley (*Rep.*), 1896.

340. **The principles & prudence of our forefathers**
—Martin Van Buren (*Dem.*), 1836.

341. **There's no indispensable man**
—Wendell Willkie (*Rep.*), 1940 (referring to his opponent, Franklin Delano Roosevelt, who was seeking an unprecedented third term as president).

342. **The Rocky Mountains echo back Frémont**
—John C. Frémont (*Rep.*), 1856 (referring to Frémont's exploits as an explorer).

343. **The same curency for the bondholder and the plowholder**
—Horatio Seymour (*Dem.*), 1868 (supporting the "Ohio idea" of paying certain war debts in greenbacks rather than gold coin).

344. **The star of the West**
—Henry Clay (*Whig*), 1844.

345. **The Territories must be free to the people**
—Abraham Lincoln (*Rep.*), 1860.

91. PRESIDENTIAL CAMPAIGNS *cont.*

346. **The Union must and shall be preserved**
—Andrew Jackson (*Dem.*), 1832 (referring to the nul-
lification controversy which tested the limits of state vs.
national power).
—John Bell (*Constitutional Unionist*), 1860.
—Stephen A. Douglas (*Dem.*), 1860.
—Abraham Lincoln (*National Unionist*), 1864.

347. **The Union now, the Union forever**
—Millard Fillmore (*Whig*), 1856.

348. **The union of Whigs for the sake of the Union**
—William Henry Harrison (*Whig*), 1840.

349. **The Union one and indivisable [*sic*]—the crisis
demands his election**
—James Buchanan (*Dem.*), 1856.

350. **The United States is rich enough to give us all a
farm**
—Abraham Lincoln (*Rep.*), 1860 (the Republican platform
supported land grants from public lands.

351. **The White House—no place for an old bachelor**
—John C. Frémont (*Rep.*), 1856 (his opponent, James
Buchanan, was a bachelor).

352. **The won't do Congress won't do**
—Harry S. Truman (*Dem.*), 1948.

353. **The worst is past**
—Herbert Hoover (*Rep.*), 1932 (referring to the economic
depression which began under Hoover).

354. **They understand what peace demands**
—Richard M. Nixon (*Rep.*), 1960.

355. **Think of America first**
—Warren G. Harding (*Rep.*), 1920 (expessing reaction
against Wilson's peace objectives).

356. **Three good terms deserve another**
—Franklin Delano Roosevelt (*Dem.*), 1944 (seeking a
fourth presidential term).

357. **$329**
—Gen. Winfield S. Hancock (*Dem.*), 1880 (referring to
profit allegedly made by the Republican candidate,
James Garfield, in the Crédit Mobilier scandal).

358. **Throw the spenders out**
—Franklin Delano Roosevelt (*Dem.*), 1932.

359. **Time for a change**
—Thomas E. Dewey (*Rep.*), 1944.

91. PRESIDENTIAL CAMPAIGNS *cont.*

360. **Time to swap horses—November 8th**
—George McClellan (*Dem.*), 1864.

361. **Tippecanoe and Morton too**
—Benjamin Harrison (*Rep.*), 1888 (Harrison was the grandson of former president William Henry Harrison, hero of Tippecanoe; Morton was B. Harrison's running mate).

362. **Tippecanoe and tariff, too**
—Benjamin Harrison (*Rep.*), 1888 (referring to his grandfather, William Henry Harrison, and to support for a high protective tariff).

363. **Tippecanoe and Tyler too**
—William Henry Harrison (*Whig*), 1840 (Harrison had won a victory over the Indians in the Battle of Tippecanoe (1811) in Indiana Territory; John Tyler was his running mate).

364. **Together—A new beginning**
—Ronald Reagan (*Rep.*), 1980.

365. **Tried and true Truman**
—Harry S. Truman (*Dem.*), 1948.

366. **Truman fights for human rights**
—Harry S. Truman (*Dem.*), 1948.

367. **Truman was screwy to build a porch for Dewey**
—Thomas E. Dewey (*Rep.*), 1948 (referring to improvements made on the White House during Truman's administration).

368. **Truth, justice and the Constitution**
—slogan of the Democratic National Convention of 1860, which was so divided it adjourned without agreeing on a presidential candidate.

369. **Twenty years of treason**
—Dwight D. Eisenhower (*Rep.*), 1952 (reflecting the viewpoint of right-wing Republicans who believed the U. S. government was under the influence of Communist sympathizers).

370. **Two good terms deserve another**
—Franklin Delano Roosevelt (*Dem.*), 1940 (referring to Roosevelt's candidacy for an unprecedented third term).

371. **Union and Constitution—preservation of the rights of the people**
—Horatio Seymour (*Dem.*), 1868.

372. **Union of States**
—John Bell (*Constitutional Unionist*), 1860.

91. PRESIDENTIAL CAMPAIGNS *cont.*

373. Universal amnesty and impartial suffrage
—Horace Greeley (*Liberal Rep.*), 1872 (referring to issues dealing with reconstruction in the South).

374. Unnecessary taxation is unjust taxation
—Grover Cleveland (*Dem.*), 1884 (Democrats supported lowering tariffs to reduce the surplus in the U. S. Treasury).

375. Untrammelled with party obligations
—Gen. Zachary Taylor (*Whig*), 1848.

376. Up with Alf, down with the alphabet
—Alf Landon (*Rep.*), 1936 (expressing opposition to numerous New Deal agencies and programs referred to by acronyms).

377. Vote as you shot
—Abraham Lincoln (*National Unionist*), 1864 (the National Union Party was a coalition of Republicans and War Democrats).
—Ulysses S. Grant (*Nat. Rep.*), 1868 (calling for loyalty to the leader of Union forces during the Civil War).

378. Vote as you shot, boys
—Rutherford B. Hayes (*Rep.*), 1876 (calling for continued loyalty to the party which prosecuted the Civil War).

379. Vote early and often
—appeared in 1848, attributed to John Van Buren, son of Free Soil candidate Martin Van Buren (used repeatedly in following elections to encourage the illegal practice of casting multiple ballots).

380. Vote for champions of the 8 hour law
—Woodrow Wilson (*Dem.*), 1916 (Wilson had supported legislation providing an eight-hour work day for certain railroad workers).

381. Vote gladly for Adlai
—Adlai Stevenson (*Dem.*), 1952.

382. Vote Kennedy for peace
—Pre-nomination campaign of Robert F. Kennedy (*Dem.*), 1968 (ended by his assassination).

383. Vote Republican—the party of Lincoln
—Richard M. Nixon (*Rep.*), 1960.

384. Vote right with Dwight
—Dwight D. Eisenhower (*Rep.*), 1952.

385. Vote straight Democratic: protect America
—Franklin Delano Roosevelt (*Dem.*), 1944.

91. PRESIDENTIAL CAMPAIGNS *cont.*

386. **Vote yourself a farm**
—Abraham Lincoln (*Rep.*), 1860 (referring to Republican support of land grants to settlers through a homestead bill).

387. **Wall Street wears a Willkie button, America wears a Roosevelt button**
—Franklin Delano Roosevelt (*Dem.*), 1940.

388. **War in the East! Peace in the West! Thank God for Wilson**
—Woodrow Wilson (*Dem.*), 1916 (referring to Wilson's success in keeping America out of World War I).

389. **Washington wouldn't! Grant couldn't! Roosevelt shan't! No third term!**
—William Howard Taft (*Rep.*), 1912 (Theodore Roosevelt had served most of McKinley's term as president after the latter's assassination and had then been elected to another term of his own; in 1912 he ran again).

390. **Washington wouldn't, Grant couldn't, Roosevelt shouldn't**
—Wendell Willkie (*Rep.*), 1940 (referring to Franklin D. Roosevelt's candidacy for an unprecedented third term as president).

391. **We are going to win the war and the peace that follows**
—Franklin Delano Roosevelt (*Dem.*), 1944.

392. **We are not going to vote away our wages**
—Benjamin Harrison (*Rep.*), 1888 (Republicans portrayed Democrats as free-traders whose policies would endanger American industry and labor).

393. **We demand a rigorous frugality in every department of the government**
—Samuel J. Tilden (*Dem.*), 1876 (responding to the corruption uncovered in the Grant administration).

394. **We demand that our customhouse taxation shall be for revenue only**
—Samuel J. Tilden (*Dem.*), 1876 (expressing opposition to excessive protective tariff).

395. **We demand the *Habeas Corpus***
—George McClellan (*Dem.*), 1864 (Lincoln had suspended the writ of habeas corpus in some instances during the Civil War).

396. **We don't want Eleanor either**
—Wendell Willkie (*Rep.*), 1940 (referring to Roosevelt's wife, Eleanor).

91. PRESIDENTIAL CAMPAIGNS *cont.*

397. **We'll vote for the Buckeye boy**
—Rutherford B. Hayes (*Rep.*), 1876 (Hayes was from Ohio, the "Buckeye State").

398. **We love him for the enemies he has made**
—Grover Cleveland (*Dem.*), 1884.

399. **We millionaires want Willkie**
—Franklin Delano Roosevelt (*Dem.*), 1940.

400. **We Polked 'em in '44; we'll Pierce 'em in '52**
—Franklin Pierce (*Dem.*), 1852.

401. **We're madly for Adlai**
—Adlai Stevenson (*Dem.*), 1952.

402. **We shall be redeemed from the rule of Nigger drivers**
—John C. Frémont (*Rep.*), 1856 (expressing the anti-slavery conviction of the Republican Party).

403. **We still like Ike**
—Dwight D. Eisenhower (*Rep.*), 1956.

404. **We want none but white men at the helm**
—John C. Breckinridge (*Southern Dem.*), 1860.

405. **We want Willkie—third term means dictatorship**
—Wendell Willkie (*Rep.*), 1940 (Roosevelt, the Democratic candidate, was seeking a third term as president).

406. **We will follow where the White Plume waves**
—James G. Blaine (*Rep.*), 1884 (Blaine was nicknamed "The Plumed Knight").

407. **What's wrong with being right?**
—Barry Goldwater (*Rep.*), 1964 (a right-wing Republican).

408. **Where were you in '32?**
—Franklin Delano Roosevelt (*Dem.*), 1936.

409. **While I am able to move I will do my duty**
—Gen. Lewis Cass (*Dem.*), 1848.

410. **White men to govern the restoration of constitutional liberty**
—Horatio Seymour (*Dem.*), 1868.

411. **Who but Hoover**
—Herbert Hoover (*Rep.*), 1928.

412. **Who but Hubert?**
—Hubert H. Humphrey (*Dem.*), 1968.

413. **Willkie for president—of Commonwealth and Southern**
—Franklin Delano Roosevelt (*Dem.*), 1940 (referring to the utilities company of which Willkie had been chief executive).

91. PRESIDENTIAL CAMPAIGNS *cont.*

414. Willkie for the millionaires—Roosevelt for the millions
> —Franklin Delano Roosevelt (*Dem.*), 1940.

415. Willkie or bust
> —Wendell Willkie (*Rep.*), 1940.

416. Win with Willkie
> —Wendell Willkie (*Rep.*), 1940.

417. Win with Wilson
> —Woodrow Wilson (*Dem.*), 1912.

418. Workingmen, don't be fooled
> —Grover Cleveland (*Dem.*), 1884 (questioning Republican claims of the benefits of a high protective tariff).

419. Workingmen's friend
> —Benjamin Butler (*Greenback party*), 1884.

420. Work with Wallace for peace
> —Henry A. Wallace (*Progressive*), 1948.

421. Would you buy a used car from this man?
> —1972 (expressing suspicion of the trustworthiness of the Republican candidate, Richard M. Nixon).

422. Would you let your sister marry this man?
> —1968 (referring to the Republican candidate, Richard M. Nixon).

423. You never had it so good
> —Herbert Hoover (*Rep.*), 1928.

92. PUBLIC SERVICE
> See also **53. GOVERNMENT SERVICE**

1. College is America's best friend
> —Council for Financial Aid to Education.

2. Give so more will live
> —Heart Fund.

3. Give them life and make it worth living
> —United Jewish Appeal.

4. Give to conquer cancer
> —American Cancer Society.

5. Help others help themselves
> —Salvation Army.

6. It's a matter of life and breath
> —American Cancer Society

7. It's the right thing to do
> —Foster Parents Plan.

8. It takes a man to help a boy
> —Big Brother.

92. **PUBLIC SERVICE** *cont.*

9. **Please! Only *you* can prevent forest fires**
—The Advertising Council.

10. **To make every community as clean as its cleanest home**
—National Clean Up Campaign Bureau.

11. **We're fighting for your life**
—American Heart Association.

93. **PUBLIC UTILITIES**

1. **A citizen, wherever we serve**
—Georgia Railway & Power Co.

2. **Ask the man from Northern Plains**
—Northern Natural Gas Co.

3. **Electricity . . . it's still hard to find a better value**
—Northeast Utilities.

4. **People you can depend on to power America's progress**
—Investor-Owned Electric Light and Power Cos.

5. **Power for progress**
—Consolidated Edison Co.

6. **Power for progress**
—The Southern Co.

7. **Service first**
—Houston Lighting and Power Co.

8. **Service is the difference**
—Century Electric Co.

9. **Taxpaying servant of a great state**
—New Jersey Public Service Electric and Gas Co.

10. **The heart of the market**
—Pennsylvania Power and Light Co.

11. **The most for your money in fuel**
—Illinois-Iowa Power Co.

12. **The power that lights and moves Alabama**
—Alabama Power Co.

13. **The power to please!**
—Florida Power Corp.

14. **This is the center of industrial America**
—Ohio Edison-Pennsylvania Power.

15. **When you make your move make sure it's a planned move**
—Central Illinois Light Co.

94. PUBLISHING
See also **85.** PERIODICALS AND NEWSPAPERS

1. **A good society is good business**
—McGraw-Hill Inc.

2. **Balanced reading for discriminating people**
—(*Circle 12 books*).

3. **Built through generations**
—(*Encyclopedia Americana*).

4. **Buy us like advertising . . . use us like salesmen**
—Home State Farm Publications.

5. **For the climate of excellence**
—Cahners Publishing Co. Inc.

6. **Kind to your pocket and pocket book**
—Pocket Books Inc.

7. **Like sending your family to college**
—(*Webster's International Dictionary*) G. & C. Merriam
Co.

8. **"Market-directed"**
—McGraw-Hill Inc.

9. **Serving America's schools, homes, commerce and industry**
—Rand McNally and Co.

10. **Serving industry constructively since 1902**
—Miller Freeman Publications.

11. **Serving man's need for knowledge . . . in many ways**
—McGraw-Hill Inc.

12. **Since 1847, the *trusted* and *authoritative* name in dictionaries**
—(*Merriam-Webster*) G. & C. Merriam Co.

13. **The accepted educational standard**
—(*Compton's Encyclopaedia*).

14. **The leading name in dictionaries since 1847**
—(*Merriam-Webster*) G. & C. Merriam Co.

15. **The live ones!**
—Cahners Publishing Co. Inc.

16. **There's a world of difference in Webster dictionaries**
—G. & C. Merriam Co.

17. **The Supreme Authority**
—(*Merriam-Webster*) G. & C. Merriam Co.

18. **The world is yours with the World Book**
—W. F. Quarrie & Co.

94. PUBLISHING *cont.*

19. **To be sure you're right . . . insist on Merriam-Webster**

           —G. & C. Merriam Co.

20. **With Time/Life Books, you've got it made**

      —(*Home Repair & Improvements*) Time-Life Inc.

21. **World's largest specialized publisher**

           —Gulf Publishing Co.

R

95. RADIO EQUIPMENT

     See also **5. AUDIO EQUIPMENT,**

         111. TELECOMMUNICATIONS

1. **A famous name in radio since 1921**

           —DeWald.

2. **Air unlox to Magnavox**

           —Magnavox Co.

3. **All that is best in radio**

           —Eagle Radio Co.

4. **Alone in tone**

        —(*receiving sets*) Magnavox Co.

5. **Always a year ahead**

           —Zenith Radio Corp.

6. **Always good company**

           —Radio Industries Corp.

7. **America's most copied radio**

           —Zenith Radio Corp.

8. **America's smart set**

           —Admiral Corp.

9. **A musical instrument of quality**

           —Philco Corp.

10. **And when you listen you'll buy this Westinghouse**

           —Westinghouse.

11. **A radio in every room; a radio for every purpose**

           —Crosley.

12. **A radio that you can play**

           —Eckhardt Corp.

13. **Arvin sets the pace, lead with Arvin**

           —Noblitt-Sparks.

95.   RADIO EQUIPMENT *cont.*

14.   **A symbol of technical excellence**
—RCA Corp.

15.   **Beautiful beyond belief in tone and styling**
—Bendix Radio Division.

16.   **Behind the panels of better built sets**
—General Radio Corp.

17.   **Believe your own ears**
—General Electric Co.

18.   **Built like a fine watch**
—Lombardi Radio Mfg. Co.

19.   **Built like a violin**
—(*Teletone radio speakers*).

20.   **Clear to the ear**
—Magnavox Co.

21.   **Comparison proves its superiority**
—Hallock & Watson Radio Corp.

22.   **Costs more, but does more**
—Zenith Radio Corp.

23.   **Every one a good one**
—Davidson Radio Corp.

24.   **Everything for the radio man**
—Midwest Radio Co.

25.   **Excellence in electronics**
—(*vacuum tubes*) Raytheon Mfg. Co.

26.   **Famous for quality the world over**
—Philco Corp.

27.   **Fits and matches the car you're driving**
—(*car radios*) Motorola Inc.

28.   **FM at its finest**
—Bendix Radio Division.

29.   **For the man who believes his own ears**
—A-C Electrical Mfg. Co.

30.   **Grand piano of the radio world**
—Fada Radio, Ltd.

31.   **Great thrill in radio by the pioneers of short-wave radio**
—Stewart-Warner Corp.

32.   **In harmony with home and air**
—Magnavox Co.

33.   **Install it, forget it**
—Kodel Radio Corp.

95. **RADIO EQUIPMENT** *cont.*

34. **Just as if you were there**
> —Borkman Radio Corp.

35. **Just plug in, then tune in**
> —(*batteryless radio sets*) Standard Radio Corp. Ltd.

36. **Known for tone**
> —(*Stradivara*) Pacific Phonograph Mfg. Co.

37. **Lambert radio invites you to rest**
> —Leon Lambert Radio Co.

38. **Listen, and you'll buy Westinghouse**
> —Westinghouse Electric Corp.

39. **Listening luxury beyond your highest hopes**
> —Bendix Radio Division.

40. **Manufacturers of world's most widely used personal communications transmitters**
> —E. F. Johnson Co.

41. **Mastery in radio**
> —Freed-Eisemann Radio Corp.

42. **Mighty monarch of the air**
> —Majestic.

43. **More pleasure per mile**
> —(*car radios*) American Bosch Corp.

44. **Most radio per dollar**
> —King-Buffalo Inc.

45. **Perfectly syntonized**
> —Hartmann Electrical Mfg. Co.

46. **Pioneers in the radio industry**
> —All-American Radio Corp.

47. **Radio builds for the years to come**
> —All-American Radio Corp.

48. **Rivaled only by reality**
> —Federal Radio Corp.

49. **Royalty of radio since 1920**
> —Air King.

50. **Sensation of radio**
> —Thermodyne Radio Corp.

51. **Smart and new from every view**
> —Rondo.

52. **The best in radio**
> —American Bosch Corp.

53. **The best in radio is better with a Bendix**
> —Bendix Radio Division.

95. **RADIO EQUIPMENT** *cont.*

54. **The blue tube with the life-like tone**
—Arcturus Radio Tube Co.

55. **The choice of noted music critics**
—All-American Radio Corp.

56. **The emblem of worth in radio**
—Kodel Radio Corp.

57. **The gold standard of radio receivers**
—J. B. Ferguson Inc.

58. **The greatest name in aircraft radio**
—Bendix Radio Division.

59. **The heart of reliable radio power**
—Raytheon Mfg. Co.

60. **The heart of your radio**
—RCA Radiotron Co.

61. **The musical instrument of radio**
—Eckhardt Corp.

62. **The name to know in radio**
—Brandes Inc.

63. **The original self-contained radio**
—Operadio Corp.

64. **The pick of the portables**
—RCA Victor.

65. **The proof is in the listening**
—Motorola Inc.

66. **The radiant name in radio**
—Magnavox Co.

67. **The radio in America's finest homes**
—Freed-Eisemann Radio Corp.

68. **The radio used by the broadcasting stations**
—Day-Fan Electric Co.

69. **The radio with the big plus value**
—General Electric Co.

70. **The real voice of radio**
—Bendix Radio Division.

71. **There is nothing finer than a Stromberg-Carlson**
—Stromberg-Carlson.

72. **The royalty of radio**
—Colin B. Kennedy Co.

73. **The sine of merit**
—Daven Radio Corp.

74. **The single six**
—Hartmann Electrical Mfg. Co.

95. **RADIO EQUIPMENT** *cont.*

   75. **The symbol of quality in radio since 1915**
      —Magnavox Co.

   76. **The thoroughbred radio**
      —Freed-Eisemann Radio Corp.

   77. **The tube to buy to satisfy**
      —Magnavox Co.

   78. **The tube with the sensible guarantee**
      —Supertron Mfg. Co.

   79. **The ultimate in radio reception**
      —MacLaren Mfg. Co.

   80. **Wake up to music**
      —General Electric Co.

96. **RAIL TRAVEL AND CARGO**
   See also **119.** TRAVEL

   1. **A dependable railway**
      —Great Northern Railway.

   2. **A good neighbor of your community**
      —Baltimore & Ohio Railroad.

   3. **All Aboard Amtrak**
      —(*Amtrak*) National Railroad Passenger Corp.

   4. **America's resourceful railroad**
      —Milwaukee Road.

   5. **America's sleepheart**
      —Chesapeake & Ohio Railroad.

   6. **Be specific, say Union Pacific**
      —Union Pacific Railroad.

   7. **Chessie knows the territory**
      —Chesapeake & Ohio Railroad.

   8. **Everywhere west**
      —Chicago, Burlington & Quincy Railroad Co.

   9. **First of the Northern Transcontinentals**
      —Northern Pacific Railway.

   10. **Four great routes for transcontinental travel**
      —Southern Pacific Railroad.

   11. **Freight Railroads are on the move**
      —American Association of Railroads.

   12. **Gateway to and from the booming west**
      —Union Pacific Railroad.

   13. **Gateway to and from your world markets**
      —Union Pacific Railroad.

   14. **Grow, grow by the rail way**
      —Association of American Railroads.

96. RAIL TRAVEL AND CARGO *cont.*

15. **Hauls more freight and handles more passengers than any other railroad in the world**
—Pennsylvania Railroad.

16. **Holiday all the way with...**
—Canadian Pacific Railway.

17. **Innovations that squeeze the waste out of distribution**
—Southern Railway Co.

18. **In partnership with all America**
—Association of American Railroads.

19. **Largest railway system in America**
—Canadian National Railroad Co.

20. **Linking 13 great states with the nation**
—Baltimore & Ohio Railroad.

21. **Look ahead. Look South**
—Southern Railway Co.

22. **Miles of travel comfort**
—Missouri-Kansas-Texas Railroad Co.

23. **Most popular route to the Rockies**
—Burlington Route.

24. **Motor coach to train side, the New York idea of travel convenience**
—Baltimore & Ohio Railroad.

25. **Motor coach train connection, a New York travel habit**
—Baltimore & Ohio Railroad.

26. **On-time-delivery is our #1 concern**
—Reading Railroad.

27. **On time every day is the Burlington way**
—Chicago, Burlington & Quincy Railroad Co.

28. **Rely on us**
—Louisville and Nashville Railroad.

29. **Retire in our sleepers instead of retiring your car**
—Baltimore & Ohio Railroad.

30. **Ride the big red cars**
—Pacific Electric Railway, Los Angeles.

31. **Road of the daily streamliners**
—Union Pacific Railroad.

32. **Road of travel luxury**
—Illinois Central Railroad.

33. **Road to the future**
—New York Central System.

96. RAIL TRAVEL AND CARGO *cont.*

34. **Route of the incomparable empire builder**
—Great Northern Railway.

35. **Safety first, friendliness, too**
—Association of American Railroads.

36. **Safety first railroad**
—Southern Pacific Railroad.

37. **Santa Fe all the way**
—Santa Fe Railroad.

38. **Saves a business day**
—(*DeLuxe Golden State Limited*) Southern Pacific Railroad.

39. **Scenic line of the world**
—Rio Grande Railroad.

40. **See America first**
—Great Northern Railway.

41. **See it all by train**
—Associated British Railways.

42. **See the FIRST of America first**
—Chesapeake & Ohio Railroad.

43. **Serves all the West**
—Union Pacific Railroad.

44. **Serving the Golden Empire**
—Southern Pacific Railroad.

45. **Serving the heart of industrial America**
—Erie Railroad.

46. **Serving the nation**
—Pennsylvania Railroad.

47. **Sleep like a kitten, arrive fresh as a daisy**
—Chesapeake & Ohio Railroad.

48. **"Southern's accent is on you"**
—Southern Railway Co.

49. **Southern serves the South**
—Southern Railway Co.

50. **Spans the world**
—Canadian Pacific Railway.

51. **Standard railroad of the south**
—Atlantic Coast Line Railroad.

52. **Thanks for using Coast Line**
—Atlantic Coast Line Railroad.

53. **The aristocrat of winter trains**
—Atlantic Coast Line Railroad.

96. **RAIL TRAVEL AND CARGO** *cont.*

54. **The B & O is the way to go**
— Baltimore & Ohio Railroad.

55. **The friendly railroad for all the family**
— Baltimore & Ohio Railroad.

56. **The Honeymoon Line**
— International Railway Co.

57. **The nation's BASIC transportation**
— Association of American Railroads.

58. **The nation's going-est railroad**
— Norfolk and Western Railway.

59. **The outstanding scenic way west**
— Missouri Pacific Railroad Co.

60. **The railroad of "creative crews"**
— Milwaukee Road.

61. **The railroad of planned progress ... geared to the nation's future**
— Rock Island Lines.

62. **"The railroad that runs by the customer's clock"**
— Nickel Plate Railroad.

63. **The railroad that's always on the move toward a better way**
— Santa Fe System Lines.

64. **The railway to everywhere in Canada**
— Canadian National Railroad Co.

65. **The road of a thousand wonders**
— Southern Pacific Railroad.

66. **The road of planned progress**
— Rock Island Lines.

67. **The route of the Black Diamond**
— Lehigh Valley Railroad.

68. **The safest, most comfortable way of going places fast**
— Pullman Co.

69. **The scenic route**
— New York Central Railroad.

70. **The seasoned traveler goes by train**
— Union Pacific Railroad.

71. **The service railroad of America**
— Chicago & Eastern Illinois Railway.

72. **The Southern serves the South**
— Southern Railway Co.

96. RAIL TRAVEL AND CARGO *cont.*

73. **The strategic middle route**
                                    —Union Pacific Railroad.

74. **The summer route you'll brag about**
                                    —Burlington Route.

75. **The wheels of transportation help turn the wheels of industry**
                                    —Union Pacific Railroad.

76. **The world's standard of quality**
                                    —New York Central Railroad.

77. **This is the way to run a railroad**
                                    —Northern Pacific Railway.

78. **To promote the American way of life, depend on the railroad**
                                    —Baltimore & Ohio Railroad.

79. **Water level route, you can sleep**
                                    —New York Central Railroad.

80. **World's most complete transportation system**
                                    —Canadian Pacific Railway.

RANGES...See **60.** HOME APPLIANCES AND EQUIPMENT

97. RECORDINGS
       See also **5.** AUDIO EQUIPMENT

1. **"Angels of the highest order"**
                                    —(*Seraphim records*) Capitol Records Inc.

2. **"Capitol" of the world**
                                    —Capitol Records Inc.

3. **Individuality graven into them**
                                    —Brunswick-Balke-Collender.

4. **Leadership through design**
                                    —Mercury Record Corp.

5. **Listen to America**
                                    —(*Decca records*).

6. **Pioneers in recording achievement**
                                    —Recordisc Corp.

7. **Recordings for the connoisseur**
                                    —Vanguard Recording Society Inc.

8. **The music America loves best**
                                    —RCA Corp.

9. **The music you want when you want it**
                                    —RCA Corp.

10. **The stars who make the hits are on RCA Victor records**
                                    —RCA Victor.

97. RECORDINGS *cont.*

11. **The world's greatest artists are NATURALLY yours on RCA Victor records**
                                        —RCA Victor.

12. **World leader in recorded sound**
                —(*Command*) ABC Records Inc.

RECORD PLAYERS ... See **5.** AUDIO EQUIPMENT

RECORDS ... See **97.** RECORDINGS

98. RECREATIONAL EQUIPMENT
See also **16.** BOATS AND BOATING EQUIPMENT,
44. FIREARMS, **45.** FISHING SUPPLIES, **56.** HEALTH
AND FITNESS, **77.** MOTORCYCLES, **108.** SPORTING
GOODS, **109.** SWIMWEAR, **118.** TOYS AND GAMES

1. **America's finest campers**
                        —Highway Cruisers Inc.

2. **America's finest camping tents**
        —(*Hoosier*) Hoosier Tarpaulin and Canvas Goods Co.

3. **America's largest builder of camping trailers**
                —Nimrod Ward Mfg. Co.

4. **America's most popular camp stove**
                —American Gas Machine Co.

5. **Cook stove and gas plant all in one**
                        —Coleman Lamp Co.

6. **"Developing products for recreation through electronic research"**
                        —Byrd Industries Inc.

7. **Fits the sport**
            —(*outdoor equipment*) Red Head Brand Co.

8. **Foremost brand in outdoor living**
                —American Thermos Products Co.

9. **Greatest name in the great outdoors. Foremost name in indoor comfort.**
                        —Coleman Co. Inc.

10. **Light, heat and cook the Coleman way**
                        —Coleman Lamp Co.

11. **Made like a gun**
                —(*Royal Enfield bicycle*).

12. **Quality requires no apology**
            —(*outdoor clothing*) Red Head Brand Co.

13. **Since 1877, America's first bicycle**
    —(*Columbia bicycles*) The Columbia Manufacturing Co.
                                                Inc.

14. **Styled for beauty, made to last**
                —(*Rollfast bicycles*).

98. RECREATIONAL EQUIPMENT *cont.*

15. The bike you'll like
—(*Yale bicycles*) Davis Sewing Machine Co.

16. The smooth way to rough it
—(*camp stoves*) Coleman Lamp Co.

REFRIGERATORS . . . See **60.** HOME APPLIANCES AND EQUIPMENT

RELISHES . . . See **29.** CONDIMENTS AND SPICES

REMEDIES . . . See **35.** DRUGS AND REMEDIES

99. RESTAURANTS
See also **47.** FOOD, MISCELLANEOUS

1. Good food is good health
—National Restaurant Association.

2. Host of the highways
—Howard Johnson Co.

3. It's worth the trip
—Dunkin' Donuts of America Inc.

4. Landmark for hungry Americans
—Howard Johnson Co.

5. McDonald's and you
—McDonald's Corp.

6. The nation's host from coast to coast
—Child's Restaurants.

7. The public appreciates quality
—Horn and Hardart restaurants, automats.

8. Travel follows good food routes
—National Restaurant Association.

9. Untouched by human hands
—Chock Full O' Nuts Restaurants.

10. What foods these morsels be
—J. N. Adams Tea Room, Buffalo, N. Y.

11. You deserve a break today
—(*McDonald's*) McDonald's Corp.

12. You want something better, you're Wendy's kind of people
—Wendy's International Inc.

100. RETAIL STORES

1. Always first quality
—J. C. Penney & Co. Inc.

2. America's most beautiful store
—Russek's, New York.

100.   RETAIL STORES *cont.*

3.   **A national institution from coast to coast**
—Browning King & Co., New York.

4.   **A nationwide institution**
—J. C. Penney & Co. Inc.

5.   **Cleveland's better food markets**
—Kroger Co.

6.   **For good eating at sensible cost**
—(*A & P Stores*) Great Atlantic & Pacific Tea Co. Inc.

7.   **For important clothes, it's Kerman Stores**
—Kerman Stores.

8.   **For stores of quality standard**
—J. Schoeneman, Inc. Baltimore, Md.

9.   **For that certain kind of woman**
—Peck and Peck.

10.   **From Maine to Texas ... and growing**
—A. Schulte, New York.

11.   **Good values consistently**
—New York Merchandise Co. Inc.

12.   **It pays to buy where you buy in safety**
—A. Jaeckel & Co.

13.   **King of them all**
—Rexall Stores.

14.   **Known for values**
—W. T. Grant Co.

15.   **Largest in the world because we serve the people best**
—United Cigar Stores.

16.   **Meet me at the fountain**
—Greenhut-Siegel-Cooper.

17.   **Meet me at the Music Box**
—Economy Drug Co., Cleveland.

18.   **No one is in debt to Macy's**
—Macy's.

19.   **On the Square**
—Klein's, New York.

20.   **Pittsburgh's Greatest Store**
—Kaufmann & Baer Co.

21.   **Rexall for reliability**
—Rexall Drug Co.

22.   **Shop at Sears and save**
—Sears, Roebuck & Co.

100. **RETAIL STORES** *cont.*

23. **Shop with people of taste**
—B. Altman & Co.

24. **Specialty shop of Originations**
—Bonwit Teller & Co.

25. **Store of individual shops**
—Franklin Simon & Co.

26. **The best always comes from Small's**
—Small's.

27. **The Friendly Store**
—Oliver A. Olson Co. Inc.

28. **The Heart of Milwaukee**
—Boston Store.

29. **The meeting place of the thrifty**
—Hunter's Variety Store, Memphis, Tenn.

30. **The oldest mail order house is today the most progressive**
—Montgomery Ward.

31. **There is one near you**
—Rexall Drug Co.

32. **There's always a new reason to shop Bradlees**
—The Stop & Shop Companies.

33. **There's more for your life at Sears**
—Sears, Roebuck & Co.

34. **There's one near you to serve you**
—Singer Sewing Center.

35. **We've got it good**
—K Mart Corp.

36. **You can't do better than Sears**
—Sears, Roebuck & Co.

37. **You never pay more at Best's**
—Best & Co.

S

SCALES . . . See **63.** INSTRUMENTS AND GAUGES

101. **SCHOOLS**

1. **America's foremost school of commercial art**
—Federal Schools.

2. **Be wise, protect your future**
—Cal-Aero Technical Institute, Glendale, Calif.

101. SCHOOLS *cont.*

 3. **Broadcasts as she bakes**
     —Radio Cooking School of America.

 4. **Earn while you learn**
     —International Correspondence Schools, Scranton, Pa.

 5. **Executive training for business leadership**
     —Woodbury College, Los Angeles.

 6. **Go to high school in bedroom slippers**
     —International Correspondence Schools, Scranton, Pa.

 7. **Originators of radio home-study training**
     —National Radio Institute.

 8. **The business leaders of today are the I. C. S. students of yesterday**
     —International Correspondence Schools, Scranton, Pa.

 9. **The West Point of Christian service**
     —Moody Bible Institute of Chicago.

 10. **The world's largest business training institute**
     —LaSalle Extension University.

 11. **University of the night**
     —International Correspondence Schools, Scranton, Pa.

 12. **We teach wherever the mails reach**
     —International Correspondence Schools, Scranton, Pa.

102. SEA TRAVEL AND CARGO
  See also **16. BOATS AND BOATING EQUIPMENT,**
  119. TRAVEL

 1. **Across the Atlantic**
     —United American Lines.

 2. **African business is our business**
     —Farrell Lines Inc.

 3. **A thousand miles of travel, a thousand thrills of pleasure**
     —Canadian Steamship Lines Ltd.

 4. **Cruising everywhere under the sun**
     —American President Lines.

 5. **For 75 years, America's link with the Orient**
     —American President Lines.

 6. **. . . Just for the sun of it**
     —T. S. Hanseatic German Atlantic Line.

 7. **Knows the Pacific**
     —Matson Lines.

 8. **Life at sea is like nothing on earth**
     —P and O Lines.

102. SEA TRAVEL AND CARGO *cont.*

   9. **Luxury and comfort with utmost safety**
                        —United States Lines Inc.

  10. **More fun per ton than any other line**
                        —Italian Line.

  11. **Niagara to the sea**
                        —Canada Steamship Lines Ltd.

  12. **Personalized service that makes the big difference**
                        —A. L. Mechling Barge Lines Inc.

  13. **Pleasure pirate pilgrimage**
                        —United American Lines.

  14. **Run away to sea with P and O**
                        —P and O Lines.

  15. **Sail a happy ship**
                        —Holland-American Line.

  16. **Sail with the British tradition wherever you go**
                        —Cunard Lines.

  17. **Sunlane cruises to Europe**
                        —American Export Isbrandtsen Lines Inc.

  18. **Sunshine belt to the Orient**
                        —Dollar Steamship Lines.

  19. **Take the sheltered route to Europe**
                        —Canadian Pacific Steamship & Railroad Co.

  20. **The "Champagne Touch"**
                        —Moore-McCormack Lines Inc.

  21. **The experience cruise line**
                        —Furness, Withy and Co. Ltd.

  22. **The lucky ones go Anchor Line**
                        —The Anchor Line.

  23. **The people who invented a nicer way to cruise**
                        —Holland-American Line.

  24. **The ships that serve Hawaii, South Seas and Australia**
                        —Matson Navigation Co.

  25. **The vacation way to Hawaii**
                        —Matson Navigation Co.

  26. **The voyage of your dreams**
                        —United American Lines.

  27. **The white Viking fleet**
                        —Swedish American Line.

  28. **The world's supreme travel experience**
                        —American President Lines.

102. SEA TRAVEL AND CARGO *cont.*

29. Unwind your way to Europe
—Italian Line.

30. When distribution is the question UBL has the answers
—Union Barge Line Corp.

SEEDS ... See **42.** FARMING SUPPLIES AND EQUIPMENT

103. SEWING AND KNITTING SUPPLIES
See also **113.** TEXTILES

1. A fastener to fit every need
—G. E. Prentice Mfg. Co.

2. A matter of pride, pleasure, and good plain sense
—(*linings*) Wm. Skinner & Sons.

3. An extra collar for a dollar
—(*League collars*) Goodman Collar Co.

4. Buttons that are MORE than buttons
—(*Costumakers*) Lidz Brothers Inc.

5. Dispels dressing discords
—(*Harmony Brand*) Federal Snap Fastener Corp.

6. Every color in the rainbow
—(*yarns*) S. W. & B. W. Fleisher Inc.

7. Extra strength that never fails you
—(*Bell thread*).

8. Guaranteed without an IF
—(*blanket binding*) Warren Weatherbone Co.

9. It's the yarn that counts
—American Yarn & Process Co.

10. It takes needles to make shirts
—L. Needles-Brooker Co.

11. Join the knit parade
—(*knitting needles*) C. J. Bates & Son.

12. Knit goods are only as good as the yarn of which they are made
—S. W. & B. W. Fleisher Inc.

13. Snap with the turtle back
—(*So E-Z snap fastener*) A. L. Clarke & Co.

14. The better the yarn the better the fabric
—Kingsport Corp.

15. The favorite home-sewing notion of the nation
—Slide Fasteners Inc.

103. SEWING AND KNITTING SUPPLIES *cont.*

16. **The laundry proof snap fastener that ends button-bother**
> —(*Gripper fasteners*) Scovill Manufacturing Co.

17. **The major zipper**
> —(*Conmar zippers*).

18. **The newest trimmings first**
> —Zucker & Josephy Inc.

19. **There are many advance styles, but there is only one Advance pattern**
> —Advance Pattern Co.

20. **The third dimension pattern**
> —Advance Pattern Co.

21. **The yarn you love to use**
> —(*Bear Brand yarn*) Bernhard Ulman Co.

22. **Turn a circle without a wrinkle**
> —(*bias fold tapes*) Friedberger-Aaron Mfg. Co.

23. **You call it a "zipper;" its real name is Prentice, the dependable slide fastener**
> —G. E. Prentice Mfg. Co.

SHAMPOO ... See **54.** HAIR CARE

104. SHAVING SUPPLIES
> See also **12.** BATH ACCESSORIES, **84.** PERFUMES AND
> FRAGRANCES, **106.** SOAP, **116.** TOILETRIES

1. **Avoid 5 o'clock shadow**
> —Gem Safety Razor Corp.

2. **Below skin level shave**
> —(*Packard electric shaver*) Lektro Products Inc.

3. **Cools and soothes as you shave**
> —F. F. Ingram Co.

4. **Easy does it**
> —(*Enders shaver*).

5. **Every shave a good shave**
> —Soap Products, Ltd.

6. **For a cooling shave**
> —F. F. Ingram Co.

7. **For a royal shave**
> —King Razor Co.

8. **For shaving without brush or lather**
> —Pryde-Wynn Co.

9. **For smooth shaves**
> —Twinplex Sales Co.

104. SHAVING SUPPLIES *cont.*

10. **For the one man in 7 who shaves every day**
     —(*Glider brushless shave*).

11. **For the shave that never fails**
     —Rock Flint Co.

12. **Get ready for the extraordinary**
     —(*Edge Extra shaving gel*) Johnson & Johnson.

13. **Get the Atra advantage**
     —(*Atra razors*) The Gillette Co.

14. **Good for its face value**
     —(*shaving cream*) Vantine & Co.

15. **Has the "edge" five ways**
     —Pal Blade Co.

16. **How to get further with father**
     —(*Seaforth shaving set*) Seaforth Corp.

17. **It lulls the skin**
     —(*shaving cream*) Coty Inc.

18. **It's quick-wetting**
     —(*Williams shaving cream*) J. B. Williams Co. Inc.

19. **Just a darn good shaving cream**
     —Commercial Laboratories.

20. **Look sharp! Feel sharp! Be sharp!**
     —(*Gillette blades*) The Gillette Co.

21. **Makes electric shaving easier**
     —(*Lectric shave lotion*) J. B. Williams Co. Inc.

22. **More practical than ever**
     —(*Old Spice shave mug refill*) Shulton Inc.

23. **More shaving comfort for your money**
     —(*Gillette blades*) The Gillette Co.

24. **Must make good or we will**
     —(*Genco razors*) Geneva Cutlery Corp.

25. **No brush, no lather, no rub-in**
     —(*Barbasol shaving cream*) Leeming/Pacquin.

26. **No pull, no pain, no sting**
     —(*Barbasol shaving cream*) Leeming/Pacquin.

27. **Nothing too good for men in service**
     —The Mennen Co.

28. **Only refill shaving stick**
     —Colgate & Co.

29. **Pal hollow ground has the "edge"**
     —Pal Blade Co.

30. **Saves shaving seconds and second shavings**
     —(*Durex razor blades*) Perma-Sharp Manufacturing Corp.

104. **SHAVING SUPPLIES** *cont.*

31. **Shave with a smile**
—Durham-Duplex Razor Co.

32. **Skin level shave**
—(*Packard electric shaver*) Lektro Products Inc.

33. **Smoother faces**
—Gem Safety Razor Corp.

34. **Softens the beard at the base**
—Colgate & Co.

35. **The ball-bearing shave**
—E. R. Squibb & Sons.

36. **The blades men swear by, not at**
—Durham-Duplex Razor Co.

37. **The brushless wonder**
—(*Benex brushless shave*).

38. **The civilized way of shaving**
—(*Schick dry razor*) Warner-Lambert Pharmaceutical Co.

39. **The close electric shave**
—(*Norelco*) North American Philips Corp.

40. **The comfort shave**
—(*Norelco*) North American Philips Corp.

41. **The four-edged razor blade**
—O. C. Craig Co., Ltd., Winnipeg.

42. **The gel that gives you more**
—(*Gillette Foaming Gel*) The Gillette Co.

43. **The gift that endears and endures**
—(*Lektro shaver*).

44. **The little barber in a box**
—American Safety Razor Corp.

45. **The mark of quality**
—(*electric shavers*) Schick Electric Inc.

46. **The only new idea in shaving since the safety razor**
—(*Vaniva shaving cream*).

47. **The quality razor of the world**
—(*Gillette safety razor*) The Gillette Co.

48. **There's something about an Aqua Velva man**
—(*Aqua Velva After Shave Lotion*) J. B. Williams Co. Inc.

49. **The shave is better when the lather stays wetter**
—(*Lifebuoy shaving cream*) Lever Bros. Co.

50. **The shave that clicks**
—King Razor Co.

51. **The woman's razor**
—Curvfit Products Co.

104.   SHAVING SUPPLIES *cont.*

52. The world's coolest shave
—(*shaving cream*) F. F. Ingram Co.

53. Where face fitness starts
—(*Williams shaving cream*) J. B. Williams Co. Inc.

54. Wilts whiskers
—(*shaving cream*) The Mennen Co.

55. You can shave in a foxhole with X-Ray
—Hamilton Preparations.

56. You can't get any closer
—(*Norelco*) North American Philips Corp.

57. You pay less for Gem Blades because you need so few
—Gem Safety Razor Corp.

SHIPPING ... See **3.** AEROSPACE, **96.** RAIL TRAVEL AND CARGO, **102.** SEA TRAVEL AND CARGO, **120.** TRUCKS AND TRUCKING INDUSTRY

SHOES ... See **48.** FOOTWEAR

SILVER ... See **67.** JEWELRY AND SILVER

SILVERWARE ... See **67.** JEWELRY AND SILVER

SKIN CARE ... See **32.** COSMETICS, **116.** TOILETRIES

105.   SMOKING ACCESSORIES
See also **115.** TOBACCO PRODUCTS

1. A classic in wood
—(*pipes*) Kaywoodie Co.

2. America's most distinguished cigarette holder
—Kirsten Pipe Co.

3. Automatically better
—(*cigarette lighters*) Ronson Corp.

4. Cooler on the draw
—(*Royal Duke pipes*) Grabow Pre-Smoked Pipes Inc.

5. Dignifying the pipe
—(*One-Up tobacco case*) Smokers Products Inc.

6. Faithfully maintaining quality at no advance in price
—Grabow Pre-Smoked Pipes Inc.

7. Filters the smoke from bowl to tip
—(*Forecaster pipe*) National Briar Pipe Co.

8. Graduate to Kaywoodie
—(*pipes*) Kaywoodie Co.

105. SMOKING ACCESSORIES *cont.*

9. **"Heart of the root" briar**
    —(*Rembrandt pipes*) National Briar Pipe Co.

10. **Hollycourt: 77.7% drier than other pipes**
    —M. Linkman & Co.

11. **It filters the smoke**
    —(*De Nicotea cigarette holder*).

12. **Look through and see**
    —(*cigarette holders*) Kirsten Pipe Co.

13. **No breaking-in with Yello-Bole**
    —(*pipe*) Kaufman Bros. & Bondy.

14. **Pathfinders in pipedom**
    —M. Linkman & Co.

15. **Press, it's lit; release, it's out**
    —(*lighters*) Ronson Corp.

16. **Ripe 'n ready for smokin' steady**
    —Grabow Pre-Smoked Pipes Inc.

17. **Smoke all you like, like all you smoke**
    —(*cigarette holders*) L. & H. Stern Co.

18. **Sweeter as the years go by**
    —(*pipes*) Kaywoodie Co.

19. **The insured pipe**
    —Wm. Demuth & Co.

20. **The last word in pipes**
    —Kaywoodie Co.

21. **The lighter that made the world lighter-conscious**
    —Zippo Mfg. Co.

22. **The lighter that works**
    —Zippo Mfg. Co.

23. **The nation's pipe**
    —Kaufman Bros. & Bondy.

24. **The oldest name in pipes**
    —House of Comoy.

25. **The people who keep improving flame**
    —(*lighters*) Ronson Corp.

26. **The pipe of distinction**
    —L. & H. Stern Co.

27. **The pipe that everybody knows**
    —Kaywoodie Co.

28. **The pipe that's broken in**
    —M. Linkman & Co.

29. **The sweetest pipe in the world**
    —Wm. Demuth & Co.

105. SMOKING ACCESSORIES *cont.*

30. The universal pipe
—Wm. Demuth & Co.

31. The up-draft lighter
—(*Lord Oxford lighters*).

32. Try Hollycourt. Why? The bowl stays dry
—(*pipes*) M. Linkman & Co.

33. You can't get a drink from a drinkless Kaywoodie
—(*pipes*) Kaywoodie Co.

34. You can't get a drink from a drinkless pipe
—Reiss-Premier Pipe Co.

106. SOAP
See also **10. BABY PRODUCTS, 12. BATH ACCESSORIES,
24. CLEANING AND LAUNDRY PRODUCTS,
104. SHAVING SUPPLIES, 116. TOILETRIES**

1. Adorns your skin with the fragrance men love
—(*Cashmere Bouquet*) Colgate-Palmolive Co.

2. A lovelier skin with just one cake
—(*Camay soap*) Procter & Gamble Co.

**3. Aren't you glad *you* use Dial? Don't you wish
everybody did?**
—Armour and Co.

4. Astonishingly good
—(*soap products*) South African Oil & Fat Industries, Ltd.

5. Best for you and baby, too
—Albert Soaps Co.

6. Beware of B. O.
—(*Lifebuoy*) Lever Bros. Co.

7. Cleans with a caress
—(*Castile soap*) Conti Products.

8. Cuts the cost of clean hands
—Soapitor Co. Inc.

9. Doctors prove Palmolive's beauty results
—(*Palmolive soap*) Colgate-Palmolive Co.

10. Dove creams your skin while you wash
—Personal Products Div., Lever Bros. Co.

11. Dove is 1/4 cleansing cream
—(*Dove*) Lever Bros. Co.

12. Finer than the finest castile
—(*Castolay*) Andrew Jergens Co.

13. For proved beauty results
—Colgate-Palmolive Co.

106. SOAP *cont.*

14. **Good morning! Have you used Pears' Soap?**
>>> —A. & F. Pears Ltd.

15. **It floats**
>>> —(*Ivory soap*) Procter & Gamble Co.

16. **It takes so little for every household use**
>>> —(*White King soap*) Spohn & Thamer.

17. **Ivory is kind to everything it touches**
>>> —(*Ivory*) Procter & Gamble Co.

18. **Keep that schoolgirl complexion**
>>> —(*Palmolive soap*) Colgate-Palmolive Co.

19. **Lux every day keeps old hands away**
>>> —(*Lux soap*) Lever Bros. Co.

20. **99 44/100% pure**
>>> —(*Ivory soap*) Procter & Gamble Co.

21. **Now better than ever for everything**
>>> —(*Ivory soap*) Procter & Gamble Co.

22. **Palmolive cares for more complexions than any other soap in the world**
>>> —(*Palmolive soap*) Colgate-Palmolive Co.

23. **Pussycat-smooth hands**
>>> —(*soap*) Newell-Gutradt Co.

24. **ReMEMber MEM**
>>> —Mem Co.

25. **Removes the grime in half the time**
>>> —(*powdered hand soap*) The Hanzo Co.

26. **The cream of olive oil soaps**
>>> —Peet Bros. Mfg. Co.

27. **The health soap**
>>> —(*Lifebuoy*) Lever Bros. Co.

28. **The lovelier soap with the costlier perfume**
>>> —(*Cashmere Bouquet*) Colgate-Palmolive Co.

29. **The luxury soap of the world**
>>> —(*Old English*) Yardley of London Inc.

30. **The perfect clue of perfect castile**
>>> —Lockwood Brackett Co.

31. **The picture of health**
>>> —(*Pine Tree soap*) Pine Tree Products Co.

32. **The skin you love to touch**
>>> —(*Woodbury's facial soap*) Andrew Jergens Co.

33. **The soap of beautiful women**
>>> —Procter & Gamble Co.

106. SOAP *cont.*

34. **The soap that agrees with your skin**
—(*Sweetheart*) Manhattan Soap Co.

35. **With the fragrance men love**
—(*Cashmere Bouquet soap*) Colgate-Palmolive Co.

36. **World's worst beauty soap. World's *best* hand soap**
—(*Lava*) Procter & Gamble Co.

37. **Your skin knows and shows the difference**
—(*Lana Oil soap*) Beaver-Remmers Co.

SOCIAL ISSUES ... See **90.** POLITICAL ISSUES

SOCKS ... See **61.** HOSIERY

SODA ... See **107.** SOFT DRINKS

107. SOFT DRINKS
See also **15.** BEVERAGES, MISCELLANEOUS, **27.** COFFEE,
110. TEA

1. **America Dry for dry America**
—(*ginger ale*) V. & E. Kohnstamm Inc.

2. **America's finest cola drink**
—Lime Cola Co.

3. **America's finest ginger ale**
—Anheuser-Busch Inc.

4. **America's finest mixer**
—(*club soda*) White Rock Products Corp.

5. **America's most modern cola**
—(*Diet-Rite*) Royal Crown Cola Co.

6. **America's No. 1 low-calorie cola**
—(*Diet-Rite*) Royal Crown Cola Co.

7. **An aristocratic beverage at a democratic price**
—(*Hires*) Crush International Inc.

8. **Base for soft drinks and desserts**
—(*Kool-Aid*) General Foods Corp.

9. **Best by taste test**
—(*Royal Crown Cola*) Nehi Corp.

10. **Buy a rack of Rooties**
—Krueger Beverage Co.

11. **Caffeine free. Never had it. Never will.**
—(*7-Up*) The Seven-Up Co.

12. **Canada's Fresh-up**
—Dominion Seven-up Co.

13. **Coke is it**
—(*Coca-Cola*) Coca-Cola Co.

107. **SOFT DRINKS** *cont.*

14. **Come alive!**
—(*Pepsi-Cola*) Pepsico Inc.

15. **Delicious and refreshing**
—Coca-Cola Co.

16. **Don't you feel good about 7-Up**
—(*7-Up*) The Seven-Up Co.

17. **Drink Coca-Cola**
—(*Coca-Cola*) Coca-Cola Co.

18. **Drink RC for quick, fresh energy**
—Royal Crown Cola Co.

19. **First aid for thirst**
—Lime Cola Co.

20. **Flavor sealed in the brown bottle**
—(*Orange Crush*) Crush International Inc.

21. **For a better tomorrow**
—(*Hires*) Crush International Inc.

22. **For occasions and all occasions**
—(*ginger ale*) Sheboygan Beverage Co.

23. **For those who think young**
—(*Pepsi-Cola*) Pepsico Inc.

24. **Fresh-up with Seven-up**
—The Seven-Up Co.

25. **Ginger ale with piquant personality**
—Clicquot Club Co.

26. **Hires to you for a better tomorrow**
—(*Hires*) Crush International Inc.

27. **Hits the spot**
—(*Pepsi-Cola*) Pepsico Inc.

28. **How can just 1 calorie taste so good!**
—(*Tab*) Coca-Cola Co.

29. **Is a toast to good health**
—(*Hires*) Crush International Inc.

30. **It had to be good to get where it is**
—Coca-Cola Co.

31. **It's the real thing**
—(*Coca-Cola*) Coca-Cola Co.

32. **Join the Pepsi generation**
—(*Pepsi-Cola*) Pepsico Inc.

33. **Kids love Kool-Aid**
—(*Kool-Aid*) General Foods Corp.

34. **Mellow as the greeting of old friends**
—(*Canada Dry ginger ale*) Canada Dry Corp.

107. SOFT DRINKS *cont.*

35. **Mixes well with any friend**
—(*Indian Hill ginger ale*).

36. **Not twice as much, but twice as good**
—Lime Cola Co.

37. **Refresh yourself**
—Coca-Cola Co.

38. **Rich in flavor**
—(*Richardson root beer*) Richardson Corp.

39. **Taste champ of the colas**
—(*Royal Crown Cola*) Nehi Corp.

40. **Taste that beats the others cold**
—(*Pepsi-Cola*) Pepsico Inc.

41. **The aristocrat of ginger ales**
—Saegertown Mineral Water Co.

42. **The drink you remember**
—(*O'Keefe's ginger ale*).

43. **The flavor-aged ginger ale**
—Clicquot Club Co.

44. **The ginger ale with the long-life bubble**
—(*Pabst*).

45. **The global high-sign**
—Coca-Cola Co.

46. **The Kola drink that's uni-blended**
—(*Nichol Kola*) H. R. Nicholson Co.

47. **The nation's cheer leader**
—Ko-Lo Corp.

48. **The pause that refreshes**
—Coca-Cola Co.

49. **The toast to good taste**
—(*Hires*) Crush International Inc.

50. **The Uncola**
—The Seven-Up Co.

51. **Things go better with Coke**
—Coca-Cola Co.

52. **Thirst come, thirst served**
—(*Goody Root Beer*) Bottlers Supply & Manufacturing Co.

53. **Those who think are proud to drink—Hires**
—(*Hires*) Crush International Inc.

54. **Tops for quality**
—(*Pepsi-Cola*) Pepsico Inc.

107. SOFT DRINKS *cont.*

55. 7-Up your thirst away
—The Seven-Up Co.

56. With real root juices
—(*Hires*) Crush International Inc.

57. You like it, it likes you
—The Seven-Up Co.

58. You're the Pepsi generation
—Pepsico Inc.

SOFTWARE ... See **28.** COMPUTER EQUIPMENT

SPICES ... See **29.** CONDIMENTS AND SPICES

108. SPORTING GOODS
See also **16.** BOATS AND BOATING EQUIPMENT,
44. FIREARMS, **45.** FISHING SUPPLIES, **56.** HEALTH
AND FITNESS, **98.** RECREATIONAL EQUIPMENT,
109. SWIMWEAR, **118.** TOYS AND GAMES

1. A better buy, by any comparison
—Safticycles Inc.

2. A national rider never changes his mount
—(*National bicycles*) Davis Sewing Machine Co.

3. And who makes great skis? Head, of course.
—Head Ski Co.

4. A progressive past. A golden future.
—Wilson Sporting Goods Co.

5. As sturdy as they are beautiful
—(*Rollfast bicycles*).

6. Authentically ski
—Ski Industries America.

7. Ball that made baseball
—A. G. Spalding & Bros.

8. Bowl where you see the Magic Triangle
—(*AMF bowling equipment*) American Machine and
Foundry Co.

9. Clubs of character for every golfer
—Vulcan Golf Co.

10. Course tested golf clubs
—Crawford, McGregor & Canby Co.

11. ... Fashioned for those who enjoy extraordinary quality
—Gerber Legendary Blades.

12. Golfcraft for the finest
—Golfcraft Inc.

108. SPORTING GOODS *cont.*

13. **Hand made to fit you**
—(*golf clubs*) Kenneth Smith.

14. **Hottest name in golf**
—Kroydon Golf Corp.

15. **King of all tees**
—(*Rex tees*) Jack Shipman.

16. **Named for the original American professionals**
—Indian Archery Corp.

17. **No. 1 name in bowling**
—Brunswick Corp.

18. **Often imitated, never duplicated**
—(*Davis tennis rackets*) Victor Sports Inc.

19. **One of the everlasting kind**
—(*golf bags*) Lowenberg Co.

20. **Play ball with Pennsylvania**
—(*rubber balls*) Pennsylvania Tire Co.

21. **Play safe with Wilco**
—(*float coat*) Willer & Son.

22. **Play to *win* with Wilson**
—Wilson Sporting Goods Co.

23. **Remember: no one is paid to play Titleist**
—(*golf balls*) Acushnet Co.

24. **Scores in every field of sport**
—(*sports equipment*) MacGregor Goldsmith Inc.

25. **Smooth, easy "floating"ride**
—Safticycles Inc.

26. **The best with the *most* on the ball**
—Adirondack Bats Inc.

27. **The brightest star in golf**
—(*Burke-Worthington*) Victor Golf Co.

28. **The greatest name in golf**
—(*golfing equipment*) MacGregor Co.

29. **The name for quality athletic goods**
—Nocona Athletic Goods Co.

30. **The name to look for**
—Golfcraft Inc.

31. **The nation's big name in archery**
—Ben Pearson Inc.

32. **The no. 1 name in billiards**
—Brunswick Corp.

33. **There's Wilson equipment for every sport**
—Thos. E. Wilson Co.

108. SPORTING GOODS *cont.*

34. They take every trick
—(*Grand Slam golf clubs*) Hillerich & Bradsby Co. Inc.

35. Wings of steel
—(*ice skates*) Nestor Johnson Mfg. Co.

36. World's finest golf clubs and accessories
—Bristol Pro-Golf Inc.

37. World's largest exclusive manufacturer of golf balls
—Plymouth Golf Ball Co.

38. World's most experienced ski maker
—Northland Ski Mfg. Co.

39. "You don't have to be a millionaire to play like one"
—Walter Hagen Golf Epuipment Co.

STATIONERY SUPPLIES . . . See **81. OFFICE EQUIPMENT AND SUPPLIES, 83. PAPER PRODUCTS, 126. WRITING INSTRUMENTS**

STEREOS . . . See **5. AUDIO EQUIPMENT**

STOCKINGS . . . See **61. HOSIERY**

STORAGE . . . See **79. MOVING AND STORAGE**

STOVES . . . See **60. HOME APPLIANCES AND EQUIPMENT**

SUNGLASSES . . . See **41. EYEGLASSES**

SWEETS . . . See **20. CANDY AND GUM**

109. SWIMWEAR
See also **26. CLOTHING, MISCELLANEOUS, 98. RECREATIONAL EQUIPMENT, 108. SPORTING GOODS**

1. Come on, you sunners
—(*Jantzen swimsuit*) Jantzen Inc.

2. Delightfully see-worthy
—(*Jordan swimsuits*).

3. Shows good form in the stretch
—(*Lastex swimsuit*) Uniroyal Inc.

T

TABLEWARE . . . See **23.** CHINA, **67.** JEWELRY AND SILVER

TAPE DECKS . . . See **5.** AUDIO EQUIPMENT

TAPES . . . See **97.** RECORDINGS

110. **TEA**
See also **15.** BEVERAGES, MISCELLANEOUS, **27.** COFFEE, **107.** SOFT DRINKS

1. **A personal blend**
—(*Mother Parker's*).

2. **Brighten up with Instant Tender Leaf Tea**
—Standard Brands Inc.

3. **Brisk flavor, never flat**
—(*Lipton's*) Thomas J. Lipton Inc.

4. **For particular people**
—Salada Tea Co.

5. **Fresh from the gardens**
—Salada Tea Co.

6. **India produces the finest tea in the world**
—India Tea Bureau.

7. **Its flavor wins favor**
—(*Tetley*) Joseph Tetley & Co. Inc.

8. **It takes less to give more flavor**
—(*Lipton's*) Thomas J. Lipton Inc.

9. **Makes good tea a certainty**
—(*Tetley*) Joseph Tetley & Co. Inc.

10. **Officially certified as the finest tea grown**
—Ming Inc.

11. **Safe-Tea First**
—Ridgeways Inc.

12. **Soothing teas for a nervous world**
—(*herb teas*) Celestial Seasonings.

13. **Tea in the finest tradition**
—(*Canterbury*) Safeway Stores Inc.

14. **The brighter tasting tea**
—(*Instant Tender Leaf*) Standard Brands Inc.

15. **The brisk tea**
—Thomas J. Lipton Inc.

110. TEA *cont.*

16. The empire's best
                                      —(*Lyon's*).

17. The most expensive tea grown
                                      —Ming Inc.

18. There's more to it
                                      —India Tea Bureau.

19. "T" stands for Tetley's—Tetley stands for finest TEA
                                      —Joseph Tetley & Co. Inc.

20. When you change to Boscul, you change for good
                                      —Wm. S. Scull Co.

21. You might as well have the best
                                      —W. S. Quimby Co.

111. TELECOMMUNICATIONS
       See also **17.** BROADCASTING, **95.** RADIO EQUIPMENT

1. All around the world
                                      —Western Union.

2. Call Sprint. Find out about it.
                              —(*Sprint long distance system*) GTE.

3. Don't write, telegraph
                                      —Western Union.

4. Don't write, telephone
                                      —Bell Telephone Co.

5. Gee! No, GTE
                                      —GTE.

6. In the twinkling of an eye
                          —(*telephone system*) Trans-Canada System.

7. Long distance is the next best thing to being there
                                      —(*Bell System*) AT&T.

8. Long distance is the shortest way home
                                      —(*Bell System*) AT&T.

9. More than a new look. A new outlook.
                                      —AT&T.

10. Obviously it must be Western Union
                                      —Western Union.

11. One policy, one system, universal service
                                      —AT&T.

12. Our ambition: ideal telephone service for Michigan
                                      —Michigan Bell Telephone Co.

13. Phone power in action
                                      —(*Bell System*) AT&T.

14. Reach out and touch someone
                                      —(*long distance calling*) AT&T.

111.   TELECOMMUNICATIONS *cont.*

15. **Serving you**
> —(*Bell System*) AT&T.

16. **Sharing greatly in America's growth**
> —General Telephone and Electronics Corp.

17. **So many times a telegram means so much**
> —Western Union.

18. **Standard of the globe**
> —(*telegraph equipment*) J. H. Bunnell & Co.

19. **Talk things over, get things done ... by long distance!**
> —(*Bell System*) AT&T.

20. **The more you hear, the better we sound**
> —AT&T.

21. **The nation's long distance phone company**
> —MCI.

22. **The phone companies' phone company**
> —American Telecommunications Corporation.

23. **The telephone people**
> —Webcor.

24. **The voice with the smile**
> —Bell Telephone Co.

25. **The voice with the smile wins the world over**
> —AT&T.

26. **Total communications from a single source through Sylvania**
> —Sylvania Electric Products Inc.

27. **Use the Bell to sell**
> —Bell Telephone Co.

28. **We bring the world closer**
> —AT&T.

29. **We're reaching out in new directions**
> —AT&T.

30. **Worldwide electronics telecommunications**
> —International Telephone and Telegraph Co.

31. **You'll be hearing from us**
> —Mura.

32. **Your anywhere, anything, anytime network**
> —AT&T.

112. TELEVISIONS
See also **38. ELECTRONICS INDUSTRY, 60. HOME APPLIANCES AND EQUIPMENT, 78. MOVIES AND ENTERTAINMENT, 122. VIDEO EQUIPMENT**

1. **A flair for elegance**
—Sylvania Electric Products Inc.

2. **A world leader in technology**
—Hitachi Sales Corporation.

3. **Built better because it's handcrafted**
—Zenith Radio Corp.

4. **Famous for quality the world over**
—Philco Corp.

5. **First with the finest in television**
—(*Dumont*) National Union Electric Corp.

6. **Get the most out of television with a Dumont Teleset**
—(*Dumont*) National Union Electric Corp.

7. **Mark of quality throughout the world**
—Admiral Corp.

8. **Sony . . . the one and only**
—Sony Corp. of America.

9. **The international one**
—Toshiba America Inc.

10. **The magnificent**
—Magnavox Co.

11. **The most expensive television set in America . . . and darn well worth it.**
—(*Curtis-Mathes*) Curtis-Mathes Sales Co.

12. **The most trusted name in television**
—RCA Corp.

13. **The quality goes in before the name goes on**
—Zenith Radio Corp.

14. **The smart set**
—(*Zenith Systems*) Zenith Radio Corp.

15. **The theatre in your home**
—U. S. Television Mfg. Corp.

16. **We'll open your eyes**
—(*RCA*) RCA Corp.

17. **Window to the world**
—U. S. Television Mfg. Corp.

113.　TEXTILES

See also **65. INTERIOR DECORATION, 103. SEWING AND KNITTING SUPPLIES**

1.　**Add a fiber from Celanese and good things get better**

　　　　　　　　　　　　　　　　—Celanese Corp.

2.　**A man you can lean on, that's Klopman**

　　　　　　　　　　　—Klopman Mills Inc.

3.　**America lives in Dacron**

　　　　　　　　　　　　　　—Du Pont.

4.　**"America's leading producer of quality canvas products"**

　　　—Fulton Cotton Mills Div., Allied Products Corp.

5.　**A name to remember, a fabric to remember**

　　　　　　　　　　—(*Brooklawn corduroy*).

6.　**Be suspicious!**

　　　　　　—(*Sanforized*) Cluett, Peabody & Co. Inc.

7.　**Comfortable, carefree cotton**

　　　　　　　　　—Cotton Producers Institute.

8.　**Contemporary fibers**

　　　　　　　　　　　　—Celanese Corp.

9.　**Continuous filament textured nylon**

　　　　　　—(*Tycora*) Textured Yarn Co. Inc.

10.　**Cotton, you can feel how good it looks**

　　　　　　　　—National Cotton Council.

11.　**Fabrics used in the most wanted women's and children's sportswear**

　　　　　　—(*Clan Crest*) Glen Raven Mills.

12.　**Fabrics with the character of quality**

　　　　　　　　—Greenwood Mills Inc.

13.　**Fine fabrics made in America since 1813**

　　　　　　　—J. P. Stevens and Co. Inc.

14.　**First in fabrics for industry**

　　　—Industrial Fabrics Div., West Point-Pepperell Inc.

15.　**Gateway to the world of fabrics**

　　　　　—(*Westgate*) Reese B. Davis and Co. Inc.

16.　**If it's Darbrook, it's durable**

　　　　　—(*silks*) Schwarzenbach Huber & Co.

17.　**It's better because it's made of Koroseal**

　　　　　　—Comprehensive Fabrics Inc.

18.　**Keeps the shape**

　　　　　　　　　　　—Pellon Corp.

113.　TEXTILES *cont.*

19.　**Linen damask, impressively correct**
　　　　　—Irish & Scottish Linen Damask Guild.

20.　**Look for the Red Ball**
　　　　　—Mishawaka Woolen Mfg. Co.

21.　**Luxury acrylic fiber**
　　　　　—(*Creslan*) American Cyanamid Co.

22.　**Nothing but nylon makes you feel so female**
　　　　　—Textiles Div., Monsanto Co.

23.　**Nothing but Spandex makes you look so female**
　　　　　—Textiles Div., Monsanto Co.

24.　**100% cotton. The fiber you can trust.**
　　　　　—National Cotton Council.

25.　**One of the oldest names in textiles ... for the
　　　newest development in synthetics**
　　　　　—Conmark Plastics Div., Cohn-Hall-Marx Co.

26.　**Rhymes with increase**
　　　　　—(*Cantrece*) Du Pont.

27.　**Sandoz thinks ahead with textiles**
　　　　　—Sandoz Chemical Works.

28.　**The extraordinary fiber**
　　　　　—(*Trevira*) Hystron Fibers Inc.

29.　**The fabric with reflex action**
　　　　　—(*Expandra*) Burlington Industries Inc.

30.　**The fiber you can trust**
　　　　　—Cotton Producers Institute.

31.　**The home furnishings fiber**
　　　　　—(*Herculon*) Hercules Inc.

32.　**The luxury of velvet with the worry left out**
　　　　　—(*Islon*) Textiles Div., Monsanto Co.

33.　**The more colorful nylon**
　　　　　—(*Caprolan*) Allied Chemical Corp.

34.　**There are imitations, of course**
　　　　　—Viyella International Inc.

35.　**The shrinkage control that lets the wool breathe**
　　　　　—American Cyanamid Co.

36.　**"Well dressed/wool dressed"**
　　　　　—American Wool Council.

37.　**World's finest cottons**
　　　　　—Supima Association of America.

38.　**Woven where the wool is grown**
　　　　　—Oregon City Woolen Mills.

113. TEXTILES *cont.*

39. Your assurance that this fabric has been pretested for performance by Celanese
>—(*Arnel*) Celanese Corp.

TIMEPIECES . . . See **124.** WATCHES AND CLOCKS

114. TIRES
>See also **8.** AUTOMOTIVE PARTS AND PRODUCTS

1. A bear for wear
>—Gillette Rubber Co.

2. America's fastest-growing tire company
>—Cooper Tire and Rubber Co.

3. Around the world on Dunlops
>—Dunlop Tire & Rubber Corp.

4. Because so much is riding on your tires
>—Michelin.

5. Best in the long run
>—B. F. Goodrich Co.

6. Broad, black, and a brute for wear
>—Cupples Co.

7. Built from the road up
>—(*Biltwell tires*).

8. Built layer on layer
>—(*Miller tires*) B. F. Goodrich Co.

9. Famous for quality
>—Brunswick Rubber Co.

10. High-performance tirepower
>—Firestone Tire and Rubber Co.

11. Lots of Flatt tires running around
>—R. A. Flatt Tire Co.

12. Makers of the safety stripe tread
>—(*Fisk*) Uniroyal Tire Co.

13. Makes a blow-out harmless
>—(*safety tubes*) Goodyear Tire and Rubber Co.

14. Means more mileage
>—Mason Tire & Rubber Co.

15. Mileage hogs
>—(*Victor tires*).

16. More people ride on Goodyear tires than on any other brand
>—Goodyear Tire and Rubber Co.

17. Most miles per dollar
>—Firestone Tire and Rubber Co.

114. **TIRES** *cont.*

18. **New dimensions in driving on the *safer* Kelly road**
    —The Kelly-Springfield Tire Co.

19. **Outcleans, outpulls, outlasts**
    —Firestone Tire and Rubber Co.

20. **Remember the horse-shoe tread**
    —(*Racine tires*).

21. **Ride the road of satisfaction**
    —(*Atlas tires*) Atlas Supply Co.

22. **Skip the rest and drive the best**
    —(*Federal tires*).

23. **Smile at miles**
    —(*Lee balloon tires*).

24. **So much more in quality for so little more in price**
    —Seiberling Tire & Rubber Co.

25. **The greatest tire name in racing**
    —Firestone Tire and Rubber Co.

26. **The most beautiful tire in America**
    —Hydro-United Tire Co.

27. **The most trustworthy tires built**
    —Oldfield Tire Co.

28. **The name that's known is Firestone—all over the world**
    —Firestone Tire and Rubber Co.

29. **The round tire that rolls 3,000 miles further**
    —(*Atlas Plycron*) General Tire and Rubber Co.

30. **Where research and development make exciting ideas**
    —General Tire and Rubber Co.

31. **You're miles ahead with General Tire**
    —General Tire and Rubber Co.

32. **Your symbol of quality and service**
    —Firestone Tire and Rubber Co.

115. **TOBACCO PRODUCTS**
    See also **105.** SMOKING ACCESSORIES

1. **Aged in the wood**
    —(*Velvet*) Liggett & Myers Inc.

2. **A honey of a tobacco**
    —(*Cookie Jar tobacco*) United States Tobacco Co.

3. **Always better, better all ways**
    —(*Philip Morris*) Philip Morris Inc.

4. **America's best tasting little cigar**
    —(*Between the Acts*) Lorillard Corp.

115. TOBACCO PRODUCTS *cont.*

5. **America's finest pipe tobacco**
   —(*Edgeworth*) House of Edgeworth.

6. **America's smoothest tobacco**
   —(*Velvet*) Liggett & Myers Inc.

7. **A pipe's best friend is fragrant Heine's blend**
   —Sutliff Tobacco Co.

8. **A *real* cigarette**
   —(*Camel*) R. J. Reynolds Tobacco Co.

9. **Aromatic in the pack, aromatic in the pipe**
   —(*Holiday tobacco*).

10. **A sensible cigarette**
    —(*Fatima*) Liggett & Myers Inc.

11. **A shilling in London, a quarter here**
    —(*Pall Mall*) American Tobacco Co.

12. **Ask Dad, he knows**
    —(*Sweet Caporal*) American Tobacco Co.

13. **Ask him why he smokes a Webster**
    —Webster Cigar Co.

14. **Ask your dealer, he knows**
    —(*cigars*) Garcia y Vega Inc.

15. **Barking Dog never bites**
    —Continental Tobacco Co.

16. **Be nonchalant, light a Deity**
    —(*Egyptian Deities*).

17. **Best for half a century, better than ever today**
    —(*Admiration cigars*) E. Regensburg & Sons.

18. **Blended right**
    —(*Winchester cigarettes*) R. J. Reynolds Tobacco Co.

19. **Buy word of millions**
    —(*King Edward cigars*).

20. **Camels agree with me**
    —R. J. Reynolds Tobacco Co.

21. **Camels suit your T-zone to a T**
    —R. J. Reynolds Tobacco Co.

22. **Champion of blends**
    —(*Sportsman pipe mixture*).

23. **Change to Bond Street for fragrant smoking**
    —(*Bond Street pipe tobacco*) Philip Morris Inc.

24. **Chesterfield King tastes great . . . tastes mild**
    —Liggett & Myers Inc.

25. **Chew Mail Pouch**
    —(*Mail Pouch chewing tobacco*) Whitehall Products Inc.

115.   TOBACCO PRODUCTS *cont.*

26.   **Come to Marlboro Country**
                    —(*Marlboro*) Philip Morris Inc.

27.   **Come to where the flavor is ... come to Marlboro country**
                    —Philip Morris Inc.

28.   **Come up to the Kool taste**
                    —Brown & Williamson Tobacco Corp.

29.   **Discover extra coolness**
                    —(*Kool*) Brown & Williamson Tobacco Corp.

30.   **Every El Dueno cigar is smooth sailing**
                    —El Dueno Cigar Co.

31.   **Every puff a pleasure**
                    —(*cigars*) Gonzalez & Sanchez Co.

32.   **Executive America's top cigar**
                    —(*Webster*) Webster Cigar Co.

33.   **Experience is the best teacher**
                    —(*Camel*) R. J. Reynolds Tobacco Co.

34.   **Famous name in tobacco for nearly 200 years**
                    —(*Old Gold*) Lorillard Corp.

35.   **Filters the smoke on the way to your throat—filters it and makes it mild**
                    —(*Pall Mall*) American Tobacco Co.

36.   **Fine tobacco is what counts in a cigarette**
                    —(*Lucky Strike*) American Tobacco Co.

37.   **First in the social register**
                    —(*cigars*) Webster-Eisenlohr Inc.

38.   **For a taste that's *Springtime fresh***
                    —(*Salem*) R. J. Reynolds Tobacco Co.

39.   **For deep-down smoking enjoyment smoke that smoke of fine tobacco—Lucky Strike**
                    —(*Lucky Strike*) American Tobacco Co.

40.   **For digestion's sake, smoke Camels**
                    —R. J. Reynolds Tobacco Co.

41.   **For real enjoyment**
                    —(*El Producto cigars*) Consolidated Cigar Corp.

42.   **For real smoking pleasure**
                    —(*Chesterfield*) Liggett Group.

43.   **For the best combination of filter and good taste Kent satisfies *best***
                    —Lorillard Corp.

44.   **For the taste that's right**
                    —(*Viceroy*) Brown & Williamson Tobacco Corp.

115. **TOBACCO PRODUCTS** *cont.*

45. **For those who want *every* puff to taste as fresh as the *first* puff!**
> —(*Montclair*) American Brands Inc.

46. **For young men and men with young ideas**
> —General Cigar Co.

47. **Four inches of a 25-cent cigar**
> —The In-B-Tween Co.

48. **Generously good**
> —(*G. W. Childs cigar*) American Cigar Co.

49. **Guard against throat-scratch**
> —(*Pall Mall*) American Tobacco Co.

50. **Have you tried a Lucky lately?**
> —(*Lucky Strike*) American Tobacco Co.

51. **Have you tried one lately?**
> —(*Robert Burns cigars*) General Cigar Co.

52. **I'd rather fight than switch**
> —(*Tareyton*) American Tobacco Co.

53. **I'd walk a mile for a Camel**
> —R. J. Reynolds Tobacco Co.

54. **I envy men the pleasant puffing of their pipes**
> —(*Tuxedo tobacco*) American Tobacco Co.

55. **If every smoker knew what Philip Morris smokers know, they'd all change to Philip Morris**
> —Philip Morris Inc.

56. **If you want a treat instead of a treatment, smoke Old Golds**
> —Lorillard Corp.

57. **I'm particular**
> —(*Pall Mall*) American Tobacco Co.

58. **It's a mighty fine pipe tobacco**
> —J. Dill Co.

59. **It's a pippin**
> —(*cigars*) H. Traiser & Co. Inc.

60. **Its blend is our secret, its fragrance your delight**
> —(*Old Briar tobacco*) United Cigar Stores.

61. **It's good because it's fresh**
> —(*Tuxedo tobacco*) American Tobacco Co.

62. **It's king-size smoking at its best, yet priced no higher than the rest**
> —(*Embassy cigarettes*).

63. **It's mild and mellow**
> —(*Revelation pipe tobacco*) Philip Morris Inc.

115. TOBACCO PRODUCTS *cont.*

64. **It's moisturized**
>—(*Raleigh*) Brown & Williamson Tobacco Corp.

65. **It's More you**
>—(*More cigarettes*) R. J. Reynolds Tobacco Co.

66. **It started me smoking cigars**
>—(*Robert Burns cigars*) General Cigar Co.

67. **It's the tobacco that counts**
>—(*Lucky Strike*) American Tobacco Co.

68. **It's toasted**
>—(*Lucky Strike*) American Tobacco Co.

69. **Ivory tips protect your lips**
>—(*Marlboro*) Philip Morris Inc.

70. **Join the first team. Reach for Winston.**
>—(*Winston cigarettes*) R. J. Reynolds Tobacco Co.

71. **Judged best by the just**
>—(*Barister cigars*) Celestino Costello Co.

72. **Judge for yourself**
>—(*Murad*) S. Anagyros Corp.

73. **Just enough!**
>—(*Montclair*) American Brands Inc.

74. **Just enough Turkish**
>—(*Fatima*) Liggett & Myers Inc.

75. **Leaf tobaccos that satisfy**
>—(*Louis Greenwald*).

76. **Lightest smoke of all**
>—(*Carlton*) American Brands Inc.

77. **LS/MFT . . . Lucky Strike means fine tobacco**
>—(*Lucky Strike*) American Tobacco Co.

78. **Luckies are gentle on my throat**
>—(*Lucky Strike*) American Tobacco Co.

79. **Luckies are kind to your throat**
>—(*Lucky Strike*) American Tobacco Co.

80. **Lucky Strike green has gone to war**
>—(*Lucky Strike*) American Tobacco Co.

81. **Make a date with Muriel**
>—(*Muriel cigars*) Consolidated Cigar Corp.

82. **Making smoking "safe" for smokers**
>—Bonded Tobacco Co.

83. **Man alive! Two for five**
>—Standard Cigar Co.

84. **Man to man, Roi-Tan, a cigar you'll like**
>—(*Roi-Tan cigars*) American Cigar Co.

115. **TOBACCO PRODUCTS** *cont.*

85. **Measure yourself for a Kelly**
—(*Kelly cigar*) American Cigar Co.

86. **Menthol-cooled**
—(*Spuds*).

87. **Mild as May**
—(*Marlboro*) Philip Morris Inc.

88. **Mildness plus character**
—Congress Cigar Co.

89. **Millions are saying "Tasting better than ever"**
—General Cigar Co.

90. **Millions of Spud smokers can't be wrong**
—(*Spuds*).

91. **More people are smoking Camels than ever before**
—R. J. Reynolds Co.

92. **Never before did a nickel buy more**
—(*cigars*) Otto Eisenlohr & Bros.

93. **Never gets on your nerves**
—(*Girard cigar*) Antonio, Roag & Langsdorg.

94. **Newport smokes fresher—and tastes better than any other menthol cigarette**
—Lorillard Corp.

95. *New* **taste,** *new* **smoking convenience ... anywhere, anytime**
—(*Roi-Tan Little Cigars*) American Brands Inc.

96. **No finer-tasting cigar at any price**
—(*Seidenberg cigars*) S. Frieder & Sons Co.

97. **No other tobacco is like it**
—(*Prince Albert tobacco*) R. J. Reynolds Co.

98. **Not a cough in a carload**
—(*Old Gold*) Lorillard Corp.

99. **Now every man can enjoy his pipe**
—Sutliff Tobacco Co.

100. **Once tried, always satisfied**
—(*Golden Virginia tobacco*).

101. **Only Viceroy has this exclusive filter**
—Brown & Williamson Tobacco Corp.

102. **Outstanding—and they are mild!**
—(*Pall Mall*) American Tobacco Co.

103. **Pall Mall's greater length travels the smoke further ... gets rid of heat and bite on the way**
—(*Pall Mall*) American Tobacco Co.

115. TOBACCO PRODUCTS *cont.*

104. **P. A. means Pipe Appeal**
—(*Prince Albert tobacco*) R. J. Reynolds Co.

105. **Players go places**
—(*Players cigarettes*) Philip Morris Inc.

106. **Product of Cuban soil and Cuban sun**
—(*La Primadora cigars*) Universal Cigar Corp.

107. **Queen of distinctive cigarettes**
—(*Helmar*) Lorillard Corp.

108. **Reach for a Lucky instead of a sweet**
—(*Lucky Strike*) American Tobacco Co.

109. **Reach for a world of flavor**
—(*Merit cigarettes*) Philip Morris Inc.

110. **Right combination, world's best tobaccos properly aged**
—(*Chesterfield*) Liggett Group.

111. **Salem softness freshens your taste**
—R. J. Reynolds Tobacco Co.

112. **Satisfies *best***
—(*Kent*) Lorillard Corp.

113. **She likes the fragrance**
—Sutliff Tobacco Co.

114. **Smart smokers smoke Seidenberg**
—(*Seidenberg cigars*) S. Frieder & Sons Co.

115. **Smells better in the pouch; smokes better in the pipe**
—(*Model pipe tobacco*) United States Tobacco Co.

116. **Smoke all 7**
—(*Viceroy*) Brown & Williamson Tobacco Corp.

117. **Smoke Omar for Aroma**
—American Tobacco Co.

118. **Sooner or later, your favorite tobacco**
—(*Sir Walter Raleigh*) Brown & Williamson Tobacco Corp.

119. **So round, so firm, so fully packed—so free and easy on the draw**
—(*Lucky Strike*) American Tobacco Co.

120. **Standard of the world**
—(*Bull Durham tobacco*) American Tobacco Co.

121. **Such popularity must be deserved**
—(*Chesterfield*) Liggett Group.

122. **Take a pouch instead of a puff**
—(*Skoal Bandits*) United States Tobacco Co.

115.   TOBACCO PRODUCTS *cont.*

123. **Take a tip from Robert Burns**
—*(cigars)* General Cigar Co.

124. **Tastes better than any other menthol cigarette!**
—*(Newport)* Lorillard Corp.

125. **Tastes great . . . yet it smokes so mild**
—*(Chesterfield)* Liggett Group.

126. **Ten to one it's a Santa Fe**
—*(cigars)* A. Sensenbrenner Sons.

127. **That pleasing cigar**
—*(Muriel)* Consolidated Cigar Corp.

128. **That's putting it MILDLY**
—*(Country Doctor pipe mixture)* Philip Morris Inc.

129. **The aristocrat of cigars**
—*(Robert Burns cigars)* General Cigar Co.

130. **The aristocrat of pipe tobacco**
—*(Old Briar)* United Cigar Stores.

131. **The best cigar in any case**
—Justin Seubert Co.

132. **The best in the Union, in pocket tins**
—*(Union smoking tobacco)* Lorillard Corp.

133. **The best tobacco makes the best smoke**
—*(Camel)* R. J. Reynolds Tobacco Co.

134. **The biteless blend**
—*(Briggs pipe mixture)* United States Tobacco Co.

135. **The brand with the grand aroma**
—Mail Pouch Tobacco Co.

136. **The choice of successful men**
—*(Blackstone cigars)* Parodi Cigar Corp.

137. **The cigar made with good judgment**
—*(Tom Keene)* General Cigar Co.

138. **The cigar that breathes**
—*(Roi-Tan cigars)* American Cigar Co.

139. **The cigar that never lasts long enough**
—*(Antonio y Cleopatra)* American Brands Inc.

140. **The filter for the taste that's right!**
—*(Viceroy)* Brown & Williamson Tobacco Corp.

141. **The first different smoking tobacco in a generation**
—*(Half & Half)* American Tobacco Co.

142. **The first new no-filter cigarette in years**
—*(York)* Lorillard Corp.

143. **The flavor's all yours**
—*(Philip Morris)* Philip Morris Inc.

115. TOBACCO PRODUCTS *cont.*

144. **The friendly smoke**
—(*Royalist cigars*) Grabowsky Bros. Inc.

145. **The holiday cigar at a week-day price**
—(*Cinco*) Bayuk Cigars Inc.

146. **The honey-cured smoke**
—Kaufman Bros. & Bondy.

147. **The makings of a nation**
—(*Bull Durham tobacco*) American Tobacco Co.

148. **The mark of quality in tobacco products**
—Brown & Williamson Tobacco Corp.

149. **The milder, better-tasting cigarette**
—(*Regent*).

150. **The national joy smoke**
—(*Prince Albert tobacco*) R. J. Reynolds Co.

151. **The *one* cigarette for everyone who smokes!**
—(*Kent*) Lorillard Corp.

152. **The one cigarette sold the world over**
—(*Melachrino*).

153. **The password is Kools**
—(*Kool*) Brown & Williamson Tobacco Corp.

154. **The perfect cigarette**
—(*Marlboro*) Philip Morris Inc.

155. **The pick of Canada's burley tobacco**
—(*Picobac*) Imperial Tobacco Co. of Canada.

156. **The pleasure is back**
—(*Barclay cigarettes*) Brown & Williamson Tobacco Corp.

157. **There's many a castle built out of cigarette smoke**
—Bonded Tobacco Co.

158. **There's something about them you'll like**
—(*Herbert Tareyton*) American Tobacco Co.

159. **The sign of a good cigar**
—United Cigar Stores.

160. **The smoke with a smile**
—(*Briggs pipe mixture*) United States Tobacco Co.

161. **The sophistocrat of cigars**
—General Cigar Co.

162. **The sum-total of smoking pleasure**
—(*Chesterfield*) Liggett Group.

163. **The taste is richer, yet the smoke is milder**
—(*Raleigh*) Brown & Williamson Tobacco Corp.

164. **The taste that's right**
—(*Viceroy*) Brown & Williamson Tobacco Corp.

115. TOBACCO PRODUCTS *cont.*

165. The tobacco of quality
                                        —(*Old Chum*).

166. The utmost in cigarettes
                                        —(*Egyptian Deities*).

167. They are the largest-selling cigarette in America
                        —(*Camel*) R. J. Reynolds Tobacco Co.

168. They cost no more
                                        —(*Regent*).

169. They respect your throat
                                        —(*Alligator*).

170. They satisfy and yet they're mild
                        —(*Chesterfield*) Liggett Group.

171. "Tobacco is our middle name"
                        —American Brands Inc.

172. "Us Tareyton smokers would rather fight than switch!"
                        —(*Tareyton*)American Brands Inc.

173. Watch his smoke
                        —(*Santa Fe cigars*) A. Sensenbrenner Sons.

174. What a whale of a difference just a few cents make
                        —(*Fatima*) Liggett Group.

175. When a feller needs a friend
                        —(*Briggs pipe mixture*) United States Tobacco Co.

176. Wherever particular people congregate
                        —(*Pall Mall*) American Tobacco Co.

177. Why be irritated? Light an Old Gold
                        —(*Old Gold*) Lorillard Corp.

178. Why not smoke the finest?
                        —(*Dunhill*) Alfred Dunhill Co. London.

179. Winston. America's Best.
                        —(*Winston cigarettes*) R. J. Reynolds Tobacco Co.

180. Winston tastes good ... like a cigarette should
                        —R. J. Reynolds Tobacco Co.

181. With men who know tobacco best, it's Luckies 2 to 1
                        —(*Lucky Strike*) American Tobacco Co.

182. With pleasure, sir!
                        —General Cigar Co.

183. With the aroma of the rose
                        —(*Rosa Aroma cigars*) C. A. Nolan.

184. World leader in luxury cigars
                        —(*Gold Label*) General Cigar Co.

115. TOBACCO PRODUCTS *cont.*

185. **You never had it this fresh!**
—(*Bright 100's cigarettes*) R. J. Reynolds Tobacco Co.

186. **You ought to meet Muriel**
—(*Muriel cigars*) Consolidated Cigar Corp.

187. **Your nose quickly knows**
—(*Tuxedo pipe tobacco*) American Tobacco Co.

188. **Your smoke comes clean**
—(*Viceroy*) Brown & Williamson Tobacco Corp.

189. **You've Come A Long Way, Baby**
—(*Virginia Slims Lights*) Philip Morris Inc.

116. TOILETRIES
See also **12. BATH ACCESSORIES, 32. COSMETICS,
34. DENTAL CARE, 54. HAIR CARE, 84. PERFUMES
AND FRAGRANCES, 104. SHAVING SUPPLIES,
106. SOAP**

1. **As easy to use as to say**
—(*Mum*) George B. Evans.

2. **As masculine as the trade mark**
—(*Royal Flush toiletries*) B. Ansehl Co.

3. **A swab by any other name is not the same**
—(*Q-tips cotton swabs*) Chesebrough-Pond's Inc.

4. **A winner with women**
—(*Quest deodorant*) Vicks Health Care.

5. **Because . . .**
—(*Modess*) Personal Products Co.

6. **Don't be half-safe. Be completely safe. Use Arrid—to
be sure.**
—(*Arrid deodorant*) Carter-Wallace Inc.

7. **HUSH takes the odor out of perspiration**
—Hush Co.

8. **Invented by a doctor—now used by millions of
women**
—Tampax Inc.

9. **Keeps you sweet as an angel**
—(*Neet deodorant*) Whitehall Laboratories.

10. **Mum helps to make a miss a hit**
—(*deodorant*) George B. Evans.

11. **MUM is the word**
—(*deodorant*) George B. Evans.

12. **Not a shadow of a doubt**
—(*Kotex*) Kimberly-Clark Corp.

116. TOILETRIES *cont.*

13. **Protects you like a man, but still treats you like a woman**
>—(*Lady Speed Stick deodorant*) The Mennen Co.

14. **Raise your hand if you're sure**
>—(*Sure deodorant*) Procter & Gamble Co.

15. **She's sure—are you?**
>—(*Odorono deodorant*) Chesebrough-Pond's Inc.

16. **Stay shower-fresh all day long**
>—(*Seaforth deodorant for men*) Seaforth Corp.

17. **Stay sweet with Hush**
>—(*deodorant*) Hush Co.

18. **The antiseptic deodorant powder**
>—Amolin Co.

19. **The dainty deodorant**
>—Eversweet Co.

20. **The finishing touch you can't afford to forget**
>—(*Seaforth deodorant for men*) Seaforth Corp.

21. **The gentler cream deodorant**
>—(*Yodora*) Norcliff Thayer Inc.

22. **The last word in gifts for men**
>—(*Courtley toiletries*).

23. **The perfect under-arm protective**
>—(*Perstik*) Feminine Products Inc.

24. **The safe-and-sure deodorant**
>—(*Etiquet*).

25. **Tussy really cares about people who care**
>—(*deodorant*) Lehn and Fink Consumer Products.

26. **Walk with comfort**
>—(*Modess*) Personal Products Co.

27. **West Point stands for good grooming**
>—(*men's toiletries*) Associated Brands.

28. **What Scandinavian men have**
>—(*Teak*) Shulton Inc.

29. **When your nose needs the softest**
>—(*Softique tissues*) Kimberly-Clark Corp.

30. **You feel so cool, so clean, so fresh . . .**
>—Tampax Inc.

31. **You work hard, you need Right Guard**
>—(*Right Guard deodorant*) The Gillette Co.

117. **TOOLS**

See also **55.** HARDWARE

1. **A file for every purpose**

—Nicholson File Co.

2. **A fine tool at a fair price**

—Capewell Mfg. Co.

3. **Bonded for life ... because they're built that way**

—Ingersoll-Rand Co.

4. **Choice of better mechanics**

—Snap-On Tools Corp.

5. **Doggone good tools**

—Duro Metal Products Co.

6. **Fingers of steel**

—(*Red Devil pliers*) Smith & Hemenway Co.

7. **For all industry**

—Snap-On Tools Corp.

8. **For industry, shop, farm and home**

—(*electric tools*) Black & Decker Mfg. Co.

9. **Go with the pick of the pros**

—Skil Corp.

10. **Hand-ee, the tool of 1001 uses**

—(*Hand-ee tool*) Chicago Wheel & Mfg. Co.

11. **It pays to use good tools**

—Vaughan & Bushnell Mfg. Co.

12. **It's all in the wheel**

—(*glass cutter*) Landon P. Smith Inc.

13. **Jack of all trades and master of plenty**

—(*Hand-ee tool*) Chicago Wheel & Mfg. Co.

14. **Keep mechanics good tempered**

—Velchek Tool Co.

15. **Keep your eye on Elliott**

—Elliott Div., Carrier Corp.

16. **Make an heirloom**

—(*woodworker's tools*) Woodcraft Supply Co.

17. **Make hard jobs easy**

—K-D Manufacturing Co.

18. **Maker of the world's first cordless electric tools**

—Black & Decker Mfg. Co.

19. ***Matched* tools for *unmatched* performance**

—Baash-Ross Div., Joy Mfg. Co.

117. **TOOLS** *cont.*

20. **O-B on a Bull Dog clamp proves the safest quality stamp**
                                        —Ohio Brass Co.

21. **On the bench since 1850**
                                        —Prentiss Vise Co.

22. **Relieves the daily grind**
                                        —Keystone Emery Mills.

23. **Right to the point**
                                —(*Yankee tools*) North Bros. Mfg. Co.

24. **Sands levels tell the truth**
                                —(*levels*) Sands Level & Tool Co.

25. **Service-backed shop equipment**
                                        —Snap-On Tools Corp.

26. **Skil makes it easy**
                                        —Skil Corp.

27. **Standard for accuracy**
                                —(*steel tapes*) Starrett Co.

28. **Standard of the industry**
                                        —Hughes Tool Co.

29. **The good mechanic's choice**
                                        —U. S. Electrical Tool Co.

30. **The hammer with a backbone**
                                        —American Hammer Corp.

31. **The jack that saves your back**
                                —(*Rees jack*) Iron City Products Co.

32. **The key to better grinding**
                                        —Black & Decker Mfg. Co.

33. **The name really means something**
                                        —Niles Tools Works Co.

34. **The right tool for the right job**
                                        —True Temper Corp.

35. **The saw most carpenters use**
                                        —Henry Disston & Sons.

36. **The small lathe for the big job**
                                        —Dalton Mfg. Co.

37. **The third hand with a mighty grip**
                                        —Prentiss Vise Co.

38. **The tool box of the world**
                                        —The Stanley Works.

39. **The tools in the plaid box**
                                        —American Saw & Mfg. Co.

117. TOOLS *cont.*

40. Toolmaker to the master mechanic
—Millers Falls Co.

41. Tools you can sell with confidence
—Marion Tool Works.

42. We want to help you do things right
—The Stanley Works.

43. World's largest manufacturer of painters' and glaziers' tools—since 1872
—Red Devil Inc.

44. Yankee tools make better mechanics
—North Bros. Mfg. Co.

TOOTHPASTE ... See **34.** DENTAL CARE

TOURISM ... See **119.** TRAVEL

118. TOYS AND GAMES
See also **10.** BABY PRODUCTS, **98.** RECREATIONAL
EQUIPMENT, **108.** SPORTING GOODS

1. A minute to learn. A lifetime to master.
—(*Othello board game*) Ideal Toy Corp.

2. BICYCLE is the card player's choice
—(*playing cards*) United States Playing Card Co.

3. Dad played marbles, too
—Akro Agate Co.

4. Engineering for boys
—(*Meccano*) Designatronics Inc.

5. For your children's sake
—(*slides, merri-go-rounds*) Merremaker Corp.

6. It is what it eats
—(*Infocom computer games*) Infocom Inc.

7. It must be good to be a Gund
—Gund Inc.

8. Ives Toys make happy boys
—Ives Mfg. Co.

9. Made by the tiny Arcadians
—Arcade Mfg. Co.

10. Made in America for American boys and girls
—(*Kiddie-Kar*) H. C. White Co.

11. Make men of boys
—Structo Mfg. Co.

12. Most trusted name in modelling
—Hawk Model Co.

118. TOYS AND GAMES *cont.*

13. "Our work is child's play"
—Fisher-Price Toys Inc.

14. Playtime Pals for the nation's kiddies
—Coronet Toy Mfg. Co.

15. Quality toys with a purpose
—(*Tinkertoys*) Toy Tinkers Div., A. G. Spalding and Bros., Inc.

16. Roller skate with three lives
—Chicago Roller Skate Co.

17. Roll on rubber
—Chicago Roller Skate Co.

18. Sane toys for healthy kids
—Lionel Toy Corp.

19. The heart's desire for every youngster
—(*Reliable dolls*).

20. The home of toys
—F. A. O. Schwartz.

21. The name for quality hobby kits
—Monogram Models Inc.

22. The skate with a backbone
—Winchester Repeating Arms Co.

23. The trains that railroad men buy for their boys
—(*Lionel*) Fundimensions.

24. Toys that are genuine
—The A. C. Gilbert Co.

25. Twice as much fun
—(*Loco-Builder electric trains*) Dorfan Co.

26. World's largest creator of preschool toys
—Fisher-Price Toys Inc.

TRACTORS . . . See 42. FARMING SUPPLIES AND EQUIPMENT

TRANSPORTATION . . . See 4. AIR TRAVEL AND CARGO, 19. BUS LINES, 96. RAIL TRAVEL AND CARGO, 102. SEA TRAVEL AND CARGO, 120. TRUCKS AND TRUCKING INDUSTRY

119. TRAVEL
See also 4. AIR TRAVEL AND CARGO, 6. AUTOMOBILE
RENTAL SERVICES, 19. BUS LINES, 36. ECONOMIC
DEVELOPMENT, 62. HOTELS AND MOTELS,
72. LUGGAGE, 79. MOVING AND STORAGE, 96. RAIL
TRAVEL AND CARGO, 102. SEA TRAVEL AND CARGO

1. **Abroad without crossing the seas**
                    —Montreal Tourist & Convention Bureau.

2. **America borders on the magnificent**
                    —Canadian Ministry of Tourism.

3. **America's dairyland**
                                        —Wisconsin.

4. **America's lake country**
                    —The Thousand Lakes Assn., St. Paul, Minn.

5. **America's most interesting state**
                    —Tennessee Dept. of Conservation.

6. **A world in itself**
                                        —New Zealand.

7. **Better yet, Connecticut**
                    —Connecticut Dept. of Economic Development.

8. **Birthplace of the nation**
    —Virginia Dept. of Conservation and Economic
                                        Development.

9. **Birth state of the nation**
                                        —Pennsylvania.

10. **Center of scenic America**
                                        —Salt Lake City.

11. **Come to Israel. Come stay with friends**
                    —Israeli Government Tourist Office.

12. **Cool off in Colorado**
                                        —Colorado.

13. **Crossroads of the Pacific**
                                        —Hawaii.

14. **Don't leave home without it**
                    —(*American Express card*) American Express Co.

15. **Don't leave home without them**
                    —(*travelers checks*) American Express Co.

16. **Double crossroads of America**
                                        —Indianapolis, Ind.

17. **Find your place in the sun**
                    —San Francisco Peninsula.

119. TRAVEL *cont.*

18. Friendly, familiar, foreign and near
—Ontario, Canada, Department of Tourism and Information.

19. Friendly land of infinite variety
—South Dakota Dept. of Highways

20. Hub of the Americas
—New Orleans.

21. I Love New York
—New York State Tourist Commission.

22. Inside the rim of adventure
—Manitoba, Canada.

23. Isle of June
—Nassau Development Board, Nassau, Bahamas.

24. Keystone of your vacation
—Pennsylvania.

25. Land of enchantment
—Department of Development, New Mexico.

26. Land of scenic splendor
—New Hampshire.

27. Mix fun and history in Virginia
—Virginia Dept. of Conservation and Economic Development.

28. Nature's paradise, man's opportunity
—State of Washington.

29. Now's the time to get away *to* it all!
—Southwest Sun Country Association.

30. Now that you've conquered the world, separate yourself from it
—Fisher's Island.

31. One management, ship and shore
—Canadian Pacific Steamship & Railroad Co.

32. See America best by car
—American Petroleum Institute.

33. See this world before the next
—Canadian Pacific Steamship & Railroad Co.

34. State of excitement
—Oregon Highway Dept.

35. The big sky country
—Montana Highway Commission.

36. The company for people who travel
—American Express Co.

119. TRAVEL *cont.*

37. **The heart of America**
                                        —Missouri.

38. **The hospitality state**
                                        —Mississippi.

39. **The land of enchantment is calling you**
                      —Vancouver, British Columbia, Canada.

40. **The land of ten thousand lakes**
                                        —St. Paul, Minn.

41. **The land that was *made* for vacations**
                      —Wisconsin Vacation and Travel Service.

42. **The place to go**
                      —Spanish National Tourist Office.

43. **The summer wonderland**
                            —Mackinac Island, Michigan.

44. **The Sunshine State**
                                        —Florida.

45. **The surprising state**
                              —State of Washington.

46. **The winter playground of America**
                              —San Antonio, Texas.

47. **The world's most beautiful island**
                                        —Jamaica.

48. **The world's playground**
                            —Atlantic City, New Jersey.

49. **Travel strengthens America**
                              —U. S. Travel Bureau.

50. **Vacationing in San Antonio is a family affair**
                —San Antonio Municipal Information Bureau.

51. **We've got your world**
                                        —Collette Tours.

52. **Where summer spends the winter**
                            —West Palm Beach, Florida.

53. **Where summer stays and the nation plays**
                                —Sarasota, Florida.

54. **Winter fun under a "summer sun"**
                                —Sun Valley, Idaho.

55. **World's greatest travel system**
                —Canadian Pacific Steamship & Railroad Co.

56. **You can't get the whole picture in just a day or two**
                —San Francisco Convention and Visitors Bureau.

119. TRAVEL *cont.*

57. You haven't seen your country if you haven't seen Alaska
—Alaska Travel Div., Department of Economic Development and Planning.

TRAVELERS CHECKS ... See **43.** FINANCIAL INSTITUTIONS AND SERVICES, **119.** TRAVEL

120. TRUCKS AND TRUCKING INDUSTRY
See also **42.** FARMING AND SUPPLIES AND EQUIPMENT, **73.** MACHINERY, **79.** MOVING AND STORAGE

1. America's greatest truck
—Mutual Truck Co.

2. Brockway, the right way
—Brockway Motor Trucks.

3. "Build a truck to do a job—change it only to do better"
—International Harvester Co.

4. Builder of trucks you can trust
—Studebaker Corp.

5. Built for business
—(*Duplex Truck*) Warner & Swasey Co.

6. Built to last longer
—(*Econoline vans*) Ford Motor Co.

7. Buy today's best truck. Own tomorrow's best trade
—Hyster Co.

8. Chevrolet is more truck ... **day in, day out**
—Chevrolet Div., General Motors Corp.

9. Dodge builds tough trucks
—(*Dodge trucks*) Chrysler Corp.

10. Leading name in truck transportation
—Consolidated Freightways Inc.

11. More than a truck line – a transportation system
—Interstate Motor Freight System.

12. No. 1 heavy-duty sales leader
—International Harvester Co.

13. Quality trucks always cost less!
—(*Chevrolet trucks*) General Motors Corp.

14. Ram Tough
—(*Dodge trucks*) Chrysler Corp.

15. Since 1900, America's hardest working truck
—Mack Trucks Inc.

16. "Speed with economy"
—Yale Express System Inc.

120. TRUCKS AND TRUCKING INDUSTRY *cont.*

17. Super service
> —T. I. M. E. Freight Inc.

18. The big brother to the railroads
> —(*Kelly-Springfield Motor Truck*).

19. "The motor carrier with more Go-How"
> —Eastern Express System Inc.

20. The only truck bodies built like a trailer
> —Fruehauf Corp.

21. The truck of continuous service
> —Maccar Truck Co.

22. The truck of proved units
> —Acme Motor Truck Co.

23. The truck of value
> —(*GMC truck*) General Motors Corp.

24. The wheels that go everywhere
> —American Trucking Associations Inc.

25. They cost more because they're worth more
> —(*Autocar*) White Motor Corp.

26. Total transportation
> —Fruehauf Corp.

27. Trucks for every purpose
> —Mack Trucks Inc.

28. Uncommon carriers
> —(*Oneida Motor Truck*).

29. Users know
> —(*Garford Motor Truck*) Consolidated Motors Corp.

30. Vital link in America's supply line
> —Transamerican Freight Lines Inc.

31. Wilson, that's haul
> —(*Wilson trucks*).

32. World leader in heavy-duty trucks
> —White Motor Corp.

33. Your best bet over the long haul
> —D. C. Trucking Co. Inc.

TYPEWRITERS . . . See **81.** OFFICE EQUIPMENT AND SUPPLIES

U

UMBRELLAS . . . See **123.** WARDROBE ACCESSORIES

121. UNDERWEAR

See also **26.** CLOTHING, MISCELLANEOUS, **61.** HOSIERY

1. A "fitting" tribute to the feminine figure
    —(*Primrose foundations*).

2. All is vanity . . . all is **Vanity Fair**
    —Vanity Fair Mills Inc.

3. As modern as tomorrow
    —Royal Worcester Corset Co.

4. Beautiful corset worn by beautiful women to make them more beautiful
    —Lily of France Corset Co.

5. Because you love nice things
    —Van Raalte Co. Inc.

6. Behind every Olga there really is an **Olga**
    —Olga Co.

7. Checks your figure but not your freedom
    —Marvelette Inc.

8. Covers the subject
    —(*foundations*) Sid Levy & Sons.

9. Don't say underwear, say **Munsingwear**
    —Munsingwear Inc.

10. Every Bali has a bow
    —Bali Brassiere Co.

11. Every mile of yarn gives an extra year of wear
    —Cooper Underwear Co.

12. Everything is under control
    —Vogue Foundations Inc.

13. Fashioned each season to fit each season's fashions
    —(*Royal Worcester corset*).

14. Fit as a fiddle
    —(*Society Girl foundations*).

15. Fits the feminine clan
    —(*girdles*) Sidley Co.

16. Flatters where it matters
    —(*Adola brassiere*) Lovable Co.

17. For the girl who knows value by heart
    —(*brassieres*) Lovable Co.

121. UNDERWEAR *cont.*

18. **For the lift of your lifetime**
                              —(*Life brassiere*) Formfit Rogers.

19. **For youthful figures of all ages**
                              —(*Lasticraft foundations*).

20. **Glamour for teen-age and queen age**
                              —(*Kabo brassiere*).

21. **Hanes makes you feel good all under**
                              —Hanes Corp.

22. **Hi-chair to hi-school**
                              —(*Nazareth*) Nazareth Mills.

23. **Hips are fashionable, fat isn't**
                              —(*girdles*) Sidley Co.

24. **Hold the bustline and you hold youth**
                              —(*La Resista corset*).

25. **If it's Madewell, it's well made**
                              —Taunton Knitting.

26. **In tune with fashion and keyed to fit**
                              —(*Lori-Lou girdles*).

27. **It's smart to conform with Reo-Form**
                              —Reo-Form Lingerie Co.

28. **It's time to Re-form**
                              —(*Helene brassiere*).

29. **It's *worth* the difference**
                              —Munsingwear Inc.

30. **Keep your eye on Maidenform**
                              —Maidenform Inc.

31. **Let Munsingwear cover you with satisfaction**
                              —Munsingwear Inc.

32. **Light as sea-foam, strong as the tide**
                              —Paris-Hecker Co.

33. **Naturally yours**
                              —Lilyette Brassiere Co.

34. **Never comes up anytime**
                              —(*foundations*) Sid Levy & Sons.

35. **Next to nothing at all**
                              —(*Du-ons*) Duofold Inc.

36. **Nicest next to you**
                              —H. W. Gossard Co.

37. **Nips the waist, not the purse**
                              —(*girdles*) Sid Levy & Sons.

38. **No hips, no hips, hooray**
                              —(*girdles*) Sid Levy & Sons.

121. **UNDERWEAR** *cont.*

39. **No woman is too stout to be stylish**
—Weingarten Bros.

40. **Puts your best figure forward**
—(*Francette corsets*) Graceform-Camlin Corset Co.

41. **Step thru, button two**
—The Sealpax Co.

42. **The anti-freeze underwear for men and boys**
—P. H. Hanes Knitting Co.

43. **The boast of the gown**
—(*Prim Miss foundations*) Sidley Co.

44. **The custom-corseted look**
—Newman & Sons Inc.

45. **The foundation of American beauty**
—(*Best Form corset*) Best Form Brassiere Co. Ltd.

46. **The house of complete corsetry**
—Kops Bros. Inc.

47. **The inner secret of outer beauty**
—(*Charm underlift brassiere*).

48. **The lift that never lets you down**
—(*Perma-Lift brassiere*) Kayser-Roth Intimate Apparel Co.

49. **There is only one Jockey**
—Jockey International Inc.

50. **There's a future for YOUR figure in Foundettes**
—(*foundations*) Munsingwear Inc.

51. **The two-piece unionsuit**
—Henderson & Erwin.

52. **The undergarment that adds charm to your outergarment**
—(*Heart's Quest*).

53. **The uplift that stays up**
—(*Surprise brassiere*) Carnival Creations Inc.

54. **They're cut to fit to fight fatigue**
—(*Reis*) Robert Reis & Co.

55. **This is the dream you can be ... with Maidenform**
—Maidenform Inc.

56. **Two buttons on the shoulder, none down the front**
—The Sealpax Co.

57. **Unaware of underwear**
—P. H. Hanes Knitting Co.

58. **Underneath it all**
—(*corsets and girdles*) Warner Bros.

121. **UNDERWEAR** *cont.*

   59. **Without the shadow of a stout**
   > —(*corsets*) Stylish Stout.

   60. **Your closest friend**
   > —(*Cupid foundations*).

UTENSILS . . . See **68.** KITCHEN PRODUCTS AND UTENSILS

V

VARNISH . . . See **82.** PAINT AND PAINTING SUPPLIES

122. **VIDEO EQUIPMENT**
> See also **78.** MOVIES AND ENTERTAINMENT,
> **112.** TELEVISIONS

   1. **In touch with tomorrow**
   > —(*video cassette recorders*) Toshiba.

   2. **It's worth it**
   > —(*video tape*) Maxell Corp.

   3. **Just slightly ahead of our time**
   > —(*video cassette recorders*) Panasonic.

   4. **Let RCA turn your television into Selectavision**
   > —(*video cassette recorders*) RCA Corp.

   5. **More games. More fun.**
   > —(*video games*) Atari.

   6. **Nobody gives you better performance**
   > —(*Fuji video tape*) Fuji Photo Film USA.

   7. **The video with a future**
   > —(*video cassette recorders*) Kenwood Electronics Inc.

W

WALLETS . . . See **123.** WARDROBE ACCESSORIES

123. **WARDROBE ACCESSORIES**
> See also **41.** EYEGLASSES, **48.** FOOTWEAR, **61.** HOSIERY,
> **67.** JEWELRY AND SILVER

   1. **A "hank" for a Yank**
   > —Bond Handkerchief Co.

   2. **A lady to her gloved finger tips**
   > —(*gloves*) Bacno Postman Corp.

123. WARDROBE ACCESSORIES *cont.*

3. A love of a glove
   —(*gloves*) Acme Glove Corp.

4. A new frame if the wind breaks it
   —(*umbrellas*) Storm Hero Umbrella Co.

5. A thorobred air in every pair
   —(*gloves*) Grewen Fabric Co.

6. Best for every purpose
   —(*Grinnel gloves*) Morrison Ricker Mfg. Co.

7. Best for your money
   —Buxton Inc.

8. Brand name of better gloves
   —(*gloves*) Aris Gloves.

9. Distinctive designs in leather accessories
   —Prince Gardner Co.

10. Every pair must please
    —(*gloves*) Wimelbacher & Rice.

11. Fit all hands and all purses
    —(*gloves*) F. T. Simmons.

12. Gloves that "go places"
    —(*gloves*) Belle Glove Co.

13. Hand in hand with fashion
    —(*mesh bags*) Whiting & Davis Co.

14. Like old friends they wear well
    —(*gloves*) Louis Meyers & Son Inc.

15. Meyers make gloves for every father's son and
    mother's daughter
    —(*Meyers gloves*) Meyers Manufacturing Co.

16. Nationally recognized as the "straw pioneer"
    —(*handbags*) Simon Bros.

17. Postman's, the gloves Milady loves
    —(*gloves*) Bacno Postman Corp.

18. Ride like a feather in your pocket
    —(*Rumpp wallets*) Aristocrat Leather Products.

19. Soft as a kitten's ear
    —(*belts*) Hews & Potter.

20. The "hanks" are coming
    —(*handkerchiefs*) Bond Handkerchief Co.

21. There's a need-keyed billfold for you
    —Amity Leather Products Co.

22. There's style and wear in every pair
    —(*Wear-Right gloves*).

123. **WARDROBE ACCESSORIES** *cont.*

    23. **The royalty of leatherware**
                    —(*Prince Gardner wallet*) Swank Inc.

    24. **They reign in the rain**
                    —(*umbrellas*) Follmer, Clogg & Co.

    25. **Tropical masterpieces**
                    —(*handbags*) Simon Bros.

    26. **Very individually yours**
                    —(*Hickok buckles*).

    27. **We shelter the world from sun and rain**
                    —(*umbrellas*) Follmer, Clogg & Co.

    28. **Where technicolor comes to life**
                    —(*straw handbags*) Simon Bros.

    29. **Why carry a cold in your pocket**
                    —(*handkerchiefs*) Pervel Corp.

    30. **Yours for Victory**
                    —(*handkerchiefs*) Bond Handkerchief Co.

124. **WATCHES AND CLOCKS**

    1. **Accurate beyond comparison**
                    —Warren Telechron Co.

    2. **A deal with Diel means a good deal**
                    —Diel Watch Case Co.

    3. **America appreciates good time**
                    —(*Ribaux watches*).

    4. **America runs on Bulova time**
                    —(*Bulova watches*) Bulova Watch Co. Inc.

    5. **America's distinguished timepiece**
                    —Harvel Watch Co.

    6. **America's "wake-up" voice**
                    —Westclox Div., General Time Corp.

    7. **Bulova Watch time, the gift of a lifetime**
                    —(*Bulova watches*) Bulova Watch Co. Inc.

    8. **Casio. Where the miracles never cease.**
                    —(*Casio watches*) Casio Inc.

    9. **Engineered for accuracy**
                    —(*Rensie watches*).

    10. **Exquisite as America's beauties**
                    —(*Rensie watches*).

    11. **Fine watchmakers since 1791**
                    —(*Girard Perregaux*) Jean R. Graef Inc.

    12. **First he whispers, then he shouts**
                    —(*Big Ben*) Westclox Div., General Time Corp.

124. WATCHES AND CLOCKS *cont.*

13. **First name in time, last word in watch styling**
—(*Omega watches*) Omega Watch Co.

14. **For a lifetime of proud possession**
—Omega Watch Co.

15. **Get time from a timepiece, but if you want a watch get a Hamilton**
—Hamilton Watch Co.

16. **Guard your time**
—Elgin National Watch Co.

17. **If you want more than time, get a Hamilton**
—Hamilton Watch Co.

18. **In rhyme with time**
—Kingston Watch Co.

19. **It remembers so YOU can forget**
—(*automatic clock*) James Clock Mfg. Co.

20. **It S-T-R-E-T-C-H-E-S and springs back**
—(*watch bands*) Speidel Corp.

21. **Keeps America on time**
—(*Big Ben*) Westclox Div., General Time Corp.

22. **Kestenmade means better made**
—(*watch bands*) Kestenman Bros.

23. **Laughs at time**
—(*Big Ben*) Westclox Div., General Time Corp.

24. **Leading maker of watches of the highest character for almost a century**
—Longines-Wittnauer Watch Co.

25. **Made in America by American craftsmen**
—Elgin National Watch Co.

26. **Makes night time plain as day**
—(*radium dial clocks*) W. L. Gilbert Clock Co.

27. **Modern masters of time**
—Seiko Time Corp.

28. **One great face deserves another**
—(*Bulova watches*) Bulova Watch Co. Inc.

29. **One of America's fine watches**
—Harvel Watch Co.

30. **One of the few great watches of the world**
—Adolphe Schwob Inc.

31. **One of the great watches of our time**
—Waltham Watch Co.

32. **Particular people prefer Hamilton**
—Hamilton Watch Co.

124. WATCHES AND CLOCKS *cont.*

33. Progress in the world of time
—Westclox Div., General Time Corp.

34. Runs accurately without winding
—(*Croton watch*) Croton Time Corp.

35. Sign of the right time
—Zodiac Watch Co.

36. Takes a licking but keeps on ticking
—Timex Corp.

37. Tells time in the dark
—(*Radiolite*) Robt. H. Ingersoll & Bro.

38. Tells time, saves time
—Hawkeye Clock Co.

39. The clocks that most people want most
—(*Heralder*) General Electric Co.

40. The jeweler's quality watch
—Vantage Products Inc.

41. The peak of Swiss watchmaking perfection
—Rado Watch Co.

42. The precision watch, America's choice
—(*Gruen watches*) The Gruen Watch Co.

43. The railroad timekeeper of America
—Hamilton Watch Co.

44. There's no better time
—(*Big Ben*) Westclox Div., General Time Corp.

45. The right choice for the right time
—Harvel Watch Co.

46. The time before your eyes
—(*auto clocks*) W. L. Gilbert Clock Co.

47. The watch for busy men
—Harvel Watch Co.

48. The watch that made the dollar famous
—Robt. H. Ingersoll & Bro.

49. The watch that times the airways
—Benrus Watch Co.

50. The watch that times the stars
—Harvel Watch Co.

51. The watch with the purple ribbon
—South Bend Watch Co.

52. The watch word of elegance and efficiency
—Elgin National Watch Co.

53. The world's most honored watch
—Longines-Wittnauer Watch Co.

124.　WATCHES AND CLOCKS *cont.*

54.　**The world's watch over time**
　　　　　　　　—Waltham Watch Co.

55.　**Timed to the stars**
　　　　　　　　—Elgin National Watch Co.

56.　**Time for a lifetime**
　　　　　　　　—(*Gotham watches*) Winton Nicolet Watch Co.

57.　**Time for a lifetime and longer**
　　　　　　　　—(*Gotham watches*) Winton Nicolet Watch Co.

58.　**Time hurries in every factory**
　　　　　　　　—(*S. Rennus time clock*).

59.　**Time in sight, day or night**
　　　　　　　　—(*radium dial clocks*) W. L. Gilbert Clock Co.

60.　**Tomorrow on every wrist**
　　　　　　　　—(*watch bands*) Speidel Corp.

61.　**Watches out for your watch**
　　　　　　　　—(*watch bands*) Speidel Corp.

62.　**Watchful of the time**
　　　　　　　　—Hawkeye Clock Co.

63.　**When something happy happens, it's Bulova time**
　　　　　　　　—Bulova Watch Co. Inc.

64.　**World's most "carefree" watch**
　　　　　　　　—(*Croton Aquamat*) Croton Time Corp.

WHISKEY ... See **71. LIQUORS**

125.　WINES
　　　　See also **14. BEER AND ALE, 15. BEVERAGES,
　　　　MISCELLANEOUS, 71. LIQUORS**

1.　**As good as gold and good for you**
　　　　　　　　—Cercle D'Or Inc.

2.　**Be considerate, serve wine**
　　　　　　　　—Wine Advisory Board, San Francisco.

3.　**Blueprint of a perfect cocktail**
　　　　　　　　—(*G & D vermouth*) United Vintners Inc.

4.　**California's premier wines**
　　　　　　　　—Almaden Vineyards Inc.

5.　**Don't stir without Noilly Prat**
　　　　　　　　—Browne Vintners Co.

6.　**Enjoy a sip of California Sunshine**
　　　　　　　　—Alta Vineyards Co.

7.　**For the great moments**
　　　　　　　　—(*Great Western champagne*) Pleasant Valley Wine Co.

125. WINES *cont.*

8. **From the finest of the vines**
    —(*Cresta Blanca*) Guild Wineries & Distilleries.

9. **From the heart of California**
    —(*Roma wines*) Guild Wineries & Distilleries.

10. **From the largest cellars in the world**
    —(*Moët champagne*) Schiefflin and Co.

11. **Here's to your health and happiness**
    —Cercle D'Or Inc.

12. **Imported from Spain, of course. True sherry is.**
    —(*Duff Gordon*) National Distillers and Chemical Corp.

13. **Made in California for enjoyment throughout the world**
    —(*Roma wines*) Guild Wineries & Distilleries.

14. **Made in the "champagne district of America"**
    —(*Gold Seal wines*) Gold Seal Vineyards Inc.

15. **Make every meal a bouquet**
    —Bisceglia Bros. Corp.

16. **Mountain grown**
    —Almaden Vineyards Inc.

17. **Mumm's the word for champagne**
    —(*Mumm champagne*) G. H. Mumm and Co.

18. **Orchard flavor in every sip**
    —(*Greystone fruit wines*) Bisceglia Bros. Corp.

19. **Pop goes the Piper**
    —(*Piper-Heidsieck champagne*) Renfield Importers Ltd.

20. **Renowned 'round the world**
    —American Wine Co.

21. **Selected from the world's greatest reserves of fine wines**
    —(*Roma wines*) Guild Wineries & Distilleries.

22. **The crest of quality wine since 1889**
    —(*Cresta Blanca*) Guild Wineries & Distilleries.

23. **The crowning achievement of vintner skill**
    —(*Roma wines*) Guild Wineries & Distilleries.

24. **The finest wines of France**
    —Barton and Guestier.

25. **The flavor secret of the finest cocktails**
    —(*Martini & Rossi vermouth*) Renfield Importers Ltd.

26. **The greatest name in wine**
    —(*Roma wines*) Guild Wineries & Distilleries.

27. **The nobility of Italian wines**
    —Marchesi L and P Antinori.

125. WINES *cont.*

28. The profit line in wine
—Bisceglia Bros. Corp.

29. The wine that celebrates food
—(*Inglenook*) International Vintage Wines.

30. The wine that tastes as good as it looks
—(*Cresta Blanca*) Guild Wineries & Distilleries.

31. The wine with the champagne taste
—Pacific Wines Inc.

32. Uncork the magic
—(*Korbel Brut Champagne*) F. Korbel & Bros. Inc.

33. We will sell no wine before its time
—(*Paul Masson*) Browne Vintners Co.

34. When you mix with CinZano, you mix with the best
—(*CinZano*) Schiefflin and Co.

35. Wines of California. Since 1882.
—(*Christian Brothers*) Fromm and Sichel Inc.

36. Winning. Worldly. Well bred.
—(*Martini & Rossi vermouth*) Renfield Importers Ltd.

37. World-famous Spanish sherries
—(*Williams and Humbert dry sack*) Julius Wile Sons and Co. Inc.

126. WRITING INSTRUMENTS
See also **81. OFFICE EQUIPMENT AND SUPPLIES**

1. All write with a Waterman Ideal Fountain Pen ... all wrong if you don't
—(*Waterman pens*).

2. Always sharp, never sharpened
—(*Eversharp pencil*) Wahl Co.

3. Always writes all ways
—Sheaffer Pen Co.

4. America's finest writing instruments since 1846
—A. T. Cross Co.

5. A pen for every purpose and a point for every hand
—Sheaffer Pen Co.

6. A pen is only as good as its point
—C. Howard Hunt Pen Co.

7. Being better is what we're all about
—(*Pentel pens*) Pentel of America Ltd.

8. Creator of advanced writing instruments
—Micropoint Inc.

126. WRITING INSTRUMENTS *cont.*

9. **Engineering with imagination**
—Scripto Inc.

10. **51 writes dry with wet ink**
—(*Parker 51*) Parker Pen Co.

11. **Fill with water, write with ink**
—(*Camel fountain pen*).

12. **Give Eversharp and you give the finest**
—(*pencils*) Wahl Co.

13. **Ink that absorbs moisture from the air**
—S. S. Stafford.

14. **Insures a new kind of faultless effortless writing**
—(*pens*) Eberhard Faber.

15. **It's a mark of distinction to own a Parker Pen**
—Parker Pen Co.

16. **It snuggles in your fingers**
—Dixon Pencil Co.

17. **Maker of the world's most wanted pens**
—Parker Pen Co.

18. **Makes its mark around the world**
—(*Waterman pens*).

19. **Masters in the art of writing**
—(*Montblanc CS-Line Pens*) Koh-I-Noor
Rapidograph Inc.

20. **Originators of the world-famous Utility ball pen**
—Lindy Pen Co. Inc.

21. **Paint with pencils**
—Eberhard Faber.

22. **Perfected wood pencils**
—Scripto Mfg. Co.

23. **Permanent as the pyramids**
—(*eternal ink*) C. M. Higgins & Co.

24. **Quality first ... from America's first penmaker**
—Esterbrook Pen Co.

25. **Right to the point**
—Conklin Pen Mfg. Co.
—Wallace Pencil Co.

26. **Rivals the beauty of the scarlet tanager**
—Parker Pen Co.

27. **Smooth as silk, strong as steel**
—Dixon Pencil Co.

28. **Spot it by the dot**
—Sheaffer Pen Co.

126. WRITING INSTRUMENTS *cont.*

29. **Tag them for good**
                                    —Gospel Pencil Co.

30. **The balanced pencil**
                                    —Swaberg Mfg. Co.

31. **The famous pencil with green and yellow plastips**
                                    —Dixon Pencil Co.

32. **The ink that never fades**
                                    —Sanford Mfg. Co.

33. **The master drawing pencil**
                                    —Joseph Dixon Crucible Co.

34. **The pen America depends on**
                                    —(*Papermate pens*) The Gillette Co.

35. **The pencil of the pros**
                                    —Scripto Mfg. Co.

36. **The pencil that uses its head**
                                    —Samuel Kanner.

37. **The pen that fills itself**
                                    —Conklin Pen Mfg. Co.

38. **The pen with the tempered point**
                                    —Wahl Co.

39. **The right point for the way you write**
                                    —Esterbrook Steel Pen Co.

40. **The sign of a lifetime**
                                    —Sheaffer Pen Co.

41. **The world's most wanted pen**
                                    —(*Parker 51*) Parker Pen Co.

42. **The yellow pencil with the red band**
                                    —Eagle Pencil Co.

43. **We've got your number**
                                    —Esterbrook Steel Pen Co.

44. **Write around the world**
                                    —Alexander Mfg. Co.

45. **Writes a strong, rich blue**
                                    —Carter's Ink Co.

46. **Writes dry with permanent ink**
                                    —(*Eversharp pens*) Wahl Co.

Index I

Slogans & Categories

Index I

Slogans & Categories

This index contains, in one alphabetic order, all of the slogans and categories listed in the text. For added convenience, slogans beginning with the words *A, An,* or *The* have been listed both by their usual form (as used in the text) and by their first significant word, with articles transposed to final position.

Categories appear in boldface type with reference given to the first page on which the listings for the category begin. All other references are to categories and slogans as numbered in the text.

A bank of personal contact, 43.1
ABC of radio satisfaction, The, 37.28
A bear for heat, 59.1
A bear for wear, 114.1
A beautiful piano with a magnificent tone, 80.1
A beautiful skin is adored, 32.1
A beer is no better than its ingredients, 14.1
A better buy, by any comparison, 108.1
A better-wearing brush for every use, 82.1
A better yield in every field, 42.1
A blend of all straight whiskies, 71.1
above-the-floor furnace, An, 58.2
Abraham Lincoln/Honest Abe of the West, 91.1
A breathless sensation, 20.1
A bright new world of electric housewares, 60.1
A brisk magazine of Parisian life, 85.1
Abroad without crossing the seas, 119.1

A bronze as strong as nickel steel, 75.1
Absorb shocks and jars, 48.1
A business journal of furnishing and decoration, 85.2
A business paper for the farm chemical industry, 85.3
A car for every purse and purpose, 7.1
A car you can believe in, 7.2
accepted educational standard, The, 94.13
Accurate beyond comparison, 124.1
Accustomed to the finest . . . you'll find it in a Beechcraft, 3.1
A chicken in every pot, a car in every garage, 91.2
A choice for a change, 91.3
A choice—not an echo, 91.4
A choice of over a million women, 60.2
A citizen, wherever we serve, 93.1
Acknowledged the world's best piano, 80.2
A classic in wood, 105.1
A Clean Home newspaper, 85.4
A clean tooth never decays, 34.1

A company of uncommon enterprise, 31.1

A complete plant food, not just a stimulant, 69.1

A complete source for fine office furniture, 81.1

Across the Atlantic, 102.1

action line, The, 18.75

Action people, 2.1

Action shoes for boys and girls, 48.2

Actually aged longer, 14.2

A cube makes a cup, 47.1

A cup for two or two for you, 60.3

A cut above the commonplace, 33.1

Add a Dutch of class to your next party, 14.3

Add a fiber from Celanese and good things get better, 113.1

added touch that means so much, The, 29.33

Adds life to years rather than years to life, 32.2

Adds miles to tire life, 8.1

Adds 70% more nourishment to milk, 15.1

Adds science to fisherman's luck, 45.1

A deal with Diel means a good deal, 124.2

A delicious health confection, 20.2

A dependable railway, 96.1

A diamond is forever, 67.1

A distinguished banking connection, 43.2

ADHESIVES, p. 31

Adlai and Estes are the bestes, 91.5

Adlai likes *me*, 91.6

Adorns your skin with the fragrance men love, 106.1

Advertise and realize, 2.2

Advertise for action, 2.3

ADVERTISING, p. 31

Advertising is the power of an idea multiplied, 2.4

Advertising that follows through to sales, 2.5

Advertising with a basic idea, 2.6

advocate of the American System, The, 91.304

A dynamic force with paper, 83.1

AEROSPACE, p. 33

Aetna, I'm glad I met ya, 64.1

Aetna-izer, a man worth knowing, The, 64.79

A famous brand in glass, 52.1

A famous camera from camera-famous West Germany, 89.1

A famous name in radio since 1921, 95.1

A fastener to fit every need, 103.1

A file for every purpose, 117.1

A finer typewriter at a fair price, 81.2

A fine tool at a fair price, 117.2

A "fitting" tribute to the feminine figure, 121.1

A flair for elegance, 112.1

A foot nearer perfection, 48.3

A foot of comfort means miles of happiness, 48.4

A fountain of youth for your skin, 32.3

African business is our business, 102.2

A friend of the family, 4.1

After every meal, 20.3

After sunset, Lightoliers, 70.1

A full meal in two biscuits, 21.1

A full package of light, 70.2

Aged by Father Time himself, 14.4

Aged extra long for extra flavor, 14.5

Aged for 8, 71.2

Aged in the wood, 115.1

agency is known by the clients it keeps, An, 2.7

A generation of worldwide acceptance, 46.1

A gentleman's drink, 71.3

A gift to remember, 20.4

A glass of Guinness is a cheerful sight, 14.6

A glorious beginning, 71.4

Aglow with friendliness, 62.1

A good broom sweeps cleaner and lasts longer, 24.1

A good business letter is always better . . . written on a Gilbert paper, 83.2

A good neighbor of your community, 96.2

A good newspaper, 85.5

A good reputation has to be earned, 60.4

A good society is good business, 94.1

A grand slam favorite, 20.5

A great name in aviation, 4.2

A great name in oil, 88.1

A great name in tackle, 45.2

A great state in which to live and work, 36.1

agreeable chewing digestant, An, 20.10

A Guinness a day is good for you, 14.7

A gun for every American shooting need, 44.1

A halo shines as bright as day around the head of Henry Clay, 91.7

A handy kitchen means living room leisure, 50.1

A "hank" for a Yank, 123.1

A hat for every face, 26.1

A heritage of quality, craftsmanship, service, 65.1

A heritage to remember, 71.5

A home away from home, 62.2

A home is known by the lawn it keeps, 69.2

A homey hotel for home folks, 62.3

A honey of a tobacco, 115.2

A hot weather hot cereal, 21.2

A house divided against itself cannot stand, 91.8

Ah, there's the rub, 35.1

A human interest newspaper, 85.6

Aids digestion, 20.6

Air-freight specialists, 4.3

Airline of the professionals, 4.4

airline run by fliers, The, 4.42

airline that knows the South Pacific best, The, 4.43

airline that measures the midwest in minutes, The, 4.44

airline that treats you like a maharajah, The, 4.45

airline with the big jets, The, 4.46

AIR TRAVEL AND CARGO, p. 35

Air unlox to Magnavox, 95.2

A journal for all who write, 85.7

A Kansas product from Kansas farms, 74.1

A King can have no more, 78.1

A lady to her gloved finger tips, 123.2

Alaska flag line, The, 4.47

A leader in dental research, 34.2

A liberal church journal, 85.8

A life preserver for foods, 60.5

A liquid finish that decorates as it preserves, 82.2

A little dab will do ya, 54.1

A little varnish makes a lot of difference, 82.3

A live picture tabloid newspaper for all the family, 85.9

A living tradition in furniture, 50.2

All Aboard Amtrak, 96.3

all-American ale, The, 14.107

All around the world, 111.1

All fresh-fruit good!, 47.2

All good things come in pears, 49.1

All I have left is a vote for Willkie, 91.9

Allis-Chalmers does its share to help *you* share in a better future, 42.2

All is vanity ... all is Vanity Fair, 121.2

All over the world BOAC takes good care of you, 4.5

all-purpose one-man crane, The, 73.30

All steel and a car wide, 8.2

All that is best, 62.4

All that is best in radio, 95.3

All that its name implies, 61.1

All that's best at lowest price, 7.3

All that the name implies, 60.6, 83.3

All the bank you'll ever need in Texas, 43.3

All the facts, no opinion, 85.10

All the flexibility of a newspaper with the coverage of a national magazine, 85.11

All the good left in, 27.1

All the new ones all the time, 26.2

All the news that's fit to print, 85.12

All the news while it is news, 85.13

All the taste without the waste, 74.2

All the way with Adlai, 91.10

All the way with J. F. K., 91.11

All the way with LBJ, 91.12

All they're cracked up to be, 49.2

All work and no play, 73.1

All write with a Waterman Ideal Fountain Pen ... all wrong if you don't, 126.1

All you can eat for a nickel, 20.7

All you need to know about paint, 82.4

All your banking under one roof, 43.4

A load for every purpose and a shell for every purse, 44.2

Alone in tone, 95.4

A lopsided diet may ruin your canary's song, 87.1

A lordly touch for simple menus, 47.3

A lovelier skin with just one cake, 106.2

A love of a glove, 123.3

Al Smith: up from the street, 91.13

aluminum ware with the smooth finish, The, 68.14

A luxury blend for the "carriage trade", 71.6

Always accurate, 63.1

Always a step ahead in style, 48.5

Always at your fingertips, 32.4

Always a year ahead, 95.5

Always better, better all ways, 115.3

Always churned from sweet cream, 33.2

Always correct, 83.4

Always first, always fair, 85.14

Always first quality, 100.1

Always first with all that's new, 48.6

Always good company, 95.6

Always in good company, 14.8

Always in good taste, 27.2

Always in the lead, 85.15

Always makes good printing better, 83.5

Always one step ahead of the weather, 18.1

Always on the level, 63.2

Always 2000 pounds to the ton, 59.2

Always reaches home, 85.16

Always refreshing, 20.8

Always reliable, 85.17

Always *right* on the job, 73.2

Always save money in the end, 58.1

Always sharp, never sharpened, 126.2

Always smoother because it's slow-distilled, 71.7

Always the same, always good, 27.3

Always the same good coffee, 27.4

Always virgin wool, 26.3

Always worth par when misfortune strikes, 64.2

Always writes all ways, 126.3

A machine for every purpose, 81.3

A magazine for all Americans, 85.18

A magazine for farm and home, 85.19

A magazine for farm women, 85.20

A magazine for southern merchants, 85.21

A magazine of better merchandising for home finishing merchants, 85.22

A magazine of good, clean humor, 85.23

A magazine only a homemaker could love, 85.24

A magazine with a mission, 85.25

A man of character, 91.14

A man's first choice, 48.7

A man who can't remember his last hailstorm is likely to get one he will never forget, 64.3

A man you can lean on, that's Klopman, 113.2

A massage for the gums, 34.3

A matter of pride, pleasure, and good plain sense, 103.2

America always, 91.15

America appreciates good time, 124.3

America borders on the magnificent, 119.2

America calls another Roosevelt, 91.16

America cannot be bought, 91.17

America Dry for dry America, 107.1

America efficient, 91.18

America for Americans—no free trade, 91.19

America has gone Budweiser, 14.9

America lives in Dacron, 113.3

America lives in R and K Originals, 26.4

American dark chaser, 70.3

America needs Eisenhower—Draft Ike in '56, 91.20

American gentlemen shoes designed for the American man, 48.8

American gentleman's whiskey since 1860, An, 71.12

American institution, An, 85.41

American institution since 1840, An, 20.11

American lady shoes designed for the American woman, 48.9

American Republicans! Beware of foreign influence! Our country first, 91.21

Americans must rule America, 91.22

American symbol of feminine charm, The, 84.22

American wages for American workingmen, 91.23

American way with Willkie, The, 91.305

American whiskey for the American taste, The, 71.90

America runs on Bulova time, 124.4

America's best-known shoes, 48.10

America's best-liked cereal assortment, 21.3

America's best-loved greeting cards, 51.1

America's best read weekly, 85.26

America's best tasting little cigar, 115.4

America's best traveling companion, 72.1

America's beverage of moderation, 14.10

America's biggest home magazine, 85.27

America's biggest selling weekly magazine, 85.28

America's biggest suburban home market, 85.29

America's business address, 62.5

America's cities are Bergstrom's forests, 83.6

America's dairyland, 119.3

America's distinguished timepiece, 124.5

America's family magazine, 85.30

America's fastest growing fuel, 59.3

America's fastest-growing tire company, 114.2

America's favorite bleach and household disinfectant, 24.2

America's favorite for thick, rich catsup, 29.1

America's favorite fun car, 7.4

America's favorite mayonnaise, 29.2

America's favorite way to fly, 4.6

America's finest basement door, 18.2

America's finest campers, 98.1

America's finest camping tents, 98.2

America's finest cola drink, 107.2

America's finest fishing rods, 45.3

America's finest fitting outercoats, 26.5

America's finest ginger ale, 107.3

America's finest mixer, 107.4

America's finest motor car for America's finest families, 7.5

America's finest pipe tobacco, 115.5

America's finest power-loomed rug, 46.2

America's finest whiskey regardless of age or price, 71.8

America's finest writing instruments since 1846, 126.4

America's first car, 7.6

America's first choice for flavor, 74.3

America's first, finest and favorite pork and beans, 47.4

America's first name in formal wear, 26.6

America's first name in lighting, 70.4

America's first truly fine small car, 7.7

America's foremost manufacturer of decorative accessories since 1890, 65.2

America's foremost producer of custom steels, 75.2

America's foremost school of commercial art, 101.1

America's friendliest factory, 7.8

America's grandest cereal assortment, 21.4

America's greatest luggage value, 72.2

America's greatest truck, 120.1

America's investment weekly, 85.31

America's lake country, 119.4

America's largest builder of camping trailers, 98.3

America's largest dairy magazine, 85.32

America's largest leasing system, 6.1

America's largest manufacturer of custom day beds and sofa beds, 13.1

America's largest manufacturer of lighting productions, 70.5

America's largest Polish newspaper, 85.33

America's largest selling high grade coffee, 27.5

America's largest selling residential locksets, 55.1

America's leading airline, 4.7

America's leading power boat magazine, 85.34

"America's leading producer of quality canvas products", 113.4

America's leading silversmiths since 1831, 67.2

America's leading washing machine, 60.7

America's lowest-priced fine car, 7.9

America's luxury whiskey, 71.9

America's magazine for the outdoorsman, 85.35

America's most beautiful store, 100.2

America's most copied radio, 95.7

America's most customer-minded oil company!, 88.2

America's most distinguished cigarette holder, 105.2

America's most distinguished motorcar, 7.10

America's most distinguished source for fine English furniture, 50.3

America's most famous bouquet, 71.10

America's most famous dessert, 47.5

America's most interesting state, 119.5

America's most luxurious motor car, 7.11

America's most modern cola, 107.5

America's most popular boats, 16.1

America's most popular camp stove, 98.4

America's most potent editorial force, 85.36

America's most recommended mover, 79.1

America's most used products away from home, 83.7

America's most useful personal planes, 3.2

America's new breakfast banquet of shredded whole wheat, 21.5

America's No. 1 gasoline, 88.3

America's No. 1 heel, 48.11

America's No. 1 low-calorie cola, 107.6

America's No. 1 Mountain Grown Coffee, 27.6

America's number 1 mover, 79.2

America's number one sportman's magazine, 85.37

America's oldest and largest showroom distributor of fine decorative furniture, 50.4

America's oldest lager beer, 14.11

America's only known-priced clothes, 26.7

America's original sparkling malt liquor, 14.12

America's physic, 35.2

America's pioneer manufacturer of prefinished metals, 75.3

America's popular year 'round breakfast, 21.6

America's premium quality beer, 14.13

America's quality magazine of discussion, 85.38

America's resourceful railroad, 96.4

America's sleepheart, 96.5

America's smartest car, 7.12

America's smartest resort hotel, 62.6

America's smartest walking shoes, 48.12

America's smart set, 95.8

America's smoothest tobacco, 115.6

America's social-light whiskey, 71.11

America's supreme dessert, 47.6

America's supreme ignition system, 8.3

America's "wake-up" voice, 124.6

Amerock makes it authentic, 18.3

A message of purity, 20.9

A midget in size, a giant in power, 69.3

A mile of silk, inspected inch by inch, 61.2

A million Americans can't be wrong, 48.13

A million and one uses, 1.1

A million in service ten years or longer, 60.8

A million yards of good will, 81.4

A minute to learn. A lifetime to master., 118.1

A miracle in the rain, 26.8

A monthly business paper for chain store executives, 85.39

A monthly magazine devoted to more profitable painting, 85.40

A more enlightened approach, 7.13

"A most remarkable airline", 4.8

A mountain of flavor in every spoonful, 27.7

A musical instrument of quality, 95.9

A "must" for every wardrobe, 26.9

An above-the-floor furnace, 58.2

An agency is known by the clients it keeps, 2.7

An agreeable chewing digestant, 20.10

An American gentleman's whiskey since 1860, 71.12

An American institution, 85.41

An American institution since 1840, 20.11

A name to remember, 18.4

A name to remember, a fabric to remember, 113.5

A name you can trust, 34.4

An apple a day is Doc Apple's way, 49.3

An aristocratic beverage at a democratic price, 107.7

A national buyword, 26.10

A national institution from coast to coast, 100.3

A national magazine for dry goods and department stores, 85.42

A national publication devoted to ship operation and shipbuilding, 85.43

A national publication for the wholesale grocer, 85.44

A national rider never changes his mount, 108.2

A nation's health is a nation's strength, 47.7

A nationwide institution, 100.4

A natural energy, food and body builder, 56.1

A natural resource company, 88.4

Anchors like a rock, 18.5

And away go troubles down the drain, 25.1

And when you listen you'll buy this Westinghouse, 95.10

And who makes great skis? Head, of course., 108.3

An emblem of security, a pledge of service, 64.4

A new frame if the wind breaks it, 123.4

A new high in whiskey smoothness, 71.13

A newspaper for everybody; it goes into the home, 85.45

A newspaper for the makers of newspapers, 85.46

A new talc with a new odor, 84.1

An extra collar for a dollar, 103.3

An extra measure of quality, 38.1

An extra quart of lubrication in every gallon, 88.5

An eye for your gas tank, 8.4

An eye to the future, an ear to the ground, 31.2

"Angels of the highest order", 97.1

An hotel of distinction, 62.7

An idea whose time has come!, 64.5

An illustrated weekly of current life, 85.47

"An inch of Pinch, please.", 71.14

An independent newspaper, 85.48

An international daily newspaper, 85.49

An international value, 83.8

Ankle-fashioned shoes, 48.14

Announcing the state of the smart, 28.1

A noble Scotch, 71.15

Another carefree Johnson, 16.2

Another clinical-strength medication from Warner-Lambert, 35.3

Another example of how Monsanto moves on many fronts to serve you, 22.1

Another fine creation by Krueger, 50.5

An ounce of prevention for everybody, everyday, 21.7

answer is wool . . . it costs less in the long run, The, 46.26

answer to all your tape needs, The, 5.33

anthracite that serves you right, The, 59.20

Anticipating tomorrow's needs today . . . , 22.2

anti-freeze underwear for men and boys, The, 121.42

antiseptic deodorant powder, The, 116.18

381

Any mail for me?, 83.9
Any Palizzio is better than no Palizzio, 48.15
Anything can happen when you wear Fame, 84.2
Anything else is a compromise, 5.1
Any time is STANDARD time, 14.14
Anywhere in the wide world, 6.2
A pen for every purpose and a point for every hand, 126.5
A pen is only as good as its point, 126.6
A penny a night for the finest light, 70.6
A personal blend, 110.1
A personalized service that comes to your home, 32.5
A pillow for the body, 13.2
A pioneer in the leasing field, 6.3
A pipe's best friend is fragrant Heine's blend, 115.7
A pip of a chip, 47.8
A pippin of a drink, 15.2
A policy for every purse and purpose, 64.6
A powerful constructive force in the development of Georgia, 85.50
Apparel without parallel, 26.11
apple a day is Doc Apple's way, An, 49.3
Applying advanced technology to bring you exciting new products, 31.3
Appollinaris mixes best with holiday spirits, 15.3
Approved by professional hair colorists, 54.2
A precious bit more than a laxative, 35.4
A printer for every need and every speed, 28.2
A profit for every investor, 66.1
A progressive past. A golden future., 108.4
A proud paper for a proud industry, 85.51
A public office is a public trust, 91.24
A quality for every purse and purpose, 13.3
A quality loaf for quality folks, 11.1
A quality name in forest products, 18.6

A radio in every room; a radio for every purpose, 95.11
A radio that you can play, 95.12
A rainbow of distinctive flavors, 71.16
A *real* cigarette, 115.8
A real magnetic horn, 8.5
A real safe, not a pretense, 81.5
Aren't you glad *you* use Dial? Don't you wish *everybody* did?, 106.3
A republic can have no colonies, 91.25
A reputation through innovation, 38.2
Are you annoyed by a drip?, 55.2
A right kind for every purpose, 82.5
aristocratic beverage at a democratic price, An, 107.7
aristocrat of American roofing, The, 18.76
aristocrat of auto jacks, The, 8.49
Aristocrat of blended Scotch-type whiskey, 71.17
aristocrat of building materials, The, 18.77
aristocrat of cigars, The, 115.129
aristocrat of electric ranges, The, 60.94
aristocrat of ginger ales, The, 107.41
aristocrat of ice creams, The, 33.37
aristocrat of liqueurs, The, 71.91
aristocrat of music magazines, The, 85.192
aristocrat of package cocoa, The, 11.48
aristocrat of pipe tobacco, The, 115.130
aristocrat of polyester neckwear, The, 26.103
aristocrat of refrigerators, The, 60.95
aristocrat of shirtings, The, 26.104
Aristocrat of the breakast table, 47.9
aristocrat of tissues, The, 83.56
aristocrat of winter trains, The, 96.53
arms that protect American farms, The, 44.20
A roller rolls and there's ice, 60.9
Aromatic in the pack, aromatic in the pipe, 115.9

Around the world on Dunlops, 114.3
A 'round the year coat, 26.12
Arrow means quality in any language, 71.18
Ars gratia artis, 78.2
Art in diamond rings, 67.3
Art in footwear, 48.16
Artistry in carpets, 46.3
A rug for every room, 46.4
Arvin sets the pace, lead with Arvin, 95.13
As a change from potatoes, 47.10
A sack of satisfaction, 11.2
A salt for every purpose, 29.3
Asbestos cannot burn, 18.7
As delicious as coffee can be, 27.8
As different as day and night, 71.19
As different from all other perfumes as you are from all other women, 84.3
As easily as the sun shines, 30.1
As easy as pointing your finger, 44.3
As easy to use as to say, 116.1
A sensible cigarette, 115.10
As fine as money can build, 7.14
As good as can be, 47.11
As good as gold and good for you, 125.1
As good as it looks, 14.15
As good as it tastes, 47.12
As good as the best you ever ate, 11.3
A shade better than the rest, 26.13
A shade is only as good as its rollers, 65.3
A shilling in London, a quarter here, 115.11
A shine in every drop, 24.3
A shoe with a talking point, 48.17
A single match is your year's kindling, 58.3
A singular experience, 71.20
Ask Dad, he knows, 115.12
Ask for K-V ... it's a known value!, 55.3
Ask him why he smokes a Webster, 115.13
A skilled hand in chemistry ... at work for you, 22.3
Ask the man from Northern Plains, 93.2
Ask the man who owns one, 7.15

Ask your dealer, he knows, 115.14
Ask your doctor, 14.16
Ask your printer, he KNOWS papers, 83.10
As masculine as the trade mark, 116.2
As modern as tomorrow, 121.3
As national as agriculture, 85.52
As necessary as brakes, 8.6
As necessary as the rain, 42.3
As of yore, 14.17
A song in every seed, 87.2
aspirin of quality, The, 35.95
A square deal all around, 91.26
A square meal from a square can, 74.4
As simple as touching the space-bar of a typewriter, quick as the action of a piano key, 60.10
As solid as the granite hills of Vermont, 64.7
As sturdy as they are beautiful, 108.5
Assurance of quality, 8.7
As sweet as love songs, 20.12
A step ahead of tomorrow, 31.4
As they eat 'em in New England, 47.13
As tonic as sunshine itself, 14.18
Astonishingly good, 106.4
A story-telling pictorial of stage, art, screen, humor, 85.53
A style for any taste, a fit for any foot, 48.18
A superb soldier—a model president, 91.27
A sure sign they're good, 48.19
A swab by any other name is not the same, 116.3
A sweater is better if it's a Huddlespun, 26.14
A sweet among sweets, 20.13
As western as the setting sun, 26.15
A symbol of technical excellence, 95.14
As you like it, 61.3
As you travel ask us, 9.1
A taste sells a case, 14.19
A team of specialists, 73.3
At home with your young ideas, 50.6
A thorobred air in every pair, 123.5
A thousand miles of travel, a thousand thrills of pleasure, 102.3

383

A time-honored name in scales, 63.3

A title on the door rates a Bigelow on the floor, 46.5

A tool for modern times, 28.3

A tower of strength, 43.5

A treasure for eating pleasure, 47.14

A true expression of heart-felt sympathy, 2.8

A truly great name among America's great whiskies, 71.21

At the crossroads of the world, 62.8

At the first sneeze, Vick's VapoRub, 35.5

At the head of the nation, 64.8

At the sign of friendly service, 9.2

A twentieth century expression of the French civilization, 7.16

At White, fine furniture making is a lost art we never lost, 50.7

At your service, 37.1

AUDIO EQUIPMENT, p. 39

A uniform & sound currency: the Sub Treasury, 91.28

Australia's round-the-world jet airline, 4.9

Authentically ski, 108.6

authority in the exciting world of beauty, The, 32.68

Authority of industry, national and international, 85.54

authority of the waterways, The, 85.193

automated answer to the paper explosion, The, 28.48

Automatically better, 105.3

Automation is economical, 28.4

AUTOMOBILE RENTAL SERVICES, p. 42

AUTOMOBILES, p. 42

automotive business paper, The, 85.194

AUTOMOTIVE PARTS AND PRODUCTS, p. 47

AUTOMOTIVE SERVICE, p. 51

automotive service shop magazine, The, 85.195

Auto stereo, 5.2

Avoid 5 o'clock shadow, 104.1

Avoid rebel rule, 91.29

Avoid "tattletale gray", 24.4

Avoid teeter-totter vitality, 15.4

A vote for Coolidge is a vote for chaos, 91.30

A vote for Roosevelt is a vote against Hoover, 91.31

À votre service, 4.35

Away with the New Deal and its inefficiency, 91.32

A wealth of value in Fortune Shoes, 48.20

A weekly for the whole family, 85.55

A weekly magazine of philately, 85.56

A weekly newspaper of insurance, 85.57

Awful fresh, 49.4

A whiskey for every taste and purse, 71.22

A winner with women, 116.4

A wipe and it's bright, 24.5

A woman never forgets the man who remembers, 20.14

A world in itself, 119.6

A world leader in technology, 112.2

A world of experience, 38.3

A world of furniture made in a way that makes a world of difference, 50.8

A world of paper products—from frozen food cartons to printing paper, 83.11

A Yale battery for every battery need, 37.2

"Babies are our business . . . our only business", 10.1

BABY PRODUCTS, p. 52

Baby's best bed builders, 10.2

Baby's milk must be safe, 33.3

"Baby talk" for a good square meal, 10.3

Back-bone of better plastering, 18.8

backbone of New York advertising, The, 2.27

Backed by a century of brewing experience, 14.20

Backed by a century-old tradition of fine craftsmanship, 60.11, 60.12

Backed by research, proved by use, 42.4

Background of beauty, 61.4

Back to Independence, 91.33

Back to normalcy, 91.34

"Bait of champions", 45.4

BAKED GOODS AND BAKING SUPPLIES, p. 52

Bakers of America's finest bread, 11.4

Bakes right because it is made right, 11.5

baking aid that nature made, The, 11.49

Balanced for perfect baking, 11.6

balanced load shells, The, 44.21

balanced pencil, The, 126.30

Balanced reading for discriminating people, 94.2

Balanced tailoring makes Timely Clothes look better—longer, 26.16

ball-bearing shave, The, 104.35

Ball that made baseball, 108.7

Baltimoreans don't say newspaper, they say SUNpaper, 85.58

bandage that breathes, The, 35.96

Banishes ironing drudgery, 60.13

bankers who do a little more for you, The, 43.43

bank for all the people, The, 43.44

bank for bankers and businessmen, The, 43.45

bank for me in '43, The, 43.46

Bank must perish, The, 91.306

bank of personal contact, A, 43.1

Bank of personal service, 43.6

bank that means business in California, The, 43.47

bank that works hardest for you, The, 43.48

bank where you feel at home, The, 43.49

bank with the international point of view, The, 43.50

Bared to its bones, it's still the "beauty", 7.17

Barking Dog never bites, 115.15

Base for soft drinks and desserts, 107.8

Basic chemicals and cost-cutting ideas, 22.4

Basic producers from mine to finished product, 22.5

Basic provider of chemicals in volume, 22.6

Basic to America's progress, 22.7

BATH ACCESSORIES, p. 55

Battery with a kick, 60.14

Bayer works wonders, 35.6

Be ale-wise, 14.21

Be all that you can be, 53.1

bear for heat, A, 59.1

bear for wear, A, 114.1

Be as regular as a clock, 35.7

Beautifies before your eyes, 82.6

Beautiful beyond belief, 7.18

Beautiful beyond belief in tone and styling, 95.15

Beautiful birch for beautiful woodwork, 18.9

Beautiful corset worn by beautiful women to make them more beautiful, 121.4

Beautiful hair, 54.3

Beautiful hair is as easy as HQZ, 54.4

beautiful piano with a magnificent tone, A, 80.1

Beautiful skies now and forever, 32.6

Beautiful skin begins with Noxema, 32.7

beautiful skin is adored, A, 32.1

beauty and distinction of custom car styling, The, 7.55

Beauty and economy burned in, 18.10

Beauty and warmth, 58.4

Beauty basis for your home, 46.6

Beauty bath for your teeth, 34.5

Beauty begins with the hair, 54.5

Beauty by the brushful, 82.7

Beauty in every box, 32.8

Beauty insurance, 54.6

Beauty *is* only skin deep; Luminiere controls the skin, 32.9

beauty laxative, The, 35.97

Beauty mark of fine Lighting, 70.7

Beauty, service and comfort, 8.8

Beauty's master touch, 32.10

Beauty that protects, 82.8

Beauty treatment for your feet, 48.21

Be bright. Feel right. Take Eno, 35.8

Because . . . , 116.5

Because it might rain, 26.17

Because it's sweet, not bitter, 47.15

Because lips that feel lifeless aren't worth a look, 32.11

Because so much is riding on your tires, 114.4

Because the music matters, 5.3

"Because there *is* a difference", 64.9

Because you love nice things, 61.5, 121.5

Be certain with Certified Milk, 33.4

Be Chic—Chew Chicks, 20.15

Be coffee-wise not coupon-foolish, 27.9

Be considerate, serve wine, 125.2

BEDS AND BEDDING, p. 56

bedspring luxurious, The, 13.26

BEER AND ALE, p. 58

Beer belongs, enjoy it, 14.22

beer for good cheer, The, 14.108

Beer is as old as history, 14.23

beer is no better than its ingredients, A, 14.1

beer of friendship, The, 14.109

Beer that grows its own flavor, 14.24

Beer that made Milwaukee famous, 14.25

beer that made Milwaukee famous, The, 14.110

beer that made the nineties gay, The, 14.111

beer that made the old days good, The, 14.112

beer that makes friends, The, 14.113

beer that's brewed the natural way, aged the natural way, The, 14.114

beer that wins awards, The, 14.115

beer with millions of friends, The, 14.116

beer with the flavor as different as day from night, The, 14.117

beer with the 4th ingredient, The, 14.118

Be finicky, 5.4

Beginning a second century of leadership, 27.10

beginning of taste, The, 23.6

Be good to your gums, 34.6

Behind every Olga there really is an Olga, 121.6

Behind the enduring institution, successful customers, 43.7

Behind the panels of better built sets, 95.16

Being better is what we're all about, 126.7

Bejeweled by Gaylin, 67.4

Be kind to your skin, 32.12

Belcraft Shirts, your bosom friend, 26.18

Believe your own ears, 95.17

Bell and Howell brings out the expert in you (automatically!), 89.2

Bell and Howell builds photographic instruments a little better than they really have to be, 89.3

Beloved by brides for almost a century, 67.5

Below skin level shave, 104.2

Bendix does the wash without you, The, 60.96

Bends with your foot, 48.22

Be nonchalant, light a Deity, 115.16

Bent like a dentist's mirror to reach more places, 34.7

Berkley Ties the world, 26.19

Be Scotch, get your money's worth, 26.20

Be seated by . . . Bemis, 55.4

Be specific, say Union Pacific, 96.6

Be sporty in '40, 61.6

best aid is first aid, The, 35.98

best always comes from Small's, The, 100.26

best and nothing but the best is labeled Armour, The, 74.22

Best anti-freeze since mink, 8.9

best at the price, The, 67.32

Best bait for fishing since fishing first began, 45.5

Best because it's pan-dried, 21.8

Best beer by far at home, club, or bar, 14.26

Best bet in Baltimore, 85.59

Best bet's Buick, 7.19

Best built, best backed American cars, 7.20

Best buy Boling, 50.9

Best buy in rye, 71.23

Best by taste test, 107.9

Best by test, 11.7

best cigar in any case, The, 115.131

best comedy in America, The, 85.196

Best cooks know foods fried in Crisco don't taste greasy!, 47.16

best cooks use aluminum, The, 68.15

best dealer in town sells Norge, The, 60.97

best drinking coffee in the world, The, 27.45

Best for baby, best for you, 10.4

Best for every purpose, 123.6

Best for half a century, better than ever today, 115.17

Best for juice and every use, 49.5

Best for rest, 48.23

Best for you and baby, too, 106.5

Best for your money, 123.7

best friend your willpower ever had, The, 56.9

Best glue in the joint, 1.2

best has a taste all its own, The, 14.119

best in radio is better with a Bendix, The, 95.53

best in radio, The, 95.52

best in tapes has "Able" on the label, The, 35.99

best in the house" in 87 lands, "The, 71.92

Best in the long run, 114.5

best in the Union, in pocket tins, The, 115.132

best known name in paper, The, 83.57

Best-known name in sterling, 67.6

best-lookin' cookin' in town, The, 74.23

best name in all-weather coats and rainwear, The, 26.105

Best nickel candy there iz-z-z, 20.16

Best of all ... it's a Cadillac, 7.21

best of the world's press, The, 85.197

best seat in the house, The, 55.31

Best-selling aerosols are powered with Freon propellents, 22.8

best that can be bought "a quarter a quart." Why pay more?, The, 88.54

best tobacco makes the best smoke, The, 115.133

Best today, still better tomorrow, 72.3

best tonic, The, 14.120

best to you each morning, The, 21.35

Best way to close an opening, 18.11

best with the *most* on the ball, The, 108.26

Best year yet to go Ford!, 7.22

Be sure, insure in INA, 64.10

Be *sure* with Pure, 88.6

Be SURE you save at a savings bank, 43.8

Be suspicious!, 113.6

Be sweeticular, 20.17

Be swept away to another world, 84.4

Be thrifty and be happy, 43.9

Be thrifty, buy quality, 88.7

Be true to your teeth or they'll be false to you, 34.8

Better always better, 60.15

Better a part-time president than a full-time phony, 91.35

Better banking, better service, better join us, 43.10

Better because it's gas ... best because it's Caloric, 60.16

Better biscuits made the better way, 11.8

Better business is our aim, 2.9

Better buy Birds Eye, 47.17

Better buy Buick, 7.23

better buy, by any comparison, A, 108.1

Better coffee every time with S & W, 27.11

Better hearing longer, 57.1

Better ideas from UOP, 88.8

Better light brings better living, 37.3

Better little shoes are not made, 48.24

Better meals by the minute, 68.1

Better medicines for a better world, 35.9

Better products at lower cost through better methods, 73.4

Better products for a better world, 60.17

Better products for man's best friend, 86.1

better spread for our daily bread, The, 47.88

Better than a mustard plaster, 35.10

Better than mayonnaise, yet costs less, 29.4

"Better than money", 43.11

Better than whisky for a cold, 35.11

better the yarn the better the fabric, The, 103.14

Better things for better living through chemistry, 22.9

Better vision for better looks, 41.1

better-wearing brush for every use, A, 82.1

Better yet, Connecticut, 119.7

better yield in every field, A, 42.1

Better your home, better your living, 50.10, 85.60

Betty's husband for president in '76, 91.36

Between wood and weather, 82.9

BEVERAGES, MISCELLANEOUS, p. 66

Be vigilant and watchful that internal dissensions destroy not your prosperity, 91.37

Beware of B. O., 106.6

Beware Of Smokers Teeth, 34.9

Beware where you buy your bee-ware, 42.5

Be wise, protect your future, 101.2

Be wiser—buy Keiser, 69.4

BICYCLE is the card player's choice, 118.2

big brother to the railroads, The, 120.18

Big-car quality at lowest cost, 7.24

big cheese of potato chips, The, 47.89

Biggest, brightest, best magazine for boys in all the world, 85.61

Biggest in the country, 85.62

biggest name in little engines, The, 37.29

biggest *should* do more. It's only right., The, 6.6

big hotel that remembers the little things, The, 62.28

big house for little shoes since 1900, The, 48.129

Big name in batteries, 37.4

big sky country, The, 119.35

Big Stick, The, 91.307

big three lines of defense, The, 8.50

bike you'll like, The, 98.15

birch line, The, 18.78

Bird takes the burden out of keeping up your home, 18.12

Birthplace of the nation, 119.8

Birth state of the nation, 119.9

biteless blend, The, 115.134

blades men swear by, not at, The, 104.36

Blended right, 115.18

Blended whiskey of character, 71.24

blend of all straight whiskies, A, 71.1

blond beer with the body, The, 14.121

blue book of the trade, The, 85.198

Blue brutes, 73.5

Blue Chip company, The, 64.80

Blue Goose stands today, as always, for quality, 49.6

blue of spotless reputation, The, 24.85

Blueprint of a perfect cocktail, 125.3

Blue Sunoco, the Over-Drive Motor Fuel, 88.9

blue tube with the life-like tone, The, 95.54

Board of 100 uses in 1000 places, 18.13

boast of the gown, The, 121.43

BOATS AND BOATING EQUIPMENT, p. 67

Body by Fisher, 7.25

Body by Soloflex, 56.2

body cosmetic, The, 32.69

B & O is the way to go, The, 96.54

Bonded for life . . . because they're built that way, 117.3

Bonds that grow in security, 66.2

boot with the muscles, The, 48.130

Borden's just has to be good, 33.5

Bores a 300-foot hole in the night, 70.8

Born in America. Worn round the world, 26.21

Born in Canada, now going great in the 48 states, 14.27

Born in 1820 . . . still going strong!, 71.25

Born of the breath of man, Waterford is life's child, 52.2

Born where a king of France was born, 71.26

Boston's most famous hotel, 62.9

bottled beer with the draught beer flavor, The, 14.122

Bowl where you see the Magic Triangle, 108.8

Boy Scouts' magazine, The, 85.199

boys in blue will see it through, The, 91.308

boy's suit built for wear, The, 26.106

Brain-built boxes, 83.12

Brains & Beauty, 28.5

Brake inspection is your protection, 8.10

branch around the corner can serve you around the world, The, 43.51

Brand name of better gloves, 123.8

brands that made tuna famous, The, 47.90

brand that always puts flavor first, The, 47.91

brand they ask for first, The, 47.92

brand with loyalty to quality, The, 26.107

brand with the grand aroma, The, 115.135

brandy of Napoleon, The, 71.93

Brayco Light makes all things clear, 70.9

Bread is your best food, eat more of it, 11.9

Break away from the ordinary, 71.27

Breakfast of champions, 21.9

Breaks the static barrier, 24.6

Breathin' brushed pigskin, 48.25

breathless sensation, A, 20.1

Bred, not just grown, 42.6

Breidt's for TIME, the part of beer you taste but never see, 14.28

Brewed in the British manner, 14.29

Brewed *only* in Milwaukee, 14.30

brew that brings back memories, The, 14.123

Brew that holds its head high in any company, 14.31

Brew with a head of its own, 14.32

brew with small bubble carbonation, The, 14.124

Bright by day, light by night, 2.10

Brightens the night, 70.10

Brighten up with Instant Tender Leaf Tea, 110.2

Brighten your home at little expense, 46.7

brighter tasting tea, The, 110.14

brightest name in aluminum, The, 18.79

brightest star in golf, The, 108.27

bright new silicates for industry, The, 22.24

bright new world of electric housewares, A, 60.1

Brilliant as the sun, 26.22

Bring back prosperity with a Republican vote, 91.38

Bring out the Hellman's and bring out the best, 29.5

Bring out your best, 14.33

Brings a touch of the tropics, 58.5

Brings happiness to homework, 60.18

Bring us together, 91.39

Brisk flavor, never flat, 110.3

brisk magazine of Parisian life, A, 85.1

brisk tea, The, 110.15

bristles are sealed, the brush will last, The, 82.62

Brite-Lite has a brilliant future, 70.11

Broad, black, and a brute for wear, 114.6

BROADCASTING, p. 68

Broadcasts as she bakes, 101.3

Brockway, the right way, 120.2

bronze as strong as nickel steel, A, 75.1

brushless wonder, The, 104.37

Brush the cobwebs from your beauty, 54.7

Brush your hair to loveliness, 54.8

budget sets the pace, The, 39.3

Budweiser . . . King of Beers, 14.34

"Build a truck to do a job—change it only to do better", 120.3

Builder of trucks you can trust, 120.4

Builders of the tools of automation, 38.4

Builders of tomorrow's feeds . . . today!, 42.7

builder's selection for unfailing protection, The, 18.80

Building business is our business, 31.5

Building for the ages, 18.14

BUILDING SUPPLIES, p. 69

Building with Chicago and the nation since 1863, 43.12

Build-in satisfaction . . . build-in Frigidaire, 60.19

Build right, with Insulite, 18.15

Builds brain, nerves and body, 15.5

Builds for the years ahead, 15.6

Build the nation securely with the nation's building stone, 18.16

Built better because it's handcrafted, 112.3

Built for a palace, priced for a cottage, 70.12

Built for business, 120.5

Built for connoisseurs of refrigeration, 60.20

Built for permanence, calibrated for performance, 3.3

Built from the road up, 114.7

Built-in quality in every shoe, 48.26

Built layer on layer, 114.8

Built like a bank vault door, 55.5

Built like a fine watch, 95.18

Built like a skyscraper, 81.6

Built like a violin, 95.19

Built like a watch, 58.6

Built like fine furniture, 18.17

Built like the finest automobile, 60.21

Built on bedrock, 2.11

Built on reputation, 16.3

Built right for over forty years, 60.22

Built stronger to last longer, 8.11

Built through generations, 94.3

Built to fit the trip, 72.4

Built to last a business lifetime, 81.7

Built to last longer, 120.6

Built to last through every trip, 72.5

Built to sustain a reputation, 50.11

Built to take it . . . beautifully, 50.12

"Built tough for you", 7.26

Built to wear without repair, 55.6

Built to weather the years, 18.18

Built with integrity, backed by service, 60.23

Bulova Watch time, the gift of a lifetime, 124.7

Burglars know no season, 64.11

Burlington, the scatter rug of beauty, 46.8

business jet that's backed by an airline, The, 3.17

business journal of furnishing and decoration, A, 85.2

business leaders of today are the I. C. S. students of yesterday, The, 101.8

business magazine of the radio industry, The, 85.200

business management magazine, The, 85.201

business paper for the farm chemical industry, A, 85.3

business paper of the electrical industry since 1892, The, 85.202

BUS LINES, p. 75

butter in Bamby makes it better, The, 20.54

butter that betters the meal, The, 33.38

Buttons that are MORE than buttons, 103.4

Buy a How searchlight today, you may need it tonight, 70.13

Buy a rack of Rooties, 107.10

Buy Castle Furniture for your castle, 50.13

Buy overalls from the inside out, 26.23

Buy protection, not policies, 64.12

Buy them by the dozen for their many uses, 49.7

Buy today's best truck. Own tomorrow's best trade, 120.7

Buy us like advertising . . . use us like salesmen, 94.4

Buy word of millions, 115.19

Buy your beauty needs from beauticians, 32.13

Buy your last refrigerator first, 60.24

By design . . . furniture distinguished for value since 1904, 50.14

By the world's largest maker of dishwasher detergents, 24.7

By this sign you shall know them, 26.24

cabinet-wood of the elect, The, 18.81

Caffeine free. Never had it. Never will., 107.11

Calendar of fashion, 48.27

California's premier wines, 125.4

Call on Central, 43.13

Call Sprint. Find out about it., 111.2

Call your Investors man—today!, 64.13

calm beauty of Japan at almost the speed of sound, The, 4.48

Camels agree with me, 115.20

Camels suit your T-zone to a T, 115.21

camera you never leave at home, The, 89.24

Cammillus has the edge, 55.7

Canada's Fresh-up, 107.12

Canada's greatest newspaper, 85.63

Canada's national farm journal, 85.64

Canada's national magazine, 85.65

Canada's national newspaper, 85.66

Candies of character, 20.18

Candies of distinctive quality, 20.19

CANDY AND GUM, p. 76

Candy has energy and taste, 20.20

Candy makers to the American nation, 20.21

candy-mint alkalizer, The, 35.100

candy mint with the hole, The, 20.55

Can lay their weight in gold, 42.8

Canned food is grand food, 47.18

Canon meets tomorrow's challenges today, 89.4

can opener people, The, 68.16

Capability has many faces at Boeing, 3.4

Capitalist tool, 85.67

"Capitol" of the world, 97.2

Carefree furniture, 50.15

car for every purse and purpose, A, 7.1

car of a thousand speeds, The, 7.56

car of no regrets, The, 7.57

car of the year in eye appeal and buy appeal, The, 7.58

Carpets of distinction, 46.9

Car plan management and leasing specialists, 6.4

Carry the weight, save freight, 18.19

Carter White Lead is concentrated paint, 82.10

car that has everything, The, 7.59

car that is complete, The, 7.60

car with a longer life, The, 7.61

car with the foundation, The, 7.62

car you can believe in, A, 7.2

Cascade eliminates drops that spot, 24.8

Casco kills colds, 35.12

Casio. Where the miracles never cease., 124.8

Cataraction, the only real figure-8 movement, 60.25

Catch them yourself or buy Fowler's, 47.19

catsup with the big tomato taste, The, 29.34

Celebrate the moments of your life, 27.12

Celebrating the future, 28.6

centaur . . . your symbol of quality, The, 71.94

Center of scenic America, 119.10

Central Pennsylvania's greatest daily, 85.68

CEREALS, p. 80

cereal you can serve a dozen ways, The, 21.36

chair of amazing comfort, The, 50.54

Chairs for all business, 50.16

chair that stands by itself, The, 50.55

Challenges the elements, 82.11

champagne of bottle beer, The, 14.125

champagne of table waters, The, 15.24

"Champagne Touch", The, 102.20

Champion of blends, 115.22

champion of internal improvements, The, 91.309

champion of popular sovereignty, The, 91.310

champion of Republicanism and the American System, The, 91.311

Change for the better with Alcoa Aluminum, 75.4

Change to Bond Street for fragrant smoking, 115.23

Change work to play three times a day, 60.26

Charcoal mellowed drop by drop, 71.28

Chases chills from cold corners, 58.7

Chases dirt, 24.9

Cheaper insurance is easier to purchase but harder to collect, 64.14

cheapest health insurance in the world, The, 35.101

Checks your figure but not your freedom, 121.7

Check with Koppers, 31.6

Cheerful as its name, 71.29

cheese most people like, The, 33.39

cheese with the paper between the slices, The, 33.40

Cheese; zest at its best, 33.6

chef's flavor in home cooking, The, 29.35

CHEMICAL INDUSTRY, p. 82

Cherished as one of the world's seven great fragrances, 84.5

Chessie knows the territory, 96.7

Chesterfield King tastes great ... tastes mild, 115.24

Chevrolet is more truck ... day in, day out, 120.8

chevron—the sign of excellence, The, 88.55

chewing gum bon bon, The, 20.56

Chew Mail Pouch, 115.25

Chewy, gooey, homemade good, 11.10

Chicago's best and cleanest paper, 85.69

Chicago's only illustrated tabloid newspaper, 85.70

chicken in every pot, a car in every garage, A, 91.2

Chief of the mouldings, 18.20

Chief of West Virginia high volatile coals, 59.4

Children cry for it, 35.13

Children like it better than milk, 15.7

children's own magazine, The, 85.203

child's magazine, The, 85.204

Chillicothe papers make the best impressions, 83.13

CHINA, p. 84

China by Iroquois for the hosts of America, 23.1

Chlorine ointment, better than iodine, 35.14

Chock Full O'Nuts is that heavenly coffee, 27.13

chocolates with the wonderful centres, The, 20.57

choice for a change, A, 91.3

choice—not an echo, A, 91.4

choice of all who know one beer from another, The, 14.126

Choice of better mechanics, 117.4

choice of businessmen lets you choose with confidence, The, 64.81

Choice of champions, 44.4

choice of champions, The, 88.56

choice of noted music critics, The, 95.55

choice of over a million women, A, 60.2

choice of professionals, The, 5.34

choice of successful men, The, 115.136

choice of the crew and the big boss, too, The, 18.82

Choice of the masters, 80.3

Choice of three generations, 55.8

choicest product of the brewer's art, The, 14.127

choice when you want quality, too, The, 81.44

choice you make once for a lifetime, The, 67.33

Choosey mothers choose Jif, 47.20

Choose your piano as the artists do, 80.4

Chronicle of current Masonic events, 85.71

Churned from sweet (not sour) cream, 33.7

cigar made with good judgment, The, 115.137

cigar that breathes, The, 115.138

cigar that never lasts long enough, The, 115.139

citizen, wherever we serve, A, 93.1

city that does things, The, 36.18

civilized way of shaving, The, 104.38

Clairol is going to make someone beautiful today, 54.9

classic in wood, A, 105.1

classic name in the building field, The, 18.83

Classics of optical precision, 89.5

Class magazine in a class by itself, 85.72

Clean around the world, 82.12

Clean clear through, 71.30

clean, convenient fuel, The, 59.21

Clean hair means a healthy scalp, 54.10

Clean Home newspaper, A, 85.4

Clean house with Dewey, 91.40

CLEANING AND LAUNDRY PRODUCTS, p. 85

cleaning people who care, The, 25.4

CLEANING SERVICES, p. 90

Cleans as it fizzes, 34.10

Cleans as it polishes, 24.10

Cleans easier, works faster, won't scratch, 24.11

Cleans in a jiff, 24.12

Cleans inside, outside and between the teeth, 34.11

Cleans like a *white tornado,* 24.13

Cleans so well so easily, and for so little, 24.14

Cleans the impossible washload, 24.15

Cleans with a caress, 106.7

Cleans without beating and pounding, 60.27

clean tooth never decays, A, 34.1

Clean up with S. O. S. It's easy, 24.16

clean way to kill dirty rats, The, 86.13

Clear heads call for Calvert, 71.31

Clear to the ear, 95.20

Cletrac way makes farming pay, The, 42.43

Cleveland runs well in England, 91.41

Cleveland's better food markets, 100.5

clocks that most people want most, The, 124.39

Close. But no lumps., 47.21

close electric shave, The, 104.39

Clothes do help you win, dry clean them oftener, 25.2

Clothes in the New York manner, 26.25

Clothes that enhance your public appearance, 26.26

CLOTHING, MISCELLANEOUS, p. 90

Clubs of character for every golfer, 108.9

Coast to coast overnight, 4.10

Coast to coast to coast, 4.11

Coast to coast, we give the most, 62.10

Coatings, colors and chemicals for industry, 82.13

coats for every wear, everywhere, The, 26.108

coat with nine lives, The, 82.63

cod liver oil with the plus value, The, 35.102

COFFEE, p. 98

coffee-er coffee, The, 27.46

Coffee from the magic mountains, 27.14

coffee of inspiration, The, 27.47

Coffee rich enough to be served in America's finest restaurants, 27.15

coffee served at the Waldorf-Astoria, The, 27.48

coffee that lets you sleep, The, 27.49

Coffee, the American drink, 27.16

coffee without a regret, The, 27.50

coffee with the flavor advantage, The, 27.51

cognac brandy for every occasion, The, 71.95

Coke is it, 107.13

Cold and silent as a winter night, 60.28

College is America's best friend, 92.1

Color cocktails for your hair with Loxol extra, 54.11

colorfast shampoo, The, 54.36

"Color Guide" tie, The, 26.109

Color or white you're always right with Martin-Senour, 82.14

Colors hair inside, as nature does, 54.12

Come alive!, 107.14

Come home, America, 91.42

Come home to comfort, 58.8

Come on, breeze, let's blow, 60.29

Come on over to the right light, 49.8

Come on, you sunners, 109.1

Come rain or fog there's no shaker-clog, 29.6

Come take a trip around our Castle, 50.17

Come to Israel. Come stay with friends, 119.11

Come to Kentucky! It's a profitable move!, 36.2

Come to Marlboro Country, 115.26

Come to Shell for answers, 9.3

Come to think of it, I'll have a Heineken, 14.35

Come to where the flavor is . . . come to Marlboro country, 115.27

Come up to the Kool taste, 115.28

Comfortable, carefree cotton, 113.7

Comfortable heat when you want it, where you want it, at a price you can afford, 58.9

comfort shave, The, 104.40
comfort shoe of tomorrow, The, 48.131
Command the powers of Adam, 28.7
Commitment to quality, 73.6
company for people who travel, The, 119.36
company for precious metals, The, 75.24
company of specialists, The, 81.45
company of uncommon enterprise, A, 31.1
company with the "know-how", The, 81.46
company with the partnership philosophy, The, 64.82
COMPAQ PLUS, the first high-performance portable personal computer, 28.8
Comparison proves its superiority, 95.21
complete authority of packaging, The, 85.205
Complete brokerage service in the world's markets, 66.3
complete family of dog and cat foods from the world leader in nutrition, The, 87.12
complete first suds detergent, The, 24.86
Complete household soap, 24.17
complete line of electric cooking apparatus, The, 60.98
complete paper house, The, 83.58
complete plant food, not just a stimulant, A, 69.1
complete source for fine office furniture, A, 81.1
Completes the feast, 11.11
COMPUTER EQUIPMENT, p. 102
Computers for people, 28.9
CONDIMENTS AND SPICES, p. 106
confection of the fairies, The, 20.58
Confections that win affections, 20.22
Confidence in every package, 28.10
Congress has no more power to make a SLAVE than to make a KING, 91.43
Connolly shoes are comfortable shoes, 48.28
Consider paper, 83.14

Consider the power of paper used with imagination, 83.15
Consistently good year after year, 42.9
Constant excellence of product, 83.16
Constantly building for community usefulness, 43.14
Constitution and the flag, one and inseparable, now and forever, The, 91.312
Constitution and the freedom of the seas, The, 91.313
Constitution and Union, 91.44, 91.45
Constitution as it is, the Union as it was, The, 91.314
Constitution & Union forever, The, 91.315
Consult your doctor about your weight problems, 56.3
Consult your physician on matters of weight control, 56.4
Contains no caffeine or other harmful stimulants, 15.8
Contemporary fibers, 113.8
Continuous filament textured nylon, 113.9
Control with Dole, 8.12
Convenient to everywhere, 62.11
convertible sofa with accordion action, The, 50.56
Cook electrically and enjoy the difference, 37.5
Cooking is just a SNAP in an Estate electric range, 60.30
Cooking up ideas, 47.22
Cook into the future with electronics from Farberware, 60.31
Cooks in nine minutes, 47.23
Cook stove and gas plant all in one, 98.5
Cooks with the gas turned off, 60.32
Cooler on the draw, 105.4
Coolest hat under the sun, 26.27
Coolidge and Dawes—Full dinner pail, 91.46
Coolidge and prosperity, 91.47
Coolidge of course, 91.48
Coolidge or chaos, 91.49
Cool off in Colorado, 119.12

Cools and soothes as you shave, 104.3

Coordinated fashions for bed and bath, 12.1

Copies for communication throughout the world, 30.2

COPYING EQUIPMENT, p. 109

Cork-lined houses make comfortable homes, 18.21

Corn-free happy feet, 35.15

corn with husk ability, The, 42.44

corn with yield ability, The, 42.45

CORPORATIONS, MISCELLANEOUS, p. 109

Correct in every weigh, 12.2

Correct mistakes in any language, 81.8

correct toothpaste, The, 34.32

correct writing paper, The, 83.59

COSMETICS, p. 112

Costs less when used, 29.7

Costs more, but does more, 95.22

Costs more, worth more, 11.12

costume jewelry of the home, The, 50.57

Cotton, you can feel how good it looks, 113.10

Could it be the real thing?, 67.7

Country charm quality, 33.8

country demands his re-election, The, 91.316

Courage, confidence, and Coolidge, 91.50

courage to change. The strength to grow, The, 42.46

Course tested golf clubs, 108.10

Courtesy, efficiency, service, 43.15

Covers Spokane and the Spokane country like the sunshine, 85.73

Covers the country intensively, 85.74

Covers the subject, 121.8

Cover the earth, 82.15

Cozy comfort for chilly days, 58.10

Crackin' good walnuts, 49.9

Cradled silence, 58.11

Craftsmen of fine solid wood furniture, 50.18

Crane beauty in the open; Crane quality in all hidden fittings, 55.9

cream of olive oil soaps, The, 106.26

Cream of the coffees, 27.17

cream of them all, The, 88.57

cream shampoo for true hair loveliness, The, 54.37

Cream's rival, 33.9

Created to carry your belongings in perfection throughout your lifetime, 72.6

Create happy hours, 78.3

Creating a new world with electronics, 38.5

. . . Creating better ways to hold things together, 55.10

Creating useful products and services for you, 38.6

Creating world-famed fishing tackle since 1893, 45.6

Creative ideas in glass, 18.22

Creator of advanced writing instruments, 126.8

Creators of dependability, 73.7

Creators of direct mail literature, 2.12

Creators of distinctive luggage, 72.7

Creators of farm wealth, 42.10

Creators of 1001 products for home decorating, 65.4

crest of quality wine since 1889, The, 125.22

Crime, corruption, Communism, and Korea, 91.51

criminal within, The, 35.103

crisp dry cold of a frosty night, The, 60.99

Crossroads of the Pacific, 119.13

crowning achievement of vintner skill, The, 125.23

crowning touch of quality, The, 18.84

crown jewel of England, The, 71.96

crown jewels of ignition, The, 8.51

Cruiser of tomorrow, 16.4

Cruising everywhere under the sun, 102.4

crystal clear gin in the crystal clear bottle, The, 71.97

Cuba must be ours, 91.52

cube makes a cup, A, 47.1

Cultivate your musical bump, 80.5

cup for two or two for you, A, 60.3

cup of southern hospitality, The, 27.52

cup that cheers, The, 15.25

Cushion every step, 48.29

custom-corseted look, The, 121.44

custom crafted shotgun, The, 44.22

customer is always No. 1, The, 6.7
"Custom of course", 65.5
cut above the commonplace, A, 33.1
Cut out for a long career, 26.28
Cuts dishpan time in half, 24.18
Cuts the cost of clean hands, 106.8
Cutting costs is our business, 81.9
Cut to fit the mouth, 20.23
Dad played marbles, too, 118.3
dainty deodorant, The, 116.19
dairy paper of the New York City
    milk shed, The, 85.206
DAIRY PRODUCTS, p. 116
Dallas is the door to Texas, 36.3,
    85.75
Dandy candy, 20.24
Danskins are not just for dancing,
    26.29
Dare you move your pictures?, 65.6
dash that makes the dish, The,
    29.36
Data General. A Generation ahead.,
    28.11
dawn of a new era in personal
    computing, The, 28.49
Daylight's only rival, 70.14
daytime fragrance, The, 84.23
Dead moths eat no holes, 86.2
dealer's own paper, The, 85.207
deal with Diel means a good deal,
    A, 124.2
Dear to your heart but not to your
    purse, 20.25
Decorates as it preserves, 82.16
Decorate with artistic lighting
    equipment, 70.15
Dedicated to excellence, 7.27
Dedicated to people on the move,
    79.3
"Dedicated to serving the families
    of the West and Hawaii . . . no one
    else", 85.76
Dedicated to the pursuit of
    excellence, 31.7
Deeds—not words, 91.53
Deep in the heart of Dixie, 85.77
Defeat the New Deal and its
    reckless spending, 91.54
Defies the elements, 82.17
Definitely Glenoit for happy
    persons, 26.30
Definitive modern furniture, 50.19
Defrosts itself, saves shut-downs,
    60.33

Deliberate witchery, 84.6
Delicious and refreshing, 107.15
Delicious, deLIGHTful, demand it,
    14.36
delicious health confection, A, 20.2
Delicious in flavor, rich in nutrition,
    47.24
deliciously perfumed hair lacquer,
    The, 54.38
delicious whole wheat cereal, The,
    21.37
Delightfully see-worthy, 109.2
Delta is ready when you are, 4.12
Dem-Ike-Crats for Eisenhower,
    91.55
Democracy is good enough for all,
    91.56
Democracy prevails throughout the
    union, 91.57
Democracy, reform, and one
    presidential term, 91.58
Democracy stands for bimetallism
    not monometallism, people not
    trusts, republic not empire, 91.59
DENTAL CARE, p. 119
dentifrice that made fine teeth
    fashionable, The, 34.33
Dependability in the field . . . safety
    for the operator, 42.11
dependability people, The, 60.100
dependable automatics, The, 60.101
Dependable in any weather, 16.5
Dependable power, absolute safety,
    73.8
dependable railway, A, 96.1
Dependable spark plugs, 8.13
Depend on Potlatch for everything
    in quality lumber, 18.23
Depression spells opportunity for
    the real investor, 66.4
desert resort by the sea, The, 62.29
Designed by women for women,
    60.34
Designed for going places in style,
    in comfort, 48.30
Designed for your industry,
    engineered for you, 73.9
Designed for your pleasure today,
    tomorrow and always, 71.32
Designed to be lived in, 26.31
Designers of innovative systems for
    the information worker, 28.12

"Designs for the world's best dressed", 26.32

Designs that dreams are made of, 65.7

Determined to serve you best, 4.13

Detroit's home newspaper, 85.78

Developers and producers of extraordinary materials, 75.5

"Developing products for recreation through electronic research", 98.6

Devoted to beauty, 32.14

Devoted to the best interests of South Florida, 85.79

Dewey is due in '48, 91.60

Dewey or don't we?, 91.61

Dewey the racket buster—New Deal buster, 91.62

diamond is forever, A, 67.1

Diamonds win hearts, 67.8

Dictate to the Dictaphone, 81.10

Die casting is the process . . . zinc, the metal, 75.6

difference is quality, The, 80.26

difference is valves, The, 7.63

different antacid, The, 35.104

Different, delicious, digestible, 47.25

Digestible as milk itself, 33.10

Dignifying the pipe, 105.5

dime that covers the world, The, 85.208

Discover extra coolness, 115.29

Discover the Dysan difference, 28.13

Discover the new in New York State, 36.4

Discover what sound is all about, 5.5

discovery company, The, 31.22

disinfecting white paint, The, 82.64

Dispels dressing discords, 103.5

Displays that move goods, 2.13

Distance is no barrier to our service, 43.16

distilled motor oil, The, 88.58

Distinctive designs in leather accessories, 123.9

Distinctive floor coverings since 1917, 46.10

distinguished banking connection, A, 43.2

Distinguished furniture for distinguished offices, 81.11

Diversified-worldwide, 31.8

Divides the road in half, 8.14

doctor in candy form, The, 35.105

doctor's prescription, The, 35.106

Doctors prove Palmolive's beauty results, 106.9

Dodge builds tough trucks, 120.9

Does a lot for you, 31.9

Does four jobs at once, 88.10

Does not harm the heart, 35.16

Doesn't scratch, 24.19

Doesn't stun 'em, kills 'em, 86.3

Does she . . . or doesn't she, 54.13

Does something for you, 26.33

Dog food of champions, 87.3

Doggone good tools, 117.5

Do it tomorrow's way . . . with gas, 59.5

dominant newspaper of the Great Northwest, The, 85.209

dominant newspaper of the rich Montreal and Quebec Province Market, The, 85.210

Dominate Philadelphia, 85.80

Don't ask for crackers, say Snow Flakes, 11.13

Don't ask for "polish," demand Brite-Lite, 24.20

Don't be a pale face, 32.15

Don't be bullied by your bowl, Bully your bowl instead, 24.21

Don't be half-safe. Be completely safe. Use Arrid—to be sure., 116.6

Don't be satisfied with less than Lennox, 58.12

Don't be vague . . . ask for Haig and Haig, 71.33

Don't bump a good man out of the White House, 91.63

Don't forget that Koveralls Keep Kids Klean, 26.34

Don't get bit, get Flit, 86.4

Don't get wet, get Palmer, 26.35

Don't go to a warm place cold, 4.14

Don't just fertilize . . . Spencerize, 42.12

Don't just tape it. TDK it., 5.6

Don't leave home without it, 119.14

Don't leave home without them, 119.15

Don't let them take it away, 91.64

Don't put it off, put it on, 82.18

Don't say beer, say Falstaff, 14.37

Don't say "paper," say "Star", 85.81

Don't say sunglasses—say C'Bon, 41.2

Don't say underwear, say Munsingwear, 121.9

Don't stir without Noilly Prat, 125.5

Don't swap horses in the middle of the stream, 91.65

Don't swap horses—stand by Hoover, 91.66

Don't tear down the Statue of Liberty! Refuse dictatorship, 91.67

Don't wait to inherit Spode, 23.2

Don't write, telegraph, 111.3

Don't write, telephone, 111.4

Don't write, Voice-O-Graph, 81.12

Don't you feel good about 7-Up, 107.16

Double action, single cost, 24.22

Double crossroads of America, 119.16

Double doom to flies and mosquitoes, 86.5

double duty searchlight, The, 70.31

Doubles your face value, 32.16

Double welt means double wear, 48.31

Doughboy does it better . . . for a wide range of industries, 31.10

Dove creams your skin while you wash, 106.10

Dove is 1/4 cleansing cream, 106.11

Downtown St. Louis at your doorstep, 62.12

Down with free trade, 91.68

drier liqueur, The, 71.98

Dries before your eyes, 82.19

Drink a bunch of quick energy, 15.9

Drink a glass of health, 15.10

Drink Coca-Cola, 107.17

Drink it and sleep, 27.18

Drink moderately, insist on quality, 71.34

Drink RC for quick, fresh energy, 107.18

Drink your apple a day, 15.11

drink you remember, The, 107.42

Drink your prunes, 15.12

Driving in its purest form, 7.28

Drop LeMay on Hanoi, 91.69

DRUGS AND REMEDIES, p. 121

Drum makers to the profession, 80.6

drum standard of the world, The, 80.27

Dry back or money back, 26.36

dry constant cold of the mountain top, The, 60.102

dry goods daily, The, 85.211

Dump the Hump, 91.70

Duraflake makes only particleboard and only the best, 18.24

Dutch name, world fame, 71.35

Duz does everything, 24.23

dynamic force with paper, A, 83.1

dynamo of Dixie, The, 36.19

Each grain salutes you, 47.26

Each week the facts add up to success, 85.82

Earn while you learn, 101.4

earth's first soft drink, The, 15.26

Easier to handle, lighter draft, more durable, 42.13

Easiest and cheapest way to heat your home, 58.13

easiest kind because skeleton lined, The, 48.132

easiest line to sell, The, 55.32

easiest name for a man to remember, The, 26.110

easiest shoe for women, The, 48.133

Easiest travel on earth, 19.1

easiest way out, The, 18.85

Easily distinguished by the yellow back, 55.11

Easy, delicious . . . versatile, nutritious, 47.27

Easy does it, 104.4

Easy doses, no fishy taste, no bad after-taste, 35.17

easy ones, The, 89.25

Easy to buy, easy to fly, 3.5

Easy to play, pay and carry, 80.7

Easy to spread, hard to beat, 18.25

Easy to thin, tint and spread, 82.20

Easy to use, 34.12

Easy to use, just shake in your shoes, 35.18

Eat candy for energy, 20.26

Eat Johnston Cookies, the taste that thrills, 11.14

Eat more apples, take less medicine, 49.10

Eats everything in the pipe, 24.24

Eats paint and bites varnish, 82.21

economical energy food, The, 47.93

ECONOMIC DEVELOPMENT, p. 129

Economy gasoline, 88.11

Eden cleans by gentle means, The, 60.103

Edited by yachtsmen for yachtsmen, 85.83

8 Companies running hard, 31.11

Elect me president—freedom and the reunion of states shall be permanently established, 91.71

Elect none but natives to office, 91.72

ELECTRICAL PRODUCTS AND SERVICES, p. 130

Electrical refrigeration, a way to better living, 60.35

electric hoist that operates in the minimum, The, 73.31

Electricity gives you matchless cooking, 37.6

Electricity . . . it's still hard to find a better value, 93.3

electric range with the safety top, The, 60.104

Electro-Copyst, a photo-copying machine for every office, 30.3

ELECTRONICS INDUSTRY, p. 132

ELEVATORS, p. 133

emblem of security, a pledge of service, An, 64.4

emblem of worth in radio, The, 95.56

empire's best, The, 110.16

EMPLOYMENT AGENCIES, p. 133

Empties with a thumb pressure, 60.36

Enchanting ladies choose Dorothy Gray, 32.17

Ends that painted look, 32.18

End the day with a smile, 81.13

Enduring as the mountains, 64.15

Enduring masterpieces, 50.20

Energy chemicals, 22.10

Energy eggs from happy hens, 47.28

Engineered for accuracy, 124.9

Engineered for longer life, 42.14

Engineered like no other car in the world, 7.29

Engineering for boys, 118.4

engineering journal of the industry, The, 85.212

engineering magazine, The, 85.213

Engineering with imagination, 126.9

Engine life preserver, 88.12

England's choicest lavender, 84.7

Enjoyable always and *all* ways, 71.36

Enjoy a sip of California Sunshine, 125.6

Enjoy the rest of your life, 13.4

envelope is the first impression, The, 83.60

Equal & full protection to American industry, 91.73

Equal rights to all, special privileges to none, 91.74

Escape from the ordinary, 7.30

Europe's foremost airline, 4.15

Europe's most helpful airline, 4.16

Even a child can tell the difference, 15.13

Even the collars and cuffs are clean, 60.37

Everlastingly beautiful, 82.22

Every Bali has a bow, 121.10

Every bite a delight, 11.15

Every bite a rarebit, 47.29

Everybody appreciates the finest, 60.38

Everybody makes terminals. Only we make Lear Sieglers., 28.14

Every business form for every form of business, 81.14

Every color in the rainbow, 103.6

Every cup's a cup of joy, 27.19

Everyday good . . . glass with flair, 52.3

Every day in some way, 49.11

Every El Dueno cigar is smooth sailing, 115.30

Every granule licks dirt 8 ways, 24.25

Every man should wear at least three straw hats, 26.37

Every mile of yarn gives an extra year of wear, 121.11

Every one a good one, 95.23

Everyone knows, if it's Caryl Richards, it is just wonderful for your hair, 54.14

Everyone needs the Sun, 64.16

Every pair is full of wear, 48.32

Every pair made to wear, 48.33

Every pair must please, 123.10

Every pair shows the care of the shoemaker's hand, 48.34

Every puff a pleasure, 115.31

Every shave a good shave, 104.5

Every style worth while, 26.38

Everything a computer's supposed to be. Except expensive., 28.15

Everything electrical for home and industry, 37.7

Everything electrical for the theatre, 37.8

Everything for the radio man, 95.24

Everything hinges on Hager, 55.12

Everything in Baltimore revolves around the Sun, 85.84

Everything is under control, 121.12

Everything's better with Blue Bonnet on it, 47.30

Everything to build anything, 18.26

Everything to wear, 26.39

Everything will come out all right, 35.19

Everything you always wanted in a beer . . . and less, 14.38

Everything you've ever wanted in a fish fillet, 47.31

Everywhere on everything, 82.23

Everywhere west, 96.8

Every woman alive wants Chanel No. 5, 84.8

Every year, more Royal typewriters are bought in America than any other brand, 81.15

Evinruding is rowboat motoring, 16.6

Excellence doubly safeguarded, 71.37

Excellence in electronics, 95.25

Excellence in software technology, 28.16

Excitement you can taste, 71.38

Exclusive makers of the original old-fashioned molasses candy in delightful modern flavors, 20.27

Executive America's top cigar, 115.32

Executive training for business leadership, 101.5

Expensive shirts ought to look it, 26.40

Experience counts: vote Nixon–Lodge for a better America, 91.75

experience cruise line, The, 102.21

Experience is the best teacher, 115.33

Expert's choice . . . since 1880, 44.5

Experts know these lamps, 70.16

Experts pronounce it best, 14.39

Express your individuality, 67.9

Exquisite as America's beauties, 124.10

Extra Care Airline, The, 4.49

extra collar for a dollar, An, 103.3

extra measure of quality, An, 38.1

extra miles are free, The, 88.59

extraordinary fiber, The, 113.28

extra quart of lubrication in every gallon, An, 88.5

Extra service without extra cost, 64.17

Extra strength that never fails you, 103.7

Eye-ease at the snap of the switch, 70.17

eye for your gas tank, An, 8.4

EYEGLASSES, p. 134

eye line of smartness, The, 61.31

eye make-up in good taste, The, 32.70

Eyes of the night, 8.15

Eyes of youth, 32.19

eye to the future, an ear to the ground, An, 31.2

Fabrics used in the most wanted women's and children's sportswear, 113.11

Fabrics with the character of quality, 113.12

fabric with reflex action, The, 113.29

Fagged? Drink a bunch of quick energy, 15.14

Faithfully maintaining quality at no advance in price, 105.6

faithfulness of an old friend, The, 37.30

Faithful to the last, 48.35

Fall in love with coffee all over again, 27.20

Famed for flavor, 21.10

Families that move the most call the world's largest mover, 79.4

Family car of the air, 3.6

Family computer history is about to be written, 28.17

family liniment, The, 35.107

family plate for seventy years, The, 67.34

famous brand in glass, A, 52.1

famous camera from camera-famous West Germany, A, 89.1

famous family of Gorton's sea foods, The, 47.94

Famous for five generations, 14.40

Famous for generations, 83.17

Famous for its its flavor, 11.16

Famous for power mowers for over 50 years, 69.5

Famous for products that really work, 24.26

Famous for quality, 114.9

Famous for quality the world over, 95.26, 112.4

Famous for their razor-sharp edges, 55.13

Famous name in pain relief, 35.20

famous name in radio since 1921, A, 95.1

Famous name in tobacco for nearly 200 years, 115.34

Famous overnight, 13.5

famous pencil with green and yellow plastips, The, 126.31

Famous shoes for women, 48.36

famous skin softener, The, 32.71

Famous. Smooth. Mellow., 71.39

fan-jet airline, The, 4.50

farmer's service station, The, 85.214

FARMING SUPPLIES AND EQUIPMENT, p. 135

Farm Implements with a future - yours!, 42.15

farm paper of service, The, 85.215

farm paper with a mission, The, 85.216

farm weekly of largest circulation and most influence, The, 85.217

fashionable fragrance, The, 84.24

Fashioned by master craftsmen, 48.37

Fashioned each season to fit each season's fashions, 121.13

... Fashioned for those who enjoy extraordinary quality, 108.11

Fashion forecasters, 48.38

Fashion in action, 26.41

Fashion loomed to last, 46.11

Fashion luggage, 72.8

Fashion-over-the-shoe, 48.39

Fashion's favored footwear, 48.40

fashion shoe, The, 48.134

Fashions in fragrance, 84.9

fastener to fit every need, A, 103.1

fastest-growing newspaper and fastest-growing city in Texas, The, 85.218

Fastest in the world, 60.39

Fast for dishes yet kind to your hands, 24.27

Father of tree surgery, 69.6

Faucets without a fault, 55.14

Faultless since 1881—The nightwear of a nation, 26.42

Faultless starch lightens laundry labor, 24.28

favorite home-sewing notion of the nation, The, 103.15

Favorite of housewives for 150 years, 11.17

Favorite shells satisfy good shooters, 44.6

Fear God and take your own part, 91.76

Feature rich, 5.7

feeder's silent partner, The, 42.47

Feeds and seeds to meet your needs, 42.16

Feel fine, go alkaline, 15.15

Feel it heal, 35.21

Feels like it's time, Cup-A-Soup time, 47.32

Feels like walking on velvet, 46.12

Feel the air cushion, 48.41

Feel the fabric and you'll feel the difference, 26.43

FEL-PRO sets the standards for the gasketing industry, 8.16

Few. The Proud. The Marines., The, 53.3

fiber you can trust, The, 113.30

Field-tested fertilizers, 42.17

54° 40' or Fight, 91.77

51 writes dry with wet ink, 126.10

Fifty per cent more wear, 26.44

57 Varieties, 47.33

50 years of brighter tasting meals, 68.2

Fights colds and sore throats, 35.22

file for every purpose, A, 117.1

Fileworthy, 85.85

Fill it to the rim with Brim, 27.21

Fill with water, write with ink, 126.11

filter for the taste that's right!, The, 115.140

Filters sun, speeds tan, 32.20

401

Filters the smoke from bowl to tip, 105.7

Filters the smoke on the way to your throat—filters it and makes it mild, 115.35

final touch to a tasty dish, The, 49.23

FINANCIAL INSTITUTIONS AND SERVICES, p. 138

Find it faster in the Yellow Pages, 2.14

Find your place in the sun, 119.17

Fine bootmakers since 1876, 48.42

Fine cabinetmakers since 1886, 50.21

Fine coffee liqueur . . . from sunny Mexico, 71.40

Fine combed, fine count percale sheets, 13.6

Fine dinnerware, 23.3

Fine fabrics made in America since 1813, 113.13

Fine fashion Jewelry, 67.10

Fine letter papers, 83.18

fine old innkeeping tradition in a modern setting", "The, 62.30

Fine photography for 40 years, 89.6

Finer seamless stockings, 61.7

Finer than the finest castile, 106.12

finer typewriter at a fair price, A, 81.2

Finest anti-knock non-premium gasoline ever offered at no extra cost, 88.13

finest chocolate in the world, The, 20.59

finest dye that money can buy, The, 24.87

finest food preparer for the home, The, 68.17

finest habit a man can have, The, 26.111

finest human hands can achieve, The, 26.112

Finest imported from Italy, 47.34

Finest in china since 1735, 23.4

finest name in sleep, The, 13.27

finest of natural cheeses—naturally from Kraft, The, 33.41

finest pads have purple bindings", "The, 81.47

finest protection available for your family, your property and your business, The, 64.83

finest wines of France, The, 125.24

Fine tobacco is what counts in a cigarette, 115.36

fine tool at a fair price, A, 117.2

Fine watchmakers since 1791, 124.11

Fine whiskey on the mild side, 71.41

Fingers of steel, 117.6

finishing touch you can't afford to forget, The, 116.20

FIREARMS, p. 141

Fire insurance is as old as the Sun, 64.18

Fire up with Firebird, 88.14

firm and fearless advocate of democracy, The, 91.317

First across the Pacific; first across the Atlantic; first throughout Latin America, 4.17

First aid for clever cooks, 29.8

First aid for the family, 35.23

First aid for thirst, 107.19

First airline in the Americas, 4.18

First always, finest all ways, 48.43

First among fine whiskies, 71.42

First and finest in copper and brass . . . Fully integrated in aluminum, 75.7

First and foremost in microfilming since 1928, 81.16

first and greatest name in electronics, The, 38.13

First because it lasts, 82.24

First, by merit, 85.86

First choice in fishing tackle hardware, 45.7

First choice in food, lodging and services nationwide!, 62.13

First choice of experience, 88.15

first computer, The, 28.50

first dental preparations made especially for children, The, 34.34

first different smoking tobacco in a generation, The, 115.141

First family in drapery hardware since 1903, 55.15

First for fast service, 8.17

First for the South, 85.87

First, from the very first, 58.14

first hands to touch it are yours, The, 33.42

First he whispers, then he shouts, 124.12

First in airfreight with airfreight first, 4.19
First in automation, 73.10
First in banking, 43.17
First in carbonless papers, 83.19
First in Chicago, 85.88
First in Cleveland, 85.89
First in creative engineering, 3.7
First in Dayton, third in Ohio, 85.90
First in dependability, 16.7
First in epoxies . . . in the age of ideas, 18.27
First in fabrics for industry, 113.14
First in fashion, 46.13
First in film news, 85.91
First in grassland farming, 42.18
First in Latin America, 4.20
First in life, first in death, 64.19
First in loans to business and industry, 43.18
First in marine propulsion, 16.8
First in outboards, 16.9
First in powered equipment since 1918, 42.19
First in quality!, 48.44
First in quality, performance, preference, 24.29
First in resources/first in capability, 88.16
First in sporting arms, 44.7
First in the farm field, 85.92
First in the field, 85.93
First in the hearts of his soldiers, 91.78
First in the social register, 115.37
First in world records, 45.8
First line in printers, The, 28.51
First magazine for women, 85.94
first name in American stationery, The, 83.61
first name in business systems, The, 81.48
First name in cast steel!, 75.8
first name in custom bedding, The, 13.28
First name in filing, 81.17
First name in paper punches, 81.18
first name in seats—the last name in quality, The, 55.33
First name in time, last word in watch styling, 124.13
First name in tire valves for original equipment and replacement, 8.18
First name in towels is the last word in sheets, 13.7
first national newspaper network, The, 85.219
first new no-filter cigarette in years, The, 115.142
First of the Northern Transcontnentals, 96.9
First on famous waters, 45.9
First on the Atlantic, 4.21
First on the finish, 82.25
First on the Pacific, 4.22
First Pennsylvania means business, 43.19
first real improvement since the spoon, The, 35.108
first really different magazine in a generation, The, 85.220
First 'round the world, 4.23
first taste tells you it's good to the last drop, The, 27.53
first taste will tell you why!, The, 71.99
First thought, first aid and Astyptodyne, 35.24
first thought in burns, The, 35.109
first thought in the morning, The, 27.54
First to last, the truth: news, editorials, advertisements, 85.95
First to serve the farmer, 42.20
First with better ways to build, 18.28
First with the features women want most, 60.40
First with the finest in television, 112.5
First with the finest in wallcoverings . . . always!, 65.8
Fish "Heddon" and fish better, 45.10
fish hook people, The, 45.20
FISHING SUPPLIES, p. 143
Fishing tackle for every kind of fishing, 45.11
Fit all hands and all purses, 123.11
Fit as a fiddle, 121.14
Fit for a golden spoon, 33.11
Fit for a king, 14.41
Fit for every foot, 48.45

Fit right, feel right, they're walk-fitted, 48.46

Fits and matches the car you're driving, 95.27

Fits on the foot like a glove on the hand, 48.47

Fits the feminine clan, 121.15

Fits the foot in action or repose, 48.48

Fits the sport, 98.7

"fitting" tribute to the feminine figure, A, 121.1

Fit to be tried, 48.49

flag of a republic forever, of an empire never, The, 91.318

flair for elegance, A, 112.1

Flat folded stationery, 83.20

Flatters where it matters, 121.16

flavor-aged ginger ale, The, 107.43

Flavor first, 49.12

flavor is sealed in the flavor bud, The, 47.95

flavor's all yours, The, 115.143

Flavor sealed in the brown bottle, 107.20

flavor secret of the finest cocktails, The, 125.25

flavor sensation that sold the nation on coffee made in the cup, The, 27.55

Flavor so delicious only your figure knows they're low calorie, 29.9

flavor you can't forget, The, 11.50

Flexible where you want it, rigid where you need it, 48.50

FLOOR COVERINGS, p. 145

floor of enduring beauty, The, 46.27

Floor with maple, beech or birch, 46.14

Florida's great home daily, 85.96

Florida's most important newspaper, 85.97

Florsheims afoot mean comfort ahead, 48.51

flour of a thousand uses, The, 11.51

flower of fine flour, The, 11.52

Flows fast, stays tough, 88.17

Flows freely, dissolves readily, develops food flavor, 29.10

Fly anywhere in Europe via Air France., 4.24

Fly the friendly skies of United, 4.25

Fly the planes that fly the U. S. Flag, 4.26

FM at its finest, 95.28

Foaming with flavor, 14.42

folding furniture with the permanent look, The, 50.58

Folks favor Fromm's flavor, 74.5

Follow the ARROW and you follow the style, 26.45

Follw the leader, he's on a Honda, 77.1

Follow the journal and you follow the oil industry, 85.98

Fond of things Italiano? Try a sip of Galiano, 71.43

Food for speed, 88.18

FOOD, MISCELLANEOUS, p. 147

Food of the gods, 47.35

Foodpower people, The, 31.23

Food producers for the world, 42.21

Food purveyors to the nation, 74.6

Food shot from guns, 21.11

food that builds bonnie babies, The, 10.7

Foot insurance for the future, 48.52

foot nearer perfection, A, 48.3

foot of comfort means miles of happiness, A, 48.4

Footwear for all occasions, 48.53

FOOTWEAR, p. 152

For a better tomorrow, 107.21

For a change, try Sohio, 88.19

For a cooling shave, 104.6

. . . for a good look, 89.7

For a good night's sleep, 35.25

For a lifetime of proud possession, 124.14

For a livelier life, 21.12

For all important occasions, wear Dura-Gloss, 32.21

For all industry, 117.7

For all kinds of insurance in a single plan, call your Travelers man, 64.20

For all you do, this Bud's for you, 14.43

For almost any product, aluminum makes it better and Kaiser aluminum makes aluminum work best, 75.9

For a man who plans beyond tomorrow, 71.44

For *any* air conditioning, 58.15

For any wear and everywhere, 48.54

For a royal shave, 104.7

For a sure tomorrow—insure enough today!, 64.21

For a taste that's *Springtime fresh,* 115.38

For beauty exercise, 20.28

For better and faster cooking, 68.3

For better eyesight, 41.3

For better living, 60.41

For better results, always use the best paper, 83.21

'forbidden' fragrance, The, 84.25

For bracing up digestion, nerves, and appetite, 21.13

For business people who think for themselves, 85.99

For busy business men, 85.100

For clean hits and clean barrels, 44.8

For comfort and pleasure all through the house, 58.16

For connoisseurs by connoisseurs, 65.9

For controlled warmth, 13.8

For deep-down smoking enjoyment smoke that smoke of fine tobacco—Lucky Strike, 115.39

Ford has a better idea, 7.31

For digestion's sake, smoke Camels, 115.40

For doctor bills, 64.22

For "dream hands," cream your hands, 32.22

Foremost brand in outdoor living, 98.8

foremost in drums, The, 80.28

For every business need, 83.22

For every floor in the house, 46.15

For every occasion of social correspondence, 83.23

Forever yours, 89.8

For every piping system, 55.16

For every room in the house, 50.22

For everything green that grows, 69.7

For everything "under the sun", 41.4

For every walk in life, 48.55, 61.8

For FAST headache help, 35.26

For freedom—Four Freedoms, 91.79

For fresher bread tomorrow, buy Taystee Bread today, 11.18

For gifts that last consult your jeweler, 67.11

For God for home and native land— the saloon must go, 91.80

For good advice . . . and good products . . . depend on your Mobil dealer, 88.20

For good and FITTING reasons, 61.9

For good eating at sensible cost, 100.6

For good food and good food ideas, 47.36

For goodness sake buy Admiration Coffee, 27.22

For goodness sake wear Buckeye Shirts, 26.46

For growing satisfaction, 69.8

For heating and cooling . . . gas is good business, 59.6

For high moments in distinguished living, 84.10

For home lovers in cities, towns, and suburbs, 85.101

For imagination in communication, look to 3M business product centers, 30.4

For important clothes, it's Kerman Stores, 100.7

For industry, shop, farm and home, 117.8

For lazy people, 34.13

For lovely lawns in sun or shade, 69.9

For matching lips and fingertips, 32.23

For men of distinction, 71.45

For men who care what they wear, 26.47

For men who know fine whiskies, 71.46

For men who measure value in terms of quality alone, 48.56

For more good years in your car, 9.4

For more than a century makers of fine furniture in traditional and modern idiom, 50.23

For more than 25 years the authority on gun cleaning, 44.9

For more than 25 years the national magazine of the furniture trade, 85.102

For occasions and all occasions, 107.22

For oil marketing, 85.103

For particular people

For particular people, 110.4
For penetrating relief get Hall's Vapor Action, 35.27
For people who love coffee, but not caffeine, 27.23
For people who travel . . . and expect to again and again, 72.9
For proved beauty results, 106.13
For quality Western lumber products, look to T, W, and J, 18.29
For quality you can *depend* on . . . *depend* on Skelgas, 88.21
For quicker meals, packed with flavor, your best bet is Universal Minute-Savor, 47.37
For real enjoyment, 115.41
For real smoking pleasure, 115.42
For relief you can trust, 35.28
For serving . . . it's Erving, 83.24
For 75 years, America's link with the Orient, 102.5
For shaving without brush or lather, 104.8
For sheer loveliness wear Chatelaine Silk Hosiery, 61.10
For silken-sheen hair easy to arrange, 54.15
For smooth shaves, 104.9
For smooth white hands tomorrow use Thine Hand Creme tonight, 32.24
For special industrial requirements, 83.25
For stores of quality standard, 100.8
For strength where the stress comes, 75.10
For superb personal movies, 89.9
For that breath-taking moment, 67.12
For that certain kind of woman, 100.9
For that "come hither" look, 32.25
For that good-looking feeling, 26.48
For that smart sun-tan look, 32.26
For the active woman of today, 48.57
For the beautiful point of view, 18.30
For the best combination of filter and good taste Kent satisfies *best*, 115.43
For the best in rest, 13.9

For the climate of excellence, 94.5
For the decorator touch, 65.10
For the elegant petite, 26.49
For the girl who knows value by heart, 121.17
For the great moments, 125.7
For the home that enjoys home life, 80.8
For the king of old-fashioneds, 71.47
For the lift of your lifetime, 121.18
For the lightest, fluffiest popcorn there's only one, Orville Redenbacher, 47.38
For the loveliest legs in the world, 61.11
For the love of Ike vote Republican, 91.81
For the man on the move, 26.50
For the man who believes his own ears, 95.29
For the man who cares, 71.48
For the men in charge, 85.104
For the nicest youngsters you know, 26.51
For the one man in 7 who shaves every day, 104.10
For the private world of the bath, 32.27
For the rest of the night, 26.52
For the REST of your life, 50.24
For these symptoms of stress that can come from success, 35.29
For the shave that never fails, 104.11
For the smart young woman, 85.105
For the smile of beauty, 34.14
For the taste that's right, 115.44
For the tummy, 35.30
For the typical American size, 26.53
For the well-dressed salad, 29.11
For the winning edge, 48.58
For the woman who dares to be different, 84.11
For the women who can afford the best. Even though it costs less, 32.28
For those friskie years, 26.54
For those letters you owe, 83.26
For those who can hear the difference, 5.8
For those who go first class, 72.10
For those who must make best impressions, 81.19

For those who really like to eat, 74.7

For those who think young, 107.23

For those who value excellence, 50.25

For those who want *every* puff to taste as fresh as the *first* puff!, 115.45

Fortune means business, 85.106

For twenty-five years, first in professional hair care, 54.16

Forward together, 91.82

Forward with Miami's oldest bank, 43.20

For Wilmington, the Carolinas, and the South, 43.21

For women whose eyes are older than they are, 32.29

For you and your town, 85.107

For you—every banking service, 43.22

For younger young men, 26.55

For young men and men who stay young, 26.56

For young men and men with young ideas, 115.46

For your children's sake, 118.5

For your pressing needs, 73.11

For your stomach's sake, 35.31

For youthful figures of all ages, 121.19

For youthful hands, to have and to hold, 32.30

foundation of American beauty, The, 121.45

Founded by merchants for merchants, 43.23

Founder of better homes in America, 85.108

fountain of youth for your skin, A, 32.3

fountain of youth, The, 15.27

four-edged razor blade, The, 104.41

Four great routes for transcontinental travel, 96.10

4-H-Club—help hustle Harry home, 91.83

Four inches of a 25-cent cigar, 115.47

Four more Roosevelt lucky years, 91.84

Four More Years, 91.85

fourth necessity, The, 64.84

fragrance of youth, The, 84.26

Freedent's the one that took the stick out of gum, and put the fresh in your breath, 20.29

Freedom to all, 91.86

Freedom to all men—war for the Union, 91.87

Free from "rings" and "shadows", 61.12

Free homes for the homeless, 91.88

Free Kansas—and the Union, 91.89

Free land, free speech and free men, 91.90

Free running, 29.12

Free soil, free men, free speech, and Frémont, 91.91

Free soil, free speech, free labor, and free men, 91.92

Free soil to a free people, 91.93

Free speech. Free press. Frémont, 91.94

Free territory for a free people, 91.95

Freight Railroads are on the move, 96.11

Fresh as a daisy, 33.12

Fresh as a spring morning, 47.39

Fresh as dewy dawn, 47.40

Fresh as the morning, 21.14

Fresh from sunshine and pure air, 74.8

Fresh from the gardens, 110.5

Fresh from the mill to you, 21.15

Fresh ideas in meat . . . from Hormel, 74.9

Fresh milk; drink it once a day, 33.13

Fresh milk; have you had your glass today?, 33.14

Fresh paint is better paint, 82.26

Fresh to you each morning, 21.16

Fresh-up with Seven-up, 107.24

friendly computer, The, 28.52

friendly drink from good neighbors, The, 27.56

Friendly, familiar, foreign and near, 119.18

Friendly land of infinite variety, 119.19

friendly railroad for all the family, The, 96.55

friendly smoke, The, 115.144

Friendly Store, The, 100.27

Friendly to the feet, 48.59

friendly way, C. P. A., The, 4.51

friendly world of Hilton, The, 62.31

friend-making work shirt, The, 26.113

friend of the family, A, 4.1

From contented cows, 33.15

From first step to fourteen years, 48.60

From flower to bee to you, 47.41

From generation to generation, 67.13, 68.4

From Maine to Texas . . . and growing, 100.10

From mill to millions, 26.57

From mine to market, 75.11

From one beer lover to another, 14.44

From pit to penthouse, 39.1

From sharp minds come Sharp products, 38.7

From the finest of the vines, 125.8

From the goodness of Louis Rich, 74.10

From the heart of California, 125.9

From the land of sky blue waters, 14.45

From the largest cellars in the world, 125.10

From the tall corn country, 74.11

From the tiniest to the mightiest, 37.9

From the Tow Path to the White House, 91.96

From the tractor people who make the big ones, 42.22

From the world's most renowned cosmetic research laboratories, 32.31

From world leaders in nutrition, 87.4

FRUITS AND NUTS, p. 162

fuel without a fault, The, 59.22

full meal in two biscuits, A, 21.1

Full of sunshine and good health, 49.13

full package of light, A, 70.2

Full powered, 88.22

Full service bank, 43.24

Functional papers, 83.27

Fur goodness sake try Kruskal, 26.58

furmost line, The, 26.114

Furnace freedom, 58.17

Furnace heat for every home, 58.18

Furniture of timeless beauty, 50.26

Furniture that's fun to live with, 50.27

FURNITURE, p. 164

Furs that reflect youth, 26.59

future belongs to those who prepare for it, The, 64.85

future is building now at Garrett, The, 3.18

future . . . without the shock, The, 28.53

gallant & successful defender of New Orleans, The, 91.319

Garrett is experience, 3.8

Gas makes the big difference, 59.7

Gasoline, not cut price guessoline, 88.23

gas range with the life-time burner guarantee, The, 60.105

gas range you want, The, 60.106

Gas, the comfort fuel, 59.8

Gateway to and from the booming west, 96.12

Gateway to and from your world markets, 96.13

gateway to the Chicago market, The, 85.221

Gateway to the Jewish market, 85.109

Gateway to the world of fabrics, 113.15

gay-hearted fragrance, The, 84.27

G-B means Great Beer, 14.46

Gee! No, GTE, 111.5

gel that gives you more, The, 104.42

Gems of the screen, 78.4

General amnesty—uniform currency—equal taxes and equal rights, 91.97

General Taylor never surrenders, 91.98

generation of worldwide acceptance, A, 46.1

Generously good, 115.48

Gen. Frank Pierce the statesman & soldier, 91.99

Genie keeps you in the driver's seat!, 55.17

Gentle as a lamb, 71.49

gentleman's drink, A, 71.3

gentlemen of the moving industry, The, 79.8

gentler cream deodorant, The, 116.21

Gently as a whisper, 18.31

Gen. Winfield Scott—first in war, first in peace, 91.100

Get a piece of the rock, 64.23

Get at that corn today, forget that ouch tomorrow, 35.32

Get brighter windows with Windex, 24.30

Get it in glass, 52.4

Get more out of life with coffee, 27.24

Get ready for the extraordinary, 104.12

Gets a hand in any land, 71.50

Gets the dirt, not the carpet, 60.42

Gets the red out, 35.33

Gets there first, 4.27

Get that golden glow with Rheingold, 14.47

Get the Atra advantage, 104.13

Get the best in the world, 64.24

Get the best things first, get Kelvinator, 60.43

Get the First National habit, 43.25

Get the most out of television with a Dumont Teleset, 112.6

Get the winning feeling, 32.32

Get time from a timepiece, but if you want a watch get a Hamilton, 124.15

Getting closer to the source, 5.9

Getting results in rural America is *Farm Journal's* business, 85.110

Get your hands on a Toyota . . . you'll never let go, 7.32

Get your man, no waiting, no walking, 81.20

GE . . . We bring good things to life, 60.44

giant of the South, The, 85.222

gift candy of America, The, 20.60

GIFTS AND GREETINGS, p. 168

Gifts long remembered, 60.45

gift that endears and endures, The, 104.43

gift to remember, A, 20.4

Ginger ale with piquant personality, 107.25

ginger ale with the long-life bubble, The, 107.44

girl with the beautiful face, The, 32.72

girl with the beautiful mouth, The, 32.73

Give-'em-Hell Harry, 91.101

Give 'em Jessie, 91.102

Give Eversharp and you give the finest, 126.12

Give her a Hoover and you give her the best, 60.46

Give light and the people will find their own way, 85.111

Give long-lasting light, bullet-fast, 70.18

Give me another Central Royal Beer, 14.48

Give Red Bands your hard job, 37.10

Gives cream and butter flavor, 33.16

Gives joy complete to women's feet, 48.61

Give so more will live, 92.2

Gives your engine an extra margin of safety, 88.24

Give the girl of your choice the ring of her choice, 67.14

Give them life and make it worth living, 92.3

Give the presidency back to the people, 91.103

Give to conquer cancer, 92.4

Give us 20 minutes and we'll give you the world, 17.1

Give Whitman's Chocolates, it's the thoughtful thing to do, 20.30

Give your cold to Contact. Real medicines for real colds., 35.34

Give your dishwasher the best, 24.31

Give your feet young ideas, 48.62

Give your guest what he wishes, 71.51

Glamour for teen-age and queen age, 121.20

Glare/Guard: A difference you can see, 28.18

GLASS AND CERAMICS, p. 168

glass of Guinness is a cheerful sight, A, 14.6

Glassware of distinction, 52.5

Gleaming armor for your floors, 24.32

Glenwood Ranges make cooking easier, 60.47

global high-sign, The, 107.45

Globe sells Boston, The, 85.223

glorious beginning, A, 71.4

Gloves that "go places", 123.12

Glowing with health, brimming with flavor, 47.42

Go as a travel adventurer, 85.112

God would not permit a Roman Catholic to be president of the United States, 91.104

Goes home and stays home, 85.113

Goes to the home, stays in the home, 85.114

Go *first class* . . . go Phillips 66, 88.25

Go 4th to win the war, 91.108

Go international . . . with all the comforts of Hilton, 62.14

Golden nugget jet service, 4.28

gold medal Kentucky bourbon since 1872, The, 71.100

gold medal whiskey, The, 71.101

gold standard of radio receivers, The, 95.57

gold standard, The, 8.52

Goldwater for president—victory over Communism, 91.105

Goldwater in 1864, 91.106

Golfcraft for the finest, 108.12

good broom sweeps cleaner and lasts longer, A, 24.1

good business letter is always better . . . written on a Gilbert paper, A, 83.2

Good candy for all the family, 20.31

Good Coffee Folks, The, 27.57

Good enough to eat, 42.23

Good feet are the foundation of good health, 48.63

Good flours make good bakers better, 11.19

Good food is good health, 99.1

Good for its face value, 104.14

Good for money wherever money means anything, 43.26

Good for tender gums, 34.15

Good habits that last a lifetime, 34.16

"good hands" people, The, 64.86

good mechanic's choice, The, 117.29

Good morning! Have you used Pears' Soap?, 106.14

good neighbor of your community, A, 96.2

good newspaper, A, 85.5

Good old Munich and it's good for you, 14.49

Good paint costs nothing, 82.27

Good papers for good business, 83.28

Good people, 40.1

"Good people to do business with", 64.25

Good Republicans don't bolt the party ticket, 91.107

good reputation has to be earned, A, 60.4

Good soap is good business, 24.33

good society is good business, A, 94.1

Good taste suggests it, 14.50

good things of life, The, 64.87

good things of milk and malt, The, 15.28

Good things to eat come from 1 Mustard St., 29.13

Good to eat and good for you, 47.43

Good to the core, 49.14

Good to the last drop, 27.25

Good to your finger tips, 32.33

Good values consistently, 100.11

Good washing wins good will, 24.34

Go to high school in bedroom slippers, 101.6

Governments derive their just powers from the consent of the governed, 91.109

GOVERNMENT SERVICE, p. 169

Go where you get choosing range, 22.11

Go with the pick of the pros, 117.9

Grace the face and stay in place, 41.5

Graduate to Kaywoodie, 105.8

Grandfather's hat, 91.110

grand old drink of the South, The, 71.102

Grand old party, good as gold, 91.111

Grandpa's pants won't fit Benny, 91.112

Grand piano of the radio world, 95.30

grand slam favorite, A, 20.5

Grantism means poor people made poorer, 91.113

Grant us another term, 91.114

grass people, The, 69.25

Grease just vanishes from pots, pans, dishes, 24.35

Great aches from little corns grow, 35.35

great American family cereal, The, 21.38

great engineers, The, 31.24

Greatest concentration in the world's richest farm region, 85.115

greatest name in aircraft radio, The, 95.58

greatest name in bourbon, The, 71.103

greatest name in building, The, 18.86

greatest name in golf, The, 108.28

greatest name in health insurance, The, 64.88

greatest name in housekeeping, The, 24.88

greatest name in socks, The, 61.32

Greatest name in the great outdoors. Foremost name in indoor comfort., 98.9

greatest name in vodka, The, 71.104

greatest name in wine, The, 125.26

greatest name in yachting, The, 16.16

greatest show on earth, The, 78.14

greatest tire name in racing, The, 114.25

Great Grapes, what a flavor, 47.44

great highway performers, The, 7.64

great name in American ceramics, The, 65.14

great name in aviation, A, 4.2

great name in oil, A, 88.1

great name in tackle, A, 45.2

Great national shoes weekly, 85.116

great newspaper of the great southwest, The, 85.224

great penetrative liniment, The, 35.110

Great people to fly with, 4.29

Great People to ship with, 4.30

great railsplitter of the West must & shall be our next president, The, 91.320

great regulator, The, 35.111

Great shoes for little Americans, 48.64

Great sound starts with the source, 5.10

great state in which to live and work, A, 36.1

Great thrill in radio by the pioneers of short-wave radio, 95.31

Greeley—Brown & reconciliation, 91.115

green cleans in-between . . . the *white* polishes bright, The, 34.35

Greeting Cards of character, 51.2

grinding, polishing and buffing authority, The, 85.225

Grover, Grover, all is over, 91.116

Grow, grow by the rail way, 96.14

Growing city within a growing city, 36.5

Growing just like Atlanta, 85.117

growing world of Libby-Owens-Ford, The, 31.25

Grows more beautiful with use, 67.15

growth company, The, 31.26

growth fund, The, 66.21

Growth leader of the aluminum industry, 75.12

Grow what you eat, 69.10

Guaranteed moth protection, 86.6

Guaranteed, the hardest working workwear, 26.60

Guaranteed without an IF, 103.8

Guard against throat-scratch, 115.49

Guardian lighting, 70.19

Guardian of American families for 80 years, 64.26

Guardian of the nation's health, 58.19

Guardians of good grooming, 54.17

Guardian will enrich and safeguard your retirement years, 64.27

Guard your mouth, 34.17

Guard your time, 124.16

Guard your youth with Youth Garde, 32.34

Guest Coffee, The, 27.58

Guest-room luxury for every bed in your house, 13.10

Guinness a day is good for you, A, 14.7

Guinness and oysters are good for you, 14.51

Gulf makes things run better, 88.26

gum with the fascinating artificial flavor, The, 20.61

gun for every American shooting need, A, 44.1

gun that knows no closed season, The, 44.23

Had enough?, 91.117

Had your iron today?, 49.15

Had your Wheaties today?, 21.17

HAIR CARE, p. 170

Hair color so natural only her hairdresser knows for sure, 54.18

hair net that sits true, The, 54.39

Half the fun of having feet, 48.65

halo shines as bright as day around the head of Henry Clay, A, 91.7

Halves the cost and doubles the satisfaction, 29.14

hammer with a backbone, The, 117.30

Hammond is the largest-selling organ in the world, The, 80.29

ham what am, The, 74.24

Hand-ee, the tool of 1001 uses, 117.10

handiest light in the world, The, 70.32

Handiest thing in the house, 35.36

Hand in hand with fashion, 123.13

Handle it mechanically, 73.12

Hand made to fit you, 108.13

handy candy, The, 20.62

handy kitchen means living room leisure, A, 50.1

Hanes knows how to please him, 61.13

Hanes makes you feel good all under, 121.21

"hank" for a Yank, A, 123.1

"hanks" are coming, The, 123.20

Happiness in every box, 20.32

happy medium, The, 85.226

Happy Motoring!, 88.27

Happy motoring, 88.28

Happy Warrior, The, 91.321

hardest hardwoods grow in the north, The, 18.87

hardest working software in the world, The, 28.54

Harding and prosperity, 91.118

Hard soft coal, 59.9

Hardware is the jewelry of the home, 55.18

HARDWARE, p. 172

Hari-kari with Barry, 91.119

Harp-maker to the world since 1889, 80.9

Harrison cooled, the mark of radiator satisfaction, 8.19

Has 'em all beat, 27.26

Hasn't scratched yet, 24.36

Has the "edge" five ways, 104.15

Has the quiet refinement of an exclusive club, 62.15

hat corner of the world, The, 26.115

hat for every face, A, 26.1

hat of silent smartness, The, 26.116

Hats made so fine that all others must be compared to them, 26.61

hat that goes with good clothes, The, 26.117

Hauls more freight and handles more passengers than any other railroad in the world, 96.15

Have a glass of Guinness when you're tired, 14.52

Have more milk 'cause milk's got more, 33.17

Have the genius to chill it, 71.52

Have you driven a Ford . . . lately?, 7.33

Have you had your fruit today?, 20.33

Have you tried a Lucky lately?, 115.50

Have you tried one lately?, 115.51

Hayes, hard money and hard times, 91.120

H & D delivers the goods, 83.29

Head for the mountains, 14.53

headlight that floodlights the road, The, 8.53

Head of the bourbon family, 71.53

head of the class, The, 14.128

Headquarters for lubricants and lubri-counsel, 88.29

HEAD work always wins over HARD work on pay day, 73.13

HEALTH AND FITNESS, p. 174

Health and growth for boys and girls, 21.18

Healthful and good, 27.27

Healthful warmth, 58.20

Health in every jar, 29.15

health soap, The, 106.27

Health without hazard, 21.19

Health . . . your happiness, our business, 15.16

Hear more, carry less, 57.2

HEARING AIDS, p. 175

heart of a good cocktail, The, 71.105

heart of America, The, 119.37

heart of a tune-up, The, 8.54

Heart of Milwaukee, The, 100.28

heart of reliable radio power, The, 95.59

heart of the market, The, 93.10

"Heart of the root" briar, 105.9

heart of your radio, The, 95.60

heart's desire for every youngster, The, 118.19

heart's in it, The, 11.53

Heat alone is not comfort, 58.21

Heat, how and when you want it, 58.22

Heat like the rays of the sun, 58.23

Heat plus beauty, 58.24

HEATING AND AIR CONDITIONING, p. 175

HEATING AND COOKING FUELS, p. 178

Heats every room, upstairs and down, 58.25

Heelproof, marproof and waterproof, 82.28

heel that won't peel, The, 48.135

heel with nine lives, The, 48.136

Heirloom quality pianos since 1896, 80.10

He kept us out of suffrage, 91.121

He kept us out of war, 91.122

He leaves the plough to save his country, 91.123

Hell no, we won't go, 90.1

Hello Central, give us Teddy, 91.124

Help Barry stamp out peace, 91.125

Help build personality, 26.62

Help Hoover help business, 91.126

Helping a nation to avoid severe colds, 35.37

... Helping people and business help themselves, 66.5

... Helping people communicate, 31.12

Help make him all the dog he's meant to be, 87.5

Help others help themselves, 92.5

Helps build strong bodies 12 ways!, 11.20

Helps nature cure your cough, 35.38

Helps you do things right, 55.19

Help yourself as you help your country, 66.6

Help yourself financially without financial help, 43.27

Help yourself to health, 21.20

Henry Clay for his country feels but Polk would stop our water wheels, 91.127

Henry Clay, the champion of a protective tariff, 91.128

Hen's only rival, 42.24

He proved the pen mightier than the sword, 91.129

Here and there it's sterling, 67.16

Here's a thrill for breakfast, 21.21

Here's to your health and happiness, 125.11

heritage of quality, craftsmanship, service, A, 65.1

heritage to remember, A, 71.5

Hermes means Swissmanship ... a step beyond craftsmanship, 81.21

hero of Buena Vista, The, 91.322

He's all right, 91.130

He saved America, 91.131

He won't change from shoes to slippers because he's enjoying Massagic comfort, 48.66

Hi-chair to hi-school, 121.22

High as the Alps in quality, 20.34

highest quality for health, The, 47.96

High fashion in fragrance from France, 84.12

high mark on leather, The, 48.137

High performance matrix printers, 28.19

High-performance tirepower, 114.10

Hips are fashionable, fat isn't, 121.23

Hires to you for a better tomorrow, 107.26

His master's voice, 5.11

History tells which line excels, 18.32

Hitch your wagon to a conteSTAR, 85.118

Hit it with a hammer, 82.29

Hits the spot, 107.27

Hits where you aim, 44.10

Holding better business with better business forms, 81.22

Hold on tight to your dreams, 27.28

Hold on to Hoover, 91.132

Holds the world together, 1.3

Hold the bustline and you hold youth, 121.24

Holiday all the way with . . . , 96.16

holiday cigar at a week-day price, The, 115.145

Holiday Inn is Number One in people pleasin', 62.16

Hollycourt: 77.7% drier than other pipes, 105.10

Holmes rugs for artistic homes, 46.16

Holophane directs light scientifically, 70.20

HOME APPLIANCES AND EQUIPMENT, p. 180

home away from home, A, 62.2

Home builders to the nation, 18.33

Home-care know-how . . . at your doorstep!, 24.37

home craft magazine, The, 85.227

home furnishings fiber, The, 113.31

home is known by the lawn it keeps, A, 69.2

home of human security, The, 64.89

home of toys, The, 118.20

home paper of the industrial worker and the farmer, The, 85.228

home with the silver lining, The, 18.88

homey hotel for home folks, A, 62.3

Honda . . . we make it simple, 7.34

Honest days with Davis, 91.133

Honest money, honest government, 91.134

honest old farmer of Chappaqua, The, 91.323

Honest wear in every pair, 48.67

Honesty at home—honor abroad, 91.135

honey-cured smoke, The, 115.146

Honeymoon Line, The, 96.56

honey of a tobacco, A, 115.2

Honor where honor's due to the hero of Tippecanoe, 91.136

Hoover and happiness, 91.137

Hoover and happiness or Smith and soup houses: which shall it be?, 91.138

Horrors of war—blessings of peace, 91.139

Hosiery fashion on five continents, 61.14

HOSIERY, p. 188

hospitality state, The, 119.38

Host of the highways, 99.2

Hot biscuits in a jiffy, 11.21

hotel of distinction, An, 62.7

HOTELS AND MOTELS, p. 190

"Hot-Line" claim service, 64.28

hotter the water, the whiter the wash, The, 58.52

Hottest name in golf, 108.14

Hot water all over the house, 58.26

Hot water at the turn of a faucet, 58.27

hot weather hot cereal, A, 21.2

Houdry means progress . . . through catalysis, 22.12

house divided against itself cannot stand, A, 91.8

house of complete corsetry, The, 121.46

house of experience, The, 75.25

house of flavor, The, 29.37

House of hospitality, 62.17

house of magic, The, 60.107

Houses painted with Carter White Lead stay painted, 82.30

house that service built, The, 83.62

How can just 1 calorie taste so good!, 107.28

How do you spell relief?, 35.39

How to get further with father, 104.16

How to make a muscle, 33.18

Hub of the Americas, 119.20

human interest newspaper, A, 85.6

Hunt for the best, 47.45

Hurts only dirt, 24.38

HUSH takes the odor out of perspiration, 116.7

Hygrade in name. Hygrade in fact, 74.12

I ask no favors & I shrink from no responsibility, 91.140

IBM . . . Dedicated to the office: where it is now and where it will be, 81.23

Ice cream for health, 33.19

Ice cream, one of the good things of life, 33.20

Ice cubes instantly, tray to glass, 60.48

ICOT . . . the data communications company, 28.20

Idea Creators, not just illustrators, 2.15

ideal complete plant food, The, 69.26

Ideal laxative for young and old, 35.40

idea whose time has come!, An, 64.5

I'd rather fight than switch, 115.52

I'd walk a mile for a Camel, 115.53

I envy men the pleasant puffing of their pipes, 115.54

If babies were born trained, they wouldn't need Diaparene Baby Powder, 10.5

If every smoker knew what Philip Morris smokers know, they'd all change to Philip Morris, 115.55

If I am re-elected president slavery must be abolished with the reunion of states, 91.141

If it doesn't sell itself, don't keep it, 60.49

If it folds . . . ask Howe, 50.28

If it is a Garland, that is all you need to know about a stove or range, 60.50

If it isn't an Eastman, it isn't a Kodak, 89.10

If it isn't P. M., it isn't an evening, 71.54

If it's an envelope, we make it, 83.30

If it's a Paramount picture, it's the best show in town, 78.5

If it's a question of cleaning/conditioning . . . ask Oakite, 24.39

If it's a Steger, it's the most valuable piano in the world, 80.11

If it's Bordens, it's got to be good, 33.21

If it's chairs . . . it's Miele!, 50.29

If it's Darbrook, it's durable, 113.16

If it's done with heat, you can do it better with gas, 59.10

If it's insurable, we can insure it, 64.29

If it's lovely to wear it's worth Ivory Flakes care, 24.40

If it's Madewell, it's well made, 121.25

If it's new, Saks has it, 48.68

If it's paper, 83.31

If it's Remington, it's right, 44.11

If it's safe in water, it's safe in Lux, 24.41

If it's Speakman, it's quality, 55.20

If Purina chows won't make your hens lay, they are roosters, 42.25

If this Gold Seal is on it — there's better meat in it, 74.13

If Weber makes it, a fish takes it, 45.12

If you can afford a washer, you can afford a Bendix, 60.51

If you can't fight, you can write, 83.32

If you could see inside oranges, you'd buy Sunkist every time, 49.16

If you don't look good, we don't look good, 54.19

If you'd walk without a care do your sleeping on Spring-Air, 13.11

If you have an instinct for quality, 72.11

If you liked Hitler, you'll love Wallace, 91.142

If you like peanuts, you'll like Skippy, 47.46

If you love words, You'll love VERBATIM, 85.119

If you prize it . . . Krylonize it, 82.31

If you're not using Vano, you're working too hard, 24.42

If you see rust, you'll know it's not aluminum, 75.13

If you think clothes don't make a difference, try walking down the street without any, 26.63

If you've got the time, we've got the beer, 14.54

If you want a change to better times, vote for Grover Cleveland, 91.143

If you want a treat instead of a treatment, smoke Old Golds, 115.56

If you want more than time, get a Hamilton, 124.17

Ignition starts with P and D, 8.20

'I' in Nixon stands for integrity, The, 91.324

I intend to fight it out on this line if it takes all summer, 91.144

I like Ike, 91.145

I like Ike but I am going to vote for Stevenson, 91.146

illustrated weekly of current life, An, 85.47

I look my best in a Hardeman

I look my best in a Hardeman,
26.64

I Love New York, 119.21

Imagination in steel for the needs
of today's architecture, 75.14

I'm extremely fond of Barry, 91.147

I'm gonna get you with the Kodak
Disc, 89.11

I'm on the water wagon now,
91.148

I'm particular, 115.57

imperial line of road machinery,
The, 73.32

"Important occasion dresses", 26.65

Important to important people,
85.120

Imported from Spain, of course.
True sherry is., 125.12

imported one, The, 71.106

Importers and makers of fine
furniture, 50.30

I'm safe with Ike, 91.149

I'm worth it, 54.20

In a word, confidence, 75.15

In a word ... it's Selig, 50.31

Incense of flowers, 32.35

inch of Pinch, please.", "An, 71.14

incomparable, The, 71.107

independent newspaper, An, 85.48

independent supplier for
independents, The, 88.60

In design and performance, always
a year ahead, 73.14

India produces the finest tea in the
world, 110.6

Indispensable to the creative
perfumer, 84.13

Individuality graven into them, 97.3

Indoor weather as you want it,
with a weatherator, 58.28

industrial bar code experts, The,
28.55

Industrious Maine, New England's
big stake in the future, 36.6

Industry is on the move to Iowa,
36.7

Industry-owned to conserve
property and profits, 64.30

Industry's friendliest climate, 36.8

industry's marketplace, The, 85.229

Industry Spokesman to CPI
management, 85.121

In electricity, it's Edison from start
to finish, 37.11

In everything you fry or bake,
47.47

Inexpensive. And built to stay that
way., 7.35

In Federation there is power, 2.16

Information. Not automation., 28.21

In garden or in fields, Schell's seeds
produce best yields, 42.26

In harmony with home and air,
95.32

In home, health, farm and industry,
science in action for you, 22.13

In Hoover we trusted, now we are
busted, 91.150

In industry world-wide, 22.14

In keeping with a fine old tradition,
62.18

Ink that absorbs moisture from the
air, 126.13

ink that never fades, The, 126.32

In metals, plastics and paper Budd
works to make tomorrow ...
today, 31.13

inner secret of outer beauty, The,
121.47

Innovation is what makes Supreme
supreme, 81.24

Innovation. Precision. Integrity.,
5.12

Innovations that squeeze the waste
out of distribution, 96.17

Innovators", "The, 31.27

In partnership with all America,
96.18

In Philadelphia nearly everybody
reads the Bulletin, 85.122

In products, performance,
purpose ... Essex measures up!,
8.21

In rhyme with time, 124.18

In San Francisco it's the Palace,
62.19

Inside the rim of adventure, 119.22

"Inspection is our middle name",
64.31

Inspired by originals for homes for
distinction, 50.32

In stainless, too, you can take the
pulse of progress at Republic,
75.16

Install confidence ... install
Thermoid, 8.22

Install it, forget it, 95.33

Instantly known when blown, 37.12

Instant news service, 66.7

In step with fashion, 48.69

instrument of the immortals, The, 80.30

INSTRUMENTS AND GAUGES, p. 192

Instruments of quality by one family for 100 years, 80.12

Instruments worthy of the masters since 1857, 80.13

Insulate as you decorate, 18.34

Insure clerical efficiency and profit protection, use multiple copy forms, 81.25

INSURANCE, p. 193

insured pipe, The, 105.19

Insures a new kind of faultless effortless writing, 126.14

Insure today to save tomorrow, 64.32

Insure your profits, use Stimpson products, 81.26

Insurors of energy systems, 64.33

Interested personal service – always – when you buy from Eastman, 22.15

INTERIOR DECORATION, p. 200

international authority on visual merchandising, The, 85.230

international daily newspaper, An, 85.49

Internationally known mark of quality, 26.66

international one, The, 112.9

international value, An, 83.8

interrupting idea, The, 2.28

In the air or outer space Douglas gets things done, 3.9

In the California manner, 48.70, 61.15

In the service of medicine for over three decades, 35.41

In the twinkling of an eye, 111.6

In touch with tomorrow, 38.8, 122.1

In tune with fashion and keyed to fit, 121.26

Invented by a doctor—now used by millions of women, 116.8

Inventor and scientist make dreams come true; the insurance man keeps nightmares from happening, 64.34

Invest in memory insurance, 83.33

Invest in rest, 13.12

INVESTMENT, p. 201

In your guts you know he's nuts, 91.151

In your heart you know he's right, 91.152

Iowa's greatest evening paper, 85.123

I propose to move immediately on your works, 91.153

Iron horse quality, 42.27

Irons while it steams, 60.52

iron with the cool blue handle, The, 60.108

Is a toast to good health, 107.29

I'se in town, honey, 11.22

Is it live? Or is it Memorex?, 5.13

Isle of June, 119.23

Isn't it worth it?, 24.43

Isn't that you behind those Foster Grants?, 41.6

Is the Telegram on your list?, 85.124

Is your refrigerator a Success?, 60.53

It beats, as it sweeps, as it cleans, 60.54

It beats the Dutch, 15.17

It can help you look younger too, 32.36

It cleans your breath while it cleans your teeth, 34.18

It costs less to pay more, 82.32

It costs no more to reach the first million first, 85.125

It deserves to be preserved, 89.12

It filters the smoke, 105.11

It floats, 106.15

It had to be good to get where it is, 107.30

It happens in two seconds, 35.42

It is accurate and it stays accurate, 63.4

It is a mark of intelligent housekeeping to possess a Simplex Ironer, 60.55

It is better and you can prove it, 33.22

It is better to have it and not need it than to need it and not have it, 64.35

It is our business to help your business, 85.126

It is profitable to produce in Massachusetts, 36.9

It is sterling, more cannot be said, 67.17

It is what it eats, 118.6

It leaves you breathless, 71.55

It lives with good taste everywhere, 14.55

It lox the sox, 61.16

It lulls the skin, 104.17

It makes a difference, 88.30

It makes a dust magnet of your dust mop or cloth, 24.44

It makes its way by the way it's made, 72.12

It might have been worse, 91.154

It more than satisfies, it agrees, 27.29

It must be good to be a Gund, 118.7

It pays to be in the news, 85.127

It pays to be particular about your oil, 88.31

It pays to buy where you buy in safety, 100.12

It pays to know when to relax, 64.36

It pays to show the name they know, 26.67

It pays to use good tools, 117.11

It puts the sunshine in your hair, 54.21

It raises the dough, 11.23

It remembers so YOU can forget, 124.19

It's a dynamite taste, 14.56

It's a life insurance policy for your engine, 88.32

It's all in fun, 84.14

It's all in the finish, 82.33

It's all in the wheel, 117.12

It's all in this little yellow box, 47.48

It's a lucky day for your car when you change to Quaker State Motor Oil, 88.33

It's always a pleasure, 71.56

It's always a shade better, 24.45

It's always coal weather, 59.11

It's always Fehr weather, 14.57

It's a mark of distinction to own a Parker Pen, 126.15

It's a matter of life and breath, 92.6

It's a mighty fine pipe tobacco, 115.58

It's a pippin, 115.59

It's a real glass of beer, 14.58

It's as good as the best and better than the rest, 29.16

It's a winner, 16.10

It's beer as beer should taste, 14.59

It's better because it's made of Koroseal, 113.17

It's better, not bitter, 14.60

It's better than it used to be, and it used to be the best, 14.61

It's blended, it's splendid, 14.62

It's blended to better your best in baking, 11.24

Its blend is our secret, its fragrance your delight, 115.60

It's bug tested, 86.7

It's built to sell when it's built of wood , 18.35

Its favor has grown through flavor alone, 29.17

It's flavoripe, 14.63

Its flavor wins favor, 110.7

It's fun to own a gift by Rival, 60.56

It's good because it's fresh, 115.61

It's good for you, America, 15.18

It's good to get home to a Guinness, 14.64

... It's good to have a great bank behind you, 43.28

Its high quality makes it economical, 27.30

It's in the bag, 29.18

It's in the fit, 26.68

It's jubilating, 14.65

It's king-size smoking at its best, yet priced no higher than the rest, 115.62

It slices, it cooks, it keeps, 33.23

It's like homemade, 47.49

It's McKinley we trust to keep our machines free of rust, 91.155

It's mild and mellow, 115.63

It's moisturized, 115.64

It's More you, 115.65

It's nature's freshness — indoors, 58.29

It's no secret ... Schilling flavor makes all the difference in the world!, 29.19

It's not a home until it's planted, 69.11

It's not Jockey brand if it doesn't have the Jockey boy, 26.69

It's not just any snack, 47.50

It snuggles in your fingers, 126.16

It's one of the three great beers, 14.66

It speaks for itself, 5.14

It splits in two, 11.25

Its purity shows in everything you bake, 11.26

It's quick-wetting, 104.18

It's scratchless, it's matchless, 24.46

"It's smart to buy right", 71.57

It's smart to choose the finest sterling, 67.18

It's smart to conform with Reo-Form, 121.27

It's still smart to be healthy, 33.24

It's sudsy, 24.47

It stands on top, 14.67

It started me smoking cigars, 115.66

It stays on the salad, 29.20

It's the finish that counts, 82.34

It's the flavor, 71.58

It's the going thing, 7.36

It's the life they lead, it's the book they read, 85.128

It's the little daily dose that does it, 35.43

It's the real thing, 107.31

It's the right thing to do, 92.7

It's the tobacco that counts, 115.67

It's the tops for kitchen tops, 24.48

It's the very finest because it's Rubee, 50.33

It's the water, 14.68

It's the woman-wise range, 60.57

It's the yarn that counts, 103.9

It's time to Re-form, 121.28

It's toasted, 115.68

It S-T-R-E-T-C-H-E-S and springs back, 124.20

It's uncanny, 47.51

It's "velveted", 71.59

It's wise to conveyorize, 73.15

It's worth it, 122.2

It's worth it ... it's Bud, 14.69

It's *worth* the difference, 121.29

It's worth the trip, 99.3

It's your guarantee of quality, 35.44

It takes a man to help a boy, 92.8

It takes Emotion to move merchandise ... Better Homes &

Gardens is PERPETUAL EMOTION, 85.129

It takes leather to stand weather, 48.71

It takes less to give more flavor, 110.8

It takes more than a flame and a casting to make a good fast-fired circulation heater, 58.30

It takes needles to make shirts, 103.10

It takes on added beauty in the shoe, 48.72

It takes so little for every household use, 106.16

It takes the best to make the best, 29.21

It tastes good because it is good, 47.52

It tastes good to the last crumb, 11.27

It washes your dandruff away, 54.22

It will tell your eyes before your eyes tell you, 63.5

It wouldn't be America without Wonder, 11.28

Ives Toys make happy boys, 118.8

Ivory is kind to everything it touches, 106.17

Ivory-mild for safety; granulated for speed, 24.49

Ivory tips protect your lips, 115.69

I Want You, 53.2

Jack of all trades and master of plenty, 117.13

jack that saves your back, The, 117.31

Jamaica's legendary liqueur, 71.60

James Buchanan—no sectionalism, 91.156

Jersey City has everything for industry, 36.10

Jet action washers, 60.58

jet that justifies itself, The, 3.19

jet with the extra engine, The, 4.52

jeweler's quality watch, The, 124.40

Jewelers to the sweethearts of America for three generations, 67.19

jewel of patent leather, The, 48.138

jewel of perfumes, The, 84.28

JEWELRY AND SILVER, p. 202

"Jewelry for the home", 70.21

Jewelry of tradition for the contemporary man, 67.20

Jewish market at its best, The, 85.231

John and Jessie forever! Hurrah!, 91.157

John Lees keeps you in trim, 18.36

John L, the best bet for every round, 14.70

Join the first team. Reach for Winston., 115.70

Join the knit parade, 103.11

Join the Pepsi generation, 107.32

Join the regulars, 35.45

Join the "regulars" with Kellogg's All-Bran, 21.22

Join with Bostik for better bonding, 1.4

Journal covers Dixie like the dew, The, 85.232

journal for all who write, A, 85.7

journal of diagnosis and treatment, The, 85.233

Judged best by the just, 115.71

Judge for yourself, 115.72

Just a darn good shaving cream, 104.19

Just a "shade" better, 18.37

Just as if you were there, 95.34

Just as you'd expect, right EVERY way, 27.31

Just enough!, 115.73

Just enough Turkish, 115.74

Just everyday things for the home made beautiful by Stevens, 13.13

Just form and fry, 47.53

... Just for the sun of it, 102.6

Just plug in, then tune in, 95.35

Just rub it on the gums, 34.19

Just rub on, inhale the vapors, 35.46

Just slightly ahead of our time, 5.15, 38.9, 122.3

Just smooth, very smooth, 71.61

Just the kiss of the hops, 14.71

Just to show a proper glow, 32.37

Just wear a smile and a Jantzen, 26.70

Kalamazoo, direct to you, 58.31

Kansas product from Kansas farms, A, 74.1

Kawasaki lets the good times roll, 77.2

Keep a roof over your head, 64.37

Keep children's feet as nature made them, 48.73

Keep cold away with Magnavox, 58.32

Keep cool with Coolidge, 91.158

Keep Dura-Gloss always on hand, 32.38

Keep faith with our sons—bring America into the League of Nations—Vote for Cox and Roosevelt, 91.159

Keep fighting, keep working, keep singing, America, 35.47

Keep going with Pep, 21.23

Keep good feet healthy, 48.74

Keep hair-conditioned, 54.23

Keep heat where it belongs, 18.38

... Keeping tradition alive, 50.34

Keep in step with Paris, 48.75

Keep in step with youth, 48.76

Keep it handy, 35.48

Keep it under your hat, 54.24

Keep kissable with Flame-Glo Lipstick, 32.39

Keep mechanics good tempered, 117.14

Keep Missouri in the center of your thinking, 36.11

Keep regular the healthful way, 49.17

Keeps a head, 14.72

Keeps America on time, 124.21

Keeps breath pure and sweet 1 to 2 hours longer, 34.20

Keeps cows contented from sunrise to sunset, 42.28

Keeps step with the weather, 58.33

Keeps the foot well, 48.77

Keeps the shape, 113.18

Keeps things to eat good to eat, 60.59

Keeps you going, 35.49

Keeps you in hot water, 58.34

Keeps your face fit, 32.40

Keeps your motor clean as a whistle, 88.34

Keeps YOU sparkling, too, 15.19

Keeps you sweet as an angel, 116.9

Keep that great GM feeling, 9.5

Keep that schoolgirl complexion, 106.18

Keep that "youthful" look with Safe-T cones, 11.29

Keep the home fire burning, 59.12

Keep the stars in your eyes, 32.41
Keep the weather out, 18.39
Keep young feet young, 48.78
Keep your bob at its best, 54.25
Keep your eye on Elliott, 117.15
Keep your eye on Maidenform, 121.30
Keep your floors beautiful always, 24.50
Keep your furniture beautiful always, 24.51
Keep your health in tune, 56.5
Keep your income coming in, 43.29
Keep your shoes beautiful always, 48.79
Kelly can do, 40.2
Kelvination, cold that keeps, 60.60
Kenwood: the sound of leadership, 5.16
Kestenmade means better made, 124.22
Keyboard of the nation, 80.14
Keyed to the mode and mood of romance, 48.80
key magazine of industry, The, 85.234
Keystone of your vacation, 119.24
key to better grinding, The, 117.32
key to happiness and success in over a million farm homes, The, 85.235
key to information center productivity, The, 28.56
Kiddies' feet are safe in Kinney's hands, 48.81
Kid flatters the foot, 48.82
Kids love Kool-Aid, 107.33
Kill lawn weeds without killing grass, 69.12
Kills ants in the nest, 86.8
Kills bugs dead, 86.9
Kills bugs wholesale, 86.10
Kills them off and keeps them off, 86.11
Kindness to hands, speed in the dishpan, 24.52
kind of a bank you will enjoy doing business with, The, 43.52
kind of clothes gentlemen wear, The, 26.118
kind real boys wear, The, 26.119
kind that keeps, The, 32.74
Kind to the eyes, 70.22

Kind to your pocket and pocket book, 94.6
King can have no more, A, 78.1
King of all tees, 108.15
king of blends, The, 71.108
King of bottled beer, 14.73
King of cheese, 33.25
king of shine for surface fine, The, 82.65
King of them all, 100.13
King of the walk, 18.40
Kitchenaid. For the way its made., 60.61
kitchen cabinet that saves miles of steps, The, 18.89
KITCHEN PRODUCTS AND UTENSILS, p. 205
Kitchen tested utensils, 68.5
Knit goods are only as good as the yarn of which they are made, 103.12
Knit to fit with the comfort foot, 61.17
knock-out fuel, nox out nox, The, 88.61
Knock out that "knock", 88.35
Knowledgeable people buy Imperial, 71.62
Known by the companies we keep, 73.16
Known by the company it keeps, 71.63
Known for tone, 95.36
Known for values, 100.14
Knows the Pacific, 102.7
Know the best by this mark, 23.5
Know your milkman, 33.26
Kodak as you go, 89.13
Kola drink that's uni-blended, The, 107.46
Kondon's kills kolds, 35.50
label mothers know and trust, The, 26.120
label to ask for, The, 26.121
Laboratory accuracy at a toolroom price, 63.6
Labor is king, 91.160
Lace papers of character, 83.34
lacquer finish that stays new, The, 82.66
lady to her gloved finger tips, A, 123.2
La grande liqueur Française, 71.64

421

Lambert radio invites you to rest, 95.37

Lamps for see-ability, 70.23

Lamps of elegance, 70.24

lamp that chases gloom and glare, The, 70.33

lamp with the 1500-hour guarantee, The, 70.34

Land for the landless, 91.161

Landmark for hungry Americans, 99.4

land of elbow room and elbow grease, The, 36.20

Land of enchantment, 119.25

land of enchantment is calling you, The, 119.39

Land of perpetual prosperity, 36.12

Land of scenic splendor, 119.26

land of ten thousand lakes, The, 119.40

land that was *made* for vacations, The, 119.41

Languid splendour set to fragrance, 84.15

lantern with the blue porcelain top, The, 70.35

largest Catholic magazine in the world, The, 85.236

Largest daily circulation in Brooklyn of any Brooklyn newspaper, 85.130

Largest evening circulation in America, 85.131

Largest immediate delivery fur house, 26.71

Largest in the northwest, 62.20

Largest in the world because we serve the people best, 100.15

Largest manufacturer of shotguns in the world, 44.12

largest multiple life insurance organization in the world, The, 64.90

Largest railway system in America, 96.19

Largest selling pain reliever, 35.51

last fits, the fit lasts, The, 48.139

Lasting impressions begin with Oxford papers, 83.35

last word in fine leather luggage, The, 72.19

last word in gifts for men, The, 116.22

last word in pipes, The, 105.20

last word in sea food, The, 47.97

Laugh at winter, 59.13

Laugh at zero, 76.1

Laugh it off with a "Jest", 35.52

Laughs at time, 82.35, 124.23

laundry does it better, The, 25.5

laundry proof snap fastener that ends button-bother, The, 103.16

LAWN AND GARDEN PRODUCTS, p. 206

lawn people, The, 69.27

LBJ for the USA, 91.162

Leadclad fences make good neighbors, 18.41

leader around the world, The, 73.33

Leader in adhesive technology, 1.5

Leader in business insurance, 64.38

Leader in computer graphics, 28.22

leader in dental research, A, 34.2

Leader in prefinished hardwoods, 18.42

leader in solid-state high-fidelity components, The, 5.35

Leaders go to Carnes for the newest in air distribution equipment, 58.35

Leadership for a change, 91.163

Leadership for the '50's, 91.164

Leadership for the '60's, 91.165

Leadership through design, 97.4

Leaders in lawn research, 69.13

Leading business and technical journal of the world in printing and allied industries, 85.132

Leading clay journal of the world, 85.133

Leading direct sellers of fine fashion jewelry, 67.21

leading journal of the Episcopal Church, The, 85.237

Leading maker of watches of the highest character for almost a century, 124.24

leading name in dictionaries since 1847, The, 94.14

Leading name in truck transportation, 120.10

Leads among the leaders of today . . . and tomorrow, 85.134

Lead the Ship 'n Shore life, 26.72

lead with the spread, The, 82.67

Leaf tobaccos that satisfy, 115.75

Learn about little women from us, 26.73

Learn the economy of quality in Solitaire Coffee, 27.32

Leather: An investment in pleasure, 50.35

leather is there in every pair, The, 48.140

Leaves that clean taste in your mouth, 34.21

Leaves you breathless, 20.35

Leave the driving to us, 19.2

Leaving the *moving* to us, 79.5

L'Echo de Paris, 48.83

leg of nations, before the court of the world, The, 61.33

Legsize stockings, 61.18

Leg-size stockings for leg-wise women, 61.19

Less than a cent's worth will flavor a cake, 29.22

Let Hertz put *you* in the driver's seat, 6.5

Let liberty be national & slavery sectional, 91.166

Let Lyon guard your goods, 79.6

Let Munsingwear cover you with satisfaction, 121.31

Let RCA turn your television into Selectavision, 122.4

Let's be done with wiggle and wobble, 91.167

Let's clean house with Ike and Dick, 91.168

Let's get another deck, 91.169

Let's keep what we've got: prosperity didn't just happen, 91.170

Let's make it for keeps, 67.22

Lets the feet grow as they should, 48.84

Lets your hair shine like the stars, 54.26

Lets your pup be your furnace man, 58.36

Lets you take weekends easy the year around, 69.14

Letters are victory weapons, 83.36

Let the furnace man go . . . forever, 58.37

Let the Gold Dust Twins do your work, 24.53

Let the "kitchen maid" be your kitchen aid, 18.43

Let them grow up in Kaynee, 26.74

Let the people rule, 91.171

Let the people speak, 91.172

Let this seal be your guide to quality, 71.65

Let us continue, 91.173

Let us encourage our own manufactures, 91.174

Let us have a clean sweep, 91.175

Let us have peace, 91.176

Let us help put Armour idea chemicals to work for you, 22.16

Let us protect your world, 64.39

Let us tan your hide, 26.75

Let well enough alone, 91.177

Let your fingers do the walking, 2.17

Let yourself go . . . Plymouth, 7.37

liberal church journal, A, 85.8

Liberté! Egalité! Fraternité!, 90.2

Liberty, equality, and fraternity, 91.178

Liberty, equality and no king, 91.179

Liberty, equality & fraternity, the cardinal principles of true democracy, 91.180

Liberty, justice and humanity, 91.181

Liberty, union, and victory, 91.182

Life at sea is like nothing on earth, 102.8

Life begins at breakfast with McLaughlin's Coffee, 27.33

Life is a movie; Cine-Kodak gets it all, 89.14

Life is swell when you keep well, 21.24

lifelong paint, The, 82.68

Lifelong security through programmed protection, 64.40

Life looks brighter, 41.7

life of leather, The, 48.141

life of paint, The, 82.69

life of the party, The, 20.63

life preserver for foods, A, 60.5

Life Savers . . . a part of living, 20.36

Lifetime office equipment, 81.27

lift that never lets you down, The, 121.48

Light as sea-foam, strong as the tide, 121.32

Light beer of Broadway fame, 14.74

lighter that made the world lighter-conscious, The, 105.21

423

lighter that works, The, 105.22
Lightest smoke of all, 115.76
Light, heat and cook the Coleman way, 98.10
Lighting from concealed sources, 70.25
Lighting over a million homes tonight, 70.26
LIGHTING PRODUCTS, p. 208
Light in the darkest corner, 82.36
light moisturizing bath oil for dry skin, The, 32.75
Light or dry, in step with the times, 71.66
Lights the home, lightens the works, 70.27
light that always shines welcome, The, 70.36
Light that never fails, 64.41
light that never fails, The, 70.37
light to live with, The, 70.38
"light" touch in automation and control, The, 38.14
Light, white and flaky, 21.25
Like a good neighbor, State Farm is there, 64.42
Like grandma's, only more so, 47.54
Like little meat pies in sauce, 47.55
Like old friends they wear well, 123.14
Like pearl temples behind the ears, 41.8
Like sending your family to college, 94.7
Like sleeping on a cloud, 13.14
Like walking on air, 48.85
Lincoln and liberty—good for another heat, 91.183
line and design for creative window planning, The, 18.90
line is drawn for the future, The, 7.65
Linen damask, impressively correct, 113.19
line of beauty, The, 70.39
line of least resistance, The, 84.29
line that moves, The, 8.55
line that's fine at cooking time, The, 68.18
line with the carbon gripper, The, 83.63
line with the go, The, 50.59
Linking 13 great states with the nation, 96.20

lipstick without the dye, The, 32.76
liquid finish that decorates as it preserves, A, 82.2
Liquid jewelry, 32.42
Liquids or solids they keep hot or cold, 68.6
LIQUORS, p. 210
Listen, and you'll buy Westinghouse, 95.38
Listening luxury beyond your highest hopes, 95.39
Listen to America, 97.5
little bank with a large circle of friends, The, 43.53
little barber in a box, The, 104.44
little dab will do ya, A, 54.1
little nurse for little ills, The, 35.112
Little piano with the big tune, 80.15
Little shoes for little devils, 48.86
little varnish makes a lot of difference, A, 82.3
Live and die with Assurance, 64.43
Live better electrically, 37.13
Live electrically and enjoy the difference, 37.14
Live in the atmosphere of an exclusive club, 62.21
Live modern for less with gas, 59.14
live ones!, The, 94.15
live picture tabloid newspaper for all the family, A, 85.9
livest lumber journal on earth, The, 85.238
Lives with good taste, 14.75
Living face make-up and living face cosmetics, 32.43
living tradition in furniture, A, 50.2
load for every purpose and a shell for every purse, A, 44.2
Localized for you, 9.6
Locks recommended by the world's leading lock experts, 55.21
log cabin candidate, the people's choice, The, 91.325
Logical locale for new business, 36.13
Long distance is the next best thing to being there, 111.7
Long distance is the shortest way home, 111.8
Longer wear in every pair, 61.20

longer you play it, the sweeter it grows, The, 5.36

Longest life by owners' records, 37.15

Longest lived micrometer that can be bought, 63.7

long-life battery for your car, The, 8.56

long line of construction machinery, The, 73.34

Long mileage Hosiery, 61.21

Look ahead. Look South, 96.21

Look ahead with lead, 75.17

Look ahead with living insurance, 64.44

Look-alikes aren't cook-alikes, 47.56

Look and listen, 81.28

Look at your shoes, others do, 48.87

Look for more from Morton, 22.17

Look for the date on the tin, 27.34

Look for the Hartmann Red on the trunk you buy, 72.13

Look for the label with the Big Red "1", 56.6

Look for the red ball, 48.88

Look for the Red Ball, 113.20

Look for the spinning wheel label, 46.17

Look for the watermark, 83.37

Look for this famous name in the oval, 33.27

look of quality, The, 65.15

Looks good from any angle, 48.89

Look sharp! Feel sharp! Be sharp!, 104.20

Looks out for you, 64.45

Look through and see, 105.12

Look to Eberhard Faber for the finest . . . first!, 81.29

Look to Libby's for perfection, 47.57

Look to Lockheed for leadership, 3.10

Look to MFG for the shape of things to come, 18.44

Look to the leader for good safe planes you can afford to buy and fly, 3.11

Look to 3M for imagination in image-making, 30.5

Loomed by American labor to beautify American homes, 46.18

lopsided diet may ruin your canary's song, A, 87.1

lordly touch for simple menus, A, 47.3

Lots of Flatt tires running around, 114.11

Lots of satisfaction, 66.8

Louisiana-Mississippi farm paper, The, 85.239

Love at first bite, 20.37

lovelier skin with just one cake, A, 106.2

lovelier soap with the costlier perfume, The, 106.28

Lovely to look at, pleasant to use, 34.22

love of a glove, A, 123.3

Lowest cost, per yard, per hour, or per mile, 42.29

Loyalty shall govern what loyalty has preserved, 91.184

LS/MFT . . . Lucky Strike means fine tobacco, 115.77

Lubrication is a major factor in cost control, 88.36

Luckies are gentle on my throat, 115.78

Luckies are kind to your throat, 115.79

lucky ones go Anchor Line, The, 102.22

Lucky Strike green has gone to war, 115.80

LUGGAGE, p. 218

luggage that knows its way around the world, The, 72.20

luggage that sets the pace for luxury, The, 72.21

Luggage you will love to travel with, 72.14

Lunch time is Guinness time, 14.76

Lux every day keeps old hands away, 106.19

Luxury acrylic fiber, 113.21

Luxury and comfort with utmost safety, 102.9

Luxury Beer, The, 14.129

luxury blend for the "carriage trade", A, 71.6

"Luxury for less", 62.22

luxury of velvet with the worry left out, The, 113.32

luxury soap of the world, The, 106.29

MACHINERY, p. 220

machine for every purpose, A, 81.3

Machines at work around the world, 73.17

Machines for total productivity, 73.18

Machines should work. People should think, 81.30

Machines that build for a growing America, 73.19

Machines that make data move, 28.23

machine to count on, The, 81.49

machine you will eventually buy, The, 81.50

Mac-It endurance, your best insurance, 55.22

Made a little better than seems necessary, 60.62

Made by masters, played by artists, 80.16

Made by OUR family for YOURS, 80.17

Made by the makers of fine furniture, 50.36

Made by the mile, sold by the foot, 18.45

Made by the tiny Arcadians, 118.9

Made for the professional!, 8.23

Made from a rare old recipe, 47.58

Made in America by American craftsmen, 124.25

Made in America for American boys and girls, 118.10

Made in America for little Americans, 26.76

Made in California for enjoyment throughout the world, 125.13

Made in Japan by fanatics, 5.17

Made in the bakery of a thousand windows, 11.30

Made in the "champagne district of America", 125.14

Made in the cup at the table, 27.35

Made in the home-made way, 29.23

Made in the milky way, 33.28

Made like a gun, 98.11

Made like, tastes like fine imported beer, 14.77

Made on honor, sold on merit, 14.78

Made stronger to wear longer, 48.90

Made stronger, wear longer, 13.15

Made strong to work hard, 83.38

Made the old-fashioned way . . . slowly . . . naturally, 14.79

Made the strongest where the wear is hardest, 61.22

Made-to-measure fit in ready-to-wear shoes, 48.91

Made to order for America's business farmer and his wife, 85.135

Made to stand the gaff, 26.77

Made to stay brighter longer, 8.24

Made with the extra measure of care, 80.18

magazine farm families depend on, The, 85.240

magazine farm people believe in, The, 85.241

magazine for all Americans, A, 85.18

magazine for all manufacturing, The, 85.242

magazine for farm and home, A, 85.19

magazine for farm women, A, 85.20

magazine for Milady, The, 85.243

magazine for parents, The, 85.244

magazine for professional builders, The, 85.245

magazine for southern merchants, A, 85.21

magazine of architectural technology, The, 85.246

magazine of a re-made world, The, 85.247

magazine of better merchandising for home finishing merchants, A, 85.22

magazine of broadcast advertising, The, 85.248

magazine of business leaders around the world, The, 85.250

magazine of business, The, 85.249

magazine of good, clean humor, A, 85.23

magazine of management, The, 85.251

magazine of methods, personnel and equipment, The, 85.252

magazine of opportunities, The, 85.253

magazine of Romance, The, 85.254

magazine of service, The, 85.255

magazine of the American market, The, 85.256

magazine of the fifth estate, The, 85.257

magazine of the hour, The, 85.258

Magazine of the paper industry, 85.136

Magazine of the radio trade, 85.137

magazine of the toiletries trade, The, 85.259

Magazine of today and tomorrow, 85.138

magazine of Western living, The, 85.260

magazine of world business, The, 85.261

magazine only a homemaker could love, A, 85.24

magazine that brings the outdoors in, The, 85.262

magazine that grew up with the industry, The, 85.263

magazine that moves the men who move the merchandise, The, 85.264

magazine with a mission, A, 85.25

magazine women believe in, The, 85.265

magic of Masland Carpets, The, 46.28

magnificent, The, 112.10

main line airway, The, 4.53

major zipper, The, 103.17

Make a date with Muriel, 115.81

Make America happen again, 91.185

Make an heirloom, 117.16

Make every meal a bouquet, 125.15

Make every plot a garden spot, 69.15

Make good foods taste better, 29.24

Make hard jobs easy, 117.17

Make insurance understandable, 64.46

Make it a habit, take "her" a bar, 20.38

Make it yourself on a Singer, 60.63

Make men of boys, 118.11

Make no mistake about figurework: call Friden, 81.31

Maker of America's number 1 cat food, 87.6

Maker of the world's first cordless electric tools, 117.18

Maker of the world's most wanted pens, 126.17

maker's name proclaims its quality, The, 14.130

Makers of fine shoes for men and women, 48.92

Makers of medicines prescribed by physicians, 35.53

Makers of the safety stripe tread, 114.12

Makers of the world's only electronic blanket, 13.16

Makers of things more useful, 37.16

maker who is proud of what he makes, uses Egyptian Lacquer, The, 82.70

Makes a better motor, keeps your motor better, 88.37

Makes a blow-out harmless, 114.13

Makes baking taste better, 11.31

Makes cotton look and feel like linen, 24.54

Makes dull faces shine, 32.44

Makes electric shaving easier, 104.21

Makes every acre do its best, 42.30

Makes every bite a banquet, 14.80

Makes every house a White House, 82.37

Makes every meal an event, 29.25

Makes every road a boulevard, 8.25

Makes eyes sparkle and mouths water, 47.59

Makes fine, better cakes, 11.32

Makes fish day a red letter day, 47.60

Makes good food taste better, 29.26

Makes good tea a certainty, 110.9

Makes hard water soft, 24.55

Makes its mark around the world, 126.18

Makes its own gas, use it anywhere, 58.38

Makes its own gravy, 87.7

Makes kids husky, 21.26

Makes life's walk easy, 48.93

Makes more loaves of better bread, 11.33

Makes night time plain as day, 124.26

Makes old things new, keeps new things bright, 24.56

Makes pancakes mother's way, 11.34

Makes products better, safer, stronger, lighter, 18.46

Makes shoes wear longer, 48.94

Makes that long haul to the curb seem shorter, 68.7

Makes the skin like velvet, 32.45

Make Sunsweet your daily good health habit, 49.18

Makes water wetter, 24.57

Makes you feel fit faster, 35.54

Makes your house a White House, 82.38

Makes your husband feel younger, too . . . just to look at you!, 54.27

Makes your teeth feel smooth as silk, 34.23

Make the capital choice, 36.14

Make the children happy, 26.78

Make the greeting sweeter, 20.39

Make the home look cheerful, 82.39

Make the White House the Dwight House, 91.186

Make the Wyse decision, 28.24

Make tomorrow pay, Standardize today, 64.47

Make warm friends, 58.39

Make your own luck with Heddon, 45.13

Make your windows avenues of health, 18.47

Make you want to walk, 48.95

Making houses into homes, 58.40

Making petroleum do more things for more people, 88.38

Making smoking "safe" for smokers, 115.82

makings of a nation, The, 115.147

Making strong the things that make America strong, 55.23

Making the world safe for baby, 50.37

Making the world sweeter, 20.40

Making things happen with petroleum energy, 88.39

Making your world a little easier, 60.64

Management publication of the housing industry, 85.139

Man alive! Two for five, 115.83

Mannesmann builds for the future, 31.14

Manning the frontiers of electronic progress, 38.10

man of character, A, 91.14

man of the hour is Eisenhower, The, 91.327

man of the hour, The, 91.326

man of the hour—Woodrow Wilson, The, 91.328

man's first choice, A, 48.7

Man's greatest food, 47.61

man's magazine, The, 85.266

man's styleful shoe on a real chassis, The, 48.142

man that can split rails can guide the ship of state, The, 91.329

Man, that's corn, 42.31

Man to man, Roi-Tan, a cigar you'll like, 115.84

Manufacturers of creative building products, 18.48

Manufacturers of quality drapery hardware since 1903, 55.24

Manufacturers of quality hardwood products since 1872, 18.49

Manufacturers of world's most widely used personal communications transmitters, 95.40

manufacturing and construction journal of the textile industry, The, 85.267

man who can't remember his last hailstorm is likely to get one he will never forget, A, 64.3

man who cares says: "Carstairs White Seal", The, 71.109

man with the plan, The, 64.91

man you can lean on, that's Klopman, A, 113.2

Many typewriters in one, 81.32

"Market-directed", 94.8

market with the "rainbow round its shoulder", The, 85.268

mark of a good roof, The, 18.91

Mark of excellence, 7.38, 67.23

mark of modern pajamas, The, 26.122

mark of quality in tobacco products, The, 115.148

mark of quality, The, 104.45

Mark of quality throughout the world, 112.7

mark of the well-built house, The, 18.92

mark of the world's most famous hat, The, 26.123

mark that is a message in itself, The, 83.64

Mar-VEL-ous for dishes, stockings, lingerie, woolens, 24.58

Maryland's Masterpiece, 14.81
massage for the gums, A, 34.3
massive men's market in print, The, 85.269
Master crafted, 55.25
Master craftsmen since 1890, 50.38
master drawing pencil, The, 126.33
master hair coloring, The, 54.40
Master jeweler, 67.24
Master of color since 1858, 82.40
Master of mathematics, 81.33
Master of road and load, 8.26
Masterpieces in plastic, 76.2
master's fingers on your piano, The, 80.31
Masters in the art of writing, 126.19
master wood of the ages, The, 18.93
Mastery in radio, 95.41
Matched tools for *unmatched* performance, 117.19
Match him, 91.187
Matchless cooking, 60.65
Matchless in outdoor excellence, 16.11
Matchless quality . . . superior service . . . enduring excellence, 60.66
material difference in building, The, 18.94
matter of pride, pleasure, and good plain sense, A, 103.2
mattress that feels so good, The, 13.29
mattress that will never grow old, The, 13.30
Maxell. It's worth it., 5.18, 28.25
Maximum capacity, 8.27
Maxwell House, too, is part of the American scene, 27.36
Mazda experience, The, 7.66
Mazola makes good eating sense, 47.62
McCarthy and peace in '68, 91.188
McCord is go . . . go with it, 8.28
McDonald's and you, 99.5
McKinley and the full dinner pail, 91.189
MDS Hero will make a hero out of you, 28.26
Meals without meat are meals incomplete, 74.14
meanest chore is a chore no more, The, 24.89

Means more mileage, 114.14
Means safety made certain, 8.29
measure of perfection, The, 71.110
Measure of quality, 47.63
Measure yourself for a Kelly, 115.85
MEATS, p. 222
meats that wear the Armour star are the meats the butcher brings home, The, 74.25
medal Scotch of the world, The, 71.111
Medicamenta vera, 35.55
meeting place of the thrifty, The, 100.29
Meeting the communications challenge of the 80's, 28.27
Meet me at the fountain, 100.16
Meet me at the Music Box, 100.17
Mellow as moonlight, 20.41
Mellow as the greeting of old friends, 107.34
Mellowed in wood to full strength, 29.27
Melts dirt away, 24.59
Mends everything but a broken heart, 1.6
Menthol-cooled, 115.86
Men wear them everywhere, 48.96
Men who build America trust this trade mark, 18.50
men will need their horses to plow with, The, 91.330
Merchandise well displayed is half sold, 2.18
merchant-minded mill with variety and reliability, The, 83.65
Meredith moves merchandise, 2.19
Merrill Lynch . . . A breed apart, 66.9
Merrill Lynch is bullish on America, 66.10
message of purity, A, 20.9
METALS INDUSTRY, p. 224
Metal, the fifth medium, 75.18
Metalurgy is our business, 75.19
Meyers make gloves for every father's son and mother's daughter, 123.15
Michigan, state of happiness for everyone, 36.15
MicroComputers for DataCommunications, 28.28
midget in size, a giant in power, A, 69.3

Mighty good shoes for boys, 48.97
Mighty monarch of the air, 95.42
Mighty monarch of the Arctic, 60.67
mighty tower—Eisenhower, The, 91.331
Mild as May, 115.87
milder, better-tasting cigarette, The, 115.149
Mildness plus character, 115.88
Mileage hogs, 114.15
mile of silk, inspected inch by inch, A, 61.2
Miles ahead, 48.98, 73.20
Miles of smiles, 88.40
Miles of travel comfort, 96.22
milk chocolate melts in your mouth. Not in your hands., The, 20.64
milk every doctor knows, The, 33.43
Milk is the fresher refresher, 33.29
Milk that cuts the cost of cooking, 33.30
Millard Fillmore for the whole country, 91.190
million Americans can't be wrong, A, 48.13
million and one uses, A, 1.1
million dollar overall, The, 26.124
million in service ten years or longer, A, 60.8
Millions are saying "Tasting better than ever", 115.89
Millions for freedom—not one cent for slavery, 91.191
Millions of Spud smokers can't be wrong, 115.90
Millions of women have their hearts set on a new Maytag, 60.68
Millions remember Doelger, a glass will tell you why, 14.82
million yards of good will, A, 81.4
Milwaukee's choice, 14.83
Milwaukee's most exquisite beer, 14.84
Minds over money, 66.11
mineral salt laxative, The, 35.113
mini-brutes, The, 7.67
minister's trade journal since 1899, The, 85.270
Minnesota brainpower builds profits, 36.16
minute to learn. A lifetime to master., A, 118.1
miracle in the rain, A, 26.8

MISCELLANEOUS, p. 226
Missing the boat? Own an Owens, 16.12
Mix 'em and match 'em, 26.79
Mixes well with any friend, 107.35
Mix fun and history in Virginia, 119.27
Mmm, Ahhh, Ohhh, Poppin' Fresh Dough, 11.35
modern aid to appetite control, The, 56.10
modern bed of coals, The, 60.109
Modern business forms for modern business systems, 81.34
modern farm paper, The, 85.271
Modern heat with oldtime fireside cheer, 58.41
modern light conditioning bulb, The, 70.40
modern magic carpet, The, 3.20
Modern masters of time, 124.27
Modern silver with the beauty of old masterpieces, 67.25
modern way to grow, The, 69.28
Moist as homemade, 47.64
Monarch out-strips them all, 18.51
monthly business paper for chain store executives, A, 85.39
monthly magazine devoted to more profitable painting, A, 85.40
MONY men care for people, 64.48
Moog means more under-car business, 8.30
Morally straight, physically strong, mentally awake, 78.6
Moral pictures most mothers approve, 78.7
More acres of corn, more corn per acre, 42.32
More and better things for more people, 60.69
More by the pair, less by the year, 48.99
more colorful nylon, The, 113.33
More corn, less cob; it's bred that way, 42.33
More cups of better coffee, 27.37
More dentists use Lavoris than any other mouthwash. Shouldn't you?, 34.24
More doors fold on Fold-Aside than any other kind!, 55.26
more enlightened approach, A, 7.13

More flavor per cup, more cups per pound, 27.38

More for the money, 2.20

More fun per ton than any other line, 102.10

More games. More fun., 122.5

More goods for more people at lower cost, 73.21

More heat, less care, 58.42

More ideas from the Armstrong world of interior design, 46.19

more living you do, the more you need Samsonite, The, 50.60

More music for the money, 80.19

More people are smoking Camels than ever before, 115.91

More people buy Cessna twins than any other make, 3.12

More people fly Cessna airplanes than any other make, 3.13

More people have bought Pipers than any other plane in the world, 3.14

More people put their confidence in Carrier air conditioning than in any other make, 58.43

More people ride on Goodyear tires than on any other brand, 114.16

More people want more aluminum for more uses than ever before, 75.20

More pleasure per mile, 95.43

More power to you, 88.41

More practical than ever, 104.22

More precious than gold for good health, 56.7

More savings with Symons, 18.52

More shaving comfort for your money, 104.23

More stars than there are in heaven, 78.8

More than a cedar chest, a piece of fine furniture, 50.39

More than a magazine, a national institution, 85.140

More than a magazine, an institution, 85.141

More than a new look. A new outlook., 111.9

More than a polish, 24.60

More than a truck line − a transportation system, 120.11

More than horse-power, 37.17

More than you expect or pay for, 64.49

More Ummm, Ummm after every crunch, 47.65

More years to the gallon, 82.41

more you eat, the more you want, The, 20.65

more you hear, the better we sound, The, 111.20

more you learn about photography, the more you count on Kodak, The, 89.26

more you look, the more you like, The, 7.68

Morning's first thought, 27.39

Morning uplift, 39.2

Mossberg for accuracy, 44.13

Most admired, most desired for cool comfort, 26.80

most asked-for brand of all, The, 47.98

most beautiful copies of all, The, 30.9

most beautiful curtains in America, The, 65.16

most beautiful kitchens of them all, The, 18.95

most beautiful tire in America, The, 114.26

most comfortable hat made, The, 26.125

most comfortable shoe in the world, The, 48.143

most complete line of firearms in the world, The, 44.24

most complete software company in the world., The, 28.57

most elegant name in cosmetics, The, 32.77

most expensive tea grown, The, 110.17

most expensive television set in America . . . and darn well worth it., The, 112.11

most experienced food processor in the world, The, 47.99

most famous name in rattan furniture, The, 50.61

Most famous name on drums, 80.20

most for your money in fuel, The, 93.11

Most heat per dollar, 58.44

most important magazine to the world's most important people, The, 85.272

most influential hardware paper, The, 85.273

most intelligent car ever built, The, 7.69

Most miles per dollar, 114.17

Most modern of lightweight typewriters, 81.35

most popular beer the world has ever known, The, 14.131

Most popular route to the Rockies, 96.23

most powerful shoe in America, The, 48.144

most prized eye cosmetics in the world, The, 32.78

most progressive name in steel, The, 75.26

Most protection when protection is most needed, 64.50

Most radio per dollar, 95.44

most remarkable airline", "A, 4.8

most respected name in fishing tackle, The, 45.21

most salable shoe in America, The, 48.145

most treasured name in perfume, The, 84.30

most trusted name in electronics, The, 38.15

most trusted name in furniture, The, 50.62

Most trusted name in modelling, 118.12

most trusted name in sound, The, 5.37

most trusted name in television, The, 112.12

most trustworthy tires built, The, 114.27

most useful magazine in metalworking, The, 85.274

most valuable piano in the world, The, 80.32

Mother's first thought for every milk need, 33.31

moth is more destructive than the flame, The, 86.14

Motion pictures are the nation's relaxation, 78.9

motor carrier with more Go-How", "The, 120.19

Motor coach to train side, the New York idea of travel convenience, 96.24

Motor coach train connection, a New York travel habit, 96.25

MOTORCYCLES, p. 226

Motorized power, fitted to every need, 37.18

motor's the thing, The, 37.31

Moulded to your foot, 48.100

Mountain grown, 125.16

mountain of flavor in every spoonful, A, 27.7

Mountain water makes the difference, 14.85

Move at the speed of sound, 5.19

Move over, Bacon, 47.66

Moves the earth, 73.22

MOVIES AND ENTERTAINMENT, p. 226

Movies make many merry moments, 78.10

MOVING AND STORAGE, p. 227

Moving with care . . . everywhere, 79.7

Mr. Nixon: how long will this new pose last?, 91.192

Mum helps to make a miss a hit, 116.10

MUM is the word, 116.11

Mumm's the word for champagne, 125.17

musical instrument of quality, A, 95.9

musical instrument of radio, The, 95.61

MUSICAL INSTRUMENTS, p. 228

music America loves best, The, 97.8

Music's most glorious voice, 80.21

music you want when you want it, The, 97.9

"must" for every wardrobe, A, 26.9

Must make good or we will, 104.24

My brand's LBJ, 91.193

My favorite son is Stevenson, 91.194

My lips are sealed with ChapStick, 35.56

My pick is Dick, 91.195

nail enamel your manicurist recommends, The, 32.79

name again . . . Nationwide Life, The, 64.92

Named for the original American professionals, 108.16

Named for those it serves, 64.51

name for quality athletic goods, The, 108.29

name for quality hobby kits, The, 118.21

name for quality, The, 49.24

name indicates the quality, The, 81.51

name is Crane, The, 31.28

name known in millions of American homes, The, 60.110

name quality made famous, The, 89.27

name really means something, The, 117.33

Name that means everything in electricity, 37.19

name that means everything in electricity, The, 60.111

name that means everything in luggage, The, 72.22

name that means MUSIC to millions, The, 5.38

name that's known is Firestone—all over the world, The, 114.28

name to know in radio, The, 95.62

name to look for, The, 108.30

name to remember, A, 18.4

name to remember, a fabric to remember, A, 113.5

name to remember in flutes, The, 80.33

name to remember in rainwear, The, 26.126

name you can trust, A, 34.4

name you can trust in margarine, The, 47.100

name you know in lamps, The, 70.41

Natick cobbler—the Galena tanner—there's nothing like leather, The, 91.332

national broadcast authority, The, 85.275

national buyword, A, 26.10

national dairy farm magazine, The, 85.276

national filling station magazine, The, 85.277

national guide to motion pictures, The, 85.278

national inspirational monthly for men and women who sell, The, 85.279

national institution from coast to coast, A, 100.3

national joy smoke, The, 115.150

Nationally famous for good taste, 14.86

Nationally recognized as the "straw pioneer", 123.16

national magazine for dry goods and department stores, A, 85.42

National magazine for mothers of infants, 85.142

national magazine of sports and recreation, The, 85.280

national magazine of the grocery trade, The, 85.281

national magazine of the hardware trade, The, 85.282

national magazine with local influence, The, 85.283

national newspaper of marketing, The, 85.284

national publication devoted to ship operation and shipbuilding, A, 85.43

national publication for the wholesale grocer, A, 85.44

national rider never changes his mount, A, 108.2

national rub down, The, 35.114

national soil sweetener, The, 42.48

national summer suit for men, The, 26.127

National voice of the shoe trade, 85.143

National weekly newspaper devoted to the fraternal interpretation of the World's current events, 85.144

national weekly of programs and personalities, The, 85.286

national weekly, The, 85.285

nation needs fixin' with Nixon, The, 91.333

nation needs Richard M. Nixon, The, 91.334

nation's BASIC transportation, The, 96.57

nation's big name in archery, The, 108.31

nation's breakfast food, The, 21.39

nation's building stone, The, 18.96

nation's business paper, The, 83.66

nation's cheer leader, The, 107.47

nation's going-est railroad, The, 96.58

nation's health is a nation's strength, A, 47.7

nation's host from coast to coast, The, 99.6

nation's innkeeper, The, 62.32

nation's largest airline, The, 4.54

nation's long distance phone company, The, 111.21

nation's pipe, The, 105.23

nation's printing papers, The, 83.67

nationwide institution, A, 100.4

Nationwide is on your side, 64.52

Nationwide system of thrifty spending, 43.30

Nationwide, worldwide depend on . . . , 4.31

natural energy, food and body builder, A, 56.1

natural language query system, The, 28.58

natural lift, The, 15.29

Naturally it's delicious . . . it's made by Bordens, 33.32

Naturally yours, 121.33

natural resource company, A, 88.4

Nature forgot vitamin D, but Dean's didn't, 33.33

Nature makes Douglas fir durable, 18.53

Nature's paradise, man's opportunity, 119.28

Nature's sweet restorer, 13.17

Neatness lasts from breakfast to bedtime, 26.81

NEC and me, 28.29

necessary two million, The, 85.287

Needs no chaser, 71.67

negative for positive results, The, 89.28

Neighbor tells neighbor, 82.42

Nestle's makes the very best, 20.42

network you can control, The, 28.59

Never Again, 90.3

Never a love so true, never a ring so cherished, 67.26

Never before did a nickel buy more, 115.92

Never before did 10¢ do so much for a woman, 32.46

Never before utensils like these, 68.8

Never comes up anytime, 121.34

Never forgets, 28.30

Never gets on your nerves, 115.93

Never lets go, 8.31

Never let your hair down, 54.28

Never neglect a break in the skin, 35.57

Never neglect the tiniest cut, 35.58

Never renew, yet ever new, 18.54

Never underestimate the power of a woman, 85.145

Never upset an upset stomach, 35.59

"Never wear a white shirt before sundown," says Hathaway, 26.82

New advances in office copying keep coming from Kodak, 30.6

new air-rolled garter, The, 61.34

new big name in beer, The, 14.132

New dimensions in driving on the *safer* Kelly road, 114.18

New England's greatest Sunday newspaper, 85.146

New England solution, The, 7.70

newest trimmings first, The, 103.18

New foods, new ideas for a better world, 47.67

new frame if the wind breaks it, A, 123.4

new high in whiskey smoothness, A, 71.13

New ideas for happier homemaking, 60.70

New ideas in automation control, 38.11

New leader in the lively art of electronics, 38.12

New leadership—Kennedy and Johnson, 91.196

new Nixon, The, 91.335

New Orleans' most famous sauce, 29.28

Newport smokes fresher—and tastes better than any other menthol cigarette, 115.94

News and management monthly of the graphic arts, 85.147

news magazine of art, The, 85.288

new smokeless coal from Old Virginia, The, 59.23

News of consequence for people of consequence, 85.148

news of the day in the newsiest way, The, 85.289

newspaper for everybody; it goes into the home, A, 85.45

newspaper for the makers of newspapers, A, 85.46

newspaper of the buying population, The, 85.290

new sparkling water, The, 15.30

new standard of performance, The, 16.17

news unbiased and unbossed, The, 85.291

newsweekly that separates fact from opinion, The, 85.292

new talc with a new odor, A, 84.1

New taste, *new* smoking convenience . . . anywhere, anytime, 115.95

New to look at, new to taste, 21.27

new way to do prestige advertising, The, 83.68

New York Agent in your community is a good man to know, The, 64.93

New York's picture newspaper, 85.149

Next best to rain, 69.16

next one tastes as good as the first, The, 14.133

Next to nothing at all, 121.35

Next to safety first, first aid, 35.60

Niagara to the sea, 102.11

Nicest next to you, 121.36

Nickel . . . its contribution is quality, 75.21

nickel lunch, The, 20.66

Niedecken Showers give refreshing hours, 18.55

Ninety golden brown biscuits from each package, 11.36

99 44/100% pure, 106.20

Nip-it with Sip-It, 35.61

Nips the waist, not the purse, 121.37

Nixon and Spiro = zero, 91.197

Nix on Ike, 91.198

Nix on Nixon, 91.199

Nixon now more than ever, 91.200

Nixon's the one, 91.201

No account too large, none too small, 43.31

No appetite control capsule works harder to help you lose weight, 56.8

No beer, no work, 91.202

No better built than Durabilt, 18.56

nobility of Italian wines, The, 125.27

noble Scotch, A, 71.15

noblest of all cabinet woods, The, 18.97

Nobody doesn't like Sara Lee, 11.37

Nobody gives you better performance, 122.6

Nobody knows chicken like the folks at Weaver, 74.15

Nobody knows more about microwave cooking than Litton, 60.71

No breaking-in with Yello-Bole, 105.13

No British pauper wages for Americans, 91.203

No brush, no lather, no rub-in, 104.25

No compromise with armed rebels— may the Union flourish, 91.204

No compromise with traitors, 91.205

No crown for Roosevelt, 91.206

No crown of thorns, no cross of gold, 91.207

No damp amps, 37.20

No emancipation, no miscegenation, no confiscation, no subjugation, 91.208

No extravagant claims, just a real good product, 71.68

No finer-tasting cigar at any price, 115.96

No fourth term either, 91.209

No Franklin the First, 91.210

No hips, no hips, hooray, 121.38

noiseless oil burner, The, 58.53

No Jewett has ever worn out, 60.72

No long waits, no short weights, 59.15

No man is good three times, 91.211

No man's debts should live after him, 64.53

No matter how diluted, it is never skimmed milk, 33.34

No matter what kind or what priced merchandise you make, the Plain Dealer alone will sell it, 2.21

No metal can touch you, 61.23

No more fireside chats, 91.212

No more slave states and no more slave territory

No more slave states and no more slave territory, 91.213

No more slave teritory, 91.214

No more sticky fingers, 32.47

no. 1 buy in the design field, The, 85.293

No. 1 heavy-duty sales leader, 120.12

no. 1 men's service magazine, The, 85.294

no. 1 name in billiards, The, 108.32

No. 1 name in bowling, 108.17

No. 1 source of gummed papers, 83.40

No North, no South, but the whole country, 91.215

No North, no South, no East, no West, nothing but the Union, 91.216

No North—no South—the Union inseperable, 91.217

No one is in debt to Macy's, 100.18

No one knows wood as good, 82.43

No other instrument so richly rewards the efforts of the beginner, 80.22

No other paint stays brighter under the sun, 82.44

No other tobacco is like it, 115.97

No "peeping Tom" can decipher the contents, 83.39

No pull, no pain, no sting, 104.26

No purer soap was ever made, 24.61

Norco way is the easiest and best way to polish silverware, 24.62

North American Aviation is at work in the fields of the future, 3.15

North American Rockwell and the future are made for you, 31.15

Northwest's only weekly farm paper, The, 85.295

No sag in any WAY, 13.18

No sash hardware installs faster than Grand Rapids Hardware, 55.27

No scotch improves the flavour of water like Teacher's, 71.69

No springs, honest weight, 63.8

No-stick cooking with no-scour clean-up, 68.9

No submission to the North, 91.218

No substitute for experience, 91.219

Not a cough in a carload, 115.98

Not a drop is sold till it's seven years old, 71.70

Not a shadow of a doubt, 116.12

No Taxation without Representation, 90.4

Nothing beats a great pair of L'eggs!, 61.24

Nothing, but nothing will tear cats away, 87.8

Nothing but nylon makes you feel so female, 113.22

Nothing but Spandex makes you look so female, 113.23

Nothing else is a Volkswagen, 7.39

Nothing else like it, 64.54

Nothing else quite measures up, 71.71

Nothing else stacks up to it, 68.10

Nothing equals stainless steel, 75.22

Nothing is better than a Verbatim response, 28.31

Nothing runs like a Deere, 69.17

Nothing tastes as good as Ritz, but RITZ, 11.38

Nothing to do but fry, 47.68

Nothing too good for men in service, 104.27

Nothing to serve but the public interest, 85.150

Nothing to shovel, nothing to explode, 58.45

Nothing was stirring but Seagram's 7 and . . . , 71.72

Notice the lighting fixtures, 70.28

Not just good . . . but wonderful, 47.69

Not made to a price, but a perfect product, 48.101

Not the biggest—but the best!, 26.83

Not the price per pair, but the cost per mile, 48.102

Not twice as much, but twice as good, 107.36

Nourishes every inch of your dog, 87.9

No watching, no turning, no burning, 60.73

No water needed, 35.62

Now better than ever for everything, 106.21

Now everybody can have Xerocopies, 30.7

Now every man can enjoy his pipe, 115.99

Now, more WEAR than EVER, 68.11

Now, no bad breath behind his sparkling smile, 34.25

No woman is too stout to be stylish, 121.39

No wonder Fleischmann's Preferred is PREFERRED, 71.73

Now's the time to get away *to* it all!, 119.29

Now that the world relies on computers it needs a computer it can rely on, 28.32

Now that you've conquered the world, separate yourself from it, 119.30

Now you'll like bran, 21.28

NR tonight, tomorrow all right, 35.63

Number ... *see also at* "no. ... ",

Number 1 in acceptance, 8.32

nuts that get noticed, The, 49.25

Oak for charm and livable character, furniture for your children's children, 50.40

O-B on a Bull Dog clamp proves the safest quality stamp, 117.20

Obviously it must be Western Union, 111.10

Ochee beverages make friends on taste, 15.20

Of America's great sources of energy, only National serves you in so many ways, 59.16

office automation computer people, The, 28.60

OFFICE EQUIPMENT AND SUPPLIES, p. 231

Office help—temporary or permanent, 40.3

Officially certified as the finest tea grown, 110.10

Official tailors to the West, 26.84

Off the rocks with Landon and Knox, 91.220

Off when it's on, on when it's off, 37.21

Of paramount importance to the housewife, 24.63

Often imitated, never duplicated, 108.18

Ohio's favorite brew since 1862, 14.87

Ohio's greatest home daily, 85.151

Oil Bank of America, The, 43.54

oil of a million tests, The, 88.62

Oil that goes farther, faster, safer, 88.42

"Okaze" your plates, "okaze" your breath, 34.26

Oklahoma's greatest newspaper, 85.152

Old Abe removed McClellan—we'll now remove Old Abe, 91.221

Old England's finest chocolates, 20.43

Old English lawn seed makes better lawns, 69.18

oldest and largest tree saving service in the world, The, 69.29

oldest farm paper in America, The, 85.296

Oldest in permanent type wall coverings, 65.11

oldest mail order house is today the most progressive, The, 100.30

oldest name in electric refrigeration, The, 60.112

oldest name in pipes, The, 105.24

oldest name in Scotch, The, 71.112

Oldest Trust Company in Connecticut, 43.32

Old floors look new in six to nine minutes, 24.64

Old friends are best, 14.88

Old Homestead Bread makes little bodies gain, 11.39

old red bandanna, The, 91.336

Once in a lifetime, 18.57

Once tried, always satisfied, 115.100

one and only one cocktail gum, The, 20.67

one and only, The, 80.34

one bed frame people ask for by name, The, 13.31

One chord is worth a thousand words, 80.23

one cigarette for everyone who smokes!, The, 115.151

one cigarette sold the world over, The, 115.152

One country, one flag, 91.222

One delicious flavor in two delicious forms, 21.29

One drive is worth a thousand words, 7.40

One flag and one Union now and forever, 91.223

One good cup deserves another, 27.40

One great face deserves another, 124.28

100% cotton. The fiber you can trust., 113.24

100% guaranteed temporary office help, 40.4

One hundred years young, 85.153

One if by day, two if by night, 50.41

One language. One solution., 28.33

One luxury all can enjoy, 14.89

One management, ship and shore, 119.31

one-man, one-hand shingle, The, 18.98

One man rule, 91.224

one more pediatricians give their own children, The, 35.115

One name in furniture everybody knows, 50.42

One of America's fine watches, 124.29

One of America's great weeklies, 85.154

One of the everlasting kind, 108.19

One of the few great watches of the world, 124.30

One of the great watches of our time, 124.31

One of the many fine products that comes from 40 years of thinking new, 18.58

One of the many quality home-improvement products made by J. M., 18.59

One of the Northwest's largest financial institutions, 43.33

One of the oldest names in textiles . . . for the newest development in synthetics, 113.25

One of the West's great newspapers, 85.155

One of the world's great hotels, 62.23

One of the world's great whiskeys, 71.74

one & only, The, 5.39

One pictograph tells more than a thousand words, 89.15

One policy, one system, universal service, 111.11

one right oil for Ford cars, The, 88.63

One shampoo convinces you, 54.29

One source, one standard—nationwide, 40.5

"one stop" creative lighting source, The, 70.42

One taste is worth a thousand words, 49.19

one that coats is the only one you need, The, 35.116

one that won't bind, The, 61.35

One third of your life is spent in bed, 13.19

one to watch for new developments, The, 22.25

one to watch, The, 7.71

one you've heard so much about, The, 58.54

Only a good cracker is fit to eat, 11.40

Only a liquid can cleanse to the depths of the pores, 32.48

Only from the mind of Minolta, 89.16

Only in a Jeep, 7.41

only instant coffee that's caffeine-free, The, 27.59

only iron that banishes ironing fatigue forever, The, 60.113

Only natural flavors last longer, naturally, 20.44

only new idea in shaving since the safety razor, The, 104.46

only 100% coverage line for cars, trucks, tractors, stationary engines, The, 8.57

Only one magazine edited for rural women exclusively, 85.156

Only refill shaving stick, 104.28

Only the best can cut it here, 78.11

Only the rich can afford poor windows, 18.60

Only three calories a squeeze, 49.20

only truck bodies built like a trailer, The, 120.20

Only Viceroy has this exclusive filter, 115.101

Only your hairdresser knows for sure, 54.30

On rearing children from crib to college, 85.157

On the bench since 1850, 117.21

"On the range", 44.14

On the right track with Jack, 91.225

On the Square, 100.19

On-time-delivery is our #1 concern, 96.26

On time every day is the Burlington way, 96.27

"Open me first", 89.17

optimum software for data center management, The, 28.61

Orchard flavor in every sip, 125.18

original and largest-selling in the world, The, 71.113

original chocolate laxative, The, 35.117

original corn flakes, The, 21.40

original drawer type freezer, The, 60.114

original masonry wall reinforcement with the truss design, The, 18.99

Original research serving the physician, 35.64

original self-contained radio, The, 95.63

Originator and perfecter of the garbage disposer, 60.74

originator of cultured pearls, The, 67.35

Originator of insulated ranges, 60.75

Originators of prefinished hardwood flooring, 46.20

Originators of radio home-study training, 101.7

Originators of the world-famous Utility ball pen, 126.20

Oshkosh, b'gosh, 26.85

other computer company, The, 28.62

ounce of prevention for everybody, everyday, An, 21.7

Our ambition: ideal telephone service for Michigan, 111.12

Our business is going to the dogs, 87.10

Our business is insuring people's dreams, 64.55

Our business is the intelligent use of computers, 28.34

Our centennial president, 91.226

Our concern is people, 64.56

Our country and our rights, 91.227

Our country needs Roosevelt for another term, 91.228

Our Dewey Special is due, 91.229

Our hand has never lost its skill, 14.90

Our readers manage the country, 85.158

Our savings are your profits, 64.57

Our state-of-the-mind is tomorrow's state-of-the-art, 5.20

Our windows reflect the way you work, 28.35

Our woofers bark, but don't bite, 5.21

Our word of honor to the public, 83.41

"Our work is child's play", 118.13

Our wurst is the best, 74.16

Outcleans, outpulls, outlasts, 114.19

Outlast the factory, 46.21

Out of the blue comes the whitest wash, 24.65

Out of the red with Roosevelt, 91.230

Out-sells because it out-shoots, 44.15

Outstanding—and they are mild!, 115.102

outstanding scenic way west, The, 96.59

Overcome skidding, nerve strain and muddy roads, 8.33

Overhead economy, 26.86

Over one billion dollars annually for industry, 66.12

Over the Atlantic and across the world, 4.32

Owned by the policyholders, 64.58

Own your share of American Business, 66.13

Pacemaker in paints, 82.45

pacemaker of gasolines, The, 88.64

Pacemakers of aviation progress, 3.16

Pacific coast magazine of motoring, The, 85.297

Packed to attract, 83.42

Packed with good taste, 20.45

Packed with the wiggle in its tail, 47.70

PAINT AND PAINTING SUPPLIES, p. 235

Paint for profit instead of expense, 82.46

Paint is at its best only when it is properly mixed, 82.47

Paints and disinfects, dries white, 82.48

Paint saves the surface, zinc saves the paint, 82.49

Paints fast as man walks, 82.50

Paint with pencils, 126.21

Paint with the two bears, it wears, 82.51

Pal hollow ground has the "edge", 104.29

Pall Mall's greater length travels the smoke further . . . gets rid of heat and bite on the way, 115.103

Palmolive cares for more complexions than any other soap in the world, 106.22

P. A. means Pipe Appeal, 115.104

Pan Am Makes the going great, 4.33

Paper engineering, 83.43

Paper is part of the picture, 83.44

Paper makers of America, 83.45

paper people, The, 83.69

PAPER PRODUCTS, p. 239

Papers for the printer who puts quality first, 83.46

paper that blazes trade trails, The, 85.298

paper that IS England, The, 85.299

Parade of Stars, 17.2

Parade of the immortals, 21.30

Particular people prefer Hamilton, 124.32

Partners in progress around the world, 43.34

party that saved the Union must rule it, The, 91.337

Pass prosperity around, 91.231

Pass the salt for better livestock, 29.29

password is Kools, The, 115.153

pass word of the road, The, 88.65

Pathfinders in pipedom, 105.14

Patient of toil/Serene amidst alarms/Inflexible in faith/ Invincible in arms, 91.232

Pat it on the face, wop it on the body, 35.65

pattern people, The, 26.128

pause that refreshes, The, 107.48

pavement that outlasts the bonds, The, 18.100

paving that's saving, The, 18.101

Peace and power with Eisenhower, 91.233

Peace at any price. Peace and Union, 91.234

Peace, freedom, abundance, 91.235

Peace, jobs, and McGovern, 91.236

Peace with dishonor, 91.237

peak of perfection, The, 71.114

Peak of quality for more than 30 years, 60.76

peak of Swiss watchmaking perfection, The, 124.41

Peak value of the year, 26.87

Peel a bite of health, 49.21

peer of beers, The, 14.134

pen America depends on, The, 126.34

pencil of the pros, The, 126.35

pencil that uses its head, The, 126.36

pen for every purpose and a point for every hand, A, 126.5

pen is mightier than the sword, The, 91.338

pen is only as good as its point, A, 126.6

Pennies more in cost . . . worlds apart in quality, 71.75

penny a night for the finest light, A, 70.6

pen that fills itself, The, 126.37

pen with the tempered point, The, 126.38

people against the bosses, The, 91.339

People have faith in *Reader's Digest,* 85.159

people movers, The, 31.29

People's Trust is the people's bank, 43.35

people who bring you the machines that *work, The,* 42.49

people who care about people who move, The, 79.9

people who invented a nicer way to cruise, The, 102.23

people who keep improving flame, The, 105.25

People who know buy Bigelow, 46.22

People who talk about good food talk about General Foods, 47.71

People you can depend on to power America's progress, 93.4

Pep for your pup, 87.11

perfect anti-freeze, The, 8.58

perfect brace that stays in place, The, 26.129

perfect candy for smart entertaining, The, 20.68

perfect cigarette, The, 115.154

perfect clue of perfect castile, The, 106.30

perfect cold cream, The, 32.80

perfected corrective shoe, The, 48.146

Perfected wood pencils, 126.22

perfect glass, The, 14.135

Perfection for new cars; protection for old cars, 88.43

Perfection in a confection, 20.46

Perfection in projection since 1909, 89.18

perfection of Scotch whisky, The, 71.115

Perfectly syntonized, 95.45

perfect powder for dentures, The, 34.36

perfect sour milk biscuit flour, The, 11.54

perfect under-arm protective, The, 116.23

Performance as great as the name, 8.34

Performance insurance, 8.35

performance line, The, 73.35

Performance speaks louder than price tags, 58.46

perfume of romance, The, 84.31

perfume of the Egyptian queens, The, 84.32

PERFUMES AND FRAGRANCES, p. 244

Perfumes of youth, 84.16

Perhaps Roosevelt is all you deserve, 91.238

PERIODICALS AND NEWSPAPERS, p. 245

Permanent as the pyramids, 126.23

Permits daylight speed at night, 8.36

personal bathroom scale, The, 12.4

personal blend, A, 110.1

Personality face powder, 32.49

Personalized cosmetic services, 32.50

personalized service that comes to your home, A, 32.5

Personalized service that makes the big difference, 102.12

personal service bank, The, 43.55

PEST CONTROL, p. 263

PET FOOD AND PRODUCTS, p. 264

PETROLEUM PRODUCTS, p. 265

Pharmaceuticals of assured accuracy, 35.66

phone companies' phone company, The, 111.22

Phone power in action, 111.13

phonograph of marvelous tone, The, 5.40

phonograph with a soul, The, 5.41

Phooey on Dewey, 91.239

PHOTOGRAPHIC EQUIPMENT, p. 270

Photographs live forever, 89.19

Photographs tell the story, 89.20

piano of international fame, The, 80.35

Pick a Perrine today!, 45.14

Picked at the fleeting moment of perfect flavor, 47.72

Picked with pride, packed with skill since 1869, 15.21

pick of Canada's burley tobacco, The, 115.155

pick of pickles, The, 29.38

Pick of the pack, picked at the peak of perfection, 47.73

pick of the portables, The, 95.64

pick o' the pines, The, 18.102

Pick the polka dot package, 74.17

picture of health, The, 106.31

pillow for the body, A, 13.2

pioneer farm journal of Western Canada, The, 85.300

Pioneering better guns and greater values since 1864, 44.16

pioneer in the leasing field, A, 6.3

pioneer of low fares to Europe, The, 4.55

Pioneers in colored glass technology, 52.6

Pioneers in hydride chemistry, 22.18

Pioneers in polycoatings, 83.47

Pioneers in recording achievement, 97.6

Pioneers in smokeless combustion, 58.47

Pioneers in the radio industry, 95.46

pipe of distinction, The, 105.26

pipe's best friend is fragrant Heine's blend, A, 115.7

pipe that everybody knows, The, 105.27

pipe that's broken in, The, 105.28

pip of a chip, A, 47.8

pippin of a drink, A, 15.2

Pittsburgh's Greatest Store, 100.20

place to go, The, 119.42

place where you keep your checking account", "The, 43.56

Play ball with Pennsylvania, 108.20

Players go places, 115.105

Play safe with Hoover, 91.240

Play safe with Wilco, 108.21

Plays all records, natural as life, 5.22

Playtime Pals for the nation's kiddies, 118.14

Play to *win* with Wilson, 108.22

Plaza pleases, The, 62.33

Please! Only *you* can prevent forest fires, 92.9

pleasure is back, The, 115.156

Pleasure pirate pilgrimage, 102.13

Plug in, I'm Reddy, 37.22

plumbing and heating weekly, The, 85.301

Plump on the Boardwalk, 62.24

plus food for minus meals, The, 21.41

Plus values, 22.19

point of penetration to the shoe market, The, 85.302

Policies "Good as Gold", 64.59

policy back of the policy, The, 64.94

policy for every purse and purpose, A, 64.6

POLITICAL ISSUES, p. 272

Polk and Texas; Clay and no Texas, 91.241

Polk and the Democratic Tariff of 1842, 91.242

Polk, Dallas, Texas, Oregon, and the Tariff of '42, 91.243

Pop goes the Piper, 125.19

Popular as music itself, 80.24

Popular at contract or auction games, 20.47

Portable phonographs of distinction, 5.23

Portable pony power, 73.23

Portable power for progress, 37.23

port of personal service, The, 36.21

possibilities are endless, The, 71.116

post everlasting, The, 18.103

Postman's, the gloves Milady loves, 123.17

Potent essence of desire to touch, 84.17

poultry authority, The, 85.303

Pour smoothness into your motor, 88.44

Powdered perfume for the complexion, 32.51

powder that penetrates between the teeth, The, 34.37

power behind the Dough, The, 11.55

Powered by Howard, 73.24

Power farming is profit farming, 85.160

Power for progress, 93.5, 93.6

powerful constructive force in the development of Georgia, A, 85.50

Powerful Software Solutions, 28.36

Power & Grace, 5.24

power is within your reach, The, 28.63

power of the pyramid is working for you, The, 64.95

power that lights and moves Alabama, The, 93.12

Power tiller of a hundred uses, 69.19

power to please!, The, 93.13

"Power to spare", 37.24

Power without powder, 44.17

PPG makes the glass that makes the difference, 18.61

Practical in design. Dependable in action., 42.34

Practical poultry paper for practical poultry people, 85.161

Praise for Biltrite comes from the heart but the comfort and long wear come from the sole, 48.103

precious bit more than a laxative, A, 35.4

Precious little aids to beauty, 54.31

Precision-built, water-tight, 16.13

Precision fishing reels since 1883, 45.15

Precision machinery since 1880, 73.25

Precision typewriters, 81.36

precision watch, America's choice, The, 124.42

Predominant with the 18 to 30 age group, 85.162

Preferred for America's most distinguished homes, 50.43

Preferred ... for mellow moments, 14.91

Preferred in fine homes for many years, 24.66

Prelude to adventure, 84.18

Prescription for your teeth, 34.27

Prescription medicines around the world, 35.67

present with a future, The, 50.64

Preserve home industries, 91.244

PRESIDENTIAL CAMPAIGNS, p. 272

Press, it's lit; release, it's out, 105.15

Press onward—enlarge the boundaries of freedom—Young Hickory, 91.245

pressure cooker people, The, 68.19

prettiest thing on two feet, The, 48.147

Prevent schoolroom slouch, 50.44

Priceless ingredient of every product is the honor and integrity of its maker, 35.68

Pride of cognac since 1724, 71.76

Prince of Ales, The, 14.136

Prince of soles, 48.104

Principles, not men, 91.246

principles & prudence of our forefathers, The, 91.340

printer company, The, 28.64

printer for every need and every speed, A, 28.2

Printers' Ink of the dental profession, The, 85.304

Probing deeper to serve you better, 7.42

problem solvers, The, 28.65

Proclaim liberty throughout the land, 91.247

Procrastination is the highest cost of life insurance. It increases both your premium and your risk, 64.60

Product of Cuban soil and Cuban sun, 115.106

Products of wood technology for construction and industry, 18.62

Products to care for your music, 5.25

products with a million friends, The, 24.90

Products you can trust from people you know, 35.69

Professional cosmetics for lovelier hair color, 54.32

professionals, The, 79.10

profit for every investor, A, 66.1

profit line in wine, The, 125.28

Progress begins with digging, 73.26

Progress for industry worldwide, 31.16

Progress in the world of time, 124.33

Progress is our most important product, 31.17

progressive past. A golden future., A, 108.4

Progressive products through chemical research, 22.20

Progress through precision, 31.18

Promise her anything but give her Arpege, 84.19

Promotes a tan while it protects your skin, 32.52

Promoting high standards in the public interest, 66.14

proof is in the listening, The, 95.65

properly balanced organic plant food, The, 69.30

Prosperity at home, prestige abroad, 91.248

Prosperity follows the plow, 85.163

Prosperity is just around the corner, 91.249

Protected where the wear comes, 67.27

Protecting the American home, 64.61

Protecting the nation — through hometown agents, 64.62

Protection and prosperity, 91.250

Protection for employer and employee, 64.63

Protection for home industries, 91.251

Protection in a new light, 64.64

Protection in depth, 64.65

Protection to all at home and abroad, 91.252

Slogans & Categories

Protection to American industry—
and no extension of slave power,
91.253

Protection to honest industry,
91.254

Protection to the working class is
an assurance of success, 91.255

Protection with profit, 64.66

Protects you like a man, but still
treats you like a woman, 116.13

Protect what you have, 64.67

Proud bird with the golden tail,
4.34

proudest name in shoes, The, 48.148

proud paper for a proud industry,
A, 85.51

Proved throughout industry for
over 40 years, 82.52

Proven best by government test,
44.18

Proven best for rest during 73 years
test, 13.20

Provident Mutual for stability,
safety, security, 64.68

Prudential has the strength of
Gibraltar, The, 64.96

prune juice with the fruit juice
appeal, The, 15.31

P. S. And it's especially great as a
hand lotion, 32.53

P. S.—Personal Service, 64.69

public appreciates quality, The, 99.7

public office is a public trust, A,
91.24

PUBLIC SERVICE, p. 299

PUBLIC UTILITIES, p. 300

Published in the heart of America:
most prosperous district of the
world, 85.164

Published to promote good farming
and right living, 85.165

PUBLISHING, p. 301

Puerto Rican mountain rum, The,
71.117

pump of compulsory accuracy, The,
73.36

Pure and white as Rainier's snows,
11.41

Pure as the mountain air, 20.48

Pure country milk with the cream
left in, 33.35

Push the button and run, 81.37

Push the button back—recline, 50.45

Pussycat-smooth hands, 106.23

Put a Burke where they lurk!, 45.16

Put a tiger in your tank, 88.45

Put errors out of business, 81.38

Put it on paper, 83.48

Put it up to men who know your
market, 2.22

Put one on, the pain is gone, 35.70

Puts its quality in writing, 81.39

Puts the "go" in ignition!, 8.37

Puts the steady hum in motordom,
8.38

Puts wings on your car, 88.46

Puts you ahead in offset
duplicating, 81.40

Puts your best figure forward,
121.40

Putting ideas to work . . . in
machinery, chemicals, defense,
fibers and films, 31.19

Putting more pleasure in sound,
5.26

Putting the "push" in America's
finest aerosols, 22.21

Putting you first, keeps us first,
7.43

Put your feet on easy street, 48.105

Put your house in the pink, 18.63

Put your lighting up to Whiting,
70.29

Put your money where the market
is, 85.166

Put your sweeping reliance on a
Bissell appliance, 60.77

Quality at your feet, 48.106

Quality brew since 1852, 14.92

quality equipment line, The, 8.59

Quality first . . . from America's first
penmaker, 126.24

Quality food products used with
confidence, 47.74

quality for every purse and purpose,
A, 13.3

quality goes in before the name
goes on, The, 112.13

quality is higher than the price,
The, 48.149

Quality is paramount to price, 35.71

quality line since eighty-nine, The,
58.55

quality loaf for quality folks, A,
11.1

Quality-made by Illinois Shade,
65.12

quality magazine of the boating field, The, 85.305

quality magazine of the radio industry, The, 85.306

quality name in air conditioning and refrigeration, The, 58.56

quality name in forest products, A, 18.6

Quality papers for industry since 1889, 83.49

"Quality parts for the auto *makers* and *owners*", 8.39

Quality product for every chocolate use, 11.42

Quality products for quality living, 18.64

quality razor of the world, The, 104.47

Quality requires no apology, 98.12

Quality seals build the reputation of professional mechanics, 8.40

Quality shows through, 50.46

Quality since 1846, 46.23

Quality. Technology. Value., 5.27

Quality . . . the best economy of all, 88.47

Quality toys with a purpose, 118.15

Quality trucks always cost less!, 120.13

Quality you can count on, 88.48

Quality you can trust, 88.49

Quality you can trust. Value you can recognize, 60.78

Queen of distinctive cigarettes, 115.107

quick brown fox, The, 81.52

quicker picker upper, The, 83.70

Quickest way to duplicate, 30.8

Quick, Henry, the Flit, 86.12

Quickly kills garden pests, 69.20

Qume printers. Your best investment in productivity., 28.37

radiant name in radio, The, 95.66

Radio builds for the years to come, 95.47

RADIO EQUIPMENT, p. 302

radio in America's finest homes, The, 95.67

radio in every room; a radio for every purpose, A, 95.11

radio that you can play, A, 95.12

radio used by the broadcasting stations, The, 95.68

radio with the big plus value, The, 95.69

rage of the college age, The, 26.130

railroad of "creative crews", The, 96.60

railroad of planned progress . . . geared to the nation's future, The, 96.61

railroad that runs by the customer's clock", "The, 96.62

railroad that's always on the move toward a better way, The, 96.63

railroad timekeeper of America, The, 124.43

RAIL TRAVEL AND CARGO, p. 306

railway to everywhere in Canada, The, 96.64

rainbow of distinctive flavors, A, 71.16

Rain or shine, it will always run, 29.30

rainy day pal, The, 26.131

Raise your hand if you're sure, 116.14

Ramis II . . . the leader by design, 28.38

Ram Tough, 120.14

ranges that bake with fresh air, The, 60.115

range with the Centra-cook top, The, 60.116

Reaches the mother through her child, 85.167

Reach for a Lucky instead of a sweet, 115.108

Reach for a world of flavor, 115.109

Reach for the Campbell's. It's right on your shelf, 47.75

Reach her when home is on her mind, 85.168

Reaching influential America, 85.169

Reach out and touch someone, 111.14

Read and preferred by construction men, 85.170

Read Time and understand, 85.171

Ready to eat, 21.31

real cigarette, A, 115.8

Real gusto in a great light beer, 14.93

real magazine of the small towns, The, 85.307

real magnetic horn, A, 8.5

Real medicine for throats too sore to ignore, 35.72

Real or reel, Royal is best, 78.12

Real restful rest on steel feathers, 13.21

real safe, not a pretense, A, 81.5

real thing from Florida, The, 15.32

real voice of radio, The, 95.70

Recline on Eclipse and the rest is easy, 13.22

Recommended by dentists surveyed 9 to 1 over all toothpastes combined, 34.28

Recommended by more dentists than any other denture cleaner, 34.29

Recordings for the connoisseur, 97.7

RECORDINGS, p. 310

record is trouble-free, The, 60.117

Record systems that talk facts fast, 81.41

RECREATIONAL EQUIPMENT, p. 311

Red apples for red cheeks, 49.22

red nylon ring of reliability, The, 18.104

Red stands out. Tastefully., 71.77

Reduce taxation before taxation reduces us, 91.256

Reduce the cost but not the heat, 59.17

Re-elect Roosevelt: his heart's with the people, 91.257

reels of champions, The, 45.22

Re-equip/Equip and profit with . . . , 8.41

Reflects good housekeeping, 68.12

Reform is necessary in the civil service, 91.258

Reform is necessary to establish a sound currency, 91.259

Refreshing as the rising sun, 20.49

Refresh, revive that sleepy skin, 32.54

Refresh yourself, 107.37

Register socially, 62.25

Reliability in rubber, asbestos, sintered metal, specialized plastics, 31.20

Relief is just a swallow away, 35.73

Relieves the daily grind, 117.22

RELy on REL for real RELief, 35.74

Rely on us, 96.28

Remember Hoover?, 91.260

ReMEMber MEM, 106.24

Remember: no one is paid to play Titleist, 108.23

Remember Pearl Harbor, 90.5

Remember Ronrico, best rum, bar none, 71.78

Remember Teapot Dome, 91.261

Remember the horse-shoe tread, 114.20

Remember the *Maine*, 90.6

Remember the name, you'll never forget the taste, 14.94

REMember this REMarkable REMedy . . . REM, 35.75

Removes the dingy film, 34.30

Removes the film of dirt and smudge, 24.67

Removes the freckles, whitens the skin, 32.55

Removes the grime in half the time, 106.25

Renowned 'round the world, 125.20

Reo Reliables . . . the powerful performers, 69.21

Repeal and prosperity, 91.262

Repeat with Roosevelt or repent with Willkie, 91.263

Repetition makes reputation, 2.23

Replace fear with cheer. Send Christmas cards this year, 51.3

Replete with hidden values, free from hidden dangers, 50.47

republic can have no colonies, A, 91.25

Repudiate the repudiators, 91.264

reputation through innovation, A, 38.2

Research in the service of medicine, 35.76

resiliency is built in the wheel, The, 8.60

Resilient floors for every need, 46.24

Resists fire and rot, 18.65

responsibility of being the best, The, 71.119

Responsiveness of a well-trained servant, 37.25

Rest assured, 13.23

Rest assured on "Shur Rest" bedding, 13.24

RESTAURANTS, p. 312

Restful ironing, 60.79

rest is easy, The, 26.137

Restituimus—"We restore"... since
1854, 64.70

retailer's daily newspaper, The,
85.309

retailer's line, The, 81.53

RETAIL STORES, p. 312

Retains all the esters, 14.95

Retire in our sleepers instead of
retiring your car, 96.29

Return the country to the people,
91.265

Reveals all your hair's natural
beauty, 54.33

Reveals the hidden beauty of your
hair, 54.34

Rexall for reliability, 100.21

Rhymes with increase, 113.26

Rich as a symphony, 71.79

Rich as butter, sweet as a nut,
11.43

Rich in flavor, 107.38

Ride like a feather in your pocket,
123.18

Ride the big red cars, 96.30

Ride the road of satisfaction, 114.21

right angle in advertising, The, 2.30

Right bearing for every car, 8.42

right business form for every form
of business", "The, 81.54

right choice for the right time, The,
124.45

Right combination, world's best
tobaccos properly aged, 115.110

Right for Sunday Morning, 26.88

right hat for real men, The, 26.138

Right in shape, temper and finish,
45.17

Right in the mixing bowl, light
from the oven, 11.44

right kind for every purpose, A,
82.5

Rightly put together to fight both
time and weather, 18.66

Right on the floor, 82.53

right paper for the purpose, The,
83.72

right point for the way you write,
The, 126.39

right road to health, The, 21.43

right spirit, The, 71.120

right tool for the right job, The,
117.34

Right to the point, 117.23, 126.25

right way to weigh right, The,
63.12

Rigid as an oak, 60.80

Rinses as it whirls, dries as it
whirls, needs no wringer, 60.81

Ripe 'n ready for smokin' steady,
105.16

rising BARometer of whiskey
preference, The, 71.121

Rivaled only by reality, 95.48

Rivals the beauty of the scarlet
tanager, 126.26

river-runt does the stunt, The,
45.23

road of a thousand wonders, The,
96.65

road of planned progress, The,
96.66

Road of the daily streamliners,
96.31

Road of travel luxury, 96.32

Road to the future, 96.33

Roaster-fresh coffee made in the
cup, 27.41

Roberts keeps you years ahead,
73.27

Roberts value keeps you years
ahead, 73.28

Robust as old rye, 71.80

rocket action car, The, 7.74

Rocky Mountains echo back
Frémont, The, 91.342

rod with the fighting heart, The,
45.24

Rolaids spells relief, 35.77

roller rolls and there's ice, A, 60.9

Roller skate with three lives, 118.16

Rollins answers the gift question,
61.25

Roll on rubber, 118.17

Roll south into summer this winter,
19.3

Rome polished copperware makes
cooking easy for the home, 68.13

roof of ages, The, 18.106

roof without a regret, The, 18.107

Roosevelt and protection, 91.266

Roosevelt and recovery, 91.267

Roosevelt and repeal, 91.268

Roosevelt for ex-president, 91.269

Roosevelt—friend of the people,
91.270

Roosevelt is robust, 91.271

Roosevelt? No! No! 1000 times NO!, 91.272

Roosevelt or ruin, 91.273

Roosevelt's way is the American way, America needs Roosevelt, 91.274

Rough and Ready: the hero of Monterrey, 91.275

Rougher on dirt, easiest on clothes, 24.68

'Round and 'round and over and over, 60.82

Round the calendar comfort, 58.48

'round the year coat, A, 26.12

round tire that rolls 3,000 miles further, The, 114.29

route of the Black Diamond, The, 96.67

Route of the incomparable empire builder, 96.34

Royal family of home fashions, 12.3

Royal releases release your worries, 78.13

royalty of lamps, The, 70.43

royalty of leatherware, The, 123.23

royalty of radio, The, 95.72

Royalty of radio since 1920, 95.49

Rubbermaid means better made, 60.83

Rub 'em, tub 'em, scrub 'em, they come up smiling, 26.89

Rub your cold away, 35.78

rug for every room, A, 46.4

Rugged as the west, 26.90

Rum, Romanism, and Rebellion, 91.276

Run away to sea with P and O, 102.14

Runs accurately without winding, 124.34

Rust-Oleum quality runs deep, 82.54

sack of satisfaction, A, 11.2

Safe and sane, 91.277

Safe and sane Cool-idge, 91.278

Safe and sound, 64.71

safe-and-sure deodorant, The, 116.24

safe antiseptic with the pleasant taste, The, 35.119

Safe as America, 66.15

Safe as sunshine, 70.30

Safe driving is a frame of mind, 8.43

Safe for every cough, 35.79

Safe for the little folks, too, 35.80

safe investment, The, 81.55

safe modern way to clean plates and bridges, The, 34.39

Safe on third, 91.279

safest, most comfortable way of going places fast, The, 96.68

safe, swift, silent "lift", The, 39.4

Safe-Tea First, 110.11

Safety first, friendliness, too, 96.35

Safety first railroad, 96.36

Safety is always the first consideration, nothing else is so important, 64.72

safe way out, The, 55.34

Sag Pruf will never let you down, 50.48

Sail a happy ship, 102.15

Sailing the South Pacific skies, 4.36

Sail with the British tradition wherever you go, 102.16

Salem softness freshens your taste, 115.111

salt cellar of America, The, 29.40

salt for every purpose, A, 29.3

Salt of the Covenant, 29.31

salt of the earth, The, 29.41

Salt of the earth, the subscribers to Needlecraft, over one million of them, 85.172

salve with a base of old-fashioned mutton suet, The, 35.120

same curency for the bondholder and the plowholder, The, 91.343

Same great whiskey today as before the war, 71.81

Same quality throughout the world, 71.82

Sandoz thinks ahead with textiles, 113.27

Sands levels tell the truth, 117.24

sandwich spread of the nation, The, 74.26

Sane toys for healthy kids, 118.18

San Francisco's leading evening newspaper, 85.173

San Francisco Style Snack Thins, The, 47.101

Sanitary, safe, durable, economical, 60.84

Sanitize your dishes sparkling clean!, 60.85

Santa Fe all the way, 96.37

Saskatchewan's only farm magazine, 85.174

SAS saves time, 28.39

Satisfies *best,* 115.112

Satisfies you, 20.50

Save America—don't save beer and wine, 91.280

Save as you spend with Christmas Club Thrifties, 43.36

Save for a sunny day, 43.37

Saves a business day, 96.38

Saves food, chills water, 60.86

Saves shaving seconds and second shavings, 104.30

Saves the face of the nation, 32.56

Save the Constitution—Thurmond for president, 91.281

Save the easy, automatic way; buy U. S. Bonds, 66.16

Save the surface and you save all, 82.55

Save what's left, 91.282

saving flour, it goes farther, The, 11.56

Saving ways in doorways since 1895, 18.67

saw most carpenters use, The, 117.35

Say it with flowers, 51.4

Say it with flowers, by wire, 51.5

Say it with pictures, 89.21, 89.22

Say Seagram's and be sure, 71.83

Say Seagram's and be sure of pre-war quality, 71.84

Say Skinless when you say frankfurters, 74.18

Scatter sunshine with greeting cards, 51.6

Scenic line of the world, 96.39

scenic route, The, 96.69

Schaefer is the one beer to have when you're having more than one, 14.96

Science of Sound, The, 5.42

Scientifically correct shoes for juveniles, 48.107

scientific corn ender, The, 35.121

SCHOOLS, p. 314

Scores in every field of sport, 108.24

Scotch that circles the globe, The, 71.122

Scotch with character, The, 71.123

Scott & Graham, union & constitution, 91.283

ScotTissue is soft as old linen, 83.50

Scott makes it better for you, 83.51

Scours the pan, not your hands, 24.69

Scratch a Democrat and you'll find a Rebel under his skin, 91.284

Scratches disappear as you polish, 24.70

Screens out burn and makes you brown, 32.57

seal mechanics see most, use most, The, 8.61

seal of certainty upon an insurance policy, The, 64.98

seam that sells the garment, The, 60.120

seasoned traveler goes by train, The, 96.70

seasoning supreme, The, 29.42

season's best and the best of seasoning, The, 29.43

SEA TRAVEL AND CARGO, p. 315

Seattle's only morning newspaper, 85.175

second best nurser in the world, The, 42.50

secret of California casualness, The, 26.139

Security is our business, 64.73

Security is the keynote today, and every day, 64.74

Security with no ifs, 43.38

See America best by car, 119.32

See America first, 96.40

Seeds of satisfaction, 69.22

Seeds you can trust, 42.35

See how much better an airline can be, 4.37

Seeing is believing, 41.9

See it all by train, 96.41

See it made, 15.22

Seen in the best of company, 26.91

See the difference, 37.26

See the FIRST of America first, 96.42

See this world before the next, 119.33

See what air-conditioning is doing now . . . See Gardner-Denver, 58.49

See what happens when you start using American ingenuity, 88.50

Segregation now, segregation
tomorrow, and segregation
forever, 91.285

Seldom equalled, never excelled,
14.97

Selected from the world's greatest
reserves of fine wines, 125.21

Sell at the decision level, 85.176

Selling and advertising to business
and industry, 85.177

Sell it in the all-day home
newspaper, 85.178

Sells easy . . . sells fast . . . makes
resales, 18.68

Sells hard wherever hardware sells,
85.179

Sell Simpson and be sure, 18.69

Send it to the dry cleaner, 25.3

"Send me a man who reads!", 83.52

Send your thoughts with special
FTD care, 51.7

Sensation of radio, 95.50

sensible cigarette, A, 115.10

sensible spectaculars, The, 7.75

Serutan spelled backwards spells
"Nature's", 35.81

Servants for the home, 60.87

Served by modern hostesses, 20.51

Serve it in silver, 67.28

Serves all the West, 96.43

"Serves you first", 64.75

Service-backed shop equipment,
117.25

Service beyond the contract, 2.24

Service first, 93.7

"Service guaranteed for life!", 45.18

Service is the difference, 93.8

service magazine, The, 85.310

service railroad of America, The,
96.71

Service that never sleeps, 75.23

Service to medicine, 35.82

Serving America's billionaires, 4.38

Serving America's schools, homes,
commerce and industry, 94.9

Serving human progress through
photography, 89.23

Serving industry constructively
since 1902, 94.10

Serving man's need for
knowledge . . . in many ways,
94.11

Serving the businessman in the blue
denim suit, 42.36

Serving the fishermen's needs for
over 100 years, 45.19

Serving the Golden Empire, 96.44

Serving the heart of industrial
America, 96.45

Serving the nation, 96.46

Serving the nation's health and
comfort, 55.28

Serving you, 111.15

Serving you around the world . . .
around the clock, 64.76

Set it and forget it, 60.88

Setting new standards in sound,
5.28

Setting you free, 28.40

Seven cents a glass, 47.76

Seven great coffees in one, 27.42

Seven leagues ahead, 60.89

7-Up your thirst away, 107.55

SEWING AND KNITTING SUPPLIES,
p. 317

shade better than the rest, A, 26.13

shade is only as good as its rollers,
A, 65.3

Shall the people rule?, 91.286

Shaped to fit like your stockings,
48.108

Shaped to your foot in action,
48.109

Sharing greatly in America's
growth, 111.16

Sharing the responsibilities of
modern medicine, 35.83

shave is better when the lather
stays wetter, The, 104.49

shave that clicks, The, 104.50

Shave with a smile, 104.31

SHAVING SUPPLIES, p. 318

Sheath the leg in loveliness, 61.26

Sheer make-up for sheer beauty,
32.58

Sheer, sheer, Berkshire, 61.27

"Sheeting action", 24.71

She has it made, 32.59

She likes the fragrance, 115.113

She's sure—are you?, 116.15

She walks in beauty, 48.110

shilling in London, a quarter here,
A, 115.11

shine in every drop, A, 24.3

shine shines through, The, 24.92

Ship from the center, not from the
rim, 36.17

ships that serve Hawaii, South Seas and Australia, The, 102.24

shirt house of America, The, 26.140

shock absorber that shifts gears, The, 8.62

shoe everybody knows, and almost everybody wears, The, 48.152

shoe of champions, The, 48.153

Shoes of character, 48.111

Shoes of worth, 48.112

Shoes that often leave everyone natty, 48.113

shoe that holds its shape, The, 48.154

shoe that's different, The, 48.155

shoe that's standardized, The, 48.156

shoe with a memory, The, 48.157

shoe with a talking point, A, 48.17

shoe with the beautiful fit, The, 48.158

shoe with the mileage, The, 48.159

shoe with the youthful feel, The, 48.160

Shop at Sears and save, 100.22

Shop with people of taste, 100.23

shortest distance between two points, The, 2.31

Short lengths, easy to eat, 47.77

Shot from guns, 21.32

shovel with a backbone, The, 55.35

Shows good form in the stretch, 109.3

Shows only the reflection, 82.56

Shrimply elegant, 47.78

shrinkage control that lets the wool breathe, The, 113.35

Sieg Heil ya'll, 91.287

Sifted through silk, 32.60

Signed, sealed, and delicious, 71.85

sign of a good cigar, The, 115.159

Sign of a healthy mouth, 34.31

sign of a lifetime, The, 126.40

sign of a new prosperity in agriculture, The, 42.51

sign of better taste, The, 15.33

sign of extra service, The, 9.7

"Sign of happy travel", 62.26

sign of paint success, The, 82.72

Sign of the leader in lawn/garden equipment, 69.23

Sign of the right time, 124.35

Signs of long life, 2.25

Silent as the rays of the sun, 58.50

silent drapery track, The, 55.36

Silent partners in famous foods, 29.32

silent servant, The, 60.121

silent servant with a hundred hands, The, 18.108

Silver with a past, a present, and a future, 67.29

simplest electric refrigerator, The, 60.122

Simplicity and a Strathmore paper, 83.53

simplified electric refrigerator, The, 60.123

Simply brush it on, 82.57

Simply say Delco, 8.44

Simply, the best, 5.29

Simply the business of homekeeping, 24.72

Simware delivers, 28.41

Since 1720, a family heritage of careful boat building, 16.14

Since 1808, a tradition in factoring and financing, 66.17

Since 1833 . . . better vision for better living, 41.10

Since 1847, the *trusted* and *authoritative* name in dictionaries, 94.12

Since 1857 . . . the standard of excellence in men's footwear, 48.114

Since 1874 stringed instrument house of the masters, 80.25

Since 1876, the servant of the well-dressed woman, 60.90

Since 1877, America's first bicycle, 98.13

Since 1886 . . . scientifically designed for practical use, 42.37

Since 1900, America's hardest working truck, 120.15

Since 1904 fine plumbing fixtures, 55.29

Since 1910, America's No. 1 scratchproof wood finish, 82.58

Since 1921 . . . the engine builders source!, 8.45

Since 1928—industry leadership in heating and air conditioning, 58.51

sine of merit, The, 95.73

single match is your year's kindling, A, 58.3

single six, The, 95.74
Sings its own praise, 61.28
singular experience, A, 71.20
Six and a half billion dollars of protection for our policyholders, 64.77
Sixteen to one, 91.288
60 million people working—why change?, 91.289
skate with a backbone, The, 118.22
skier's tailor since 1929, The, 26.141
skilled hand in chemistry . . . at work for you, A, 22.3
skill is in the can, The, 82.73
Skil makes it easy, 117.26
Skin level shave, 104.32
skin you love to touch, The, 106.32
Skip the rest and drive the best, 114.22
Skol tan keeps you "outdoor lovely", 32.61
Slate—consider its uses, 18.70
Slavery is a moral, social, and political wrong, 91.290
Sleeping on a Sealy is like sleeping on a cloud, 13.25
Sleep like a kitten, arrive fresh as a daisy, 96.47
Slip into a Bradley and out-of-doors, 26.92
Slipper-free where the foot bends, 48.115
Slippers of merit, 48.116
Slow aged for finer flavor, 14.98
small business that got big serving small business, The, 64.99
Small cost for great richness, 18.71
smaller fine car, The, 7.76
small lathe for the big job, The, 117.36
Smart and new from every view, 95.51
Smart Desk from IBM, The, 28.66
smartest thing on two feet, The, 61.37
smart set, The, 112.14
Smart shoes for beautiful feet, 48.117
Smart smokers smoke Seidenberg, 115.114
Smart, smooth, sensibly priced, 71.86
Smart to be seen in, smarter to buy, 7.44

Smells better in the pouch; smokes better in the pipe, 115.115
Smile at miles, 114.23
smile follows the spoon, The, 33.44
Smith Barney. They make money the old-fashioned way . . . they earn it., 66.18
Smoke all 7, 115.116
Smoke all you like, like all you smoke, 105.17
Smoked with hickory, 74.19
Smoke Omar for Aroma, 115.117
smoker's friend, The, 34.40
Smoke that never varies from fires that never die, 74.20
smoke with a smile, The, 115.160
SMOKING ACCESSORIES, p. 321
Smooth as a kitten's ear, 18.72
Smooth as silk, but not high hat, 71.87
Smooth as silk, strong as steel, 126.27
Smooth, easy "floating"ride, 108.25
Smoother faces, 104.33
Smoothest powders in the world, 32.62
Smooth sailing with Old Anchor Beer, 14.99
smooth tooth paste, The, 34.41
smooth way to rough it, The, 98.16
snapshots you'll want tomorrow, you must take today, The, 89.29
Snap with the turtle back, 103.13
sniffling, sneezing, coughing, aching, stuffy head, so you can rest medicine, The, 35.122
soap of beautiful women, The, 106.33
Soap! Soap! Blaine's only hope, 91.291
soap that agrees with your skin, The, 106.34
SOAP, p. 323
So beautifully practical, 60.91
Socially, America's first motor car, 7.45
sock America wears to work, The, 61.38
So easy, a child can steer it, 42.38
Soft and silky as a kitten's purr, 26.93
Soft as a kitten's ear, 123.19
Soft as kitten's ears, 26.94
SOFT DRINKS, p. 325

Softens the beard at the base, 104.34

Softness is Northern, 83.54

Soft shoes for hard wear, 48.118

Soft shoes for tender feet, 48.119

So gentle for children, so thorough for grown-ups, 35.84

... So glamorous you have to be *told* they're hypo-allergenic, 32.63

So good you want a second cup, 27.43

So high in fashion ... so light in weight, 72.15

Sold by more dealers than any other brand, 8.46

Sold by the carload, used by the drop, 24.73

Sole of fashion, 48.120

Solid and true, walnut clear through, 50.49

Solid as the continent, 64.78

Solid comfort seating, 50.50

Solid silver where it wears, 67.30

So long as the rig is on the location, 85.180

Solution of the power problem, 59.18

So many times a telegram means so much, 111.17

Sombre silver dulls more than the dinner, 24.74

Some like 'em big, some like 'em little, 47.79

Someone's always looking at your luggage, 72.16

Something more than a beer, a tradition, 14.100

Some things speak for themselves, 14.101

Something to crow about, 24.75, 42.39

So much more in quality for so little more in price, 114.24

So new! So right! So obviously Cadillac!, 7.46

song in every seed, A, 87.2

Son of his grandfather, 91.292

Sony ... the one and only, 112.8

Sooner or later, your favorite tobacco, 115.118

So-o soft, so-o smooth, so-o comfortable, 26.95

Soothes. Cleanses. Refreshes., 35.85

Soothing teas for a nervous world, 110.12

sophistocrat of cigars, The, 115.161

So round, so firm, so fully packed— so free and easy on the draw, 115.119

sound approach to quality, The, 5.43

sound investment, The, 80.36

Sound money, expansion, protection, prosperity, 91.293

Sound money—good markets, 91.294

sound of excellence!, The, 5.44

Sound shapers have no equal, 5.30

soup most folks like best, The, 47.102

South America's greatest newspaper, 85.181

Southern cakes for southern tastes, 11.45

Southern Fertilizers for the southern farmer, 42.40

Southern Ohio's greatest newspaper, 85.182

"Southern's accent is on you", 96.48

Southern serves the South, 96.49

Southern serves the South, The, 96.72

South Florida's east bank, 43.39

South's greatest newspaper, The, 85.311, 85.312

South's most famous confection, The, 20.69

South's oldest makers of fine furniture, The, 50.66

South's standard newspaper, The, 85.313

South's supreme hotel, 62.27

sovereign wood, The, 18.109

Spans the world, 96.50

Sparkling hair that thrills men, 54.35

Special chemicals for industry, 22.22

Specialists in children's good shoes since 1892, 48.121

Specialists in digital technology, 28.42

Specialists in farmstead mechanization, 42.41

Specialists in filing supplies and equipment since 1894, 81.42

Specialists in financing, 66.19

Specialists in international jet service to Texas or South America, 4.39

Specialists in making water behave, 22.23

Specialists in process and energy control, 31.21

Specialists in seating—and seating only—since 1927, 50.51

Specialists in skin care, 32.64

Specialty shop of Originations, 100.24

specialty steel company, The, 75.28

Specify Spicer, 8.47

Speedbird service, 4.40

Speed recovery—re-elect Hoover, 91.295

Speed. Simplicity. Versatility., 81.43

"Speed with economy", 120.16

Speedy is its middle name, 35.86

Spendable everywhere, 43.40

Spend the difference, 7.47

Spirited new scent of the sixties, 84.20

spokesman for the independent paint dealer, The, 85.314

SPORTING GOODS, p. 328

Sports isn't just fun and games, 85.183

sportsman's car, The, 7.77

sportsman's whiskey, The, 71.124

Sportswear for sportsmen, 26.96

Spot it by the dot, 126.28

spotlight car of the year, The, 7.78

Spray "Jake" for safety sake, 69.24

Spray that cleans windows without water, 24.76

Spreads like good news, 24.77

square deal all around, A, 91.26

square meal from a square can, A, 74.4

Standard for accuracy, 117.27

standard of residential lighting, The, 70.44

Standard of the globe, 111.18

Standard of the industry, 117.28

Standard of the plotting industry, 28.43

Standard of the world, 7.48, 115.120

Standard railroad of the south, 96.51

Stand pat, 91.296

Stand Pat with Nixon, 91.297

Stand up for America—Wallace-LeMay, 91.298

Star is Kansas City and Kansas City is the Star, The, 85.315

star of the West, The, 91.344

stars who make the hits are on RCA Victor records, The, 97.10

Start enjoying life, 85.184

starter that is built to order, The, 8.63

Starts the day in Detroit, 85.185

Starts with a quarter turn, 16.15

Start the day right with Yale Coffee, 27.44

Start with—stay with Knox, 47.80

Start with the finish, 82.59

Start with the "heart" where farmers are worth 2 for 1, 85.186

State of excitement, 119.34

state of the art now, The, 89.30

state's greatest newspaper, The, 85.316

Static is stuck on you, 24.78

Stay crisp in milk or cream, 21.33

Stay fit for fun with Phillips, 35.87

Stay fresh for years, 37.27

Stay pretty in the sun, 32.65

Stay put, 48.122

Stay-satisfactory range, 60.92

Stays dustless until the last shovelful, 59.19

Stay shower-fresh all day long, 116.16

Stays on till you take it off, 32.66

Stay sweet with Hush, 116.17

Steady America, 91.299

steels with the Indian names, The, 75.29

step ahead of tomorrow, A, 31.4

Step inside a Yankee Barn. You many never want to live in a house again., 18.73

Step into a Fortune, your key to a wealth of satisfaction, 48.123

Step out with a Stetson, 26.97

Step thru, button two, 121.41

Sterling of lasting good taste, 67.31

sterling of leatherware, The, 72.24

Sticks like a barnacle, 48.124

Stick with Roosevelt, 91.300

stiff brim straw with the soft brim fit, The, 26.142

Stir up the Campbell's . . . soup is good food, 47.81

St. Louis' largest daily, 85.187
Stop all unnecessary taxation, 91.301
Stops rust!, 82.60
Stop that leak in the toilet tank, 55.30
Stop that tickle, 35.88
Stop window washing, 24.79
Store of individual shops, 100.25
store that never closes, The, 60.124
story-telling pictorial of stage, art, screen, humor, A, 85.53
STP is the racer's edge, 88.51
straight-talk tire people, The, 8.64
strained foods baby really likes, The, 10.8
Strained for babies, chopped for young children, 10.6
strategic middle route, The, 96.73
Strategic solutions to storing, sharing and moving data, 28.44
Stratus: Continuous processing, 28.45
Strength . . . in a glass by itself, 14.102
Strength is the foundation of all good baking, 11.46
Strength, safety, service, 43.41
Strength, safety, style and speed, 7.49
Strike three F. D. you're out, 91.302
strong arm of industry, The, 73.38
Strong enough to stand on, 50.52
Stronger than dirt, 24.80
Stronger than the law, 48.125
Strong for work, 26.98
Strong where strength is needed, 73.29
Studio sound for the home, 5.31
Sturdy to the last, 48.126
Style authority in wrought iron, 50.53
Styled for beauty, made to last, 98.14
Styled for the stars, 41.11
Styled for young fellows, worn by all fellows, 26.99
Styled in California, applauded by all America, 46.25
style for any taste, a fit for any foot, A, 48.18
style leader, The, 7.79

Styles for every room in the house, 65.13
Style that stays, 48.127
Style without extravagance, 26.100
Such popularity must be deserved, 115.121
Suds in a jiffy, 24.81
sugar free taste of sugar, The, 56.11
Sugar's got what it takes, 47.82
summer route you'll brag about, The, 96.74
summer wonderland, The, 119.43
sum-total of smoking pleasure, The, 115.162
Sunbrite, the cleanser with a spotless reputation, 24.82
Sunlane cruises to Europe, 102.17
sun never sets on Hammondtanks, The, 18.110
Sunshine belt to the Orient, 102.18
sunshine of the night, The, 70.45
Sunshine State, The, 119.44
superb soldier—a model president, A, 91.27
superfine small car, The, 7.80
superior brake fluid, The, 8.65
superior interior, The, 18.111
Super service, 120.17
Superstar power for more car power, 88.52
support of a nation, The, 61.39
Support 'the Little Giant' who has proved himself the greatest statesman of the age, 91.303
Supreme Authority, The, 94.17
Supreme in the laundry industry, 85.188
supreme structural wood of the world, The, 18.112
Sure is strong, 24.83
sure sign they're good, A, 48.19
Sure to delight your appetite, 47.83
surprise of Formica products, The, 65.17
surprising state, The, 119.45
Surround your life with fragrance, 84.21
swab by any other name is not the same, A, 116.3
sweater is better if it's a Huddlespun, A, 26.14
sweet among sweets, A, 20.13
Sweeten it with Domino, 47.84
Sweeter as the years go by, 105.18

sweetest pipe in the world, The, 105.29

Swift relief follows the swallow, 35.89

SWIMWEAR, p. 330

Swisscare. Worldwide, 4.41

Switch to Dodge and save money, 7.50

Symbol of accuracy since 1870, 44.19

Symbol of quality, 18.74

symbol of quality in radio since 1915, The, 95.75

symbol of technical excellence, A, 95.14

Systematic saving spells success, 43.42

"Table Grade" Margarine, 47.85

Tag them for good, 126.29

Tailored to taste, 14.103

Take a pouch instead of a puff, 115.122

Take a tip from Robert Burns, 115.123

Take it easy and breezy, 48.128

Take it slow, it's rarin' to go, 88.53

Takes a licking but keeps on ticking, 124.36

Takes the burns out of broiling, 60.93

Takes the guessing out of dressing, 26.101

Takes the "lug" out of luggage, 72.17

Take stock in America, 66.20

Takes TOIL out of toilet cleaning, 24.84

Take the sheltered route to Europe, 102.19

Take the Studebaker third degree road test, 7.51

Take to water like a duck, 61.29

Take two, pain's through, 35.90

Take your travel lightly, 72.18

Taking charge, 7.52

Talk of the town, 20.52

Talk things over, get things done ... by long distance!, 111.19

Talk to the right people in the right places, 85.189

Tandem. NonStop transaction processing., 28.46

tang of good old ale, The, 14.138

Tangy as old Scotch, 71.88

tapeway to stereo, The, 5.45

Tartan lets you TAN, never burn, 32.67

Taste as good as they make you feel, 35.91

Taste champ of the colas, 107.39

taste is richer, yet the smoke is milder, The, 115.163

taste of the nation, The, 14.139

Tastes better than any other menthol cigarette!, 115.124

taste sells a case, A, 14.19

Tastes great ... yet it smokes so mild, 115.125

Tastes so good and so good for you, 21.34

Tastes twice as good as ever before, 47.86

taste tells, The, 74.27

Taste that beats the others cold, 107.40

taste that sets the trend, The, 85.317

taste that's right, The, 115.164

Taste the difference, 33.36

Taste the magic, 71.89

Taste the taste, 74.21

Taste without waist, 14.104

taste your dog's been fishing for, The, 87.14

Tate-made is Rite-made, 26.102

Taxpaying servant of a great state, 93.9

Taylor instruments mean accuracy first, 63.9

TEA, p. 331

Teaching a nation to avoid severe colds, 35.92

Teaching the millions to buy, 2.26

Tea in the finest tradition, 110.13

team of specialists, A, 73.3

Team of steel, 42.42

technology leader in data communications, The, 28.67

Technology never felt so comfortable, 7.53

TELECOMMUNICATIONS, p. 332

telephone people, The, 111.23

Teletype: value sets us apart, 28.47

TELEVISIONS, p. 334

Tell it in the morning, tell it in the *Philadelphia Inquirer*, 85.190

Tells time in the dark, 124.37

Tells time, saves time, 124.38

Tell the truth, 63.10

Temperatures made to order, 8.48

tender-textured gelatin, The, 47.103

Ten to one it's a Santa Fe, 115.126

Territories must be free to the people, The, 91.345

Test drive total performance '65, 7.54

Tested in the waters of the world, 82.61

tested treatment for infectious dandruff, The, 35.123

Texas' oldest newspaper, 85.191

text book of the confectionery trade, The, 85.318

TEXTILES, p. 335

Thanks for using Coast Line, 96.52

That Bud . . . that's beer!, 14.105

That eyes may see better and farther, 41.12

That good Pittsburgh candy, 20.53

That Kruschen feeling, 35.93

That marvelous mixer, 15.23

That old-time ale with the old-fashioned flavor, 14.106

That ole southern flavor, 11.47

That pleasing cigar, 115.127

That reminds me, 83.55

That's all. Nothing else., 35.94

That's all you need to know about stockings, 61.30

That's Italian, 47.87

That's life, 5.32

That's putting it MILDLY, 115.128

The ABC of radio satisfaction, 37.28

The accepted educational standard, 94.13

The action line, 18.75

The added touch that means so much, 29.33

The advocate of the American System, 91.304

The Aetna-izer, a man worth knowing, 64.79

The airline run by fliers, 4.42

The airline that knows the South Pacific best, 4.43

The airline that measures the midwest in minutes, 4.44

The airline that treats you like a maharajah, 4.45

The airline with the big jets, 4.46

The Alaska flag line, 4.47

The all-American ale, 14.107

The all-purpose one-man crane, 73.30

The aluminum ware with the smooth finish, 68.14

The American symbol of feminine charm, 84.22

The American way with Willkie, 91.305

The American whiskey for the American taste, 71.90

The answer is wool . . . it costs less in the long run, 46.26

The answer to all your tape needs, 5.33

The anthracite that serves you right, 59.20

The anti-freeze underwear for men and boys, 121.42

The antiseptic deodorant powder, 116.18

The aristocrat of American roofing, 18.76

The aristocrat of auto jacks, 8.49

The aristocrat of building materials, 18.77

The aristocrat of cigars, 115.129

The aristocrat of electric ranges, 60.94

The aristocrat of ginger ales, 107.41

The aristocrat of ice creams, 33.37

The aristocrat of liqueurs, 71.91

The aristocrat of music magazines, 85.192

The aristocrat of package cocoa, 11.48

The aristocrat of pipe tobacco, 115.130

The aristocrat of polyester neckwear, 26.103

The aristocrat of refrigerators, 60.95

The aristocrat of shirtings, 26.104

The aristocrat of tissues, 83.56

The aristocrat of winter trains, 96.53

The arms that protect American farms, 44.20

The aspirin of quality, 35.95

theatre in your home, The, 112.15

The authority in the exciting world of beauty, 32.68

The authority of the waterways, 85.193

The automated answer to the paper explosion

The automated answer to the paper explosion, 28.48

The automotive business paper, 85.194

The automotive service shop magazine, 85.195

The backbone of New York advertising, 2.27

The baking aid that nature made, 11.49

The balanced load shells, 44.21

The balanced pencil, 126.30

The ball-bearing shave, 104.35

The bandage that breathes, 35.96

The bankers who do a little more for you, 43.43

The bank for all the people, 43.44

The bank for bankers and businessmen, 43.45

The bank for me in '43, 43.46

The Bank must perish, 91.306

The bank that means business in California, 43.47

The bank that works hardest for you, 43.48

The bank where you feel at home, 43.49

The bank with the international point of view, 43.50

The beauty and distinction of custom car styling, 7.55

The beauty laxative, 35.97

The bedspring luxurious, 13.26

The beer for good cheer, 14.108

The beer of friendship, 14.109

The beer that made Milwaukee famous, 14.110

The beer that made the nineties gay, 14.111

The beer that made the old days good, 14.112

The beer that makes friends, 14.113

The beer that's brewed the natural way, aged the natural way, 14.114

The beer that wins awards, 14.115

The beer with millions of friends, 14.116

The beer with the flavor as different as day from night, 14.117

The beer with the 4th ingredient, 14.118

The beginning of taste, 23.6

The Bendix does the wash without you, 60.96

The best aid is first aid, 35.98

The best always comes from Small's, 100.26

The best and nothing but the best is labeled Armour, 74.22

The best at the price, 67.32

The best cigar in any case, 115.131

The best comedy in America, 85.196

The best cooks use aluminum, 68.15

The best dealer in town sells Norge, 60.97

The best drinking coffee in the world, 27.45

The best friend your willpower ever had, 56.9

The best has a taste all its own, 14.119

The best in radio, 95.52

The best in radio is better with a Bendix, 95.53

The best in tapes has "Able" on the label, 35.99

"The best in the house" in 87 lands, 71.92

The best in the Union, in pocket tins, 115.132

The best known name in paper, 83.57

The best-lookin' cookin' in town, 74.23

The best name in all-weather coats and rainwear, 26.105

The best of the world's press, 85.197

The best seat in the house, 55.31

The best that can be bought "a quarter a quart." Why pay more?, 88.54

The best tobacco makes the best smoke, 115.133

The best tonic, 14.120

The best to you each morning, 21.35

The best with the *most* on the ball, 108.26

The better spread for our daily bread, 47.88

The better the yarn the better the fabric, 103.14

The big brother to the railroads, 120.18

The big cheese of potato chips, 47.89

The biggest name in little engines, 37.29

The biggest *should* do more. It's only right., 6.6

The big hotel that remembers the little things, 62.28

The big house for little shoes since 1900, 48.129

The big sky country, 119.35

The Big Stick, 91.307

The big three lines of defense, 8.50

The bike you'll like, 98.15

The birch line, 18.78

The biteless blend, 115.134

The blades men swear by, not at, 104.36

The blond beer with the body, 14.121

The blue book of the trade, 85.198

The Blue Chip company, 64.80

The blue of spotless reputation, 24.85

The blue tube with the life-like tone, 95.54

The boast of the gown, 121.43

The body cosmetic, 32.69

The B & O is the way to go, 96.54

The boot with the muscles, 48.130

The bottled beer with the draught beer flavor, 14.122

The Boy Scouts' magazine, 85.199

The boys in blue will see it through, 91.308

The boy's suit built for wear, 26.106

The branch around the corner can serve you around the world, 43.51

The brands that made tuna famous, 47.90

The brand that always puts flavor first, 47.91

The brand they ask for first, 47.92

The brand with loyalty to quality, 26.107

The brand with the grand aroma, 115.135

The brandy of Napoleon, 71.93

The brew that brings back memories, 14.123

The brew with small bubble carbonation, 14.124

The brighter tasting tea, 110.14

The brightest name in aluminum, 18.79

The brightest star in golf, 108.27

The bright new silicates for industry, 22.24

The brisk tea, 110.15

The bristles are sealed, the brush will last, 82.62

The brushless wonder, 104.37

The budget sets the pace, 39.3

The builder's selection for unfailing protection, 18.80

The business jet that's backed by an airline, 3.17

The business leaders of today are the I. C. S. students of yesterday, 101.8

The business magazine of the radio industry, 85.200

The business management magazine, 85.201

The business paper of the electrical industry since 1892, 85.202

The butter in Bamby makes it better, 20.54

The butter that betters the meal, 33.38

The cabinet-wood of the elect, 18.81

The calm beauty of Japan at almost the speed of sound, 4.48

The camera you never leave at home, 89.24

The candy-mint alkalizer, 35.100

The candy mint with the hole, 20.55

The can opener people, 68.16

The car of a thousand speeds, 7.56

The car of no regrets, 7.57

The car of the year in eye appeal and buy appeal, 7.58

The car that has everything, 7.59

The car that is complete, 7.60

The car with a longer life, 7.61

The car with the foundation, 7.62

The catsup with the big tomato taste, 29.34

The centaur . . . your symbol of quality, 71.94

The cereal you can serve a dozen ways, 21.36

The chair of amazing comfort, 50.54

The chair that stands by itself, 50.55

The champagne of bottle beer, 14.125

The champagne of table waters, 15.24

The "Champagne Touch", 102.20

The champion of internal improvements, 91.309

The champion of popular sovereignty, 91.310

The champion of Republicanism and the American System, 91.311

The cheapest health insurance in the world, 35.101

The cheese most people like, 33.39

The cheese with the paper between the slices, 33.40

The chef's flavor in home cooking, 29.35

The chevron—the sign of excellence, 88.55

The chewing gum bon bon, 20.56

The children's own magazine, 85.203

The child's magazine, 85.204

The chocolates with the wonderful centres, 20.57

The choice of all who know one beer from another, 14.126

The choice of businessmen lets you choose with confidence, 64.81

The choice of champions, 88.56

The choice of noted music critics, 95.55

The choice of professionals, 5.34

The choice of successful men, 115.136

The choice of the crew and the big boss, too, 18.82

The choicest product of the brewer's art, 14.127

The choice when you want quality, too, 81.44

The choice you make once for a life-time, 67.33

The cigar made with good judgment, 115.137

The cigar that breathes, 115.138

The cigar that never lasts long enough, 115.139

The city that does things, 36.18

The civilized way of shaving, 104.38

The classic name in the building field, 18.83

The clean, convenient fuel, 59.21

The cleaning people who care, 25.4

The clean way to kill dirty rats, 86.13

The Cletrac way makes farming pay, 42.43

The clocks that most people want most, 124.39

The close electric shave, 104.39

The coats for every wear, everywhere, 26.108

The coat with nine lives, 82.63

The cod liver oil with the plus value, 35.102

The coffee-er coffee, 27.46

The coffee of inspiration, 27.47

The coffee served at the Waldorf-Astoria, 27.48

The coffee that lets you sleep, 27.49

The coffee without a regret, 27.50

The coffee with the flavor advantage, 27.51

The cognac brandy for every occasion, 71.95

The colorfast shampoo, 54.36

The "Color Guide" tie, 26.109

The comfort shave, 104.40

The comfort shoe of tomorrow, 48.131

The company for people who travel, 119.36

The company for precious metals, 75.24

The company of specialists, 81.45

The company with the "know-how", 81.46

The company with the partnership philosophy, 64.82

The complete authority of packaging, 85.205

The complete family of dog and cat foods from the world leader in nutrition, 87.12

The complete first suds detergent, 24.86

The complete line of electric cooking apparatus, 60.98

The complete paper house, 83.58

The confection of the fairies, 20.58

The Constitution and the flag, one and inseparable, now and forever, 91.312

The Constitution and the freedom of the seas, 91.313

Slogans & Categories

The Constitution as it is, the Union as it was, 91.314
The Constitution & Union forever, 91.315
The convertible sofa with accordion action, 50.56
The corn with husk ability, 42.44
The corn with yield ability, 42.45
The correct toothpaste, 34.32
The correct writing paper, 83.59
The costume jewelry of the home, 50.57
The country demands his re-election, 91.316
The courage to change. The strength to grow, 42.46
The cream of olive oil soaps, 106.26
The cream of them all, 88.57
The cream shampoo for true hair loveliness, 54.37
The crest of quality wine since 1889, 125.22
The criminal within, 35.103
The crisp dry cold of a frosty night, 60.99
The crowning achievement of vintner skill, 125.23
The crowning touch of quality, 18.84
The crown jewel of England, 71.96
The crown jewels of ignition, 8.51
The crystal clear gin in the crystal clear bottle, 71.97
The cup of southern hospitality, 27.52
The cup that cheers, 15.25
The custom-corseted look, 121.44
The custom crafted shotgun, 44.22
The customer is always No. 1, 6.7
The dainty deodorant, 116.19
The dairy paper of the New York City milk shed, 85.206
The dash that makes the dish, 29.36
The dawn of a new era in personal computing, 28.49
The daytime fragrance, 84.23
The dealer's own paper, 85.207
The deliciously perfumed hair lacquer, 54.38
The delicious whole wheat cereal, 21.37
The dentifrice that made fine teeth fashionable, 34.33

The dependability people, 60.100
The *dependable* automatics, 60.101
The desert resort by the sea, 62.29
The difference is quality, 80.26
The difference is valves, 7.63
The different antacid, 35.104
The dime that covers the world, 85.208
The discovery company, 31.22
The disinfecting white paint, 82.64
The distilled motor oil, 88.58
The doctor in candy form, 35.105
The doctor's prescription, 35.106
The dominant newspaper of the Great Northwest, 85.209
The dominant newspaper of the rich Montreal and Quebec Province Market, 85.210
The double duty searchlight, 70.31
The drier liqueur, 71.98
The drink you remember, 107.42
The drum standard of the world, 80.27
The dry constant cold of the mountain top, 60.102
The dry goods daily, 85.211
The dynamo of Dixie, 36.19
The earth's first soft drink, 15.26
The easiest kind because skeleton lined, 48.132
The easiest line to sell, 55.32
The easiest name for a man to remember, 26.110
The easiest shoe for women, 48.133
The easiest way out, 18.85
The easy ones, 89.25
The economical energy food, 47.93
The Eden cleans by gentle means, 60.103
The electric hoist that operates in the minimum, 73.31
The electric range with the safety top, 60.104
The emblem of worth in radio, 95.56
The empire's best, 110.16
The engineering journal of the industry, 85.212
The engineering magazine, 85.213
The envelope is the first impression, 83.60
The experience cruise line, 102.21
The *Extra Care* Airline, 4.49
The extra miles are free, 88.59

461

The extraordinary fiber, 113.28
The eye line of smartness, 61.31
The eye make-up in good taste, 32.70
The fabric with reflex action, 113.29
The faithfulness of an old friend, 37.30
The family liniment, 35.107
The family plate for seventy years, 67.34
The famous family of Gorton's sea foods, 47.94
The famous pencil with green and yellow plastips, 126.31
The famous skin softener, 32.71
The fan-jet airline, 4.50
The farmer's service station, 85.214
The farm paper of service, 85.215
The farm paper with a mission, 85.216
The farm weekly of largest circulation and most influence, 85.217
The fashionable fragrance, 84.24
The fashion shoe, 48.134
The fastest-growing newspaper and fastest-growing city in Texas, 85.218
The favorite home-sewing notion of the nation, 103.15
The feeder's silent partner, 42.47
The Few. The Proud. The Marines., 53.3
The fiber you can trust, 113.30
The filter for the taste that's right!, 115.140
The final touch to a tasty dish, 49.23
"The fine old innkeeping tradition in a modern setting", 62.30
The finest chocolate in the world, 20.59
The finest dye that money can buy, 24.87
The finest food preparer for the home, 68.17
The finest habit a man can have, 26.111
The finest human hands can achieve, 26.112
The finest name in sleep, 13.27
The finest of natural cheeses— naturally from Kraft, 33.41

"The finest pads have purple bindings", 81.47
The finest protection available for your family, your property and your business, 64.83
The finest wines of France, 125.24
The finishing touch you can't afford to forget, 116.20
The firm and fearless advocate of democracy, 91.317
The first and greatest name in electronics, 38.13
The first computer, 28.50
The first dental preparations made especially for children, 34.34
The first different smoking tobacco in a generation, 115.141
The first hands to touch it are yours, 33.42
The First line in printers, 28.51
The first name in American stationery, 83.61
The first name in business systems, 81.48
The first name in custom bedding, 13.28
The first name in seats—the last name in quality, 55.33
The first national newspaper network, 85.219
The first new no-filter cigarette in years, 115.142
The first real improvement since the spoon, 35.108
The first really different magazine in a generation, 85.220
The first taste tells you it's good to the last drop, 27.53
The first taste will tell you why!, 71.99
The first thought in burns, 35.109
The first thought in the morning, 27.54
The fish hook people, 45.20
The flag of a republic forever, of an empire never, 91.318
The flavor-aged ginger ale, 107.43
The flavor is sealed in the flavor bud, 47.95
The flavor's all yours, 115.143
The flavor secret of the finest cocktails, 125.25

The flavor sensation that sold the nation on coffee made in the cup, 27.55

The flavor you can't forget, 11.50

The floor of enduring beauty, 46.27

The flour of a thousand uses, 11.51

The flower of fine flour, 11.52

The folding furniture with the permanent look, 50.58

The Foodpower people, 31.23

The food that builds bonnie babies, 10.7

The 'forbidden' fragrance, 84.25

The foremost in drums, 80.28

The foundation of American beauty, 121.45

The fountain of youth, 15.27

The four-edged razor blade, 104.41

The fourth necessity, 64.84

The fragrance of youth, 84.26

The friendly computer, 28.52

The friendly drink from good neighbors, 27.56

The friendly railroad for all the family, 96.55

The friendly smoke, 115.144

The Friendly Store, 100.27

The friendly way, C. P. A., 4.51

The friendly world of Hilton, 62.31

The friend-making work shirt, 26.113

The fuel without a fault, 59.22

The furmost line, 26.114

The future belongs to those who prepare for it, 64.85

The future is building now at Garrett, 3.18

The future ... without the shock, 28.53

The gallant & successful defender of New Orleans, 91.319

The gas range with the life-time burner guarantee, 60.105

The gas range you want, 60.106

The gateway to the Chicago market, 85.221

The gay-hearted fragrance, 84.27

The gel that gives you more, 104.42

The *gentlemen* of the moving industry, 79.8

The gentler cream deodorant, 116.21

The giant of the South, 85.222

The gift candy of America, 20.60

The gift that endears and endures, 104.43

The ginger ale with the long-life bubble, 107.44

The girl with the beautiful face, 32.72

The girl with the beautiful mouth, 32.73

The global high-sign, 107.45

The Globe sells Boston, 85.223

The gold medal Kentucky bourbon since 1872, 71.100

The gold medal whiskey, 71.101

The gold standard, 8.52

The gold standard of radio receivers, 95.57

The Good Coffee Folks, 27.57

The "good hands" people, 64.86

The good mechanic's choice, 117.29

The good things of life, 64.87

The good things of milk and malt, 15.28

The grand old drink of the South, 71.102

The grass people, 69.25

The great American family cereal, 21.38

The great engineers, 31.24

The greatest name in aircraft radio, 95.58

The greatest name in bourbon, 71.103

The greatest name in building, 18.86

The greatest name in golf, 108.28

The greatest name in health insurance, 64.88

The greatest name in housekeeping, 24.88

The greatest name in socks, 61.32

The greatest name in vodka, 71.104

The greatest name in wine, 125.26

The greatest name in yachting, 16.16

The greatest show on earth, 78.14

The greatest tire name in racing, 114.25

The great highway performers, 7.64

The great name in American ceramics, 65.14

The great newspaper of the great southwest, 85.224

The great penetrative liniment, 35.110

The great railsplitter of the West must & shall be our next president, 91.320

The great regulator, 35.111

The *green* cleans in-between ... the *white* polishes bright, 34.35

The grinding, polishing and buffing authority, 85.225

The growing world of Libby-Owens-Ford, 31.25

The growth company, 31.26

The growth fund, 66.21

The Guest Coffee, 27.58

The gum with the fascinating artificial flavor, 20.61

The gun that knows no closed season, 44.23

The hair net that sits true, 54.39

The hammer with a backbone, 117.30

The Hammond is the largest-selling organ in the world, 80.29

The ham what am, 74.24

The handiest light in the world, 70.32

The handy candy, 20.62

The "hanks" are coming, 123.20

The happy medium, 85.226

The Happy Warrior, 91.321

The hardest hardwoods grow in the north, 18.87

The hardest working software in the world, 28.54

The hat corner of the world, 26.115

The hat of silent smartness, 26.116

The hat that goes with good clothes, 26.117

The headlight that floodlights the road, 8.53

The head of the class, 14.128

The health soap, 106.27

The heart of a good cocktail, 71.105

The heart of America, 119.37

The heart of a tune-up, 8.54

The Heart of Milwaukee, 100.28

The heart of reliable radio power, 95.59

The heart of the market, 93.10

The heart of your radio, 95.60

The heart's desire for every youngster, 118.19

The heart's in it, 11.53

The heel that won't peel, 48.135

The heel with nine lives, 48.136

The hero of Buena Vista, 91.322

The highest quality for health, 47.96

The high mark on leather, 48.137

The holiday cigar at a week-day price, 115.145

The home craft magazine, 85.227

The home furnishings fiber, 113.31

The home of human security, 64.89

The home of toys, 118.20

The home paper of the industrial worker and the farmer, 85.228

The home with the silver lining, 18.88

The honest old farmer of Chappaqua, 91.323

The honey-cured smoke, 115.146

The Honeymoon Line, 96.56

The hospitality state, 119.38

The hotter the water, the whiter the wash, 58.52

The house of complete corsetry, 121.46

The house of experience, 75.25

The house of flavor, 29.37

The house of magic, 60.107

The house that service built, 83.62

The ideal complete plant food, 69.26

The 'I' in Nixon stands for integrity, 91.324

The imperial line of road machinery, 73.32

The imported one, 71.106

The incomparable, 71.107

The independent supplier for independents, 88.60

The industrial bar code experts, 28.55

The industry's marketplace, 85.229

The ink that never fades, 126.32

The inner secret of outer beauty, 121.47

"The Innovators", 31.27

The instrument of the immortals, 80.30

The insured pipe, 105.19

The international authority on visual merchandising, 85.230

The international one, 112.9

The interrupting idea, 2.28

Their choice every time, 87.13

The iron with the cool blue handle, 60.108

The jack that saves your back, 117.31

The jet that justifies itself, 3.19

The jet with the extra engine, 4.52

The jeweler's quality watch, 124.40

The jewel of patent leather, 48.138

The jewel of perfumes, 84.28

The Jewish market at its best, 85.231

The Journal covers Dixie like the dew, 85.232

The journal of diagnosis and treatment, 85.233

The key magazine of industry, 85.234

The key to better grinding, 117.32

The key to happiness and success in over a million farm homes, 85.235

The key to information center productivity, 28.56

The kind of a bank you will enjoy doing business with, 43.52

The kind of clothes gentlemen wear, 26.118

The kind real boys wear, 26.119

The kind that keeps, 32.74

The king of blends, 71.108

The king of shine for surface fine, 82.65

The kitchen cabinet that saves miles of steps, 18.89

The knock-out fuel, nox out nox, 88.61

The Kola drink that's uni-blended, 107.46

The label mothers know and trust, 26.120

The label to ask for, 26.121

The lacquer finish that stays new, 82.66

The lamp that chases gloom and glare, 70.33

The lamp with the 1500-hour guarantee, 70.34

The land of elbow room and elbow grease, 36.20

The land of enchantment is calling you, 119.39

The land of ten thousand lakes, 119.40

The land that was *made* for vacations, 119.41

The lantern with the blue porcelain top, 70.35

The largest Catholic magazine in the world, 85.236

The largest multiple life insurance organization in the world, 64.90

The last fits, the fit lasts, 48.139

The last word in fine leather luggage, 72.19

The last word in gifts for men, 116.22

The last word in pipes, 105.20

The last word in sea food, 47.97

The laundry does it better, 25.5

The laundry proof snap fastener that ends button-bother, 103.16

The lawn people, 69.27

The leader around the world, 73.33

The leader in solid-state high-fidelity components, 5.35

The leading journal of the Episcopal Church, 85.237

The leading name in dictionaries since 1847, 94.14

The lead with the spread, 82.67

The leather is there in every pair, 48.140

The leg of nations, before the court of the world, 61.33

The lifelong paint, 82.68

The life of leather, 48.141

The life of paint, 82.69

The life of the party, 20.63

The lift that never lets you down, 121.48

The lighter that made the world lighter-conscious, 105.21

The lighter that works, 105.22

The light moisturizing bath oil for dry skin, 32.75

The light that always shines welcome, 70.36

The light that never fails, 70.37

The light to live with, 70.38

The "light" touch in automation and control, 38.14

The line and design for creative window planning, 18.90

The line is drawn for the future, 7.65

The line of beauty, 70.39

The line of least resistance, 84.29

The line that moves, 8.55

The line that's fine at cooking time, 68.18

The line with the carbon gripper

The line with the carbon gripper, 83.63

The line with the go, 50.59

The lipstick without the dye, 32.76

The little bank with a large circle of friends, 43.53

The little barber in a box, 104.44

The little nurse for little ills, 35.112

The live ones!, 94.15

The livest lumber journal on earth, 85.238

The log cabin candidate, the people's choice, 91.325

The longer you play it, the sweeter it grows, 5.36

The long-life battery for your car, 8.56

The long line of construction machinery, 73.34

The look of quality, 65.15

The Louisiana-Mississippi farm paper, 85.239

The lovelier soap with the costlier perfume, 106.28

The lucky ones go Anchor Line, 102.22

The luggage that knows its way around the world, 72.20

The luggage that sets the pace for luxury, 72.21

The Luxury Beer, 14.129

The luxury of velvet with the worry left out, 113.32

The luxury soap of the world, 106.29

The machine to count on, 81.49

The machine you will eventually buy, 81.50

The magazine farm families depend on, 85.240

The magazine farm people believe in, 85.241

The magazine for all manufacturing, 85.242

The magazine for Milady, 85.243

The magazine for parents, 85.244

The magazine for professional builders, 85.245

The magazine of architectural technology, 85.246

The magazine of a re-made world, 85.247

The magazine of broadcast advertising, 85.248

The magazine of business, 85.249

The magazine of business leaders around the world, 85.250

The magazine of management, 85.251

The magazine of methods, personnel and equipment, 85.252

The magazine of opportunities, 85.253

The magazine of Romance, 85.254

The magazine of service, 85.255

The magazine of the American market, 85.256

The magazine of the fifth estate, 85.257

The magazine of the hour, 85.258

The magazine of the toiletries trade, 85.259

The magazine of Western living, 85.260

The magazine of world business, 85.261

The magazine that brings the outdoors in, 85.262

The magazine that grew up with the industry, 85.263

The magazine that moves the men who move the merchandise, 85.264

The magazine women believe in, 85.265

The magic of Masland Carpets, 46.28

The magnificent, 112.10

The main line airway, 4.53

The major zipper, 103.17

The maker's name proclaims its quality, 14.130

The maker who is proud of what he makes, uses Egyptian Lacquer, 82.70

The makings of a nation, 115.147

The man of the hour, 91.326

The man of the hour is Eisenhower, 91.327

The man of the hour—Woodrow Wilson, 91.328

The man's magazine, 85.266

The man's styleful shoe on a real chassis, 48.142

The man that can split rails can guide the ship of state, 91.329

The manufacturing and construction journal of the textile industry, 85.267

The man who cares says: "Carstairs White Seal", 71.109

The man with the plan, 64.91

The market with the "rainbow round its shoulder", 85.268

The mark of a good roof, 18.91

The mark of modern pajamas, 26.122

The mark of quality, 104.45

The mark of quality in tobacco products, 115.148

The mark of the well-built house, 18.92

The mark of the world's most famous hat, 26.123

The mark that is a message in itself, 83.64

The massive men's market in print, 85.269

The master drawing pencil, 126.33

The master hair coloring, 54.40

The master's fingers on your piano, 80.31

The master wood of the ages, 18.93

The material difference in building, 18.94

Thematic advertising, 2.29

The mattress that feels so good, 13.29

The mattress that will never grow old, 13.30

The Mazda experience, 7.66

The meanest chore is a chore no more, 24.89

The measure of perfection, 71.110

The meats that wear the Armour star are the meats the butcher brings home, 74.25

The medal Scotch of the world, 71.111

The meeting place of the thrifty, 100.29

The men will need their horses to plow with, 91.330

The merchant-minded mill with variety and reliability, 83.65

The mighty tower—Eisenhower, 91.331

The milder, better-tasting cigarette, 115.149

The milk chocolate melts in your mouth. Not in your hands., 20.64

The milk every doctor knows, 33.43

The million dollar overall, 26.124

The mineral salt laxative, 35.113

The mini-brutes, 7.67

The minister's trade journal since 1899, 85.270

The modern aid to appetite control, 56.10

The modern bed of coals, 60.109

The modern farm paper, 85.271

The modern light conditioning bulb, 70.40

The modern magic carpet, 3.20

The modern way to grow, 69.28

The more colorful nylon, 113.33

The more living you do, the more you need Samsonite, 50.60

The more you eat, the more you want, 20.65

The more you hear, the better we sound, 111.20

The more you learn about photography, the more you count on Kodak, 89.26

The more you look, the more you like, 7.68

The most asked-for brand of all, 47.98

The most beautiful copies of all, 30.9

The most beautiful curtains in America, 65.16

The most beautiful kitchens of them all, 18.95

The most beautiful tire in America, 114.26

The most comfortable hat made, 26.125

The most comfortable shoe in the world, 48.143

The most complete line of firearms in the world, 44.24

The most complete software company in the world., 28.57

The most elegant name in cosmetics, 32.77

The most expensive tea grown, 110.17

The most expensive television set in America . . . and darn well worth it., 112.11

The most experienced food processor in the world, 47.99

The most famous name in rattan furniture, 50.61

The most for your money in fuel, 93.11

The most important magazine to the world's most important people, 85.272

The most influential hardware paper, 85.273

The most intelligent car ever built, 7.69

The most popular beer the world has ever known, 14.131

The most powerful shoe in America, 48.144

The most prized eye cosmetics in the world, 32.78

The most progressive name in steel, 75.26

The most respected name in fishing tackle, 45.21

The most salable shoe in America, 48.145

The most treasured name in perfume, 84.30

The most trusted name in electronics, 38.15

The most trusted name in furniture, 50.62

The most trusted name in sound, 5.37

The most trusted name in television, 112.12

The most trustworthy tires built, 114.27

The most useful magazine in metalworking, 85.274

The most valuable piano in the world, 80.32

The moth is more destructive than the flame, 86.14

"The motor carrier with more Go-How", 120.19

The motor's the thing, 37.31

The musical instrument of radio, 95.61

The music America loves best, 97.8

The music you want when you want it, 97.9

The nail enamel your manicurist recommends, 32.79

The name again . . . Nationwide Life, 64.92

. . . The name for fine rattan furniture, 50.63

The name for quality, 49.24

The name for quality athletic goods, 108.29

The name for quality hobby kits, 118.21

The name indicates the quality, 81.51

The *name* is Crane, 31.28

The name known in millions of American homes, 60.110

The name quality made famous, 89.27

The name really means something, 117.33

The name that means everything in electricity, 60.111

The name that means everything in luggage, 72.22

The name that means MUSIC to millions, 5.38

The name that's known is Firestone—all over the world, 114.28

The name to know in radio, 95.62

The name to look for, 108.30

The name to remember in flutes, 80.33

The name to remember in rainwear, 26.126

The name you can trust in margarine, 47.100

The name you know in lamps, 70.41

The Natick cobbler—the Galena tanner—there's nothing like leather, 91.332

The national broadcast authority, 85.275

The national dairy farm magazine, 85.276

The national filling station magazine, 85.277

The national guide to motion pictures, 85.278

The national inspirational monthly for men and women who sell, 85.279

The national joy smoke, 115.150

The national magazine of sports and recreation, 85.280

The national magazine of the grocery trade, 85.281

The national magazine of the hardware trade, 85.282

The national magazine with local influence, 85.283

The national newspaper of marketing, 85.284

The national rub down, 35.114

The national soil sweetener, 42.48

The national summer suit for men, 26.127

The national weekly, 85.285

The national weekly of programs and personalities, 85.286

The nation needs fixin' with Nixon, 91.333

The nation needs Richard M. Nixon, 91.334

The nation's BASIC transportation, 96.57

The nation's big name in archery, 108.31

The nation's breakfast food, 21.39

The nation's building stone, 18.96

The nation's business paper, 83.66

The nation's cheer leader, 107.47

The nation's going-est railroad, 96.58

The nation's host from coast to coast, 99.6

The nation's innkeeper, 62.32

The nation's largest airline, 4.54

The nation's long distance phone company, 111.21

The nation's pipe, 105.23

The nation's printing papers, 83.67

The natural language query system, 28.58

The *natural* lift, 15.29

The necessary two million, 85.287

The negative for positive results, 89.28

The network you can control, 28.59

The new air-rolled garter, 61.34

The new big name in beer, 14.132

The New England solution, 7.70

The newest trimmings first, 103.18

The new Nixon, 91.335

The news magazine of art, 85.288

The new smokeless coal from Old Virginia, 59.23

The news of the day in the newsiest way, 85.289

The newspaper of the buying population, 85.290

The new sparkling water, 15.30

The new standard of performance, 16.17

The news unbiased and unbossed, 85.291

The newsweekly that separates fact from opinion, 85.292

The new way to do prestige advertising, 83.68

The New York Agent in your community is a good man to know, 64.93

The next one tastes as good as the first, 14.133

The nickel lunch, 20.66

The nobility of Italian wines, 125.27

The noblest of all cabinet woods, 18.97

The noiseless oil burner, 58.53

The no. 1 buy in the design field, 85.293

The no. 1 men's service magazine, 85.294

The no. 1 name in billiards, 108.32

The Northwest's only weekly farm paper, 85.295

The nuts that get noticed, 49.25

The office automation computer people, 28.60

The Oil Bank of America, 43.54

The oil of a million tests, 88.62

The oldest and largest tree saving service in the world, 69.29

The oldest farm paper in America, 85.296

The oldest mail order house is today the most progressive, 100.30

The oldest name in electric refrigeration, 60.112

The oldest name in pipes, 105.24

The oldest name in Scotch, 71.112

The old red bandanna, 91.336

The one and only, 80.34

The one and only one cocktail gum, 20.67

The one bed frame people ask for by name, 13.31

The *one* cigarette for everyone who smokes!, 115.151

The one cigarette sold the world over, 115.152

The one-man, one-hand shingle, 18.98

The one more pediatricians give their own children, 35.115

The one & only, 5.39

The one right oil for Ford cars, 88.63

The "one stop" creative lighting source, 70.42

The one that coats is the only one you need, 35.116

The one that won't bind, 61.35

The one to watch, 7.71

The one to watch for new developments, 22.25

The one you've heard so much about, 58.54

The only instant coffee that's caffeine-free, 27.59

The only iron that banishes ironing fatigue forever, 60.113

The only new idea in shaving since the safety razor, 104.46

The only 100% coverage line for cars, trucks, tractors, stationary engines, 8.57

The only truck bodies built like a trailer, 120.20

The optimum software for data center management, 28.61

The original and largest-selling in the world, 71.113

The original chocolate laxative, 35.117

The original corn flakes, 21.40

The original drawer type freezer, 60.114

The original masonry wall reinforcement with the truss design, 18.99

The original self-contained radio, 95.63

The originator of cultured pearls, 67.35

The other computer company, 28.62

The outstanding scenic way west, 96.59

The pacemaker of gasolines, 88.64

The Pacific coast magazine of motoring, 85.297

The paper people, 83.69

The paper that blazes trade trails, 85.298

The paper that IS England, 85.299

The party that saved the Union must rule it, 91.337

The password is Kools, 115.153

The pass word of the road, 88.65

The pattern people, 26.128

The pause that refreshes, 107.48

The pavement that outlasts the bonds, 18.100

The paving that's saving, 18.101

The peak of perfection, 71.114

The peak of Swiss watchmaking perfection, 124.41

The peer of beers, 14.134

The pen America depends on, 126.34

The pencil of the pros, 126.35

The pencil that uses its head, 126.36

The pen is mightier than the sword, 91.338

The pen that fills itself, 126.37

The pen with the tempered point, 126.38

The people against the bosses, 91.339

The people movers, 31.29

The people who bring you the machines that *work,* 42.49

The people who care about people who move, 79.9

The people who invented a nicer way to cruise, 102.23

The people who keep improving flame, 105.25

The perfect anti-freeze, 8.58

The perfect brace that stays in place, 26.129

The perfect candy for smart entertaining, 20.68

The perfect cigarette, 115.154

The perfect clue of perfect castile, 106.30

The perfect cold cream, 32.80

The perfected corrective shoe, 48.146

The perfect glass, 14.135

The perfection of Scotch whisky, 71.115

The perfect powder for dentures, 34.36

The perfect sour milk biscuit flour, 11.54

The perfect under-arm protective, 116.23

The performance line, 73.35

The perfume of romance, 84.31

The perfume of the Egyptian queens, 84.32

The personal bathroom scale, 12.4

The personal service bank, 43.55

The phone companies' phone company, 111.22

The phonograph of marvelous tone, 5.40

The phonograph with a soul, 5.41

The piano of international fame, 80.35

The pick of Canada's burley tobacco, 115.155

The pick of pickles, 29.38

The pick of the portables, 95.64

The pick o' the pines, 18.102

The picture of health, 106.31

The pioneer farm journal of Western Canada, 85.300

The pioneer of low fares to Europe, 4.55

The pipe of distinction, 105.26

The pipe that everybody knows, 105.27

The pipe that's broken in, 105.28

The place to go, 119.42

"The place where you keep your checking account", 43.56

The Plaza pleases, 62.33

The pleasure is back, 115.156

The plumbing and heating weekly, 85.301

The plus food for minus meals, 21.41

The point of penetration to the shoe market, 85.302

The policy back of the policy, 64.94

The port of personal service, 36.21

The possibilities are endless, 71.116

The post everlasting, 18.103

The poultry authority, 85.303

The powder that penetrates between the teeth, 34.37

The power behind the Dough, 11.55

The power is within your reach, 28.63

The power of the pyramid is working for you, 64.95

The power that lights and moves Alabama, 93.12

The power to please!, 93.13

The precision watch, America's choice, 124.42

The present with a future, 50.64

The pressure cooker people, 68.19

The prettiest thing on two feet, 48.147

The Prince of Ales, 14.136

The principles & prudence of our forefathers, 91.340

The printer company, 28.64

The Printers' Ink of the dental profession, 85.304

The problem solvers, 28.65

The products with a million friends, 24.90

The professionals, 79.10

The profit line in wine, 125.28

The proof is in the listening, 95.65

The properly balanced organic plant food, 69.30

The proudest name in shoes, 48.148

The Prudential has the strength of Gibraltar, 64.96

The prune juice with the fruit juice appeal, 15.31

The public appreciates quality, 99.7

The Puerto Rican mountain rum, 71.117

The pump of compulsory accuracy, 73.36

The quality equipment line, 8.59

The quality goes in before the name goes on, 112.13

The quality is higher than the price, 48.149

The quality line since eighty-nine, 58.55

The quality magazine of the boating field, 85.305

The quality magazine of the radio industry, 85.306

The quality name in air conditioning and refrigeration, 58.56

The quality razor of the world, 104.47

The quick brown fox, 81.52

The quicker picker upper, 83.70

The radiant name in radio, 95.66

The radio in America's finest homes, 95.67

The radio used by the broadcasting stations, 95.68

The radio with the big plus value, 95.69

The rage of the college age, 26.130

The railroad of "creative crews", 96.60

The railroad of planned progress ... geared to the nation's future, 96.61

"The railroad that runs by the customer's clock", 96.62

The railroad that's always on the move toward a better way, 96.63

The railroad timekeeper of America, 124.43

The railway to everywhere in Canada, 96.64

The rainy day pal, 26.131

The ranges that bake with fresh air, 60.115

The range with the Centra-cook top, 60.116

The real magazine of the small towns, 85.307

The real thing from Florida, 15.32

The real voice of radio, 95.70

There *are* imitations—be sure the brand is *Tabasco,* 29.39

There are imitations, of course, 113.34

There are many advance styles, but there is only one Advance pattern, 103.19

There are no dudes in our duds, 26.132

There are no finer shoes, 48.150

There can be no compromise with quality, 26.133

The record is trouble-free, 60.117

The red nylon ring of reliability, 18.104

The reels of champions, 45.22

There IS a difference in hearing aids, 57.3

There is as much satisfaction in the brewing of a good beer as in the drinking of it, 14.137

There is beauty in every jar, 32.81

There is no finer sterling silver than Fine Arts, 67.36

There is no ration on letters, 83.71

There is no saturation point for honest value, 7.72

There is no substitute for experience, 60.118

There is no substitute for quality, 88.66

"There is nothing better in the market", 71.118

There is nothing finer than a Stromberg-Carlson, 95.71

There is one best in everything, 18.105

There is one near you, 100.31

There is only one In-A-Dor bed, the Murphy, 13.32

There is only one Jockey, 121.49

There is only one "old faithful", 72.23

There's a difference in farm papers, 85.308

There's a Ford in your future, 7.73

There's a future for YOUR figure in Foundettes, 121.50

There's a Hotpoint electric range for every purse and purpose, 60.119

There's a Jewel for every use, 82.71

There's a Lee for every job, 26.134

There's always a new reason to shop Bradlees, 100.32

There's a meal in every Muffet, 21.42

There's a Merton cap or hat for every sport, 26.135

There's a need-keyed billfold for you, 123.21

There's a quality about a home with Henredon, 50.65

There's a Tycos or Taylor Thermometer for every purpose, 63.11

There's a world of difference in Webster dictionaries, 94.16

There's beauty in every drop, 34.38

There's double wear in every pair, 48.151

There should be a Lee in your future, 73.37

The resiliency is built in the wheel, 8.60

There's longer wear in every pair, 61.36

There's many a castle built out of cigarette smoke, 115.157

There's more for your life at Sears, 100.33

There's more to it, 110.18

There's no beating deep heating, 35.118

There's no better time, 124.44

There's no better way to protect your investment, 68.20

There's no indispensable man, 91.341

There's no obligation . . . except to those you love, 64.97

There's not a cleaner like it, 24.91

There's no telling who uses it, 54.41

There's one near you to serve you, 100.34

The responsibility of being the best, 71.119

There's power in every drop, 88.67

There's simply nothing else quite like it under the sun, 69.31

There's something about an Aqua Velva man, 104.48

There's something about them you'll like, 26.136, 115.158

There's style and wear in every pair, 123.22

The rest is easy, 26.137

There's Wilson equipment for every sport, 108.33

The retailer's daily newspaper, 85.309

The retailer's line, 81.53

The right angle in advertising, 2.30

"The right business form for every form of business", 81.54

The right choice for the right time, 124.45

The right hat for real men, 26.138

The right paper for the purpose, 83.72

The right point for the way you write, 126.39

The right road to health, 21.43

The right spirit, 71.120

The right tool for the right job, 117.34

The right way to weigh right, 63.12

The rising BARometer of whiskey preference, 71.121

The river-runt does the stunt, 45.23

The road of a thousand wonders, 96.65

The road of planned progress, 96.66

The rocket action car, 7.74

The Rocky Mountains echo back Frémont, 91.342

The rod with the fighting heart, 45.24

The roof of ages, 18.106

The roof without a regret, 18.107

The round tire that rolls 3,000 miles further, 114.29

The route of the Black Diamond, 96.67

The royalty of lamps, 70.43

The royalty of leatherware, 123.23

The royalty of radio, 95.72

The safe-and-sure deodorant, 116.24

The safe antiseptic with the pleasant taste, 35.119

The safe investment, 81.55

The safe modern way to clean plates and bridges, 34.39

The safest, most comfortable way of going places fast, 96.68

The safe, swift, silent "lift", 39.4

The safe way out, 55.34

The salt cellar of America, 29.40

The salt of the earth, 29.41

The salve with a base of old-fashioned mutton suet, 35.120

The same curency for the bondholder and the plowholder, 91.343

The sandwich spread of the nation, 74.26

The San Francisco Style Snack Thins, 47.101

The saving flour, it goes farther, 11.56

The saw most carpenters use, 117.35

The scenic route, 96.69

The Science of Sound, 5.42

The scientific corn ender, 35.121

The Scotch that circles the globe, 71.122

The Scotch with character, 71.123

The seal mechanics see most, use most, 8.61

The seal of certainty upon an insurance policy, 64.98

The seam that sells the garment, 60.120

The seasoned traveler goes by train, 96.70

The seasoning supreme, 29.42

The season's best and the best of seasoning, 29.43

The second best nurser in the world, 42.50

The secret of California casualness, 26.139

The sensible spectaculars, 7.75

The service magazine, 85.310

The service railroad of America, 96.71

The shave is better when the lather stays wetter, 104.49

The shave that clicks, 104.50

The shine shines through, 24.92

The ships that serve Hawaii, South Seas and Australia, 102.24

The shirt house of America, 26.140

The shock absorber that shifts gears, 8.62

The shoe everybody knows, and almost everybody wears, 48.152

The shoe of champions, 48.153

The shoe that holds its shape, 48.154

The shoe that's different, 48.155

The shoe that's standardized, 48.156

The shoe with a memory, 48.157

The shoe with the beautiful fit, 48.158

The shoe with the mileage, 48.159

The shoe with the youthful feel, 48.160

The shortest distance between two points, 2.31

The shovel with a backbone, 55.35

The shrinkage control that lets the wool breathe, 113.35

The sign of a good cigar, 115.159

The sign of a lifetime, 126.40

The sign of a new prosperity in agriculture, 42.51

The sign of better taste, 15.33

The sign of extra service, 9.7

The sign of paint success, 82.72

The silent drapery track, 55.36

The silent servant, 60.121

The silent servant with a hundred hands, 18.108

The simplest electric refrigerator, 60.122

The simplified electric refrigerator, 60.123

The sine of merit, 95.73

The single six, 95.74

The skate with a backbone, 118.22

The skier's tailor since 1929, 26.141

The skill is in the can, 82.73

The skin you love to touch, 106.32

The small business that got big serving small business, 64.99

The smaller fine car, 7.76

The small lathe for the big job, 117.36

The Smart Desk from IBM, 28.66

The smartest thing on two feet, 61.37

The smart set, 112.14

The smile follows the spoon, 33.44

The smoker's friend, 34.40

The smoke with a smile, 115.160

The smooth tooth paste, 34.41

The smooth way to rough it, 98.16

The snapshots you'll want tomorrow, you must take today, 89.29

The sniffling, sneezing, coughing, aching, stuffy head, so you can rest medicine, 35.122

The soap of beautiful women, 106.33

The soap that agrees with your skin, 106.34

The sock America wears to work, 61.38

The sophistocrat of cigars, 115.161

The sound approach to quality, 5.43

The sound investment, 80.36

The sound of excellence!, 5.44

The soup most folks like best, 47.102

The Southern serves the South, 96.72

The South's greatest newspaper, 85.311, 85.312

The South's most famous confection, 20.69

The South's oldest makers of fine furniture, 50.66

The South's standard newspaper, 85.313

The sovereign wood, 18.109

The specialist in plate steels, 75.27

The *specialty* steel company, 75.28

The spokesman for the independent paint dealer, 85.314

The sportsman's car, 7.77

The sportsman's whiskey, 71.124

The spotlight car of the year, 7.78

The standard of residential lighting, 70.44

The Star is Kansas City and Kansas City is the Star, 85.315

The star of the West, 91.344

The stars who make the hits are on RCA Victor records, 97.10

The starter that is built to order, 8.63

The state of the art now, 89.30

The state's greatest newspaper, 85.316

The steels with the Indian names, 75.29

The sterling of leatherware, 72.24

The stiff brim straw with the soft brim fit, 26.142

The store that never closes, 60.124

The straight-talk tire people, 8.64

The strained foods baby really likes, 10.8

The strategic middle route, 96.73

The strong arm of industry, 73.38

The style leader, 7.79

The sugar free taste of sugar, 56.11

The summer route you'll brag about, 96.74

The summer wonderland, 119.43

The sum-total of smoking pleasure, 115.162

The sun never sets on Hammondtanks, 18.110

The sunshine of the night, 70.45

The Sunshine State, 119.44

The superfine small car, 7.80

The superior brake fluid, 8.65

The superior interior, 18.111

The support of a nation, 61.39

The Supreme Authority, 94.17

The supreme structural wood of the world, 18.112

The surprise of Formica products, 65.17

The surprising state, 119.45

The sweetest pipe in the world, 105.29

The symbol of quality in radio since 1915, 95.75

The tang of good old ale, 14.138

The tapeway to stereo, 5.45

The taste is richer, yet the smoke is milder, 115.163

The taste of the nation, 14.139

The taste tells, 74.27

The taste that sets the trend, 85.317

The taste that's right, 115.164

The taste your dog's been fishing for, 87.14

The technology leader in data communications, 28.67

The telephone people, 111.23

The tender-textured gelatin, 47.103

The Territories must be free to the people, 91.345

The tested treatment for infectious dandruff, 35.123

The text book of the confectionery trade, 85.318

The theatre in your home, 112.15

The things we do to make you happy, 4.56

The third dimension pattern, 103.20

The third hand with a mighty grip, 117.37

The thoroughbred radio, 95.76

The three-cent quality medium of America's greatest market, 85.319

The Tiffany of the bolt and nut business, 55.37

The time before your eyes, 124.46

The toaster you've always wanted, 60.125

The toast of the coast, 14.140

The toast to good taste, 107.49

The tobacco of quality, 115.165

The tone heard 'round the world, 80.37

The tool box of the world, 117.38

The tools in the plaid box, 117.39

The toothsome paste, 34.42

The touch of tomorrow in office living, 81.56

The toughest job you'll ever love, 53.4

The tower of strength in Dixie, 64.100

The tractor people, Allis-Chalmers, 42.52

The trade magazine for independents, 85.320

The trade paper of the home, 85.321

The trade paper of the tire industry, 85.322

The trains that railroad men buy for their boys, 118.23

The traveler's world, 85.323

The trend to dictaphone swings on, 81.57

The truck of continuous service, 120.21

The truck of proved units, 120.22

The truck of value, 120.23

The true old-style Kentucky bourbon, 71.125

The trunk with doors, 72.25

The truth without courting favor or fearing condemnation, 85.324

The tube to buy to satisfy, 95.77

The tube with the sensible guarantee, 95.78

The tuned car, 7.81

The 21st century company, 31.30

The two most trusted names in meat, 74.28

The two-piece unionsuit, 121.51

The ultimate in radio reception, 95.79

The unbeatable way to jet home, 4.57

The Uncola, 107.50

The undergarment that adds charm to your outergarment, 121.52

The unhurried whiskey for unhurried moments, 71.126

The Union must and shall be preserved, 91.346

The Union now, the Union forever, 91.347

The union of Whigs for the sake of the Union, 91.348

The Union one and indivisable [sic]—the crisis demands his election, 91.349

The United States is rich enough to give us all a farm, 91.350

The universal car, 7.82

The universal pipe, 105.30

The "unstoppables", 7.83

The up-draft lighter, 105.31

The uplift that stays up, 121.53

The user friendly company, 28.68

The utmost in cigarettes, 115.166

The utmost in lubrication, 88.68

The utmost in luxury at moderate prices, 61.40

The vacation way to Hawaii, 102.25

The varnish invulnerable, 82.74

The varnish that won't turn white, 82.75

The very best buy is the whiskey that's dry, 71.127

The *very* best in floor care products, 60.126

The very best in temporary help, 40.6

The *very* good washer, 60.127

The video with a future, 122.7

The vital 1/4 of your costume, 61.41

The voice of authority, 85.325

The voice of the cathedrals, 80.38

The voice of the master barber, 85.326

The voice with the smile, 111.24

The voice with the smile wins the world over, 111.25

The voyage of your dreams, 102.26

The walk of the town, 48.161

The washable shoes, 48.162

The washday miracle, 24.93

The washer with the backbone, 60.128

The watch for busy men, 124.47

The watch that made the dollar famous, 124.48

The watch that times the airways, 124.49

The watch that times the stars, 124.50

The watch with the purple ribbon, 124.51

The watch word of elegance and efficiency, 124.52

The way the best lemons sign their name, 49.26

The way to a man's heart, 29.44

The way to get there, 4.58

The weed exterminator, 69.32

The weekly journal of the electrical industry, 85.327

The weekly news magazine, 85.328

The weigh to profits, 63.13

The welcome partner, 20.70

The West Point of Christian service, 101.9

The West's great national magazine, 85.329

The West's great paper, 85.330

The wheels of transportation help turn the wheels of industry, 96.75

The wheels that go everywhere, 120.24

The whiskey of the gourmet, 71.128

The whiskey that grew up with America, 71.129

The whiskey that speaks for itself, 71.130

The whiskey with no regrets, 71.131

The whiskey you feel good about, 71.132

The White House—no place for an old bachelor, 91.351

The white line is the Clorox line, 24.94

The white Viking fleet, 102.27

The Wilson label protects your table, 74.29

The wine that celebrates food, 125.29

The wine that tastes as good as it looks, 125.30

The wine with the champagne taste, 125.31

The winter playground of America, 119.46

The wipe-clean wall covering, 65.18

The woman's razor, 104.51

The woman who uses it, knows, 24.95

The wonder rug of America, 46.29

The won't do Congress won't do, 91.352

The wood eternal, 18.113

The world is smaller when you fly a Beechcraft, 3.21

The world is yours with the World Book, 94.18

The world knows no better Scotch, 71.133

The world leader in tape technology, 5.46

The world over, 35.124

The world's best climate makes the world's best rum, 71.134

The world's best table water, 15.34

The world's coolest shave, 104.52

The world's fastest cook stove, 60.129

"The world's finest", 80.39

The world's finest bourbon since 1795, 71.135

The world's finest name in silver care, 24.96

The world's "first family" of changers and tape decks, 5.47

The world's greatest artists are NATURALLY yours on RCA Victor records, 97.11

The world's greatest Catholic monthly, 85.331

The world's greatest industrial paper, 85.332

The world's greatest newspaper, 85.333

The world's greatest travel publication, 85.334

The world's largest airline, 4.59

The world's largest and finest, 47.104

The world's largest business training institute, 101.10

The world's largest independent airline, 4.60

The world's largest independent manufacturer of computer interfaces, 28.69

The world's largest manufacturer of fine kitchen cabinets, 18.114

The world's most beautiful china, 23.7

The world's most beautiful island, 119.47

The world's most beautiful organs, 80.40

The world's most broadly based electronics company, 38.16

The world's most honored watch, 124.53

The world's most precious simulated pearls, 67.37

The world's most wanted pen, 126.41

The world's 100,000-mile durability champion, 7.84

The world's only tourists' magazine, 85.335

The world's playground, 119.48

The world's safest safe, 81.58

The world's smartest collar, 26.143

The world's standard of quality, 96.76

The world's supreme travel experience, 102.28

The world's textile authority, 85.336

The world's watch over time, 124.54
The worst is past, 91.353
They all speak well of it, 62.34
They almost talk to you, 85.337
They always eat better when you remember the soup, 47.105
They are the largest-selling cigarette in America, 115.167
The yarn you love to use, 103.21
They better your aim, 44.25
They cost more because they're worth more, 120.25
They cost no more, 115.168
They cure the tickle, 35.125
They do things for your legs, 61.42
The year 'round insecticide, 69.33
The yellow pencil with the red band, 126.42
They express success, 81.59
They fit, 61.43
They fit royally, 26.144
They hold their shape, 26.145
They just don't wilt, 11.57
They keep a-running, 37.32
They last longer, 83.73
They make ordinary occasions special, 49.27
They moo for more, 42.53
They must be good, 49.28
They must make good or we will, 26.146
They neither crimp your roll nor cramp your style, 48.163
The young man's magazine, 85.338
The young point of view in shoes, 48.164
They're cut to fit to fight fatigue, 121.54
They're Grrrr-eat!, 21.44
They reign in the rain, 123.24
They're not just breadcrumbs, 47.106
They're smackin' good, 47.107
They respect your throat, 115.169
They're tops for the bottoms, 48.165
They're wear-conditioned, 61.44
They're wonderful so many ways, 49.29
They satisfy and yet they're mild, 115.170
They show when they blow, 37.33
They take every trick, 108.34

They understand what peace demands, 91.354
They've got to be Stetson to be snappy, 48.166
They walk with you, 48.167
They wear and wear and wear, 46.30
They win your feet, 48.168
Things go better with Coke, 107.51
things we do to make you happy, The, 4.56
Think, 81.60
Think ahead—think SCM, 81.61
Think before you drink, say Seagram's and be sure, 71.136
Think copper, 75.30
Think of America first, 91.355
Think of it first, 2.32
Think original, think Dellinger, 46.31
Think system, 45.25
third dimension pattern, The, 103.20
third hand with a mighty grip, The, 117.37
Thirst come, thirst served, 14.141, 107.52
33 fine brews blended into one great beer, 14.142
This is a good place for a Stickup, 24.97
This is living . . . this is Marriott, 62.35
This is no place for "second best", 29.45
This is the center of industrial America, 93.14
This is the dream you can be . . . with Maidenform, 121.55
This is the walnut age, 49.30
This is the way to run a railroad, 96.77
This one means business, 3.22
thorobred air in every pair, A, 123.5
thoroughbred radio, The, 95.76
Those heavenly carpets by Lees, 46.32
Those in the know ask for Old Crow, 71.137
Those who think are proud to drink—Hires, 107.53
Thoughtfully designed with a woman in mind, 24.98

thousand miles of travel, a thousand thrills of pleasure, A, 102.3

three-cent quality medium of America's greatest market, The, 85.319

Three good terms deserve another, 91.356

$329, 91.357

Three magazines in one, 85.339

Thrift brings happiness, 43.57

Through pictures to inform, 85.340

Throw the spenders out, 91.358

Thundering power in the eye of the market, 85.341

Tide's in, dirt's out, 24.99

Tiffany of the bolt and nut business, The, 55.37

time before your eyes, The, 124.46

Timed to the stars, 124.55

Time for a change, 91.359

Time for a lifetime, 124.56

Time for a lifetime and longer, 124.57

time-honored name in scales, A, 63.3

Time hurries in every factory, 124.58

Time in sight, day or night, 124.59

Time it when you take it, 35.126

Time to swap horses—November 8th, 91.360

Time will tell, wear Sundial Shoes, 48.169

Time works wonders, 71.138

Tintex tints in the rinse, 24.100

Tints gray hair any shade, 54.42

Tippecanoe and Morton too, 91.361

Tippecanoe and tariff, too, 91.362

Tippecanoe and Tyler too, 91.363

TIRES, p. 337

title on the door rates a Bigelow on the floor, A, 46.5

toaster you've always wanted, The, 60.125

toast of the coast, The, 14.140

toast to good taste, The, 107.49

Toast to your taste, every time, 60.130

"Tobacco is our middle name", 115.171

tobacco of quality, The, 115.165

TOBACCO PRODUCTS, p. 338

To be sure you're right . . . insist on Merriam-Webster, 94.19

To better serve the Golden West, 64.101

To bid you good morning, 47.108

To bring you permanent cooking satisfaction, 68.21

To build a stronger nation, 85.342

Today's finest—designed for tomorrow's needs, 89.31

Today's ideas . . . engineered for tomorrow, 73.39

Today's most scientific shoes, 48.170

Today's need for tomorrow is life insurance, 64.102

To feel new power, *instantly*, install new Champions now and every 10,000 miles, 8.66

To fly high in the morning, take Phillips at night, 35.127

To get a letter, write a letter, 83.74

Together—A new beginning, 91.364

Together, we can find the answers., 28.70

To gladden hearts and lighten labor, 22.26

To greater vision through optical science, 41.13

To grow healthy hair, keep your scalp clean, 54.43

To heat right, burn our anthracite, 59.24

TOILETRIES, p. 348

To keep happy, keep well, 21.45

To keep teeth clean use Saltine, 34.43

To lighten the burden of womankind, 60.131

To make every community as clean as its cleanest home, 92.10

To measure is to economize, 63.14

Tomorrow is a friend of Dunbar, 50.67

Tomorrow on every wrist, 124.60

Tomorrow's car today, 7.85

Tomorrow's medicines from today's research, 35.128

Tomorrow's skin care—today, 32.82

Tomorrow's software. Here today., 28.71

Tomorrow's software today, 28.72

tone heard 'round the world, The, 80.37

Tone the sunlight with window shades just as you tone the electric light with lamp shades, 65.19

Tonight at bedtime, 35.129

Too good to forget, 14.143

tool box of the world, The, 117.38

tool for modern times, A, 28.3

Toolmaker to the master mechanic, 117.40

tools in the plaid box, The, 117.39

Tools you can sell with confidence, 117.41

TOOLS, p. 350

Tooth powder in paste form, 34.44

toothsome paste, The, 34.42

Top of the morning, 21.46

To promote the American way of life, depend on the railroad, 96.78

Tops everything for lasting beauty, 65.20

Tops for quality, 107.54

Tops the meal, 15.35

To sell millions, tell millions, 2.33

Total communications from a single source through Sylvania, 111.26

Total performance, 7.86

Total quality, 80.41

Total transportation, 120.26

Touches the spot, 35.130

touch of tomorrow in office living, The, 81.56

Tough as the hide of a rhinoceros, 82.76

toughest job you'll ever love, The, 53.4

To uphold your sox, trousers and dignity, 61.45

tower of strength, A, 43.5

tower of strength in Dixie, The, 64.100

TOYS AND GAMES, p. 352

Toys that are genuine, 118.24

tractor people, Allis-Chalmers, The, 42.52

trade magazine for independents, The, 85.320

trade paper of the home, The, 85.321

trade paper of the tire industry, The, 85.322

Traditionally preferred throughout our land, 74.30

Trailways serves the nation at "scenery level", 19.4

trains that railroad men buy for their boys, The, 118.23

Transos envelope the world, 83.75

TRAVEL, p. 354

Travel begins with Everwear, 72.26

traveler's world, The, 85.323

Travel follows good food routes, 99.8

Travel light, travel right, 72.27

Travel strengthens America, 119.49

Travel with Everwear; Everwear travels everywhere, 72.28

Treasured American glass, 52.7

treasure for eating pleasure, A, 47.14

trend to dictaphone swings on, The, 81.57

Tried and true Truman, 91.365

Trim is in, 47.109

Triply protected for oven-time freshness, 11.58

Tropical masterpieces, 123.25

Tropical suit that "breathes" fresh air, 26.147

truck of continuous service, The, 120.21

truck of proved units, The, 120.22

truck of value, The, 120.23

TRUCKS AND TRUCKING INDUSTRY, p. 357

Trucks for every purpose, 120.27

true expression of heart-felt sympathy, A, 2.8

True in every sound, 5.48

true old-style Kentucky bourbon, The, 71.125

True salesmanship in print, 2.34

True stories from real life, 85.343

True to its tone, 23.8

truly great name among America's great whiskies, A, 71.21

Truman fights for human rights, 91.366

Truman was screwy to build a porch for Dewey, 91.367

Trunks may come and trunks may go, but Everwear goes on forever, 72.29

trunk with doors, The, 72.25

Trust Band-Aid brand to cover you better, 35.131

Trust in Phillips is world-wide, 76.3

Trust the Midas touch, 9.8

Trust us to make it work for you, 66.22

Trust your car to the man who wears the star, 9.9

Truth, justice and the Constitution, 91.368

truth without courting favor or fearing condemnation, The, 85.324

Try Hollycourt. Why? The bowl stays dry, 105.32

Try it a week; you'll use it for life, 74.31

Try them on for sighs, 61.46

"T" stands for Tetley's—Tetley stands for finest TEA, 110.19

tube to buy to satisfy, The, 95.77

tube with the sensible guarantee, The, 95.78

tuned car, The, 7.81

Tune the meal and tone the system, 49.31

Turn a circle without a wrinkle, 103.22

Turns night into day, 70.46

Turns sidewalks into soft carpets, 48.171

Tussy really cares about people who care, 116.25

Tussy really cares about the sorcery, 84.33

12 kinds—better than most people make, 71.139

twentieth century expression of the French civilization, A, 7.16

21st century company, The, 31.30

Twenty years of treason, 91.369

Twice a day and before every date, 34.45

Twice as much fun, 118.25

Twin names in quality towels, 12.5

Two buttons on the shoulder, none down the front, 121.56

Two feet of comfort in every step, 48.172

Two good terms deserve another, 91.370

200 extra miles of lubrication, 88.69

Two layers of softness . . . and one is purest white, 83.76

two most trusted names in meat, The, 74.28

two-piece unionsuit, The, 121.51

Two scotches of exceptional character, 71.140

Typewriter leader of the world, 81.62

Uh, Oh, better get Maaco, 9.10

ultimate in radio reception, The, 95.79

Unaware of underwear, 121.57

unbeatable way to jet home, The, 4.57

Unchallenged for quality, 7.87

Uncola, The, 107.50

Uncommon carriers, 120.28

Uncork the magic, 125.32

undergarment that adds charm to your outergarment, The, 121.52

Underneath it all, 121.58

Under the old town clock, 43.58

UNDERWEAR, p. 359

unhurried whiskey for unhurried moments, The, 71.126

uniform & sound currency: the Sub Treasury, A, 91.28

Union and Constitution—preservation of the rights of the people, 91.371

Union must and shall be preserved, The, 91.346

Union now, the Union forever, The, 91.347

Union of States, 91.372

union of Whigs for the sake of the Union, The, 91.348

Union one and indivisable [sic]—the crisis demands his election, The, 91.349

Unique in all the world, 7.88

United Moves the people that move the world, 79.11

United States is rich enough to give us all a farm, The, 91.350

Univac is saving a lot of people a lot of time, 28.73

Universal amnesty and impartial suffrage, 91.373

universal car, The, 7.82

universal pipe, The, 105.30

University of the night, 101.11

"Unlocking new concepts in architectural hardware since 1839", 55.38

Unmistakably . . . America's premium quality beer, 14.144

Unnecessary taxation is unjust taxation, 91.374

"unstoppables", The, 7.83

Unsurpassed to help your car last, 88.70

Untouched by human hands, 20.71, 99.9

Untrammelled with party obligations, 91.375

Unwind your way to Europe, 102.29

up-draft lighter, The, 105.31

uplift that stays up, The, 121.53

Up up and away, 4.61

Up with Alf, down with the alphabet, 91.376

Use BOST, and get a good paste in the mouth, 34.46

Used by more men today than any other hair tonic, 54.44

Use-engineered for cleaning, protecting and processing, 22.27

Useful products for family living, 60.132

Use redwood, it LASTS, 18.115

user friendly company, The, 28.68

Users know, 120.29

Use the Bell to sell, 111.27

Use the wheat and spare the meat, 11.59

"Us Tareyton smokers would rather fight than switch!", 115.172

utmost in cigarettes, The, 115.166

utmost in lubrication, The, 88.68

utmost in luxury at moderate prices, The, 61.40

Vacationing in San Antonio is a family affair, 119.50

vacation way to Hawaii, The, 102.25

Value-engineered papers from the mills of Mosinee, 83.77

Value engineering favors zinc, 75.31

"Value" is a *good* word for Benefit Trust Life., 64.103

varnish invulnerable, The, 82.74

varnish that won't turn white, The, 82.75

Venida rules the waves, 54.45

Verified insulation performance, 18.116

very best buy is the whiskey that's dry, The, 71.127

very best in floor care products, The, 60.126

very best in temporary help, The, 40.6

very good washer, The, 60.127

Very individually yours, 123.26

Veteran reel for veteran fisherman, 45.26

VIDEO EQUIPMENT, p. 362

video with a future, The, 122.7

Visual . . . See for yourself, 28.74

Vital link in America's supply line, 120.30

vital 1/4 of your costume, The, 61.41

Vitamins you can trust, 56.12

Vitrified pottery is everlasting, 52.8

voice of authority, The, 85.325

Voice of quality, 82.77

voice of the cathedrals, The, 80.38

Voice of the dairy farmer, 33.45

voice of the master barber, The, 85.326

voice with the smile, The, 111.24

voice with the smile wins the world over, The, 111.25

Vote as you shot, 91.377

Vote as you shot, boys, 91.378

Vote early and often, 91.379

Vote for champions of the 8 hour law, 91.380

vote for Coolidge is a vote for chaos, A, 91.30

vote for Roosevelt is a vote against Hoover, A, 91.31

Vote gladly for Adlai, 91.381

Vote Kennedy for peace, 91.382

Vote Republican—the party of Lincoln, 91.383

Vote right with Dwight, 91.384

Vote straight Democratic: protect America, 91.385

Vote yourself a farm, 91.386

voyage of your dreams, The, 102.26

Wakes up your hair, 54.46

Wake up lazy gums with Ipana and massage, 34.47

Wake up to music, 95.80

Wake up your liver, 35.132

walk of the town, The, 48.161

Walk with comfort, 116.26

Walls of character, 18.117

Wall Street wears a Willkie button, America wears a Roosevelt button, 91.387

WARDROBE ACCESSORIES, p. 362

Wares that men wear, 26.148

War in the East! Peace in the West! Thank God for Wilson, 91.388

Warm as sunshine, light as floating clouds, 13.33

Warmth works wonders, 35.133

Warm toes in Fox River Hose, 61.47

washable shoes, The, 48.162

washday miracle, The, 24.93

Wash easier, dry faster, absorb more, wear longer, 10.9

Washer of tomorrow is the Barton of today, 60.133

washer with the backbone, The, 60.128

Washes and dries without a wringer, 60.134

Washington wouldn't! Grant couldn't! Roosevelt shan't! No third term!, 91.389

Washington wouldn't, Grant couldn't, Roosevelt shouldn't, 91.390

Wash them any way you like, we guarantee the size, 61.48

WATCHES AND CLOCKS, p. 364

Watches out for your watch, 124.61

Watches your weight, 63.15

watch for busy men, The, 124.47

Watchful of the time, 124.62

Watch Highson ... for progress through creative research, 22.28

Watch his smoke, 115.173

watch that made the dollar famous, The, 124.48

watch that times the airways, The, 124.49

watch that times the stars, The, 124.50

Watch the Fords go by, 7.89

Watch the wear, 26.149

watch with the purple ribbon, The, 124.51

watch word of elegance and efficiency, The, 124.52

Watch your children thrive on it, 33.46

Watch your feet, 48.173

Water level route, you can sleep, 96.79

Water-proofed against sogginess, 34.48

Waterproofs everything, 82.78

way the best lemons sign their name, The, 49.26

way to a man's heart, The, 29.44

way to get there, The, 4.58

We aim to humanize the science of insurance, 64.104

wealth of value in Fortune Shoes, A, 48.20

We are Dodge, an American Revolution, 7.90

We are driven, 7.91

We are going to win the war and the peace that follows, 91.391

We are not going to vote away our wages, 91.392

We are what others pretend to be, 26.150

We are your movie star, 78.15

Wear Kayser, you owe it to your friends, 61.49

Wears like a pig's nose, 26.151

Wear tested for your comfort, 48.174

Weather armour for homes, 82.79

Weathers our weather, 82.80

"Weavers of the world's finest netting", 45.27

We believe in the power of the printed word, 83.78

We bring the world closer, 111.28

We brush aside all competition, 50.68

We build excitement, 7.92

We can help you here and now. Not just hereafter., 64.105

We care about color, 46.33

We challenge comparison, 80.42

We cover the earth with drugs of worth, 35.134

We demand a rigorous frugality in every department of the government, 91.393

We demand that our customhouse taxation shall be for revenue only, 91.394

We demand the *Habeas Corpus,* 91.395

Wed in the wood, 71.141

We don't insure status ... only quality, 26.152

We don't make computers. We make them better., 28.75

We don't want Eleanor either, 91.396

weed exterminator, The, 69.32

Weekends were made for Michelob, 14.145

weekly for the whole family, A, 85.55

weekly journal of the electrical industry, The, 85.327

weekly magazine of philately, A, 85.56

weekly news magazine, The, 85.328

weekly newspaper of insurance, A, 85.57

We evolved the styles that the world admires, 72.30

We fool the sun, 18.118

Weigh the loads and save the roads, 63.16

weigh to profits, The, 63.13

We know what we CAN 'cause we can what we grow, 15.36

We know where you're going, 4.62

Welcome aboard, 4.63

Welcomed in the best homes, 71.142

welcome partner, The, 20.70

Welcome to Miller time, 14.146

"We like it here", 36.22

"Well dressed/wool dressed", 113.36

We'll make you believe in signs, 2.35

We'll open your eyes, 112.16

We'll rest our case on a case, 14.147

We'll vote for the Buckeye boy, 91.397

We'll wait. Grant's 8, 71.143

We love him for the enemies he has made, 91.398

We make networks work, 28.76

We make the addition easy, 28.77

We make the right decisions, 28.78

We make your systems fault tolerant from end to end, 28.79

We millionaires want Willkie, 91.399

We move families, not just furniture, 79.12

We pamper passengers throughout mid-central U.S.A., 4.64

We pave the way to save delay, 81.63

We Polked 'em in '44; we'll Pierce 'em in '52, 91.400

We're cooking at the table now, 60.135

We're fighting for your life, 92.11

We're madly for Adlai, 91.401

We're reaching out in new directions, 111.29

We're synergistic, 31.31

We're the guys who get the information around ... PIW ... the interconnect people, 38.17

We roast it, others praise it, 27.60

We shall be redeemed from the rule of Nigger drivers, 91.402

We shall overcome, 90.7

We shelter the world from sun and rain, 123.27

We sparked the revolution, 28.80

We stick up for everybody, 2.36

We still like Ike, 91.403

West Point of Christian service, The, 101.9

West Point stands for good grooming, 116.27

We stretch your budget. Not the truth., 28.81

West's great national magazine, The, 85.329

West's great paper, The, 85.330

Westvaco inspirations lead to new value in paper and packaging, 83.79

We take better care of your car, 88.71

We take the nut very seriously, 49.32

We take the world's greatest pictures, 89.32

We take you there, 5.49

We teach wherever the mails reach, 101.12

We took the splash out of the kitchen, 55.39

We try harder, 6.8

We understand how important it is to listen, 31.32

We've earned the trust of American Business, 4.65

We've got it good, 100.35

We've got your number, 126.43

We've got your world, 119.51

We've just begun to grow, 31.33

We want none but white men at the helm, 91.404

We want to help you do things right, 55.40, 117.42

We want Willkie—third term means dictatorship, 91.405

We want you to hear more music, 5.50

We will follow where the White Plume waves, 91.406

We will sell no wine before its time, 125.33

We work to keep you safe, 64.106

What a whale of a difference just a few cents make, 115.174

Whatever you do, eat Krumbles, 21.47

What foods these morsels be, 99.10

What I'm really giving you is a part of me, 51.8

What next from Alcoa!, 75.32

What Scandinavian men have, 116.28

What's happening. In business. To business., 85.344

What's new for tomorrow is at Singer today, 31.34

What's wrong with being right?, 91.407

What the big boys eat!, 21.48

What you want is a Wollensack, 5.51

Wheat shot from guns is elegant eatin', 21.49

wheels of transportation help turn the wheels of industry, The, 96.75

wheels that go everywhere, The, 120.24

When a feller needs a friend, 115.175

When all soaps fail, Flash cleans, 24.101

When appearance counts, 26.153

When a Studio Girl enters your home a new kind of beauty brightens your life, 32.83

When better cars are built, Buick will build them, 7.93

When distribution is the question UBL has the answers, 102.30

When E. F. Hutton talks, people listen, 66.23

Whenever a recipe calls for gelatine, think of Knox, 47.110

Whenever good impressions count, rely on carbonizing papers by Schweitzer, 83.80

When in Broderick suits your class is dressed, each girl's inspired to play her best, 26.154

When it comes to cooking for dogs—Rival has no rival, 87.15

When it rains, it pours, 29.46

When it's a Shamrock, you've got the best, 60.136

When it's Domino Sugar, you're *sure* it's *pure!*, 47.111

When its the sound that moves you, 5.53

When it's time to change, get a Glenwood Range, 60.137

When it's wet it's dry, 29.47

When nature forgets, remember EX-LAX, 35.135

When nature won't, Pluto will, 35.136

When only the best will do, say Uncle, 47.112

When something happy happens, it's Bulova time, 124.63

When the mercury soars, keep happy, 60.138

When the sun goes down, 26.155

When you care enough to send the very best, 51.9

When you change to Boscul, you change for good, 110.20

When you crave good candy, 20.72

When you get a shot, you get a duck, with Super X, 44.26

When you like your music enough, 5.53

When you make your move make sure it's a planned move, 93.15

When you mix with CinZano, you mix with the best, 125.34

When you need the best, call the best, 40.7

When you pay for quality, why not get the finest, 48.175

When you're out to beat the world, 48.176

When your nose needs the softest, 116.29

When you say Budweiser, you've said it all, 14.148

When you take cold, take lemons, 49.33

When you think of asbestos, think of Johns-Manville, 18.119

When you would serve the best, 71.144

Where advertising pays it stays—and grows, 85.345

485

Where all street cars meet, 43.59
Where banking is a pleasure, 43.60
Where beautiful young ideas begin, 32.84
Where better goldfish are grown, 87.16
Where big ideas turn into aluminum extrusions, 75.33
Where big things are happening, 36.23
Where bold new ideas pay off for profit-minded farmers, 42.54
Where departments unite to make service right, 83.81
Where *experience* guides *exploration,* 22.29
Where face fitness starts, 104.53
Where flame technology creates new products, 22.30
Where food grows finest, there Libby packs the best, 47.113
Where free enterprise is still growing, 36.24
Where friend meets friend, 7.94
Where good cheer abides, 62.36
Where good government is a habit, 36.25
Where great ideas are meant to happen, 31.35
Where ideas unlock the future, 31.36
Where imagination leads, 28.82
Where important people turn to say important things, 85.346
Where nature helps industry most, 36.26
Where new ideas take shape in aluminum, 75.34
Where only the best will do, 27.61
Where only the plane gets more attention than you, 4.66
Where people and ideas create security for millions, 64.107
Where people make the difference, 43.61
Where pride of craftsmanship comes first, 50.69
Where quality is a family tradition, 42.55
Where quality is a tradition, 18.120, 62.37
Where quality is built in, not added on, 7.95

Where quality is produced in quantity, 55.41
Where quality is traditional, 83.82
Where quality makes sense, 85.347
Where research and development make exciting ideas, 114.30
Where research is planned with progress in mind, 88.72
Where service and software come together, 28.83
Where southern hospitality flowers, 62.38
Where summer spends the winter, 119.52
Where summer stays and the nation plays, 119.53
Where technicolor comes to life, 123.28
Where telling the world means selling the world, 85.348
Where the action is!, 45.28
Where the best costs less, 62.39
Where the big idea is innovation, 75.35
Where the data movement started and startling moves are made, 28.84
Where the nicest people meet the nicest things, 60.139
Where there's life ... there's Bud, 14.149
Where the Solutions Come First, 28.85
Where the sun never sets on an unfilled order, 2.37
Where thrift meets style, 48.177
Where today's theory is tomorrow's remedy, 35.137
Wherever money is handled or records are kept, 81.64
Wherever particular people congregate, 115.176
Wherever shafts move, 88.73
Wherever wheels turn or propellers spin, 37.34
Wherever you go, there it is, 71.145
Wherever you go you look better in Arrow, 26.156
Wherever you look ... you see Budd, 31.37
Where were you in '32?, 91.408
Where what's happening gets its start, 22.31

Where what you want to know comes first, 17.3

Where your dollar works harder . . . grows bigger!, 66.24

Where your "resort dollar" buys more, 62.40

Where your sealing is unlimited, 18.121

Where you save *does* make a difference, 43.62

While I am able to move I will do my duty, 91.409

While there is Life there is hope, 85.349

whiskey for every taste and purse, A, 71.22

whiskey of the gourmet, The, 71.128

whiskey that grew up with America, The, 71.129

whiskey that speaks for itself, The, 71.130

whiskey with no regrets, The, 71.131

whiskey you feel good about, The, 71.132

White House—no place for an old bachelor, The, 91.351

white line is the Clorox line, The, 24.94

White men to govern the restoration of constitutional liberty, 91.410

Whiter, finer, softer, Carter, 82.81

white Viking fleet, The, 102.27

Who but Hoover, 91.411

Who but Hubert?, 91.412

Who changed it?, 73.40

Wholesale floor coverings of distinction, 46.34

Wholesome sweets for children, 20.73

Why be irritated? Light an Old Gold, 115.177

Why carry a cold in your pocket, 123.29

Why fool around with anyone else?, 4.67

Why go anywhere else?, 9.11

Why not smoke the finest?, 115.178

Wide range of therapeutic usefulness, 35.138

Wide-track, 7.96

Wide world of entertainment, 17.4

Wieland's extra pale is always extra good, 14.150

Will cure a cold in one night, 35.139

Willkie for president—of Commonwealth and Southern, 91.413

Willkie for the millionaires—Roosevelt for the millions, 91.414

Willkie or bust, 91.415

Will not kink, 61.50

Wilson label protects your table, The, 74.29

Wilson, that's haul, 120.31

Wilts whiskers, 104.54

Windblown through silk, 32.85

Window beauty is Andersen, 18.122

Window to the world, 112.17

WINES, p. 367

Wines of California. Since 1882., 125.35

wine that celebrates food, The, 125.29

wine that tastes as good as it looks, The, 125.30

wine with the champagne taste, The, 125.31

Wings of steel, 108.35

Wings of the morning, 27.62

winner with women, A, 116.4

Winning and holding good will, 7.97

Winning. Worldly. Well bred., 125.36

Winston. America's Best., 115.179

Winston tastes good . . . like a cigarette should, 115.180

Winter fun under a "summer sun", 119.54

winter playground of America, The, 119.46

Win their way by their play, 5.54

Win with Willkie, 91.416

Win with Wilson, 91.417

wipe and it's bright, A, 24.5

wipe-clean wall covering, The, 65.18

Wipe 'em out, don't stir 'em up, 86.15

Wipe off the dust, 65.21

Wipes off dirt and grease, as easy as dusting, 24.102

Wise men seek wise counsel, 64.108

With all the grace and beauty of its name, 80.43

With an engine you'll never wear out, 7.98

487

With everything American, tomorrow is secure, 64.109

With Graflex, the payoff is in the picture, 89.33

With men who know tobacco best, it's Luckies 2 to 1, 115.181

Without grounds for complaint, 27.63

Without the shadow of a stout, 121.59

With pleasure, sir!, 115.182

With real root juices, 107.56

Withstands the test of time, 18.123

With that sweet smoke taste, 74.32

With the aroma of the rose, 115.183

With the fragrance men love, 106.35

With Time/Life Books, you've got it made, 94.20

With youth, first impressions last, 85.350

Wizard of wash, 24.103

woman never forgets the man who remembers, A, 20.14

woman's razor, The, 104.51

woman who uses it, knows, The, 24.95

wonder rug of America, The, 46.29

Won its favor through its flavor, 21.50

won't do Congress won't do, The, 91.352

wood eternal, The, 18.113

Wood that nature armed against decay, 18.124

Wood that weathers every storm, 18.125

Wood that you would and should use, 18.126

Words to go to sleep by, 13.34

Word to the wives is sufficient, 29.48

Work clothing that conquers hard wear, 26.157

Work horse of the world, 7.99

Working for today, planning for tomorrow, 60.140

Working funds for industry, 66.25

Workingmen, don't be fooled, 91.418

Workingmen's friend, 91.419

Work with Wallace for peace, 91.420

World champions of worth!, 42.56

World-famous Spanish sherries, 125.37

world in itself, A, 119.6

world is smaller when you fly a Beechcraft, The, 3.21

world is yours with the World Book, The, 94.18

world knows no better Scotch, The, 71.133

World leader in heavy-duty trucks, 120.32

World leader in luxury cigars, 115.184

World leader in recorded sound, 97.12

world leader in tape technology, The, 5.47

world leader in technology, A, 112.2

World leader on highway and speedway, 8.67

world of experience, A, 38.3

world of furniture made in a way that makes a world of difference, A, 50.8

world of paper products—from frozen food cartons to printing paper, A, 83.11

world over, The, 35.124

world's best climate makes the world's best rum, The, 71.134

World's best seller, 85.351

world's best table water, The, 15.34

World's biggest seller!, 77.3

World's champion ammunition, 44.27

world's coolest shave, The, 104.52

World's Fair feet, 48.178

world's fastest cook stove, The, 60.129

world's finest bourbon since 1795, The, 71.135

World's finest cottons, 113.37

World's finest golf clubs and accessories, 108.36

World's finest mink, 26.158

world's finest name in silver care, The, 24.96

World's finest petrochemical products, 88.74

World's finest reproductions, 67.38

world's finest", "The, 80.39

world's "first family" of changers and tape decks, The, 5.48

World's first family of jets, 3.23

World's first mass produced tractor, 42.57

World's first—world's finest, 88.75

World's foremost heavy-duty ignition line, 8.68

World's foremost rebuilders of automotive parts, 8.69

World's friendliest airline—Panagra, 4.68

world's greatest artists are NATURALLY yours on RCA Victor records, The, 97.11

world's greatest Catholic monthly, The, 85.331

world's greatest industrial paper, The, 85.332

world's greatest newspaper, The, 85.333

World's greatest table makers, 50.70

world's greatest travel publication, The, 85.334

World's greatest travel system, 119.55

World's largest air cargo carrier, 4.69

world's largest airline, The, 4.59

world's largest and finest, The, 47.104

World's largest builder of organs and pianos, 80.44

world's largest business training institute, The, 101.10

World's largest charter airline, 4.70

World's largest creator of preschool toys, 118.26

World's largest exclusive fly line manufacturer, 45.29

World's largest exclusive manufacturer of golf balls, 108.37

world's largest independent airline, The, 4.60

world's largest independent manufacturer of computer interfaces, The, 28.69

World's largest maker of tufted carpets and rugs, 46.35

World's largest maker of V-Belts, 8.70

World's largest manufacturer of fine carbonizing papers, 83.83

world's largest manufacturer of fine kitchen cabinets, The, 18.114

World's largest manufacturer of glass tableware, 52.9

World's largest manufacturer of household electric heating appliances, 58.57

World's largest manufacturer of mirrors, 65.22

World's largest manufacturer of painters' and glaziers' tools—since 1872, 117.43

World's largest manufacturer of staplers for home and office, 81.65

World's largest mattress maker, 13.35

World's largest newspaper, 85.352

World's largest producer of automotive wheels, hubs and drums, 8.71

World's largest producer of bath scales, 12.6

World's largest producer of non-powder guns and ammo, 44.28

World's largest roof truss system, 18.127

World's largest selling air conditioners, 58.58

World's largest specialized publisher, 94.21

World's leading direct-by-mail vitamin and drug company, 56.13

World's leading padlock manufacturers, 55.42

world's most beautiful china, The, 23.7

world's most beautiful island, The, 119.47

world's most beautiful organs, The, 80.40

world's most broadly based electronics company, The, 38.16

World's most "carefree"watch, 124.64

World's most comfortable mattress, 13.36

World's most complete line of sporting arms and accessories, 44.29

World's most complete transportation system, 96.80

World's most dependable air freight service, 4.71

World's most economical motor oil, 88.76

World's most experienced airline, 4.72

World's most experienced ski maker, 108.38

world's most honored watch, The, 124.53

World's most perfect high fidelity components, 5.55

world's most precious simulated pearls, The, 67.37

World's most respected accordion, 80.45

World's most wanted lure, 45.30

world's most wanted pen, The, 126.41

World's most wonderful phonograph, 5.56

World's number one weed killers, 69.34

World's oldest and largest manufacturer of electric blankets, 60.141

world's 100,000-mile durability champion, The, 7.84

world's only tourists' magazine, The, 85.335

World's outstanding boxing magazine, 85.353

world's playground, The, 119.48

World's safest low-priced car, 7.100

world's safest safe, The, 81.58

World's second largest manufacturer of cameras and films, 89.34

world's smartest collar, The, 26.143

world's standard of quality, The, 96.76

World's strongest padlocks, 55.43

world's supreme travel experience, The, 102.28

World standard, 3.24

world's textile authority, The, 85.336

world's watch over time, The, 124.54

World's worst beauty soap. World's *best* hand soap, 106.36

Worldwide electronics telecommunications, 111.30

World-wide engineering, manufacturing and construction, 31.38

World-wide voice writing service, 81.66

Worn with pride by millions, 48.179

worst is past, The, 91.353

Worth a guinea a box, 35.140

Worth changing brands to get, 88.77

Worthy of the name, 60.142

Worthy to become heirlooms, 68.22

Wouldn't you really rather have a Buick?, 7.101

Would you buy a used car from this man?, 91.421

Would you let your sister marry this man?, 91.422

Woven where the wool is grown, 113.38

Woven with a warp of honesty and a woof of skill, 46.36

Write around the world, 126.44

Write often, write cheerfully, WRITE, 83.84

Writes a strong, rich blue, 126.45

Writes dry with permanent ink, 126.46

WRITING INSTRUMENTS, p. 369

Writing papers that create an impression, 83.85

Writing paper that welcomes the pen, 83.86

Written so you can understand it, 85.354

Wrought from solid silver, 67.39

Wurlitzer means music to millions, 80.46

Yale battery for every battery need, A, 37.2

Yale marked is Yale made, 55.44

Yamaha—the way it should be, 77.4

Yankee tools make better mechanics, 117.44

yarn you love to use, The, 103.21

Year in, year out, the perfect servant, 60.143

year 'round insecticide, The, 69.33

Years ahead in the science of flight, 3.25

Years from now you'll be glad it's Norge, 60.144

Years of wear in every yard, 46.37

yellow pencil with the red band, The, 126.42

"Yes, I know . . . Marie Brizard", 71.146

You bet your Life Savers, 20.74

You call it a "zipper;" its real name is Prentice, the dependable slide fastener, 103.23

You can bank on a Frank, 80.47

You can bank on Bankers, 64.110

You can be sure if it's Westinghouse, 31.39

You can be sure of Shell, 88.78

You can count on Continental to take care of you, 75.36

You can count on Kemper care under the Kemper flag, 64.111

You can depend on it, 88.79

You can depend on the integrity and quality of Smith-Douglass, 42.58

You can depend on the name, 33.47

You can do it better with gas, 59.25

You can get all types of insurance under the Travelers umbrella, 64.112

You can have your cake and drink it, too, 11.60

You can pay more, but you can't buy more, 81.67

You can shave in a foxhole with X-Ray, 104.55

You can't buy a multigraph unless you need it, 30.10

You can't describe it until you've tried it, 27.64

You can't do better than Sears, 100.36

You can't get a drink from a drinkless Kaywoodie, 105.33

You can't get a drink from a drinkless pipe, 105.34

You can't get any closer, 104.56

You can't get the whole picture in just a day or two, 119.56

You can't knock the crease out, 26.159

You can trust the man who sells this brand, 74.33

You can't wear out their looks, 48.180

You cook better automatically with a Tappan, 60.145

You deserve a break today, 99.11

"You don't have to be a millionaire to play like one", 108.39

You eat it with a smile, 33.48

You *expect* more from Standard and you *get* it., 88.80

You feel so cool, so clean, so fresh . . . , 116.30

You feel you've had something worth drinking when you've had a Guinness, 14.151

You get more out of Hampden, 14.152

You get the good things first from Chrysler Corp., 7.102

You have a friend at Chase Manhattan, 43.63

You haven't seen your country if you haven't seen Alaska, 119.57

You just know she wears them, 61.51

You know it's fresh, it's dated, 29.49

You know the quality when it's King-Fisher made, 13.37

You like it, it likes you, 107.57

You live better automatically with Tappan, 60.146

You'll always be glad you bought a General Electric, 60.147

You'll appreciate the flavor, 27.65

You'll be ahead with Chevrolet, 7.103

You'll be ahead with Nash, 7.104

You'll be hearing from us, 111.31

You'll fall in love with Jersey Maid, 33.49

You'll find the woman's touch in every Purex product, 24.104

You look like you just heard from Dean Witter, 66.26

You may dent the wood, but the varnish won't crack, 82.82

You might as well have the best, 27.66, 110.21

You need an oil this good, 88.81

You never had coffee like this before, 27.67

You never had it so good, 91.423

You never had it this fresh!, 115.185

You never have to lift or tilt it, 60.148

You never heard it so good, 5.57

You never pay more at Best's, 100.37

Young America spreads it on thick, 47.114

Younger by design, 26.160

young man's magazine, The, 85.338

young point of view in shoes, The, 48.164

You ought to be in pictures, 85.355

You ought to meet Muriel, 115.186

You pay less for Gem Blades because you need so few, 104.57

You press the button, we do the rest, 89.35

Your air commuter service in 12 busy states, 4.73

Your anywhere, anything, anytime network, 111.32

Your assurance of quality in tape components, 5.58

Your assurance that this fabric has been pretested for performance by Celanese, 113.39

Your best bet over the long haul, 120.33

Your best food from the sea, 47.115

Your biggest bargain in cleanliness, 24.105

Your canary may be overfed, yet undernourished, 87.17

Your closest friend, 121.60

Your complexion's best friend, 32.86

Your daily dentist, 34.49

You're always safe with Baker's Magdolite, 35.141

You're asking for a good sock, 61.52

You're better off with Bostitch, 81.68

You're better off with Pan Am, 4.74

You're in good hands with Allstate, 64.113

You're in the money, 76.4

You're miles ahead with General Tire, 114.31

You're money ahead when you paint with White Lead, 82.83

You're money ahead with a Maytag, 60.149

You're not just flying. You're flying the friendly skies., 4.75

You're not just playing, you're learning, 28.86

You're sure of yourself in Phoenix, 61.53

You're the Pepsi generation, 107.58

You're tuned to 88 ... WCBS ... All news radio, 17.5

You're twice as sure with Frigidaire, 60.150

Your face never had it so clean!, 32.87

Your feet are worth Fortunes, 48.181

Your feet are your fortune, 48.182

Your first taste tells you and sells you, 14.153

Your friend, 48.183

Your friend in the home, on the highway, where you work, 64.114

Your future is our business today, 64.115

Your guardian for life, 64.116

Your Hartford agent does more than he really has to, 64.117

Your helping hand when trouble comes, 64.118

Your investment success is our business, 66.27

Your key to hospitality, 71.147

Your kitchen companion since 1899, 68.23

Your legs will thank you, 61.54

Your letterhead is the voice of your business, 83.87

Your life plan deserves expert guidance, 64.119

Your money goes farther in a General Motors car., 7.105

Your morning is as good as your mattress, 13.38

Your mouth will sing its praises, 34.50

Your nose quickly knows, 115.187

Your one-source solution to every filing problem, 81.69

Your peace of mind is worth the premium, 64.120

Your personal pedestal, 48.184

Your personal plane IS HERE, 3.26

Your printer's performance starts with fine papers, 83.88

Yours for a good morning, 21.51

Yours for growing satisfaction, 69.35

Yours for leisure, 60.151

Yours for Victory, 123.30

Your shoulders will thank you, 26.161

Your skin knows and shows the difference, 106.37

Your smoke comes clean, 115.188

Your strongest line of defense against gum disease, 34.51

Your symbol of quality and service, 114.32

Your teeth are only as healthy as your gums, 34.52

Your way of life depends upon your day of work, 42.59

Your windows are the lamps which light your rooms by day, 18.128

You save with paper, 83.89

You sleep ON it, not IN it, 13.39

You've Come A Long Way, Baby, 115.189

You've got the card, 43.64

You walk on cushions when you walk in Osteo-path-iks, 48.185

You want it. You got it., 4.76

You want something better, you're Wendy's kind of people, 99.12

You work hard, you need Right Guard, 116.31

Ze dash zat makes za dish, 29.50

Index II

Source Information

Index II

Source Information

This index contains, in one alphabetic order, all source information—product, company, individual, and institutional names—listed in the text. All items are indexed by first significant word or (where applicable) surname.

Aamco Transmissions, 9.11
Abbott Laboratories, 22.6
ABC Records Inc., 97.12
A. B. C. Super Electric, 60.7
Abilene Flour Mills, 11.36, 11.47
Abilene Flour Mills Co., 11.21
Abrasive Industry, 85.225
Ace combs, 54.10
A-C Electrical Mfg. Co., 95.29
Acme Appliance Mfg. Co., 55.26
Acme Glove Corp., 123.3
Acme Motor Truck Co., 120.22
Acme White Lead & Color Works, 82.72
Acushnet Co., 108.23
Adam Computers, 28.7
Adams Tea Room, J. N., Buffalo, N. Y., 99.10
ADC, 5.30
Addressograph-Multigraph Corp., 31.12, 81.9
Adirondack Bats Inc., 108.26
Adler elevator shoes, 48.184
Adler socks, 61.29, 61.48
Adler & Sons, David, 26.153
Administrative Management, 85.252
Admiral Corp., 95.8, 112.7
Admiration cigars, 115.17
Admiration soapless shampoo, 54.46
Adola brassiere, 121.16

Advance Pattern Co., 103.19, 103.20
Advertising Age, 85.120, 85.284
Advertising Council., The, 92.9
Aeolian Vocalion, 5.56
Aero Mayflower Transit Co. Inc., 79.1
Aeronca, 3.26
Aerowax, 24.64
Aetna Brewing Co., 14.18, 14.106
Aetna Life & Casualty, 64.1, 64.56, 64.69, 64.79, 64.81
Agfa-Gevaert Inc., 89.34
Agricultural Publishers Association, 85.163
Ahrend Co., D. H., 2.12
Aid-A-Walker shoes, 48.100
Aim toothpaste, 34.16
Airborne Freight Corp., 4.71
Air Canada, 4.1
Air Express, 4.27
Air France, 4.24, 4.35, 4.59, 4.62
Airhart, J. S., 35.66
Air-India, 4.45
Air King, 95.49
Airline honey, 47.41
Airlines of the U. S., 4.26
Air New Zealand, 4.43
Air Step shoes, 48.160, 48.171
Airtex Products Inc., 8.32
Aiwa, 5.7

Ajax, 24.13
Ajax all-purpose cleaner, 24.92
Ajax detergent, 24.80
Akai, 5.57
Akro Agate Co., 118.3
Alabama Power Co., 93.12
Aladdin Co., 18.33
Aladdin Laboratories Inc., 45.14
Aladdin Mfg. Co., 70.26
Alamac Hotel, Atlantic City, N. J., 62.24
Alaska Airlines Inc., 4.28
Alaska Refrigerator Co., 60.5
Alaska Travel Div., Department of Economic Development and Planning, 119.57
Albers Bros. Milling Co., 21.51
Alberto-Culver Co., 24.78, 54.33
Alberto VO5 hairspray, 54.33
Albert Soaps Co., 106.5
Alcoa, 75.20
Alexander Bros., 48.137
Alexander Mfg. Co., 126.44
Algoma Panel Co., 18.71
Alkaid, 35.100
Alka-Seltzer, 35.29, 35.73, 35.86
All-American Premium Beer, 14.16
All-American Radio Corp., 95.46, 95.47, 95.55
Allan Mfg. Co., 45.7
Allegheny Airlines Inc., 4.73
Allegheny Industrial and Chemical Co., 22.24
Allen, 7.76
Allen & Co., S. L., 69.10
Allen Mfg. Co., 58.2, 58.41
Allen's Foot Ease, 35.18
Allen-Spiegel Shoes, 48.185
Alliance Mfg. Co. Inc., 55.17
Allied Chemical Corp., 22.7, 22.21, 113.33
Allied Drug Products, 35.65
Allied Mills Corp., 42.7
Allied Van Lines Inc., 79.2, 79.4, 79.12
Alligator, 115.169
Alligator Co., The, 26.105
Alligator rainwear, 26.12
Allis Co., Louis, 37.17
Allis-Chalmers Mfg. Co., 42.2, 42.22, 42.52, 73.34
Allstate Insurance Co., 64.86, 64.113
All-Steel Equipment Inc., 81.44
Allsweet margarine, 47.92, 47.98

Almaden Vineyards Inc., 125.4, 125.16
Almay, 32.63
Alonzo, 35.4
Alpha Micro, 28.15, 28.81
Alta Vineyards Co., 125.6
Altman & Co., B., 100.23
Aluminum Co. of America, 75.4, 75.20, 75.32
Aluminum Goods Mfg. Co., 68.12
aluminum ware, 68.4
Aluminum Ware Association, 68.15
Amana Refrigeration Inc., 60.11, 60.12
AMC/Renault, 7.71
Amend Co., Fred W., 20.31
Amerdent mouth wash, 34.31
Amerdent tooth paste, 34.21
"America Fore" Insurance & Indemnity Group, 64.12
America Motors Corp., 7.104
American, 85.138
American Agricultural Chemical Co., 42.23, 42.39
American Airlines Inc., 4.4, 4.7, 4.10
American Association of Railroads, 96.11
American Baby, 85.142
American Beauties, 85.53
American Bosch Corp., 95.43, 95.52
American Boy, 85.61
American Brands Inc., 115.45, 115.73, 115.76, 115.95, 115.139, 115.171, 115.172
American Brass Co., 75.30
American Broadcasting Co., 17.4
American Broom & Brush Co., 24.1
American Cancer Society, 92.4, 92.6
American Can Co., 47.18
American Chain Co., 8.33
American Chewing Products Corp., 20.5, 20.15, 20.47, 20.49, 20.51, 20.70
American Chicle Co., 35.27, 35.39, 35.77
American Cigar Co., 115.48, 115.84, 115.85, 115.138
American Coffee Co., 27.19
American Cyanamid Co., 22.13, 24.14, 65.13, 82.33, 113.21, 113.35
American Dairy Association, 33.6, 33.17, 33.29, 33.45
American Distilling Corp., 71.97
American ElectrICE Corp., 60.123

American Engineering Co., 73.31
American Export Isbrandtsen Lines Inc., 102.17
American Express, 43.64
American Express card, 43.64, 119.14
American Express Co., 43.40, 66.11, 119.14, 119.15, 119.36
American Farming, 85.216
American Fruit Growers, 49.6
American Gas Association, 59.5, 59.6, 59.7, 59.10, 59.14, 59.25
American Gas Machine Co., 58.10, 58.23, 60.129, 70.3, 70.35, 98.4
American Girl Service, 40.3
American Hammer Corp., 117.30
American Hard Rubber Co., 54.10
American Hardware Mutual Insurance Co., 64.21
American Heart Association, 92.11
American Home, 85.168
American Home Foods Inc., 47.55
American Home Products Corp., 24.66
American Honda Motor Co. Inc., 7.34, 7.65, 77.1, 77.3
American Ice Co., 59.12
American Independent, 91.172, 91.286, 91.299
American Insurance Co., 64.109
American Latex Products Corp., 13.4
American Laundry Machinery Co., 25.2, 25.3
American Legion Monthly, 85.18
American Machine and Foundry Co., 108.8
American Machinist, 85.274
American Magazine, 85.346
American Manganese Bronze Co., 75.1
American Motors Corp., 7.18, 7.27, 7.49, 7.75, 7.95
American Mutual Insurance, 64.118
American Mutual Liability Insurance Co., 64.57, 64.63
American National Bank, 43.29
American Nickeloid Co., 75.3
American Optical Co., 41.3, 41.10
American Painter and Decorator, 85.40
American Party, 91.22
American Petroleum Institute, 119.32

American Photocopy Equipment Co., 30.2
American Poultry Advocate, 85.161
American President Lines, 102.4, 102.5, 102.28
American Press Association, 85.74
American Register Co., 83.20
American Republican Party, 91.21, 91.72
American Rice Products Co., 47.12
American Safety Razor Corp., 104.44
American Saint Gobain Corp., 18.22
American Saw & Mfg. Co., 117.39
American Sea Green Slate Co., 18.76
American Seating Co., 50.44
American Standard, 55.28
American Sugar Refining Co., 47.84, 47.111
American Tar & Chemical Co., 18.80
American Telecommunications Corporation, 111.22
American Telephone & Telegraph Co., *see* AT&T
American Thermos Products Co., 98.8
American Tobacco Co., 115.11, 115.12, 115.35, 115.36, 115.39, 115.49, 115.50, 115.52, 115.54, 115.57, 115.61, 115.67, 115.68, 115.77, 115.78, 115.79, 115.80, 115.102, 115.103, 115.108, 115.117, 115.119, 115.120, 115.141, 115.147, 115.158, 115.176, 115.181, 115.187
American Trucking Associations Inc., 120.24
American United Life Insurance Co., 64.82
American Walnut Mfrs. Assn., 18.81, 18.97, 49.30
American Weekly, 85.283
American Wine Co., 125.20
American Woman, 85.307
American Wool Council, 113.36
American Writing Paper Co., 83.72
American Yarn & Process Co., 103.9
American Zinc Institute, 75.31
America's Banks, 43.38
Amerikorn, 21.39
Amerock Corp., 18.3
AMF bowling equipment, 108.8
Amity Leather Products Co., 123.21

Amoco Chemicals Corp., 22.31
Amolin Co., 116.18
Amtrak, 96.3
Amway Corp., 24.37
Anacin analgesic, 35.51
Anaconda, 75.30
Anagyros Corp., S., 115.72
Anchor Hocking Glass Corp., 52.3, 52.9
Anchor Line., The, 102.22
Andersen Corp., 18.60, 18.122
Anderson Chemical Co. Inc., 22.23
Angelus lipstick, 32.25
Angelus marshmallows, 20.9
Anglo-American Mill Co., 11.16
Anglo-California Trust Co., 43.55
Anheuser-Busch Inc., 14.9, 14.23, 14.33, 14.34, 14.43, 14.53, 14.55, 14.69, 14.73, 14.75, 14.100, 14.101, 14.105, 14.119, 14.131, 14.136, 14.145, 14.148, 14.149, 107.3
Ansehl Co., B., 116.2
Anthracite Mining Association, 59.24
anti-glare panels, 28.18
Anti-Prohibition, campaign of 1932, 91.202, 91.263
Antonio, Roag & Langsdorg, 115.93
Antonio y Cleopatra, 115.139
Antrol, 86.8
Antrol Laboratories, 69.20, 86.8
Apex Coal Corp., 59.2
Apex vacuum cleaner, 60.76
A. P. Parts Corp., 8.46
Appollinaris carbonated water, 15.3
April Showers perfume, 84.26
A & P Stores, 100.6
Aqua Velva After Shave Lotion, 104.48
Aqua Velva cream, 32.40
Arbogast Co., Inc., Fred, 45.4
Arcade Mfg. Co., 118.9
Architectural and Engineering News, 85.127
Architecture, 85.310
Arch Preserver shoes, 48.77
Arcraft Broom Co., 24.63
Arctic electric fan, 60.138
Arcturus Radio Tube Co., 95.54
Arden, Elizabeth, 32.65
Ar-ex Products Inc., 32.76
Argosy, 85.294
Aris Gloves, 123.8

Aristocrat Leather Products, 72.24, 123.18
Arizona Republican, Phoenix, 85.316
Armour & Co., 22.16, 24.61, 74.3, 74.22, 74.23, 74.24, 74.25, 106.3
Armour Grain Co., 11.34
Armour's fertilizer, 42.30
Armstrong Cork Co., 46.15, 46.19, 46.30
Armstrong Cork & Insulation Co., 18.21
Armstrong flutes, 80.33
Armstrong Inc., Collin, 2.30
Arnel, 113.39
Arno Adhesive Tapes Inc., 35.99
Arnold Co., J. L., 2.31
Arrid deodorant, 116.6
Arro-lock shingles, 18.50
Arrow Liquors Co., 71.18, 71.50
ArtCarved Inc., 67.5
ArtCarved rings, 67.5
Art Digest, The, 85.288
Artificial Intelligence Corp., 28.58
Artistic Lighting Equipment Association, 70.15
Artkraft Sign Co., 2.25
Arvin Industries Inc., 31.35, 58.16
A-1 sauce, 29.36, 29.50
Asbestos Brake Lining Assn., 8.10
asbestos pads, 24.48
Asbestos Shingle, Slate and Sheathing Co., 18.7
Ashaway Line and Twine Mfg. Co., 45.8
ashcans, 60.84
Ashcraft-Wilkinson Co., 42.53
Ashland Oil and Refining Co., 88.60
Associated Brands, 116.27
Associated British Railways, 96.41
Associated Lighting Industries, 70.28
Associated Seed Growers, 42.6, 69.2, 69.8, 69.9, 69.22
Associated Tile Mfrs., 18.54
Associates Investment Co., 66.19
Association of American Railroads, 96.14, 96.18, 96.35, 96.57
Astyptodyne Chemical Co., 35.24
Atari, 28.9, 122.5
Athol Machine & Foundry Co., 73.29
Atlanta Biltmore, Atlanta, Ga, 62.27, 62.38

Atlanta Journal, 85.232
Atlantic City, New Jersey, 119.48
Atlantic Coast Line Railroad, 96.51, 96.52, 96.53
Atlantic Drier & Varnish Co., 82.8, 82.78
Atlantic Products Corp., 72.27
Atlantic Richfield Refining Co., 88.38, 88.39
Atlas Plycron, 114.29
Atlas Plywood Corp., 18.19
Atlas Supply Co., 114.21
Atlas tires, 114.21
Atra razors, 104.13
AT&T, 2.1, 2.3, 2.14, 2.17, 111.7, 111.9, 111.11, 111.13, 111.14, 111.15, 111.19, 111.20, 111.25, 111.28, 111.29, 111.32
Audio Devices Inc., 5.14
Audiotape, 5.14
Audio Technica, 5.12
Aunt Jemima pancake flour, 11.22
Aurora toilet paper, 83.76
Austin, Nichols and Co. Inc., 71.119, 71.143
Autocar, 120.25
automatic treadle-operated door, 18.85
Automotive Daily News, 85.13
Autonetics Div., North American Rockwell Corp., 38.10
Auto Owners Insurance Co., 64.49, 64.51
Auto-Pneumatic Action Co., 80.31
Avianca, 4.18
Avis Inc., 6.8
Avon cosmetics, 32.5
Avon Liquors Company, 71.38
Avon Products Inc., 32.5
Aztec Brewing Co., 14.140
Baash-Ross Div., Joy Mfg. Co., 117.19
Babbitt Inc., B. T., 24.5
Baby Bear Products Corp., 11.1, 11.50
baby chicks, 42.8
Baby Ruth candy bar, 20.7
Bacardi Imports Inc., 71.36, 71.58, 71.69, 71.115, 71.120
Bachman Chocolate Mfg. Co., 20.59
Bacno Postman Corp., 123.2, 123.17
bacon, 74.30, 74.32
Baer Bros., 82.51
Baggies trash bags, 68.7

Bailey's Irish Cream liqueur, 71.89
Baker, Frentress & Co., 66.2
Baker Bros. Inc., 73.16
Baker Importing Co., 27.50
Baker's cocoa, 11.17, 11.42
Baker's Magdolite, 35.141
Balart Co., Alexander, 27.63
Baldwin Co., D. H., 80.36
Baldwin National Bank & Trust Co., 43.9
Baldwin Piano & Organ Co., 80.4
Bali Brassiere Co., 121.10
Ballantine, 14.135
Balm-o-Lem, 32.3
Baltimore Copper Paint, 82.25
Baltimore Luggage Co., 72.2, 72.8, 72.11
Baltimore News-Post, 85.113
Baltimore & Ohio Railroad, 96.2, 96.20, 96.24, 96.25, 96.29, 96.54, 96.55, 96.78
Baltimore Salesbook, 81.14, 81.22, 81.34
Baltimore Sun, 85.58, 85.84
Baltzer boats, 16.5
Band-Aid, 35.58, 35.131
Bankers Accident Insurance Co., 64.110
Bankers Life Insurance Co. of Nebraska, 64.87
Bankers Trust Co., 43.5, 43.26
Bank of America, 43.17
Bank of Bay of Biscayne, 43.20
Bank of the Southwest, 43.50
Bank of the United States, 43.2
Barbasol shaving cream, 104.25, 104.26
Barber Asphalt Co., 18.123
Barber's Journal, 85.326
Barbey's Inc., 14.129
Barclay and Co. Ltd., Jas, 71.41
Barclay cigarettes, 115.156
Barister cigars, 115.71
Barr & Co., W. M., 82.21
Barrett Co., The, 42.40
Barrington Hall, 27.50
Barron-Anderson Co., 26.5
Barrthea garters and suspenders, 61.45
Barton and Guestier, 125.24
Barton Corp., 60.133
Barton Salt Co., 29.40
Barwick Industries Inc., E. T., 46.35

Bassett Furniture Industries Inc., 50.6

Baston Co. Inc., J. R., 61.3

Bates Shoe Co., 48.115

Bates & Son, C. J., 103.11

Battery Div., Sonotone Corp., 37.23

batteryless radio sets, 95.35

Bauer & Black, 35.121

Bausch & Lomb Optical Co., 41.12, 41.13

Bavarian Brewing Co., 14.15

Bavarian Motor Works, 7.77

Bayer aspirin, 35.6, 35.16, 35.42

Bayuk Cigars Inc., 115.145

B. B. Chemical Div., United Shoe Machinery Corp., 1.4

Beach Soap Co., 24.86

Beacon Falls Rubber Co., 48.130

Beam Distilling Co., James B., 71.135

Bear Brand yarn, 103.21

Beardsley's Sons, J. W., 47.53

Bearing Co. of America, 8.42

Bear Mfg. Co., 8.41

Beau, 85.266

Beautyrest, 13.36

Beaver-Remmers Co., 106.37

Beaver-Remmers-Graham Co., 32.12

Beech Aircraft Corp., 3.1, 3.21

Beechalex laxative, 35.40

Beecham Products Inc., 35.8, 35.102, 35.111, 35.140, 54.1

Beecham's pills, 35.111, 35.140

Beechnut, 27.40

Beech-nut gum, 20.6, 20.8

Beechnut Packing Co., 20.62

Beefeater gin, 71.37, 71.96, 71.106

Beich, Paul F., 20.16

Bekins Van and Storage Co., 79.10

Belcraft Shirt Co., 26.18

Belding-Hall Electric Corp., 60.22, 60.33

Bell, John, 91.45, 91.216, 91.373

Bell Aircraft Corp., 3.16, 3.20

Bell and Howell Co., 89.2, 89.3

Belle Glove Co., 123.12

Belle-Sharmeer, 61.18

Belle-Sharmeer hosiery, 61.19

Bellevue Stratford, Philadelphia, 62.23

Bell Helicopter Co., 3.24

Bell & Howell Co., 89.9

Bell's Blended scotch, 71.2

Bell System, 111.7, 111.8, 111.13, 111.15, 111.19

Bell Telephone Co., 111.4, 111.24, 111.27

Bell thread, 103.7

Bemis Mfg. Co., 55.4

Bendix Aviation Corp., 3.3, 3.7

Bendix Corp., 31.36

Bendix Radio Division, 95.15, 95.28, 95.39, 95.53, 95.58, 95.70

Bendix washer, 60.51, 60.96

Benedict Mfg. Co., 67.28

Benefax, 56.12

Benefit Trust Life Insurance, 64.103

Beneke Corp., 55.33

Benex brushless shave, 104.37

Benjamin Electric Mfg. Co., 37.16, 60.94

Benrus Watch Co., 124.49

Bergmann Shoe Mfg. Co., 48.141

Bergman, Theo, 48.144

Bergstrom Paper Co., 83.6

Berkeley Square Clothes, 26.155

Berkley Knitting Co., 26.19

Berkshire International Corp., 61.14

Berkshire Knitting Mills, 61.2, 61.11, 61.27

Berman and Associates Inc., Jules, 71.40

Bernhard Ulman Co., 103.21

Berry Bros. & Co., 71.3

Beryllium Corp., The, 75.5

Beseler Co., Charles, 89.31

Best & Co., 100.37

Best Foods, 29.5

Best Foods Div., Corn Products Co., 47.100

Best Foods Div., CPC International Inc., 29.45

Best Form Brassiere Co. Ltd., 121.45

Best Form corset, 121.45

Best Pleat Nip-tite, 65.10

Best Seed Co., 69.15

Betsy Ross spinet, 80.1

Better Bedding Alliance of America, 13.12

Better Cheddars, 47.101

Better Homes & Gardens, 85.27, 85.29, 85.101, 85.128, 85.129

Better Vision Institute, 41.1

Between the Acts, 115.4

Bewley's flour, 11.2

bias fold tapes, 103.22

Bi-Car Gum Co., 20.10
Big Ben, 124.12, 124.21, 124.23, 124.44
Big Brother, 92.8
Bigelow-Sanford Inc., 46.5, 46.22
Biggs Antique Co. Inc., 50.38
Big Horn, 27.60
Bilco Co., 18.2
bill posters, 2.36
Billy the Kid slacks, 26.107
Biltmore Hotel, 62.4
Biltrite Rubber Co., 48.103
Biltwell tires, 114.7
Biolac, 10.3
bird seed, 87.2
Birds Eye Div., General Foods Corp., 47.17
Bird & Son Inc., 18.12, 18.83, 18.98, 46.4
Birmingham News, 85.311
Bisceglia Bros. Corp., 125.15, 125.18, 125.28
Biscuit & Cracker Mfrs. Assn., 11.40
Bishman Mfg. Co., 8.59
Bishop Candy Co. Inc., 20.27
Bishop Industries Inc., 32.28
Bismarck Hotel, Chicago, 62.37
Bisquick, 11.52
Bissell Carpet Sweeper Co., 60.36, 60.77
Black, H. & L., 26.139
Black and White, 71.123, 71.140
Black and White face powder, 32.35
Black & Decker Mfg. Co., 63.16, 117.8, 117.18, 117.32
Black Flag insect spray, 86.7
Black Label beer, 14.104
Black Mfg. Co., 26.90
Black Silk Stove Polish Works, 24.3
Blackstone cigars, 115.136
Blaine, James G., 91.68, 91.160, 91.203, 91.245, 91.407
Blank and Co. Inc., Frederic, 65.11
blanket binding, 103.8
Blatz, 14.84, 14.137
Bliss Medical Co., 35.4
Blistex Inc., 32.11
Blistex lip balm, 32.11
Block Drug Co. Inc., 34.28, 34.29, 34.39, 35.25, 35.110
Blu-Cold refrigerators, 60.4
Bluebird Appliance Co., 60.18
Blue Co. Inc., John, 42.37

Blue Jay corn plaster, 35.35
Blue Moon Silk Hosiery Co., 61.20
Blue Reprint machines, 30.1
Blue Ribbon mayonnaise, 29.15
Blue Shield, 64.22
Blue Streak, 8.68
Blumenthal Co., F., 48.47
BMW, 7.77
bobby pins, 54.25
body repair, 9.10
Boeing Co., 3.4, 3.23
Bolens Div., FMC Corp., 42.19
Boling Chair Co., 50.9, 50.16
Bols liqueurs, 71.35
Bon Ami cleanser, 24.36
Bon Ami Co., 24.36
Bonded Floors Co., 46.24
Bonded Tobacco Co., 115.82, 115.157
Bond Handkerchief Co., 123.1, 123.20, 123.30
Bond Street pipe tobacco, 115.23
Bon Merito rum, 71.117
Bonnart Inc., Sam, 26.1
Bonne Bell Inc., 32.87
Bonwit Teller & Co., 100.24
Boot and Shoe Recorder, 85.116, 85.143, 85.302
Borden Chemical Div., Borden Inc., 1.2
Borden Inc., 27.67, 33.5, 33.11, 33.21, 33.22, 33.30, 33.32, 33.35, 33.46, 33.47
Borden's instant, 27.67
Borden's Prescription Prods., 10.3
Borg-Warner Corp., 31.24, 60.144
Borkman Radio Corp., 95.34
Bosch Corp., 8.3, 8.6
Boss, B. S., 32.2
Bost Inc., 34.9, 34.40, 34.46
Bostitch Div., Textron Inc., 81.68
Boston Confectionery Co., 20.63
Boston Globe, 85.223
Boston Herald., 85.345
Bostonian, 48.34
Bostonian Shoe Co., 48.46
Boston Store, 100.28
Boston Traveler, 85.45
Boston Varnish Co., 82.57
Boston Woven Hose Co., 61.50
Bost tooth paste, 34.40
Botany shirts, 26.43

Bottlers Supply & Manufacturing
Co., 107.52
Bounty paper towels, 83.70
Bowdil Co., The, 73.2
Bowlene, 24.98
Boyle Co., A. S., 24.32, 56.5, 86.7
Boyle-Midway, 24.70, 24.89
Boys' Life, 85.199
Bozeman Canning Co., 47.79
Brach, 20.68
Brach & Sons., B. J., 20.68
Bradley Knitting Co., 26.92
Bradley & Vrooman Co., 82.26,
82.27, 82.73
brake linings, 8.29
Brandes Inc., 95.62
Braniff Airways Inc., 4.39
Brauer Bros. Shoe Co., 48.110
Braumeister beer, 14.83
Bray Screen Products, 70.9
Brearley Co., The, 12.2, 12.6
Breck Inc., John H., 54.3
Breckinridge, John C., 91.52, 91.56,
91.218, 91.227, 91.405
Breidt Brewing Co., 14.5, 14.28,
14.114, 14.117, 14.118
Breon Laboratories Inc., 10.5
Brewer's Best, 14.132
Brewery Corp. of America, 14.139
Brewing Corp. of America, 14.104,
14.128
Breyer's ice cream, 33.36
Brick and Clay Record, 85.133
brick-oven beans, 47.13
Bridgeport luggage, 72.12
Briggs pipe mixture, 115.134,
115.160, 115.175
Brighton Wide-Web garters, 61.54
Bright 100's cigarettes, 115.185
Brillion Iron Works Inc., 42.15
Brim decaffeinated, 27.21
Brisacher & Staff, Emil, 2.23
Bristol-Myers Co., 34.14, 34.15,
34.47, 35.94, 35.113, 54.22
Bristol Pro-Golf Inc., 108.36
Britelite Co., 24.20, 24.56, 70.11
British European Airways, 4.15
British Overseas Airways Corp., 4.5,
4.32, 4.40
British Petroleum Co., London,
88.18
Broadcast Redi-Meat, 74.4
Brockenridge Brewing Co., 14.99
Brockton Footwear Inc., 48.114

Brockway Motor Trucks, 120.2
Broderick Co., Tom, 26.154
Brokaw-Eden Mfg. Co., 60.103
Bromo Seltzer, 35.26, 35.54
Brooke Bond Foods, 27.38
Brookfield, 33.39
Brooklawn corduroy, 113.5
Brooklyn Standard Union, 85.130
Brooklyn Varnish Co., 82.7
Brown Co., 83.69
Browne Vintners Co., 125.5, 125.33
Brown-Forman Distillers Corp.,
71.7, 71.35, 71.118, 71.125
Brown Friar whiskey, 71.68
Brown & Haley, 20.24
Browning Arms Co., 44.7, 45.3
Browning King & Co., New York,
100.3
Brown Instrument Co., 63.14
Brown Medicine Co., 35.139
Brown pyrometers, 63.14
Brown & Sharpe Mfg. Co., 55.8
Brown Shoe Co., 48.89, 48.106,
48.158, 48.164, 48.171
Brown & Williamson Tobacco Corp.,
115.28, 115.29, 115.44, 115.64,
115.101, 115.116, 115.118, 115.140,
115.148, 115.153, 115.156, 115.163,
115.164, 115.188
Bruce Co., E. L., 18.42
Bruckmann Co., 14.65
Bruning Co., Chas, 30.9
Brunswick-Balke-Collender, 97.3
Brunswick Corp., 16.8, 16.11, 108.17,
108.32
Brunswick Rubber Co., 114.9
Bryan, William Jennings, 91.25,
91.59, 91.74, 91.109, 91.171, 91.181,
91.207, 91.287, 91.289, 91.313,
91.319
Bryant Heater Co., 58.3, 58.8, 58.36
Brylcreem, 54.1
BSR (USA) Ltd., 5.47
Buchanan, James, 91.44, 91.156,
91.350
Buckeye Aluminum Co., 68.14
Buckeye Producing Co., 14.49, 14.95
Buckeye Shirt Co., 26.46
Bucyrus-Erie Co., 73.6
Budd Co., 31.13, 31.29, 31.37
Bud Light, 14.33, 14.119
Budweiser, 14.9, 14.23, 14.34, 14.43,
14.55, 14.69, 14.73, 14.75, 14.100,
14.105, 14.131, 14.148

Buescher Band Instrument Co., 80.16
Buhner Fertilizer Co., 42.3
Buick, 7.17, 7.19, 7.23, 7.81, 7.93, 7.101
Building Construction, 85.246
Building Supply News, 85.126, 85.207
Bulldog paint remover, 82.21
Bulldog Venetian blind cleaner, 24.45
Bull Durham tobacco, 115.120, 115.147
Bulletin, The, 85.80
Bully toilet bowl cleaner, 24.21
Bulova Watch Co. Inc., 124.4, 124.7, 124.28, 124.63
Bulova watches, 124.4, 124.7, 124.28
bumpers, 8.2, 8.50
Bunnell & Co., J. H., 111.18
Bunte Bros., 35.88
Burdett Shoe Co., 48.76
Burke-Worthington, 108.27
Burk Inc., Ben, 71.11, 71.67
Burleigh Brooks Inc., 89.5
Burlington Industries Inc., 61.29, 61.48, 113.29
Burlington Route, 96.23, 96.74
Burnham Inc., E., 32.48
Burnham & Morrill Co., 47.13
Burns Cuboid Co., 48.63
Burson Knitting Co., 61.17
Busch, 14.53
Busch Pale Dry, 14.136
Bushmill's whiskey, 71.74, 71.80, 71.88
Business Advertising Agency, 2.9
Business Jets Div., Pan American World Airways Inc., 3.17
business machines, 81.43
Business Week, 85.176
Business Week magazines, 85.325
Bussman Mfg. Co., 70.32
Buster Boy Suit Co., 26.79
Butler, Benjamin, 91.420
butter, 33.2, 33.12
butterscotch, 20.12, 20.13
Butzer Packing Co., 74.1
Buxton Inc., 123.7
Byer-Rolnick, 26.125
Byers Machine Co., 73.30
Byrd Industries Inc., 98.6
cable television movie service, 78.15
Cabot Corp., 22.30

Cadbury's Ltd., 20.43
Cadillac, 7.21, 7.46, 7.48, 7.87
Cahners Publishing Co. Inc., 94.5, 94.15
Cal-Aero Technical Institute, Glendale, Calif, 101.2
Cal Comp, 28.22, 28.42, 28.43
California cling peaches, 49.29
California Computer Products Inc., 28.22, 28.42, 28.43
California Packing Corp., 15.31, 27.31, 27.42
California Prune & Apricot Growers, 15.12, 49.13
California Redwood Assn., 18.65, 18.115
California Walnut Growers Assn., 49.2, 49.9
Caloric Corp., 60.16, 60.106
Calumet Baking Powder Co., 11.7
Calvert blended whiskey, 71.31, 71.45
Camay soap, 106.2
Camel, 115.8, 115.33, 115.133, 115.167
Camel fountain pen, 126.11
cameras, 89.10, 89.13, 89.17
Cameron Machine Co., 73.3
Cameron nylons, 61.26
Cammillus Cutlery Co., 55.7
Campana Balm, 32.71
Campana Corp., 32.16, 32.71, 32.86
Campbell foods, 47.22
Campbell's corn flakes, 21.14
Campbell Soup Co., 47.3, 47.42, 47.75, 47.81, 47.102, 47.105
Campbell's soups, 47.3, 47.42
camp stoves, 98.16
Canada Dry Corp., 107.34
Canada Dry ginger ale, 107.34
Canada Health Foods Ltd., 56.1
Canada Steamship Lines Ltd., 102.11
Canadian Club, 71.92
Canadian Ministry of Tourism, 119.2
Canadian National Railroad Co., 96.19, 96.64
Canadian Pacific Air Lines, 4.51
Canadian Pacific Railway, 96.16, 96.50, 96.80
Canadian Pacific Steamship & Railroad Co., 102.19, 119.31, 119.33, 119.55

Canadian Steamship Lines Ltd., 102.3
Canadian Westinghouse Co., 37.7
Candy and Ice Cream, 85.318
candy mint, 20.25
Canfield Oil Co., 88.61
Cannon Mills Co., 12.3, 13.7
Cannon Oiler Co., 68.6
Cannon towels & sheets, 13.7
Canon Inc., 89.4
Canterbury, 110.13
Cantrece, 113.26
CāPac, 8.27, 8.35
Capewell Mfg. Co., 117.2
Capitol Records Inc., 97.1, 97.2
Capper's Farmer, 85.241
Caprolan, 113.33
Caradco Inc., 18.48
Carbola Chemical Co., 82.48, 82.64
Cardine Hat Co., 26.27
Carey Salt Co., 29.48, 34.8
Carhartt, Hamilton, 26.57
Caritol, 35.17
Carling National Breweries Inc., 14.27, 14.56, 14.60, 14.81
Carling's ale, 14.27, 14.60
Carlisle Chemical Works Inc., 22.22
Carlisle Shoe Co., 48.147
Carlton, 115.76
Carnation Albers cereals, 21.51
Carnation Co., 33.15, 33.43, 87.4, 87.8, 87.12
Carnes Corp., 58.35
Carnival Creations Inc., 121.53
Carolina Mirror Corp., 65.22
Carpenter-Morton, 82.34
Carpenter Steel Co., The, 75.15
car radios, 95.27, 95.43
Carrier Corp., 58.43
car speakers, 5.2, 5.21
Carstairs Bros., 71.24, 71.48, 71.109
car stereos, 5.1, 5.19, 5.27, 5.52
Carter, Jimmy, 91.163
Carter Carburetor Corp., 8.38
Carter's Compound Extract, 35.139
Carter's Ink Co., 126.45
Carter & Sons, H. W., 26.149
Carter's pills, 35.132
Carter-Wallace Inc., 35.132, 116.6
Carter White Lead Co., 82.10, 82.20, 82.30, 82.67, 82.81
cartridges, (audio) 5.4, 5.12, 5.34; (firearms) 44.11
Carven Parfums, 84.12

Cascada SA, 11.33
Cascade, 24.8, 24.31, 24.71
Casco Co., 35.12
Cashmere Bouquet, 106.1, 106.28
Cashmere Bouquet soap, 106.35
Cashmere Bouquet talcum, 32.69
Casio Inc., 124.8
Casio watches, 124.8
Cass, Gen. Lewis, 91.180, 91.247, 91.314, 91.410
cassette decks, 5.32
cassettes, 5.6
Cassini Inc., Oleg, 61.7
Castile soap, 106.7
Castle Furniture Co., 50.13, 50.17
Castolay, 106.12
Caswell-Massey Co., 24.74
Caswell Mfg. Co., 5.23
Cataract washer, 60.25
Caterpillar Tractor Co., 73.19
Cat's Paw, 48.136
catsup, 29.34
CBS radio network, 17.3
Ceco Weatherstrip Co., 18.39
Cedar Rapids Block Co., 18.99
Celanese Corp., 113.1, 113.8, 113.39
Celebrated Products Sales, 32.8, 32.49
Celestial Seasonings, 110.12
Celotex Corp., 18.91
Central Breweries Inc., 14.48, 14.133
Central Illinois Light Co., 93.15
Central National Bank & Trust Co., 43.13
Central Oil & Gas Stove Co., 58.24, 58.42
Central Soya Co. Inc., 31.23, 42.36
Central Trust & Savings Co., 43.49
Century Electric Co., 37.32, 93.8
Cercle D'Or Inc., 125.1, 125.11
Certified Milk Producers of Southern California, 33.4
Certigrade Red Cedar Shingles, 18.34
Cessna Aircraft Co., 3.6, 3.12, 3.13
Chain Store Age, 85.39
Challenge Foods Co., 33.3
Challenge milk, 33.3
Chambers Corp., 60.32, 60.75
Champale, 14.12
Champion Animal Food Co., 87.10
Champion Mfg. Co. Inc., 70.7
Champion Papers Inc., 83.14, 83.15

Champion Spark Plug Co., 8.13, 8.54, 8.66
Chanel Inc., 84.8, 84.30, 84.31
Chanel No. 22, 84.31
Channel Chemical Co., 24.10, 24.88
Chap Stick, 35.56
Chap Stick Co., 32.64
Charles of the Ritz Group Ltd., 32.6, 84.4
Charleston Mattress Mfg. Co., 13.9
Charlton Co., 50.41, 50.56
Charm underlift brassiere, 121.47
Chartreuse, 71.52
Chase Brass & Copper, 60.135
Chase Manhattan Bank, 43.18, 43.63
Chase & Sanborn, 27.10, 27.34
Chattanooga, Tenn, 36.19
Cheek-Neal Coffee Co., 27.1, 27.5, 27.36, 27.53
Chemical Bank, New York, 43.48
Chemical Div., General Mills Inc., 22.19
Chemicals Inc., 24.42
Chemical Week, 85.121
Cheney Talking Machine Co., 5.36
Cheramy Inc., 84.16
Cherristock, 71.91
Chesapeake & Ohio Railroad, 96.5, 96.7, 96.42, 96.47
Chesebrough-Pond's Inc., 32.32, 35.36, 35.38, 35.79, 54.44, 116.3, 116.15
Chess, Mary, 84.21
Chesterfield, 115.42, 115.110, 115.121, 115.125, 115.162, 115.170
Chevrolet, 7.3, 7.24, 7.43, 7.52, 7.60, 7.94, 7.103
Chevrolet Div., General Motors Corp., 120.8
Chevrolet trucks, 120.13
Chicago American, 85.5
Chicago, Burlington & Quincy Railroad Co., 96.8, 96.27
Chicago & Eastern Illinois Railway, 96.71
Chicago Engineering Works, 73.13
Chicago Musical Instrument Co., 80.33
Chicago Paper Co., 83.58
Chicago Rawhide Mfg. Co., 8.40, 8.61
Chicago Roller Skate Co., 118.16, 118.17

Chicago Steel Post Co., 18.5
Chicago Tribune, 85.333
Chicago Wheel & Mfg. Co., 117.10, 117.13
Chicken of the Sea tuna, 47.29, 47.60, 47.90
Chiffon soap flakes, 24.61
Child Life, 85.167, 85.203
Children, 85.244
Children's Tylenol, 35.115
Childs cigar, G. W., 115.48
Child's Restaurants, 99.6
children's suits, 26.120
Chillicothe Paper Co., 83.13
Chivers & Sons Ltd., 47.9
Chloraseptic, 35.72
Chlorax, 34.41
Chock Full O' Nuts, 27.13
Chock Full O' Nuts Corp., 27.13
Chock Full O' Nuts Restaurants, 99.9
chocolate malted milk, 33.46
Christian Brothers, 125.35
Christian Herald, 85.141
Christian Science Monitor, Boston, 85.49
Christmas Club, 43.30, 43.36
Chrysler, 7.14
Chrysler Corp., 7.14, 7.20, 7.37, 7.50, 7.72, 7.90, 7.100, 7.102, 120.9, 120.14
Chuckles, 20.31
Church Div., C. F. American Standard Inc., 55.31
Churchman., The, 85.8, 85.237
CIBA Products Co., 18.27
cigarette holders, 105.12, 105.17
cigars, 115.14, 115.31, 115.37, 115.59, 115.92, 115.123, 115.126
Cincinnati Elec. Prods. Co., 37.20
Cincinnati Enquirer, 85.114
Cincinnati Post, 85.182
Cinco, 115.145
Cincom Systems Inc., 28.16
Cinemax, 78.15
CinZano, 125.34
Circle 12 books, 94.2
Cities Service Co., 22.10, 88.4
Citizens & Southern Bank, 43.31
Citizens Trust Co., 43.16
Citrus World Inc., 15.36
Clabber Girl baking powder, 11.44
Clairex Corp., 38.14
Clairol hair color, 54.30

Clairol Inc., 32.59, 32.72, 32.73, 54.9, 54.13, 54.18, 54.27, 54.30, 54.36
Clan Crest, 113.11
Clapp's baby foods, 10.6
Clarion, 5.19
Clark Co., D. L., 20.48
Clark Distilling Corp., James, 14.70, 71.34
Clarke & Co., A. L., 103.13
Clark Harp Mfg. Co., 80.7
Clark's Teaberry gum, 20.45
Clay, Henry, 91.7, 91.21, 91.72, 91.73, 91.127, 91.128, 91.174, 91.256, 91.310, 91.312, 91.345
cleaner, 24.46
Cleveland, Grover, 91.24, 91.112, 91.143, 91.277, 91.292, 91.302, 91.337, 91.375, 91.399, 91.419
Cleveland Plain Dealer, 2.21
Cleveland Press, 85.89
Cleveland-Sandusky Brewing Corp., 14.107
Cleveland Tractor Co., 42.29, 42.38, 42.43
Cleveland Trust Co., 43.44
Clicquot Club Co., 107.25, 107.43
Climalene Co., The, 24.98
Clinical Lab, 34.34
Clinton Carpet Co., 46.12
Clorox bleach, 24.2, 24.29, 24.94
Clorox Co., 24.2, 24.29, 24.94
club soda, 107.4
Cluett, Peabody & Co. Inc., 26.45, 26.156, 113.6
coaxial cable, 38.17
Coca-Cola, 107.13, 107.17, 107.31
Coca-Cola Co., 107.13, 107.15, 107.17, 107.28, 107.30, 107.31, 107.37, 107.45, 107.48, 107.51
Cocker Machine and Foundry Co., 73.33
cocktail mixes, 71.113
cocoanut oil shampoo, 54.6
Cocomalt, 15.1
codfish cakes, 47.53
Codo Mfg. Co., 83.63
Codville Co. Ltd., 11.23
Coffee Products of America, 27.29
Coffield washer, 60.37
Coins of All Nations, 76.4
Coldspot freezers, 60.124
ColeCo., 28.7, 28.17
Coleman Co. Inc., 98.9

Coleman Lamp Co., 58.38, 60.108, 70.6, 70.36, 70.45, 98.5, 98.10, 98.16
Colfanite Prods. Co., 82.2
Colgate & Co., 104.28, 104.34
Colgate dental cream, 34.18, 34.25
Colgate-Palmolive Co., 24.6, 24.13, 24.15, 24.58, 24.80, 24.92, 32.69, 34.18, 34.25, 34.45, 54.34, 54.35, 54.37, 68.7, 106.1, 106.9, 106.13, 106.18, 106.22, 106.28, 106.35
Colgate Ribbon dental cream, 34.45
College Humor, 85.196
Collette Tours, 119.51
Collier's, 85.285
Collins Radio Co., 38.3
Colombo Inc., Leopold, 50.30
Colonial Chemical Corp., 86.10
Colonial Products Co., 18.114
Colophane Corp., 82.16
Colorado, 119.12
Colorado Chemical Co., 34.19
coloring, 29.32
Colt 45 Malt Liquor, 14.56
Colt Patent Fire Arms Mfg. Co., 44.3, 44.18
Columbia, 85.236
Columbia bicycles, 98.13
Columbia Broadcasting System Inc., 17.3
Columbia Casualty Co., 64.35
Columbia Graphophone Co., 81.10, 81.57
Columbia Manufacturing Co. Inc., The, 98.13
Columbia Mills Inc., 18.128, 65.19
Columbia Pictures Corp., 78.4
Columbia Protektosite Co., 76.2
Columbus Dispatch, 85.151
Columbus-Union Oil Cloth Co., 65.18
Combe Inc., 54.41
Combustion Engineering Inc., 31.16
Comet Rice Co., 21.25
Comfort Magazine, 85.235
Command, 97.12
Commercial Appeal and *Evening Appeal,* Memphis, 85.77
Commercial Appeal, Memphis, 85.312
Commercial Credit Co., 66.5
Commercial Laboratories, 104.19
Commercial Photo Service Co., 89.22

Commodore, 28.52
Common Brick Mfrs. Assn. of America, 18.10
Commonwealth, 7.62
Commonwealth Shoe & Leather Co., 48.34, 48.127
Community silver, 67.22
Compaq Computer Corporation, 28.8
Comprehensive Fabrics Inc., 113.17
Comptone Co., 41.9
Compton's Encyclopaedia, 94.13
computer systems, 28.77
Comtrex Cold Reliever, 35.94
Concord, 5.1
condensed milk, 33.30
Conewango Furniture Co., 50.59
Confections Inc., 20.46
Congoleum, 46.37
Congoleum Corp., 46.7, 46.27, 46.37
Congoleum rugs, 46.7
Congress Cigar Co., 115.88
Conklin Pen Mfg. Co., 126.25, 126.37
Conmark Plastics Div., Cohn-Hall-Marx Co., 113.25
Conmar zippers, 103.17
Connecticut Dept. of Economic Development, 119.7
Connecticut General Life Insurance Co., 64.107
Connecticut Mutual Life Insurance Co., 64.80
Connecticut Valley Brewing Co., 14.29
Conn Inc., C. G., 80.5
Connolly Shoe Co., 48.5, 48.28
Conn Organ Corp., 80.8
Connor Lumber and Land Co., 18.49
Conoco, 88.27
Conoco Inc., 88.53
Consolidated Aluminum Corp., 75.12
Consolidated Cigar Corp., 115.41, 115.81, 115.127, 115.186
Consolidated Edison Co., 93.5
Consolidated Freightways Inc., 120.10
Consolidated Motors Corp., 120.29
Consolidated Vultee, 3.2, 3.5
Consolidated yachts, 16.16

Conso Products Co., Div. Consolidated Foods Corp., 65.4, 65.10
Constitutional Unionist, 91.216, 91.373
Constitutional Union party, 91.45
Constitution, Atlanta, 85.313
Construction Methods and Equipment, 85.170
Consumers Public Power District, 37.3
Contac cold capsules, 35.49
Contac cold medicine, 35.34, 35.44
Contac cough capsules, 35.108
Continental Air Lines Inc., 4.8, 4.34
Continental Baking Co. Inc., 11.20
Continental Distilling Corp., 71.30, 71.122
Continental Envelope Corp., 83.62
Continental Jewelry Co., 67.9
Continental Oil Co., 88.27
Continental Steel Corp., 75.36
Continental Tobacco Co., 115.15
Continental Trailways Bus System, 19.1, 19.4
Conti Products, 106.7
Contoure Laboratories, 32.13
Converse Rubber Co., 48.98, 48.176
Cookie Jar tobacco, 115.2
Cookson Co., 18.11
Coolidge, Calvin, 91.14, 91.46, 91.47, 91.48, 91.49, 91.50, 91.53, 91.158, 91.177, 91.279
Coon Co., W. B., 48.91, 48.170
Cooper Laboratories, 34.48
Cooper Lamps Inc., Frederick, 70.24
Cooper & Nephews Inc., William, 86.11
Cooper Tire and Rubber Co., 114.2
Cooper Underwear Co., 121.11
Copeland Products, 60.143
Coppers Engineering Corp., 73.9
Coppertone Corp., The, 32.15
Coppes Bros. & Zook, 18.17
Corby's, 71.41
Cordova guitars, 80.18
Corega Chemical Co., 34.36
Corning Glass Works, 68.2, 68.3
Corning Ware, 68.2
Corn Kix, 21.27
Corn Products Co., 47.62
Corn Products Refining Co., 47.24
corn salve, 35.15, 35.32

Coronado Hotel, The, St. Louis, 62.18
Coronet Toy Mfg. Co., 118.14
corsets, 121.58, 121.59
Corvair, Monza, 7.64
Cosmair Inc., 54.20
Costello Co., Celestino, 115.71
Costumakers, 103.4
Cotton, 85.267
Cotton Producers Institute, 113.7, 113.30
cottonseed meal, 42.53
Coty, 32.82
Coty Div., Chas. Pfizer and Co. Inc., 84.11
Coty Inc., 104.17
Coty 24 Hour lipstick, 32.66
cough drops, 35.88, 35.101
Council for Financial Aid to Education, 92.1
Council meats, 74.2, 74.8
Counselor bathroom scales, 12.2, 12.6
Country Doctor pipe mixture, 115.128
Country Gardens Inc., 47.14
Country Gentleman, 85.271
Courtley toiletries, 116.22
Courvoisier cognac, 71.93
Coventry Inc., Sarah, 67.10, 67.21
Cowden Mfg. Co., 26.157
Cowles Detergent Co., 24.34
Cox, James M., 91.159
CPC International Inc., 24.54, 29.2, 47.46, 47.51, 47.59
C-P Fittings Div., Essex Wire Corp., 8.21
Crabbs Taylor Reynolds Elevator Co., 42.16
Crackerjack Co., 20.9
Crackerjacks, 20.65
Craig Co., Ltd., O. C., Winnipeg, 104.41
Crane Co., 31.28, 55.9, 55.16
Crane & Co. Inc., 83.64
Crane's, 33.37
Crane's papers, 83.64
Crawford, McGregor & Canby Co., 108.10
Cream of Rice, 21.34
Cream of Wheat, 21.38, 21.46
Creole pralines, 20.69
Crescent Mfg. Co., 27.65
Creslan, 113.21

Cresta Blanca, 125.8, 125.22, 125.30
Crisby Frisian Fur Co., 26.75
Crisco shortening, 47.47
Crocker-Citizens National Bank, 43.47
Crocker Hamilton Papers Inc., 83.88
Cromar Co., The, 46.20
Crop Life, 85.3
Crosley, 95.11
Crosman Arms Co., 44.17, 44.23
Cross Co., A. T., 126.4
Cross Co., The, 73.10
Crosse & Blackwell, 29.38
Crossett Co., L. A., 48.93
Croton Aquamat, 124.64
Croton Time Corp., 124.34, 124.64
Croton watch, 124.34
Crown Central Petroleum Corp., 88.49
Crown & Headlight, 26.23
Crown Overall Mfg. Co., 26.124
Crush International Inc., 107.7, 107.20, 107.21, 107.26, 107.29, 107.49, 107.53, 107.56
Crystal washer, 60.131
Cubs cereal, 21.5, 21.12
Cudahy Packing Co., 24.9, 24.19, 74.27
Cullman Products Corp., 18.36
Cumberland Brewing Co., 14.85
Cunard Lines, 102.16
Cup-A-Soup, 47.32
Cupid foundations, 121.60
Cupples Co., 114.6
Curity diapers, 10.9
Currick, Leiken & Bandler, 26.24
Currier Mfg. Co., 81.63
Curtis Industries Inc., Helene, 32.75, 32.83, 32.84
Curtis Candy Co., 20.7, 20.21
Curtis Hotel, Minneapolis, 62.20
Curtis-Mathes, 112.11
Curtis-Mathes Sales Co., 112.11
Curvfit Products Co., 104.51
Cushman Mfg. Corp., H. T., 50.27
Cushman's Sons Inc., 20.54
Cutler Desk Co., 81.59
Cutty Sark Whiskey, 71.3
Czechoslovak Glass Products Co., 52.5
Daggett & Ramsdell, 32.74, 32.80
Daily Forward, New York, 85.109
Daily Metal Trade, 85.289
Daily Mirror, New York, 85.9

Daily News, 85.88, 85.90, 85.149
Daily News Record, 85.211
Dainty flour, 11.26
Dairy Farmer, The, 85.32
Dairymen's League News, 85.206
Daisy/Heddon Div., Victor
    Comptometer Corp., 44.28
Da-Lite Screen Co. Inc., 89.18
Dallas Morning News, 85.75
Dallas, Texas, 36.3
Dalton Mfg. Co., 117.36
Daly, Charles, 44.22
Dana Perfumes Corp., 84.3, 84.25
Danish and Blue Cheese, 33.1
Danskin Inc., 26.29
D'Arcy Advertising Co., 2.4
Data General Corp., 28.11
Datapoint Corp., 28.80
Dataproducts Corporation, 28.64
Datasouth Computer Corporation,
    28.19
Data Switch, 28.79
Dated Mayonnaise Inc., 29.49
Datsun, 7.63, 7.91
Daven Radio Corp., 95.73
Davey Tree Expert Co., 69.6, 69.29
Davidow Suits Inc., 26.121
Davidson Radio Corp., 95.23
Davis, John W., 91.30, 91.133,
    91.135, 91.262
Davis and Co. Inc., Reese B., 113.15
Davis Cabinet Co., 50.18
Davis Co., R. B., 15.1
Davis-Howland Oil Corp., 88.29
Davis Sewing Machine Co., 98.15,
    108.2
Davis tennis rackets, 108.18
Day-Fan Electric Co., 95.68
Daystrom Furniture Div., Daystrom
    Inc., 50.12
Dayton Spice Mills Co., 27.3
Dazey Products Co., 68.16, 68.23
D-Con Co. Inc., 86.13
D-Con mouse and rat killer, 86.13
D. C. Trucking Co. Inc., 120.33
Dean Foods Co., 33.8
Dean Medicine Co., 35.125
Dean Milk Co., 33.33
Dean Witter Reynolds, 66.26
DeBeers Consolidated Mines Ltd.,
    67.1
Decca records, 97.5
Decision Data Computer
    Corporation, 28.78

Decker, Alfred, 26.56, 26.93
Deere and Co., 69.14
Deere Tractors, John, 69.17
Deering Coal & Wood Co., 59.20
Delco battery, 37.34
Delco Products, 37.34
Delineator, 85.108
Dellinger Inc., 46.31
Del Monte, 15.31, 27.31, 27.42
Del Monte Corp., 47.91, 49.8, 49.12
Del Monte fruit cocktail, 47.91
Del Monte Light fruit, 49.8
Delta Air Lines Inc., 4.12, 4.46
Deltah Inc., 67.38
DeLuxe Golden State Limited, 96.38
Demuth & Co., Wm, 105.19, 105.29,
    105.30
De Nicotea cigarette holder, 105.11
Dennison Mfg. Co., 83.40
Dental Hi-gene Products Inc., 34.17
Dental Lab. Prods. Co., 34.3
deodorant, 116.10, 116.11, 116.17,
    116.25
Department of Development, New
    Mexico., 119.25
Derby Foods Inc., 29.8
Derby steak sauce, 29.8
Dermassage, 32.53
Designatronics Inc., 118.4
Desks Inc., 81.1
Des Moines Capital, 85.150
Desq software, 28.35
Detecto, 12.4
Detroit Life Insurance Co., 64.19
Detroit News, 85.15, 85.78
Detroit Times, 85.290
deviled ham, 74.21, 74.26
DeWald, 95.1
Dewar's, 71.111
Dewey, Thomas E., 91.33, 91.40,
    91.60, 91.61, 91.62, 91.83, 91.224,
    91.229, 91.283, 91.360, 91.368
DeWitt Clinton Hotel, Albany, N.
    Y., 62.34
Dexatrim weight loss capsules, 56.8
Dexter Corp., 22.20
DH 125, The, 3.22
Diamond Crystal salt, 29.10
Diamond Crystal Salt Co., 29.10
Diamond Walnut Growers, 49.25
Dickinson Clothes Inc., 26.87
Dictograph Products Corp., 81.20
Diebold Safe Co., 81.37, 81.41
Diel Watch Case Co., 124.2

Dierks Forests Inc., 18.120
Diet-Rite, 107.5, 107.6
Dietz Co., R. E., 70.30
Dif Corp., 24.12, 24.18
Digby Inc., 26.159
Digby slacks, 26.159
Dillard Paper Co., 83.31
Dill Co., J., 115.58
Dill Co., The, 35.19
Discwasher Inc., 5.25
disks, 28.13, 28.25, 28.30, 28.31
Display World, 85.230
Disston & Sons, Henry, 117.35
Ditchburn Boats Ltd., 16.3
Ditto duplicator, 30.8
Dixon Crucible Co., Joseph, 126.33
Dixon Pencil Co., 126.16, 126.27, 126.31
Dodge, 7.50, 7.72, 7.90
Dodge trucks, 120.9, 120.14
Doelger, 14.82
Doe Oil Burner, 58.11
Dole Valve Co., 8.12
Dollar Steamship Lines, 102.18
DOM B and B, 71.98
DOM Benedictine, 71.64
Domestic Engineering, 85.301
Dominion Seven-up Co., 107.12
Donald Duck orange juice, 15.36
Doniger & Co., 26.20
Donnatal medicine, 35.138
Dorfan Co., 118.25
Doris Miller Clothes, 26.48
Dorman and Co., N., 33.40
Dorr-Oliver Inc., 31.38
Dot snappers, 26.122
Double Rotary Sprinkler Co., 69.16
Doughboy Industries Inc., 31.10
Doughnut Corp. of America, 47.25
Douglas, Stephen A., 91.304, 91.311
Douglas Aircraft Co. Inc., 3.9
Douglas Co., W. L., 48.10
Douglas Shoe Co., W. L., 48.154
Dove, 106.11
Dow aromatics, 84.13
Dow Chemical Co., 22.26, 68.20, 84.13
Dow Corning Corp., 22.29
Dower Lumber Co., 18.26
Dow Jones and Co., 66.7
Downtowner Corp., 62.26
Dozier & Gay Paint Co., 82.39
Drackett Co., The, 24.30, 24.44, 24.76

drain pipe cleaner, 24.24
Drake Bakeries Inc., 11.3
Drake's cake, 11.3
Dravo Corp., 31.1
Dr. Chas. E. Shiffer shampoo, 54.29
Dr. Edward's Olive tablets, 35.97
Drene shampoo, 54.26
Dreskin cosmetics, 32.16
dressings, 35.69
Drew Furniture Co., 50.46
Drexel Enterprises Inc., 50.62
Drexel Heritage Furnishings, 50.10
Dreyfous & Lang, 26.100
Dr. Hand's teething lotion, 34.19
Drilling, 85.180
Dr. Lyons, 34.33
Dr. Miles Medical Co., 35.11
Dr. Price's vanilla, 29.7
Dr. Scholl's Odor Eaters, 48.58
Drug Products Co., 35.41
Dr. West's toothbrushes, 34.48
Dryden Rubber Co., 48.151
Dry Goods Merchants Trade Journal, 85.42
DuBarry, 32.77
Dubois Chemicals, 22.27
Dubuque ham, 74.11
Dubuque Packing Co., 74.11
Duff Gordon, 125.12
Duff Mfg. Co., 8.49
Duffy-Mott Co. Inc., 15.33
Dumont, 112.5, 112.6
Dunbar Furniture Corp., 50.67
Duncan Coffee Co., 27.22, 27.52
Duncan Hines cake mixes, 47.64
Duncan Hines cookie mix, 11.10
Dunhill, 115.178
Dunhill Co., Alfred, London, 115.178
Dunhill Temporaries, 40.7
Dunkin' Donuts of America Inc., 99.3
Dunlop Tire & Rubber Corp., 114.3
Dunn & McCarthy Inc., 48.12, 48.61
Dun's Review and Modern Industry, 85.201
Duofold Inc., 121.35
Du-ons, 121.35
Duplex Lighting Works of General Electric, 70.38
Duplex Truck, 120.5
Duplicator Manufacturing Co., 30.8

Du Pont, 8.9, 8.58, 22.8, 22.9, 44.8, 44.11, 54.8, 68.9, 82.35, 113.3, 113.26
duPont and Co., Francis I., 66.27
Durabilt Steel Locker Co., 18.56
Dura Corp., 81.43
Duraflake Co., 18.24
Durant Star, 7.85
Dura Pictures Corp., 89.12
Durex razor blades, 104.30
Durham-Duplex Razor Co., 104.31, 104.36
Durham Hosiery Mills Inc., 61.22
Duro Metal Products Co., 117.5
Dur-O-Wal, 18.99
Dutch Boy, 82.41
Duz washing powder, 24.23, 24.27
Dykstra's Food Service, 74.10
Dynamo detergent, 24.15
Dysan Corp., 28.13
Eagle Pencil Co., 126.42
Eagle Radio Co., 95.3
Eagle whiskey, 71.108
Earhart luggage, Amelia, 72.11
Earhart Luggage Co., Amelia, 72.16
Earl's Court Collection, 50.32
Early & Daniel Co., 42.47
Early Times bourbon, 71.7, 71.125
Eastern Airlines Inc., 4.6, 4.13, 4.14, 4.37
Eastern Express System Inc., 120.19
Eastham & Co., P. W., 27.57
Eastman Chemical Products Inc., 22.15
Eastman Kodak Co., 30.6, 81.40, 89.7, 89.8, 89.10, 89.11, 89.13, 89.14, 89.17, 89.23, 89.25, 89.26, 89.29, 89.35
Eaton Co., Charles A., 48.42
Eaton, Crane & Pike Co., 83.59
Eatonic Remedy Co., 35.31
Eaton Paper Co., 83.4, 83.9, 83.17, 83.18, 83.32, 83.36, 83.71, 83.74, 83.84
Eaton, Yale and Towne Inc., 31.3
Eckhardt Corp., 95.12, 95.61
Eclipse Sleep Products Inc., 13.5, 13.22, 26.95
Econoline vans, 120.6
Economics Laboratory Inc., 24.7, 24.77, 24.105
Economy Drug Co., Cleveland, 100.17
Edelbrew, 14.24

Edge Extra shaving gel, 104.12
Edgeworth, 115.5
Ediphone, 81.66
Edison, 5.41
Edison Chemical Co., S. M., 32.53
Edison Electric Institute, 37.13
Edison Mfg. Co., 60.45
Edison-Splitdorf spark plugs, 8.34
Edison-Splitdorf Corp., 37.11, 58.57, 60.119
Educator shoes, 48.84, 48.156
Edwards & Co., J., 48.71, 48.177
Edwards shoes, 48.129
Egyptian Deities, 115.16, 115.166
Egyptian Lacquer Mfg. Co., 82.22, 82.70
Ehlers, Albert, 27.38
Ehlers Inc., Albert, 27.17
Eichler, 14.42
Einhorn Bros., 26.136
Eisenhower, Dwight D., 91.20, 91.35, 91.51, 91.55, 91.63, 91.81, 91.117, 91.145, 91.149, 91.168, 91.186, 91.234, 91.328, 91.332, 91.370, 91.385, 91.404
Eisenlohr & Bros., Otto, 115.92
Elam Mills Inc., 11.53
Elastic Stop Nut Corp. of America, 18.104
Elder Co. Inc., 60.52
Elder Mfg. Co., 26.28
El Dueno Cigar Co., 115.30
Electrasol, 24.7
Electrical Record, 85.202
Electrical World, 85.327
Electric Battery Co., 8.56
ElectrICE, 60.123
Electric Hoist Manufacturers' Association, 73.38
electric motors, 37.9, 37.17, 37.32
Electro-Copyst, 30.3
Electro-Kold Corp., 60.122
Electrol Inc., 58.13
Electrolux Corp., 60.66
Electronic Data Systems, 28.34
Electronics, 85.229
Electro-Voice Inc., 5.24, 5.28
Elephant Memory Systems, 28.30
Elgin National Watch Co., 124.16, 124.25, 124.52, 124.55
Eljer Plumbingware Div., Wallace-Murray Corp., 55.25, 55.29
Elkay Products Corp., 69.24
Elkhorn cheese, 33.42

Ellesse clothing, 26.11
Ellesse U.S.A. Inc., 26.11
Elliott Div., Carrier Corp., 117.15
Elmer's Glue All, 1.2
El Penn Motor Oil Co., 88.57
El Producto cigars, 115.41
Elto outboard motors, 16.15
Embassy cigarettes, 115.62
Emeralite desk lamp, 70.22
Emeraude, 84.11
Emery Worldwide, 4.65
Emhart Corp., 44.16, 44.29
Emir, 84.3
Emkay Inc., 6.3
Empire Brush Works, 82.12
Empire Furniture Corp., 50.69
Empire Scientific Corp., 5.55
Employers' Group Insurance, 64.91
Employers Liability Assurance
  Corp., 64.108
Employers Mutual Liability
  Insurance Co. of Wisconsin, 64.25
Employers Mutual of Wausau, 64.46
Enco, 88.45
Enco Div., Humble Oil and
  Refining Co., 88.16
Encyclopedia Americana, 94.3
Enders shaver, 104.4
Endicott Johnson Corp., 48.13
Endust, 24.44
Englander Co. Inc., 13.27
Enjay Chemical Co. Div., Humble
  Oil and Refining Co., 22.2
Enna Jetticks, 48.12
Eno laxative, 35.103
En-Ve Inc., 32.9
Enzel-of-Paris Inc., 48.75
EPI, 5.9
Epiphone Inc., 80.26
equalizers, 5.30, 5.31
Equitable Life Assurance Society of
  the United States, 64.44
Equitable Life Insurance Co., 64.8
Erie Railroad, 96.45
Erlanger Brewery, 14.141
Erving Paper Mills, 83.24
ESB Inc., 37.4, 37.27
Esquire socks, 61.37
Essley Shirt Co., 26.81
Esso, 9.7
Estate Stove Co., 58.25, 60.30,
  60.57, 60.115
Esterbrook Pen Co., 126.24

Esterbrook Steel Pen Co., 126.39,
  126.43
Etiquet, 116.24
Euclid Road Machinery Co., 73.22
Eureka Co., The, 60.42, 60.151
Eureka vacuum cleaner, 60.42,
  60.151
Eureka Williams Co., 60.126
Evans, George B., 116.1, 116.10,
  116.11
Evans Products Co., 18.75
evaporated milk, 33.35
Evening Graphic, New York, 85.6
Evening Journal, New York, 85.131
Evening Post, 85.69
Evening Tribune, Des Moines,
  85.123
Eveready batteries, 37.24, 37.26
Eveready Nurser, 42.50
Ever Ready Calendar Mfg. Co.,
  83.55
Eversharp pencil, 126.2
Eversharp pens, 126.46
Eversweet Co., 116.19
Evervess, 15.30
Everybody's Daily, Buffalo, 85.33
Evinrude Motor Co., 16.6, 16.9
Evyan Ltd., 84.6, 84.17, 84.18
Excello, 26.40
Ex-Lax, 35.45, 35.117, 35.135
Ex-Lax Distributing Co. Inc., 35.45,
  35.117, 35.135
Expandra, 113.29
Expositor., The, 85.270
Extension Magazine, 85.331
Exxon Corp., 28.53, 86.4, 86.12,
  88.28, 88.48
Exxon office systems, 28.53
E. Z. garters, 61.35
E-Z polish, 24.95
Fab, 24.6
Faber, Eberhard, 81.29, 81.39,
  126.14, 126.21
Factor & Co., Max, 32.26, 32.68
Factory, 85.242, 85.251
Factory Mutual Insurance Co.,
  64.30
Fada Radio, Ltd., 95.30
Fairbank Co., N. H., 24.53, 24.55
Fairbanks-Morse, 63.3
Fairchild-Wood Visaphone Corp.,
  81.28
Fairfax, 12.5
Fairy Foot, 48.146

Falfurrias Dairy Co., 33.38
Falk American Potato Flour Corp., 11.49
Falstaff, 14.127
Falstaff Brewing Corp., 14.13, 14.37, 14.127, 14.144
Family Circle, 85.24
Family Herald and Weekly Star, 85.64
Fan·Jet Falcon, 3.17
Farberware, 60.31
Farberware Ultra Chef, 60.31
Fargo-Hallowell Shoe Co., 48.60, 48.90
Farmers Deposit Bank, 43.7
Farmer's Wife, 85.20, 85.156
Farmer, The, 85.295
farm feed, 42.4
Farm Journal, 85.62, 85.92, 85.110, 85.240
Farm Life, 85.52
Farnsworth Hoyt Co., 48.94
Farrell-Cheek Steel Co., 75.8
Farrell Lines Inc., 102.2
Fashionable Dress, 85.243
Father John's medicine, 35.106
Father & Son shoes, 48.13
Fatima, 115.10, 115.74, 115.174
faucet washer, 55.11
Faultless Nightwear Corp., 26.42
Faultless Starch Co., 24.28
Faust Shoe Co., 48.86
Fay Inc., Leslie, 26.53
Fedders Corp., 58.58
Federal Advertising Agency, 2.16, 2.22, 2.28
Federal Cartridge Corp., 44.6
Federal Express, 4.67
Federal Mill, 11.19
Federal-Mogul Corp., 8.17
Federal Radio Corp., 95.48
Federal Schools, 101.1
Federal Snap Fastener Corp., 103.5
Federal tires, 114.22
Fehr Brewing Co., Frank, 14.57
Feldman Co. Inc., Manuel, 46.34
Fellowship Forum., The, 85.144
Fels Naphtha soap, 24.4
Felton, Sibley & Co., 82.24, 82.44
Felt Products Mfg. Co. Inc., 8.16
Feminine Products Inc., 116.23
Fenner, Beane, & Co., 66.3
Ferguson Farm Equipment, H., 42.51

Ferguson Inc., J. B., 95.57
Fernstrom Storage and Van Co., 79.9
Ferry-Morse Seed Co., 42.35
F. & F. Laboratories Inc., 35.100
Fiberglas insulation, 18.63
Fiber Glass Div., PPG Industries Inc., 18.46
Fibreboard Corp., 46.25
Ficks Reed Co., 50.61
Fidelity National Bank & Trust Co., 43.58
Fieldcrest Mills Inc., 12.1, 13.8
Field & Flint Co., 48.155
Field & Stream, 85.35, 85.37
Fife Products Corp., 32.56
Filko Ignition, 8.51
Fillmore, Millard, 91.37, 91.190, 91.215, 91.235, 91.348
Film Daily, 85.91
Financial World, 85.31
Finch & Co., J. S., 71.132
Finck & Co., W. M., 26.151
Fine Arts sterling silver, 67.36
Fir Door Institute, 18.53
Fireman's Fund Insurance Co., 64.2, 64.34, 64.83
Firestone luggage, 72.3
Firestone Tire and Rubber Co., 114.10, 114.17, 114.19, 114.25, 114.28, 114.32
First National Bank at Pittsburgh, 43.25
First National Bank, Boston, 43.37
First National Bank of Chicago, 43.12
First National Bank of Pleasanton, 43.53
First National Bank of Tampa, 43.39
First National City Bank, 43.11, 43.34
First Pennsylvania Banking and Trust Co., 43.19
First Trust & Deposit Co., 43.6
Fisher automobile bodies, 7.25
Fisher Flouring Mills Co., 11.24, 11.59, 21.2
Fisher Nut Company, 49.32
Fisher-Price Toys Inc., 118.13, 118.26
Fisher's Island, 119.30
fish hooks, 45.17
fishing tackle, 45.23

Fish Net & Twine Co., 45.19
Fisk, 114.12
Fisk, Clinton B., 91.80
Fitch shampoo, 54.22
Fitzpatrick Bros., 24.38
Fix-All Liquid Cement Co., 1.1, 1.6
Fizzadent Corp., 34.10
Flame-Glo Cosmetics, 32.39
Flamingo gas heaters, 58.5
Flanagan Nay Brewery, 14.58
Flash Chemical Co., 24.101
Flatt Tire Co., R. A., 114.11
Flavor flour, 11.16
Flax-li-num Insulating Co., 18.92
Fleer Corp., F. H., 20.56
Fleischmann Co., 11.9
Fleischmann Distilling Corp., 71.73,
  71.99, 71.123, 71.140
Fleisher Inc., S. W. & B. W., 103.6,
  103.12
Fletcher's Castoria, 35.13
Fletcher Works Inc., 60.128
Fleurette frocks, 26.136
Flexo-Products Div., McClellan
  Industries, 45.16
Flint Paint & Varnish Ltd., 82.17
float coat, 108.21
Flock Brewing Co., 14.67
Florence heaters, 58.24, 58.42
Florida, 119.44
Florida Citrus Commission, 15.32
Florida Citrus Exchange, 49.31
Florida Power Corp., 93.13
Florists Association, 2.8
Florists Telegraph Delivery
  Association, 51.5
Florists Transworld Delivery
  Association, 51.7
Florsheim Shoe Co., 48.18, 48.43,
  48.51, 48.54, 48.56, 48.87, 48.92,
  48.96, 48.132, 48.175
flour, 11.41, 11.53
Fly-Ded insect spray, 86.5
Fly-Foon Co., The, 86.3
Flying Tiger Line Inc., 4.3, 4.19
FMC Corp., 31.19
FOCUS software, 28.33, 28.56
Foley Mfg. Co., 68.5
Folger and Co., 27.6, 27.7, 27.14,
  27.30, 27.51, 27.54
Folger's, 27.6, 27.7, 27.14, 27.30,
  27.51, 27.54
Folger's instant, 27.15
Follmer, Clogg & Co., 123.24, 123.27

Food Suppliers Inc., 11.26
Foot Lift Plow, E. B., 42.13
Foot-Joy, 48.114
Foot Saver shoes, 48.108
Forbes, 85.67, 85.100
Ford, 7.47, 7.82
Ford, Gerald R., 91.36
Ford Authorized Leasing System,
  6.1
Ford & Co., Luther, 24.73, 24.85
Ford gas gauge, 8.4
Ford Motor Co., 7.4, 7.10, 7.13, 7.22,
  7.31, 7.33, 7.36, 7.40, 7.47, 7.53,
  7.54, 7.73, 7.79, 7.82, 7.84, 7.86,
  7.88, 7.89, 120.6
Ford Motor Co. Research
  Laboratories, 7.42
Ford Tempo, 7.53
Ford Tractor Div., Ford Motor Co.,
  42.57
Forecaster pipe, 105.7
Forest City Brewing, 14.126
Forhan's Co., 34.52
Formby's wood finishing products,
  82.43
Formfit Rogers, 121.18
Formica Corp., 65.17
Fort Howard Paper Co., 83.7
Fortune, 85.104, 85.250
Fortune Magazine, 85.106
Fortune shoes, 48.123
Forum, 85.38
Foss Mfg. Co., 55.11
Foster Grant Co., 41.6, 41.11
Foster Parents Plan, 92.7
Foster Rubber Co., 48.136
Foundation for Commercial Banks,
  43.24, 43.56
foundations, 121.8, 121.34, 121.50
Founders Furniture Inc., 50.19
4C Breadcrumbs, 47.106
Four Roses Distillers Co., 71.6, 71.8,
  71.10, 71.12, 71.81
Four Roses whiskey, 71.8, 71.10,
  71.81
Fourth Estate, 85.46
Fowler Sea Products Co., 47.19
Foxboro Co., The, 31.21
Fox Brewing Co., Peter, 14.50
Fox River Hose, 61.47
Foy Paint Co., 82.42
Frailey Prods, 32.24
Fraker Coal Co., 59.1
Francette corsets, 121.40

Frank Co., Wm, 80.47
Frankfort Distilleries, 71.90
Franklin County Dist. Co., 71.114
Franklin Mint, 76.4
Franklin Pottery, 52.8
Franklin Simon & Co., 100.25
Franz Butter-Nut bread, 11.43
Fraser and Johnston Co., 58.51
Frederick Advertising & Display
  Co., 2.35
Freed-Eisemann Radio Corp., 95.41,
  95.67, 95.76
Freedent chewing gum, 20.29
Freeman, Edw, 72.19
Freeman Mfg. Co., 26.132
Freeman Publications, Miller, 94.10
Freeman Shoe Corp., 48.179
Free Press, 85.185
Frémont, John C., 91.71, 91.89,
  91.91, 91.94, 91.102, 91.157, 91.254,
  91.343, 91.352, 91.403
French Battery Co., 37.28
French Co., The R. T., 29.13, 87.1,
  87.2, 87.17
French dressing, 29.20
French Lick Springs Co., 35.2,
  35.136
Freon, 22.8
Fresh Milk Industry, 33.14
Fresh Milk Industry of Southern
  California, 33.13
Friden Div., Singer Co., 81.31
Friedberger-Aaron Mfg. Co., 103.22
Frieder & Sons Co., S., 115.96,
  115.114
Friedman & Sons., S., 82.11
Frigidaire, 60.19, 60.58, 60.85
Frigidaire refrigerators, 60.150
Friskies, 87.4, 87.12
Friskies Buffet cat food, 87.8
Frito-Lay Inc., 47.50
Fromm and Sichel Inc., 125.35
Fromm Bros., 74.5
Frontex shirts, 26.15
Frost Fishing Tackle Co., 45.12
Frozen Foods Magazine, 85.263
Fruehauf Corp., 120.20, 120.26
Fruit Dispatch Co., 49.21
Fuji Photo Film USA, 122.6
Fuji video tape, 122.6
Fuller Brush Co., 24.72
Fuller Co., H. B., 1.3, 1.5
Fullerton Electric Co., 70.10

Fulton Cotton Mills Div., Allied
  Products Corp., 113.4
Fundimensions, 118.23
Funke, 20.22
Funk G. Hybrids, 42.9
Furness, Withy and Co. Ltd., 102.21
Furniture Record, 85.22, 85.102
furs, 26.58, 26.75
Fusion Inc., 28.4
Gabrieleen Co., 54.5
Gaines dog food, 87.9
Galion Iron Works and Mfg. Co.,
  The, 73.20
Gallagher & Burton whiskey, 71.6
Galveston News, 85.191
garage-door openers, 55.17
Garcia Corp., The, 45.18
Garcia y Vega Inc., 115.14
Gardco Paint Co., 82.36
Garden Way Research, 69.31
*Garden Way Sun Room/Solar
  Greenhouse,* 69.31
Gardner-Denver Co., 58.49
Garfield, James, 91.96
Garford Motor Truck, 120.29
Garneau Co. Inc., Joseph, 71.95
Garrett AiResearch, The Garrett
  Corp., 3.8, 3.18
Gary Safe Co., 81.55
Gas Station Topics, 85.277
gas water heaters, 58.26, 58.52,
  58.55
Gates Rubber Co., 8.70
Gay Diversion perfume, 84.18
Gaylin Jewelry Co., 67.4
G & D vermouth, 125.3
Geartronics Corp., 73.7
Gehl Bros. Mfg. Co., 42.55
Gelusil, 35.104
Gem Crib and Cradle Co., 10.2
Gem Safety Razor Corp., 104.1,
  104.33, 104.57
Genco razors, 104.24
General Brewing Corp., 14.72
General Cigar Co., 115.46, 115.51,
  115.66, 115.89, 115.123, 115.129,
  115.137, 115.161, 115.182, 115.184
General Electric Co., 8.24, 28.65,
  31.17, 37.9, 37.18, 38.13, 60.6, 60.8,
  60.34, 60.40, 60.41, 60.44, 60.87,
  60.107, 60.130, 60.147, 95.17, 95.69,
  95.80, 124.39
General Foods Corp., 11.17, 11.32,
  11.42, 15.8, 15.29, 21.7, 21.21,

21.24, 21.29, 21.33, 27.12, 27.18, 27.21, 27.23, 27.25, 27.58, 27.59, 29.26, 29.44, 47.5, 47.54, 47.71, 47.86, 87.7, 87.9, 107.8, 107.33
General Foods International Coffees, 27.12
General Ledger, 28.10
General Mills Inc., 11.52, 21.9, 21.17, 21.27, 21.31, 21.48, 47.67
General Motors Corp., 7.1, 7.3, 7.9, 7.17, 7.19, 7.21, 7.23, 7.24, 7.25, 7.30, 7.38, 7.43, 7.46, 7.48, 7.52, 7.59, 7.60, 7.64, 7.67, 7.74, 7.81, 7.87, 7.92, 7.93, 7.94, 7.96, 7.101, 7.103, 7.105, 8.44, 9.5, 31.2, 60.19, 60.58, 60.69, 60.85, 60.150, 120.13, 120.23
General Radio Corp., 95.16
General Refrigeration Co., 60.102
General Telephone and Electronics Corp., 111.16
General Time Corp., 124.33
General Tire and Rubber Co., 114.29, 114.30, 114.31
Genesco Inc., 26.39, 48.134, 48.157, 48.174
Genesee Brewing Co., 14.103
Genetron, 22.21
Geneva Cutlery Corp., 104.24
Geo. Dunham washer, 60.81
Geon Vinyls, 18.94
George Washington, 27.35
Georgiana frocks, 26.10
Georgian and Sunday American, The, Atlanta, 85.50, 85.117
Georgia-Pacific Corp., 31.26
Georgia Railway & Power Co., 93.1
Gerber Legendary Blades, 108.11
Gerber Products Co., 10.1
Gesture, Anthony, 26.83
Getty Refining & Marketing Co., 88.43
Gevaert film, 89.28
Ghirardelli Chocolate Co., 15.7
Ghirardelli's hot chocolate, 15.7
Ghisholt Machine Co., 73.18
Gibbard furniture, 50.49
Giese Bros. Coal Co., 59.19
Gilbert & Barker Mfg. Co., 58.44
Gilbert Clock Co., W. L., 124.26, 124.46, 124.59
Gilbert Co., The A. C., 118.24
Gilbert Paper Co., 83.2
Gilbert Shoe Co., 48.74

Gilbey's vodka, 71.86
Gillette blades, 104.20, 104.23
Gillette Co., The, 104.13, 104.20, 104.23, 104.42, 104.47, 116.31, 126.34
Gillette Foaming Gel, 104.42
Gillette Rubber Co., 114.1
Gillette safety razor, 104.47
ginger ale, 107.1, 107.22
Girard cigar, 115.93
Girard Perregaux, 124.11
girdles, 121.15, 121.23, 121.37, 121.38, 121.58
Glamorene Products Corp., 24.26
Glass Containers Manufacturers Institute, 52.4
Glaxo, 10.7
Gleason Tiebout Glass, 70.46
Glenbrook Laboratories, 34.33, 35.6, 35.13, 35.16, 35.42, 35.62, 35.84, 35.87, 35.127
Glenmore Distilleries Co., 71.46, 71.128, 71.141, 71.142
Glenoit Mills Inc., 26.30
Glen Raven Mills, 113.11
Glenwood Range Co., 60.47, 60.137
Glidden Co., 82.23, 82.45
Glider brushless shave, 104.10
Globe Brewing Co., 14.63, 14.122
Globe-Democrat, 85.187
Globe Laboratories, 24.84
Globe Mach. & Stamping Co., 76.1
Globe radiator shutters, 76.1
Globe-Wernicke Co., The, 81.56
GLO soapy scouring pads, 24.69
GMC truck, 120.23
GM service, 9.5
Goding Shoe Co., 48.139
Goebel Brewing Co., 14.86
Gold Bond, 18.28, 18.58
Gold Dust Corp., 24.47
Gold Dust soap powder, 24.55
Golden Fleece Corp., 83.56
Golden Virginia tobacco, 115.100
Golden Wedding, 71.132
Gold Label, 115.184
Gold Seal Vineyards Inc., 125.14
Gold Seal wines, 125.14
Goldwater, Barry, 91.3, 91.4, 91.105, 91.147, 91.152, 91.408
Golfcraft Inc., 108.12, 108.30
Golfer's Magazine, 85.334
Gonzalez & Sanchez Co., 115.31
Good Furniture Magazine, 85.2

Good Hardware, 85.282
Good Looks Merchandising, 85.259
Goodman Collar Co., 103.3
Goodrich Co., B. F., 8.64, 18.94,
  48.19, 114.5, 114.8
Goodrich General Products Co.,
  26.8
Goodrich-Gulf Chemicals Inc., 22.25
Goodyear service, 9.4
Goodyear Tire and Rubber Co., 9.4,
  114.13, 114.16
Goody Root Beer, 107.52
Gordon's gin, 71.105, 71.116
Gorham Div., Textron Inc., 67.2,
  67.6
Gorton Corp., The, 47.68
Gorton-Pew Fisheries Co., 47.94
Gorton's codfish cakes, 47.68
Gospel Pencil Co., 126.29
Gossard Co., H. W., 121.36
Gotham watches, 124.56, 124.57
Gottschalk-Humphrey, 2.7
Gould Storage Battery Co., 37.15,
  37.21
Goya Guitars Inc., 80.39
Grabow Pre-Smoked Pipes Inc.,
  105.4, 105.6, 105.16
Grabowsky Bros. Inc., 115.144
Grace Bros., 14.46
Graceform-Camlin Corset Co.,
  121.40
Graef Inc., Jean R., 124.11
Graflex Inc., 89.33
Grain Growers Guide, Winnipeg,
  Canada, 85.19
Granco Steel Products Co., 75.14
Grand Rapids Hardware, 55.27
Grand Slam golf clubs, 108.34
Granger & Co., 27.2, 27.39
Grant, Ulysses S., 91.114, 91.144,
  91.153, 91.176, 91.184, 91.187,
  91.233, 91.265, 91.285, 91.331,
  91.333, 91.338
Grant Co., W. T., 100.14
Grantley sunglasses, 41.11
Grape Nuts, 21.29
Grape Nuts Flakes, 21.21, 21.29
Gratz Brewing Co., Wm, 14.79
Gravely Motor Plow & Cultivator
  Co., 69.3
Gravy Train dog food, 87.7
Gray, Dorothy, 32.52, 32.54, 32.57
Gray & Davis Inc., 70.27

Gray & Dudley Co., 60.142
Great American Insurance Co.,
  64.62
Great Atlantic & Pacific Tea Co.
  Inc., 100.6
Great Northern Railway, 96.1,
  96.34, 96.40
Great Waters of France Inc., 15.26
Great Western champagne, 125.7
Great West Life Assurance Co.,
  64.66, 64.77, 64.115
Grecian Formula 16, 54.41
Greeley, Horace, 91.115, 91.178,
  91.324, 91.339, 91.374
Greene Bros. Inc., 70.21
Green Giant Co., 47.72
Green Giant peas, 47.72
Greenhut-Siegel-Cooper, 100.16
Greenpoint-Southern Co., 13.24
Greenwood Mills Inc., 113.12
Greeting Card Association, 51.3,
  51.6
Grennan Cake Co., 11.15
Grenville Inc., 84.32
Grewen Fabric Co., 123.5
Grey Advertising Agency, 2.29
Greyhound Lines Inc., 19.2, 19.3,
  79.5
Greystone fruit wines, 125.18
Griggs Cooper Co., 27.37
Grinnel gloves, 123.6
Gripper fasteners, 103.16
Grisby-Grunow, 60.67
Griswold Mfg. Co., 68.18
Groceries, 85.44
Grocery Store Products Co., 21.34
Grolsch Importers Inc., 14.3
Grolsch lager, 14.3
Gross Co., B. & E. J., 67.3
Ground Gripper Shoe Co., 48.143
Grover's Sons Co., J. J., 48.119
Gruen Watch Co., The, 124.42
Gruen watches, 124.42
GTE, 111.2, 111.5
Guarantee Liquid Measure Co., 63.1
Guardian Life Insurance Co., 64.26,
  64.27, 64.116
Guardian Light Co., 70.19
Gude's Inc., 48.70, 61.15
Guiflani & Bro., A., 47.34
Guild Wineries & Distilleries, 125.8,
  125.9, 125.13, 125.21, 125.22,
  125.23, 125.26, 125.30

Source Information

Guinness-Harp Corp., 14.6, 14.7, 14.51, 14.52, 14.64, 14.76, 14.102, 14.151
Guinness Stout, 14.6, 14.7, 14.51, 14.52, 14.64, 14.76, 14.102, 14.151
Guittard Chocolate Co., 11.60
Gulbransen Industries Inc., 80.43
Gulf and Western Industries Inc., 31.30
Gulf Coast Lumberman, 85.238
Gulf Oil Corp., 88.26, 88.74
Gulf Publishing Co., 94.21
gummed paper moistener, 81.4
Gumpert & Co., S., 15.10
Gum-rub, 34.3
Gund Inc., 118.7
Gundlach & Co, Esmond, 33.20
Gutta Percha rubbers, 48.33
G & W Distillers, 71.110
Haas & Howell, 2.24
Hachmeister Lind Chemical Co., 18.117
Haeger Potteries Inc., 65.14
Haffenreffer & Co., 14.138
Hagen Golf Epuipment Co., Walter, 108.39
Hager Hinge Co., 55.12
Hagerty and Sons, Ltd. Inc., W. J., 24.96
Haig & Haig, 71.133
Hale Rubber Co., Alfred, 48.104
Half & Half, 115.141
Halliburton travel cases, 72.6
Hallmark Cards Inc., 51.8, 51.9
Hallock & Watson Radio Corp., 95.21
Hall's Mentho-Liptus, 35.27
Halo shampoo, 54.34
Hamilton Brown Shoe Co., 48.8, 48.9
Hamilton Cosco Inc., 60.132
Hamilton Preparations, 104.55
Hamilton & Sons, W. C., 83.28
Hamilton Watch Co., 124.15, 124.17, 124.32, 124.43
Hamm Brewing Co., Theo, 14.45, 14.91
Hammer Blow Tool Co., 8.31
Hammermill Paper Co., 83.37, 83.41, 83.57
Hammerschlag Refining Co., 14.1
Hammond Cedar Co., 18.72
Hammond Iron Works, 18.110

Hammond Organ Co., 80.21, 80.22, 80.29, 80.34
Hammond Typewriter Co., 81.32
Hamm's, 14.45
Hamm's beer, 14.91
Hampden Brewing Co., 14.152
Hampden Specialty Products Co., 50.50
Hancock, Gen. Winfield S., 91.27, 91.358
Hancock Companies, John, 64.105
Hand-ee tool, 117.10, 117.13
Handy and Harman, 75.24
Handy Chair & Table Co., 50.11
Hanes Corp., 61.13, 121.21
Hanes Knitting Co., P. H., 121.42, 121.57
Hang Ten clothing, 26.152
Hanley & Kinsella Coffee Co., 27.8, 27.61
Hanover Fire Insurance Co., 64.4
Hanseatic German Atlantic Line., T. S., 102.6
Hanzo Co., The, 106.25
Harbor Master, 26.17
Hardeman Hat Co., 26.64
Harding, Warren G., 91.34, 91.118, 91.167, 91.300, 91.356
Hardware Age, 85.179, 85.273
Hardware Mutual Casualty Co., 64.94
Hardwood Bros., 88.54
Hardwood Mfrs. Institute, 18.109
Harlan Insurance Co., 64.5
Harman-Kardon Inc., 5.20, 5.35, 5.50
Harmony Brand, 103.5
Harmony vitamins, 56.5
Harper's Bazaar, 85.72, 85.317
Harrisburg Telegraph, 85.68
Harrison, Benjamin, 91.19, 91.23, 91.41, 91.110, 91.116, 91.251, 91.252, 91.293, 91.362, 91.363, 91.393
Harrison, William Henry, 91.58, 91.123, 91.136, 91.326, 91.349, 91.364
Harrison Radiator Corp., 8.19
Harrison Radiator Div., General Motors Corp., 8.48
Harter Corp., 50.51
Hartford Conn. Trust Co., 43.32
Hartford Fire Insurance Co., 64.98
Hartford Inc., E. V., 8.25

Hartford Insurance Group., The, 64.39, 64.117
Hartford Steam Boiler Inspection and Insurance Co., 64.31, 64.33
Hartmann Electrical Mfg. Co., 95.45, 95.74
Hartmann Trunk Co., 72.13
Hart-Parr Co., 42.10, 42.21
Harvard Brewing Co., 14.17
Harvard Mfg. Co., 13.31
Harvel Watch Co., 124.5, 124.29, 124.45, 124.47, 124.50
Haserot Co., The, 27.4, 47.83
Hathaway Co., C. F., 26.82
Havoline motor oil, 88.30
Hawaii, 119.13
Hawes floor wax, 24.66
Hawker Siddeley Group Ltd., 3.22
Hawkeye Clock Co., 124.38, 124.62
Hawk Model Co., 118.12
Hawthorne Roofing Tile Co., 18.107
Hayes, Rutherford B., 91.29, 91.134, 91.226, 91.309, 91.379, 91.398
Haynes Automobile Co., 7.6
Haynes Co., Wm. S., 80.37
Haynes-Hunt Corp., 8.8
Hazel Bishop, 32.28
Hazelnut Liquor, 71.38
Head Ski Co., 108.3
Healthaids Inc., 35.7, 35.81
Health Waters Inc., 15.24
Hearst's Magazine, 85.25
Heart Fund, 92.2
Heart's Quest, 121.52
Hecker H-O Co. Inc., 11.56
Heddon's Sons, James, 45.10, 45.13, 45.23, 45.24
Hegel Furniture Co., 50.68
Heileman Brewing Co. Inc., 14.84, 14.137
Hein and Kopins Inc., 13.28
Heineken, 14.35
Heinz catsup, 29.1
Heinz Co., H. J., 29.1, 29.24, 29.27, 29.43, 47.21, 47.33
Heinz Home Style gravy, 47.21
Heirloom Sterling, 67.13
Helene brassiere, 121.28
Heller and Co., Walter E., 66.12, 66.25
Hellman Inc., Richard, 29.15, 29.23
Hellmann's, 29.2
Hellmann's mayonnaise, 29.5, 29.45
Helmar, 115.107

Henderson & Erwin, 121.51
Henredon Furniture Industries Inc., 50.25, 50.65
Herald and Examiner, 85.221
Heralder, 124.39
Herald Knitwear Co., 26.14
Herald-Tribune, New York, 85.95
Herbert Tareyton, 115.158
Hercules bed spring, 13.21
Hercules Inc., 113.31
Herculon, 113.31
Heritage Furniture Inc., 50.2
Herrick Refrigerator Co., 60.95
Herschell-Spillman Motor Co., 37.31
Hertz Corp., 6.2, 6.5, 6.6
Hesston Corp. Inc., 42.56
Heublein cocktails, 71.139
Heublein Inc., 29.36, 29.50, 71.2, 71.55, 71.57, 71.104, 71.139
Heurich Brewing Co., 14.31, 14.124
Hewlett-Packard Co., 28.40, 38.1
Hewlett-Packard personal computers, 28.40
Hews & Potter, 123.19
Hickok buckles, 123.26
Higgins & Co., C. M., 126.23
Highland Scotch Mist, 71.57
High Point decaffeinated, 27.20
Highson Chemical Co., 22.28
Highway Cruisers Inc., 98.1
Hillerich & Bradsby Co. Inc., 108.34
Hillsdale Nurseries, 69.11
Hilo Varnish Corp., 82.6, 82.19
Hilton Hotels Corp., 62.5, 62.14, 62.31
Hinde & Dauch Paper Co., 83.29, 83.42
Hiram Walker bourbon, 71.145
Hires, 107.7, 107.21, 107.26, 107.29, 107.49, 107.53, 107.56
Hitachi Sales Corporation, 112.2
Hoard's Dairyman, 85.276
Hobart Corp., 68.17
Hobart Manufacturing Co., 60.61
Hoffman, Arthur W., 47.35
Hoffmann & Billings, 18.55
Hogan Systems, 28.71
Hoke gauges, 63.6
Holiday Inns of America Inc., 62.13, 62.16, 62.30, 62.32
Holiday tobacco, 115.9
Holland-American Line, 102.15, 102.23
Holland Furnace Co., 58.21, 58.39

Holland House Brands Inc., 71.113
Holley Carburetor Co., 8.39
Hollingshead Corp., 24.79
Holmes & Edwards Silver Co., 67.16, 67.27, 67.30
Holmes & Son, Archibold, 46.16
Holophane Glass Co., 70.20
Home Appliance Corp., 58.22
Home Life Insurance Co., 64.6
Home Repair & Improvements, 94.20
Home State Farm Publications, 94.4
Homocea, Ltd., England, 35.130
Honda, 7.34, 77.1, 77.3
Honda Civic Hatchback, 7.65
Honeywell, 28.62, 28.70
Hood River Apple Growers Assn., 49.22
Hood rubbers, 48.19
Hoosier, 98.2
Hoosier Mfg. Co., 18.89, 18.108
Hoosier Tarpaulin and Canvas Goods Co., 98.2
Hoover, Herbert, 91.2, 91.38, 91.66, 91.126, 91.132, 91.137, 91.138, 91.154, 91.170, 91.241, 91.250, 91.296, 91.354, 91.412, 91.424
Hoover Co., The, 60.46, 60.54
Hoover vacuum cleaner, 60.46, 60.54
Hopkins & Son, F. L., 32.10
Hoppe Inc., F. A., 44.9
Horlick's Malted Milk Corp., 15.4, 15.27, 15.28
Hormel and Co., Geo. A., 74.9
Horn and Hardart restaurants, automats, 99.7
Horn Luggage Co., 72.10, 72.18
Hornung Brewing Co., Jacob, 14.26, 14.115
Horst Co., F. F., 24.62, 82.65
Hortex Mfg. Co., 26.107
Horton Pilsener, 14.61
Hotel Astor, New York, 62.8
Hotel Delmonico, New York, 62.25
Hotel Fort Shelby, Detroit, 62.1
Hotel Grunewald, 20.69
Hotel Lincoln, New York, 62.17
Hotel New Yorker, New York, 62.39
Hotels Mayfair and Lennox, St. Louis, 62.12, 62.21
Hotel Touraine, Buffalo, New York, 62.36
Hotpoint, 60.40
Hotpoint appliances, 60.45, 60.87

Hotpoint ranges, 60.34
Houbigant, 32.58
Houbigant Inc., 32.58, 84.26
Houdry Process and Chemical Co., 22.12
House and Home, 85.139
House Beautiful, 85.60, 85.347
House of Comoy, 105.24
House of Edgeworth, 115.5
House of Tre-Jur, 84.22, 84.29
House of Worsted-Tex, 26.26
House of Wrisley Inc., 32.27
house slippers, 48.23
Houston Lighting and Power Co., 93.7
Houston Post-Dispatch, 85.218
Houze Glass Corp., 52.6
Howard Industries Inc., 73.24
Howard Johnson Co., 99.2, 99.4
Howard Paper Co., 83.66
Howard Paper Mills Div., St. Regis Paper Co., 83.67
Howe Folding Furniture Inc., 50.28
Howell Electric Motors Co., 37.10
How Lamp & Mfg. Co., 70.13
HPM Div., Koehring Co., 73.35
HQZ Laboratories, 54.4
Huber Brewing Co., 14.83
Hudson, 7.18, 7.49
Hudson National Inc., 56.13
Hughes, Charles Evans, 91.15, 91.18, 91.76
Hughes, E. Griffiths, 35.93
Hughes Aircraft Co., 38.5
Hughes Tool Co., 117.28
Hulman & Co., 11.44
Humble Oil and Refining Co., 88.45
Hummel Co., A. C., 81.4
Humphrey, Hubert H., 91.70, 91.197, 91.413
Humphrey Co., 58.27, 58.34
Hunt Co., F. C., 5.54
Hunter's Variety Store, Memphis, Tenn., 100.29
Hunter whiskey, 71.12
Hunt Pen Co., C. Howard, 126.6
Hunt-Wesson Foods Inc., 29.34, 47.38, 47.45
Hush Co., 116.7, 116.17
Hush Puppies, 48.25
Hutton, E. F., 66.23
Huyler's Inc., 20.60
Hyde Park Breweries Assn., 14.4, 14.97, 14.116

Hydraulic Press Mfg. Co., 73.11
Hydro-United Tire Co., 114.26
Hygienic Productions, 78.6, 78.7
Hygrade Food Products Co., 74.12
Hygrade Sylvania Corp., 70.2, 70.16
Hyster Co., 120.7
Hystron Fibers Inc., 113.28
Hyvis motor oil, 88.37
Iberia Air Lines of Spain, 4.58, 4.66
IBM, 28.1, 28.3, 28.66, 81.23, 81.30, 81.60
Ice Capades, 78.11
Icelandic Airlines, 4.55
ICOT Corp., 28.20
Idaho Potato Growers Inc., 47.56
Ideal Leather Case Co., 72.30
Ideal Toy Corp., 118.1
Ideas Inc., 2.32
Ilco headlight, 8.15
Illinois Baking Corp., 11.29
Illinois Central Railroad, 96.32
Illinois-Iowa Power Co., 93.11
Illinois National Bank, 43.27
Illinois Refrigerator Co., 60.86
Illinois Shade Div., Slick Industrial Co., 65.12
Illustrated News, 85.70
Imperial, 71.107
Imperial Auto Insurance, 64.28
Imperial Candy Co., 20.17
Imperial Furniture Co., 50.70
Imperial Oil Co., 88.35
Imperial Tobacco Co. of Canada, 115.155
Imperial whiskey, 71.59
In-B-Tween Co., The, 115.47
Inc. Magazine, 85.99
Inc. Publishing Co., 85.99
Independent Insurance Agents, 64.75
Indiana Dept. of Commerce, 36.24
Indiana Lamp Corp., 8.15, 8.53
Indiana Limestone, 18.16
Indiana Limestone Quarrymen's Assn., 18.77, 18.96
Indianapolis, Ind, 119.16
Indianapolis Star, 85.14
Indianapolis Tent & Awning Co., 18.118
Indian Archery Corp., 108.16
Indian Hill ginger ale, 107.35
Indian Packing Corp., 74.2, 74.8
Indian Refining Co., 88.30
India Tea Bureau, 110.6, 110.18

Industrial Fabrics Div., West Point-Pepperell Inc., 113.14
Industrial Management, 85.213
Industrial Marketing, 85.177
Industrial News, 85.228
Inecto Inc., 54.12
Infocom computer games, 118.6
Infocom Inc., 118.6
Information Builders Inc., 28.33, 28.56
Ingersoll & Bro., Robt. H., 124.37, 124.48
Ingersoll-Rand Co., 117.3
Inglenook, 125.29
Ingram Co., F. F., 32.37, 32.81, 104.3, 104.6, 104.52
Ingram's rouge, 32.37
Inland Mfg. Co., 60.48
Inland Printer, 85.132
In-Sink-Erator Mfg. Co., 60.74
Instant Postum, 15.29
Instant Sanka, 27.59
Instant Tender Leaf, 110.14
Insulite Co., The, 18.15
Insulite Div., Minnesota and Ontario Paper Co., 18.68
Insurance Co. of North America, 64.10, 64.67
Insured Savings and Loan Associations, 66.24
Intellect software, 28.58
Interlan Inc., 28.76
Interlude, 85.220
Intermec, 28.55
International Business Machines, see IBM
International Coffee Co., 27.26
International Correspondence Schools, Scranton, Pa, 101.4, 101.6, 101.8, 101.11, 101.12
International Duplex Coat Co., 26.108
International Harvester Co., 42.20, 42.46, 42.49, 120.3, 120.12
International Management, 85.261
International Mutoscope Corp., 81.12
International Nickel Co., 75.10, 75.21
International Paper Co., 83.8, 83.11, 83.52, 83.78
International Playtex Corp., 34.22
International Railway Co., 96.56

International Salt Co., 29.3, 29.6, 29.18, 29.29
International Shoe Co., 48.2, 48.27, 48.38, 48.65
International Silver Co., 67.29, 67.34, 67.39
International Telephone and Telegraph Co., 111.30
International Vintage Wines, 125.29
Interstate cotton oil, 47.88
Interstate Motor Freight System, 120.11
Interstate Trust Co., 43.1
Interwoven Stocking Co., 61.32
Intimate, 84.5
Investor-Owned Electric Light and Power Cos., 93.4
Investors Diversified Services Inc., 64.13
Iona Mfg. Co., 60.78
Iowa Development Commission, 36.7
Ipana, 34.14, 34.15
Irish & Scottish Linen Damask Guild, 113.19
Iron Age, 85.332
Iron City Beer, 14.80
Iron City Products Co., 117.31
Iron Trade Review, 85.54
Iroquois China Co., 23.1
Iroquois Electric Refrigeration Co., 60.99
Irving Trust Co., 43.45
Irwill Knitwear Corp., 26.31
Iselin and Co. Inc., William, 66.17
Islon, 113.32
Israeli Government Tourist Office, 119.11
Italian Line, 102.10, 102.29
Ithaca Gun Co. Inc., 44.5
ITT Continental Baking Co. Inc., 11.28
Ivaline-Foralyn, 88.63
Iver-Johnson Arms and Cycle Works, 44.20
Ives Mfg. Co., 118.8
Ivory, 106.17
Ivory Flakes, 24.40
Ivory Snow, 24.49, 24.52
Ivory soap, 106.15, 106.20, 106.21
I. W. Harper bourbon, 71.56, 71.100, 71.101
Izod Lacoste, 26.150
Jack Daniels Distillery, 71.28

Jackes-Evans Mfg. Co., 58.5
Jackson, Andrew, 91.57, 91.305, 91.307, 91.320, 91.347
Jackson China Co., 23.5
Jack Tar Togs, 26.89
Jacob Ruppert, 14.112
Jacobs Bros. Co. Inc., 12.4
Jacobson & Sons, F., 26.140
Jacques Mfg. Co., 11.55
Jaeckel & Co., A., 100.12
Jamaica, 119.47
James Bros., 20.23
James Clock Mfg. Co., 124.19
Jameson & Son, John, 71.70
Jamestown Upholstery Co., 50.54
Jantzen Inc., 26.70, 26.96, 109.1
Jantzen swimsuit, 109.1
Japan Air Lines, 4.48
Jarcons Bros. Inc., 63.15
Jarman, 48.174
Jarman Shoe Co., 48.59
Jax Brewing Co., 14.109
Jays Foods Inc., 47.8
Jays potato chips, 47.8
J & B scotch, 71.75
Jeep, 7.99
Jeep CJ-7, 7.41
Jeep Corp., 7.41, 7.99
Jefferson, Thomas, 91.179
Jeffrey Mfg. Co., 73.12
Jell-o, 47.5, 47.86
Jenn-Air Corp., 60.91
Jennison-Wright Co., 18.101, 46.21
Jensen, 5.52
Jergens Co., Andrew, 106.12, 106.32
Jeris hair tonic, 54.43
Jersey City, N. J., 36.10
Jersey Maid Ice Cream Co., 33.49
Jests Inc., 35.52
Jewell Refrigerator Co., 60.24
Jewel Paint & Varnish Co., 82.9, 82.53
Jewett Refrigerator Co., 60.72
Jewish exhortation, 90.3
Jif peanut butter, 47.20
Jif soap flakes, 24.81
Jobbers Overall Co., 26.98
Jockey International Inc., 121.49
Jockey Menswear Div., Coopers Inc., 26.69
John Jameson whiskey, 71.70
John Martin's Book, 85.204
Johnnie Walker Red Label scotch, 71.25, 71.61, 71.77

Johnnie Walker scotch, 71.82, 71.144

Johns-Manville Corp., 18.59, 18.105, 18.119

Johnson, 16.2, 16.7

Johnson, Lyndon B., 91.12, 91.106, 91.119, 91.125, 91.151, 91.162, 91.173, 91.193

Johnson, Read & Co., 2.11

Johnson Co., E. F., 95.40

Johnson Co., S. T., 58.6

Johnson Iron Horse gas engine, 73.23

Johnson & Johnson, 34.51, 35.58, 35.60, 35.71, 35.98, 35.131, 104.12

Johnson & Johnson Baby Products Co., 10.4

Johnson & Johnson dental floss, 34.51

Johnson Mfg. Co., Nestor, 108.35

Johnson Reels Inc., 45.9

Johnson's baby powder, 10.4

Johnson "sea-worthy" boats, 16.13

Johnson & Son Inc., S. C., 86.9

Johnston and Murphy, 48.157

Johnston Co., R. A., 11.14

Joint Coffee Trade Publicity Committee, 27.16

Jordan swimsuits, 109.2

Jordeau Inc., Jean, 32.3

Joyce & Co., W. B., 64.17

Joy Mfg. Co., 73.17

Judge, 85.226

Julian, George W., 45.5

Julian & Hokenge Co., 48.52, 48.117

Jumping-Jacks Shoes Inc., 48.118

June Dairy Products Co., 33.2, 33.12

Jung & Wulff Co., 15.35

Juvenile Shoe Corp., 48.149

JVC America Inc., 5.49

Kabo brassiere, 121.20

Kaffee Hag Corp., 27.27, 27.49

Kahlua, 71.40

Kahn Tailoring Co., 26.118

Kaiser, 7.55

Kaiser Aluminum and Chemical Corp., 75.9

Kaiser-Frazer Corp., 7.55

Kaiser Jeep Corp., 7.83

Kalamazoo Stove Co., 58.31

Kanner, Samuel, 126.36

Kansas City Kansan, 85.107

Kansas City Post, 85.164, 85.324

Kansas City Star, 85.315

Karastan Rug Mills, 46.2, 46.29

Karastan rugs, 46.29

Karges Furniture Co., 50.21

Karry-lite luggage, 72.17

Kasco Mills, 42.4

Kasko Distillers Corp., 71.23

Katz, Samuel, 26.71

Kaufman Bros. & Bondy, 105.13, 105.23, 115.146

Kaufmann & Baer Co., 100.20

Kawasaki Motors Corp., 77.2

Kay Musical Instrument Co., 80.19

Kaynee Co., The, 26.74

Kayser gloves and hosiery, 61.9

Kayser-Roth Corp., 26.40, 61.49

Kayser-Roth Glove Co. Inc., 61.9

Kayser-Roth Hosiery Co. Inc., 61.30, 61.37, 61.46, 61.53

Kayser-Roth Intimate Apparel Co., 121.48

Kaywoodie Co., 105.1, 105.8, 105.18, 105.20, 105.27, 105.33

KC baking powder, 11.55

K-D Manufacturing Co., 117.17

Keds Corp., 48.153, 48.162

Keene Corp., 31.33

Keener Rubber Inc., 81.51

Keep-Kool, 26.127

Keepsake diamond ring, 67.26

Keikhaefer Mercury, 16.8

Keiser Mfg. Co., 69.4

Keith Co., George E., 48.128, 48.148

Keith Furnace Co., 58.1

Keith Highlanders, 48.148

Kelley Island Lime & Transport Co., 42.48

Kellogg Co., The, 21.3, 21.4, 21.16, 21.19, 21.20, 21.22, 21.23, 21.30, 21.35, 21.40, 21.41, 21.44, 21.45, 21.47, 21.50

Kellogg's All-Bran, 21.19, 21.41, 21.45

Kellogg's Sugar Frosted Flakes, 21.44

Kelly cigar, 115.85

Kelly Services Inc., 40.2, 40.4, 40.5

Kelly-Springfield Motor Truck, 120.18

Kelly-Springfield Tire Co., The, 114.18

Kelsey-Hayes Co., 8.71

Kelvinator Co., 60.15, 60.20, 60.43, 60.60, 60.88, 60.112, 60.117, 60.118

Kemper Insurance Co., 64.111
Kendall Co., The, 35.35
Kendall Refining Co., 88.56, 88.70
Ken-La Farms, 42.8
Ken-L-Biskit, 87.3, 87.5
Ken-L-Products Div., Quaker Oats Co., 87.3, 87.5
Kennedy, John F., 91.11, 91.165, 91.196, 91.199, 91.225
Kennedy, Robert F., 91.383
Kennedy Co., Colin B., 95.72
Kent, 115.112, 115.151
Kent brushes, 54.7
Kenton Pharmacal Co., 54.42
Kentucky, Commonwealth of, 36.23
Kentucky Dept. of Commerce, 36.2
Kentucky Tavern, 71.46, 71.128
Kenwood Electronics Inc., 5.16, 5.43, 5.53, 122.7
Kerman Stores, 100.7
Kerr Bros., 20.12, 20.13
Kessler's blended whiskey, 71.87
Kestenman Bros., 124.22
Keyspray, 24.67
Keystone Chemical Co., 24.67, 86.14
Keystone Emery Mills, 32.44, 117.22
Kiddie-Kar, 118.10
Kid Group, 48.82
Kiel Furniture Co., 50.20
Kilgen & Son, George, 80.3
Kimball International, 80.13, 80.14, 80.41
Kimberly-Clark Corp., 83.1, 116.12, 116.29
Kimco Auto Products Inc., 8.69
Kinder-Garten shoes, 48.32
King-Buffalo Inc., 95.44
King Edward cigars, 115.19
King-Fisher Mattress Co., 13.37
King Motor Car, 7.57
King Razor Co., 104.7, 104.50
Kings Brewery, 14.41
Kingsport Corp., 103.14
Kingston Watch Co., 124.18
King whiskey, 71.47
Kinnear Corp., 18.67
Kinney Co., G. R., 48.3, 48.45, 48.81
Kinsey, 71.126
Kirstein & Sons, E., 41.5
Kirsten Pipe Co., 105.2, 105.12
Kitchenaid appliances, 60.61
Kitchenaid mixer, 68.17
Kitchen Bouquet Inc., 29.35
Kitchen Klenzer, 24.38

Kitchen Kompact Inc., 18.78
Kleinert's Rubber Co., 26.67
Klein's, New York, 100.19
Klopman Mills Inc., 113.2
K Mart Corp., 100.35
Knabe & Co., Wm, 80.2
Knape & Vogt Mfg. Co., 55.3
Knapp and Tubbs Inc., 50.4
Knapp-Monarch Co., 60.38
Knorr soups, 47.51
Knox Gelatine Co., Chas, 47.80, 47.96, 47.110
Knox the Hatter, 26.61, 26.115
Kobrand Corp., 71.37, 71.96, 71.106
Kodak Disc camera, 89.11
Kodak Ektalith, 81.40
Kodel Radio Corp., 95.33, 95.56
Koh-I-Noor Rapidograph Inc., 126.19
Kohler and Campbell Inc., 80.10
Kohler Mfg. Co., 35.15, 35.32
Kohler Swiss Chocolate Co., Peter Cailler, 20.34
Kohnstamm Inc., V. & E., 107.1
Ko-Lo Corp., 107.47
Kondon Mfg. Co., 35.50
Kool, 115.29, 115.153
Kool-Aid, 107.8, 107.33
Koolfoam pillows, 13.4
Koorc Spat shoes, 48.113
Kopper Gas & Coke Co., 59.13
Koppers Co. Inc., 31.6
Kops Bros. Inc., 121.46
Korbel & Bros. Inc., F., 125.32
Korbel Brut Champagne, 125.32
Koroseal raincoat, 26.8
Kotex, 116.12
Kozy Komfort Shoe Mfg. Co., 48.116
Kraft & Bros., J. L., 33.42
Kraft Foods, 29.4, 47.2, 47.36
Kraft Inc., 33.10, 33.23, 33.27, 33.36, 33.41, 47.48
Krause Milling Co., Chas. A., 21.39
Kreml shampoo, 54.15
Kreolite floors, 46.21
Kroehler Mfg. Co., 50.8, 50.42
Kroger Co., 100.5
Krohn Feckheimer Co., 48.21, 48.22, 48.145
Kroydon Golf Corp., 108.14
Krueger, 14.32, 14.39, 14.66
Krueger Beverage Co., 107.10
Krueger Metal Products Co., 50.5

Krushen salts, 35.43
Kruskal and Kruskal, 26.58
Krylon Dept., Borden Chemical Co., 82.31
Kuehnle-Wilson, 82.18
Kwikset Div. Emhart Corp., 55.1
Kyanize, 82.57
La Barge Mirrors Inc., 65.15
La Belle Iron Works, 75.11
Lack Carpet Co., 46.8
Ladies Home Journal, 85.145, 85.265
Lady Baltimore, 72.2, 72.8
Lady Borden ice cream, 33.11
Lady Crosby diamond rings, 67.12
Lady Speed Stick deodorant, 116.13
Laird, Schober & Co., 48.16
Lake Central Airlines Inc., 4.64
Lamar Life Insurance Co., 64.100
Lambert-Hudnut Mfg. Labs Inc., 32.77
Lambert Pharmacal Co., 34.5, 34.12, 34.13, 34.27, 35.22, 35.119, 35.123
Lambert Radio Co., Leon, 95.37
Lampe Shoe Co., 48.69
Lamson & Hubbard Co., 26.116
Lana Oil soap, 106.37
Landers, Frary & Clark, 47.37, 68.1
Land O' Lakes Creameries Inc., 33.7
Landon, Alf, 91.17, 91.54, 91.169, 91.220, 91.377
Lane Co., The, 86.6
Lane Furniture, 50.32
Lang Brewery, Gerhard, 14.20
Langenberg Hat Co., 26.138
Langenburg Mfg. Co., 58.20
Langendorf United Bakeries, 11.4
Langrock Clothing Co., 26.112, 26.133
Lan-O-Tone Products, 54.24
Lansing Sound Inc., James B., 5.5
Lanvin-Charles of the Ritz Inc., 84.19
La Prensa, 85.181
La Presse, 85.210
La Primadora cigars, 115.106
La Resista corset, 121.24
Largman Gray Co., 61.36
Larson, Jr. Co., L. P., 20.35
LaSalle Extension University, 101.10
Lasergrafix 1200 printer, 28.82
Lastex swimsuit, 109.3
Lasticraft foundations, 121.19

Latchford Glass Co., 52.1
Latrobe Steel Co., 75.28
Latterman Shoe Mfg. Co., 48.53
Laucks Inc., I. F., 82.59
Laughter, 85.23
Laundry Age, 85.188
Laundryette Mfg. Co., 60.134
Laundry Industry of Seattle, 25.5
Laura Secord candy, 20.73
Lava, 106.36
Lavoris, 34.24
La Vor Products Co., 47.76
Lawrence Leather Co., 48.138
Leadclad Wire Co., 18.41
Lead Industries Association, 75.17, 82.83
League collars, 103.3
Lear Siegler Inc., 28.14
Lectric shave lotion, 104.21
Lee balloon tires, 114.23
Lee Co. Inc., H. D., 26.60, 26.84, 26.134
Lee Data Corp., 28.12
Lee Foods, Sara, 11.37
Leek and Sons Inc., C. P., 16.14
Lee Machinery Corp., 73.37
Lee-Marion Co., 70.39
Lee Mercantile Co., H. D., 26.44
Leeming/Pacquin, 35.33, 104.25, 104.26
Lee & Perrin's sauce, 29.33
Lees and Sons Co., James, 46.32
Lee's Magnesia, 35.129
Lee-Strauss Co. Inc., 35.129
Lee tires, 8.43
Lee work clothes, 26.134
Leggett, F. H., 29.25
L'eggs pantyhose, 61.24
L'eggs Products Inc., 61.24
Legion Magazine, 85.134
Lehigh Mfg. Co., 60.4
Lehigh Valley Railroad, 96.67
Lehn and Fink Consumer Products, 24.43, 32.17, 84.33, 116.25
Leisy Brewing Co., 14.2, 14.87
Lektro Products Inc., 104.2, 104.32
Lektro shaver, 104.43
Lelong Parfums Corp., Lucieu, 84.10
Lemar lamps, 70.39
Lennox Industries Inc., 58.12, 58.29, 58.48
Lenox Inc., 67.26
Lentheric, 84.15, 84.23

Leopold, Solomon & Eisendrath,
26.55
Lever Bros. Co., 24.35, 24.41, 34.16,
34.20, 34.30, 104.49, 106.6, 106.11,
106.19, 106.27
Levi Strauss & Co., 26.34
Levy & Sons, M. S., 26.142
Levy & Sons., Sid, 121.8, 121.34,
121.37, 121.38
Levy's Sons, Chas., 26.99
Lewis and Son., William, 80.25
Lewis Co., G. B., 42.5
Lewis-Howe Co., 35.91
Libby, McNeil & Libby, 47.57,
47.99, 47.113
Libby-Owens-Ford Co., 31.25
Liberty, 85.55
Liberty Carillon, 80.38
Liberty Cherry & Fruit Co., 49.23
Liberty Magazine, 85.26
Liberty Mutual Insurance Co.,
64.65, 64.106, 64.114
Liberty Orchards Co., 20.58
Liberty Prods., 18.45
Lidz Brothers Inc., 103.4
Liebmann Breweries, 14.47, 14.59,
14.147
Life, 85.36, 85.340, 85.349
Life brassiere, 121.18
Lifebuoy, 106.6, 106.27
Lifebuoy shaving cream, 104.49
Life International, 85.348
Life Magazine, 85.184
Life Savers, 20.36, 20.55, 20.74
Life Savers Inc., 20.6, 20.8, 20.36,
20.74
Life Stride, 48.164
Liggett Group, 115.42, 115.110,
115.121, 115.125, 115.162, 115.170,
115.174
Liggett & Myers Inc., 115.1, 115.6,
115.10, 115.24, 115.74
Liggett's chocolates, 20.57
lighters, 105.15, 105.25
Lightolier Inc., 70.1, 70.4
Lilli-Ann Corp., 26.49
Lilly and Co., Eli, 35.67
Lilyette Brassiere Co., 121.33
Lily of France Corset Co., 121.4
Lime Cola Co., 107.2, 107.19, 107.36
Lincoln, Abraham, 91.1, 91.8, 91.65,
91.86, 91.87, 91.88, 91.90, 91.95,
91.141, 91.161, 91.166, 91.182,
91.183, 91.191, 91.204, 91.205,

91.214, 91.230, 91.238, 91.248,
91.253, 91.255, 91.291, 91.316,
91.321, 91.330, 91.346, 91.351,
91.378, 91.386
Lincoln Candies Inc., Mary, 20.38
Lincoln Continental, 7.10
Lincoln Zephyr, 7.79
Lindsay Ripe Olive Co., 47.104
Lindy Pen Co. Inc., 126.20
Linit laundry starch, 24.54
Linkman & Co., M., 105.10, 105.14,
105.28, 105.32
Lionel, 118.23
Lionel Toy Corp., 118.18
Lion Oil Refining Co., 88.59
Lipton Inc., 47.32, 47.109
Lipton Inc., Thomas J., 110.3,
110.8, 110.15
Lipton Inc., Thos. J., 29.9
Lipton's, 110.3, 110.8
Liquidometer Corp., The, 63.2
Listerine, 35.22, 35.119, 35.123
Listerine tooth paste, 34.5, 34.12,
34.13, 34.27
Lite, 14.38
Lithographers National Association,
2.5
Little America frozen foods, 47.39
Little Yankee, 48.64
Litton Microwave ovens, 60.71
Litton Systems Inc., 60.71
Livingstone's oats, 21.15
Lockheed Corp., 3.10, 3.25
Lockwood Brackett Co., 106.30
Loco-Builder electric trains, 118.25
Loftis Bros. & Co., 67.8, 67.19
Logan, Jonathan, 26.17
Log Cabin syrup, 29.44
Loma Linda Food Co., 47.7
Loma Plant Food, 69.7
Lombardi Radio Mfg. Co., 95.18
London Life Insurance Co., 64.59
Long-Bell Lumber Co., 18.6, 18.103
long distance calling, 111.14
Longines-Wittnauer Watch Co.,
124.24, 124.53
Look, 85.30, 85.256
Loose-Wiles Biscuit Co., 11.25
Lord Oxford lighters, 105.31
Lord & Thomas, 2.34
Lorillard Corp., 115.4, 115.34,
115.43, 115.56, 115.94, 115.98,
115.107, 115.112, 115.124, 115.132,
115.142, 115.151, 115.177

Lori-Lou girdles, 121.26
Lorrie Deb Corp., 26.65
Lorr Laboratories, 32.4, 32.21, 32.38, 32.42, 32.46
Los Angeles Bureau of Power and Light, 37.6
Los Angeles, California, 36.26
Los Angeles Evening Herald, 85.48
Los Angeles Examiner, 85.224
Lotus Development Corp., 28.54
Lotus software, 28.54
Louis Greenwald, 115.75
Louis Rich cold cuts, 74.10
Louisville and Nashville Railroad, 96.28
Lovable Co., 121.16, 121.17
Loving Care, 54.27
Lowenberg Co., 108.19
Lowry Coffee Co., 27.45
Lubeck Brewing Co., 14.113
Lucas & Co., John, 82.32
Lucky Strike, 115.36, 115.39, 115.50, 115.67, 115.68, 115.77, 115.78, 115.79, 115.80, 115.108, 115.119, 115.181
Ludlum Steel Co., 75.29
Ludwig Drum Co., 80.6, 80.20, 80.27
Luft-Tangee Inc., 32.18
Lukens Steel Co., 75.27
Lumaghi Coal Co., 59.9
Lunt Silversmiths, 67.31
Lunt silverware, 67.31
Lustberg-Nast Co., 26.22
Lustray shirts, 26.22
Lustre-Cream shampoo, 54.35, 54.37
Lux soap, 24.41, 106.19
Luzier Inc., 32.50
Lyman Gun Sight Corp., 44.25
Lyon-Healy Co., 80.9
Lyon's, 110.16
Lyon Van Lines Inc., 79.6
Lysol disinfectant spray, 24.43
Maaco Enterprises Inc., 9.10
Maas Co., Julian, 2.13
macaroni, 47.10, 47.23, 47.77, 47.93
Maccar Truck Co., 120.21
MacFarlane Nut Co., 49.4, 49.19
MacGregor Co., 108.28
MacGregor Goldsmith Inc., 108.24
Mackinac Island, Michigan, 119.43
Mack Trucks Inc., 120.15, 120.27
MacLaren Mfg. Co., 95.79
Maclean's Magazine, 85.65

Maclean's Magazine, Toronto, 85.140
M/A-COM Linkabit Inc., 28.59
Macy's, 100.18
Mademoiselle, 48.134
Mademoiselle, 85.105
Made-Rite flour, 11.5
Magee Carpet Co., 46.11, 46.17, 46.18, 46.36
Magic Chef Inc., 60.105
Magill-Weinsheimer, 83.39
Magnavox Co., 58.32, 95.2, 95.4, 95.20, 95.32, 95.66, 95.75, 95.77, 112.10
Mahogany Assn. Inc., 18.93
Maid-Easy Cleansing Products Corp., 24.103
Maidenform Inc., 121.30, 121.55
Mail Pouch chewing tobacco, 115.25
Mail Pouch Tobacco Co., 115.135
Maine Dept. of Economic Development, 36.6
Maine Development Commission, 47.61
Majestic, 95.42
Major Equipment Co., 37.8
Majorca, 67.37
Malady & MacLauchlan, 81.25
Malleable Iron Range Co., 60.92
Mallory Hat Co. Inc., 26.117
Malta Mfg. Co., 18.90
Maltcao, 15.6
Manhattan Industries Inc., 26.66
Manhattan Soap Co., 106.34
Manitoba, Canada, 119.22
Mannesmann-Export Corp., 31.14
Man-O-West slacks and pants, 26.132
Manpower Inc., 40.6
Manufacturers Hanover Trust Co., 43.28
Manufacturers Liability Insurance Co., 64.104
Manufacturers News, 85.234
Manufacturers Trust Co., 43.15
Maple Flooring Mfrs. Assn., 46.14
Maple Island Inc., 33.24
Maraca rum, 71.66
Marathon Div., American Can Co., 83.54, 83.76
Marchant Calculating Machine Co., 81.33
Marchesi L and P Antinori, 125.27
Marcus-Lesoine Inc., 54.25

margarine, 47.30, 47.62
Marinello, 32.43
Marine Review, 85.43
Marion Power Shovel Co., 73.26
Marion Tool Works, 117.41
Marlboro, 115.26, 115.69, 115.87, 115.154
Marlboro shirts, 26.80
Marlin Firearms Co., 44.1, 44.19
Marmon Motor Car Co., 7.7
Marquette Mfg. Co., 8.4
Marriott Motor Hotels Inc., 62.35
Mars Candy Company, 20.64
Marshall mattress, 13.23
Marsh Furniture Co., 50.1
Mars Inc., 20.50
Marston & Brooks Co., 48.67
Martel cognac, 71.95
Martex, 12.5
Martinelli & Co., S., 15.11
Martini & Rossi vermouth, 125.25, 125.36
Martin & Martin, 24.95
Martin outboard motors, 16.17
Martin Reel Co., 45.15
Martin-Senour Co., 82.14, 82.40, 82.77
Marvelette Inc., 121.7
Marvella Inc., 67.7
Maryland Assurance Corp., 64.43
Maryland Pharmaceutical Co., 35.74, 35.75
Masland and Sons, C. H., 46.28
Mason Clothes, 26.51
Mason Fibre Co., 18.38
Mason Tire & Rubber Co., 114.14
Massachusetts, Commonwealth of, 36.9
Massachusetts Development & Industry Comm, 36.13
Massagic air cushion shoes, 48.1
Mass. Co-operative Bank League, 43.46
Masstor Systems Corp., 28.44
Master Lock Co., 55.5, 55.42, 55.43
Master Mix feeds, 42.36
Mathematica Products Group, Martin Marietta Data Systems Co., 28.38
Mathews Industries Inc., 75.18
Matson Lines, 102.7
Matson Navigation Co., 102.24, 102.25

Matsushita Electric Corp. of America, 5.42, 38.9
Matthews Co., 42.27
Maxell Corp., 5.18, 5.33, 28.25, 122.2
Max Factor make-up, 32.26
Maxima, 5.21, 5.27
Maxwell House, 27.5, 27.25, 27.53
Maybelline Co., 32.70, 32.78
Mayer Shoe Co., F., 48.57
Mayfair House, New York, 62.7, 62.15
Mayflower, 79.1
May Oil Burner Corp., 58.37
mayonnaise, 29.11, 29.23
Maytag Co., 60.49, 60.68, 60.100, 60.101, 60.149
Maytag washer, 60.49
Mazda auto lamps, 8.24
Mazda Motors of America, 7.66, 7.68
Mazola, 47.100
Mazola salad oil, 47.59
M/B Designs Inc., 65.7
McAn Shoe Co., Thom, 48.183
McCall's, 85.94, 85.339
McCallum Hosiery Co., 61.51
McCarthy, Eugene, 91.103, 91.188
McCawley & Co. Inc., 26.113
McClellan, George, 91.78, 91.139, 91.208, 91.221, 91.223, 91.315, 91.361, 91.396
McClintock Co., 2.36
McClure's, 85.254
McCord Corp., 8.28
McCormack & Dodge Corp., 28.72
McCormick and Co. Inc., 27.62, 29.17, 29.37
McCormick & Co., 69.33
McDonald's, 99.11
McDonald's Corp., 99.5, 99.11
McFadden & Co., H. G., 70.22
McGovern, George, 91.42, 91.185, 91.237
McGraw-Edison Co., 60.98
McGraw-Hill Inc., 85.325, 94.1, 94.8, 94.11
McGregor-Doniger Inc., 26.50
MCI, 111.21
McIlhenny Co., 29.39, 29.42
McKesson & Robbins, 32.67, 34.37, 71.43
McKinley, William, 91.111, 91.155, 91.189, 91.222, 91.249, 91.295, 91.340

McKinney Mfg. Co., 55.18
McLaughlin's, 27.33
McLaughlin-Sweet Inc., 48.131
McNeil Consumer Products Co.,
    35.28, 35.115
MDB Systems Inc., 28.69
Mead Corp., The, 83.45
Mead Johnson and Co., 56.4
Meakin & Ridgway, 23.7
Mears Heel Co., F. W., 48.135
Meccano, 118.4
Mechling Barge Lines Inc., A. L.,
    102.12
Medisalt, 34.8
Medtech Laboratories Inc., 35.106
Meese Inc., 60.136
Meiselbach Mfg. Co. Inc., 45.26
Melachrino, 115.152
Melba Mfg. Co., 32.62
Melbroke ties, 26.94
Meldan Co. Inc., 50.34
Mellon National Bank, 43.4
Melville Shoe Corp., 48.55, 48.152,
    48.167
Mem Co., 106.24
Memorex Corp., 5.13
Memorex recording cassettes, 5.13
Menace perfume, 84.6
Mendel-Drucker, 72.1
Menley & James Laboratories,
    35.34, 35.44, 35.49, 35.108
Mennen Co., The, 104.27, 104.54,
    116.13
Mentholatum Co., The, 35.112,
    35.118
Mentholatum Deep Heating Rub,
    35.118
Mercedes-Benz, 7.29
Mercedes-Benz of North America
    Inc., 7.29
Merchandising Co., The, 35.56
Merchants Coffee Co. of New
    Orleans, 27.9
Merchants Journal and Commerce,
    85.21
Merchants National Bank, 43.23
Merchant Tailors Society, 26.111
Merckens Chocolate Co., 15.6
Merck, Sharp and Dohme Div.,
    Merck and Co. Inc., 35.137
Mercury, 7.13
Mercury Comet, 7.84
Mercury outboard motor, 16.11
Mercury Record Corp., 97.4

Meredith Publishing Co., 2.19
Merit cigarettes, 115.109
Merit Clothing Co., 26.33
Merremaker Corp., 118.5
Merriam, H. W., 48.107
Merriam Co., G. & C., 94.7, 94.12,
    94.14, 94.16, 94.17, 94.19
Merriam Shoe Co., 48.126
Merriam-Webster, 94.12, 94.14, 94.17
merri-go-rounds, 118.5
Merrill Lynch Pierce Fenner and
    Smith, 66.9, 66.10
Mersman Tables, 50.57
Merton & Co., C. S., 26.135
Metal Hydrides Inc., 22.18
Metal Ware Corp., 60.3
Metalworking News, 85.341
Metrecal, 56.4
Metro-Goldwyn-Mayer, 78.2, 78.8
Metropolis Brewery of New Jersey,
    Inc., 14.12
Metropolitan Furniture Adjusters,
    81.46
Metropolitan Life Insurance Co.,
    64.36, 64.41, 64.84, 64.97
Metropolitan Newspapers, New
    York, 85.219
Meyer Bros. Drug Co., 35.134
Meyers gloves, 123.15
Meyers Manufacturing Co., 123.15
Meyers & Son Inc., Louis, 26.38,
    123.14
Miami Herald, 85.97
Miami Margarine Co., 47.85
Miami Realty Co., 66.8
Michelin, 114.4
Michelob, 14.101, 14.145
Michigan, 36.15
Michigan Bell Telephone Co.,
    111.12
Michigan Business Farmer, 85.215
Michigan Seating Co., 50.22
Michigan Stove Co., 60.50
Mickelberry Corp., 74.16
Mickelberry's sausage, 74.16
Micom Systems Inc., 28.28
Micropoint Inc., 126.8
Midas Mufflers, 9.8
Midway Chemical Co., 24.64, 24.90,
    86.5
Midwest Radio Co., 95.24
Miele Inc., Ralph A., 50.29
Miessner Piano Co., 80.15

Mifflin, McCambridge Co., The, 35.114

Mifflin alcohol, 35.114

Mikimoto Inc., K., 67.35

Miles Laboratories Inc., 24.16, 35.29, 35.73, 35.86, 56.6

Milk Products Div., Pet Inc., 56.3

Milky Way Co., 20.72

Miller, 14.54, 14.146

Miller Brewing Co., 14.30, 14.38, 14.54, 14.125, 14.146

Miller High Life, 14.30, 14.125

Miller luggage, 72.4

Miller-Morton Co., 86.15

Millers Falls Co., 117.40

Miller tires, 114.8

Millis Advertising Co., 2.26

Milner Hotels, 62.10

Milo hose, 61.50

Milwaukee Corrugating Co., 18.8

Milwaukee Journal, 85.86

Milwaukee Lace Paper Co., 83.34

Milwaukee Paper Co., 83.12

Milwaukee Road, 96.4, 96.60

Milwaukee Tank Works, 73.36

Min-A-Gro Corp., 87.11

Mineral Refining & Chemical Co., 82.37

Ming Inc., 110.10, 110.17

Mini-Max hearing-aid devices, 57.1

Minneapolis Bedding Co., 13.18

Minneapolis Knitting Works, 26.120

Minneapolis-Moline Inc., 42.14

Minneapolis Steel & Machinery Co., 42.42

Minneapolis Tribune, 85.209

Minnesota Dept. of Business Development, 36.16

Minnesota Mining and Manufacturing Co., 30.4, 30.5

Minolta Corp., 89.6, 89.16, 89.27

Minolta X100 camera, 89.16

Minox Chemical Corp., 35.14

Minox Corp., 89.1, 89.24

Mint Products Co., 20.55

Minute Model Gulbransen piano, 80.43

Minwax Co., 82.58

Miracle Whip salad dressing, 29.4

Mirawal Co., 18.64

Mirro aluminum, 68.12

Mirro Aluminum Co., 75.25

Mishawaka Rubber Co. Inc., 48.88

Mishawaka Woolen Mfg. Co., 113.20

Mississippi, 119.38

Missouri, 119.37

Missouri Commerce and Industrial Development Commission, 36.11

Missouri-Kansas-Texas Railroad Co., 96.22

Missouri Pacific Railroad Co., 96.59

Mistol rub, 35.78

Mittman Co., M., 13.1

M & M Candies, 20.64

Mobil Oil Corp., 9.2, 88.20

Model pipe tobacco, 115.115

Modern Farming, New Orleans, 85.239

Modern Machine Shop, 85.166

Modern Medicine, 85.233

Modern Packaging, 85.205

Modern Priscilla, Boston, 85.321

Modess, 116.5, 116.26

Moe-Bridges Co., 70.12

Moeller Co., A. E., 63.10

Moët champagne, 125.10

Mohasco Corp., 46.6

Mohawk Data Sciences, 28.26

Mohawk rugs and carpets, 46.6

Mojud, 61.30

Molded Fiber Glass Companies Inc., 18.44

Monarch Cleaner Corp., 24.91

Monarch Knitting Co., Ltd., 61.8

Monarch Life Insurance Co., 64.40

Monarch Metal Weatherstrip Co., 18.51

Monet Jewelers, 67.24

Money Making, 85.253

Monitor Stove Co., 58.18

Monmouth Hosiery Mills, 61.44

Monogram Models Inc., 118.21

Monroe Auto Equipment Co., 8.67

Monroe Calculating Machine Co., 81.7

Monsanto Co., 22.1

Montag, Inc., Div. Westab Inc., 83.85

Montana Highway Commission, 119.35

Montauk Paint Mfg. Co., 82.5

Montblanc CS-Line Pens, 126.19

Montclair, 115.45, 115.73

Montclair Laboratories, 32.30

Montgomery Inc., J. A., 64.29

Montgomery Ward, 100.30

Montreal Daily Star, 85.63

Montreal Tourist & Convention Bureau, 119.1
Monumental Life Insurance Co., 64.64
Moody Bible Institute of Chicago, 101.9
Moog Industries Inc., 8.30
Moore Business Forms Inc., 81.54
Moore Corp., The, 58.30, 60.2, 60.93
Moore-McCormack Lines Inc., 102.20
Moore's Hi-Lo broiler, 60.93
More cigarettes, 115.65
Morey Mercantile Co., 27.32
Morgan Co., The, 82.74
Moroney Inc., James, 71.75
Morrison Ricker Mfg. Co., 123.6
Morrison Tractor, 42.59
Morris Plan Insurance Society, 64.53
Morse & Rogers, 48.169
Morton Chemical Co., 22.17
Morton Salt Co., 29.41, 29.46
Mosinee Paper Mills Co., 83.77
Mossberg and Sons Inc., O. F., 44.13
Mother Parker's, 110.1
Mothersill's seasick remedy, 35.124
Moth-Tox, 86.2
Motorite, 88.69
Motor Land, 85.297
Motor, New York, 85.194
Motorola Inc., 38.12, 95.27, 95.65
Motor Service, 85.195
Motorstoker Corp., 58.45
Mottahedeh and Sons, 65.9
Mott's apple juice, 15.33
Mountain Valley Water, 15.16
Moving Picture World, 85.93
Mr. John, 26.32
Mrs. Day's Ideal Baby Shoe Co., 48.24, 48.101
Mrs. Paul's fish fillets, 47.31, 47.52
Mrs. Paul's Kitchens, 47.31, 47.52
Mrs. Stewart's bluing, 24.73, 24.85
Mueller Co., C. F., 47.10, 47.23, 47.77
Mueller Mfg. Co., H., 55.6, 55.14
Muffets Corp., 21.42
Multigraph Co., 30.10
Mum, 116.1
Mumm and Co., G. H., 125.17
Mumm champagne, 125.17

Munsingwear Inc., 121.9, 121.29, 121.31, 121.50
Mura, 111.31
Murad, 115.72
Murchison National Bank, 43.21
Muriel, 115.127
Muriel cigars, 115.81, 115.186
Murine Co. Inc., 35.85
Murphy Dor Bed Co., 13.32
Murphy Paint Co., 82.68
Murphy & Saval Co., 48.83
Murray Corp., 8.55
Musebeck Shoe Co., 48.49, 48.165, 48.182
Muskegon Piston Ring, 8.45
Mustad & Sons, O., 45.17, 45.20
Mustang, 7.4
Musterole, 35.10
Mutual Life Assurance of Canada, 64.58
Mutual of New York, 64.48
Mutual of Omaha Insurance Co., 64.88
Mutual Products Co. Inc., 81.18
Mutual Truck Co., 120.1
Myers & Sons, D., 48.26
Mystic Cream Co., 32.45
Mystic foam upholstery cleaner, 24.14
Nabisco Inc., 21.38, 21.46, 47.101
Nacho Cheese Doritos, 47.50
NAHB Journal of Homebuilding, 85.245
Narragansett Brewing Co., 14.32, 14.39, 14.66, 14.78, 14.135
Nash, 7.104
Nason Paint Co., 82.46
Nassau Development Board, Nassau, Bahamas, 119.23
Nathan & Co., Ltd., Jos., London, 10.7
National Airlines Inc., 4.11
National Association of Ice Cream Mfrs., 33.19
National Association of Straw Hat Mfrs., 26.37
National Automotive Parts Association, 8.7
National Bank of Tulsa, 43.54
National bicycles, 108.2
National Biscuit Co., 11.11, 11.38, 11.57, 21.5, 21.12, 21.36
National Blank Book Co., 81.53

National Briar Pipe Co., 105.7, 105.9
National Broadcasting Co., 17.2
National Car Rental System Inc., 6.7
National Cash Register Co., 28.6, 81.64, 83.19
National City Bank, 43.51
National City Savings Bank & Trust Co., 43.41
National Clean Up Campaign Bureau, 92.10
National Coffee Council, 27.28
National Confectioners' Assn., 20.26
National Contest Bulletin, 85.118
National Cotton Council, 113.10, 113.24
National Dairy Products, 33.18
National Distilleries, 71.51
National Distillers and Chemical Corp., 71.19, 71.21, 71.39, 71.53, 71.85, 71.86, 71.103, 71.137, 125.12
National Distillers Products Corp., 71.108
National Fiberstock Envelope Co., 83.73
National fruit cake, 11.11
National Geographic Magazine, 85.125
National Gypsum Co., 18.28, 18.58
National Investors Corp., 66.21
National Jewelers Publicity Association, 67.11
National Life Insurance Co., 64.61
National Life Insurance Co. of Vermont, 64.7
National LP-Gas Market Development Council, 59.16
National Lumber Manufacturers Association, 18.35
National Machine Tool Builders Assn., 73.21
National Meter Co., 63.4
National Mills Div., U. S. Industries, 61.43
National Mortar & Supply Co., 18.25
National Oak Lumbermen's Assn., 18.125, 18.126
National Oats Co., The, 21.26
National Oil Co., 88.73
National Oil Fuel Institute Inc., 88.79
National Paint Co., 82.63

National Paving Brick Mfrs., 18.100
National Petroleum News, 85.103
National Plastics Products Co., 65.20
National Pneumatic Co., 18.85
National Premium beer, 14.81
National Presto Industries Inc., 68.19
National Radiator Co., 58.4
National Radio Institute, 101.7
National Railroad Passenger Corp., 96.3
National Rain Bird Sales and Engineering Corp., 69.28
National Refining Co., 88.41, 88.62
National Refrigerating Co., 60.121
National Restaurant Association, 99.1, 99.8
National Screw and Mfg. Co., 55.10
National Slate Assn., 18.70
National Surety Co., 64.120
National Transitads Inc., 2.33
National Underwriter, 85.57
National Union Electric Corp., 112.5, 112.6
National X-Ray Reflector Co., 70.25
Nation's Business, 85.344
Nationwide Insurance Co., 64.52, 64.92
Naturalizer shoes, 48.89, 48.158
Nature's Remedy laxative, 35.63
Nature-Tread Mfg. Co., 48.95
Nawa Co., The, 54.23
Nazareth, 121.22
Nazareth Mills, 121.22
NEC Information Systems Inc., 28.29
Needlecraft Magazine, 85.172
Needles-Brooker Co., L., 103.10
Neet deodorant, 116.9
Nehi Corp., 107.9, 107.39
Nekoosa-Edwards Paper Co., 83.21, 83.22, 83.25
Nelson Knitting Co., 61.38
Neolite soles, 48.120
Neosho Nurseries, 69.35
Neo-Syn Co., 35.89, 35.90
Nescafe, 27.41, 27.55
Nestle Co. Inc., 20.42, 27.41, 27.55
Nestle Color Tint, 54.2
Nestle Hairlac, 54.38
Nestle-LeMur Co., 54.2, 54.38
Nestle's chocolates, 20.42

Nettleton Co., A. E., 48.112, 48.150
Networking Microplexer, 28.67
Nevamar, 65.20
Newark Evening News, 85.16
Newell-Gutradt Co., 106.23
Newell Mfg. Co., 55.15
New England Fish Co., 47.70
New First National Bank, 43.14
New Hampshire, 119.26
New Holland Div., Sperry Rand
    Corp., 42.18, 42.34, 42.41
New Idea Farm Equipment Co.,
    42.54
New Jersey Egg Market Committee,
    47.28
New Jersey Public Service Electric
    and Gas Co., 93.9
New Jersey Zinc Co., 18.57, 82.49
Newman & Sons Inc., 121.44
New Orleans, 119.20
Newport, 115.124
Newskin Co., 35.57
News-Post, 85.59
News Week, 85.208
Newsweek, 85.292
New-Syn Co., The, 35.80
New York Central Railroad, 96.69,
    96.76, 96.79
New York Central System, 96.33
New York Commercial, 85.298
New York Edison, 37.1
New Yorker, New York, 62.28
New York Life Insurance Co., 64.38,
    64.72, 64.93
New York Merchandise Co. Inc.,
    100.11
New York State Dept. of
    Commerce, 36.4
New York State Tourist
    Commission, 119.21
New York Stock Exchange, 66.14
New York Stock Exchange
    Members, 66.13
New York Sunday American.,
    85.178
New York Times, 85.12
New Zealand, 119.6
Niagara Searchlight Co., 70.8
Nichol Kola, 107.46
Nichols Aluminum Co., 18.79
Nicholson Co., H. R., 107.46
Nicholson File Co., 117.1
Nickel Plate Railroad, 96.62
Nikon cameras, 89.32

Nikon Inc., 89.32
Niles Tools Works Co., 117.33
Nimrod Ward Mfg. Co., 98.3
Nippon Kokan, 75.26
Nissan Motor Corp., 7.63, 7.91
Nixon, Richard M., 91.39, 91.75,
    91.82, 91.85, 91.192, 91.195, 91.200,
    91.201, 91.219, 91.298, 91.325,
    91.334, 91.335, 91.336, 91.355,
    91.384, 91.422, 91.423
Noblitt-Sparks, 95.13
Nocona Athletic Goods Co., 108.29
Noctil, 24.25
No-Ease Co., 41.8
Nogar Clothing Mfg. Co., 26.77
Nolan, C. A., 115.183
Noname Hat Mfg. Co., 26.91
Noned Corp., 48.109
Nopco Chemical Co., 22.3
Norcliff Thayer Inc., 35.30, 35.63,
    116.21
Norcross Inc., 51.1
Norelco, 60.1, 104.39, 104.40, 104.56
Norfolk and Western Railway, 96.58
Norfolk, Va, 36.18
Norge, 60.144
Norge Co., 60.9, 60.17, 60.65, 60.97,
    60.140
Norge ranges, 60.65
North American Aviation Inc., 3.15
North American Life, 64.78
North American Philips Corp., 60.1,
    104.39, 104.40, 104.56
North American Rockwell Corp.,
    3.19, 31.15
North American Van Lines Inc.,
    79.8
North British & Mercantile
    Insurance Co., 64.37
North Bros. Mfg. Co., 117.23,
    117.44
North Carolina Dept. of
    Conservation, 36.25
Northcool suits, 26.147
North East Electric Co., 8.5, 37.25,
    37.30
Northeast Utilities, 93.3
Northern Electric Co., 60.141
Northern Hard Maple Mfrs., 18.87
Northern Hemlock Mfrs. Assn., 18.9
Northern Insurance Co., 64.74
Northern Machinery Co., 58.33
Northern Natural Gas Co., 93.2

Northern Pacific Railway, 96.9, 96.77
Northland Ski Mfg. Co., 108.38
North Memphis Coal Co., 59.15
Northwest Airlines Inc., 4.38, 4.50
Northwest Envelope Co., 83.30
Northwestern Mutual Life Insurance Co., The, 64.9
Northwest Paper Co., 83.5
Nor'West Farmer, Winnipeg, 85.165, 85.300
Norwich-Eaton Pharmaceuticals, 35.59, 35.72, 35.109
Norwich Pharmacal Co., 35.116
No-Sha-Do hosiery, 61.12
Novelty Mills Co., 11.41
Novelty Rubber Sales Co., 61.34
Noxell Corp., 32.7, 35.21
Noxema skin cream, 32.7, 35.21
N-tane, 88.53
Nu-Art Laboratories, 32.1
Nulyne Laboratories, 34.41
Numark, 5.31
Nunn-Bush Shoe Co., 48.14, 48.37, 48.44
Nunn, Bush & Weldon Shoe Co., 48.35
Nunziola accordion, 80.45
Nupercainal, 35.128
Nutone Inc., 60.110
Nutrasweet, 56.11
Nut Tootsie Rolls, 20.40
Nyquil cold medicine, 35.122
Nytol, 35.25
Oakhurst Co., 35.78, 35.97
Oakite Products Inc., 24.39
Oakland, 7.97
Oakland Motor Car Co., 7.97
Oakland Tribune, 85.155
Oak Service Bureau, Hardwood Institute, 50.40
O'Brien Varnish Co., 82.3, 82.38
Occident flour, 11.12
Ocean Spray Cranberries Inc., 15.18
Ocean Spray cranberry drinks, 15.18
O-Cedar polish, 24.10
O-Cedar products, 24.88
Ochee Spring Water Co., 15.20
Oculens sunglasses, 41.9
Odol Corp., 88.67
Odorono deodorant, 116.15
Ohio Brass Co., 18.32, 18.66, 18.82, 117.20

Ohio Butterine Co., 33.28
Ohio Edison-Pennsylvania Power, 93.14
Ohio Salt Co., 29.31
Ohio State Journal, Columbus, 85.291
Oil and Gas Journal, 85.98
Oil City Brewing Co., 14.40
Oil-Elec-Tric Engineering Corp., 58.11
Oil Field Engineering, 85.212
Oil of Olay, 32.36
Oilray Safety Heater Inc., 58.9
O'Keefe's ginger ale, 107.42
Oklahoma City, 36.12
Olay Corp., 32.36
Old Briar, 115.130
Old Briar tobacco, 115.60
Old Chum, 115.165
Old Colony Brewing Co., 14.21
Old Colony Co-operative Bank, 43.42
Old Colony Envelope Co., 83.82
Old Crow, 71.21, 71.39, 71.103, 71.137
Old Dutch cleanser, 24.9, 24.19
Old English, 106.29
Old English household cleaner, 24.102
Old English No Rubbing Wax, 24.32
Old English powdered cleaner, 24.59
Old English scratch removing polish, 24.70
Oldetyme Distilling Co., 71.130, 71.131
Old Export beer, 14.85
Oldfield Tire Co., 114.27
Old Fitzgerald, 71.147
Old Forester bourbon, 71.118
Old Gold, 115.34, 115.98, 115.177
Old Grand-Dad bourbon, 71.53
Old Homestead Bakery, 11.39
Old Overholt whiskey, 71.19
Old Poindexter whiskey, 71.114
Old Reliable, 27.3
Oldsmobile, 7.30, 7.59, 7.74
Old Spice shave mug refill, 104.22
Old Sunny Brook whiskey, 71.29
Olds & Whipple, 69.1, 69.26, 69.30
Old Taylor whiskey, 71.85
Old Thompson whiskey, 71.141
Old York cereal, 21.43

Olga Co., 121.6
Oliver typewriter, 81.2
Olivetti Corp., 28.5, 81.50, 81.62
Olivetti M20 personal computer,
28.5
Olson Co. Inc., Oliver A., 100.27
Olsten Temporary Services, 40.1
Olympia, 14.68
Olympia Brewing Co., 14.68
Olympia Div., Inter-Continental
Trading Corp., 81.36
Omaha Public Power District, 36.20
Omega Oil, 35.110
Omega Watch Co., 124.13, 124.14
Omega watches, 124.13
One-a-Day vitamins, 56.6
103 Degree Incubator Co., 42.24
Oneida Ltd., 67.13, 67.22, 67.23
Oneida Motor Truck, 120.28
O'Neil Oil Co., 88.44
One-Up tobacco case, 105.5
Onondaga Pottery Co., 23.8
Ontario, Canada, Department of
Tourism and Information, 119.18
Opel Kadett, 7.67
Operadio Corp., 95.63
Opler Inc., E. & A., 11.48
Optical Coating Laboratory Inc.,
28.18
Oral Hygiene, 85.304
Orange Crush, 107.20
Oregon City Woolen Mills, 113.38
Oregon Highway Dept, 119.34
Oregon-Washington-California Pear
Bureau, 49.1
Oriental cream, 32.10
original-Ohner adding machine,
81.49
Original Ry-Krisp Co., 47.43
Orphos Co., 34.32
*Orville Redenbacher Gourmet
Popping Corn,* 47.38
Osborn Mfg. Co., 82.1
Oshkosh Overall Co., 26.85, 26.146
Ostermoor & Co., 13.20
O'Sullivan Industries Inc., 5.29
O'Sullivan Rubber Co., 48.11
Otard cognac, 71.26
Otarion singlepack hearing aid,
57.2
Othello board game, 118.1
Otis Clapp & Son, 34.23
Otis Elevator Co., 39.1, 39.2, 39.3
Outboard Marine Co., 16.2, 16.7

Outdoor Recreation, 85.262
Outlook, 85.47
Ovaltine, 15.5
Owen Magnetic Motor Car, 7.56
Owens Brush Co., 54.17
Owens-Corning Fiberglas Corp.,
18.63, 18.116
Owens Yacht Co., 16.12
Oxford Filing Supply Co., 81.17
Oxford Paper Co., 83.35
Oxydol, 24.17
Oxydol soap, 24.68
Oyster Growers & Dealers Assn.,
47.97
Oyster Growers of North America,
47.115
Ozark Air Lines Inc., 4.44
Ozark Fisheries, 87.16
Pabco linoleums, 46.25
Pabst, 107.44
Pabst Blue Ribbon, 14.62
Pabst Corp., 14.62, 14.120, 14.123,
14.130, 14.142
Pacific Brewing & Malting Co.,
14.19, 14.150, 14.153
Pacific Coast Biscuit Co., 11.13
Pacific Egg Producers, 47.40
Pacific Electric Railway, Los
Angeles, 96.30
Pacific Northern Airlines, 4.2, 4.47
Pacific Northwest Fruits Inc., 49.3,
49.14
Pacific Phonograph Mfg. Co., 95.36
*Pacific Rural Press and California
Farmer,* San FrancisCo., 85.268
Pacific Wines Inc., 125.31
Packard, 7.15, 7.45
Packard electric shaver, 104.2,
104.32
Page Mill Co., Thomas, 11.54
Paillard Inc., 81.21
Paint and Varnish Association,
82.55
Painter Carpet Mills, Inc., Div.
Collins and Aikman, 46.3
Paint Logic, 85.314
Pakistan International Airlines,
4.29, 4.30
Palace Hotel, 62.19
Pal Blade Co., 104.15, 104.29
Palizzio Inc., 48.15
Pall Mall, 115.11, 115.35, 115.49,
115.57, 115.102, 115.103, 115.176
Palm Beach Times, 85.79

Palmer Asbestos & Rubber Corp., 26.35

Palmolive soap, 106.9, 106.18, 106.22

Pan-American Coffee Bureau, 27.24, 27.56

Pan American-Grace Airways Inc., 4.68

Pan American World Airways Inc., 4.17, 4.20, 4.21, 4.22, 4.23, 4.33, 4.69, 4.72, 4.74

Panasonic, 5.15

Panasonic, 38.9

Panasonic, 122.3

P and D Mfg. Co., 8.20

P and O Lines, 102.8, 102.14

Paper Center Inc., 83.43

Papermate pens, 126.34

paper towels, 83.38

Paper Trade Journal, 85.136

Paquins hand cream, 32.22

Parade Magazine, 85.355

Paradyne Corp., 28.27

Paramount Pictures Corp., 78.1, 78.5

Parents, 85.157

Parfums Corday Inc., 84.2

Paris garters, 61.23, 61.39

Paris-Hecker Co., 121.32

Paris Nights, 85.1

Park & Tilford, 71.9

Park & Tilford candy, 20.11, 20.52

Park & Tilford Distillers Co., 71.9, 71.22

Park Central Hotel, New York, 62.2

Parke, Davis & Co., 35.9, 35.53, 35.55

Parker 51, 126.10, 126.41

Parker House, 62.9

Parker Pen Co., 126.10, 126.15, 126.17, 126.26, 126.41

parlor furnace, 58.2, 58.41

Parodi Cigar Corp., 115.136

Partola, 35.105

Partola Products Co., 35.105

Pasmantier Inc., 23.4

Pasmore's 2-minute aid, 35.126

Patcraft Mills Inc., 46.9, 46.13

Pat-&-Wop, 35.65

Paul Jones whiskey, 71.1, 71.127

Paul Masson, 125.33

Peace Corps, 53.4

Pears Ltd., A. & F., 106.14

Pearson Inc., Ben, 108.31

Peavey Co., 11.12

Peck and Peck, 100.9

Peckham-Foreman, 26.145

Pediforme shoes, 48.30

Peerless Plumbers Corp., 55.2

Peet Bros. Mfg. Co., 106.26

Pellon Corp., 113.18

Pencil Specialty Co., 2.2

Pendleton Woolen Mills, 26.3

Penetro, 35.120

Pen Metal Co. Inc., 18.4

Penn Electric Switch Co., 58.17

Penney & Co. Inc., J. C., 100.1, 100.4

Penn Fishing Tackle Mfg. Co., 45.22

Penn Maryland whiskey, 71.79

Penn Mutual Underwriter Insurance, 64.119

Pennsylvania, 119.9, 119.24

Pennsylvania Power and Light Co., 93.10

Pennsylvania Railroad, 96.15, 96.46

Pennsylvania Tire Co., 108.20

Pennzoil Co., 88.17, 88.24, 88.42

Pentax cameras, 89.30

Pentax Corporation., The, 89.30

Pentel of America Ltd., 126.7

Pentel pens, 126.7

Peoples Fire Insurance Co., 64.71

People's Popular Monthly, 85.227

People's Trust & Guaranty Co., 43.35

Pep Bran Flakes, 21.23

Pepperell sheets, 13.10

Pepsico Inc., 107.14, 107.23, 107.27, 107.32, 107.40, 107.54, 107.58

Pepsi-Cola, 107.14, 107.23, 107.27, 107.32, 107.40, 107.54

Pepsodent, 34.30

Pepsodent antiseptic, 34.20

Pepto-Bismol, 35.59, 35.116

Pequot sheets, 13.15

Perfection clothes, 26.119

Perfection Foods Co., 87.13

Perfection Stove Co., 58.7

Perkin-Elmer, 28.85

Perma-Lift brassiere, 121.48

Perma-Sharp Manufacturing Corp., 104.30

Permatex Co. Inc., 8.23

Perrier, 15.24, 15.26

Personal Products Co., 116.5, 116.26

Personal Products Div., Lever Bros. Co., 106.10

Perstik, 116.23
Pertussin, 35.38, 35.79
Pervel Corp., 123.29
Petelco Div., Pyle-National Co.,
　70.42
Peterson, Howell and Heather, 6.4
Peters Shoe Co., 48.140
Pet Inc., 20.14, 20.30
Pet Milk Co., 33.16, 33.34
Pfister Associated Growers, 42.31,
　42.32, 42.33, 42.44, 42.45
Pfizer and Co. Inc., Chas, 32.66,
　32.82
Pflueger, 45.2
PHAZE Information Machines
　Corp., 28.77
Philadelphia Brand Cream Cheese,
　33.27
Philadelphia Carpet Co., 46.23
Philadelphia Evening Bulletin,
　85.122
Philadelphia Gas Works Co., 59.8
Philadelphia Inquirer., 85.190
Philadelphia Insulated Wire Co.
　Inc., 38.17
Philadelphia Record, 85.17
Philadelphia Seed Co., 69.18
Philadelphia whiskey, 71.5
Philco Corp., 95.9, 95.26, 112.4
Philip Morris, 115.3, 115.143
Philip Morris Inc., 20.45, 115.3,
　115.23, 115.26, 115.27, 115.55,
　115.63, 115.69, 115.87, 115.105,
　115.109, 115.128, 115.143, 115.154,
　115.189
Philips cocoa, 15.17
Phillips-Jones Corp., 26.143, 26.144
Phillips' Milk of Magnesia, 35.84,
　35.87, 35.127
Phillips' Milk of Magnesia tablets,
　35.62
Phillips Petroleum Co., 88.25
Phillips Research Laboratories, 76.3
Phillips-Van Heusen Corp., 26.160
Phoenix Hosiery Co., 61.21
Phoenix of Hartford Insurance Co.,
　64.70
Phoenix Vita Bloom hosiery, 61.53
Photographer's Association of
　America, 89.19, 89.20
Photoplay, 85.257
Photoplay Magazine, 85.162, 85.278
Photoswitch Div., Electronics Corp.
　of America, 38.11

Physical Culture, 85.342
Pickering and Co. Inc., 5.8
Picobac, 115.155
Pictograph Corp., 89.15
Pictorial Review, 85.337
Piel Bros. Inc., 14.36, 14.74, 14.77,
　14.89
Piel's, 14.36
Pierce, Franklin, 91.99, 91.401
Pierce-Arrow Motor Car Co., 7.5
Pigments and Chemicals Div.,
　National Lead Co., 82.41
Pillsbury Co., The, 11.6, 11.35
Pinch scotch, 71.4
Pine Tree Products Co., 106.31
Pine Tree shampoo, 54.21
Pine Tree soap, 106.31
Pioneer Audio Systems, 5.3
Pioneer Electronics (USA) Inc., 5.3
Pioneer mints, 20.1
Pioneer Suspender Co., 26.47,
　26.161, 61.54
Piper Aircraft Corp., 3.11, 3.14
Piper-Heidsieck champagne, 125.19
Pittsburgh Brewing Co., 14.80,
　14.143
Pittsburgh Garter Co., 61.16
Plant Co., Thos. G., 48.36
Planters Cheese Balls, 47.65
Planter's Nut & Chocolate Co.,
　20.66
Planters Peanuts, 47.65, 49.24, 49.27
PlastiCraft motorboat, 16.10
Playa de Cortes, Guaymas, MexiCo.,
　62.29
Players cigarettes, 115.105
Plaza Hotel, New York, 62.33
Pleasant Valley Wine Co., 125.7
Plough Inc., 32.35, 35.10, 35.120
Pluto Water, 35.2, 35.136
Plymouth, 7.20, 7.37, 7.100
Plymouth Golf Ball Co., 108.37
P. M. whiskey, 71.54
PN-700 washing powder, 24.57
Pocket Books Inc., 94.6
Poinsettia Ice Cream Co., 33.44
Polar Frosted Foods, 47.73
Polaroid Corp., 41.2
Polident, 34.28, 34.29, 34.39
Polk, James K., 91.77, 91.242,
　91.243, 91.244, 91.246
Polk Miller Products Co., 86.1
Pomiac gasoline, 88.22
Pompeian beauty products, 32.85

Pompeian Inc., 32.85, 84.1
Pond Co., A. H., 67.14
Ponderosa Mouldings Inc., 18.20
Pontiac, 7.9, 7.92, 7.96
Pope and Talbot Inc., 18.62
Poppin' Fresh Dough, 11.35
Popular Mechanics, 85.354
Porsche, 7.28
Portable Elevator Mfg. Co., 60.114
Port Authority of the City of St. Paul, 36.14
Porter Co. Inc., H. K., 73.40
Post-Dispatch, St. Louis, Mo, 85.85
Post Intelligencer, 85.175
Post's Bran Chocolates, 20.2
Post's Bran Flakes, 21.7, 21.24
Post Toasties, 21.33
Postum, 15.8
Postum Cereal Co. Inc., 20.2, 21.28
Potlatch Forests Inc., 18.23, 18.74
Potosi Brewing Co., 14.92, 14.108, 14.111
Potter & Moore, 84.7
Poultry Tribune, 85.303
Powell Muffler Co., 8.11
Power Boating, 85.34
Power Farming, 85.160
Powermatic Inc., 73.39
Powers Products Co., John Robert, 32.29
PPG Industries Inc., 18.61, 22.4, 48.33
Pratt & Lambert, 82.28, 82.29, 82.56, 82.82
Pratt & Whitney, 63.6
Preference by L'Oreal hair color, 54.20
Preis & Co., J. J., 26.106
Premier salad dressing, 29.25
Premier warm air heater, 58.28
Prentice Mfg. Co., G. E., 103.1, 103.23
Prentiss Vise Co., 117.21, 117.37
Press-Telegram, Long Beach, California, 85.4
Presteline, 60.104
Prest-O-Lite, 60.14
Prestolite Co., The, 60.14
Prestone, 8.58
Prime soap, 24.86
Prim Miss foundations, 121.43
Primrose foundations, 121.1
Prince Albert tobacco, 115.97, 115.104, 115.150

Prince Gardner Co., 123.9
Prince Gardner wallet, 123.23
Princesse de Conde chocolates, 20.4
Princess Pat Ltd., 32.14
Pringle's Cheesum, 47.89
Printing Magazine, 85.147
Printronix, 28.2, 28.51
Procter & Gamble Co., 11.10, 24.8, 24.17, 24.23, 24.27, 24.31, 24.33, 24.40, 24.49, 24.52, 24.68, 24.71, 24.93, 24.99, 27.15, 27.20, 47.16, 47.20, 47.47, 47.64, 47.74, 47.89, 83.70, 106.2, 106.15, 106.17, 106.20, 106.21, 106.33, 106.36, 116.14
Proctor Electric Co., 60.13, 60.113, 60.148
Prodex Div., Koehring Co., 73.14
Product Engineering, 85.293
Prof. Research Labs, 34.49
Progressive Farmer, 85.217, 85.264
Progressive Grocer, The, 85.281
Prohibition, campaign of 1932, 91.148, 91.281
Pro-phy-lac-tic Brush Co., 34.1, 34.6, 34.35
Pro-phy-lac-tic toothbrush, 34.1, 34.6
Provident Life and Accident Insurance Co., 64.89
Provident Mutual Life Insurance Co., 64.68
Prudential Insurance Co., 64.23, 64.54, 64.85, 64.96
Pryde-Wynn Co., 104.8
Public Services of Indiana Inc., 36.8
Puerto Rican, 71.134
Puffed Wheat, Puffed Rice, 21.11
Pullman Co., 96.68
Pulvex flea powder, 86.11
Punch, London, 85.299
Pure Oil Co., The, 88.6, 88.14, 88.77
Purex Corp., 24.4, 24.104
Puritan Stationery Co., 83.61
Purity Bakeries, 11.18
Purity Cheese Co., 33.25
Purity Condiments Inc., 29.30
Purity Oats Co., 21.10
Purity salt, 29.30
Purolator Courier, 4.76
Puss 'n Boots, 87.6
Pussywillow face powder, 32.60
Pyle Driver, 5.10
Pyrex cookware, 68.3

Pyrograph Advertising Sign Corp., 2.10
Qantas, 4.9
Q-tips cotton swabs, 116.3
Quadram System, 28.75
Quaker Maid candies, 20.39
Quaker Maid Co., 47.93
Quaker Oats Co., 11.22, 21.6, 21.11, 21.13, 21.32, 21.49, 87.6
Quaker State motor oil, 88.81
Quaker State Oil Refining Corp., 88.5, 88.12, 88.15, 88.33, 88.81
Quality ice cream, 33.24
Quality Micro Systems Inc., 28.82
Quarrie & Co., W. F., 94.18
Quarterdeck Office Systems, 28.35
Queen Quality shoes, 48.36
Queens Health salt, 29.16
Queenston Limestone, 18.14
Quest deodorant, 116.4
Quimby Co., W. S., 27.66, 110.21
Qume Corp., 28.37
Racine tires, 114.20
Radbill Oil Co., 88.76
radiant heater, 58.38
Radio Age, 85.258
Radio Broadcast, 85.306
Radio Cooking School of America, 101.3
Radio Corporation of America, *see* RCA Corp.
Radio Digest, 85.275
Radio Guide, 85.286
Radio Industries Corp., 95.6
Radiolite, 124.37
Radio Merchandising, 85.137
Radio Retailing, 85.200
Radio Shack, 28.49
Radi-Oven, 60.38
Rado Watch Co., 124.41
Radways & Co., 35.133
Radway's Ready Relief, 35.133
Raelin Prods, 34.21, 34.31
Rag Content Paper Mfrs., 83.87
Ragu Foods Inc., 47.87
Ragu Spaghetti Sauce, 47.87
Raid, 86.9
Railway Age, 85.154
Rain & Hail Insurance Bureau, 64.3, 64.32
Raleigh, 115.64, 115.163
Ralston Purina Co., 21.18, 42.25, 47.29, 47.60, 47.90
Ramada Inns Inc., 62.22

Ramis II software, 28.38
Ram Knitting Mills, 26.152
R and K Originals Inc., 26.4
Rand McNally and Co., 94.9
Ranier, 7.12
Rapala Div., Nordic Enterprises Inc., 45.30
Rapid Mfg. Co., 70.37
Rapid Oats, 21.8
Rap-I-Dol Mfg. Co., 54.40
Rapids-Standard Co. Inc., 73.15
Rath Packing Co., 74.19
Rauchbach-Goldsmith Co., 72.14, 72.22, 72.26, 72.28, 72.29
Rauh & Co., S., 48.23
Raybestos-Manhattan Inc., 31.20
Rayette-Faberge Inc., 54.16
Raylo Corp., 24.60
Raynorshyne Products, 24.50, 24.51, 48.79
Ray Oil Burner Co., 58.14
Ray-O-Vac batteries, 37.4, 37.27, 37.28
Raytheon Mfg. Co., 95.25, 95.59
RCA, 112.16
RCA Corp., 5.11, 5.37, 38.15, 38.16, 95.14, 97.8, 97.9, 112.12, 112.16, 122.4
RCA Radiotron Co., 95.60
RCA Victor, 95.64, 97.10, 97.11
RCA Whirlpool, 60.127
Reade Mfg. Co., 69.32
Reader's Digest, 85.159, 85.351
Readi-cut houses, 18.33
Reading Railroad, 96.26
Reagan, Ronald, 91.365
Real Silk Hosiery Mills, 61.40
Rebbor candies, 20.20
Reckitt & Colman Ltd., 24.65
Reckitt's blue, 24.65
Recordak Corp., 81.16
Recordisc Corp., 97.6
Red Book, 85.247
Red Cedar Lumber Mfrs. Assn., 18.124
Red Cedar Shingle and Handsplit Shale Bureau, 18.84
Red Cross shoes, 48.21, 48.22, 48.145
Red Devil Inc., 117.43
Red Devil pliers, 117.6
Reddy Communications, 37.5, 37.14, 37.22
Reddy Kilowatt, 37.5, 37.14, 37.22

Red Goose shoes, 48.2, 48.65
Red Gum Products Co., 34.42
Red Head Brand Co., 98.7, 98.12
Red Jacket Coal Sales Co., 59.4,
   59.23
Red-line-in, 48.94
Reed and Barton, 67.18
Reed Ltd., 65.6
Reed Service Inc., 66.1
Rees jack, 117.31
Reflex slicker, 26.131
Regal salt, 29.12
Regatta yacht paints, 82.25
Regensburg & Sons, E., 115.17
Regent, 115.149, 115.168
Reichardt Cocoa & Chocolate Co.,
   15.13, 15.25
Reis, 121.54
Reis & Co., Robert, 121.54
Reiss-Premier Pipe Co., 105.34
Reliable dolls, 118.19
Reliance Electric and Engineering
   Co., 38.4
Reliance State Bank, 43.10
Rembrandt pipes, 105.9
Remington Arms Co., 55.13
Remington Office Systems Div.,
   Sperry Rand Corp., 28.48
Remington Rand, 81.3, 81.48
Remington shells, 44.8
Remoulade, 29.28
Remy-Martin cognac, 71.76, 71.94
Renault, 7.16
Renault Inc., 7.16, 7.71
Renfield Importers Ltd., 71.4, 71.14,
   71.33, 71.76, 71.94, 71.116, 71.133,
   125.19, 125.25, 125.36
Rennus luggage, 72.5
Rennus, S. time clock, 124.58
Rensie watches, 124.9, 124.10
Reo-Form Lingerie Co., 121.27
Resistol self-conforming hats, 26.125
Revelation pipe tobacco, 115.63
Revere Copper and Brass Inc., 75.7
Revere-Wollensack Div., Minnesota
   Mining and Mfg. Co., 5.51
Revlon Inc., 32.23, 32.31, 32.79, 84.5
Rexall Drug Co., 100.21, 100.31
Rexall Stores, 100.13
Rex tees, 108.15
Reyner & Bros. Inc., 20.53
Reynolds Aluminum Supply Co.,
   75.23
Reynolds Corp., 18.88

Reynolds lifetime aluminum, 68.8
Reynolds Metals Co., 68.8, 75.13,
   75.34
Reynolds Tobacco Co., R. J., 115.8,
   115.18, 115.20, 115.21, 115.33,
   115.38, 115.40, 115.53, 115.65,
   115.70, 115.91, 115.97, 115.104,
   115.111, 115.133, 115.150, 115.167,
   115.179, 115.180, 115.185
Rheem Mfg. Co., 58.40
Rheingold, 14.59
Rhinelander Refrigerator Co., 60.62
Rhino enamel, 82.76
Rhode Island, 36.1
Rhodes Co., J. H., 24.69
Ribaux watches, 124.3
Rice Council, 47.27
Rice & Hutchins, 48.84, 48.156
Richard Ginori, 23.4
Richard Hudnut Sportsman, 84.20
Richards Inc., Caryl, 54.14
Richardson Boat Co., 16.4
Richardson Corp., 107.38
Richardson-Merrell Inc., 82.43
Richardson Ranger, 16.4
Richardson & Robbins, 47.6
Richardson root beer, 107.38
Richland Shoe Co., 48.20, 48.123,
   48.181
Richter, E. A., 89.21
Riddle Co., E. N., 70.44
Ridgeways Inc., 110.11
Riegel Paper Corp., 83.65
Right Guard deodorant, 116.31
Ringling Brothers and Barnum &
   Bailey Circus, 78.14
Ring, The, 85.353
Rinso, 24.35
Rio Grande Railroad, 96.39
Rising Paper Co., 83.10
R. I. Tool Co., 55.37
Rit Products Corp., 24.87
Rittenhouse Hotel, Philadelphia,
   62.11
Ritz-Carlton, Atlantic City, N. J.,
   62.6
Ritz crackers, 11.38, 11.57
Rival Mfg. Co., 60.56
Rival Pet Foods Div., Associated
   Products, Inc., 87.15
road machinery, 73.20
Robert Burns cigars, 115.51, 115.66,
   115.129
Roberts Co., 73.27, 73.28

Roberts, Johnson & Rand, 48.125
Roberts & Mander, 60.116
Robertson Factories Inc., 65.16
Robin Hood, 21.8
Robin Hood flour, 11.33
Robins Co. Inc., 56.7
Robins Co. Inc., A. H., 35.138
Roche-Bobois Furniture, 50.35
Rock Flint Co., 104.11
Rock Island Lines, 96.61, 96.66
Roger & Gallet, 84.9
Rogers Mfg. Co., Wm, 67.32
Rohr Corp., 31.7
Roi-Tan cigars, 115.84, 115.138
Roi-Tan Little Cigars, 115.95
Rolaids antacid, 35.39, 35.77
Rollfast bicycles, 98.14, 108.5
Rollins Hosiery Mills, 61.25, 61.41,
   61.42
Roma wines, 125.9, 125.13, 125.21,
   125.23, 125.26
Rome Co., 13.26
Rome Mfg. Co., 68.13, 68.21, 68.22
Romweber Industries, 50.26, 50.43
Rondo, 95.51
Ronnoco Coffee Co., 27.64
Ronrico Corp., 71.78
Ronson Corp., 105.3, 105.15, 105.25
Roosevelt, Franklin Delano, 91.16,
   91.31, 91.79, 91.84, 91.108, 91.131,
   91.150, 91.231, 91.258, 91.261,
   91.264, 91.266, 91.268, 91.269,
   91.271, 91.272, 91.274, 91.275,
   91.280, 91.301, 91.357, 91.359,
   91.371, 91.386, 91.388, 91.392,
   91.400, 91.409, 91.414, 91.415
Roosevelt, Theodore, 91.26, 91.124,
   91.228, 91.232, 91.267, 91.294,
   91.297, 91.308
Roosevelt Savings Bank, 43.57
Root Co., A. I., 47.41
Rosa Aroma cigars, 115.183
Rosenberg & Brand, 61.28
Roser Co., 54.45
Ross Inc., Will, 35.69
Ross Mfg. Co., 55.30
Rotarian, The, 85.255
Roth Co., C. H., 61.6
Rothschild Bros. Hat Co., 26.2
Roto-Rooter Corp., 25.1
Rototiller, 69.19
Round-the-Clock, 61.43
Roux Labs Inc., 54.32
Royal, 47.103

Royal Banquet whiskey, 71.17,
   71.142
Royal Blend, 27.2, 27.39
Royal Crown Cola, 107.9, 107.39
Royal Crown Cola Co., 107.5, 107.6,
   107.18
Royal Crystal fuse plug, 37.12
Royal Duke pipes, 105.4
Royal Easy Chair Co., 50.45
Royal Electric Co., 37.12
Royal Enfield bicycle, 98.11
Royal Flush toiletries, 116.2
Royalist cigars, 115.144
Royal Pictures, 78.9, 78.10, 78.12,
   78.13
Royal Typewriter Co. Inc., 81.13,
   81.15, 81.35, 81.67
Royal typewriters, 81.13, 81.15,
   81.67
Royal Worcester corset, 121.13
Royal Worcester Corset Co., 121.3
Royster Guano Co., F. S., 42.17
Rubbermaid Inc., 60.83, 68.10
Rubee Furniture Mfg. Corp., 50.33
Rubsam & Horrmann, 14.88, 14.94,
   14.134
Ruby Lighting Corp., 70.5
Rudofker's Sons, 26.6
Rueckheim Bros. & Eckstein, 20.65
Rugged luggage, 72.23
Rumford baking powder, 11.58
Rumford Chemical Works, 24.25
Rumford Co., The, 11.58
Rumpp luggage, 72.24
Rumpp wallets, 123.18
Runstop hosiery, 61.41
Ruppert, 14.98
Rusco windows, 18.1
Russek's, New York, 100.2
Russell, Bursdall & Ward Bolt &
   Nut Co., 55.23
Russell Co., R. C., 18.1
Russel Motor Axle Co., 8.26
Russwin-Emhart Corp., 55.38
Rust Craft Greeting Cards Inc.,
   51.2
Rust-Oleum Corp., 82.52, 82.54,
   82.60
Rust Sash and Door Co., 18.18
Ruud Heater Co., 58.46
Ruud Mfg. Co., 58.26, 58.52, 58.55
rye, 71.30
Saab, 7.69
Saab-Scania of America Inc., 7.69

Sabena Belgian World Airlines, 4.16
Sabreliner, 3.19
Sackman Bros., 26.78
Saegertown Mineral Water Co., 107.41
SAE Two, 5.44
Saf-De-Lite Sales Corp., 8.14, 8.36
Safe-Cabinet Co., 81.58
Safeway Stores Inc., 110.13
Safticycles Inc., 108.1, 108.25
Sagner Inc., 26.147
Sag Pruf furniture foundation, 50.48
Saks Shoe Corp., 48.68
Salada Tea Co., 110.4, 110.5
Salem, 115.38
Sales Affiliates Inc., 32.41, 32.43, 32.88, 54.11
Sal Hepatica, 35.113
Saltine Co., 34.43
Salt Lake City, 119.10
Salvation Army, 92.5
Samson folding table, 50.52
Samsonite Corp., 50.60, 72.20, 72.21
San Antonio Municipal Information Bureau, 119.50
San Antonio, Texas, 119.46
Sandoz Chemical Works, 113.27
Sandoz Inc., 35.64
Sands Level & Tool Co., 117.24
Sanford Mfg. Co., 126.32
Sanford Truss Inc., 18.127
Sanforized, 113.6
San Francisco Call, 85.173
San Francisco Convention and Visitors Bureau, 119.56
San Francisco Peninsula, 119.17
Sani-flush, 24.89
Sanitas wall covering, 65.13, 65.21
Sanka, 27.18
Sanka decaffeinated, 27.23
Sansui, 5.26
Santa Fe cigars, 115.173
Santa Fe Railroad, 96.37
Santa Fe System Lines, 96.63
Sanyo, 5.32
Sarasota, Florida, 119.53
Saratoga Vichy Spring Co., 15.15
Sardis Luggage Co., The, 72.9
Sargent & Co., 18.31
SAS Institute Inc., 28.39
Saskatchewan Farmer, Regina, 85.174
Sassoon, Vidal, 54.19

Satinwax, 24.77
Saturday Evening Post, 85.41
Savage Arms Corp., 44.12, 44.24, 60.10, 60.39, 60.79
Savage ironer, 60.10, 60.79
Savarin, 27.43, 27.46, 27.48
Savings and Loan Foundation Inc., The, 43.62
Savings Bank Association, 43.8
Sawyer Biscuit Co., 11.8
Sawyer-Massey, 73.32
Schaefer, 14.11, 14.96
Schaefer Brewing Co., F. & M., 14.11, 14.90, 14.96
Scheirich Co., H. J., 18.95
Schell's seeds, 42.26
Schenley Industries Inc., 71.56, 71.91, 71.100, 71.101, 71.105, 71.111
Schick dry razor, 104.38
Schick Electric Inc., 104.45
Schieffelin and Co., 32.63, 47.1, 125.10, 125.34
Schiefflin and Co., 71.52, 71.134, 71.146
Schield Mfg. Co., Wm, 24.83
Schilling coffee, 27.62
Schilling Div., McCormick and Co. Inc., 29.19
Schlitz, 14.93
Schlitz Brewing Co., Jos, 14.25, 14.71, 14.93, 14.110
Schneider lenses, 89.5
Schoeneman, Inc., J., Baltimore, Md, 100.8
Scholastic Magazines, 85.350
Scholl Inc., 48.58, 48.173
Schonbrunn & Co. Inc., S. A., 27.43, 27.46, 27.48
Schrader's Son, A., 8.18
Schulte, New York, A., 100.10
Schwabacher Bros., 27.47
Schwabacher-Frey Stationery Co., 83.81
Schwartz Bros. Dress Co., 26.68, 26.73
Schwartz, F. A. O., 118.20
Schwarzenbach Huber & Co., 113.16
Schweitzer Div., Peter J., Kimberly-Clark Corp., 83.80, 83.83
Schwob Inc., Adolphe, 124.30
Scientific Anglers Inc., 45.25, 45.29
SCM Corp., 81.52, 81.61
Scolding Locks Corp., 54.28

Scoldy Lox bobby pin, 54.28
scotch, 71.14, 71.143
scotch whiskey, 71.49
Scott, Gen. Winfield, 91.100, 91.284
Scott and Co., O. M., 69.13, 69.25, 69.27
Scott Paper Co., 83.38, 83.46, 83.50, 83.51
Scott's emulsion, 35.102
Scovill Manufacturing Co., 31.9, 103.16
screws, 55.22
Scripps-Howard, 85.111
Scripto Inc., 126.9
Scripto Mfg. Co., 126.22, 126.35
Scull Co., Wm. S., 110.20
Sea Dog dog food, 87.14
Seaforth Corp., 104.16, 116.16, 116.20
Seaforth deodorant for men, 116.16, 116.20
Seaforth shaving set, 104.16
Seagram & Sons Inc., J. E., 71.31, 71.32, 71.44, 71.45, 71.63, 71.83, 71.84, 71.136, 71.138
Seagram Co. Ltd., The, 71.87
Seagram's 7, 71.72
Seagram's Canadian V.O., 71.63
Seagram's Distillers, 71.27, 71.72
Seagram's V.O., 71.27
Seagram's whiskey, 71.138
Sea Island Mills, 26.104
Seale-Lilly Ice Cream Co., 33.48
Sealpax Co., The, 121.41, 121.56
Sealtex, 35.96
Sealy Inc., 13.14, 13.25, 13.38
Sealy mattress, 13.14
Sealy Mattress Co., 13.2
Searle & Co., G. D., 35.76, 56.11
Sears, Roebuck & Co., 60.124, 66.22, 100.24, 100.33, 100.36
Sears Financial Network, 66.22
Seattle Community Adv., W., 36.5
Seattle First National Bank, 43.33
Secord Candy Shops Ltd., Laura, 20.73
Sego, 56.3
Sego Milk Products Co., 33.9
Seiberling Tire & Rubber Co., 114.24
Seidenberg cigars, 115.96, 115.114
Seidner's Mayonnaise, 29.11
Seiko Time Corp., 124.27
Seinsheimer Co., H. A., 26.119

Selastic Co., 82.62
Selby Shoe Co., 48.178
Selectron International Co., 5.7
Selig Mfg. Co. Inc., 50.31
Selznick Pictures Corp., 78.3
Semet-Solvay Co., 59.22
Senate beer, 14.31
Senchal perfume, 84.4
Sensenbrenner Sons, A., 115.126, 115.173
Sentry Insurance Co., 64.45, 64.99
Seraphim records, 97.1
Sergeant's, 86.1
Sergeant's flea powder, 86.15
Serta Inc., 13.34, 13.39
Serta Perfect Sleeper mattress, 13.34, 13.39
Serutan laxative, 35.7, 35.81
Service Industries, 24.57
Servicemaster, 25.4
Seubert Co., Justin, 115.131
Seven Seas slacks, 26.83
7-Up, 107.11, 107.16
Seven-Up Co., The, 107.11, 107.16, 107.24, 107.50, 107.55, 107.57
Sewell Cushion Wheel Co., 8.60
Seymour, Horatio, 91.97, 91.217, 91.257, 91.344, 91.372, 91.411
Shaft-Pierce Shoe Co., 48.31, 48.73, 48.121
Shallcross Co., 81.19
Sharon Steel Corp., 75.2
Sharp Electronics Corp., 38.7
Shaw-Walker Co., 81.6, 81.27
Sheaffer Pen Co., 126.3, 126.5, 126.28, 126.40
Shearson/American Express, 66.11
Sheboygan Beverage Co., 107.22
Shelby Shoe Co., 48.77
Sheldon Axle & Spring Co., 8.50
Shell Oil Co., 9.3, 88.10, 88.78
Sherwin-Williams Co., 82.4, 82.13, 82.15
Sherwood Bros., 88.40
Shipman, Jack, 108.15
Ship 'n Shore Inc., 26.72
Shirriff's Lushus jelly, 47.95
Shirriff's marmalade, 47.58, 47.108
Shirriff's vanilla, 29.22
Shortback's, 48.108
Shredded Wheat, 21.36
Shredded Wheat Co., 21.1
Shulton Inc., 104.22, 116.28
Shure, 5.4

Shyde, Gertrude, 32.19
Sidley Co., 26.129, 61.33, 121.15, 121.23, 121.43
Sidley cords, 26.130
Silent Automatic Corp., 58.53
Silent Gliss Inc., 55.24, 55.36
Silent Glow Oil Burner Corp., 58.50
Silverglo Lamps Inc., 70.14, 70.17, 70.33
Simmons, F. T., 123.11
Simmons U.S.A, 13.16, 13.17, 13.19, 13.35, 13.36
Simon Bros., 48.161, 123.16, 123.25, 123.28
Simon Manges and Son Inc., 46.33
Simons Mfg. Co., E., 26.137
Simplex ironer, 60.55
Simplex Mfg. Co., 48.78
Simplicity Patterns Co. Inc., 26.128
Simpson Timber Co., 18.69
Simware Inc., 28.41
Sinclair Consolidated Oil Corp., 88.34
Sinclair Oil Corp., 88.1
Singer Co., 31.8, 31.34, 60.63
Singer Sewing Center, 100.34
Singer sewing machine, 60.63
Singing, 85.192
Sip-It cough remedy, 35.61
Sir Walter Raleigh, 115.118
Sitroux Importing Co., 54.39
Sizzlean, 47.66
Skelly Oil Co., 88.21, 88.66, 88.68
Ski Industries America, 108.6
Skil Corp., 117.9, 117.26
Skinner & Sons., Wm, 103.2
Skippy peanut butter, 47.46
Skoal Bandits, 115.122
Skol sun oil, 32.61
Skylark fragrance, 84.14
Slide Fasteners Inc., 103.15
Slim-Mint Gum, 56.9, 56.10
Slingerland Drum Co., 80.28
Sloan's, 35.107
Sloan's instant balm, 35.20
Sloan's liniment, 35.48
Sloat & Scanlon, 66.4
Slocomb Co., J. T., 63.7
Slumber Chair, 50.24
S. M. A. Corp., 35.17
Small's, 100.26
Smart Set, 85.343
Smart Shoe Co., Bob, 48.163
Smead Mfg. Co., The, 81.69

Smirnoff vodka, 71.55, 71.104
Smith, Alfred E., 91.13, 91.104, 91.322
Smith, Kenneth, 108.13
Smith, Kline & French Co., 35.95
Smith & Hemenway Co., 117.6
Smith Barney, 66.18
Smith Beads, Lew, 65.5
Smith Bros., 35.101
Smith Corp., A. O., 58.19
Smith-Douglass Div., Borden Chemical Co., 42.58
Smithfield Ham & Products Co. Inc., 74.7
Smith Inc., Landon P., 117.12
Smith Paper Co., H. P., 83.47
Smith Shoe Co., J. P., 48.180
Smokers Products Inc., 105.5
Snap-On Tools Corp., 117.4, 117.7, 117.25
Snarol, 69.20
Snellenburg Cloth Co., 26.127
Snickers candy bars, 20.50
Snyder's Sani-Bilt Furniture, 50.47
Soapitor Co. Inc., 106.8
Soap Products, Ltd., 104.5
Society Brand clothes, 26.56, 26.93
Society for Electrical Development, 60.35
Society Girl foundations, 121.14
Society of American Florists, 51.4
Socony-Vacuum Co., 88.3
Sodiphene Co., 35.23
So E-Z snap fastener, 103.13
Sofa-niter, 50.41, 50.56
Softique tissues, 116.29
Soft Sense skin lotion, 32.47
Software AG of North America Inc., 28.36
Software International, General Electric Information Services Co., 28.10
Sohmer & Co., 80.17, 80.23
Soilax, 24.105
Solex Co., Ltd., 70.34
Soloflex home fitness system, 56.2
Solomon Knitting Mills., R., 26.76
Somerset Importers Ltd., 71.20, 71.25, 71.61, 71.77, 71.82, 71.112, 71.144
Somerville Co., 35.1
Sonneborn & Co., Henry, 26.7
Sonoco Products Co., 83.49

Sony Corp. of America, 5.39, 5.45, 112.8

S. O. S. Magic scouring pads, 24.16

Soup Di Pasta, 47.49

South African Oil & Fat Industries, Ltd., 106.4

South Bend Tackle Co., Div. Gladding Corp., 45.6, 45.11

South Bend Watch Co., 124.51

South Dakota Dept. of Highways, 119.19

Southern Agriculturist, Nashville, 85.222

Southern Biscuit Works, 11.45

Southern Comfort Corp., 71.102

Southern Comfort mattress, 13.9

Southern Comfort whiskey, 71.102

Southern Co., The, 93.6

Southern Cypress Mfrs. Assn., 18.113

Southern Pacific Railroad, 96.10, 96.36, 96.38, 96.44, 96.65

Southern Pine Assn., 18.112

Southern Planter, Richmond, 85.296

Southern Railway Co., 96.17, 96.21, 96.48, 96.49, 96.72

Southwest Sun Country Association, 119.29

Spalding & Bros., A. G., 108.7

Spanish National Tourist Office, 119.42

Sparkies, 21.49

Sparton refrigerator, 60.28

Speakman Co., 55.20

Specialty Salesman Magazine, 85.279

Speidel Corp., 124.20, 124.60, 124.61

Spencer Chemical Div., Gulf Oil Corp., 42.12

Spencer, Kellogg & Sons, 82.69

Sperry Corp., 28.21, 31.32

Sperry Footwear, 48.124

Sperry Rand Corp., 28.50, 28.73, 31.31

Spicer Div., Dana Corp., 8.47

Spiegel Neckwear Co. Inc., 26.94

Spode Inc., 23.2

Spohn & Thamer, 106.16

Spokesman-Review, 85.73

Sponsor, 85.248

Spoor Co., Russell H., 2.18

Sportleigh briefer coat, 26.9

Sportlife, 85.280

Sports Illustrated, 85.82, 85.183

Sportsman pipe mixture, 115.22

Spot Bottle whiskey, 71.67

Spree Togs for children, 26.54

Spring-Air, 13.29

Spring Air Co., The, 13.11, 13.29

Springfield Tool Co., 82.47

Springs Mills Inc., 13.15

Sprint long distance system, 111.2

Spuds, 115.86, 115.90

Square and Compass, 85.71

Squibb & Sons, E. R., 35.47, 104.35

Squibb Beech-Nut Inc., 34.2

Squibb Corp., 34.4, 34.7, 35.68

Squibb toothbrush, 34.7

Stacy-Adams Co., 48.102, 48.139

Stadium clothes, 26.62

Stafflight, 72.9

Stafford., S. S., 126.13

Stakmore Co. Inc., 50.55, 50.58

Stamps, 85.56

Standard Accident Insurance Co., 64.11, 64.14

Standard Brands Inc., 27.10, 27.34, 47.30, 47.103, 110.2, 110.14

Standard Brewing Co., 14.8, 14.14

Standard Cigar Co., 115.83

Standard Diary Co., 83.33

Standard Electric Stove Co., 60.26

Standard Envelope Mfg. Co., 83.60

Standard Life Insurance Co., 64.47

Standard Motor Parts Inc., 8.68

Standard Oil Co., 88.19

Standard Oil Co. of California, 88.55

Standard Oil Div., American Oil Co., 9.1, 88.50, 88.71, 88.80

Standard Products Co., 18.121

Standard Radio Corp. Ltd., 95.35

Standard Textile Products Co., 65.21

Standard Tool and Mfg. Co., 73.4

Stange Co., 29.32

Stanlabs Inc., 35.83

Stanley hardware, 55.19, 55.40

Stanley Home Products Inc., 60.139

Stanley Works, The, 55.19, 55.40, 117.38, 117.42

Stanton, 5.34

Starcraft Co., 16.1

Stardust Hotel and Golf Club, 62.40

Star ham, 74.24

Sta-Rite Hair Pin Co., 54.31

Starrett Co., 117.27

State Farm Insurance Co., 64.42

Static Guard, 24.78
Stationers Loose Leaf Co., 83.3
Staybestos Mfg. Co., 8.29
Staze Inc., 34.26
Stearns Coal & Lumber Co., 59.11
Stearns-Knight, 7.11
Steero cubes, 47.1
Steger & Sons, 80.11, 80.32
Stein Co., A. G., 61.23, 61.39
Steiner & Son, 26.52
Steinway & Sons, 80.30, 80.35
Steinwender-Stoffregen Coffee Co., 27.44
Stereopticon lantern slides, 89.21
sterling, 67.33
Sterling Faucet Co., 55.41
Sterling salt, 29.29
Sterling Silversmiths of America, 67.17
Sterling Software Marketing, 28.68, 28.83
Stern Co., L. & H., 105.17, 105.26
Sterno Corp., 59.21
Stetson Co., John B., 26.21, 26.86, 26.88, 26.97, 26.123
Stetson Shoe Co., 48.99, 48.166
Stevens and Co. Inc., J. P., 113.13
Stevens arms, 44.16
Stevens & Co. Inc., 13.6, 13.13
Stevenson, Adlai, 91.5, 91.6, 91.10, 91.146, 91.194, 91.198, 91.382, 91.402
Stewart Hartshorn Co., 65.3
Stewart-Warner Corp., 8.2, 95.31
Stickup room deodorant, 24.97
Stiffel Co., The, 70.43
Stillman Co., 32.55
Stimpson computing scale, 81.26
Stimpson Computing Scale Co., 63.12, 63.13
Stinson, 3.2, 3.5
Stitzel-Walker Distillery Inc., 71.147
Stix-Altman-Weiner Inc., 48.80
St. John, John P., 91.130
St. Johns Silk Co., 61.10, 61.31
St. Joseph Lead Co., 75.6
St. Louis, Mo., 36.17
St. Louis Star, 85.81
Stokely, 10.8
Stokely-Van Camp Inc., 47.4
stokers, 58.40
Stone Bros., 26.148
Stop & Shop Companies, The, 100.32

storage batteries, 8.44
Storm Hero Umbrella Co., 123.4
Story and Clark Piano Co., 80.12, 80.40
Stouffer Foods, 47.11
stoves, 60.2, 60.32
Stow and Davis Furniture Co., 81.11
St. Paul, Minn, 119.40
St. Paul Insurance Co., The, 64.76
STP Corp., 88.51
STP oil treatment, 88.51
Stradivara, 95.36
Strathmore Paper Co., 83.44, 83.53, 83.68
Strathmore Products Co., 32.33
Stratus, 28.32, 28.45
Streit Mfg. Co., C. F., 50.24
Stride Rite Corp., The, 48.129
Stroh Brewing Co., The, 14.44
Stroh's, 14.44
Stromberg-Carlson, 95.71
Strong, Carlisle & Hammond Co., 55.22
Strong, Cobb & Co., 20.1, 20.25
Structo Mfg. Co., 118.11
Struthers Mfg. Co., 8.62
Strutwear nylons, 61.46
Studebaker, 7.44, 7.58, 7.78
Studebaker Corp., 7.8, 7.44, 7.51, 7.58, 7.78, 120.4
Studebaker-Packard Corp., 7.15, 7.45
Stuhmer Co., Geo. F., 11.27
Sturdee folding ironing table, 60.80
Style-Mart suit, 26.33
Styleplus, 26.7
Stylish Stout, 121.59
Subaru, 7.35, 7.70
Subaru of America Inc., 7.35, 7.70
Successful Farming, 85.115, 85.135, 85.158, 85.186, 85.214, 85.308
Success Mfg. Co., 60.53
Suchard chocolate bars, 20.37
Sugar Information Inc., 47.82
suits, 26.49
Summit Sales Co., 71.1, 71.127
Sunbeam Corp., 60.23
Sunbrite cleanser, 24.11, 24.22
Sunday Advertiser, Boston, 85.146
Sunday American, 2.27
Sun Insurance Co., 64.16, 64.18
Sunkist fresh fruit drinks, 15.22
SunKist Fruit Rolls, 20.33

Sunkist Growers Inc., 15.22, 20.33, 49.5, 49.7, 49.16, 49.17, 49.20, 49.26, 49.33

Sunkist oranges, 49.20

Sun Life Insurance Co., 64.50

Sun-Maid Raisin Growers Assn., 49.15

Sunny Smile Products Co., 34.44

Sun Oil Co., 88.9, 88.23, 88.47, 88.58, 88.65

Sunray DX Oil Co., 88.2

Sunset, 85.76, 85.260, 85.329

Sunshine Biscuits, 11.30

Sunshine Biscuits Inc., 11.30

Sunshine Chemical Co., John, 24.24

Sunshine Ice Co., 60.59

Sunsweet Growers Inc., 49.18, 49.28

Sun Valley, Idaho, 119.54

Sunworthy wallpapers, 65.6

Super-Cyclone, 37.29

Superior Hat Co., 26.13

Superior Industries Inc., 75.33

Supertron Mfg. Co., 95.78

Supima Association of America, 113.37

Supreme Equipment & Systems Corp., 81.24

Supreme Polish Co. Ltd., 24.75

Sure deodorant, 116.14

Surpass Leather Co., 48.72

Surprise brassiere, 121.53

suspenders, 26.129

Sutliff Tobacco Co., 115.7, 115.99, 115.113

Sutra lotion, 32.20

Swaberg Mfg. Co., 126.30

Swank Inc., 67.20, 123.23

Swans Down, 11.32

Swedish American Line, 102.27

Sweet Caporal, 115.12

Sweetheart, 106.34

Sweet Message chocolates, 20.71

Sweets Co. of America, 20.40

S & W Fine Foods, 27.11

Swift & Co., 22.14, 24.11, 24.22, 24.46, 24.82, 33.39, 47.66, 47.92, 47.98, 74.6, 74.17, 74.20, 74.28, 74.30, 74.31, 74.32, 74.33

Swift's Premium, 74.28, 74.33

Swingline Inc., 81.65

Swiss Air Transport Co. Ltd., 4.41

Sylvania Electric Products Inc., 111.26, 112.1

Symons Mfg. Co., 18.52

Syracuse China Corp., 23.6

Syroco Div., Dart Industries Inc., 65.2

System, 85.249

Tab, 107.28

Tabasco sauce, 29.39, 29.42

Tabu, 84.25

Taft, William Howard, 91.107, 91.278, 91.327, 91.390

Tak-hom-a-biscuit, 11.25

Tampa Daily Times, 85.96

Tampa Electric Co., 60.109, 63.5

Tampax Inc., 116.8, 116.30

Tandem Computers Inc., 28.46

Tandy personal computers, 28.49

Tangee lipstick, 32.18

Tanners Council of America, 48.82

Tanqueray gin, 71.20

Tappan Co., 60.145, 60.146

Tareyton, 115.52, 115.172

Tartan sun oil, 32.67

Tarter, Webster and Johnson Div., American Forest Products Corp., 18.29

Tate Mfg. Co., 26.102

Tater flakes, 47.107

Tater-Flakes Co., The, 47.107

Taunton Knitting, 121.25

Tavern Weekly, 85.51

Taylor, Gen. Zachary, 91.98, 91.140, 91.276, 91.323, 91.376

Taylor, J. & J., 81.5

Taylor and Co., W. A., 71.60, 71.93, 71.124

Taylor Co., Thos. P., 61.35

Taylor Instrument Co., 63.9, 63.11

TDK Electronics Corp., 5.6, 5.46

Teac, 5.17

Teachers Scotch, 71.58, 71.69, 71.115, 71.120

Tea & Coffee Trade Journal, 85.198

Teak, 116.28

Tecate, 14.121

Tecate Importers, 14.121

Tech beer, 14.143

Technics, 5.42

Teel mouth wash, 34.38

Teeple Shoe Co., 48.17, 48.97

Teflon, 68.9

Tek toothbrush, 34.22

Teletone radio speakers, 95.19

Teletype Corp., 28.23, 28.47, 28.84

Templar, 7.80

1006 lotion, 32.87

Tender Touch, 32.75
Ten High whiskey, 71.13
Tenneco Inc., 31.5
Tennessee Corp., 22.5
Tennessee Dept. of Conservation, 119.5
Tennessee Furniture Corp., 50.36, 50.39
Tennessee Tool Works, 82.50
Tetley, 110.7, 110.9
Tetley & Co. Inc., Joseph, 110.7, 110.9, 110.19
Tetlow Co., Henry, 32.60
Texaco Inc., 9.6, 9.9, 88.36, 88.52, 88.64
Texaco Sky Chief, 9.6
Texaco Super unleaded gasoline, 88.52
Texas Instruments Inc., 28.75, 28.86, 38.6
Texas National Bank of Commerce of Houston, 43.3
Textile Div., The Kendall Co., 10.9
Textiles Div., Monsanto Co., 113.22, 113.23, 113.32
Textile World, 85.336
Textured Yarn Co. Inc., 113.9
Theobald Industries, 74.14
Thermador Electrical Mfg. Div., Norris Industries Inc., 60.89
Thermodyne Radio Corp., 95.50
Thermogas Inc., 59.3
Thermoid Div., H. K. Porter Co. Inc., 8.22
thermostatic blankets, 13.8
Thilmany Pulp and Paper Co., 83.27
Thomaston Mills Inc., 13.3
Thomaston sheets, 13.3
Thomasville Furniture Industries Inc., 50.14
Thompson Co., J. Walter, 2.6, 2.20
Thompson Medical Co. Inc., 56.8, 56.9, 56.10
Thorpe awnings, 18.37
Thousand Lakes Assn., The, St. Paul, Minn., 119.4
Three Feathers, 71.42, 71.121
Three Minute cereals, 21.26
Thunderbird, 7.40, 7.88
Thurmond, J. Strom, 91.282
Tia Maria, 71.60
Tide, 24.93, 24.99
Tide Water Oil Co., 88.11, 88.46

Tiffin Products Inc., 20.19
Tilden, Samuel J., 91.113, 91.120, 91.175, 91.259, 91.260, 91.394, 91.395
Timbertone Decorative Co. Inc., 65.8
Time, 85.189, 85.272, 85.328
T. I. M. E. Freight Inc., 120.17
Time-Life Inc., 85.171, 85.184, 94.20
Timely Clothes Inc., 26.16
Time magazine, 85.171
Timeplex Inc., 28.67
Times, Los Angeles, 85.352
Times-Picayune, New Orleans, 85.87
Times Square Trust Co., 43.22
Timex Corp., 124.36
Timex/Sinclair, 28.63
Timken Roller Bearing Co., 73.1
Tinkertoys, 118.15
Tintex Co. Inc., 24.100
Tire Rebuilders News, 85.320
Tires, 85.322
Tirometer Valve Corp., 8.1
Toastmaster, 60.98
Toledo Scale Co., 63.8
Tom Keene, 115.137
Topcon Super D, 89.31
Topps Chewing Gum Inc., 20.44
Topps gum, 20.44
Torfeaco bedding, 13.33
Torginol of America Inc., 46.1
Toro, 69.5
Toronto-Dominion Bank, 43.61
Toronto Globe, 85.66
Torrington Co., 31.18, 31.27
Toshiba, 122.1
Toshiba America Inc., 38.8, 112.9
Tourist, 85.335
Tower Co., A. J., 26.131
Toyota Motor Distributors Inc., 7.26, 7.32
Toy Tinkers Div., A. G. Spalding and Bros., Inc., 118.15
Train & McIntyre Ltd., 71.15, 71.49
Traiser & Co. Inc., H., 115.59
Trane Co., 58.15
Trans America Insurance Company, 64.55, 64.95
Transamerican Freight Lines Inc., 120.30
Trans-Canada System, 111.6
Transcontinental & Western, 4.42
Transo Envelope Co., 83.75

Trans Union Corp., 31.11
Trans World Airlines Inc., 4.31, 4.56, 4.61
Travel Adventures, 85.112
Travelers Insurance Co., 64.20, 64.90, 64.112
Travelo knit jackets and vests, 26.145
Treasure Isle Inc., 47.78
Treganowan, Ernest, 46.10
Trevira, 113.28
Triangle Raincoat Co., 26.126
Tribune, Salt Lake City, 85.330
Trico fuse, 37.33
Trico Mfg. Co., 37.33
Tri-Lok Co., 18.40
Trimble Nurseryland Furniture Inc., 50.37
Trim Cup-A-Soup, 47.109
Tri-Parel Corp., 26.54
Trommers, 14.74, 14.77
Troy Engine & Machine Co., 73.8
True, 85.269
True Shape Hosiery Co., 61.1
True Story, 85.287
True-Taste mayonnaise, 29.14
True Temper Corp., 45.1, 117.34
Truman, Harry S., 91.64, 91.101, 91.240, 91.290, 91.353, 91.366, 91.367
Trust Co. of Georgia, 43.60
Tryce Mfg. Co. Inc., 42.11
Tucker & Dorsey Mfg. Co., 60.80
Tulsa World, 85.152
Tums, 35.30, 35.91
Tungsten Contact Mfg. Co., 8.37
Turnbull Elevator Co., 39.4
Tuxedo feeds, 42.47
Tuxedo pipe tobacco, 115.187
Tuxedo tobacco, 115.54, 115.61
T. V. Guide, 85.28
Tweedie Boot Top Co., 48.122
Twin City Milk Producers Association, 33.26
Twinplex Sales Co., 104.9
Tycora, 113.9
Tydol, 88.11, 88.46
Tylenol pain reliever, 35.28
Ullman Studios, Martin, 2.15
Uncle Ben's Foods, 47.26, 47.112
Uncle Ben's Inc., 47.63
Uncle Ben's rice, 47.112
Underwood Co., Wm, 74.26
Underwood typewriters, 81.50, 81.62

Underwood, William, 74.21
Unguentine, 35.109
Union Barge Line Corp., 102.30
Union brass faucet, 55.39
Union Brass & Metal Manufacturing, 55.39
Union Carbide Agricultural Products Co., 69.12, 69.34
Union Carbide Consumer Products Co., 37.26
Union Carbide Corp., 31.22, 37.24
Union Central Life Insurance Co., The, 64.60
Union Fork & Hoe, 55.35
Union Oil Co., 88.13, 88.69
Union Pacific Railroad, 96.6, 96.12, 96.13, 96.31, 96.43, 96.70, 96.73, 96.75
Union smoking tobacco, 115.132
Unique luggage, 72.7
Uniroyal Inc., 48.39, 109.3
Uniroyal Tire Co., 114.12
United Air Lines Inc., 4.25, 4.49, 4.53, 4.54, 4.63, 4.75
United American Lines, 102.1, 102.13, 102.26
United California Bank, 43.43
United-Carr Inc., 26.122
United Cigar Stores, 100.15, 115.60, 115.130, 115.159
United Electric Co., 60.27
United Jewish Appeal, 92.3
United Mfg. Co., 13.30
United Mink Producers Assn., 26.158
United of Omaha, 64.73
United Prune Growers of California, 49.11
United Retail Candy Stores, 20.32
United Shoe Mfrs., 48.168
United States Borax and Chemical Corp., 22.11
United States Cartridge Co., 44.10
United States Daily, Washington, D. C., 85.10, 85.11, 85.169
United States Gypsum Co., 18.86
United States Lines Inc., 102.9
United States Playing Card Co., 118.2
United States Savings Bonds, 66.6, 66.15, 66.16
United States Shoe Co., 48.48, 48.50
United States Steel Corp., 75.22, 75.35

United States Tobacco Co., 115.2,
115.115, 115.122, 115.134, 115.160,
115.175
United Van Lines Inc., 79.7, 79.11
United Vintners Inc., 125.3
Unity Mutual, 64.101
Univac, 28.50
Universal Cigar Corp., 115.106
Universal Oil Products Co., 88.8,
88.72
Universal Pad and Tablet Corp.,
The, 81.47
Universal Paper Products Co., 83.89
University Computing Co., 28.57
Univis glasses, 41.7
Upson Board, 18.111
Upson Co., The, 18.13, 18.111
Urdang Inc., Laurence, 85.119
U.S. Army, 53.1, 53.2
U.S. Bakery, 11.43
U.S. Brewers Assn., 14.10
U.S. Brewers Foundation, 14.22
U.S. Cartridge Co., 44.2
U.S. Electrical Tool Co., 117.29
U. S. Gaytees rubbers, 48.39
U.S. Marines, 53.3
U.S. National Bank, 43.52
U.S. News and World Report,
85.148
Usol Fly Spray, 42.28
U.S. rallying cry during Spanish-
American War, 90.6
U.S. rallying cry during
Revolutionary War, 90.4
U.S. rallying cry during World War
II, 90.5
U.S. Savings Bonds, 66.20
U.S. Television Mfg. Corp., 112.15,
112.17
U.S. Travel Bureau, 119.49
U.S. Van Lines Inc., 79.3
UTA French Airlines, 4.36
Utica, 13.6
Utica Heater Co., 58.47, 58.54
Utica Trust & Deposit Co., 43.59
Utley Paint Co., 82.80
Utz & Dunn Co., 48.133
Val-A-Pak luggage, 72.27
Valentine & Co., 82.75
Valier & Spies Milling Co., 11.31,
11.46
Valspar Corp., 82.61, 82.79
Valspar paints, 82.61, 82.79
Value Computing Inc., 28.61

Valvoline Oil Co., Div. Ashland Oil
and Refining Co., 88.7, 88.32,
88.75
Vanadium-Alloys Steel Co., 75.19
Van Buren, Martin, 91.28, 91.43,
91.92, 91.93, 91.213, 91.317, 91.318,
91.341, 91.380
Vancouver, British Columbia,
Canada, 119.39
Vanguard Recording Society Inc.,
97.7
Van Heusen, 26.160
Vanity Fair Mills Inc., 121.2
Vanity hats, 26.91
Vaniva shaving cream, 104.46
Van Munching & Co. Inc., 14.35
Van Raalte Co. Inc., 61.5, 121.5
Vantage Products Inc., 124.40
Vantine & Co., 104.14
VapoRub, 35.5, 35.46
Varsity, 85.338
Vaseline, 35.36, 54.44
Vaseline Intensive Care Lotion,
32.32
Vaughan & Bushnell Mfg. Co.,
117.11
Veedol oil, 88.43
Velchek Tool Co., 117.14
Vel soap, 24.58
Velveeta, 33.10, 47.48
Velveola Souveraine face powder,
32.51
Velvet, 115.1, 115.6
Ventura Travelward Inc., 72.15
Venture, 85.323
Verbatim Corp., 28.31
VERBATIM, *The Language
Quarterly,* 85.119
Vernon Div., Metlox Mfg. Co., 23.3
Vernonware, 23.3
Viceroy, 115.44, 115.116, 115.140,
115.164, 115.188
Vick Chemical Co., 34.24, 35.5,
35.37, 35.46, 35.92, 35.122
Vicks Health Care, 116.4
Victor-American Fuel Co., 59.17
Victor Computer Corp., 81.38
Victor Golf Co., 108.27
Victor Manufacturing and Gasket
Co., 8.57
Victor Sports Inc., 108.18
Victor Talking Machine Co., 5.48
Victor tires, 114.15

Victory Sports Net Div., The
Fishnet and Twine Co., 45.27
Vietnam-era draft resisters, 90.1
Viking Glass Co., 52.7
Viking of Minneapolis Inc., 5.58
Viko Furniture, 50.15
Vi-lets, 20.56
Virginia Dept. of Conservation and
Economic Development, 119.8,
119.27
Virginia Fruit Juice Co., 15.2
Virginia Horticultural Society, 49.10
Virginia Maid Hosiery Mills Inc.,
61.4
Virginia Mirror Co., 65.1
Virginia Slims Lights, 115.189
Visine eye drops, 35.33
Visking Corp., 74.18
Visonik, 5.2
Visual Technology Inc., 28.74
Vita Glass Corp., 18.47
Vitanola Talking Machine Co., 5.22,
5.40
Vivaudou Inc., V., 84.24
Viyella International Inc., 113.34
Vogan Candy Co., 20.41
Vogue Foundations Inc., 121.12
Volkswagen, 7.39
Volkswagen of America Inc., 7.28,
7.39
Volman Lawrence Co., 48.111
Volvo of America Corp., 7.2
Von Duprin Div., Vonnegut
Hardware Co. Inc., 55.34
Vose & Sons Piano Co., 80.42
Vulcan Golf Co., 108.9
Wabash Appliance Corp., 70.40
Wadsworth Howland, 82.71
Wagner Electric Corp., 8.63, 8.65,
60.29
Wagner Mfg. Co., 68.4
Wahl Co., 83.48, 126.2, 126.12,
126.38, 126.46
Wakefield Brass Co., F. W., 70.31
Walker, W. H., 48.172
Walker & Co., W. H., 48.159
Walker Inc., Hiram, 71.13, 71.16,
71.59, 71.62, 71.71, 71.92, 71.107,
71.145
Walker-Knaier Shoe Corp., 48.146
Walker's DeLuxe bourbon, 71.71
Walk-Over Koolies, 48.128
Wallace, George C., 91.69, 91.172,
91.286, 91.299

Wallace, Henry A., 91.236, 91.421
Wallace & Co., 20.18
Wallace Pencil Co., 126.25
Wallace Shoe Co., 48.32
Wallace Silversmiths, 67.15, 67.25,
67.33
Waltham Watch Co., 124.31, 124.54
Wander Co., 15.5
Wang Laboratories Inc., 28.60
Wang VS computers, 28.60
Ward Foods Co., 47.69
Warner & Co., W. R., 35.20, 35.48,
35.107
Warner Bros., 121.58
Warner-Lambert Pharmaceutical
Co., 35.3, 35.26, 35.54, 35.104,
84.20, 104.38
Warner & Swasey Co., 73.25, 120.5
Warren Co., S. D., 83.16
Warren's chewing gum, 20.67
Warren Telechron Co., 124.1
Warren Weatherbone Co., 103.8
Washington, State of, 119.28, 119.45
Washington powder, 24.18
Washington Shoe Mfg. Co., 48.40
Washwear, 26.28
Wassmuth-Endicott Co., 18.43
Waterford crystal, 52.2
Waterman pens, 126.1, 126.18
Waters-Genter Co., 60.73, 60.125
Watkins Co., R. L., 54.6
Watson Mfg. Co. Inc., 81.45
Watson sterling, 67.25
Waukesha mineral water, 15.23
wax, 24.90
Wayne feeds, 42.7
Wayne Gossard Corp., 61.18
WCBS Radio, 17.5
Wear-Ever aluminum, 68.11
Wear-Ever Aluminum Inc., 68.11
Wear-Right gloves, 123.22
Weatherbee, 26.126
Weaver Chicken Rondelets, 74.15
Weaver Inc., 74.15
Webcor, 111.23
Weber & Heilbroner, 26.25
Webster, 115.32
Webster Cigar Co., 115.13, 115.32
Webster-Eisenlohr Inc., 115.37
Webster's International Dictionary,
94.7
Weed Co., Lewis M., 26.36
Weedone, 69.12, 69.34

Weingarten Bros., 121.39
Weis Mfg. Co., The, 81.42
Weiss & Klau Co., 24.48
Welch grape juice, 15.9, 15.14, 15.21
Welch Grape Juice Co., 15.9, 15.14, 15.21, 47.15, 47.44, 47.114
Weldon Roberts Rubber Co., 81.8
Wellman-Seaver-Morgan Co., 59.18
Wells Mfg. Corp., 8.27, 8.35
Wells-Treister Co., 26.114
Wembley Ties Inc., 26.101, 26.103, 26.109
Wendy's International Inc., 99.12
West Bend Co., The, 60.70
West Branch cedar hope chest, 50.64
Westclox Div., General Time Corp., 124.6, 124.12, 124.21, 124.23, 124.33, 124.44
West Coast Lumbermen's Assn., 18.106
Westcott, 7.61
Westcott Motor Car Co., 7.61
Western Air Lines Inc., 4.52, 4.57
Western Cartridge Co., 44.4, 44.15, 44.26, 44.27
Western Co., The, 34.11
Western Electric, 57.3
Western Life Insurance Co., 64.15, 64.102
Western Mfrs. Assn., 18.102
Western Newspaper Union, 2.37
Western Union, 111.1, 111.3, 111.10, 111.17
Westgate, 113.15
Westinghouse, 37.19, 60.111, 95.10
Westinghouse Electric Corp., 31.39, 70.23, 70.41, 95.38
Westminster, New York., The, 62.3
Westminster socks, 61.52
West Palm Beach, Florida, 119.52
West Point Pepperell, 12.5, 13.10
Westvaco Corp., 83.79
Wexler and Co., David, 80.18
Weyenberg Shoe Mfg. Co., 48.1, 48.7, 48.29, 48.41, 48.62, 48.66, 48.85, 48.105
Wheatena Co., The, 21.37
Wheaties, 21.9, 21.31, 21.48
Wheel Horse Products Co., 69.5, 69.21, 69.23
Whelen Engineering Company Inc., 38.2
Whirlpool appliances, 60.64

Whirlpool Corp., 60.64, 60.127
Whirlpool washer, 60.21, 60.82
White & Wyckoff Mfg. Co., 83.23, 83.26, 83.86
White Co., H. C., 118.10
White Consolidated Industries Inc., 60.90
Whitecraft Inc., 50.63
White Furniture Co., 50.66
Whitehall Laboratories, 116.9
Whitehall Labs Div., American Home Products Co., 35.51
Whitehall Products Inc., 115.25
White House evaporated milk, 33.31
White King soap, 106.16
White Motor Corp., 120.25, 120.32
White of Mebane, 50.7
White Rock Products Corp., 15.19, 15.34, 107.4
White Rock water, 15.19, 15.34
White Seal whiskey, 71.48
White sewing machine, 60.90
White Shoulders perfume, 84.17
White Stag Mfg. Co., 26.141
Whiting Co., H. S., 70.29
Whiting & Davis Co., 123.13
Whitman's chocolates, 20.14, 20.30
Whiz, 20.16
Whiz mirror and glass cleaner, 24.79
Wicker Bros., 30.1
Widdicomb Co., John, 50.23
Wilbur-Suchard Choc. Co., 20.37
Wild Turkey bourbon, 71.119
Wile Sons and Co. Inc., Julius, 71.64, 71.65, 71.98, 125.37
Willcox & Gibbs Sewing Machine Co., 60.120
Willer & Son, 108.21
Williams and Humbert dry sack, 125.37
Williams Co. Inc., J. B., 32.40, 32.61, 54.15, 104.18, 104.21, 104.48, 104.53
Williams Gun Sight Co., 44.14
Williamson Shoe Co., Ault, 48.4
Williams shaving cream, 104.18, 104.53
Willkie, Wendell, 91.9, 91.32, 91.67, 91.206, 91.209, 91.210, 91.211, 91.212, 91.239, 91.270, 91.273, 91.303, 91.306, 91.342, 91.391, 91.397, 91.406, 91.416, 91.417
Willsonite sunglasses, 41.4

Willys-Knight, 7.98
Willys-Overland Inc., 7.11, 7.98
Wilmington, Del., 36.21
Wilson, Woodrow, 91.121, 91.122, 91.129, 91.329, 91.381, 91.389, 91.418
Wilson and Co. Inc., 74.13, 74.29
Wilson Bros., 26.110
Wilson Co., Thos. E., 108.33
Wilson Sporting Goods Co., 108.4, 108.22
Wilson trucks, 120.31
Wimelbacher & Rice, 123.10
Winarick Inc., Ar, 54.43
Winchester cigarettes, 115.18
Winchester flashlight, 70.18
Winchester Repeating Arms Co., 44.21, 118.22
Windex window cleaner, 24.30, 24.76
Wine Advisory Board, San Francisco, 125.2
Winona Oil Co., 88.22, 88.63
Winship & Sons, 72.25
WINS Radio, 17.1
Winston cigarettes, 115.70, 115.179
Winter & Co., 80.24
Winthrop Shoes, 48.6
Winton Nicolet Watch Co., 124.56, 124.57
Wisconsin, 119.3
Wisconsin Div. of Economic Development, 36.22
Wisconsin Vacation and Travel Service, 119.41
Wish Bone salad dressing, 29.9
Wiss & Sons, J., 55.32
Witt Cornice Co., 60.84
Wix Corp., 8.52
Wm. Penn whiskey, 71.110
Wolf's Head Oil Refining Co. Inc., 88.31
Wolf Tailoring, 26.63
Wolverine World Wide Inc., 48.25
Woman's Digest, 85.197
Women's Wear, 85.309
Wonder Bread, 11.20, 11.28
Wood and Hogan, 50.3
Woodbury College, Los Angeles, 101.5
Woodbury's facial soap, 106.32
Woodco Corp., 18.30
Woodcraft Supply Co., 117.16

Woodhull, Goodale & Bull Inc., 26.62
Woodward and Sons Inc., Lee L., 50.53
Wool Carpets of America, 46.26
Worcester Salt Co., 29.21, 29.47
Worcester Salt tooth paste, 34.50
Work Boat, The, 85.193
Workmen's Circle Call, 85.231
World Airways Inc., 4.60, 4.70
World Fire and Marine Insurance Co., 64.24
World, New York, 85.319
World-Telegram, New York, 85.124
Worthington Pump & Machinery Corp., 73.5
Wrangler's, 26.41
Wren Co., Jenny, 11.51
Wright Co., A. E., 29.20
Wright & Co., E. T., 48.142
Wright's silver cream cleaner, 24.74
Wrigley Jr. Co., William, 20.3, 20.28, 20.29, 20.61
Wrigley's gum, 20.3, 20.28, 20.61
Writer's Monthly, 85.7
Wurlitzer Co., 80.44, 80.46
Wurlitzer phonograph, 5.38
Wyeth Laboratories Div., American Home Products Corp., 35.82
Wyse Technology, 28.24
Xerox Corp., 30.7
Yachting, 85.83, 85.305
Yale bicycles, 98.15
Yale Electric Corp., 37.2
Yale Express System Inc., 120.16
Yale & Towne, 55.21, 55.44
Yamaha Motor Corp., U. S. A., 77.4
Yankee Barn Homes, 18.73
Yankee Toffee, 20.24
Yankee tools, 117.23
Yankiboy play clothes, 26.78
Yardley of London Inc., 84.15, 84.23, 84.27, 106.29
Ybry Inc., 84.28
Yellow Pages, 2.1, 2.3, 2.17
Yodora, 116.21
York, 115.142
York Chemical Co., 42.1
York Corp., 58.56
Young Distilling Co., Alexander, 71.129
Youth Garde Moisturizer, 32.34
Youth's Companion, 85.153
Yuban, 27.58

Zapon Co., 82.66
Z-Bec Vitamins, 56.7
Zebco Div., Brunswick Corp., 45.21, 45.28
Zenith Radio Corp., 95.5, 95.7, 95.22, 112.3, 112.13, 112.14
Zenith Systems, 112.14
Zerex, 8.9

Zimmerman-Scher Co., 26.59
Ziplock storage bags, 68.20
Zippo Mfg. Co., 105.21, 105.22
Zodiac Watch Co., 124.35
Zono pads, 35.70
Zoom, 21.2
Zoom 8, 89.27
Zucker & Josephy Inc., 103.18